JOINT ECONOMIC COMMITTEE
CONGRESS OF THE UNITED STATES

COMPARISONS OF THE UNITED STATES AND SOVIET ECONOMIES

Papers Submitted by Panelists Appearing
Before the
Subcommittee on Economic Statistics

PARTS I - III
(1959)

GREENWOOD PRESS, PUBLISHERS
NEW YORK 1968

First Greenwood reprinting, 1968

Library of Congress catalogue card number: 69-10164

PRINTED IN THE UNITED STATES OF AMERICA

COMPARISONS OF THE UNITED STATES AND SOVIET ECONOMIES

Papers Submitted by Panelists Appearing
Before the
Subcommittee on Economic Statistics

JOINT ECONOMIC COMMITTEE
CONGRESS OF THE UNITED STATES

Printed for the use of the Joint Economic Committee

JOINT ECONOMIC COMMITTEE

(Created pursuant to sec. 5(a) of Public Law 304, 79th Cong.)

PAUL H. DOUGLAS, Illinois, *Chairman*
WRIGHT PATMAN, Texas, *Vice Chairman*

SENATE

JOHN SPARKMAN, Alabama
J. W. FULBRIGHT, Arkansas
JOSEPH C. O'MAHONEY, Wyoming
JOHN F. KENNEDY, Massachusetts
PRESCOTT BUSH, Connecticut
JOHN MARSHALL BUTLER, Maryland
JACOB K. JAVITS, New York

HOUSE OF REPRESENTATIVES

RICHARD BOLLING, Missouri
HALE BOGGS, Louisiana
HENRY S. REUSS, Wisconsin
FRANK M. COFFIN, Maine
THOMAS B. CURTIS, Missouri
CLARENCE E. KILBURN, New York
WILLIAM B. WIDNALL, New Jersey

RODERICK H. RILEY, *Executive Director*
JOHN W. LEHMAN, *Clerk*

SUBCOMMITTEE ON ECONOMIC STATISTICS

RICHARD BOLLING, Missouri, *Chairman*

JOHN SPARKMAN, Alabama
J. W. FULBRIGHT, Arkansas
PRESCOTT BUSH, Connecticut
JACOB K. JAVITS, New York

HALE BOGGS, Louisiana
FRANK M. COFFIN, Maine
THOMAS B. CURTIS, Missouri

JOHN W. LEHMAN, *Economist*
JAMES W. KNOWLES, *Economist*

LETTERS OF TRANSMITTAL

September 28, 1959.

Hon. Paul H. Douglas,
Chairman, Joint Economic Committee,
U.S. Senate, Washington, D.C.

Dear Senator Douglas: Transmitted herewith is part I of a series of papers submitted by the panelists invited to appear before the Subcommittee on Economic Statistics in connection with the subcommittee's current study of "Comparisons of the United States and Soviet Economies." Additional papers will be submitted in part II, which will contain the remainder of the general presentations, and in part III, which will present papers in summary and conclusion.

This study is being conducted in accordance with instructions from the full committee as announced in the Joint Economic Committee's report on the 1959 Economic Report of the President. The study grows out of previous work of the Joint Economic Committee during the 83d and 85th Congresses.

It should be recognized, as was stated in the earlier studies, that the problems of making comparisons between any two national economies are exceedingly complex and even more so when those economies are at different stages of development and have different policy objectives. Such limitations are carefully set forth in the papers of the opening panel and will be further assessed by the panelists preparing the summary and conclusions.

The papers are presented in advance of the subcommittee's hearings in accordance with the Joint Economic Committee's usual practice in order to provide members of the subcommittee and the participating panelists an opportunity to examine thoroughly the analyses and findings in preparation for the discussions at the hearings.

Richard Bolling,
Chairman, Subcommittee on Economic Statistics.

September 25, 1959.

Hon. Richard Bolling,
Chairman, Subcommittee on Economic Statistics,
House of Representatives, Washington, D.C.

Dear Representative Bolling: Transmitted herewith is part I of the series of papers submitted by the panelists invited to appear before the Subcommittee on Economic Statistics at the hearings to be held November 16–20. The papers are arranged by panel topics in the order in which they are scheduled for discussion at the hearings. Part II, containing the papers of panelists appearing in the latter part of the hearings dealing with the subjects of "National Income and Product," "Foreign Economic Activities," and the "Evaluation of the Russian Economic Threat by Private Policymakers" will be submitted within 2 weeks. Part III, containing the papers on summary and policy implications will be submitted in early November.

The papers are presented as submitted by the panelists, without deletions.

JOHN W. LEHMAN,
Economist, Subcommittee on Economic Statistics.

CONTENTS

PROBLEMS OF SOVIET-UNITED STATES COMPARISONS

POPULATION AND LABOR FORCE

INDUSTRY

TRANSPORTATION

TABLES

AGRICULTURE

LEVELS OF LIVING AND INCENTIVES IN THE SOVIET AND UNITED STATES ECONOMIES

COMPARISONS OF THE UNITED STATES AND SOVIET ECONOMIES

PROBLEMS OF SOVIET-UNITED STATES COMPARISONS

(By Hans Heymann, Jr., Economics Division, the Rand Corp., Washington, D.C.)

Introduction: Nature of the Problem

As the Joint Economic Committee launches into the third of its biennial comparative studies of Soviet economic growth, it seems most fitting that our attention be focused at the very outset on what is probably the most elusive and critical issue with which any comparison must deal, namely that of method and concept: how adequate are the yardsticks we must employ, how commensurable are the features we wish to compare, and how clearly can we define the purposes which the comparisons are intended to serve? These questions are, of course, not new and, in part, they have been intelligently discussed in the two previous studies in this series.[1] It seems most appropriate, nevertheless, that we take another look at these problems at this time. For in the interim since the publication of the last study there have been several developments which lend these questions new interest and urgency.

First, the Soviet authorities have seen fit to release considerably more statistical information about their own economy in the last 3 years than they have in the preceding 20. Innumerable statistical handbooks have made their appearance, covering major economic sectors, industries, and regions of the U.S.S.R.,[2] and the Soviet periodical literature is now also more generously festooned with statistical tabulations and compendia. It may be well to ask, then, whether this new flood of data constitutes a qualitative as well as a quantitative improvement in the information at our disposal, or whether it is merely more of the same mixture of ill-defined fact and propagandistic distortion to which we have been so frustratingly subjected in the past.

A second development is the growing Soviet preoccupation with economic comparisons. Since about the middle of last year, and particularly coincident with the launching of the new 7-year plan, the long-held and prestige-laden Soviet objective of "catching up with

[1] See, for example, the interesting analysis of the limitations and pitfalls of national income comparisons undertaken in the 1955 study ("Trends in Economic Growth: A Comparison of the Western Powers and the Soviet Bloc," ch. VIII, pp. 54–59) and the discussion of conceptual and statistical problems in the 1957 study ("Soviet Economic Growth: A Comparison With the United States," pp. 7–9).

[2] Partial listings of the new handbooks have been compiled by John P. Hardt in the American Economic Review, June 1958, pp. 472–473, and by Michael Kaser in Soviet Studies, January 1959, p. 319 ff.

America" has been rapidly transformed by Khrushchev from a mere propaganda slogan into something approaching a national obsession. "Economic competition" has become the watchword and the attention of Soviet economists has been increasingly directed toward economic developments in the West and toward comparisons of the economic progress of the two leading contestants, the United States and the U.S.S.R. While engaging in a veritable orgy of comparisons of their own, Soviet economists have now also become unhappily aware of the comparisons being made by their American "bourgeois" colleagues and have subjected these to violent and tendentious criticism in a dreary succession of articles and books.[3] These Soviet criticisms are, of course, not inspired by any love of truth or respect for scholarship; they condemn passionately and reject wholesale whatever we say that may tend to question the perfect wisdom of Soviet policies or the inevitable superiority of Soviet institutions. But our comparisons have not always been above reproach, and some of the Soviet criticisms cannot be entirely laughed off. But whether we take them seriously or dismiss them as propaganda, it is well to be aware of the fact, now more than ever, comparisons of the sort we are making have become subjects of bitter international controversy. In order to avoid both the emotional and the statistical traps, it would be well for us to lean over backward to recognize the ambiguities of our data, to acknowledge the temperamental nature of our yardsticks and to be conscious of the complexities of our criteria.

Finally, and perhaps most important, we are beginning to show more concern about the purposes and perspectives that international comparisons should serve. We are beginning to ask ourselves some searching questions about the meaning of the economic competition with the U.S.S.R. We have begun to suspect that Khrushchev's simplistic objective of catching up with us in the production of goods may be admirably suited to his purposes, but that such a competition hardly defines our own aims and may, in fact, distract our attention from the real issues. Evidently, Khrushchev would like nothing better than to turn the entire international arena into a gigantic racetrack on which all contestants must accept his ground rules, assume his handicaps, and compete for his goals. But his production race is not necessarily a meaningful contest for us and perhaps we should not even be running on the same track. What is the true nature of the competition? What are the measures of comparison that are appropriate to our tasks and that will correctly identify our opportunities and dangers? Is it the speed of Soviet economic growth that threatens our security or is it the direction and efficiency of its disposition? Can we measure Soviet economic strength by its total output, or is it the skill with which the output is used that accounts for the Soviet threat? Questions such as these concerning the criteria and values that should guide our comparisons lie at the very heart of our problem. There is a strong temptation to ignore these issues and

---

[3] Interestingly, much of this criticism is directed at the 1957 Joint Economic Committee report "Soviet Economic Growth * * *." For a sample of these critiques, see V. Kuvarin and A. Mikhailov, "A New Attempt To Distort the Picture of Soviet Economic Growth," Voprosy Ekonomiki No. 11, November 1957, p. 136 ff.; A. Kozlov, "Some Attempts To Distort the Facts Concerning the Development of the Soviet Economy," Voprosy Ekonomiki, No. 4, April 1958, p. 100 ff.; S. Kheinman, "Bourgeois Economists on Soviet Industry," Voprosy Ekonomiki, No. 5, May 1958, p. 87 ff.; more recently, the Gosplan U.S.S.R. Institute of Economic Research has devoted an entire book to tnis subject, under thetitle "Ekonomicheskol sorevnovanie mezhdu SSSR i SShA. Kritika vzgliadov Amerikanskikh burzhuaznykh ekonomistov" (The economic contest between the U.S.S.R. and United States: A critique of the views of American bourgeois economists), Moscow, 1959.

to proceed mechanically with our comparisons, letting others worry about what they mean; or, at the other extreme, to give up in despair and avoid comparisons altogether.[4] But if comparisons are to be made, their usefulness, in the final analysis, will depend on our ability to throw some light on precisely these issues.

In a brief general discussion such as this, divorced from the actual comparisons themselves, it is, of course, possible to examine only a few of these issues and to treat them only in highly summary fashion. This paper will begin by reviewing, very briefly, some of the purely technical problems arising from the inadequacies of the data, and their limited coverage; it will then turn to some broader questions of comparability arising from differences in structure over time and space; and, finally, it will touch upon one or two of the larger issues of perspective and focus upon which the significance of the comparisons so largely depends.

Limitations of Data and Tools

USABILITY OF STATISTICS

The increasing availability of Soviet statistics in recent years has been a source of both encouragement and frustration to Western scholars who had long been treated to a Soviet diet of virtual statistical starvation. The new data, published in the form of official manuals and tabulations presented sporadically in the periodical press, touch upon many important aspects of Soviet economic life, fill some gaping voids, afford us greater opportunities for checking internal consistency, and provide a somewhat more rounded picture of Soviet economic development than could be obtained prior to 1956. But the new data are still a long way indeed from meeting what would be considered in the Western World as minimum acceptable standards of statistical adequacy.[5] The data still exhibit large gaps and omissions in reporting, widespread internal inconsistencies and discrepancies, and an almost ludicrous lack of documentation, definition, or other explanatory notes; all this adds up to an overall statistical situation that resembles a jigsaw puzzle with a fuzzy picture and at least half the pieces missing.

In lashing out at Soviet statistics, it may be well to bear in mind that Western statistics, too, have their deficiencies and limitations, and that governments and individuals everywhere are prone to select, manipulate, or withhold data so as to present a "special" interpretation of the facts. But in the democratic West, misrepresentation and distortion tends to be kept within reasonable bounds by the open clash of ideas, by the public airing of scholarly controversy, and by the checks and balances of responsible government. In the Soviet case these controls and disciplines are absent and there are other serious impediments to the presentation of a reliable, balanced, and undistorted statistical image of Soviet reality.

---

[4] The U.S. education mission to the U.S.S.R. recently published a report of its observations of Soviet education, but carefully abstained from any comparisons on the ground that "the objectives of education in the two countries are so different as to make comparisons misleading.' (U.S. Office of Education, "Soviet Commitment to Education, Report of the First Official U.S. Education Mission to the U.S.S.R.," Bulletin 1959 No. 16, Washington, D.C.).

[5] For a critique of the new data, see Naum Jasny, "The Soviet 1956 Statistical Handbook: A Commentary," Michigan State University Press, 1957; Harry Schwartz, "The Renaissance of Soviet Statistics," Review of Economics and Statistics, May 1958, p. 122 ff.; and Robert L. Allen, "A Note on Soviet Foreign Trade Statistics," "Soviet Studies," April 1959, p. 360 ff.

One of these impediments has its origin in the very nature of what Gregory Grossman calls the Soviet command economy. Unlike a market economy, a command economy allocates resources not through a market mechanism but by direct production orders from the center to the enterprises. The flow of information in such an economy is, therefore, somewhat similar to the system of commands and execution that prevails in a military organization and is quite unlike the casual information reporting typical of a market economy. The principle of authority and subordination that pervades Soviet economic administration has important and often negative consequences for the reliability of the production statistics and other records of performance that the Soviet "subordinates" report to their superiors. For, as Grossman so aptly puts it, "authority breeds deception, and commands elicit simulation." [6] Deception and simulation take the form of statistical manipulations by both workers and management in Soviet enterprises, who, because of the rigorous structure of incentives and penalties under which they operate are pulled in the direction of writeups of output and simulation of plan fulfillment. "Borrowing" output from succeeding periods, the inclusion of spoilage and substandard goods in reports of finished output and the devaluation of the product assortment produced all tend to impair the numerical accuracy of the data reported to the Soviet authorities by their subordinates. But while there is much evidence of data distortion and even falsification of this sort, there are also definite limits placed on such opportunities for misreporting and, by and large, it may be reasonable to assume that the relative magnitude of distortion from this source is not fatal for our purposes.

But the distortion of the information reported to the Soviet authorities is the lesser of the impediments to statistical adequacy. A much more serious problem for us is the distortion of the facts about the Soviet economy reported by the Soviet authorities in their publications. This is a very different kind of distortion which takes the form not of numerical falsification, but of a concerted effort to mislead the reader by withholding and suppressing data, by partial and selective release, by deliberate ambiguity in description, and by biased choice of bases for comparison. The reasons for this systematic Soviet effort to deprive and to deceive are twofold: first, an almost compulsive preoccupation with preserving military secrecy which, in Soviet practice, is defined much more comprehensively than almost anywhere else in the world, and second, a vital political and ideological stake in presenting a special kind of image of the Soviet economy both to its own citizens and to the world at large. Thus the imperatives of national security and propaganda combine to produce a sadly incomplete and distorted picture of Soviet reality, shielding from our view both some of the most successful and some of the poorest performing sectors of the economy, and presenting us with the formidable problem of interpreting data that are often of unknown reliability and are sometimes actually known to distort what they claim to represent. Much of the energy of Western scholars, therefore, has had to be diverted from the important study of the causes and effects of Soviet economic expansion to a painstaking reconstruction of independent appraisals of its actual speed and extent. Moreover, however neces-

[6] Gregory Grossman, "Soviet Statistics of Physical Output of Industrial Commodities: Their Compilation and Quality." (Draft of a forthcoming study to be published by the National Bureau of Economic Research, Inc., New York.)

sary the sacrifice has been, this diversion of valuable human resources to the dreariest sort of detective work could, at best, yield alternative answers that are suggestive, but can never fully resolve the uncertainties and ambiguities of the raw data on which all such reappraisals must ultimately rest. In short, despite its recent easing, the restrictive and propagandistic Soviet information policy continues to impose on us a heavy burden of statistical compilation and interpretation and succeeds in seriously impeding our ability to reconstruct a reliable balanced, and undistorted statistical image of Soviet progress.

THE PROBLEM OF AGGREGATION

A quite different kind of problem in making comparisons arises from the inherent limitations of the economist's tools of measurement. It is easy enough for us to measure changes in output of individual, homogeneous commodities, or services. Thus, growth in steel output can be revealed with reasonable precision when measured in metric tons, production of refrigerators when counted in number of units, and the availability of housing can be reflected at least with quantitative accuracy in terms of square meters of floor space. But as soon as we begin to ask more comprehensive questions—such as: How much has total industrial production increased? to what extent has the level of consumption improved? what has been the rate and direction of investment?—we run head on into the "index number problem." For the answers to such questions depend on the synthetic measure we use to combine the various different products or services involved into a single generalized product or service. This means that we must decide on the relative importance, the "weights," that we should assign to the individual components of our generalized measure or "index," while combining them. But there are a number of possible weighting systems that can be employed and a variety of mathematical formulas that might be used in constructing the index, each yielding significantly different answers to the same question. And the divergences in the results tend to be greatest when an economy is experiencing rapid growth, undergoing radical structural changes, and following an uneven path of development, as has been the Soviet experience over much of its 30 years of industrialization history.

An injudicious or reckless choice of weighting procedure and form of an index can lead to enormous bias in results. The official Soviet index of industrial output is often cited as a particularly horrible example of such methodological distortion. Its upward bias has been due, at different times, to at least four different causes: (1) being a gross-value index, its system of price weights (which includes materials costs) has tended to give much greater prominence to the fastest growing "material intensive" components of the index than would have resulted from "value added" weights (which exclude materials costs); (2) gross-value weighting has also meant "double counting" of intermediate products in successive stages of processing, yielding an inflated figure for the absolute volume of output in any given year; (3) the weight-base used by the index until 1950 was the fixed price structure of the year 1926–27, which is remote in time and which is bound to yield a much higher overall index than would have emerged if mid-industrialization or postindustrialization prices had been used; and (4) new goods that were not produced in the base year were allowed to enter the index at the prices of the first year of series production, thus overweighting these new products both because of the general price inflation that had occurred and because of higher early production costs.

Confronted with such an obvious and perhaps intentional pattern of bias, Western scholars have tried to discover possible shortcuts for measuring Soviet industrial growth independently. These shortcuts took the form of selecting one or a small number of economic indicators and accepting their rate of advance as approximations to the growth of industry as a whole. For example, the consumption of minerals and the railroad freight turnover in ton-kilometers were used as indicators on the grounds that they reproduce the trend of industrial output quite faithfully in the United States. Or, on a more subtle plane, an attempt was made to use as indicators the growth rates of fuel, steel, and power consumption, combining these into a formula that gave the nearest approximation to the growth rates of total manufacturing in 15 Western countries.[7] But all of these simplifications, while they circumvent the worst of the index number problems, do have one defect in common: they assume that the functional relationships that can be observed in the United States or in the West between the chosen indicators and total output also prevail in the U.S.S.R., an assumption that is both questionable and unverifiable.

Given the limitations of these shortcuts, a number of Western scholars have undertaken the arduous and risky task of trying for an independent reconstruction of the record of Soviet industrial expansion by compiling as many individual commodity series as possible and then aggregating them by means of certain chosen weights. For the Western observer, looking at the Soviet economy from the other side of a very thick curtain, the attempt to estimate industrial growth by accounting separately for each of its innumerable components and then selecting an acceptable method of combining them into a single index, encounters formidable difficulties of measurement in general and dilemmas of aggregation in particular. The reliability of such indexes is inevitably impaired by our inability to achieve a representative product coverage relative to the total product mix and by the impossibility of knowing for sure what weights it would be proper to attach. There is no real way of resolving these difficulties; it is possible only to reduce their impact by measuring in a number of ways, by constructing different index forms and by experimenting with a variety of systems of weights. In the final analysis, the degree of success achieved depends in large measure on the care and circumspection with which the results are analyzed and used.

Differences Over Time and Space

So far we have discussed and lamented the more narrowly technical difficulties of comparison occasioned by the deficiencies of the data and the limitations of our tools of measurement. We turn now briefly to a quite different but related category of pitfalls that are placed in our path, namely, those arising from the profound diversities and disparities that exist between the two economies over time and space. There is, first, the uniqueness of the direction and path of economic growth followed by the U.S.S.R.; second, the dearth of what might be

[7] See Francis Seton, "The Tempo of Soviet Industrial Expansion," paper read before the Manchester Statistical Society, Jan. 9, 1957.

called normal periods of development in Soviet history, undisturbed by natural or manmade disasters; and third, the less advanced stage and level of economic maturity attained by the Soviet economy relative to that of the United States. Since these differences can easily distort the meaning of our comparisons, a brief comment on each may be in order.

First, the special character of Soviet economic growth. The great unevenness of Soviet economic development becomes immediately and strikingly apparent to any Western visitor to the U.S.S.R. One is struck by the degree to which the economically efficient, the technologically modern exist side by side with the inefficient and backward; by the extent to which some segments of the economy have been radically transformed in the course of the last 30 years, while others have remained virtually stagnant. This unevenness of development is, of course, the result largely of consciously adopted policies and priorities. For since the industrialization drive began, Soviet resources and energies have been mobilized as in no other country toward the attainment of two goals: industrial power and military might. This has meant not only that Soviet industry underwent swift and radical changes as a whole, but also that growth rates diverged widely from one branch of industry to another. The "primacy of heavy industry" resulted in enormous increases in the output of producers' and military goods, but in only very modest increases in manufactured consumers' goods. Broad general indexes of industrial production, consequently, are not very revealing instruments for reconstructing a balanced record of Soviet growth, since they conceal from us these important structural disparities. Moreover, for technical reasons which need not be explored here, such indexes may be greatly affected in their numerical value by the course of expansion that the economy followed and may show a greater or lesser rate of growth than in fact occurred. These measurement difficulties are not, of course, confined to the field of industry. They confront us with equal intensity in many other fields, particularly in the sphere of living standards, where structural changes have been, if anything, even more perplexing. For rapid urbanization in a peasant country involves radical changes in the mode of life, and causes large shifts in the composition of urban consumption.

The Soviet urban dweller, for example, has available to him now much more of the social amenities, urban services, and modern manufactured consumers goods, but he has benefited little, if at all, from any increase (per capita) in housing, clothing, or the more highly nutritive foodstuffs. And so far as peasants are concerned, their levels of consumption may well have shown no increase at all since the beginning of collectivization. With such an uneven record and given the enormous shifts which have occurred, our statistical yardsticks tend to become warped and any overall judgment on trends in per capita consumption become extremely hazardous.

A second problem of comparison over time and space is the absence, in Soviet economic history, of anything that might be called a moderately long period of undisturbed development. The first dozen years or so of the Soviet era were turbulent, indeed, being marked by war, revolution, and civil war, followed by economic collapse from which the system did not recover until 1928. Only then did the regime's industrialization drive as such take off. And Soviet industrialization itself was anything but a smooth and steady process. The first 8 years, from 1928 through 1936, represent a most intense and hectic example of the early stages of "forced industrialization," during which both the growth achieved and the mistakes made were enormous. These years established the institutional framework and the basic locational pattern of the economy. The years 1937 through 1940, however, were the years of the great purges and the gradual mobilization for war, which diverted manpower increments from the labor force to the army and shifted resources from investment to defense; growth during these years, consequently, was more or less consciously sacrificed to the needs of security. World War II, beginning in 1941, was of course a major economic calamity for the U.S.S.R., from which it took until about 1950 to recover fully.

Perhaps the most "normal" period of modern Soviet growth has been the years since 1950, which have been years of steady though gradually slowing expansion of the sort which Walt W. Rostow might describe as "the homestretch on the drive to maturity." But this is a very brief and recent span of history which hardly provides us a sufficiently long perspective to permit us to establish a meaningful long-term record of accomplishment or to make any judgments about the growth-generating capacity of the Soviet economy. The unfortunate fact of the matter is that, no matter how hard we try, we are simply not able to compute or distill a satisfactory long-term trend out of such an erratic and heterogeneous period of history, and synthetic attempts in this direction tend to be deceptive and misleading.[8] A truly balanced historical perspective of the long-term Soviet growth performance relative to our own is likely always to elude us; but to the extent that we are interested in prediction, our best hope lies in more intense observation of the more or less normal subperiods of Soviet economic development, in a continuing analysis of rates of growth in the most recent period and in a careful consideration of those new trends and developments on the Soviet scene that are most likely to make for acceleration or retardation of its future growth.

I have mentioned a third impediment to our comparisons over time and space, namely the disparity in the levels of economic maturity attained by the two economies. Our difficulty here stems largely from the fact that we understand relatively little about the general process of economic development, the evolution which Simon Kuznets calls "the spread of the industrial system across the face of the earth".[9] Since the process is still incomplete and we ourselves are still experiencing its constant changes, we are simply too close to it, too enmeshed in it, to be able fully to comprehend its origins, to trace the speed and direction of its course, and to discern its possible destinations. In a general way we recognize that the Soviet economy is still today in an earlier phase of economic development than that of the United States. Its "takeoff" occurred perhaps 50 years later than

[8] My alarm here is not occasioned solely by calculations that treat the entire Soviet era or the Soviet industrialization era as a single period, in the manner of G. Warren Nutter who selects 1913–55 and 1928–55 as significant periods of Soviet experience for comparison with the United States. (See his interesting article "Soviet Economic Growth," in Science, vol. 130, No. 3370, July 31, 1959.) My reservations apply also, though with much less force, to calculations that seek to eliminate entirely the abnormal periods, concentrating only on more or less undisturbed periods of growth, as in G. Grossman's ingenious telescoping of the Soviet plan era into 22 "effective years" of growth. (See his "Thirty Years of Soviet Industrialization," Soviet Survey, October 1958.)

[9] S. Kuznets, "Notes on the Study of Economic Growth," items, vol. 13, No. 2, June 1959.

that of the United States[10] and it is now beginning to attain a stage of maturity through which the United States had passed some decades earlier. But it is drawing abreast of the mature industrial societies of the West at an infinitely more advanced level of technology and in a fundamentally different social and political setting than that which prevailed in any earlier period of history and one wonders to what extent we can rely on the West's historical precedent to guide our analysis of the Soviet development course.

Has the Soviet economy so far followed the U.S. pattern of structural evolution or does it tend to diverge from it? Is Soviet society as a whole likely to become bored with the miracle of industrialization? Does the process of moving toward maturity contain with in it the seeds of its own modification? Does it generate a trend toward lower growth rates and higher mass consumption? These questions have no easy answers, but they are directly relevant to any comparison of Soviet development with our own, to any attempt to explain the high growth tempos of the past and to our efforts to gage the prospects for future growth or retardation.

We should like to know, for example, whether the high "growth-effectiveness" of investment that we have observed in the Soviet world in the past is likely to be a temporary or a durable phenomenon. We recognize that the Soviet economy, as is true for any latecomer, has enjoyed some advantages from its youth and backwardness. Its fixed capital stock was built relatively recently and is still quite young. A smaller proportion of its gross investment, therefore, has had to be used for replacement than is necessary in the older industrial countries of the West. How will the growth-generating capacity of Soviet investment be affected by a steadily rising burden of maintenance, wear and tear, and obsolescence? Similarly, will diminishing returns set in when the richer and more readily accessible reserves of ores and fuels have been "creamed" and it becomes necessary for the Soviet economy to dig deeper and to go farther afield? Is the past neglect of transport expansion and of unproductive investments such as housing finally beginning to catch up with the Soviet planners and forcing them to divert investment away from the growth-inducing sectors? Perhaps most important, can science and technology alter the pattern? The Soviet economy has benefited immensely, as a latecomer, from the big unapplied backlog of technology that has been available to it. A mature economy, being out at the margin of technology, can in each year draw only on the new technology that it created, say, in the previous year. A latecomer can bring the entire backlog of technology to bear much more rapidly than it had been created.

The ability to utilize the technology of other nations on a mass scale, to take over in their entirety complex readymade techniques and designs under conditions unencumbered by patent laws or other proprietary restrictions has been a tremendous accelerating force for Soviet economic progress. Has the Soviet economy now reached the point of diminishing returns in the borrowing of ideas from abroad or is there much more scope for fruitful copying of Western experience? How do we go about analyzing the distinctive role that science and technology has played and can play in modern economic growth? At

[10] Walt W. Rostow, in a summary of his Cambridge University lectures on economic growth published by The Economist, August 15, 1959, and August 22, 1959, identifies the "takeoff" period for Russia as 1890 to 1914 and that for the United States as 1843 to 1860.

our present stage of knowledge, unfortunately, confident answers to these questions are not within our grasp.

PERSPECTIVE AND FOCUS OF THE COMPARISONS

There seems to be a tendency, in our comparisons between Soviet and United States economic progress, to focus all of our attention on the relative levels of output that the two countries have attained, and to neglect the relative capabilities for using this output that the two countries may possess. Our comparisons tend to dwell at length on the physical problems of production, on the availability of resources and their efficient utilization, and on other factors that determine the relative output capacity, the production successes of the two competitors, but they are little concerned with the tasks and purposes which the output is intended to serve. We worry much about the rapidity of Soviet growth, but rarely inquire into its relevance. Too many of our comparisons assume the form of a kind of numbers racket, in which charts are drawn up of the volume of production in the two countries, with the lines ominously crossing at some more or less distant point in the future. Implicitly we are expected to groan each time the scoreboard shows another Soviet advance and to quaver whenever Soviet output moves closer to ours by another notch. But do such gains in output really represent a significant improvement of the Soviet power position relative to our own, or is it merely a matter of our being outpointed in some meaningless parlor game devised in the Kremlin?

The answer to this question is not entirely clear cut. In an indirect way, surely, there is a relationship between the expansion of a nation's total output and the facts of international relations. A steadily growing volume of production enables a nation, if it so chooses, to divert an ever larger quantity of its economic goods to uses that are designed to enhance its national power and to be worrisome to its opponents—to an enlarged military effort, for example, or to an expanded politico-economic offensive. In this sense, then, economic growth represents a potential power asset; but before this potential can be translated into actual power, further decisions are required about how the added resources are to be allocated. In the Soviet case, of course, given its obsession with the pursuit of national power, it is not difficult to imagine the directions in which these allocation decision will go.

There is also another sense in which Soviet economic growth, as an end in itself, can affect the power balance on the current international scene. The Soviet leaders have made an international symbol out of their ambition to catch up with America in per capita production by 1970. The impact of this symbol could be quite powerful. Not that even Khrushchev expects seriously to achieve such parity of output in any meaningful sense by 1970. He could hardly be that unrealistic. But the exact timing of the "triumph" may be of no consequence, so long as the relative trends continue in the Soviet favor. It is not the sudden tipping of the scales, but the steady and progressive diminution of the U.S. lead that would tend to be most demoralizing to the West and that would give an immense boost to Soviet prestige.

Moreover, such rapid Soviet economic progress would exercise fascination and appeal in the vast parts of the world where speedy economic development has become virtually a prerequiste to political survival. The spectacle of a Soviet economy successfully pursuing rapid economic growth with a sense of utmost urgency is bound to hold strong attractions for the less developed countries and would lend conviction to the Soviet claim that, in the age of industrialism its own style of planned economy is superior to the market economy of the West and that its example constitutes a relevant model of economic development for all of the underdeveloped world.

But aside from these rather indirect effects of economic growth on a nation's power position, it is probably fair to say that the rate of growth offers no meaningful standard for practical power calculations. To the extent that we look to our economic comparisons for insights into larger national policy issues, we must go well beyond the problems of relative rates of growth or relative levels of output, and consider the far more complex questions of how effectively the output is enlisted to advance the national interest and what tasks the output is intended to serve. National power, clearly, does not rest on total output, but on the efficiency and consistency with which a nation is able to use its output to advance its policy objectives. In a comparison of national power, what counts is not parity of output but parity of performance, since even a nation with a much smaller output capacity, a greatly inferior resource base, can easily outperform another, if it is willing to divert a larger proportion of its resources to its national aims, or if it is able to use its resources more efficiently, or if its tasks are simpler and more limited.

Thus, a direct comparison of economic magnitudes, without consideration of these larger contextual matters, can often be quite misleading. A good example of this is our occasional attempts to compare Soviet military expenditures with our own in terms of the relative share of its gross national product that each country devotes to these purposes. How little light such a comparison throws on the relative "adequacy" of these allocations or on relative defense "capabilities" is not always fully appreciated. At best, such a comparison is a measure of relative effort; it can tell us something of the resource burden imposed by the military effort on each country; it does not necessarily reflect the relative output of defense goods. Thus it measures resource "input," but not "yield." Depending on the relative productivity of resources in the two countries, a given share of resource input into defense production may yield a much larger share of defense output in one country than in the other, and our GNP percentage comparison might give us a quite mistaken impression of the relative quantity of defense goods produced. But even if we were able, somehow, accurately to compare the relative quantity of defense output and the size of the military forces of the two countries, it would still be a far cry from a meaningful picture of relative "capabilities." For in order to say anything about the military worth or effectiveness of these forces, we would have to consider the immensely complex strategic factors of any given military situation, the relative efficiency of each country's weapons choice, the role of allies, and much else.

The mere fact, for example, that the Soviet leaders are able to maintain an almost impenetrable blanket of secrecy and concealment over much of their defense activity creates, all by itself, a fundamental imbalance in the military requirements of the United States versus those of the U.S.S.R., imposing a much heavier defense production burden on us, and enabling them to devote a larger share of their resources to the arena of research and development, to which much of the contest for military superiority has now shifted. No amount of direct quantitative economic comparison, clearly, would help us with problems such as these.

Other examples could be cited to illustrate the profound differences in the political tasks and objectives of the two countries and their significance for our comparisons. But perhaps the essential point has been made: A superior U.S. production capacity does not automatically denote superior U.S. national power, nor does the political impact of Soviet resources depend on its achieving parity of output with us. For both countries, it is the effectiveness of the actual performance that counts and this must be measured in the multidimensional framework of a society's will and skill in applying its resources to its national tasks.

PROBLEMS OF UNITED STATES-SOVIET ECONOMIC COMPARISONS

(By Robert W. Campbell, Department of Economics, University of Southern California)

Introduction—Statement of Findings

The purpose of the present paper is to explain in a general way and illustrate with examples some of the most important difficulties involved in making comparisons of the economies of the United States and the Soviet Union. The past decade and a half of research has greatly increased the amount of solid evidence we possess concerning the comparative performance of these two economies. At the same time, however, it has also added greatly to the sophistication of economists concerning the pitfalls that await those who seek to appraise the relative performance of two economies so different as these.

The authors of the substantive comparisons that follow are well aware of these problems and it is not unlikely that some of them will be touched on in the course of the comparisons made. The paper is in no way intended as a critique of their efforts. Nevertheless it seems worth while to give some explicit, prefatory attention to the obstacles that complicate such undertakings. The current world situation has led to widespread recognition by the American people of the need to know more about the relative status of these two economies. Intelligent action on our part in many areas of public policy requires that we know how big Soviet output is in comparison with our own, how effectively the Soviet Union uses its resources by our standards, how fast their output and productivity are increasing, and what allocations the Soviet leaders make of their output.

The following discussion is intended to remind those who ask such questions as these of the limitations on the certainty and precision with which they must content themselves in the answers, and to emphasize the sort of questions they should always raise in evaluating the statistical comparisons offered in answer. By giving separate attention to this subject, it will be possible to make some generalizations about the nature of the problems in a way that is not possible in the substantive comparisons, and to discuss how they can sometimes be dealt with.

The obstacles to United States-Soviet economic comparisons may be said to comprise several distinct orders. It will be helpful to discuss them under three main headings as follows:

(1) The availability and interpretation of statistical data;
(2) The index number problems;
(3) The danger of comparing isolated indicators out of context.

The availability and interpretation of statistical data.—One of the most frustrating problems facing anyone who tries to make United States-Soviet comparisons is in securing the raw materials for his effort, namely the statistical data. This difficulty is most often presented by the Soviet side of the comparison rather than the American, although there are also instances where U.S. data make comparisons difficult. The deficiences of Soviet statistics have often been recited. Although the Soviet system generates a huge volume of statistical information, the amount actually released by the Government is limited in amount, the meaning of data in terms of its coverage or definition is often left unexplained, figures are presented in a misleading way with the aim of serving propaganda purposes or ideological pretensions. In many cases, particularly in the case of complex economic indicators, such as output indexes or aggregative magnitudes the Soviet statements are completely unreliable.

The amount of economic data published by the Soviet Government has varied greatly over time. In the years before the industrialization drive, and even for some time after the beginning of the 5-year plans in the early thirties, statistical information was relatively abundant. Subsequently, however, it dwindled in amount until by the end of the thirties only isolated scraps were published. This mania for secrecy continued until Stalin's death in 1953. Since then the publication policy for statistical information has changed drastically, and the amount of information released has been greatly increased. There have now appeared a larger number of statistical handbooks; the periodical economic literature has begun to include some discussion of real problems based on real data. One now even finds serious monographs discussing individual aspects of the economy which contain actual data that has not yet been blessed with the official imprimatur of release in an official speech or document. Of course, the Soviet statistical output is still only a tiny trickle compared to the mass of economic data that is available for the U.S. half of economic comparisons. A suggestive measure of this difference in volume is found in the size of the major statistical sources concerning the industry of the two countries. The Soviet statistical handbook for industry contains a little less than 35,000 bits of data.

Many of these, however, represent mere recapitulations of absolute data in percentage form, so that the actual amount of information is not much over 30,000 bits.[1] Volume II of the U.S. census of manufactures, by contrast, contains something more of the order of half a million numbers. Moreover, the Soviet source completely ignores a number of important categories of statistics. As far as the handbook is concerned, there is no such thing as an industrial labor force or a nonferrous metals industry, although there are many pages of information on such uninteresting matters as the geographic distribution of the production of gypsum, lime, brick, slate, tile, and timber. The distorted perspective of the handbook means that much of the information it contains is not very useful. Of course, much additional statistical information on Soviet industry can be culled from other Soviet sources, though proportionately these are much less rich sources than similar ones in the United States. The example of industrial statistics is representative of the whole gamut of information and suggests how asymmetrical are the sources of information underlying comparisons.

A second aspect of the information problem has to do with the interpretation of the data which the Soviet Government does vouch-

[1] "Tsentral'noe Statisticheskoe Upravlenie," Promyshlennost' SSSR, Moscow, 1957.

safe us. The statistical sources for industry again provide a suggestive comparison. All the text and explanatory notes in the Soviet handbook would not add up to more than about seven pages, whereas the census of manufactures contains several hundred pages of explanation. Moreover, in the U.S. source the lavish use of detailed breakdowns helps greatly to clarify the composition and scope of the data.

The importance of clarity in statistical definitions warrants additional explanation. The difficulty is that it is possible for a notion which appears on the surface to be perfectly straightforward to be defined in a number of different ways and hence ambiguous in meaning unless the scope is clearly stated. Many of these apparently simple concepts actually have a number of dimensions that make alternative definitions conceivable. When one sets out to embody even such a notion as the output of electric power in numbers drawn from the actual workings of an economy, decisions must be made as to what producers will be included, at what point output will be measured, and so forth. This point can be illustrated with examples drawn from an actual exercise in comparison. Suppose that it is desired to compare the total industrial output of the United States with that of the Soviet Union, and it is decided to approach this problem by determining the relative outputs for as exhaustive a list of commodities as we can manage. The final step would be to weight these separate comparisons of output by some notion of the relative importance of each commodity (such as value added or employment) to obtain a single index expressing the overall relative output. In table I a few of the commodities that would be included in such a comparison have been listed and columns (1) and (2) show the outputs of these commodities in each country as given in the Soviet industrial handbook, and the Statistical Abstract of the United States. Column (3) shows the ratio of Soviet output to U.S. output.

TABLE I.—*Comparison of selected commodity outputs in the United States and Soviet Union*

	Year	Unit of measure	United States	U.S.S.R.	U.S.S.R. as percent of United States
Electric power	1957	Billion kilowatt-hours	716.0	209.5	29.3
Coal	1956	Million short tons	529.8	472.1	89.1
Cotton cloth	1957	Million linear yards	9,563.0	6,119.0	64.0
Oil	1956	Million metric tons	364.0	83.8	23.0
Natural gas	1956	Billion cubic feet	10,082.0	483.0	4.8
Lumber	1957	Million board-feet	37,698.0	32,204.0	85.4

The specialist on the Soviet economy will immediately suggest many corrections that will have to be made in these numbers before they can be used as the raw material for a comparison of industrial output. For example, the first item on the list—electric power—is defined in the Soviet Union as the total output of power produced by the generators, gross of the amounts used or lost within the generating plant itself, whereas the U.S. figure is net of this amount. Fortunately the Russians tell us how much of the power generated goes for the needs of the stations themselves, so that it is possible to correct the Soviet figure to U.S. terms in this dimension. When the correction is made, it changes the comparison markedly, reducing Soviet output from 29.3 percent of U.S. output to 27.5 percent. There are uncertainties in some other dimensions as well, however. In both countries electric power is produced both by specialized utility plants, and by industrial plants for their own use. The output of most of these nonutility plants is included in the total for both countries, but the cutoff point is apparently not the same in both cases. For the United States the output of industrial plants covers only those with a capacity of 100 kilowatts and over, but it is clear from the statistics in Promyshlennost' SSSR, page 176, that the Soviet figure includes the production of plants much smaller than this. This difference again involves an appreciable fraction of output—namely, about 2.1 percent of total Soviet output in 1955.

For coal, the next item in the list, even cursory examination of the sources raises a suspicion that there may be an important difference in coverage. The U.S. figure is defined as mine shipments, mine sales, or marketable production, including consumption by producers. This seems to imply that it is measured after preparatory processes such as cleaning and sorting, and one breakdown in the Statistical Abstract of the United States gives a figure of 58.7 percent as the percentage of total production mechanically cleaned. The Soviet figure, on the other hand, may well involve measurement before these processes. Some 26 percent of Soviet coal output was sent to beneficiation plants in 1955, and in the process underwent a reduction in volume of 11.9 percent. So total output after processing was 3.08 percent less than the figure shown in table I. A second difference is that the U.S. figure for bituminous coal output covers mines with an annual output of 1,000 tons or more. It seems probable that the Soviet total would not make such an exclusion, though there are no data to indicate how important this difference in scope would be.

This possible divergence in the meaning of the coal figure also serves as a reminder that even though the output of many commodities is measured in physical units, comparison in these terms may be deceptive, since the commodity may not be at all homogenous with respect to quality or some other dimension. This problem becomes most important when one is dealing with highly fabricated products, but is also serious even with commodities which seem to have easily indentifiable physical measures, such as those in table I. For instance, the figures on output of cotton cloth, given in table I in lineal yards as commonly measured in the statistics of both countries, are not at all comparable, since the average width of cotton goods produced in the United States is slightly over 40 inches, whereas it is slightly under 30 inches in the Soviet Union.

In the case of coal and electric power, the explanations in Soviet statistical sources are clear enough to make one aware of the differences in concept, though for neither country are the data detailed enough to permit bringing both figures to a common concept. For many commodities, however, the degree of comparability cannot be so easily ascertained. Output figures for the next two items on the list, i.e., oil and natural gas, are easily found in Soviet sources, but when U.S. sources are consulted for comparable data, it turns out that the petroleum extraction industry has another important output, namely, natural gasoline and natural gas liquids, equal in volume to about 10 percent of the crude oil output. These products are undoubtedly much less important in Soviet operations but must surely exist. Since they are not mentioned in the statistical source, one wonders whether they are perhaps included somehow in the oil output figure.

The notion of lumber output appears superficially to be a fairly simple idea, and the fact that the figures for both the United States and the Soviet Union are expressed in terms of physical volume is comforting. But even the briefest survey of U.S. statistical sources will disclose a number of alternative figures for lumber output differing slightly from each other in concept and accordingly in amount. To which of these concepts does the Soviet figure correspond? Moreover, if the breakdown given in the census of manufactures are examined a number of possible differences in concept immediately suggest themselves. The U.S. output figures cover sawmills and planing mills, and includes both rough and finished lumber. Since the U.S. figures are collected on an establishment basis, there is probably some double counting of lumber sawed in one plant and finished in another. To what extent is this true of the Soviet total? Furthermore, suppose a Soviet enterprise both rough-saws and finishes lumber; is its output measured in terms of the volume of the finished or unfinished wood? Careful study may succeed in unearthing answers to these questions, but the answers are not at all obvious from the statistical sources themselves, from handbooks on industrial statistical procedure or from the more generally available books dealing with the economics, planning, and administration of the lumber industry.

It should be admitted that definitions are not always presented along with statistics in the more general U.S. statistical publications. Nevertheless it is almost always possible to find in easily accessible sources detailed explanations of what a given statistic covers and how it has been derived. The difficulty of doing this for the U.S.S.R. often introduces an air of uncertainty into comparisons such as those in table I.

The existence of differences between the concepts underlying Soviet and U.S. economic data should not be surprising. Comparison of the statistics of any two countries will always reveal similar inconsistencies. They flow out of differences in the organization of the economy, different statistical traditions, divergent preoccupations among those who collect statistics. Statistics are often a byproduct of some concern other than economic analysis and their definition is controlled in part by competing objectives and expediencies. What is peculiar to Soviet statistical practice, however, is the great premium which the Russians place on the propaganda use of economic indicators, and in the service of this end concepts are sometimes deliberately defined in a misleading way. This propaganda objective is one of the explanations for their secretiveness concerning the actual definitions of the statistical material they publish. The propaganda uses of Soviet economic statistics also mean that definitions are sometimes changed to mask failure or exaggerate gains. The most infamous example of such a change is the shift from the "barn yield" concept to the "biological yield" concept of grain output in the thirties, adopted to make grain output appear larger than it actually was. Even though it was possible to find out from Soviet sources that this change in definition had been made, the appropriate correction to achieve comparability with a barn-yield concept remained unknown. Not until Khrushchev's speech to the plenary session of the Central Committee in December 1958, was it revealed precisely how great the difference was. The figures he cited for 1952, i.e., barn yield as 30 percent less than the biological yield, involved a bigger difference than had commonly been estimated. A more recent example of the subversion of intertemporal and international comparability to propaganda objectives is the change in the definitions of meat and milk output. Khrushchev has made catching up with the United States in meat and milk production one of the important goals of his agricultural program, and to make the fulfillment of this goal easier, the scope of the definitions of meat and milk output has been broadened beyond past definitions and beyond the American concepts.

The examples discussed so far all involve a very simple class of economic magnitudes, namely, physical outputs. The possible differences in concept that can confound comparison in such cases are multiplied many fold when one turns to more complex statistical indicators. Any attempt at qualification of such complicated concepts as gross national product accounts, labor force and employment statistics, or output indexes, offers so many conceivable alternatives in conceptualization, and involves so many expediencies in implementing the concept with data, that it may be impossible to make any reasonably accurate reconciliation of the actual numbers that the statistical systems of the two countries actually generate. The Soviet concept of national income is far different from that accepted in most capitalist countries, for instance. Although we know in a general way many of the differences between the United States and Soviet concepts in this case, there are still many unanswered questions concerning the Soviet definitions, such as how they make the division of total output into an "accumulation fund" and a "consumption fund," for example. For many of these complicated indicators, the differences in concept and the uncertainty of interpretation are so great that economists outside the Soviet Union have traditionally rejected Soviet data and resorted to independent calculations from basic data.

Deficiencies in the statistical raw materials on which comparisons are based are not confined to the Soviet Union. There are also cases where the U.S. side of a comparison may be obscure. Inventory statistics may be cited as a single illustration. Recent data on Soviet inventories have included a number of breakdowns that make it possible to ascertain fairly well the range of items that are included in the Soviet inventory concept, and our knowledge of Soviet accounting practices makes it possible to state more or less precisely how inventory values are calculated. In many ways the U.S. inventory figures [2] are more detailed than the Soviet ones, but variations in the accounting practices of individual firms makes it impossible to state with certainty just how comprehensive these figures are in terms of the items included and the basis of valuation. It may well be that there is a difference in the scope of the inventory concept and as a result comparisons using these data may be misleading.

Finally, it frequently happens that the concepts relevant to some comparison in which we are vitally interested are not well enough defined to be embodied very satisfactorily in actual statistical data in either country. The vagueness of what is being measured means that the definitions used in generating the data are chosen somewhat

[2] For an explanation of the uncertainties involved in the meaning of U.S. inventory statistics, see George M. Cobren, "The Nonfarm Business Inventory Component," in National Bureau of Economic Research Studies in Income and Wealth, vol. XII, pp. 381–400.

arbitrarily. For example, speculation about the relative efforts of the United States and the Soviet Union in science and in research has recently become a popular enterprise in economic comparison. As one of the main ingredients of technical progress both in military and civilian applications, the amount of research is supposed to be a powerful influence on our respective power and growth possibilities. The Russians, incidentally, are also interested in this comparison. In the United States, this aspect of national economic activity has been labeled research and development, and some statistics purporting to show how many dollars worth of research and development are being carried out have been published in recent years. These statistics have been strongly criticized, however, as arbitrary in definition and vague in meaning. After all, this is a very new concept and effort, and those who report such expenditures at the local level face many unsettled questions in deciding how much research and development their firm does.

The Russians call this activity science, and in the past few years Soviet leaders have quoted a figure showing a global total for this magnitude. This Soviet figure, however, represents more a reflection of certain budgetary and administrative conventions than any well-defined concept of effort devoted to the expansion of knowledge and improvement of technology. The uncertainty in any comparison of the Soviet and American research efforts, therefore, is not so much due to the fact that the specific content of the respective ruble and dollar amounts differs, as to the fact that neither of these amounts measures very exactly just what we would like to measure.

The discussion above has concentrated on the obstacles to obtaining comparable statistical raw materials as a basis for comparative studies of the United States and Soviet economies. To restore a balanced perspective, it should be added in concluding this section that most of these problems can be dealt with tolerably well. Finding data and establishing their meaning is the expected task of any economist who sets out to make comparisons of the two economies. Given experience and enough time he can usually settle such issues as those described with an acceptable margin of error. These are obstacles that will succumb to knowledge, and the recent increase in Soviet statistical output is beginning to clarify some former mysteries. So far, however, the problem has only been ameliorated, not eliminated. When a researcher is unable to deal with some data problem satisfactorily, he has a duty to present his figures with an appropriate statement of reservations. Similarly, those who make use of the comparative studies that are made must know that such problems exist, that they cannot always be settled completely satisfactorily, and that comparisons made in this situation are always subject to some qualifications. Hence, they should always ask for the qualifications and alternative interpretations along with the answers.

The index number problem.—The second order of obstacles to international economic comparisons comprises a number of variants of what is known as the index number problem. These obstacles differ from those discussed earlier by the fact that they do not result simply from ignorance but rather from a number of unanswered, and perhaps unanswerable questions of theory and conceptualization. They are therefore more intractable than those discussed in the previous section. The index number problem arises whenever one tries to compare relatively large aggregates either between countries or over time. Most of the questions which international economic comparisons are designed to answer involve the comparative measurement of such large aggregates. The question of relative American and Soviet economic strength, for example, is usually posed as the size of Soviet output relative to our own, as measured by some indicator such as gross national product. Or people may ask for comparisons of smaller but still very heterogeneous components of this aggregate. It is common, for example to ask how well off the average Soviet consumer or industrial worker is relative to his opposite number in the United States. Those who are responsible for making U.S. defense policy would like to know how the Soviet military effort compares with our own in terms of its overall size. Making comparisons in these aggregative terms is the only way to escape getting lost in a host of contradictory details.

Economic aggregates such as those listed above can be measured only in value terms. The diverse physical goods and services encompassed in American or Soviet gross national product can be expressed in a single figure only through using the common denominator of monetary value. Hence, if it is desired to compare Soviet and American gross national product it is necessary to find some conversion factor, some exchange rate, that permits one to translate the rubles of one into the dollars of the other, or vice versa. Unfortunately, however, it so happens that the value of a ruble, expressed in how many dollars worth of output can be bought with it, varies markedly depending on the kind of product or service that is being considered. The structure of relative prices in the two countries is very different, so that the value of a ruble compared to a dollar is far greater in the purchase of some items than of others. This difference between the Soviet and American price structure is the result of many separate factors, including differences in the scarcities of the resources going into different commodities, the differential degree to which the Russians have caught up with American technology in different sectors of the economy, and the peculiarities of Soviet accounting, pricing, and fiscal practices. Hence any even moderately aggregative magnitude contains components for which the appropriate dollar-ruble conversion ratios diverge widely. The problem is to find an average ratio appropriate to the conversion of the aggregate we are interested in. The approach that springs immediately to mind is to average the individual conversion ratios, weighted by the relative importance of the various components of the aggregate.

The problem, however, is that the relative importance of the components is different in the two countries. As a result, there is a choice of weighting patterns and a choice of conversion ratios. The problem can be illustrated by the simple numerical example shown in the following table, in which the gross national product of two countries is compared. This example outrages reality in assuming that all gross national product is directed either to consumption or to military purposes, but this oversimplification makes the nature of the problem easier to see. We have called the two countries the United States and the Soviet Union, although the magnitudes shown for the gross national product and its components in each case are completely arbitrary. The proportions between consumption and military uses, however, and the implied difference in the price structures of the two countries are plausible reflections of reality. Columns (1) and (2) show the composition of the gross national product in each country measured in its own prices. Column (3) shows the value of a ruble in dollars in the purchase of the goods included in the respective components of the gross national product. Using these figures as conversion ratios, it is possible to calculate the size of each country's gross national product in the currency of the other. The results are shown in columns (4) and (5). There are now enough totals so that the gross national product can be compared either in dollars or in rubles, but a glance at the figures shows that the result will not be the same for both comparisons. When the output of both countries is measured in United States prices, Soviet output appears to be one-third as large as that of the United States, but if a comparison is made in Soviet prices, Soviet output turns out to be only 28.5 percent of American.

TABLE II.—*Schematic illustration of the index number problem*

	U.S.S.R. (in billion rubles) (1)	United States (in billion dollars) (2)	Conversion rate (dollars per ruble) (3)	U.S.S.R. (in billion dollars) (4)	United States (in billion rubles) (5)
Consumption	100	40	.10	10	400
Military expenditure	20	5	.25	5	20
Total	120	45		15	420

NOTE.—Soviet output as a percentage of United States output:
In rubles: 120÷420=28.6 percent.
In dollars: 15÷45=33.3 percent.

What is the reason for this difference in the two answers? A rigorous explanation would involve going into the complexities of index number construction, but the essence of the mechanism at work can be explained as follows. Pricing in rubles is equivalent to converting total gross national product at an exchange rate of 10.71 cents per ruble, 10.71 being the average of the separate ruble-dollar price ratios, weighted in proportion to the relative magnitudes of the components of U.S. gross national product as they would look to a Russian. Valuation in dollars, on the other hand, amounts to the use of a conversion ratio of 12.5 cents per ruble, 12.5 being the average of 10 and 25, weighted by the relative importance of consumption and military expenditures as they would look to one accustomed to American prices.

The same mechanism can also be explained in somewhat different terms though with equivalent meaning. In the U.S. price system, consumer goods are priced cheaper relative to military goods than in the Soviet price system. We have indicated this difference in price structure in table II in an approximate illustrative way by the exchange rates shown in column (3). These conversion rates imply that a dollar's worth of consumer goods would be worth 10 rubles in the Soviet Union, but a dollar's worth of military goods would be worth only 4 rubles. Ruble valuation of the output of either country will therefore magnify the significance of the consumption component of its gross national product and diminish the significance of the military component, compared with valuation in dollars. Since the composition of Soviet gross national product differs from the U.S. pattern

46283—59—pt. 1——3

by its relatively higher emphasis on military expenditure, it will look bigger relative to the U.S. total when both are seen in the light of a price system which prices military goods relatively high and consumption goods relatively low (i.e., the dollar price system) than in the light of one that has high prices for consumer goods and low prices for military goods (the ruble price system).

This ambiguity of answers in international comparisons is not uncommon. Whenever the price structures and the composition of aggregates vary between countries, different answers about the relative size of the aggregates will be obtained, depending on which country's prices are used. The greater the differences in price relationships and in composition, the greater will be the difference between the alternative answers. There are appreciable differences between the alternative measures of relative size of gross national product even when the U.S. is compared with countries with relatively high productivity and modern technologies such as Great Britain or Germany.[3] When comparisons are attempted between the United States and countries where allocation and price structures are more radically different, such as Italy or the Soviet Union, the degree of indeterminacy is even greater.

What guidance can be offered the person who finds that the answer to his simple question about the relative size of the United States and Soviet economies is given in the form of an indeterminate range? In terms of the example in table II, is the figure of 33.3 percent or 28.6 percent the "correct" figure for the size of the Soviet gross national product relative to our own? The answer to this puzzle turns on the fact that the two numbers represent answers to two different questions. The comparison made in rubles (i.e., the one showing the Soviet gross national product as 28.6 percent of American) answers the question "How big is Soviet output?" if it is assumed that it was as hard for them to produce a given collection of consumer goods relative to, say, a missile, as in the United States. The figure ot 33.3 percent answers the question "How big was it?" if we assume that in the United States a given basket of consumer goods was priced as high relative to a missile as in the Soviet Union. One might argue that neither of these questions is "realistic." The relative prices of consumer goods and military goods are not the same in both countries. The questioner did not intend it should be pretended they were when he asked how big Soviet output was relative to ours. This is perhaps true enough, but the researcher is forced to such expediencies in trying to make the comparison at all. The problem is that what appeared on the face of it to be a straightforward question; namely, "How big is Soviet output relative to our own?" really begs important issues, issues which the statistician must settle explicitly when he gets down to the mechanics of formulating a numerical answer. And though one may object that the way the statisticians have traditionally settled these issues (i.e., by seeing Soviet cutput in the light of U.S. value relationships or U.S. output in terms ot Soviet scarcity relationships), he will find it difficult to suggest any more satisfactory approach. In a fundamental sense the two aggregates are not directly comparable, and the traditional approach has

[3] See Milton Gilbert & Associates, "Comparative National Products and Price Levels," Paris, 1958, OEEC, for illustrations of the differences that alternative pricing makes in comparing U.S. output with some countries of Western Europe.

at least the virtue of marking out the limits that one might reasonably wish to set conceptually.

The above example is only one variant of the index number problem; even when comparisons involve much smaller aggregates than gross national product the same difficulty arises. In the numerical example of table II, for instance, it was assumed that a ruble is worth 10 cents in the purchase of consumption goods and 25 cents in buying the inputs of a military program. But how can a conversion ratio for such a component of gross national product be arrived at in the first place? Each of these aggregates (i.e., consumption and military expenditures) is itself a heterogeneous collection of goods and services, the composition of which varies between the two countries. Furthermore, the purchasing power of a ruble in terms of dollars is very different as between, say shelter and bread or between the maintenance of a soldier and the building of a missile. This means that one would have to choose among alternative weighting systems in order to compute conversion ratios for the separate components of gross national product before the problem of gross national product comparison could even be formulated as in table II. The existence of a range of possible values for the conversion ratio applicable to consumption or to military goods means that the range between the extremes of relative gross national product magnitudes would be even greater.

Another well-known variant of the index number problem arises in the calculation of rates of growth of various economic magnitudes such as industrial output, consumption levels, labor productivity, or others. In such problems it is necessary to determine the relative size of a given aggregate (e. g., consumption or industrial output) at two different points in time. Characteristically, the composition and the price structures for such aggregates change over time. (In the Soviet Union the changes in composition and price relationships have been exceptionally great.) The problem is formally identical with that of international comparisons of aggregates, and the same indeterminacy arises. In this case, however, there are good grounds for arguing that extremes at the ends of the range of possible answers flowing from different weighting systems can be ignored and something like the geometric mean of the extremes taken as an acceptable measure of the rate of growth. The sharp difference in weighting patterns chosen from points far distant in time is a function of how far apart the terminal dates of the comparison are. By looking at shorter periods, the changes in structure and price relationships are found to be less important, and the range of estimates of growth is greatly reduced.

What implications does the index number problem hold for those who seek to make reliable comparisons of the United States and Soviet economies? (1) First, the existence of this problem allows a certain degree of subjective latitude to the person making a comparison. In comparing aggregates, or in measuring rates of growth in each system he has a choice of many alternative weighting systems, with no clearly, defined theory to indicate that one of them is better than the other. Despite this uncertainty, however, it is more or less customary to present answers as if they could be expressed in a single number. This is what we are accustomed to in statistical measures of our own economic performance, and those who ask for economic comparisons in the first place expect exact answers. People who want to determine policy on the basis of comparative studies that are made should take a somewhat critical point of view toward whatever numbers they are offered, and must understand how certain decisions made in the course of the calculations are reflected in the results. A corollary implication is that they should not fix on any one extreme figure among the many that are presented, but be prepared to think in terms of a range.

(2) A second implication is that the vagueness which flows from the index number problem can often be reduced somewhat by greater purposiveness in the comparisons that are made. As the one who asks for a comparison makes his question more precise and defines its purpose more clearly, it will generally be possible to find a reasonable basis for choosing among alternatives in concept and in weighting systems. Global comparisons such as the relative size of United States and Soviet total output have their uses, and there are good and sufficient reasons why they will continue to be made.

However, it often turns out that such comparisons are only a prelude to some more specific comparisons that the questioner is really interested in. For instance one common objective is to determine the relative economic power of the two countries in some sense, say their ability to support military programs, or their capability to engage in foreign trade and extend foreign aid. To answer such a question, it is tempting to take a figure on Soviet GNP in dollars from somewhere, apply to it the percentage share going to military purposes, perhaps from some other study, and get two figures expressed in dollars. Such a procedure is treacherous. At best it can give a very indeterminate answer. Choosing from the extremes at either end of the figures available for GNP in dollars and the share devoted to military purposes, one can get an absurdly wide range of estimates of Soviet military spending in dollars. This approach is at its worst when the figure on the percentage of GNP devoted to military uses comes from a calculation different in concept from the one underlying the total accepted for GNP. If the question is about relative size of the military effort, then it is much more useful to make this comparison directly. This makes it possible to work with smaller aggregates, which are less heterogeneous as far as price relatives and composition are concerned than GNP as a whole. The degree of vagueness inherent in the index number problem is therefore reduced. The latter approach may also stimulate one to think out more clearly just how to measure the power created by a given military budget, and suggest principles for adding up Soviet men and hardware for comparison with American that are more reasonable than those implicit but not clearly understood in the roundabout method of applying a percentage to a GNP figure in dollars.

Another common exercise in these comparisons is to ask how soon the Russians will catch up with us in GNP or in some element of it such as industrial output. By estimating the relative size of the chosen economic indicator at the present time, and then projecting each of them forward at some rate of growth a date for the Russian catching up emerges. Because of the wide range of relative sizes that one can start with, and the wide choice of growth rates (reflecting in both cases the index number problem) it is possible to determine a period for the catching up process varying from a decade and a half to four or five decades. What is the purpose of a question that cannot be answered more definitely than that? Part of the indeterminacy comes from the fact that it is not clear what the comparison is aimed to show. If the question one ultimately wants to answer is something like "how soon will Soviet machinery output be great enough to cover a program of investment, trade, and military expenditure such as ours, then it might be more nearly answerable with an acceptable degree of exactness.

Dangers in comparing isolated indicators out of context.—The third order of obstacles to meaningful comparisons of the American and Soviet economies involves the possibility of misinterpreting fairly specific indicators through ignoring important features of the context. If the index number problem makes the comparison of large aggregates difficult, at the other extreme differences in organization, in technology, and in resource availabilities often make comparisons of very narrowly defined magnitudes or overly specific indicators misleading. The Soviet and American economies differ from each other markedly in administrative structure, in the resource endowment within which each must operate, and in technology. Consequently the significance of a given economic indicator often varies between them.

In their zeal to make some comparison appear better than it really is, the Russians are frequently guilty of overlooking such differences. For instance Khrushchev has worked hard to make expansion of Soviet per capita butter production to the U.S. level a symbol of catching up with the United States in general. Apart from the question of differing attitudes of the two populations toward fats in their diets, this comparison overlooks the fact that butter production in the United States is supplemented by an output of margarine 3 percent greater than the production of butter itself, whereas in the Soviet Union the output of margarine is only 70 percent of butter output.[4]

Another such prestige output which they have elevated to the status of a symbol is the output of sugar. Soviet propagandists are fond of comparing sugar output in the two countries. For instance, in one of the standard statistical handbooks for agitators,[5] the production of sugar in the two countries is shown as 17 kilograms in the Soviet Union and 12 kilograms in the United States. This figure appears to be accurate enough as far as it goes, but what it fails to mention is that while Soviet sugar output is augmented by imports only to the extent of about 2 percent, U.S. domestic output is far overshadowed by imports so that per capita consumption is more nearly 45 kilograms than 12.[6]

Another common example is the preoccupation with individual commodity outputs, such as steel or electric power output, as general indicators of "industrial base," which in turn is thought of as being some indicator of relative Soviet military potential, or ability to implement other strategic objectives such as foreign aid capital accumulation or growth. What this comparison overlooks is the radically different pattern of consumption of these two products in the two countries. Consumer goods, such as automobiles and home

---

[4] These figures are taken from Statistical Abstract of the United States, 1958 edition, pp. 674 and 681, and V. P. Zotov, Pishchevaia promyshlennost' Sovetskogo Soiuza, Moscow, 1958, pp. 169–170.

[5] I. A. Ioffe, Strany sotsializma i kapitalizma v. tsifrakh, (The Countries of Socialism and Capitalism in Figures) Moscow, 1957.

[6] These figures are from Statistical Abstract of the United States, p. 671, V. P. Zotov, Pishchevaia promyshlennost' SSSR, p. 170, and Ministerstvo Vneshnei torgovli SSSR, Vneshniaia torgovlia Soiuza SSR za 1957 god, Moscow, 1958, pp. 21 and 33.

appliances take a vastly higher proportion of United States, than of Soviet steel output. Similarly with electric power output; the Soviet output of 231 billion kilowatt-hours in 1957 compared to the American output of 716 billion kilowatt-hours seems to suggest that the productive capacity of the Soviet economy must be strongly restricted by the lack of this vital ingredient of productivity. Again, however, the pattern of utilization is very different. Only a tiny fraction of Soviet power output goes for such uses as household consumption, and municipal and commercial lighting, whereas a very large share of U.S. power output is devoted to these purposes. Hence it is erroneous to consider the relative outputs as a reliable indicator of industrial power.

One of the common areas of concern for people who are making these comparisons is the productivity of the Soviet economy, that is the amount of output they get per unit of the resources at their disposal. The rationale of such comparisons is a belief that productivity has something to do with the relative efficiency of the two economies. Here, however, a different context of technology and of resource endowments greatly beclouds the meaning of specific productivity comparisons. One of the most commonly studied indicators is labor productivity. Such studies always show that output per Soviet worker in any area of the economy is considerably below output per worker in the United States. The Russians themselves claim that output per worker in industry is about half the U.S. level, although this is the kind of comparison that is suspect because of the index number problem discussed earlier. The calculation presupposes some estimate of the relative size of United States and Soviet industrial output, and the great variety of possible weighting schemes means that such comparisons have to be examined very skeptically. In a number of individual branches of the economy, where it is possible to find more or less homogeneous physical measures of output, output per worker can be easily enough compared, however. The result of such comparisons is to show a great range of comparative labor productivity, but despite the variation from case to case, such comparisons show clearly that output per worker is far lower in the Soviet Union than in the United States.

It is but a short step from comparisons such as these to the conclusions that the Soviet economy is extremely wasteful and inefficient. This is a conclusion that is often drawn, but one that is by no means warranted on the evidence of comparative labor productivity. In general this low labor productivity is far less a reflection of inefficiency or waste than of the different resource situation confronting the Russian planners, a resource situation fundamentally different from ours. Soviet industrialization has taken place against the background of an abundance of manpower. The planners have faced a situation where it was never any problem to secure additional labor. The real difficulty was in finding the capital to create new capacity, new factories in which the labor could be employed. It was therefore economically sensible for them to use labor lavishly, substituting it whenever possible for capital goods, and bringing in more workers whenever it was possible by doing so to squeeze a bit more output out of existing enterprises. The result of such a policy was to make output per worker low, but it was still the correct thing to do in the light of the abundance of labor.

The low productivity of the Soviet industrial labor force can be explained alternatively as the low level of mechanical assistance which the Soviet worker has at his disposal. A good summary indicator of the amount of mechanical power which the worker has to assist him in loing his job is the amount of electrical power consumed per worker. Consumption of electric power per industrial worker in the Soviet Union is less than half the American level, and this factor alone goes a long way toward explaining why Soviet industrial labor productivity is so much below ours. It should be emphasized, again, however, that the failure of the Soviet planners to supply their workers with as much mechanical assistance as American workers enjoy does not necessarily imply a mistake in planning. Given the population situation and the amount of capital that could be accumulated, the Soviet planners have found that they could expand the industrial labor force much more easily than they could build more generating plants and other power facilities to increase the mechanical assistance provided for the worker.

The difference in resource endowments distorts other indicators in the opposite direction. Because of the intensive utilization of capacity the output per machine or per other unit of capital is much higher than in the United States. One of the best known examples is the high productivity of capital in Soviet railroad transportation. The Russians have a much higher output of freight turnover per mile of track and per freight car than we do in the United States—something over three times as much freight turnover per mile of track and almost three times as much freight turnover per ton of freight car capacity. Another industry in which Soviet equipment productivity is much higher is in blast furnace operation. Measuring the blast furnace capacity by the total internal volume of the blast furnace and output in tons, in turns out that the Russians get on the average 1.25 tons of pig iron per cubic meter of blast furnace capacity, whereas American producers get only 0.92 ton. It should be added that the productivity of blast furnaces is a function of their size, with larger furnaces being appreciably more productive per cubic meter of space than small furnaces are. Since American furnaces are rather larger on the average than Soviet furnaces, the higher productivity of Soviet furnaces is all the more notable.

Soviet economists are very fond of making such comparisons of capital productivity and concluding that they prove the greater efficiency of their economic system and the chaotic wastefulness of capitalism. This conclusion is as dubious as the reverse one that we sometimes make on the basis of labor productivity comparisons. The high rate of utilization of capital equipment makes sense for the Soviet Union but not for the United States. The relative abundance and cheapness of capital in this country makes it rational for a firm to provide itself generously with capacity.

The argument above should not be understood as implying that the American and Soviet systems are equally efficient in making use of the different resource endowments which each enjoy. The point is rather that the difference in relative scarcities of the basic factors of production makes productivity comparisons a very ambiguous kind of evidence on this score, though superficially they seem so suggestive of relative efficiencies. To what extent the difference in some productivity indicator is evidence of inefficiency and to what extent a reflection of different resource availabilities is a question that can be answered with certainty, if at all, only by a detailed scrutiny of many other aspects of the context.

Even when the influence of such radically different scarcity relationships is absent, more subtle differences in the parameters which confront decision makers and in technology may mean that technological indicators must be interpreted carefully. For instance in a comparative study of the electric power industry of the two countries, one question that would immediately draw attention to itself would be the expenditure of fuel per kilowatt-hour of electric power produced. The electric power industry is engaged essentially in the transformation of the heat energy of fuel into electric energy, and so this ratio is an important indicator of its technological perfection. There is no particular statistical problem to such a comparison—this is an important operating indicator used in the planning and administration of the electric power industry and it is a statistic the Russians collect and publish. Data of the same form can easily be calculated for the U.S. power industry. But as the comparison of the two industries went further, it would soon be found that one of the important differences between the United States and Soviet power industries is that Soviet generating equipment includes an appreciable proportion of installations in which some of the waste heat is captured and used for heating purposes. The generation of electric power inevitably involves the loss of some heat—it is impossible to convert all the energy in the fuel into electrical energy. The Russians use a considerable amount of this heat. Americans use it very little. In computing the fuel consumption per kilowatt-hour of electric power, the Russians assign a significant amount of the fuel burned in power stations (i.e., about 16 percent) to the heating operations.[7]

When it comes to choosing a fuel expenditure ratio for comparison with the American should one use the one cited by the Russians or one corrected to include all fuel burned in electric power stations? There are objections to either alternative. There would be little justification for basing the comparison on the total fuel burned since the Russians are correct in implying that this fuel is not one of the costs of power. It is true that most of this heat could not be converted to electric power even if they did not have the alternative use for it. Nevertheless they do have a use for it, and have made a choice of equipment which will permit them to capture it and avoid burning fuel in conventional installations for heating purposes. In the light of the alternatives open to them, then they are correct in saying that part of the fuel is really chargeable to heating rather than power generation. On the other hand we hesitate to use the Soviet fuel expenditure ratio as they present it because of doubts about the correctness of the amount of the fuel they assign to heating. The allocation between the two purposes is made on the basis of an engineering convention rather than on the basis of what a sophisticated economist would consider correct. What it comes down to is that the power industry in the two countries employs two slightly different technologies, and as a result fuel expenditure per kilowatt-hour of power is an indicator with a slightly different meaning in the two countries. Even apart from this difficulty, other qualifications would have to be considered before this indicator could be taken as a measure

[7] This percentage can be calculated from data given in Promyshlennost' S.S.S.R.

of the relative efficiency of the Soviet Union and American power industries. Fuel expenditure per kilowatt-hour is a function of various design parameters of the equipment, such as the temperature and pressure of the steam. Rational decisions on these parameters are very sensitive to the costs of fuel relative to costs of the other inputs that go into the original construction and the operation of generating stations. Hence relatively small differences in price structure might mean that rational or "efficient" decisions would result in a different fuel expenditure ratio in the two countries.

A final illustration of the treacheries of comparing economic indicators torn from different contexts is provided by investment in the two countries. It has been a commonplace to explain the rapid rate of growth of the Soviet economy as flowing in part from the high rate of investment in the Soviet Union. The Soviet planners have been able to keep down consumption levels and in consequence devote a larger share of current output to building new production capacity than the United States does. To embody this argument in statistics, one commonly resorts to a comparison of the share of GNP devoted to investment purposes. Once attention is focused on this mode of analysis, actual statistical comparisons of investment in absolute terms or as a share of GNP are productive of considerable confusion. Investment as a percentage of GNP turns out to be not so radically different in the two countries, and this bolsters the suspicion that maybe the Soviet economy is not growing as fast as we have been led to believe. It also prompts the comforting thought that if small reallocations of Soviet GNP away from investment should take place the Russians will lose whatever advantage relative to the U.S. economy they may have had in the past. This confusion comes from focusing attention on gross investment as an explanation of growth rather than net investment which is the concept that covers the net additions to productive capacity. We have traditionally emphasized gross rather than net investment in our national income accounting and analysis because of the difficulty of measuring net investment meaningfully, and indeed for some international comparisons gross investment might serve well enough. Because the Soviet and American economies are so different with respect to the size and age of their capital stock and the rate of growth, however, the share of gross investment that represents real net additions to productive capacity is much greater for the Soviet Union than for the United States.

Conclusion.—The task of this paper has been to discuss the problems involved in United States-Soviet economic comparisons. It would be a source of great chagrin to the author if this listing of obstacles should be taken as a justification for a belief that it is hopeless or pointless to undertake such comparisons. With respect to the first problem, data availability, the limitations of what can be accomplished has certainly not yet been reached. Indeed the rate of flow of data has increased recently much faster than our efforts to make use of it. Also the possible approaches for clearing up obscurities in the meaning of Soviet statistics are greater than may have been implied. The index number problem is not peculiar to United States-Soviet comparisons alone, but actually affects many measurement problems within our own economy. It is only that the attention of economists has been directed toward these difficulties in comparison and measurement most strongly in the comparative study of the

United States and Soviet economies because intertemporal and international differences in economic structure are more striking when we try to evaluate their performance relative to ours than in many other kinds of problems that economists deal with. Likewise our preoccupation with the interpretation of data comes from the fact that the Russians are particularly persistent in choosing concepts that complicate comparability of economic indicators.

In this connection a final important implication of the discussion should be pointed out. The Russians are truly compulsive in making comparisons of their economy with ours, and in the process they turn all the ambiguities discussed above to good account in exaggerating their achievements relative to ours. They ignore important differences in the concepts underlying comparisons, choose weighting systems that present their achievements in the best possible light, and emphasize indicators the comparability of which is violated by differences in the context. All these misinterpretations can, of course, also be employed by those who would underemphasize Soviet economic performance. With a greater respect for truth than the Russians we should take pains to point out the errors involved in the Soviet comparisons, and with perhaps greater sophistication about the pitfalls of international economic comparisons we should be able to avoid the dangers of accepting misleading evaluations of Soviet economic performance from either end of the spectrum.

POPULATION AND LABOR FORCE

THE POPULATION OF THE SOVIET UNION

(By John F. Kantner, Foreign Manpower Research Office, U.S. Bureau of the Census)

Chapter 1. General Summary

The interrelationships between population and economic organization are numerous and complex. It scarcely exaggerates the matter to assert that for every population of a given size and structure there is a narrowly limited set of economic forms and arrangements which will work. Therefore, provided one has the information, treatments of the connections between demographic and economic phenomena can be as encyclopedic as time and inclination allow.

In seeking a basis for selection for this discussion, two problems of the current Soviet scene appeared to stand out as vitally related to the economic position of the U.S.S.R. now and in the future. These are the problem of labor supply and the growth prospects for the Soviet population over the next 15 years. Chapter 2 presents an analysis of the problem of labor supply and chapter 3 develops some of the implications of differing growth prospects and attempts to discern from very fragmentary evidence and trend in Soviet fertility. In discussing each of these topics comparisons with the United States are frequently made. To bring all comparative data together for convenient reference, a final chapter of basic U.S.-U.S.S.R. demographic comparisons has been added. An appendix is also included which provides some of the basic demographic information currently available on the Soviet Union.

Soviet economic development until recently has not been handicapped by a population surplus such as threatens to erase the economic gains of the underdeveloped countries of the present period. The Soviet Union presents a chronicle of catastrophic population losses which have kept the long-term growth rate (excluding population gains through annexation) below 1 percent per year. At the same time, however, the population in the age range considered, in Soviet usage, to cover the "able-bodied population" (16–59 years of age) has steadily increased in proportion to the total population.

The Second World War left the Soviet Union with a shortage of some 20 million men. For this and other reasons, a larger proportion of women are employed than in almost any other industrial country in the world and this proportion has declined only slightly since the end of the war. Having a delayed impact on the labor force is the enormous birth deficit of the war. Net additions to the working-age population currently run around 1 million persons annually or only about half the number 2 or 3 years earlier. Then those being added were persons born before the war. This number may drop to less than 100,000 per year in the near future, causing an even more critical manpower problem for the current 7-year plan (1959–65) than was faced by the abortive sixth 5-year plan (1956–60).

In years to come the numerical imbalance between men and women will be alleviated as more and more of the able-bodied population comes to consist of persons born since the end of the war. There will be also a sharp upturn in the number of annual additions to the population of working age after 1963. In spite of this, the growth of the population of working age during the period of the 7-year plan will amount to only about half of the 12 million increase in employment called for in the plan. The Soviet Government seems to be counting on three other principal sources to augment its labor supply: The household economy, the educational system, and the agricultural population. The prospects for obtaining additional labor force from each of these sources are to a large extent contingent upon the success of other parts of the Government's program. In particular, the extent to which the agricultural population can make up the greater part of the deficit will be determined, partially at least, by the success of efforts to modernize agricultural production, introduce substitutes for agricultural products, complete a vast urban housing program, consolidate the collective farms, and so on.

Expansion of the labor force by drawing upon the household economy and altering the school programs would increase the flow of people into production. The recent changes in the educational system will divert to the labor force most of those now enrolled in the last 2 years of general education. Generally these are children 15 and 16 years old. Recent surveys of persons entering the labor force from the household economy indicate that most of the men and about two-thirds of the women are under 20 years of age. The qualitative changes contemplated in Soviet education are designed to provide new members for the labor force whose training is more in keeping with the requirements of industry. The planned blending of study and productive work should also help to meet the planned labor force requirements. Soviet planners face a problem in giving proper direction to the rural to urban migration flow which is to be an important source of new industrial labor. Their efforts to move population to new industrial centers in the east have not been fully successful, and much of the limited success achieved is attributable to the forced evacuation of the population during the war years. The preference of migrants for the large old industrial towns has resulted in a substantial misallocation of labor since these places have not been favored in the allocation of new investment. The Soviet Union, therefore, faces a dual manpower problem, first the problem of size, and second the problem of efficient territorial distribution of labor. Its gigantic 7-year construction program may be of tremendous significance in the solution.

Looking beyond the 7-year plan, the outlook is for continued correction of the low ratio of men to women. The working-age population will also increase in proportion to the total population, but the rate at which this takes place will depend upon the trend of Soviet fertility. Since the proportion of persons over 60 years of age is increasing steadily, a substantial drop in fertility will be required if the population aged 16 to 59 years is to comprise as large a proportion of the total population in 1975 as it now does.

The nature of many other developments depends upon the trend in fertility. This is true even with respect to changes which are inherent in the present structure of the population.

The prospective trend in fertility is difficult to predict, however, since there are tendencies operating in both directions. Tentatively, the opinion is advanced that the combined effect of rural-urban migration, the diffusion of secular attitudes toward reproduction, and the spread of the practice of contraception will outweigh other tendencies toward an increase in average family size.

Among the more significant demographic comparisons which can be made between the U.S.S.R. and the United States, the following deserve to be noted:

1. Because of the enormous war losses sustained by the Soviet Union, its population now exceeds that of the United States by only 18 percent, whereas before the war, the margin was 46 percent.

2. The current natural increase of the Soviet Union is somewhat greater than that of the United States due principally to the lower Soviet death rate. The annual increase of the two countries is about equal because of immigration to this country.

3. The extent to which the two countries will differ in size in the future depends largely upon the trend in fertility. According to current projections, should the countries follow opposite courses the difference in size in 1975 might be as low as 4 million (Soviet fertility down; U.S. fertility up) or as high as 65 million (Soviet fertility up; U.S. fertility down).

4. The low Soviet death rate, which is currently below that of the U.S., is partly attributable to a favorable age composition and may increase somewhat in the future. It is clear, however, that the Soviet Union has participated substantially in the worldwide revolution in medicine and health.

5. The number of children in the ages to be attending elementary and secondary school, the group which will provide the coming generation of scientists and technicians, is nearly the same in the U.S.S.R. and the United States. In the United States, enrollment rates in higher education are mounting rapidly; in the U.S.S.R., the policy, at least for the short run, is to prevent expansion in higher education.

6. The number of Soviet men of military age (18–34) will remain relatively stationary over the next 15 years. The present numerical superiority which the U.S.S.R. has relative to the United States, will decline from about 11 million to about 3.5 million during that time.

7. By 1975 the United States will have nearly as many persons of university age (18–22) as the U.S.S.R. The U.S.S.R. now has some 22 million in this age group compared to 12 million in the United States.

8. During the period of the Soviet 7-year plan (1959–65), the population of working age (15–59) will increase by around 6.7 million in the U.S.S.R. and by more than 10 million (1958–65) in the United States.

9. The Soviet population 60 years of age and over will increase from 17 million to more than 30 million by 1975. In absolute terms this is a slightly larger group than the United States will have at that time. As a proportion of the total population, the U.S. figure is greater.

10. Expected changes in population composition among persons of the age to occupy the middle grade and senior positions in the economy suggest that by 1975 career advancement will be relatively easier in the U.S.S.R. than in the United States.

Chapter 2. Population and Labor Supply

THE ROLE OF DEMOGRAPHIC FACTORS DURING THE FIRST 40 YEARS OF SOVIET DEVELOPMENT

The Soviet Union, at least until World War II, never had a population problem in the sense that it lacked sufficient manpower or that its rate of population growth was greater than its rate of economic development.[1] It is true that prerevolutionary levels of economic activity were not regained until around 1926, by which time the population had increased (over 1914) by 4.7 percent, or nearly 7 million. But even during the post-World War I period, when both the economy and the population were recovering from its impact, the rate of economic development very likely exceeded the rate of population increase. The problems of the opening decade of Soviet rule are more accurately attributed to failures of economic and administrative organization than to the pressure of population on resources.

Since the institution of the 5-year plan in 1928, the rate of population increase has never threatened to overtake the rate of overall economic growth.[2] The fact is, rather, that to a considerable extent the Soviet Union's rapid industrialization was achieved by the profligate use of manpower. To achieve a sevenfold increase of industrial production between 1928 and 1956, the number of industrial-production workers in Soviet industry was increased nearly fivefold, or by 14,684,000 workers.[3] The United States, on the other hand, attained more than a sevenfold increase in the output of manufactured goods between 1935 and 1956 with less than a doubling of the number of production workers in manufacturing.[4] The concern in the U.S.S.R. with raising

[1] The Soviet Government is committed to the position that under communism there can be no such thing as a population problem. According to Marxian theory, the problem of too many people is an infirmity of capitalist societies which cannot occur under a Socialist allocation of resources. No one was worried in Marx's day about too few people.

[2] This conclusion is secure even though there is wide variation in measures of Soviet national product Even the most conservative indexes increase at several times the rate of population increase. With respect to that part of the national product allocated to consumption by households, the situation is somewhat modified but the conclusion remains the same. During the first two 5-year plans, population growth just about kept pace with household consumption, although according to Chapman's calculations the real income of urban workers and employees actually fell during these years. However, consumption by civilian households during the last completed postwar 5-year plan—1951–55—increased at a rate about four times the rate of population increase. For discussions of Soviet national product see Gregory Grossman's article in Abram Bergson (ed.), "Soviet Economic Growth," Row, Peterson & Co., 1953, pp. 1–23; Oleg Hoeffding and N. Nimitz, "Soviet National Income and Product 1949–55," the Rand Corp., Santa Monica, Calif., Apr. 6, 1959; and Paul Studenski, "The Income of Nations," New York University Press, 1958, ch. 25; for estimates of changes in the real income of urban workers and employees, see Janet G. Chapman, "Real Wages in the Soviet Union, 1928–52," Review of Economics and Statistics, vol. XXXVI, No. 2, May 1954.

[3] Demitri B. Shimkin and Frederick A. Leedy, "Soviet Industrial Growth—Its Costs, Extent, and Prospects" in Automotive Industries, Jan. 1, 1958, p. 51, table 1; for the number of industrial-production personnel see Tsentral'noye statisticheskoye upravleniye pri sovete ministrov S.S.S.R., "Narodnoye khozyaystvo S.S.S.R. v 1956 godu (The National Economy of the U.S.S.R. in 1956)," Moscow, 1957, pp. 204–205.

[4] U.S. Department of Commerce, Bureau of the Census, "Statistical Abstract of the United States 1958," table No. 1020, p. 774.

labor productivity [5] through more efficient deployment of the labor force,[6] through plant specialization, increased mechanization and automation undoubtedly reflects a growing realization that the manpower pool is getting low and that new practices designed to improve labor utilization are in order.[7]

To insist that the Soviet Union has not encountered a population problem would be unrealistic from any point of view except that of economic development. The costs of development in human terms have been high. The human costs of the First World War, the revolution and famine during the early years of Soviet rule can be measured in terms of 12 million excess civilian deaths, 2 million refugees, and a birth deficit [8] of nearly 10 million. Direct military losses of some 2 million during World War I were thus only a minor part of the levy of those frightful years.[9]

The dozen years between the first and second national censuses in 1926 and 1939 encompassed the collectivization of agriculture and the liquidation of the wealthier or more independent peasants. The human costs of this period were also very large, running perhaps as high as 20 million. This figure includes the deaths of about 5 million persons who would have survived if more normal rates of mortality had prevailed and a birth deficit of about 15 million.[10] Births were limited through family separations and general interference with the process of family formation and also through abortions, which in 1934 and 1935 in some of the larger cities amounted to more than twice the number of live births. The Government responded in 1936 with a ban on nontherapeutic abortions, with the result that the number of certified abortions dropped by 97 percent between the first half of 1936 and the second half of 1937.[11] Following this action, and with the restoration of more settled conditions, the birth rate climbed rapidly toward its former level.

By far the most catastrophic period in the chronicle of Soviet demographic development was the period of World War II. Judging from estimates of the number of survivors of the prewar population in 1950, the loss of life between 1940 and 1950 among persons born before 1940 may be placed at somewhat more than 45 million. Had prewar

[5] Soviet levels of labor productivity are lower than the United States, the degree of difference varying greatly by economic sector. A recent article published in the U.S.S.R. on this subject makes the following comparison of Soviet and U.S. productivity for 1957:

Branch:	*U.S.S.R. productivity as percent of U.S.*
Industry	50
Construction	59
Transportation	33
Agriculture	20–25

See A. Aganbegyan, "Catching and Overtaking the U.S.A. in the Level of Labor Productivity," Sotsialisticheskyy trud (Socialist Labor), No. 4, April 1959, p. 19.

[6] Writing in Sovetskaya Rossiya, June 18, 1959, A. Abramov complained: "* * * it is well known to Gosplan that at times, and despite the objections of enterprises, young specialists are sent who were not requested. This can be explained simply. More of some specialists are trained than are needed and vice versa * * *. A precise, scientifically based method for determining the country's future needs for specialists is required. But neither Gosplan U.S.S.R., Gosplan R.S.F.S.R., nor the Ministry of Higher Education, U.S.S.R. is engaged in this complex problem."

[7] Undoubtedly it reflects also longstanding Soviet practice continually agitating on any point that may increase output.

[8] The term "birth deficit" is merely a handy reference for the difference between the actual number of births in a given period when fertility is low and the number which would have been expected under "normal" rates of reproduction.

[9] See Frank Lorimer, "The Population of the Soviet Union," League of Nations, Geneva, 1946, pp. 36–41.

[10] Lorimer, op. cit., pp. 112–137.

[11] Between 1922 and 1936, abortions were free and legal in the Soviet Union, so long as they were certified to have been performed under proper medical and sanitary conditions. For additional discussion, see Lorimer, op. cit., pp. 126–130.

death rates prevailed throughout the decade, only some 20 to 25 million deaths might have been expected.

The population under 10 years in 1950 was relatively small, partly because Soviet birth rates during the years 1940–49 were quite low, on the average, and partly because high infant and child mortality was characteristic throughout most of the nation during this period. The estimated number of children born during 1940–44 who survived to 1950 was about the same as the number of survivors of persons born during 1930–34, a period already noted to have been characterized by very low fertility. Altogether some 9 to 15 million children would have been born had there been no war.[12]

From the viewpoint of economic development, the question can be raised whether the losses just outlined have not, in fact, been an important positive factor in Soviet economic growth. To such a hypothetical question only a hypothetical answer can be given, since it is likely that with a different demographic past the course of social and economic change in the Soviet Union would have been altogether different. Nevertheless, it is interesting to note that since the advent of the period of state planning in 1928, the rate of increase in GNP (gross national product) has been well ahead not only of the actual rate of population growth but ahead also of the rate of population growth which might have been expected under normal conditions. A faster rate or population growth, however, would have called for greater diversion of the national product to household consumption and a reorganization of the whole matrix of economic activity. This would have resulted in a dampening of the rate of increase in GNP so long as the greatly increased emphasis on armaments was maintained. A retarded rate of industrial growth, and a consequent reduction of economic opportunities in cities would have presented the Soviet Government with a host of new problems.

POPULATION COMPOSITION

The notion that in the past the Soviet Union has never been faced with a population problem can be examined further by looking at the age composition of the Soviet population. Over the past 30 or more years—during most of which centralized state planning has been in effect—the population has been characterized by an increasing proportion of persons in the ages of maximum productivity [13] and a corresponding decline in young dependents (table 1). The decline in the percentage under 15 years of age has more than offset the slow but steady increase in the percentage 60 years of age and over. Even after the figures on the population 16 to 59 years old are reduced to allow for youths in school and in military service, the remaining population—that is the group potentially available for employment—comprised a higher proportion of the total population in 1959 than in 1926.[14]

---

[12] For a more extended discussion of changes in population during this period, see U.S. Department of Commerce, Bureau of the Census, "Estimates and Projections of the Population of the U.S.S.R.: 1950 to 1976" by Arthur A. Campbell and James W. Brackett, International Population Report Series P-95, No. 52, app. A.

[13] The age interval 16 to 59 is shown in table 1 since this is the range covered by the Soviet designation of the "able-bodied" population which includes men between the ages of 16 and 59 and women 16 to 54 years.

[14] In 1959 the combined total of persons in the final 3 grades of secondary school, in higher education, in tekhnikums, and in military service amounted to approximately 10,000,000. The comparable figure for 1926 was slightly over 1,000,000

TABLE 1.—*Percent distribution of the population of the U.S.S.R. by age for selected years, 1926–1975*

(Figures for 1965–75 are projections by the U.S. Bureau of the Census)

Age	1926	1940	1950	1959	1965	1970	1975
All ages	100.0	100.0	100.0	100.0	100.0	100.0	100.0
Under 15 years	37.3	35.2	31.0	29.2	31.2	29.9	28.3
15 to 29 years	29.1	26.9	28.6	26.3	23.5	22.3	23.6
30 to 44 years	16.6	20.6	19.7	20.6	21.3	22.9	20.2
45 to 59 years	10.3	10.6	13.6	15.7	14.2	14.0	16.0
60 years and over	6.7	6.7	7.0	8.2	9.8	10.9	11.9
16 to 59 years	53.5	56.2	60.1	61.2	56.0 59.0	54.7 59.8	55.1 61.0

Source: 1926: Tsentral'noye statisticheskoye upravleniye SSSR. Vsesoyuznaya perepis' naseleniya, 1926 g. (All-Union Census of Population, 1926), Vol. 17, Moscow, 1929, pp. 46–48.

1940: U.S. Bureau of the Census. Estimates and Projections of the Population of the U.S.S.R.: 1950 to 1976 by Arthur A. Campbell and James W. Brackett. International Population Reports, Series P–95, No. 52.

1950–1965: Estimates prepared by Foreign Manpower Research Office. U.S. Bureau of the Census. These estimates are revisions of the Campbell-Brackett estimates taking account of the preliminary results of the 1959 Soviet census released in Izvestiya, May 10, 1959. The effect of the revision is to alter the balance between males and females. It has a negligible effect on the age distribution.

1970–1975: U.S. Bureau of the Census. Op. cit. The two figures given for each year represent a range resulting from the effect of differences in assumptions regarding fertility. The lower percentage is associated with a high fertility assumption; the high percentage figure assumes that Soviet fertility will decline within the next 10 years to a level similar to the low point reached by the United States in the 1930's. Age intervals represented by single figures rather than a range have been estimated on the basis of the assumption of a continuation of present estimated fertility rates.

In what sense, then, can it be said, as it sometimes is, that in the past several years the Soviet Union has been faced with a labor shortage? The answer lies in the fact that the term "labor shortage" is a many-faceted concept. Given demographic magnitudes in themselves do not necessarily cause or solve labor shortages. Relative to economic objectives, relative to prevailing levels of labor productivity, relative to traditional patterns of labor force participation and, too, relative to numbers, there may be a labor shortage. References to Russia's labor shortage began to be heard at the time of the abortive sixth 5-year plan (1956–60) which called for an increase over 5 years of 6.6 million in the State-employed labor force.[15] For this period, as table 2 shows, the estimated net increase in the population 16 to 59 years was approximately 7 million, or only slightly more than the number required by the plan. This slight margin is quite inadequate to take care of manpower drains of the educational system and the military establishment, of replacements for nonstate agriculture, and to allow for persons who either voluntarily or involuntarily do not take civilian employment. It is not easy to state this manpower drain in quantitative terms, although it is not difficult to demonstrate that the number is substantial. For example, in the 1956–57 school year there were approximately 1.5 million students enrolled in the 10th and 11th grades of the general schools.

[15] That is, the "workers and employees" (rabochiye i sluzhashchiye), Izvestiya, Jan. 15, 1956.

TABLE 2.—*Estimated population of the U.S.S.R., 16 to 59 years of age: 1956–66*

(Figures for 1960–66 are projections by the U.S. Bureau of the Census)

[In thousands]

Year	Population 16 to 59 years	Population change during preceding year		Population 18 and 19 years	Population 16 and 17 years
1956	121,923	------		8,500	9,200
1957	124,094	2,171		9,300	8,500
1958	126,090	1,996		9,100	8,000
1959	127,709	1,619	7,160	8,400	7,600
1960	128,813	1,104		7,900	6,800
1961	129,083	270		7,600	5,700
1962	129,144	61		6,800	4,800
1963	129,386	242	5,633	5,700	4,900
1964	130,298	912		4,800	5,800
1965	131,914	1,616		4,800	7,300
1966	133,342	1,428		5,800	7,900

Source: Estimates prepared by the Foreign Manpower Research Office, U.S. Bureau of the Census.

Under normal matriculation and progression, most of these would be 16 years of age and therefore should not be counted among the available labor supply increment for that year. In addition, an undetermined number, perhaps a third or more, of the 1.2 million 2d, 3d, and 4th year tekhnikum students should also be regarded as unavailable. Most of these would enter the labor force in a year or two and some—over 200,000 in recent years—would enter institutions of higher education for periods up to 5 years. Even with the falling enrollments of the past few years, we would expect for the period as a whole a drain into educational channels alone of at least 2 million.[16] Diversions into other channels are impossible to estimate at present. In general we would anticipate that about three-fourths of the population of working age would participate in the labor force.[17] Thus, out of a net change of 7 million persons in the age group 16–59, a little more than 5 million would be found in the labor force. The planned increase of 6.6 million in state employment would have to be met in part therefore through transfers within the labor force, by cutting back on educational enrollment, by increasing the rate of military demobilization over the rate of recruitment and by general measures to reduce the number of persons of working age who were economically inactive. Without question, the sixth 5-year plan had to cope with a stringent labor supply situation.

Before following this problem of labor supply into the future, we should consider one other critical aspect of current demographic conditions in the U.S.S.R.—the shortage of males. A moderate deficit of males is characteristic of populations relatively closed to migration, which have attained high levels of longevity. In such populations the numerical superiority of males resulting from a greater number of male than female births is gradually dissipated with advancing age, since women tend to live longer than men. Thus, in the United States

[16] In considering the total Soviet labor balance the fact that these drains are offset to some extent by persons entering the labor force from the educational system, the military service, etc., is a relevant consideration. Here, however, we are comparing labor force requirements with the increments expected through natural increase of the population 16–59 years of age. Present information is not sufficient to permit a comparison of the flow in and out of the labor force of persons of working age.

[17] 1957 is the last year for which there is enough information to estimate the size of the civilian labor force. In that year there were 53,148,000 persons employed in State enterprises [see Tsentral'noye statisticheskoye upravleniye pri sovete ministrov SSSR, USSR v tsifrakh (The U.S.S.R. in Figures), Gosstatizdat, Moscow, 1958, p. 313]. Cooperative employment was 1,200,000 (ibid., p. 308) and collective farmers plus persons engaged in hunting and fishing is estimated at around 37 million. Thus, the sum of these amounts to nearly 75 percent of the estimated population between the ages of 16 and 59.

today, some 35 years after the last large wave of immigration, there are approximately 98 men for every 100 women. The sex ratio in the U.S.S.R. has been well below this level throughout the Soviet period, reaching a low point immediately after World War II. The ratio for 1950 shown in table 3 represents in absolute terms a shortage relative to females of 23.5 million males. By 1959, this male deficit had declined to 20.8 million—still an extremely high figure.

TABLE 3.—*Males per 100 females in the U.S.S.R., all ages and ages 15 to 59 years, selected years, 1926–75*

Year	All ages	Ages 15-59	Year	All ages	Ages 15-59
1926	93	90	1959	82	77
1940	92	91	1965	85	81
1950	77	68	1975	87	87

Source: Same as for table 1.

The relative size of the male deficit is even greater within the population 15 to 59 years of age. In absolute terms it amounted to 21 million males in 1950 and to 17 million males in 1959. As time passes, the trough in the male age distribution will move along the age scale so that the problem of a male deficit changes qualitatively as well as quantitatively. The problem in 1950 took its character from the fact that over 70 percent of the male deficit occurs in the age range 20 to 44 years. This had important qualitative implications not only for the labor supply but for the social structure generally—especially for the rates of family formation and reproduction. By 1959 the population having the heavy male deficit had grown older and had its greatest effect upon the ages between 30 and 54 years. Balance among the sexes had largely been restored below age 30, that is among those in the ages of maximum fertility and among those who for the first time enter the civilian labor force and the military forces.

The Soviet "solution" to its male deficit by way of extraordinarily high participation of women in the labor force is well known and is an interesting demonstration of the extent to which adaptable social organization can dull the edge of demographic forces. In 1957, the latest year for which there are full comparative data, we estimate that women composed 53 percent of the Soviet labor force whereas in the United States, which itself has experienced somewhat of a revolution in regard to the employment of women, 32 percent of the "experienced civilian labor force" consisted of women.[18] The differences are even more striking in individual branches of the economy as the comparisons in table 4 illustrate:

[18] U.S. Bureau of the Census, Annual Report on the Labor Force, 1957, series P–50, No. 86, p. 8. The concept "experienced civilian labor force" refers to persons who were employed or looking for work during the week of the employment survey, provided the latter had previously had a job. The estimate for women in the Soviet labor force is based upon participation rates reported for State employment which accounts for slightly more than half the labor force (see Tsentral'noye statisticheskoye upravleniye pri sovete ministrov SSSR, "SSSR v tsifrakh (The U.S.S.R. in Figures)," Moscow, 1958, pp. 336–337) and upon crude estimates for the cooperative and private spheres of employment. The estimate for total and for female labor on collective farms—which is the predominant female occupation—was based upon reports of the number of labor days earned by Soviet collective farmers and the assumption that the participation of men and women in this work would resemble the situation reported for the Ukraine where about one-fourth of the collective farmers are found.

TABLE 4.—*Percent of total employment comprised of females, for selected economic branches, U.S.S.R. and United States, 1957*

Industry group	U.S.S.R.[1]	United States[2]
Industry[3]	45	26
Construction	31	3
Agriculture[4]	59	19
Transportation and communication	32	18
Trade and supply[5]	65	39
Government and administration[6]	51	27

1 Tsentral'noye statisticheskoye upravleniye pri sovete ministrov, "SSSR v tsifrakh (The U.S.S.R. in Figures)," Moscow, 1958, pp. 336–337.
2 U.S. Bureau of the Census, "Annual Report on the Labor Force, 1957," series p–50, No. 86, p. 8.
3 In Soviet usage "Industry" includes forestry, fishing, and mining in addition to manufacturing. The figure for the United States given here refers to manufacturing only.
4 Soviet agriculture includes collective and state farmers, personnel of machine tractor stations, and persons engaged in private subsidiary agriculture. The U.S. figure includes wage and salary workers in agriculture, self-employed workers and unpaid family workers.
5 The U.S.S.R. figure covers persons employed in "trade, public catering, and material technical supply." The U.S. approximation to this is "wholesale and retail trade."
6 The Soviet figure includes the administrative apparatus of the state, cooperative organizations and pubic organizations other than public health and education. The U.S. figure is for public administration.

Although the high labor force participation rates of Soviet women may be viewed as a response to both a war-produced shortage of males and more recently to a general shortage of manpower, it must be recognized that Russian women have traditionally been active in the economy. The evidence indicates, moreover, that during the past decade or so the Soviet Union has not solved its growing manpower needs by increased dependence on the employment of women. There appears, in fact, to have been a decline since the war in the degree to which women have participated in the labor force,[19] most likely as a result of an increase in proportion of women—especially urban women—who are married. Instead, the problem has been met by shifting manpower among different sectors of the economy, most significantly from collectivized and private agriculture to the state sector—to the accompaniment of a large rural to urban movement of population.

It would appear that between 1950 and 1959 rural to urban migration furnished at least half of the 16 or so million increase in state employment which, excluding state farm and machine tractor station employment, is mostly urban.[20] The still vast rural population of the U.S.S.R. will undoubtedly continue to be an important source of manpower as the net flow of new manpower slows to a trickle in the years immediately ahead.

It now appears that Russia's demographic past is beginning to have practical consequences. For almost 40 years nothing which could be called purely a population problem had slackened the pace of economic development unless it might be the postwar shortage of men. But even this shortage has not been wholly negative in effect since it has

19 "SSSR v tsifrakh," op. cit., pp. 336–337.
20 Urban increase from 1950 to 1959 amounted to about 28 million, of which 11 or 12 million would have resulted from a surplus of births over deaths (assuming an annual rate of natural increase of 17 per thousand). Thus, net urban migration (plus some administrative changes) would have added 16 or 17 million to the urban population of which perhaps 9 million would have entered the urban labor force. The net change in the urban labor supply (population 16–59) by very rough approximation might be placed at 8 or 9 million (the proportionate urban share of total net change in the population 16–59). The sharp increase in teenage school enrollment would cut into the number available to the labor force but there may have been a compensating return to the civilian labor force of demobilized servicemen. Whatever the resultant of these exchanges it seems that the combination of rural-urban migration and natural additions to the labor supply might have provided 17 or 18 million persons to fill the manpower demands of a growing urban economy. For state employment, which constitutes the bulk of urban employment, the increase between 1950 and 1959 is very likely close to 16 million.

built up a body of skills and work habits among a large part of the female population of the U.S.S.R. and at the same time, through its probable depressing effect on the birth rate, has kept the number of dependents and the consumption demands on the economy below the level they might otherwise have reached. As the birth cohorts of the war years have begun to enter the working ages—since 1956—the growth of the labor supply has slowed markedly and fallen behind the requirements set by Gosplan. The main solutions to a problem of this sort are to draw a larger proportion of the potential labor supply into the labor force or to obtain additional manpower for more favored sections of the economy by internal reorganization of the employed labor force.[21] The latter course has been followed by the Soviet Union since the war, notably so in the case of the diversion of labor from nonstate agriculture into urban state employment. There is no evidence up to the present of any substantial increase in the proportion of the potential labor supply which is active in the labor force, although, as we shall see, plans to this end are being actively considered in the Soviet Union.

THE PROBLEM AHEAD—SOLUTIONS

I. Contraction of the household and private economies

The manpower demands of the current Soviet 7-year plan (1959–65) are even greater than those of the defunct plan 6. At the same time, the estimated net additions to the overall labor supply are approaching a nadir (table 2). How are the Soviets to make ends meet? Both the question and the answer were given shortly after the plan was announced:

> In the present 7-year plan the growth of production and the projected decrease in the length of work time requires an increase of 11.5 million persons in the number of workers and employees. What sources are available to us for increasing the army of working persons? Of course, the number of the population in able-bodied ages is increasing. But this is insufficient. It is necessary to enlist for work in production and in the area of cultural and personal services persons engaged in the household and private subsidiary economy.[22]

A more precise specification of this group which is to fill the manpower gap can be gained from the annual labor resource balance compiled by the Central Statistical Administration of the U.S.S.R. According to the balance, the group is a residual obtained by subtracting both students in the "able-bodied ages" and employed persons from total "labor resources," the latter consisting of physically fit, civilian men and women 16–59 and 16–54, respectively, plus older and younger persons who are regularly employed. Making up the residual, therefore, would be housewives, domestics, persons in various lines of private employment and the unemployed, including youths who have completed 7-year or 10-year school and are looking for work for the first time or are simply unemployed. M. Ya. Sonin, a prominent Soviet economist, maintains, perhaps with a touch of hyperbole, that there are millions of people in this group who can and should be drawn into employment in the socialized economy.[23]

---

[21] Other remedies, such as increased hours of work, increased work norms, the use of "volunteer" labor on weekends and holidays, etc., are available also. One of these measures, the increase in worktime, has apparently been discarded. Provided labor productivity is not adversely affected, it is planned to reduce the length of the workday from 8 to 7 hours in the course of the 7-year plan.

[22] B. Braginskiy: "The Achievements of October," Trud (Labor), Jan. 22, 1959, p. 2.

[23] M. Ya. Sonin, "On Actual Questions of the Multiplication of Labor Resources in the U.S.S.R.," Voprosy sotsialisticheskogo vosproizvodstva (Problems of Socialist Reproduction), ed. by Ya. A. Kronrod, Moscow, 1958, pp. 262–268.

Of this group, which we assume is the group earmarked in Trud, women without small children, who spend their time keeping house, would be among those most eligible for employment. It is not surprising, therefore, that the central statistical administration keeps close watch on this group by means of a special "female labor account" which separates women in the able-bodied age group by marital status and provides information on such items as the number with children of preschool age, the number who use Government crèches and nurseries, the number employed "only in housekeeping," etc.[24]

Information of this sort provides Government planners with a more accurate notion of the number of women who might be made available to the labor force with presumably the least discouraging consequences. It also furnishes some guidance as to the adequacy of the child-care facilities for working mothers, the shortage and poor quality of which appear to be current barriers to fuller labor force participation of Soviet women.[25]

Sonin, quoted above, describes a survey taken in February-March 1955, which revealed that there is also a significant number of youths who have completed their schooling and are looking for work for the first time. He concludes that labor recruitment methods must be improved to draw these youths into useful work more quickly since they have been well drained and would be valuable additions to the work force. The situation is becoming more and more critical, he warns, since the number of graduates from 10-year schools is increasing while the facilities in higher schools are not.

II. Draining the schools

The recent Soviet educational reforms are often mentioned in connection with the problem of supplying supplementary labor. One of the central provisions of the new educational program is a cutting back of full-time enrollment in the upper grades of the secondary level (formerly grades 8 to 10) and the diversion of students into production. Lenin is cited on the subject of the inseparability of work and study to give this unpalatable move the backing of orthodoxy. The old system of 7 years of compulsory schooling has been changed to require 8 years of schooling for all children. As before, there will be 3 additional years of noncompulsory secondary education (now grades 9 to 11 instead of 8 to 10) which students may complete either as evening or correspondence students in "schools for working and rural youth" or as full-time students of the new vocational schools which are to be substituted for the old general schools. Students in schools for working and rural youth will be full-time members of the labor force subject to the limitations put on their hours of work because of

---

[24] L. E. Minz, "Methodological Problems of Labor Balance Sheet Construction and the Importance of Investigating Levels and Factors Pertaining to Labor Input" in Reports Made by Soviet Scientists to the 31st Session of the International Statistical Institute, Academy of Sciences of the U.S.S.R., Moscow, 1958. The amount of information which Soviet planners have at their disposal for labor planning is impressive. In addition to overall labor balance sheets for the urban and rural population, there are balance sheets for each economic region and branch of industry, separate balance sheets of labor on collective and state farms and, as we have seen, a special balance sheet for female labor. Supplementing these are balance sheets of "free disposable time" developed from time-budget surveys conducted by the Central Statistical Administration. These time-budget surveys are conducted on a sample basis among workers, employees, collective farmers, and other groups of the population and indicate available free time (time not used in working, eating, or sleeping) according to sex, age, residence, occupation, length of workday, and social group subdivided into (*a*) time for household and other work, (*b*) attendance at schools, courses, lectures, (*c*) time used at home for studies and self-improvement, (*d*) sports, (*e*) visits to cinemas, theaters, houses of culture, and other cultural institutions, (*f*) time spent with children, including help in children's studies, (*g*) rest time spent in walks, conversations, entertainment of friends, etc., (*h*) other forms of time expenditure. Very little technical information is available relative to the representativeness, reliability, or precision of the sample.

[25] Significant in this regard is the planned expansion of boarding schools for elementary and secondary education. The planned enrollment in these schools for 1965 is 2.5 million. Some of these schools will provide 8 years, some 11 years, of instruction, depending upon local conditions.

age. Students in vocational schools will work 2 days a week in local enterprises or in school workshops if training facilities in local industry are inadequate. The time thus spent in productive labor does not count toward the "work experience" which most students are required to have for admission to higher education. A graduate of the proposed 8-year schools will be able to complete his secondary education also by enrolling in a tekhnikum either as a full-time day student, as an evening student, as a correspondence student, or as a working student carrying a reduced course load It is planned that 25 to 30 percent of tekhnikum students will be day students enrolled on a full time basis- In their final year (third or fourth) full-time tekhnikum students will be required to work a regular 46-hour week in their chosen trade or specialty.

During a transitional period of 3 to 5 years, the old system of secondary education will be retained in certain areas on a scale sufficient to insure the uninterrupted flow of candidates for higher education. After that the new system will be in operation. Under it preference in gaining admission to schools of higher education will be given to students who have completed their secondary education with a good competitive standing and who have accumulated 2 years of work experience (provided they are under 35 years of age and provided, doubtless, that they get the support of the Komsomol, trade union, party, and management representatives—all of whom have a hand in selecting the candidates).[26]

There is thus little doubt that, for the short run at least, the "reforms" will augment the flow to the labor force through a pruning back of enrollment at all levels beyond the first 8 years of schooling. The number to be gained is difficult to estimate, but most likely will be considerably less than the number of 9 and 10 graders currently enrolled. Excluding working youth and adults the number presently enrolled in grades 9 and 10 is thought to be around 2.5 million.[27] As the plan is set up for the transitional period, a certain minimum 9 to 10 grade enrollment will be maintained, thus putting the maximum estimate of the number to be added to the labor force at something less than 2½ million. As an estimate of net additions to the civilian labor force, this figure should be further qualified in terms of the number who will be mobilized by the armed forces, the number who for various reasons remain out of the labor force, and the numbers of persons presently in the labor force who will leave it to enter school on the basis of their work experience. Finally, there is a large discount due to the fact that the man-hour contribution of persons in these ages is less than their contribution to the size of the payroll.

This scheme to inject more young people into the labor force may well be a short-run expedient. The new educational program worked out for the Russian Republic (RSFSR), which often takes the lead in implementing new policy lines, anticipates that by 1965 the enrollment in the upper grades of the new vocational schools will be roughly double the enrollment in the upper grades of the present secondary

[26] Eighty percent of the enrollment in institutions of higher education is to be reserved for students who have had at least 2 years of work experience. Izvestiya, June 4, 1958.

[27] This figure was obtained very crudely by subtracting an estimate for the number of students in eighth grade from the number enrolled in grades 8 to 10 in the 1957–58 school year (excluding working and rural youth and adult enrollees). General corroboration of such a figure is to be found in Khrushchev's address to the Presidium of the Central Committee of the party (published in Narodnoye obrazovaniye, No. 10, October 1958, p. IV), in which he explains that the plan to send youth to work after 8 years of education will add 2 to 3.5 million young people to the work force in the near future of which 40 percent will come from cities and the rest from rural areas.

system.[28] If this were to be the general pattern for the U.S.S.R., it would present a greater claim against the potential labor pool of persons 15–17 years of age than could be compensated for by the twice-weekly work contribution of vocational school students or by the moderate rise expected in the size of the age group.

The Soviet educational reforms, therefore, should not be interpreted solely as a device to solve the labor shortage of the 7-year plan in quantitative terms alone. Reports of young people unable to find employment suggest that there may be substance to the widely heard complaint that Soviet schools have been turning out an unacceptably high proportion of young people who are unprepared for the jobs available to them and disdainful of manual labor. Perhaps more important is the fact that managers of Soviet enterprises with their eye constantly on output and productivity are reportedly reluctant to hire these young people because of the short workday which is mandatory for personnel under 18 years of age.[29] Thus, the strong polytechnical emphasis and the combination of work and study in the new program are as much remedies for the qualitative deficiencies in the present system as they are devices for directly [30] infusing manpower into the labor force. A more direct explanation of the educational reforms than as a desperate quest for manpower is suggested by the facts shown in table 5 which indicate the nature of the logjam which has developed as enrollment and graduations from the high schools have increased many times more rapidly than admissions to universities and institutes of higher education.[31] To avoid tremendous waste of effort and frustration, either the higher educational facilities would have to be expanded, or else higher school education would have to be confined to a select few. In view of the heavy investment strain of the 7-year plan it is not surprising that for the short run the second alternative was chosen.

---

[28] Uchitel'skaya gazeta, April 1959, p. 1.

[29] "As is known, only a lesser part (of graduates from secondary schools) will be accepted into higher and secondary special educational institutions. The major part must be drawn into industry and agriculture. As a rule there is a reluctance to hire the young graduates in industrial plants and factories, regardless of specific instruction of the party and the Government. Young people who have not reached 18 years and who, according to law, have a right to a reduced workday, have special difficulties. Preference is also given to young boys; girls have more difficulty getting hired." (Editorial in Pravda, Sept. 25, 1957.)

[30] Several features of the reform, the effectiveness of which cannot be evaluated, seem designed to give the student a more productive role in the household economy and possibly, thereby, facilitate the release of some adult members.

[31] The downturn in enrollment (grades 8-10) and 10th grade graduations may be due to a combination of smaller age cohorts (children born during the war), an increased dropout rate attributable to discouragement over the possibility of admission to higher education (see Izvestiya, July 16, 1958, p. 2), and to the passing of persons whose education was delayed by the war.

TABLE 5.—*Enrollment in grades 8–10, graduates from the 10th grade, and 1st time enrollment in institutions of higher education, U.S.S.R.: Selected school years 1940–41—1958–59*

[In thousands]

School year	Enrollment in grades 8–10 [1]	Graduates from 10th grade [1]	First-time enrollment in institutions of higher education [2]
1940–41	2,558	(3)	162
1945–46	1,091	(3)	176
1949–50	1,151	276	210
1950–51	1,836	(3)	238
1951–52	2,789	394	256
1952–53	3,900	552	261
1953–54	5,220	972	282
1954–55	5,958	1,196	299
1955–56	6,159	1,400	286
1956–57	6,135	1,500	264
1957–58	5,570	1,600	(3)
1958–59	(3)	1,400	245

[1] As is customary, Soviet statistics for 10th grade students include the relatively small number who in a few areas attend an 11th grade.
[2] Excluding enrollment in correspondence courses.
[3] Not available.

Source: Enrollment in grades 8-10: 1945–46—1949–50 and 1951–52—1954–55 from Tsentral' noye statisticheskoye upravleniye pri sovete ministrov SSSR. Kul' turnoye stroitel'stvo SSSR (Cultural Construction of the U.S.S.R.), Moscow, 1956, p. 122 adjusted (except 1949–50) to include enrollment in schools for working youth and adults, ibid., pp. 156–157; 1940–41, 1950–51, 1955–56, and 1956–57 from Tsentral'noye statisticheskoye * * * Narodnoye khozyaystvo SSSR v 1956 godu (National Economy of the U.S.S.R. in 1956), Moscow: Gosstatizdat, 1957, p. 244. Enrollment in schools for working and rural youth and adults for 1945–46 from ibid., p. 248. 1957–58 from SSSR v tsifrakh (U.S.S.R. in Figures), Moscow: Gosstatizdat, 1958, p. 349.

Graduates from 10th grade: For 1956–59 figures reported in following sources:
1955–56—Izvestiya, Aug. 2, 1956.
1956–57—Pravda, Jan. 27, 1958.
1957–58—Trud, Jan. 16, 1959.
1958–59—Pravda, July 14, 1959.
For earlier years figures computed from linked percentages.
First-time enrollment in institutions of higher education:
Data exclude enrollment in correspondence courses and come from the following sources:
1940–41—1955–56 from Kul'turnoye stroitel'stvo * * *, op. cit., p. 203.
1956–57 from Narodnoye Khozyaystvo * * *, op. cit., p. 251.
1958–59 from V. P. Yelyutin, U.S.S.R. Minister of Higher Education, statement released June 19, 1958.

III. Rural-urban migration

The 12 million additional workers which the Soviet Union needs to carry out its 7-year plan are largely nonagricultural workers. Although the plan contemplates that production on collective and state farms is to be 70 percent greater in 1965 than in 1958,[32] labor productivity in agriculture is supposed to nearly double.[33] Taken at face value these figures imply that approximately 5 million persons might be released from agriculture, the great majority, if not all, coming from collective farms. This group plus the 5.6 million expected from the growth of the able-bodied population (table 2) would take care of more than 90 percent of the planned growth of the state employment and would leave only a million or so to be gleaned from households, street corners, schoolyards, military posts, and the many unsocialized niches in the economy.

[32] "Kontrol'nyye tsifry razvitiya narodnogo khozaystva SSSR na 1959–1965 godu (Control Figures for the Development of the National Economy of the U.S.S.R. From 1959 to 1965)," an address of N.S. Khrushchev to the XXI Congress of the C.P.S.U., Moscow: Gospolitizdat, 1958, p. 52.
[33] Kontrol'nyye tsifry * * *," op. cit., p. 59. The plan calls for a doubling of labor productivity on collective farms and a 55 to 60 percent increase for state farms. The mean increase, weighted by the present number of collective and state farmers, is around 95 percent.

However, since the rural-urban movement is to be largely voluntary [34] and since the increased productivity of farm labor depends upon the success of ambitious plans (i.e., nearly doubling the present tractor and combine park; [35] quadrupling the supply of electric power to agriculture; [36] tripling the output of chemical fertilizers; [37] changing the geographic pattern of crop production [38] and completing a prodigious housing and construction program,[39] it is apparent that the recruitment of labor from rural areas is not going to be an easy solution to the Soviet manpower shortage.

There is no doubt that great advances in labor productivity are possible for Soviet agriculture. From his studies of labor input in wheat production, V. S. Nemchinov has concluded that the 1952–53 level of mechanization in the North Caucasus achieved a two-third reduction in labor input required with the use of horse and manual power. According to his calculations, employment of the latest techniques in this area would reduce labor input requirements to less than 8 percent of the requirement under man-horse technology.[40] On his trip through the black earth belt of the Ukraine in the spring of 1959, Khrushchev deplored the great amount of hand labor still used on the farms and was particularly displeased at the sight of girls using shovels to winnow grain. He complained that "tens of thousands of young people are sent annually to harvest crops in the new lands in place of machines which would cut the labor force needed and the cost of production to a fraction." The problem then is not one of a lack of opportunities for increasing labor productivity, but one of the magnitude and cost of the effort which has been scheduled for the short space of 7 years.[41]

POPULATION REDISTRIBUTION

To achieve the ends of a plan for economic expansion, labor of the right kind must not only be found but also directed to its proper destination.

Economic change in the U.S.S.R. in the past has been associated with a massive movement of people to cities and a moderate but perceptible shift of population from west to east. Movement of population to the east—to the ore and coal deposits of the Urals and western Siberia, to the oilfields in the southeast—was a claimed accomplishment of the first 5-year plan and has been a feature of all Soviet plans since then as a means of rationalizing the distribution of productive forces in the country.

[34] This is not to say that a variety of pressures may not be applied to push population out of rural areas, e.g., gradual liquidation of the collective farmer's private plots and livestock holdings, steps to increase the farmer's dependence on money wages, etc. Not to be overlooked either are the transfers of rural youth under the labor reserve program and the organized labor draft.

[35] SSSR v tsifrakh, op. cit., p. 179 and "Kontrol'nyye tsifry * * *," op. cit., p. 58.

[36] Ibid., p. 58.

[37] Ibid., p. 33.

[38] Ibid., p. 53. This shift in crop areas is premised on the reliability of output from the new grain areas in the submarginal steppe lands of Kazakhstan, the Urals and Western Siberia which, together in 1956 accounted for more than half of the area under grain crops in the U.S.S.R. See "sel'skoye khozyaystvo SSR (Agriculture in the U.S.S.R.)," sel'khozgiz, Moscow, 1958, p. 170.

[39] Because of the Soviet emphasis on industrial growth, we assume that the various plan targets which have been cited are felt to be necessary to achieve the planned level of productivity in agriculture and the consequent release of farm labor.

[40] Minz, op. cit., p. 47.

[41] Writing in the August 1959 issue of the propaganda magazine USSR published by the Soviet Embassy in Washington, Mark Postolovsky asserts that "the intensive farm mechanization called for by the plan" will ease the present situation on the collective and state farms which now "could use considerably more workers than they have." Thus he expects "that there will be some movement of workers to the cities to swell the industrial labor total."

The eastward movement has required continued prodding by the Government, which in some periods has had to resort to special incentives, appeals to patriotism, and to the imposition of quotas, to get the required number of migrants. Despite these measures there has always been a large backwash of migrants to their far more congenial communities in the west. Wartime evacuation to the Urals and to areas east of the Urals was responsible for important additions to both the population and the economic base of these regions. The population of the Urals region, of western and eastern Siberia, and of the Far East increased by nearly 10 million between 1939 and 1959. From an analysis of changes in the size of the employed population, Newth has concluded that "the greater part of the expansion of the eastern regions took place during and just after the war." [42] Newth was referring to the period from 1939 to 1956. Since 1956 the growth of the eastern regions has not been significantly greater than that of the rest of the country.

Consideration is now being given to overhauling the devices which the Soviet Government used before and since the war to provide pioneers for the territory beyond the Urals. According to the Soviet economist Sonin, the organized draft (nabor) of labor, the resettlement of families and entire villages by the Resettlement Administration, and the training program of the state labor reserves, no longer function effectively and new techniques are needed. Sonin endorses the recently innovated "public appeal" whereby the party and the Government "appeal" to organizations such as the Komsomol' and trade unions and to the public at large, to volunteer and to send "volunteers" for permanent migration to Siberia or Central Asia.[43]

The difficulty in attracting and holding migrants in the east is undoubtedly related to the inadequate provision of housing, transportation, consumer goods, and the entire range of municipal and cultural services. For years there have been appeals to local industrial organizations and cooperatives to aid in providing essential amenities, but the problem still remains. The higher level of nominal wages paid in the east is not sufficient to keep real wages on a par with those in the western part of the Union.[44]

The movement of population to cities poses a different problem for the Soviet Government. Partly for ideological considerations (the metropolis is an ugly manifestation of the unleashing of the profit motive), and partly to avoid the diversion of investment from direct production, Soviet planners have endeavored to check migration to the very large cities (Moscow, Leningrad, Kiyev, etc.), At the same time, they have tried to channel movement to the growing industrial cities and away from older urban centers which have not figured in Soviet plans for economic expansion. In both respects they have failed. Even within its unrealistically restricted boundaries, Moscow has now exceeded the limit of 5 million persons decreed for it when the plan for Greater Moscow was adopted in 1935. Movement to the older cities has also continued, and has resulted in a surplus of labor there and shortages elsewhere. More graphically, according to Sonin, there are millions of people who do not participate in the socialized economy [45] as a result of misdirected migration.

[42] J. A. Newth, "Some Trends in the Soviet Population, 1939 to 1956 (with particular reference to the RSFSR)," Soviet Studies, No. 3, January 1959.

[43] Sonin, op. cit., pp. 269–281.

[44] Ibid., p. 281.

[45] Ibid., p. 262.

To meet its manpower objectives the Soviet Government must not only release labor for transfer within the economy but must also develop more efficient ways of transferring it to the places where it is needed. Unless steps are taken to make the new industrial centers more attractive to migrants, the ban on new construction and industrial expansion in the old industrial centers—seemingly preferred by migrants—may result only in slowing the urban flow of rural migrants. The solution to this problem, therefore, may lie in still one more Gargantuan fact—the Soviet plan to increase the square meters of urban housing during the 7-year plan period by an amount nearly equal to that erected during all previous plans. This would represent a 60-percent increase over the 1958 housing inventory. If actually accomplished, and if properly allocated, this effort could be crucial in determining both the extent and direction of future rural-urban movement.

SUMMARY AND CONCLUSIONS

There is ample evidence that after a long period of treating labor as an abundant resource, the Soviet Union must now cope with an acute shortage of replacements for its labor force. This problem is in direct consequence of the drastically reduced birth rates of the war years. Also a legacy of World War II is a large deficit of men in the ages over 30. To achieve the mobilization of its labor resources required by planned economic expansion, the U.S.S.R. must resort to fuller utilization of its labor supply and to even more transfers of labor between sectors of the economy.

Transfers between economic sectors are an inevitable concomitant of economic expansion and involve the cityward migration of population as well as job mobility. In spite of efforts to channel this movement, the flow of rural to urban migration in the U.S.S.R. has not coincided perfectly with the flow of capital investment. Migrants have shown a preference for the older and larger cities, and have tended to shun the new industrial complexes in the eastern regions of the country. This has compounded the labor shortage in areas vitally involved in the plan for economic growth.

Various expedients are being considered in the Soviet Union to deal with these problems. In the short run the program of school reorganization will undoubtedly augment the labor force. The attempt to obtain additional manpower from the household economy figures prominently in Soviet discussions but its probable success is difficult to assess. To a certain extent the success achieved in drawing people from households into production depends upon the success of other specific programs, e.g., the construction of nurseries, the effectiveness of the home-chore features of the new educational program. It depends also on the trend in such unpredictable parameters as the marriage rate, the level of real income, and so on. The single most important source of added industrial labor is likely to be the collective farm, provided the urban housing program is carried forward and provided the expected gains in agricultural labor productivity are achieved.

This by no means exhausts the alternatives open to Soviet planners. These are the "solutions" to the manpower problem which have been discussed publicly and they have in common the fact that they require minimum reliance on coercion. Thus, it should not be overlooked that, as in the past, the U.S.S.R. may employ more direct, more forceful measures to assure the necessary labor input. Hours of work could be increased (or not reduced as scheduled), work norms could be increased, "voluntary" labor contributions could harden its corvée exactments, pension rates could fail to respond to the push of inflation, etc. A balanced consideration of the problem demands that we recognize alternatives of this sort, even though at the moment there is no evidence that the Soviet regime has any of these particular schemes in mind.[46]

There are other alternatives open to Soviet planners by which they might reach many of their economic goals in spite of a labor shortage. These consist of the whole complex apparatus of direct controls and priority systems, developed by modern nations for allocation of the factors of production. Finally, of course, there is the alternative of general retrenchment and revision of economic objectives. This course, under the concealment of spurious statistics, is one for which the observer of the Soviet economy must continually be alert.

Chapter 3. Fertility and Population Growth

Given the weaknesses of our methods for making population estimates and projections, long views are particularly hazardous. But given the lumbering pace of economic and technological change in which a decade or more may be required to let the present unwind, long views are necessary. Thus, we might look at demographic trends in the U.S.S.R. over the next 15 years or so, bearing in mind that the figures we shall be examining are nothing more than estimates of the present composition of the Soviet population projected on the basis of assumptions about the future course of fertility and mortality in the U.S.S.R.

The Soviet Union is already looking beyond the end of the present 7-year plan to 1975. By that time some of its fondest hopes with regard to passing the United States in production and to matching us in per capita consumption are to be realized. Both of these goals are dependent upon the course of demographic change in the U.S.S.R. over the next 15 years.

The future level of per capita consumption in the Soviet Union is obviously difficulty to foresee when projected populations for 1975 range between 248 and 281 million.[47] This difference of 33 million consumers, which of course is purely hypothetical, results entirely from differing assumptions about the present level and future trend of Soviet fertility. The larger total is based on the assumption that by 1966 Soviet fertility will have risen to a relatively high level (comparable to that reached and passed in the United States around 1954) and remain at that level until 1975). The lower figure assumes that by 1966 Soviet fertility will decline to a relatively low level

[46] There are some very interesting recent developments in the Soviet Union which may be related in part to the labor shortage and which belong to the collection of inherent, semicoercive techniques: The decree prohibiting, as of Oct. 1, 1959, the keeping of privately owned cattle by residents of large cities (except in certain eastern areas) may well be designed, among other things, to force a large part of the 3 million or so urban dwellers who are engaged in the "private subsidiary economy" into the State labor force. Of interest also is the extensive formation of volunteer guard units for police duty during their free time, This may actually be, as it is claimed, an effective means of combating vandalism and delinquency. It is almost certainly a factor also in the recently announced 40 percent reduction in the regular constabulary forces.

[47] U.S. Department of Commerce, Bureau of the Census, "Estimates and Projections of the Population of the U.S.S.R.: 1950 to 1976," by Arthur A. Campbell and James W. Brackett, International Population Reports, Series P-95, No. 52, table 2.

(close to that of the United States during the depression years of the 1930's) and remain there until 1975.

Differing rates of growth result not only in differences in population size but also in differences in population composition. Differences in population composition entail differences in the pattern of consumption and the economic potential of the population.

The Soviet pattern of consumption (and of investment and production) in 1975 will vary greatly, for example, depending upon whether the number of children under 5 years of age should be around 30 million (under the high fertility assumption) or less than 20 million (under the low fertility assumption).[48] Similarly, the problems confronted by the Soviet school system and the channeling of Government investment would not be the same with 47 million children of school age (7–14) as with 33 million children.

When the relationship of one population group to another is considered, and the implications traced out into the social fabric one is struck by the far-reaching significance of differences in rates of population growth. For example, the availability of women for the labor force, the nature of the demand for housing, the level of average family income, the general mobility of the population—to mention just some of the consequences—will all be influenced by whether in 1975 the estimated 45 million Soviet women 20–45 years of age have 42 million children of preschool age (under 7 years) or only 28 million.

Not all significant demographic changes stem directly from current growth rates. Some are inherent in the structure of the present population, and represent the unfolding of past demographic dynamics. Among the more important demographic developments which appear significant from the point of view of the future of Soviet society and its general posture relative to the United States are the following:

1. The number of men in the U.S.S.R. of prime military age (20–34) is expected to remain fairly stationary and to decline as a percentage of the total population between 1960 and 1975. The numerical superiority over the United States which now stands at around 10 million men is expected to drop to around 2.5 to 3 million.

2. The Soviet population of university age (18–22) will decline between 1960 and 1975 from around 23 million to about 21.5 million. In the United States, there will be an upsurge in this age group from around 12 million to nearly 20 million.

3. There should be some increase in future opportunity for career advancement in the U.S.S.R. among those in middle grade positions. At the present time the number of persons 40–49 years of age is nearly equal to the number 50–59 years of age. By 1975, however, for every 10 persons in the younger age group, there will be only 6 persons 50–59 years of age. The trend in the United States is the other way and so will it be in the U.S.S.R. after 1975.

4. The population 60 years of age and over is expected to increase in the Soviet Union from around 17 million to more than 30 million by 1975. This will have a large impact upon the Soviet social security program and upon society generally. In absolute terms this population will be larger in the U.S.S.R. than in the United States, but relative to the size of the working

[48] Campbell and Brackett, op. cit.

age population the Soviet Union will have fewer elder citizens than the United States has presently.

The exact manner in which the impact of these demographic facts will be registered depends upon many other circumstances—many of them nondemographic. It is equally certain that the impact will be shaped in part by the rate of population growth. The growth of population affects not only the numerical relationships among subcategories of the population, but entails a functional and spatial reorganization of the population which alters the entire setting in which economic, social, and even demographic change take place. The most significant determinant of the future rate of growth of the Soviet population is the trend in fertility. Soviet mortality rates are relatively low and can be expected to improve. Their affect on the character of the future Soviet population, however, appears to be much less problematic than in the case of fertility.

TRENDS IN SOVIET FERTILITY

The object of our speculation here is Soviet fertility and not the Soviet birthrate. The latter is merely the ratio of births to total population and thus subject to fluctuation as the composition of the population changes, even though the inherent pattern of fertility may remain stable. Fertility, as we regard it here, is a more refined measure of the rate at which the population of a given age and sex composition produces children.[49] We can, in fact, state the question with any degree of refinement we may choose, but the answer at the present time can only be given in the form of a discussion of the hypothetical effect of selected factors on Soviet fertility. Among the relevant factors are those which might be expected to alter the rates of reproduction among Soviet women of given ages, viz the urban drift of the population, social change in backward areas of the U.S.S.R., changes in the proportion of the population which is married, attitudes toward family limitation, the availability of birth control techniques, the effect of an official pronatalist policy, and so on.

The very meager information on these factors and the fact that they sometimes work in opposite directions make their analysis involved and the outcome tentative. To some it may appear to be wholly inconclusive. In our opinion, however, there is reason to believe that the net effect may be toward a reduction in fertility. This is too important a question to treat by mere assertion, however, and thus the remainder of this chapter is devoted to a discussion of the pieces of information on which our conclusion is based.

In the U.S.S.R., as in the United States, rural fertility appears to be higher than urban fertility. Our evidence for this rests largely on Soviet assertions that such is the case [50] and on reports that rural birthrates are higher than urban rates despite the fact that the presumably greater shortage of men in the countryside would tend to reduce the proportion of married women and thus reduce fertility. This factor is of diminishing significance, however, since there is no longer a serious imbalance between the sexes in the most fertile years

[49] Fertility measures are frequently further refined to exclude the influence of marital status, previous reproductive history, ethnic group, and other variables. Since these variables are not controlled in our population projections, we shall treat them as extraneous to the present discussion of fertility.

[50] Sonin, *op. cit.*, p. 259.

(under 32). Also significant is the fact that the recent Soviet campaign to encourage the use of contraception (as a substitute for abortion) is directed primarily toward the women worker in urban areas. In an effort to reduce the cost and lost time [51] associated with abortions, women's consultation units and "rooms of personal hygiene" have been established in maternity hospitals and as part of the medical section of industrial establishments and urban enterprises. These are used extensively for disseminating contraceptive information and the sale of contraceptive devices. While the Soviet interest in contraception has increased significantly in the last few years, it should not be overlooked that as far back as 1936 Soviet doctors gave free advice on contraception and that drugstores continued to stock contraceptives even after the antiabortion decrees of 1936.[52] The differential practice of contraception has been mentioned as a factor in differential urban and rural married fertility as far back as the last century.[53]

Supporting high rural fertility would be the force of the rural large family tradition and perhaps also differences in the rate of illegitimacy.[54] To the extent that the large family tradition has survived in rural Russia, urban movement and urbanization of parts of the countryside would tend to reduce general age-sex specific fertility. With about 60 percent of Soviet families living in rural areas, and with nearly one-quarter of the births contributed by areas where the birth rate stands at 30 or more per thousand, the possible reduction in fertility is large.

Evidence concerning the trend in large families is very meager and uncertain. Families having six or more members constituted 13 percent of the urban families of the U.S.S.R. at the time of the 1926 census. According to sample data of the Central Statistical Administration and the Institute of Residential Housing, urban families with six or more members now constitute 8 percent [55] of all urban families. At the time of the Soviet Union's entry into the war, the annual number of fifth or higher order births was something over 200,000,[56] in contrast to 350,000 in the United States in 1940. This provides a rough indication of a weakening of the large family pattern. Of more recent date, we may note that between 1950 and 1956 the number of mothers receiving stipends for five or more children increased by approximately 6 percent [57] while the number of women

[51] Certified abortions are recognized as justification for work leave and compensation. The same benefits are extended in the case of miscarriage, self-induced abortions which occur within 196 days of conception, and under certain conditions to uncertified abortions that result in prolonged illness.

[52] Abortions were legalized in the U.S.S.R. in November 1955. Since that time there has been a growing interest in contraception but only as a substitute for a greater evil—abortion. The subject of contraception received considerable attention at the National Conference of Gynecologists and Obstetricians in December 1957, and in the spring of 1959 the first All-Union Conference on Contraception was held. According to the findings of the U.S.S.R. Ministry of Public Health toward the end of 1958, the variety, reliability, and quantity of contraceptives were found wanting. Considerable research is now underway throughout the U.S.S.R. and more is called for in the program of medical research for the 1958–55 period.

[53] S. A. Novosel'skiy, "Voprosy demograficheskiy i sanitornoy statistiki" (Problems of Demographic and Sanitary Statistics), Moscow, 1958, p. 73. Contraception was not unknown in rural areas. On their annual visits to market towns Ukrainian peasant women purchased contraceptive sponges at the pharmacies and a study conducted before the war indicated that among peasants in the Ukraine, coitus interruptus was widespread. See Norman E. Himes, The Medical History of Contraception," Williams and Wilkins Co., 1936, pp. 174–175 and 178.

[54] The Government policy toward illegitimacy is one of official tolerance and material support to unwed mothers. Public opinion, judged by the tone of official remonstrations, is less tolerant although S. A. Novosel'skiy has demonstrated that formerly (1926–27 in Leningrad) there were very marked differences among social classes in the incidence of illegitimacy. See S. A. Novosel'skiy, op. cit., p. 177.

[55] B. R. Rubanenko, address to the plenum session of the Academy of Construction and Architecture of the U.S.S.R. on Problems of Residential Construction, May 15–20, 1957, in "Zhilishchnoye stroitel'stvo (Residential Construction)," Moscow, 1958, pp. 25–27.

[56] Izvestiya, July 8, 1945.

[57] Tsentral'noye statisticheskoye upravleniye * * *, "Dostizheniya sovetskoy vlasti za 40 let v tsifrakh (Achievements of Soviet Power Over 40 Years in Figures)," Gosstatizdat, Moscow, 1957, p. 350.

in the age group 25–40, the approximate age group in question, increased by almost 9 percent. All of these observations are consistent with a decline in the large Soviet family, at least in urban areas,[58] and this in turn would suggest some decline in fertility among women in the more advanced ages of the childbearing period.

An increase in fertility involving lower birth orders could of course compensate for a decline in the number and average size of large families. To an important degree, a trend of this type would depend upon the proportion of women married and upon the incidence of childlessness among married couples. With respect to the first factor we know nothing beyond the fact that the marriage rate is currently relatively high.[59] We can expect, however, that the married population will become a larger proportion of the total as the imbalance between the sexes wears away. Fragmentary evidence indicates that the stillbirth rate and the proportion of sterile marriages in the U.S.S.R. is within range of the values for the United States. Barring significant medical advances, very little increase in fertility is to be expected from reduction of stillbirths or sterility. It is also improbable, taking the experience of other countries as a guide, that fertility will be increased in consequency of the tax levied on single men and childless couples.[60] Officially, the tax is not justified in terms of its pronatalist effects but as a source of revenue for the program to encourage families with three or more children.[61] Some pronatalist intent is suggested, however, by the fact that the tax is aimed at urban men and married women in the reproductive ages.

Putting all the fragments together, there seems some basis for expecting a continuation of the decline in fertility which appears to have set in already among the higher birth orders. The legalization of abortion and the consequent effort to discover and promote improved methods of contraception provide the mechanism. The rural-urban movement of the population, and the general spread of secular attitudes to the country, provide the motivational setting. An increase in the relative number of married couples is one of the most apparent tendencies working in the opposite direction. Insofar as this is conditioned by the numerical imbalance between men and women, it appears to be a factor which has spent its force. An improvement in housing conditions, and a decrease in the average

[58] Among collective farm families the decline between 1940 and 1956 in the relative number of their members under 15 years of age has been much more rapid than for the country as a whole. See "Narodnoye khozyaystvo * * *," op. cit., p. 218. This is not necessarily evidence of a decline in rural fertility as defined here, since in addition to the wartime birth deficit, the figure is affected by differentials in migration and other factors which are independent of the pattern of fertility.

[59] Fluctuations in the Soviet marriage rate could occur as the result of the legalization of de facto marriages. Under current divorce legislation the number of such marriages is believed to be large. Their legalization would have little or no effect on fertility.

[60] The tax is set at 6 percent of income with graduated reductions provided in the case of incomes under 450 rubles per month. Single women, students, military personnel, invalids, parents whose children were lost in the war, and certain other groups are exempted. The tax falls largely on urban residents and upon men between the ages of 20 and 50 and married women 20 and 45.

[61] Among the provisions to encourage large families are:

1. Grants and subsidies for the birth of a child who has three or more living siblings. These continue until the youngest child reaches 5 years of age. One-time grants are given for the birth of a third child having two living siblings.

2. Employed women who raised five or more children to the age of 8 are entitled to pensions at the age of 50 after 15 years of service.

3. Kindergarten and nursery fees are reduced 50 percent for families with four or more children; families with three children and monthly income less than 400 rubles, by 50 percent; families with three children and monthly income less than 800 rubles, by 35 percent; families with two children and monthly income of less than 600 rubles by 25 percent.

4. Awards and medals of varying degrees beginning with the 2d Degree Medal of Motherhood which is awarded for bearing and raising 5 children, up to the Order of Mother Heroine which is bestowed, with a diploma from the Presidium of the Supreme Soviet, for bearing and raising 10 children.

age at marriage as a result of a drop in the average age at which young people will become income earners under the new educational program, would both tend to raise the marriage rate and thus the fertility rate. The resolution of these conflicting tendencies cannot be foreseen at the moment. The high proportion of rural population and the fact that improved contraceptive methods should become more widely accessible, appear to outweigh other considerations and lead to the expectation of a further decline in Soviet fertility.

Chapter 4. Basic Demographic Comparisons Between the U.S.S.R. and the United States

INTRODUCTION

Preliminary results from the recent population census of the U.S.S.R., together with certain related information, afford the best opportunity in 20 years for comparing the population of the U.S.S.R. and the United States. The two countries have followed quite divergent courses during these years, with the result that in some respects they are less alike than before the war. In other respects, notably in total population, these two countries have become more alike. The following review of current information on the population of the U.S.S.R. points up some of these similarities and contrasts. Until more complete data are available, however—data such as those which are to be ready around the end of 1959 [62]—analysis is necessarily limited and conclusions correspondingly tentative.

I. TOTAL SIZE AND GROWTH

A. The size of the total population

Before the war the population of the U.S.S.R. within its present boundaries was larger by 46 percent than the population of the United States. Today, however, the Soviet population exceeds that of the United States by only 18 percent, even though throughout most of the postwar period official statistics show a more rapid rate of natural increase for the U.S.S.R. than for the United States.

Table 6.—*Total population of the U.S.S.R. and United States and percent increase 1939–59* [1]

Country	Population		Percent increase, 1939–59
	1939	1959	
U.S.S.R.	[2] 190.7	[2] 208.8	9.5
United States	[3] 131.0	[4] 177.2	35.3
U.S.S.R. / United States	1.46	1.18	

[1] In this and subsequent tables, data for Alaska and Hawaii are not included.
[2] Izvestiya, May 10, 1959. The 1959 population as reported to the nearest thousand is 208,826,000.
[3] U.S. Department of Commerce, Bureau of the Census, "Statistical Abstract of the United States, 1958," p. 5, No. 2.
[4] Interpolation between estimated population in 1957: ibid.; and average of projected values for 1969, ibid., p. 6, No. 3.

[62] The release o fpreliminary data is to be followed by more detailed tabulations of the same items plus data on such matters as age and sex, nationality, native language, marital status, educational attainment, social group, and means of subsistence, occupation, and type of economic activity.

The explanation of the very low rate of growth of the U.S.S.R. population is of course the heavy losses and deficit of births inflicted on the Soviet Union by the war.

B. Evaluation of total population

The total population reported by the Soviet census is lower than many observers had expected. The senior engineer and executive officer of the Central Statistical Administration's machine accounting division, D. K. Zhak, in discussing plans for tabulating census results, anticipated a population in the neighborhood of 215 million.[63] The announced total also is more than a million short of the population that would have been reached if the officially estimated population of 200.2 million in 1956 [64] had grown according to the officially reported rates of natural increase. And since the 1956 figure, especially its urban component, has been characterized as possibly too low [65] there seemed to be good reason to expect a figure larger than 210 million.

Aside from these prior expectations, there are no unchallengable grounds for rejecting the census results. An examination of the preparations for the census and the plans for its conduct reveals no obvious shortcomings but rather shows a thoroughgoing concern for completeness of coverage.[66] The most likely major exclusion, the military, are stated to be included in the figures that have been released.

If past experience can be relied on, we should not expect major revisions of the preliminary census total.

c. Growth of the Soviet population

The United States is not expected to attain a population as large as the present Soviet population before 1970.[67] The future growth of both countries will be largely a matter of natural increase,[68] that is, an excess of births over deaths. Unlike the United States during its period of basic industrial development. the U.S.S.R. has not been able to rely upon immigration to supply its manpower needs but has had to raise its own. In its 40-year history the U.S.S.R. has acquired approximately 20 million persons through annexation—all since 1939—and a number of these have entered into the streams of eastward migration within the country. Coincidently, this figure is close to the number of immigrants who entered the United States during the 40 years prior to the passage of the restrictive immigration legislation of 1924.

---

[63] D. K. Zhak, "Mekhaniziroyannaya razrabotka materialov perepisey naseleniya S.S.S.R. (Mechanical Processing of the Material From the U.S.S.R. Census of Population)," Moscow, 1958, p. 116.

[64] Tsentral'noye statisticheskoye upravleniye pri Sovete Ministrov S.S.S.R., Narodnoye khozyaystvo S.S.S.R. (National Economy of the U.S.S.R.)," Moscow, 1956, p. 17.

[65] M. Ya. Sonin, "Ob aktual'nykh voprosakh vosproizvodstva trudovykh resursov S.S.S.R. (On Actual Problems of the Reproduction of Labor Resources in the U.S.S.R.)," in "Voprosy sotsialisticheskogo vosproizvodstva (Problems of Socialist Reproduction), Moscow," 1958, p. 258. In this source Sonin refers to total population only. In another source he stated his belief that the urban population was too low.

[66] On the first canvass of the population 207,752,000 persons were enumerated; this was followed by a second visit which added another 285,000 persons to the total. Finally, a checking out of schedules which had been filled out for persons who were temporarily absent at the time of the enumerator's visit yielded an additional 789,000.

[67] The average of the four series of Bureau of the Census projections of the total population for 1970 is 211,006,000. Series III projection for 1970 is 208,199,000 and assumes a moderate decline in the level of fertility, U.S. Department of Commerce, Bureau of the Census, "Statistical Abstract of the United States, 1958," pp. 6-7. The population projected for the U.S.S.R. in 1970 falls in the range between 237 and 259 million. See U.S. Department of Commerce, Bureau of the Census, "Estimates and Projections of the Population of the U.S.S.R.: 1950 to 1976, by Arthur A. Campbell and James W. Brackett, series P-95, No. 52, Washington, 1959.

[68] Since the war net annual immigration to the United States has fluctuated between 150,000 to 350,000 per year. The U.S.S.R. has not reported any statistics on immigration. It has put forth considerable effort in recent years to persuade emigres to return from abroad, but it seems unlikely that this would be a major source of growth in the future.

1. *Natural increase.*—In 1957 the rate of natural increase in the Soviet Union was 17.5 per thousand, compared to 15.7 per thousand in the United States. These may be compared to natural increase rates of 13.4 and 8.6, respectively, for 1940 (see table 7). Thus, while growth rates for both countries have risen, the U.S. rate has shown a greater increase. In 1940, for example, the rate of natural increase in the United States amounted to only 64 percent of the rate in the Soviet Union, while in 1957 it was 90 percent (see table 8).

Interestingly, rises in the growth rate for the respective countries stem basically from different origins. In the U.S.S.R. both birth and death rates have declined, but the decline in the death rate has been much greater than the decline in the birth rate. In the United States, on the other hand, while the death rate declined somewhat, a modest rise (30 percent) in the birth rate was the major contribution to the higher growth rates. Neither the U.S.S.R. nor the U.S. rates of natural increase are high when contrasted to many of the world's underdeveloped countries, but they are more than double the rates for the countries of Western Europe, largely because of the difference in birth rates.

Taking reported rates at face value and leaving out war years, the U.S.S.R. natural increase rate shows no decided trend either downward or upward during the Soviet period. The present level is slightly above the rate in 1913 but the tendency between 1913 and 1940 was in the other direction. The only way to guess at the prospective course of natural increase, therefore, is to examine its two components: the death rate and the birth rate.

TABLE 7.—*Vital rates of the U.S.S.R. and the United States: Selected years, 1913–57*

Year	U.S.S.R.				United States			
	Rate per 1,000 population			Infant mortality rate [1]	Rate per 1,000 population			Infant mortality rate [1]
	Birth	Death	Natural increase		Birth	Death	Natural increase	
1913	47.0	30.2	16.8	273	[2] 29.5	[2] 13.2	[2] 16.3	[2] 99.9
1940	31.7	18.3	13.4	184	19.4	10.8	8.6	47.0
1950	26.5	9.6	16.9	81	24.1	9.6	14.5	29.2
1951	26.8	9.6	17.2	84	24.9	9.7	15.2	28.4
1952	26.4	9.3	17.1	75	25.1	9.6	15.5	28.4
1953	24.9	9.0	15.9	68	25.0	9.6	15.4	27.8
1954	26.5	8.9	17.6	68	25.3	9.2	16.1	26.6
1955	25.6	8.2	17.4	60	25.0	9.3	15.7	26.4
1956	25.0	7.5	17.5	47	25.2	9.4	15.8	26.0
1957	25.3	7.8	17.5	45	25.3	9.6	15.7	26.3

[1] Deaths of infants under 1 year of age per 1,000 births.
[2] Rates for 1915. Death rate for 1913 is 13.8.

Source: U.S.S.R.: Vestnik Statistiki, No. 10, 1958, p. 93, United States: Various editions of Statistical Abstract of the United States.

TABLE 8.—*Comparison of vital rates for the U.S.S.R. and the United States: 1940 and 1957*

Country	1940			1957		
	Birth	Death	Natural increase	Birth	Death	Natural increase
1940 rate=100:						
U.S.S.R.	100	100	100	80	43	131
United Sattes	100	100	100	130	89	183
U.S.S.R. rate=100:						
U.S.S.R.	100	100	100	100	100	100
United States	61	59	64	100	123	90

Source: Table 7.

2. *The death rate.*—The death rate of 7.5 per thousand which was reported along with the census results is not the lowest in the world as claimed, but is nevertheless an impressively low rate. It represents real gains in Soviet science, medicine, and sanitation, and also reflects a favorable age and sex structure of the population.

If the United States death rates [69] for individual age-sex groups are assumed for the population of the U.S.S.R.,[70] a death rate of 6.4 per thousand results. Comprising this with the U.S.S.R. crude rate of 7.5 strongly suggests lower mortality for specific age and sex groups in the United States than in the Soviet Union.

Additional evidence that mortality in the U.S.S.R. has not reached the level of the United States comes from a comparison of infant mortality rates, one of the most sensitive indicators of the general level of health in a population. The Soviet infant mortality rate as reported for 1957 (45 per thousand live births) [71] exceeds that of the United States (26) by 73 percent. It is about the level of the prewar U.S. rate and very close to the present rates for Italy and Japan. Nevertheless, a rate of 45 per thousand for the U.S.S.R. represents a striking decline from its prewar level of 184 per thousand, which is higher than the rates currently reported for any of the underdeveloped countries of the world. It is clear that the U.S.S.R. has partaken fully of the worldwide revolution in medicine and public health. This is clear also from the life expectancy figures which have been released. The expectation of life at birth reported for the U.S.S.R. in 1955–56 [72] was 63 years for males and 69 years for females. In the United States, male life expectation attained a comparable level in 1941, but the average length of life for females did not reach 69 years until after the war. Since the end of the war 3 years have been added to the average length of life of U.S. males; the average length of life of U.S. females has been stretched by 5 years. The expectation of life at birth for the United States in 1956 was 67 years for males and 73 years for females. Thus, although the U.S.S.R. has not yet achieved the low levels of mortality of the United States, the picture from the official figures is of impressive gains.

---

[69] Rates for 1955 were used. See United Nations Demographic Yearbook, 1957.

[70] The population used for this exercise was an estimated distribution for 1958 prepared by the Foreign Manpower Research Office, Bureau of the Census. The structure of this estimated population is consistent with all known facts about the Soviet population but there is, of course, no guarantee that it is a completely accurate reproduction.

[71] Vestnik statistiki (Statistical Herald), No. 10, 1958, p. 93.

[72] Dostizheniya sovetskoy vlasti za sorok let v tsifrakh (Accomplishment of the Soviet regime over 40 years, in figures), Moscow, 1957, p. 345. Very little is known about the data from which these life expectancy values were computed. The construction of new Soviet life tables is planned for 1961 using data from the recent population census.

Another relevant aspect of the mortality situation in the U.S.S.R. is the amount of variation in the death rate between different parts of the country. In 1955 the crude death rate [73] varied from a low of 6.6 in the Republic of Georgia to 11.9 for Estonia.[74] Crude death rates in the United States in the same year exhibit an almost identical range of variation: 6.6 for Utah to 11.7 for New Hampshire. Age appears to be a factor in explaining these variations in both cases, although for the Soviet Union our only measure of age composition is the ratio of voters—persons 18 years of age and over—to total population. Thus, the relatively high death rate for Estonia would seem to be associated with the fact that almost 8 out of 10 persons in that republic are 18 years of age or older. In the Republic of Georgia, where the lowest death rate is found, approximately 6 out of 10 are 18 years and over. The difference between the extreme death rates in the United States is also associated with difference in age. In New Hampshire 67 percent of the population is 18 years and over while in Utah the figure is 58 percent.[75]

A more important point, however, is the fact that if we eliminate from consideration the two areas of the Soviet Union with the highest death rates and the oldest populations—Estonia and Latvia [76]—the death rates for all the remaining areas are below the lowest ever reached by the United States. With the differences between the two countries in infant mortality and average length of life favoring the United States, the indicators again point to a young population as a principal ingredient in the low Soviet death rates. Inaccuracies in the statistics themselves cannot be dismissed as a reason for the low death rates reported by the U.S.S.R. We have no definite information, however, that would lead us to believe that deaths are less accurately reported than the population figures to which they are related.

With no high death rate areas susceptible to easy victories, the future course of the Soviet death rate would seem to be an upstream struggle against an aging population, for the declines in age-specific mortality which are to be expected cannot be counted on to fully counteract a trend toward a higher crude death rate. This trend will be reinforced by a balancing out of the number of men and women in the population. Death rates are higher among men than women, and thus the present deficit of U.S.S.R. males acts to hold down the general death rate.[77] As the gap between the number of men and women closes, the crude rate will tend to rise.

3. *The birth rate.*—The announced Soviet birth rate (25 births per thousand population) is very close to that which has been recorded for the United States in recent years. Both the Soviet and United States birth rates have been fairly stable since 1950. The difference is that the U.S.S.R. birth rate has never regained its prewar level whereas the current U.S. rate is as high as any that has been recorded since before World War I. Very different demographic dynamics,

---

[73] A crude rate is based upon the total number of events of some type occurring to a stated population during a given period of time. Refined rates measure events among more restricted populations in order to exclude the influence of certain variables.

[74] Rates for Uzbekistan and Turkmenistan are not available.

[75] U.S. Department of Commerce, Bureau of the Census, "Estimate of the Civilian Population by Broad Age Groups for States and Selected Outlying Areas: July 1, 1957," Current Population Reports, Series P-25, No. 194. The difference in age composition between these two States is more clearly brought out by comparing the population 65 years and over: New Hampshire, 11.1 percent; Utah, 6.3 percent.

[76] Latvia's death rate in 1955 was 10.5. Seventy-two percent of the population of Latvia was 18 years of age and over. In both the ratio of deaths to total population and the ratio of voters to total population Latvia ranks second to Estonia.

[77] For more on the age and sex composition of the Soviet population, see section III below.

therefore, underlie the surface similarity of the United States and U.S.S.R. crude birth rates.

In the United States, for example, there is relatively little geographic variation in the crude rates outside of several States in the South and Southwest where the birth rate exceeds 30 per thousand.[78] These States, however, currently account for only 5 percent of the births. In the U.S.S.R., on the other hand, much greater geographic variation in the birth rate is encountered. Areas with birth rates greater than 30 in 1955 accounted for nearly one-quarter of all births. Younger populations, balanced sex ratios, and higher age-specific fertility rates are no doubt all involved in these high birth rates. Most of the high birth rate areas in the U.S.S.R. are found in the republics of central Asia and Transcaucasia. Continued social and economic change in these areas can be expected to have a downward effect on the birth rate.

As in the United States, so it is in the Soviet Union that the birth rates in rural areas are higher than in urban areas. In this connection, therefore, it is important to note that about 60 percent of Soviet families are rural families.[79] It is nearly the reverse in the United States, where in 1957 over 60 percent of the families were urban.[80] As Soviet farmers continue to move to the city and as the countryside becomes urbanized, a tendency toward lower birth rates is expectable.

Marriage in the U.S.S.R. has to contend with a difficult housing situation—more of a barrier perhaps in urban than in rural places. Perhaps equally important in its effect on the proportion married is the imbalance between the sexes. As it affects the birth rate, however, this is of diminishing importance since the sexes in the most fertile years (under 32) are now stated to be equal. The marriage rate of 12 per thousand is relatively high (the U.S. rate in 1957 was 8.9) and undoubtedly reflects this balance of the sexes in the marriageable ages. The marriage rate and the birth rate do not always move together and it is risky, therefore, to put any emphasis on the probable future decline in the Soviet marriage rate.[81]

To forecast the results of the various factors impinging on the birth rate is hazardous.[82] There is much high fertility potential to be reduced in central Asia and among rural families. However, the great unknowns are the relative number of married persons now and in the future, and the extent to which arbitrary family limitation will be practiced in the future.[83]

If we can assume that the Soviet birth rate already reflects the impact of an increased marriage rate and an increase in the proportion of the population married, the net effect from all other influences would be toward a lower crude birth rate in the future.

[78] "Statistical Abstract," op. cit., p. 58.

[79] "Planovoye khozyaystvo (Planned Economy)," No. 6, 1955, p. 55.

[80] "Statistical Abstract," op. cit., p. 47. The percentage reported is 63.3. This is an understatement of the urban proportion since it refers only to places which were urban in 1950.

[81] The nature of the Soviet marriage rate is not perfectly clear since the handling of common-law marriages is unknown. There is besides, perhaps, some tendency toward inflation in the rate since marriage certificates are useful in obtaining housing allocations in certain areas.

[82] For a discussion of the factors which might be expected to influence future Soviet fertility, see ch. 3.

[83] Abortions have been legalized in the Soviet Union since 1955. No stipulations other than proper medical and sanitary safeguards are made. Abortions have been reported to exceed 30 percent of the live births in recent years. Concern over the high rate of abortions appears to have stimulated serious Soviet interest in contraception. See report of Abraham Stone in Science, vol. 127, May 16, 1958.

D. Summary of growth prospects

Only the most tentative and cautious conclusions about the future rate of natural increase can be drawn from a consideration of the present birth and death rates reported for the U.S.S.R. There is some reason, however, to expect an increase in the overall death rate due to the aging of the population and an expectable increase in the proportion of males in the population. Such an increase would most likely be moderated by a further decline in age-specific mortality, but if the present reported levels of infant mortality and life expectation are correct, such gains would have a minor effect on the total number of deaths. There is not enough information for a convincing analysis of Soviet fertility. However, the large proportion of rural families and the high birth rates of the underdeveloped areas within the Soviet Union are threats to a sustained, high level of the national birth rate.

With a slight rise in the death rate and some decline in fertility, the natural increase rate of the Soviet Union could easily fall below that of the United States at the present time. More importantly, however, the implication of a diminished rate of natural increase for the U.S.S.R., and even of a closer correspondence in the overall size of the Soviet Union and the United States, depends upon the ecological and social organization of each population aggregate.

II. REDISTRIBUTION OF THE POPULATION

Changes in the geographic distribution of the Soviet population between 1939 and 1959 reflect two major trends—movements from west to east and from rural territory to urban areas. Both movements continue trends established in the previous intercensal period, 1926–39. Like comparable movements in the United States, they indicate a nation undergoing rapid industrialization and making adjustments to utilize its resources more fully.

A. Total population

The census results show some striking increases in the population of Eastern regions of the U.S.S.R. A gain of 70 percent was reported for the total population of the Far East, 32 percent for eastern Siberia, 33 percent for the Urals, 53 percent for Kazakhstan, and 42 percent for Kirgiziya—as compared with an increase of 9.5 percent in the total. Despite these high rates of increase, however, the absolute shift of population from west to east has been quite moderate. Seventy percent of the Soviet population now lives west of the Urals. Before the war, the population in this part of the country, which constitutes only 21 percent of the total area, was 76 percent of the total (table 9).

TABLE 9.—*Percentage distribution of the area and population of the U.S.S.R., by western and eastern regions, 1939 and 1959*

Region	Area	Population					
		Total		Urban		Rural	
		1939	1959	1939	1959	1939	1959
Total	100.0	100.0	100.0	100.0	100.0	100.0	100.0
West of the Urals	21.0	75.5	69.8	76.1	68.6	75.2	70.9
Urals and east	78.9	24.5	30.2	23.9	31.4	24.8	29.1

Source: Area—Informatsionno-statisticheskiy otdel prezidiuma verkhovnogo soveta SSSR. SSSR Administrativno-territorial'noye deleniye soyuznykh respublik na 1 yanvarya 1958 goda (U.S.S.R. Administrative-Territorial Divisions of the Union Republics on Jan. 1, 1958), Moscow, 1958, pp. 13–483.
1939 Population—Izvestiya, May 10, 1959; Tsentral'noye statisticheskoye upravleniye. Sovetskaya torgovlya (Soviet Trade), Moscow, 1957, pp. 312–332.
1959 Population—Izvestiya, May 10, 1959.

The only three regions which showed a decrease in population between the censuses were the central European part of the R.S.F.S.R. (around Moscow), Belorussia, and Lithuania. Of these three, the central European region was the big loser, with a net loss of 3.2 million.

A rough comparison of this west-east shift in the U.S.S.R. to population shifts in the United States between 1940 and 1957 indicates that the movement of the Soviet population to the east has been greater than the westward movement in the United States (table 10). In 1940, 69 percent of the population lived east of the Mississippi in 29 percent of the total area. By 1957 the proportion of the population east of the Mississippi had dropped slightly to 67 percent.

TABLE 10.—*Percentage distribution of the area and population of the United States, east and west of the Mississippi River: 1940, 1950, and 1957*

Region	Area	Population						
		Total			Urban		Rural	
		1940	1950	1957	1940	1950	1940	1950
Total	100.0	100.0	100.0	100.0	100.0	100.0	100.0	100.0
East of the Mississippi	29.1	69.2	68.1	67.0	74.0	70.4	63.1	64.6
West of the Mississippi	70.9	30.8	31.9	33.0	26.0	29.6	36.9	35.4

Source: Area—U.S. Bureau of the Census, "Statistical Abstract of the United States: 1958." (79th edition), Washington, D.C., p. 160. Population—Ibid., pp. 10, 13, and 23. 1957 data are provisional figures for July 1.

These figures do not reveal the dramatic increase which occurred in the Pacific region (comprising California, Oregon, and Washington), which increased by 8.7 million between 1940 and 1957, or by more than 89 percent. This was a much larger increase than was registered by any of the Soviet economic regions; the largest gain there was 70 percent for the Far East. Other regions of the United States which showed marked gains were the Mountain region, 54 percent; South Atlantic, 38 percent; and East North Central, 32 percent.

Two conclusions thus emerge: (1) Certain areas within the U.S.S.R.—especially those east of the Urals—have exhibited remarkable rates of growth since the prewar period in spite of only a moderate increase of the total population. These rates of increase have been equaled by several areas in the United States during roughly the same period; (2) the rapid growth of the Soviet east has produced a very moderate eastward shift in the population. In the United States, using the traditional east-west dividing line of the Mississippi, differential regional growth has not appreciably affected the prewar east-west population balance.

The eastward shift of some 16 million persons between 1939 and 1959 occurred as the result of both migration and natural increase, their relative importance being difficult to evaluate. Millions of people were moved to the Urals and other eastern areas during the war, and many never returned to their homes. Thousands of servicemen demobilized since World War II have also settled in the east. The greatest source of migration, however, has been the planned—often forced—resettlement of both families and single persons from the cities and villages of the European west to the new lands of the east. Soviet sources carry daily reports of families—often thousands of families—who have undertaken a pioneering venture beyond the Urals. A certain number of these migrants return to their former homes, but it seems clear that large numbers have become permanent residents in the east.

Other factors producing the population shift have been the relatively smaller civilian war losses of the regions east of the Urals, and a higher rate of natural increase which characterized these areas before and since the war.

It is probable that the eastward shift of the Soviet population will continue for some time. The current 7-year plan contains provisions for an accelerated development of the east, and a planned flow of both industrial and agricultural labor to take part in the new programs is to be expected. This, together with higher rates of natural increase, should produce a steady, gradual shift of Soviet population to the east.

B. Urban population

The urban population of the U.S.S.R. increased from 60.4 to 99.8 million between 1939 and 1959, a gain of more than 65 percent. Compared with the increase of 9.5 percent in the total population, this is an impressive change. It bespeaks a torrential flow of population from rural to urban areas as a concomitant of rapid industrialization.

Nevertheless, the process of urbanization in the U.S.S.R. has slowed down markedly in comparison with that of the previous intercensal period, 1926–39. Both the annual increment to the urban population and the annual rate of increase are below comparable figures for the earlier period. Between 1939 and 1959 the average annual increment to the urban population was 2.0 million, or half a million less than the annual average increment of 2.5 million between 1926 and 1939. The annual rate of increase, 1939–59, was 3.3 percent, while the rate for the period 1926–39 was 9.4 percent. In the most recent period the absolute annual average increase of the Soviet urban population seems to have attained its prewar level but the rate of increase is still around half the average prewar rate despite the fact that the annual increase in the index of industrial output is higher now than before the war.

The Soviet urban population at present is slightly greater than the U.S. urban population at the time of the 1950 census, but probably only about three-fourths of the present urban population of the United States.[84] Stated in terms of the numbers of persons leading a nonagricultural way of life, the differences between this country and the U.S.S.R. are even more extreme. Approximately 85 percent of rural families in the U.S.S.R. are farm families whereas in the United States the figure is 35 percent.[85] Thus, while the urban population of the United States probably exceeds the urban population of the Soviet Union by about one-fourth, the estimated nonagricultural population of the United States is one-third greater than that of the U.S.S.R.

The shift of the Soviet urban population to the east has been comparable to that of the total population, as is shown by the data in table 9. Although there have been some tremendous increases in the number of urban residents in eastern regions, 68.6 percent of the Soviet urban population still lives west of the Urals.

In all of the eastern regions of the R.S.F.S.R. the urban population increased more than 100 percent—including a gain of nearly 150 percent in the Far East. The republics of central Asia showed similar gains—Kirgizia and Tadzhikstan both had increases of more than 150 percent—while the urban population of Kazakhstan grew by 141 percent.

Increases in the western areas were smaller, percentagewide, but greater in numbers of persons. All of the western regions registered urban population increases of more than 30 percent, with a 36.6 percent growth in the populous center, around Moscow, and much larger increases in the smaller Baltic and Transcaucasian republics.

The growth of urban population in the U.S.S.R. has been the result of three processes: Migration, administrative action, and natural increase. Although the exact share of the increase attributable to each source is not known, it is certain that migration from rural areas has played the greatest role. Since the 1920's there has been a steady flow in this direction, and the rural reservoir is still large.

Administrative action, or a change from rural to urban status by decree, has been another important factor, particularly in the last few years. Between 1939 and 1959 there was a net increase of 1,857 urban places in the U.S.S.R.—503 new cities and 1,354 new urban-type settlements. Of these, 128 cities and 499 settlements were added in the 3 years between January 1956 and January 1959.[86]

The Soviet Union has a greater number of cities with a population above 50,000 than the United States, 299 in 1959 compared with 232 in the United States in 1950.[87] Of these, the U.S.S.R. had 25 in the size group of 500,000 and above, and the United States had 18. There has been little change in this comparison since before World War II, when the U.S.S.R. had 221 cities with a population of 50,000 or more, and the United States had 199.

C. Rural population

The other side of the picture of population change in the Soviet Union is the decrease of the rural population. During the intercensal period the number of rural inhabitants dropped by nearly 21 million,

[84] According to recent estimates by Resources for the Future, Inc., the U.S. urban population in 1960 will be 126,600,000, or 70.5 percent of the total U.S. population.

[85] Based on data in U.S. Bureau of the Census, ' Statistical Abstract of the United States: 1957" (78th edition), Washington, D.C., 1957, p. 15; and Tsentral'noye statisticheskoye upravleniye pri sovete ministrov SSSR, Narodnoye khozyaystvo SSSR v 1956 godu (National Economy of the U.S.S.R. in 1956), Moscow, 1957, pp. 19, 105, and 203.

[86] Narodnoye khozyaystvo, op. cit., p. 33, and Izvestiya, May 10, 1959.

[87] Izvestiya, May 10, 1959, and "Statistical Abstract," op. cit., p. 19.

or by 16 percent of the total in 1939. As a proportion of the total population, it declined from 68 percent in 1939 to 52 percent in 1959.

Rural inhabitants in the United States, on the other hand, increased by 7.9 percent between 1940 and 1950, or from 57.2 to 61.8 million—using the 1940 concept of urban. (If the 1950 definition of urban were used for both 1940 and 1950 the increase in rural population would be somewhat less.) This is consistent with the longtime trend for rural population in the United States which has shown an increase in every decade since the earliest years despite losses in some of the Central States. Unlike the U.S.S.R., where for at least 30 years rural areas have lost population to urban areas, the U.S. rural population, through natural increase and immigration, has managed to supply people to the cities and still increase in size.

The continuing Soviet efforts to develop agriculture in the east, and especially the "virgin lands" campaign which began in 1954, have involved the movement of hundreds of thousands of persons to the east. In 1956 it was announced that more than 350,000 persons had settled in the "virgin lands," [88] and since that time the movement of both single persons and families has continued. Nevertheless, the shift of rural population eastward has not been great.

It was only in Kazakhstan and in three central Asiatic republics (Uzbek, Tadzhik, and Kirgiz) that the rural population increased. In all eastern regions of the R.S.F.S.R. the rural population decreased. The conclusion which these data suggest is that a large share of the Soviet eastward migration has gone to urban areas, and that within the eastern regions themselves there has been an extensive rural-urban movement.

In the west, all regions but one lost rural population between 1939 and 1959. The Moldavian Republic showed an increase of 5.5 percent, but the losses in other areas ranged up to a high of 31 percent in the center, around Moscow.

The slight geographic shift eastward of the U.S. rural population between 1940 and 1950—from 63 to 65 percent east of the Mississippi—was of a fundamentally different nature than the eastward shift of the rural population of the U.S.S.R. American farmers west of the Mississippi did not open up new agricultural areas in the east but became part of the rural-urban movement within their own areas and to other parts of the country. The number of farms and acres of harvested cropland have generally declined in the eastern part of the United States.

III. POPULATION COMPOSITION

A. The sex ratio

One of the most significant disclosures of the Soviet census is the low proportion of males in the total population. Females outnumber males by 20 million, a greater imbalance than is shown in any earlier Soviet census.

[88] New York Times, Apr. 8, 1956.

TABLE 11.—*Males per 100 females, U.S.S.R. and United States, selected years*

Year	Males per 100 females	
	U.S.S.R.	United States
1926	93.4	103.1
1939	91.9	100.8
1959	81.9	[1] 98.0

[1] Includes Armed Forces overseas.

The low sex ratio of 1926 reflects the losses and birth deficits of World War I and the Revolution. To this was added the effects of the calamitous period of collectivization of the 1930's, which depressed the ratio even further in 1939. The present nadir of the sex ratio—the lowest reported for any country in the world except East Germany—is a simple measure of the demographic cost of World War II. Low birth rates during World War II and the longer average length of life of women have been secondary contributors to the low Soviet sex ratio.

B. Age composition

No direct 1959 census information on the age structure of the Soviet population has so far been released. The number of persons 18 years of age and over enumerated in the census has not yet been announced. An approximation to the size of this group is given by the number of voters [89] registered for the March 1959 elections.

The ratio of voters (approximately 137 million) to total population when compared with ratios of the same type for earlier years reveals an upward tendency, denoting a decline in the relative size of the preadult population as well, perhaps, as an aging of the adult population due to the increase in the average length of life: [90]

TABLE 12.—*The ratio of registered voters to total population in the U.S.S.R.: Selected years*

Year:	*Voters per 100 of the population*	Year—Continued	*Voters per 100 of the population*
1939	55	1955	63
1950	62	1958	65
1951	62	1959	65

The only other available indication of the current age composition of the Soviet population is the statement that there are an equal number of males and females under 32 years of age.[91] This is possibly a statement that should not be taken too literally, for in addition to a probable rounding error, it is likely that the number of women reporting themselves as under 32 is somewhat inflated due to the almost universal tendency among women toward polite understatement of age. In general, however, the statement makes sense, since it is the population under 32 that escaped the heaviest mortality of the last war.

The population 18 to 31 years of age in 1959 was born during the years from 1928 to 1941. These are years for which we have some

[89] Legal voting age in the U.S.S.R. is 18.

[90] Nondemographic factors such as the political amnesties of 1953–56 have helped to increase this ratio but do not appear capable of explaining it.

[91] Izvestiya, May 10, 1959.

information about births, and if our guesses about the deaths suffered by this group are not too bad, we would expect approximately 53 million persons in the age group 18–31 in 1959. Those 32 and above would therefore equal 84 million (137 million voters minus 53 million 18–31 years of age).

Putting these pieces together with the reported total number of males and females, we arrive at the surprising—and of course very tentative—conclusion that in the ages 32 and above there were more than 5 women for every 3 men (see table 13).[92] The implied sex ratio of 60 is more than 10 points below that for East Germany, indicating, if true, that the decimation of Soviet troops exceeded that of any other belligerent. The common observation of women doing men's work in the U.S.S.R. needs no further confirmation than the figures here cited.

TABLE 13.—*Estimated current sex ratios by age for the U.S.S.R. and the United States*

Age	Males per 100 females		Age	Males per 100 females	
	U.S.S.R. 1959	United States, 1960		U.S.S.R. 1959	United States, 1960
All ages	82	98	45 to 49 years	53	95
			50 to 54 years	62	96
Up to 4 years	105	104	55 to 59 years	64	94
5 to 9 years	104	104	60 to 64 years	60	91
10 to 14 years	104	104	65 to 69 years	58	88
15 to 19 years	104	103	70 years and over	51	79
20 to 24 years	104	102	Under 15 years	104	104
25 to 29 years	91	99	15 to 59 years	77	98
30 to 34 years	80	97	60 years and over	56	85
35 to 39 years	60	96	32 years and over	60	93
40 to 44 years	50	96			

Source: United States. U.S. Bureau of the Census, "Illustrative Projections of the Population of the United States, by Age and Sex, 1960 to 1980," by Meyer Zitter and Jacob S. Siegel, "Current Population Reports," series P-25, No. 187.
U.S.S.R.: See table 1.

By adding some more tentative figures to those already considered we get the following broad profile of the Soviet population in 1959 which can be contrasted with current estimates for the United States:

[92] The detailed distribution by age in table 12 and in table F of the appendix has been obtained by adjusting earlier estimates to conform to the new census information. For a full description of the procedures by which the detailed estimates are made, see Campbell and Brackett, op cit.

TABLE 14.—*Estimated age distribution of the population of the U.S.S.R. and the United States: 1959*

[Absolute figures in millions]

Age	U.S.S.R.		United States [1]	
	Number	Percent	Number	Percent
All ages	208.8	100.0	180.1	100.0
0 to 6 years	[2] 33.0	15.8	27.6	15.3
7 to 17 years	[3] 38.8	18.6	36.7	20.4
18 to 31 years	[4] 53.0	25.4	32.7	18.2
32 years and over	[5] 84.0	40.2	83.1	46.1

[1] Estimates for 1960. See "Statistical Abstract, 1958," op. cit., pp. 6–7.
[2] Survivors of estimated births 1953–58. See U.S. Bureau of the Census, "Estimates and Projections of the Population of the U.S.S.R.: 1950 to 1976," series P–95, No. 52.
[3] Residual. Children enrolled in grades 1–10, the vast bulk of whom are in the age group 7 to 17, are estimated to have numbered approximately 30 million in 1959. The implied school participation rate $\frac{30.0}{38.8}=0.77$ is reasonable.
[4] Estimated survivors of births, 1928–41. See U.S. Bureau of the Census, op. cit.
[5] Registered voters in 1959 all-union elections minus estimated population, 18–31.

The preschool population of the U.S.S.R. is approximately 20 percent greater than that of the United States, according to our rough calculations. This is about as might be expected from a comparison of the estimated number of births in the two countries in recent years. In 1956, estimated births in the U.S.S.R. exceeded the number of U.S. births by 19.6 percent.

The number of children now receiving their elementary and secondary training (ages 7–17), among whom are the coming generation of scientists and technicians, is not greatly different between the two countries. The reason, of course, is that this group includes those born between 1942 and 1946 when the birth rate was relatively high in the United States and extremely low in the Soviet Union.

Comparison within the young adult age groups (18 to 31) must be made very cautiously since there are reasons to believe that the Soviet figure may be exaggerated.[93] There seems little question, however, that the draft-age population in the Soviet Union exceeds that of the United States by a greater margin than is suggested by the differences in the total population. This does not necessarily mean that the pool of manpower available for military services is that much larger in the U.S.S.R. The relative scarcity of older men requires industry and agriculture to draw upon these men. The greater need for industrial and agricultural manpower in the Soviet Union, due to a lower level of labor productivity, also necessarily increases labor demand.

Comparison of numbers in the final age group is nearly meaningless because of the vast differences in sex composition. To a considerable extent, this already maimed group in the Soviet Union is the one on which the present generation of school children must depend. And they must depend for the most part upon those under 50—the group most seriously affected by the war and among whom the proportion of married families with both parents present will undoubtedly be

[93] If the sex ratio for ages 32 and over is raised, the population 32 and over will be increased and the number 18–31 would have to fall in order to be compatible with the total number of voters. This would imply that our estimate of the survivors of births, 1928–41 was too high. This is a readily admitted possibility since the mortality of the war period is still very unclear.

low. For these age groups in the United States in 1957 married persons comprised over 80 percent—a qualitatively and quantitatively different dependency situation.

We might expand this discussion of the "working age" population by drawing upon more detailed estimates of the age and sex composition of the Soviet population prepared by the U.S. Buréau of the Census. These estimates suggest that the Soviet population of "working age," taken here to be 15 to 59 years, numbered almost 131 million in 1959, 57 million men and 74 million women (see table 15). The U.S. population in this group numbered about 99 million divided about equally between men and women.

TABLE 15.—*Comparison of the "working age" population (15 to 59 years) for the U.S.S.R. and the United States: 1958/1959 and 1965/1966*

[In thousands]

Group	Soviet Union			United States		
	Population		Percent change	Population		Percent change
	Jan. 1, 1959	Jan. 1, 1966		July 1, 1958	July 1, 1965	
Both sexes	130, 887	137, 628	5. 2	98, 596	109, 054	10. 6
Male	56, 785	61, 911	9. 0	48, 744	53, 966	10. 7
Female	74, 102	75, 717	2. 2	49, 850	55, 088	10. 5

Source: United States, 1958: Appendix tables E and F and Statistical Abstract of the United States, 1959, p. 24.

By 1966, the projections point to a working-age population of about 138 million for the U.S.S.R. and 109 million for the United States. While the male population in this age range in the Soviet Union is expected to show a greater increase than the female portion (9 percent for males compared to only 2.2 percent for females), it is not expected to grow as much as that for the United States (10.7 percent for males, 10.5 percent for females).

To the extent that these estimates of the Soviet age distribution have any validity—and in certain respects, as we have noted, they are not unreasonable—they tend to confirm the overall census total. That is, they can be accommodated by it. This is not to say that there may not be an error of several million in the reported totals. It does, however, reinforce our earlier conclusion that there is no compelling reason to reject the results which have so far been released. More than that we cannot say until more data become available.

APPENDIX A. SELECTED DATA ON THE POPULATION OF THE U.S.S.R.

The following tables contain recent data on the population of the U.S.S.R. One table for the United States has been provided for comparative purposes. The tables are included as general background and reference materials.

TABLE A.—*Population of the U.S.S.R., by urban-rural residence, selected years, 1913–59*

[Absolute figures in millions]

Year	Population			Percent urban
	Total	Urban	Rural	
1913				
Current boundaries	159.2	28.1	131.1	18
Boundaries prior to Sept. 17, 1939	139.3	24.7	114.6	18
1926				
Population census of Dec. 17, 1926 (boundaries prior to Sept. 17, 1939)	147.0	26.3	120.7	18
1939				
Population census of Jan. 17, 1939 (boundaries prior to Sept. 17, 1939)	170.6	56.1	114.5	331
Estimate, including western oblasts of the Ukraine and Byelorussia, plus Moldavia, Lithuania, Latvia, and Estonia [1]	190.7	60.4	130.3	32
1956				
Estimate as of April 1956	200.2	87.0	113.2	43
1959				
Population census of Jan. 15, 1959	[2] 208.8	99.8	109.0	48

[1] The expanded figure for 1939 (190.7) is treated in Soviet discussions as comparable to the 1959 census figure (208.8). This suggests that the former figure may therefore include the areas annexed after the war (Tannu-Tuva, Southern Sakhalin, and East Prussia).

[2] Of which 207,752,000 were originally enumerated, 285,000 added subsequently as a result of the post-enumeration control canvass, and 789,000 added following the checking of control sheets.

Source: The Central Statistical Administration's release of May 10, 1959, in Izvestiya; and Tsentral'noye statisticheskoye upravleniye. Narodnoye khozyaystvo S.S.S.R. v 1956 godu (National Economy of the U.S.S.R. in 1956). Moscow: Gosudarstvennoye Statisticheskoye Izdatel'stvo, 1957, p. 17.

TABLE B.—*Population of the U.S.S.R., by Union Republic and urban-rural residence 1939 and 1959*

[Data relate to current boundaries. Absolute figures in thousands]

Republic	Population						Percent urban	
	Jan. 17, 1939			Jan. 15, 1959				
	Total	Urban	Rural	Total	Urban	Rural	1939	1959
U.S.S.R.	190,678	60,409	130,269	208,826	99,782	109,044	32	48
R.S.F.S.R.	108,379	36,296	72,083	117,494	61,477	56,017	33	52
Ukrainian S.S.R.	40,469	13,569	26,900	41,893	19,130	22,763	34	46
Belorussian S.S.R.	8,910	1,855	7,055	8,060	2,475	5,585	21	31
Uzbek S.S.R.	6,336	1,470	4,866	8,113	2,720	5,393	23	34
Kazakh S.S.R.	6,094	1,690	4,404	9,301	4,069	5,232	28	44
Georgian S.S.R.	3,540	1,066	2,474	4,049	1,696	2,353	30	42
Azerbaydzhan S.S.R.	3,205	1,157	2,048	3,700	1,765	1,935	36	48
Lithuanian S.S.R.	2,880	659	2,221	2,713	1,045	1,668	23	39
Moldavian S.S.R.	2,452	328	2,124	2,880	639	2,241	13	22
Latvian S.S.R.	1,885	663	1,222	2,094	1,173	921	35	56
Kirgiz S.S.R.	1,458	270	1,188	2,063	692	1,371	19	34
Tadzhik S.S.R.	1,484	249	1,235	1,989	645	1,337	17	33
Armenian S.S.R.	1,282	366	916	1,768	884	884	29	50
Turkmen S.S.R.	1,252	416	836	1,520	698	822	33	46
Estonian S.S.R.	1,052	355	697	1,196	674	522	34	56

Source: Izvestiya, May 10, 1959.

TABLE C.—*Number and population of urban places in the U.S.S.R. by size class and type of urban place, 1939 and 1959*

[Data relating to current boundaries]

Size class and type of urban place	Number of urban places		Population (in millions)	
	1939	1959	1939	1959
Total	2,759	4,616	60.4	99.8
Under 3,000	467	849	.9	1.6
3,000 to 5,000	531	887	2.1	3.5
5,000 to 10,000	757	1,288	5.3	9.2
10,000 to 20,000	501	810	7.0	11.3
20,000 to 50,000	315	483	9.6	15.1
50,000 to 100,000	99	151	7.1	10.6
100,000 to 500,000	78	123	15.6	24.4
500,000 and over	11	25	12.8	24.1
Cities	1,191	1,694	51.2	82.6
Under 3,000	70	94	.1	.2
3,000 to 5,000	104	128	.4	.5
5,000 to 10,000	233	284	1.7	2.2
10,000 to 20,000	304	440	4.4	6.4
20,000 to 50,000	292	449	9.1	14.2
50,000 to 100,000	99	151	7 1	10.6
100,000 to 500,000	78	123	15.6	24.4
500,000 and over	11	25	12.8	24.1
Urban-type settlements	1,568	2,922	9.2	17.2
Under 3,000	397	755	.8	1.4
3,000 to 5,000	427	759	1.7	3.0
5,000 to 10,000	524	1,004	3.6	7.0
10,000 to 20,000	197	370	2.6	4.9
20,000 and over	23	34	.5	.9

Source: Izvestia, May 10, 1959.

TABLE D.—*Population of the U.S.S.R., by sex, according to censuses of 1926, 1939, and 1959*

[Territory as of census date. Absolute figures in millions]

Census date	Population			Percent of total population		Sex ratio [1]
	Total	Male	Female	Male	Female	
Dec. 17, 1926	147.0	71.0	76.0	48	52	93.4
Jan. 17, 1939	170.6	81.7	88.9	48	52	91.9
Jan. 15, 1959	208.8	94.0	114.8	45	55	[2] 81.9

[1] Males per 100 females.
[2] An equal number of males and females is reported for ages under 32 years.

Source: Izvestiya, May 10, 1959.

TABLE E.—*Projected population of the United States, by age and sex: July 1, 1960 and 1965*

[In thousands Including Armed Forces overseas but excluding Alaska and Hawaii]

Age	1960			1965		
	Both sexes	Male	Female	Both sexes	Male	Female
All ages	180, 126	89, 112	91, 014	195, 747	96, 637	99, 110
Under 5 years	19, 991	10, 184	9, 807	21, 243	10, 828	10, 415
5 to 9 years	19, 159	9, 782	9, 377	20, 837	10, 637	10, 200
10 to 14 years	17, 217	8, 795	8, 422	19, 216	9, 806	9, 410
15 to 19 years	13, 406	6, 804	6, 602	17, 267	8, 803	8, 464
20 to 24 years	11, 311	5, 703	5, 608	13, 502	6, 808	6, 694
25 to 29 years	10, 946	5, 449	5, 497	11, 459	5, 736	5, 723
30 to 34 years	11, 878	5, 860	6, 018	11, 068	5, 493	5, 575
35 to 39 years	12, 434	6, 084	6, 350	11, 914	5, 871	6, 043
40 to 44 years	11, 549	5, 647	5, 902	12, 374	6, 042	6, 332
45 to 49 years	11, 050	5, 390	5, 660	11, 389	5, 541	5, 848
50 to 54 years	9, 796	4, 790	5, 006	10, 741	5, 185	5, 556
55 to 59 years	8, 372	4, 058	4, 314	9, 340	4, 487	4, 853
60 to 64 years	7, 238	3, 447	3, 791	7, 759	3, 657	4, 102
65 to 69 years	5, 877	2, 747	3, 130	6, 395	2, 920	3, 475
70 years and over	9, 902	4, 372	5, 530	11, 243	4, 823	6, 420

Source: U.S. Bureau of the Census, "Illustrative Projections of the Population of the United States, by Age and Sex, 1960 to 1980," by Meyer Zitter and Jacob S. Siegel, current population reports, series P-25, No. 187. The distributions shown are those for series II. This series postulates the continuation of fertility at the 1955-57 level

TABLE F.—*Estimated and projected population of the U.S.S.R., by age and sex: Jan. 1, 1959 and 1966*

[In thousands]

Age	1959			1966		
	Total	Male	Female	Total	Male	Female
Total	208, 826	94, 012	114, 814	233, 714	107, 674	126, 040
Under 5 years	24, 402	12, 506	11, 896	25, 285	12, 973	12, 312
5 to 9 years	21, 717	11, 080	10, 637	24, 440	12, 518	11, 922
10 to 14 years	14, 755	7, 511	7, 244	22, 903	11, 689	11, 214
15 to 19 years	19, 217	9, 787	9, 430	17, 993	9, 155	8, 838
20 to 24 years	19, 716	10, 049	9, 667	15, 481	7, 870	7, 611
25 to 29 years	16, 114	7, 668	8, 446	21, 402	10, 888	10, 514
30 to 34 years	19, 795	8, 813	10, 982	15, 507	7, 579	7, 928
35 to 39 years	12, 898	4, 834	8, 064	19, 293	8, 864	10, 429
40 to 44 years	10, 306	3, 454	6, 852	15, 262	6, 191	9, 071
45 to 49 years	12, 503	4, 336	8, 167	10, 181	3, 515	6, 666
50 to 54 years	11, 097	4, 250	6, 847	11, 539	3, 850	7, 689
55 to 59 years	9, 241	3, 594	5, 647	10, 970	3, 999	6, 971
60 to 64 years	6, 391	2, 392	3, 999	9, 180	3, 508	5, 672
65 to 69 years	4, 409	1, 625	2, 784	6, 365	2, 350	4, 015
70 years and over	6, 265	2, 113	4, 152	7, 913	2, 725	5, 188

Source: Foreign Manpower Research Office. U.S. Bureau of the Census. The total given for 1959 is that reported in the preliminary results of the Soviet census of population taken as of Jan. 15, 1959. The age and sex distribution for 1959 is estimated on the basis of numerous fragments of information; 1966 population is a projection of the 1959 figures on the assumption of no change in the present fertility level. The 2 dates chosen are those which span the current Soviet 7-year plan.

COMPARISONS OF THE UNITED STATES AND SOVIET ECONOMIES: THE LABOR FORCE

(By Warren W. Eason, Princeton University)

A comparison of two countries such as the Soviet Union and the United States in the matter of a vital component of total economic activity such as the "labor force" raises many fundamental questions. On the one hand, there are the "statistical" questions, of definition and concept, and of the reliability, comparability and meaning of various quantitative indexes. On the other hand, there are the larger questions directed toward evaluating the "effectiveness with which human resources are utilized"—in two economic systems which differ as to ends and means but which are faced with the common problem of bringing manpower into phase with the changing requirements of an industrialized society. Furthermore, since the Soviet Union and the United States are seen increasingly "in competition" with one another in the economic sphere, questions on the labor force, as well as others, tend to be viewed in the light of their implications with respect to the outcome of this competition.

In its most basic form, the problem of the labor force common to both the United States (over its history) and the Soviet Union is the general problem of labor in industrialization, the problem of transforming ordinary manpower from "primitive tillers of the soil into a disciplined industrial labor force," committed to a "drastically new way of life";[1] and the problem of developing cadres of skilled and higher level manpower, i.e., "personnel with the skill necessary to formulate and execute developmental policies,"[2] to handle positions of management, planning, and research.

These demands of a developing economy quite evidently involve both quantitative and qualitative changes in the labor force, which may be conveniently categorized under four headings:

(1) The number of persons available for productive work, by age and sex (i.e., the "labor force" in the basic sense of the word);

(2) The level and distribution of skills and experience;

(3) Distribution by the major characteristics of the demand for labor (e.g., job requirements, time and seasonal patterns of work, geographical location, industry, etc.);

(4) Effectiveness or efficiency in given work situations.

These are what might be called the four dimensions of the labor force, and set the terms on which the Soviet Union and the United States will be compared in the present paper.

At the same time, it must be recognized that the contribution of labor to economic performance is not an absolute and isolated matter; in other words, a certain sense of relevance must be kept in mind. Even if we could quantify or otherwise delineate "labor" as such, proper interpretation and evaluation of the results would depend,

[1] W. Galenson, ed., "Labor and Economic Development" (New York: John Wiley & Sons, 1959), p. 2.
[2] Ibid., p. 15.

for example, on the particular stage of economic development we were considering, as well as on the availability and effectiveness of other resources, such as "capital" and "land."

Furthermore, these relationships are more than in the nature of a static comparison. They reflect an underlying, continuing process of change and adjustment. For this reason, it is essential in the final analysis to take account of the organizational and structural framework within which methods, practices, and policies with respect to the utilization of human resources work themselves out. In other words, it is necessary to examine the "web of rules" [3] which serves in any industrialized system to relate the elements of labor to each other and to the other parts of the system.

This is the broad outline suggested by a comparison of the "labor force" in the Soviet Union and the United States. Unfortunately, neither the size of this paper nor the level of our understanding of many of the questions will permit a comprehensive survey at the present time. By the same token, however, it should be possible to touch upon some major issues and at the same time to keep the larger outline in mind. The approach will be to consider each of the four dimensions of the labor force listed above in turn, and then to make some concluding observations.

LABOR FORCE TRENDS

The first dimension of the labor force refers to the number of persons, by age or sex, who work or who want to work for pay or profit, or who contribute without pay to the principal productive effort of the head of the household. Such measures of the total labor force of the Soviet Union and the United States, for selected years beginning with 1860, are summarized in table 1. The U.S. figures are from the dicennial censuses through 1930 and the monthly survey of the labor force beginning with 1940. The U.S.S.R. figures are estimates based on data from several censuses, as well as on available noncensus data. Projections of the labor force from 1960 to 1975 are based on assumptions that will be set forth below.[4]

In sheer numbers, the Soviet Union has been frequently characterized in terms of a manpower "pool" which is abundant relative to other resources, including arable land and capital equipment, and which is rapidly growing. The United States, on the other hand, at least from a historical point of view, has been portrayed as a country of labor "scarcity," manifest particularly in the incentives traditionally offered to immigration.

---

[3] C. Kerr and A. Siegel, "The Structuring of the Labor Force in Industrial Relations: New Dimensions and New Questions," Industrial and Labor Relations Review, vol. VIII, No. 2, January 1955, pp. 162-163.

[4] Details on the Soviet data themselves and on methods and concepts for this section of the paper may be found in W. W. Eason, "Soviet Manpower: The Population and Labor Force of the U.S.S.R.," an unpublished Ph. D. thesis on deposit with Columbia University.

TABLE 1.—*The total labor force of the U.S.S.R. and United States, by sex, estimated, 1860–1955, and projected, 1960–75* [1]

Year [2]	Both sexes			Males			Females			Females percent of both sexes	
	U.S.S.R. [3]	United States [4]	United States percent of U.S.S.R.	U.S.S.R.	United States	United States percent of U.S.S.R.	U.S.S.R.	United States	United States percent of U.S.S.R.	U.S.S.R.	United States
	Thousands	*Thousands*		*Thousands*	*Thousands*		*Thousands*	*Thousands*			
1860	35,500	10,500	29.6								
1900	64,400	28,800	44.7	35,400	23,500	66.3	29,000	5,300	18.3	45.0	18.4
1928	85,100	46,700	54.9								
1930	88,500	48,900	55.3	47,400	38,100	80.4	41,100	10,800	26.3	46.4	22.1
1940	105,300	55,700	53.0	58,400	41,500	71.1	46,900	14,200	30.3	44.5	25.5
1950	105,300	64,500	61.3	51,900	45,900	88.4	53,400	18,600	34.8	50.7	28.8
1955	111,600	67,700	60.7	58,000	47,600	82.1	53,600	20,100	37.5	48.0	29.6
1960	114,800	73,200	63.8	62,100	49,900	80.4	52,700	23,200	44.0	45.9	31.7
1965	117,100	79,200	67.6	65,800	53,000	80.5	51,300	26,200	51.1	43.8	33.1
1970	123,100	86,200	70.0	72,000	56,800	78.9	51,100	29,400	57.5	41.5	34.1
1975	130,600	93,400	71.5	79,400	60,900	76.7	51,200	32,500	63.5	39.2	34.8

[1] Data for the U.S.S.R. are derived from sources and by methods set forth in W. W. Eason, "Soviet Manpower: The Population and Labor Force of the U.S.S.R.", unpublished Ph. D. thesis on deposit with Columbia University, adjusted to conform to the preliminary results of the 1959 Soviet census, Pravda, May 10, 1959.

Data for the United States are from C. D. Long, "The Labor Force Under Changing Income and Employment" (Princeton: Princeton University Press, 1958), pp. 285–287 and 316–317; for 1928 only from data in S. Lebergott, "Annual Estimates of Unemployment in the United States, 1900–1954," in C. D. Long, ed., "The Measurement and Behavior of Unemployment" (Princeton: Princeton University Press, 1957, p. 215; and Bureau of the Census, "Projections of the Labor Force in the United States, 1955 to 1975," Current Population Reports Series P–50, No. 69, October, 1956, pp. 12–13.

[2] As of January, for U.S.S.R.; April, 1860–1930, first quarterly average, 1940–55, and annual average, 1960–75, for United States.

[3] Territory for 1860–1930 is Soviet pre-1939; territory for 1940–75, present.

[4] U.S. data through 1930 are from censuses; from 1940–55, according to current population surveys.

With respect to the earlier periods of industrialization in the two countries, this comparison is essentially valid. In more recent years, however, the difference has been sharply narrowed, largely due to basic changes in the structure of resource relationships in the Soviet Union. Since the beginning of the industrialization drive in 1928 the capital stock has increased and modern technology has been introduced on a wide scale, with the result that labor productivity has increased measurably. From this source alone, one can speak of a rise in the "capital-labor" ratio since 1928, or a decline in the "abundance" of labor relative to capital.

But there is a further movement in the same direction, particularly important at the present time, which is attributable to demographic forces. Partly because of the catastrophic effects of World War II, but also due to a relatively greater decline in the birth rate than death rate in peacetime, the overall rate of population growth (other than through territorial annexation) since 1928 has considerably declined. The first effect on the rate of growth of the labor force was felt as a result of the war itself, through the premature death of more than 20 million adults.[5] The second effect is being felt now, and will be felt in the future, with the entry into the working and reproductive ages of persons born during the war, when birth rates were low and infant mortality rates high.

Assuming unchanged labor force participation rates by age and sex (about which more below), the incidence of mortality during the war, as shown in table 1, had the direct effect of holding the total labor force to approximately the same level in 1950 (105 million) as it was in 1940, whereas in the absence of war the number would have increased by more than 10 million.

From 1950 to 1955, on the other hand, there was an increase in the labor force of more than 6 million, reflecting the entry into the working ages of individuals who were born before the war, when the birth rate was relatively high, and who were consequently young enough to escape some of the hazards of the war.

At present and over the next few years, the dominant effect is a rather sharp slowing down in the rate of growth of the labor force, due to the entry of the "war babies" into the working ages. This is largely the reason why the Soviet labor force in table 1 displays between 1955 and 1965 only one-half of the average absolute increase that it does between 1950 and 1955.[6] Beginning approximately with 1965, however, because of the lower peacetime birth rates of recent years, the absolute increase of the labor force should return to earlier levels, although the increase relative to the total population will be somewhat lower.

These are very significant developments toward accelerating the reduction in the relative "abundance" of manpower that was already taking place in the course of Soviet industrialization. At the same time, it would be a mistake to exaggerate the implications, or to overstate the case in terms of an overall labor "shortage."

In the first place, the Soviet labor force is still increasing, although the rate of increase has been temporarily cut in half. More important

[5] W. W. Eason, "The Soviet Population Today: An Analysis of the First Results of the 1959 Census," Foreign Affairs, vol. 37, No. 4, July 1959, pp. 598–606. Needless to say, not all of those who died prematurely would have been in the labor force in any event.

[6] The 5-year intervals on which these estimates are based are selected for estimating convenience, so that the years cited cannot have the connotation of annual estimates.

is the fact that the "labor problem" in economic development is really a question of the changes which must be brought about in the "qualitative" dimensions of the labor force. To a certain extent, sheer numbers of persons and the increase therein can serve the cause of rising production. However, the ultimate goals of rising productivity per worker (and rising living standards per capita) demand that sooner or later there be "qualitative" changes in the labor force, lest the full fruits inherent in the accumulation of capital, the advancement of technology, and the increased complexity of economic organization, be foregone. What a slowing down in the rate of increase of the number in the labor force entails is a quickening of the need to bring about the "qualitative" changes which are necessary if overall economic goals are to be met.

Broad relationships of this type may very well lie behind what is apparent in Soviet circles as a heightened concern at this very time for improving the effectiveness of manpower utilization, from the ordinary worker through higher level technical and managerial personnel. Soviet planners and administrators have always been concerned with these problems, it is true, but the results until recently have been well below levels of manpower efficiency attained in the more advanced industrial countries. This is understandable, given the magnitude of the problem, the time factor, and the possibility heretofore of relying more on quantity than on quality. The present indication is of more persistent and pervasive efforts to raise the qualitative indexes. Attention to these questions will be given below.

Some final observations on the influence of population growth on labor force trends in the two countries may be made on the basis of a direct comparison of the data in table 1. The outstanding characteristic of the comparison is the amount by which the rate of increase of the U.S. labor force has exceeded that of the Soviet Union (and imperial Russia, on Soviet territory). Between 1860 and 1955, the Soviet labor force increased by about 3 times, from 35 to 112 million, while the labor force of the United States increased by 6 times, from 11 to 68 million. In other words, the U.S. labor force was in 1860 equal to 30 percent of the Soviet labor force, and in 1955, 60 percent. Furthermore, if the assumptions on which the respective projections to 1975 are based are at all "predictive," the U.S. labor force by that time will equal approximately 70 percent of the Soviet.

Tending to raise the rate of growth of the U.S. labor force relative to that of the Soviet Union since 1860 were the waves of immigration of the 19th and early 20th centuries. Tending to lower the Soviet rate of growth were the effects of World Wars I and II and of the Civil War of 1918–20, together with the decline in population growth during the early 1930's.

These particular considerations are more than enough to account for the implied demographic effects on relative labor force growth rates, because the overall pattern of peacetime birth and death rates (until the 1950's), taken by itself, actually shows an earlier decline in the rate of natural increase of the population in the United States than in the Soviet Union, as an integral part of the process of industrialization which began much earlier in the United States.

Since about 1950, crude birth and death rates and the rate of natural increase of the population have been quite similar in the two countries, but this may be a somewhat misleading identity from the standpoint of its effect on the labor force. In the first place, as pointed out above, relative rates of growth of the respective labor forces in the immediate future will be quite different due to the influence of the war, another way of saying that beneath the pattern of similar birth and death rates lies a rather different population structure by age and sex. This fact partly explains the increase in the U.S. labor force from 61 percent of the Soviet in 1955 to 68 percent in 1965, but the remainder of the explanation is the assumption of declining labor force participation rates in the Soviet Union after 1950 (about which more below).

The assumption of declining labor force participation rates is also probably the major (if not entire) explanation for the fact that from 1965 to 1970 the U.S. labor force percent of the Soviet rises at all. In other words, from demographic causes alone one would expect the rates of increase of the respective labor forces to be more or less similar in this period, due to the entry into the working ages of persons born beginning with 1950, when birth rates were similar.

After about 1975, however, the participation rates may very well move once again "in favor" of the United States, as far as purely demographic considerations are concerned. The reason lies in the possible pattern of birth rates over the immediate future, since it is these age groups that will provide the new workers in about 15 or 20 years. On the assumption that fertility rates with respect to women of childbearing ages remain more or less unchanged for each country, over the coming years the birth rate in the Soviet Union will almost certainly fall below that of the United States. This is because the relatively small age-groups born during the war are now entering the reproductive ages in the Soviet Union, while the opposite is true in the United States.

Up to this point the discussion has been almost entirely concerned with the relationship of population growth to labor force trends. The implication is that in the long run the two are more or less synonymous, i.e., that questions of overall labor supply are ultimately questions of population. At any moment in time, however, the size of the total labor force is also a function of the percentage of the population in the labor force, by age and sex, a consideration which also contributes in minor degree to longrun trends. More important, changes in the percentage of the population in the labor force with respect to a given country are significant for what they reveal about attitudes toward work and leisure in response to changes in income and other variables. Soviet data are extremely inadequate for a comparison with the United States on these grounds, but some general observations may nevertheless be made.

Reproduced in table 2 are selected percentage relationships between the population and the labor force with respect to ages 14 and over in the United States and 16 and over in the Soviet Union. (The difference in age coverage introduces a minor difficulty in making this comparison, but is not readily eliminated on the basis of available data.)

The percentage for the United States is consistently below the corresponding figure for the Soviet Union, and is also essentially stable. This stability may be seen as well in the U.S. data for earlier years,[7]

[7] C. D. Long, "The Labor Force Under Changing Income and Employment" (Princeton: Princeton University Press, 1958).

and stands as the net effect of a rising percentage of females and falling percentage of older men and youths in the labor force, the percentage of males in the prime working ages in the labor force remaining about constant.

TABLE 2.—*The percentage of the population of the U.S.S.R. and U.S.A. in the labor force, ages 16 and over (U.S.S.R.) and 14 and over (U.S.A.), by sex, estimated and reported, 1926–55, and hypothetical, 1960–75* [1]

Year	Both sexes		Males		Females	
	U.S.S.R.	U.S.A.	U.S.S.R.	U.S.A.	U.S.S.R.	U.S.A.
1926	81.2		92.9		70.8	
1930		53.9		84.1		24.3
1940	79.9	55.9	95.5	83.9	66.3	28.2
1950	78.2	58.3	95.6	84.4	66.6	33.1
1955	76.2	58.0	95.0	82.3	62.8	34.5
1960	74.2	57.9	94.5	81.0	59.2	35.9
1965	71.8	57.7	93.3	79.3	55.3	37.2
1970	69.8	58.0	92.5	78.7	51.8	38.5
1975	68.2	58.8	91.8	78.9	48.6	39.8

[1] Sources of data are the same as in table 1.

Compared to other countries of the world, a very large percentage of the Soviet population has always been engaged in "economic activity." In Imperial Russia, a predominantly agricultural economy, the principal production unit of which was the individual household organized into villages and operating under the general control of the landed estate, virtually all able-bodied persons of both sexes participated in primary economic activity at least part of the year. This condition is generally appreciated, but statistical confirmation rests almost entirely with the Soviet census of 1926, taken just before the start of the industrialization drive and the collectivization of agriculture. The census shows 81 percent of the population age 16 and over in the labor force, compared to 55 percent of the U.S. population age 14 and over in 1930.

Under conditions of the industrialization drive, the percentage of the population dependent on nonagricultural occupations increased (see table 5, below), but this may not have reduced significantly the percentage of the population in the labor force. Unfortunately, comprehensive figures on the total labor force of the U.S.S.R., except for the control figures as of 1931, have not become available since the 5-year plans began. The results of the 1937 census were officially abrogated shortly after the census was taken,[8] and although tabulation was subsequently completed,[9] were never published. Releases from the 1939 census, on the other hand, have been confined to population data with partial detail, including a classification by "social groups" which is only of indirect aid in deriving labor force figures. The preliminary results of the 1959 census include no data on the labor force.

In short, with the exception of the 1931 data, Soviet estimates of the total labor force during the plan years have never been published. In the absence of adequate data, therefore, any indication of the changes in the relationship between the population and the labor force must be to a certain extent speculative.

[8] Izvestiia, September 26, 1937.

[9] F. Lorimer, "The Nature of Soviet Population and Vital Statistics," The American Statistician, April–May, 1953, pp. 7–11.

Under conditions of the plan years, certain factors would appear to have increased the percentage of the population in the labor force and others to have decreased it; but on balance, the effect was probably to decrease the percentage to some degree. Tending to increase it would be (1) the efforts of the Soviet Government to get the maximum proportion of the adult population into the labor force, although considering the high proportion already existing on the eve of the plans, there are decided limits in this direction; (2) the increase in the population age 16 to 59 relative to other groups; and (3) possibly the indirect effects of the fall in real wages, which were low before the plans and which have apparently remained below the 1938 level until as recently as 1952.[10] Tending to decrease it would be (1) the increase in school attendance, although this would be more a case of reducing the average number of days worked during the year, since many young people (especially on farms) would continue to be in the labor force for at least part of the year; and (2) the large-scale migration of females from rural to urban areas.

On the basis of these general considerations, amplified and supported by indirect and fragmentary evidence, the percentage of the Soviet population in the labor force—by age and sex and rural and urban areas—was derived for 1939–40. The results of this estimate, with respect to the population age 16 and over, are reproduced in table 2.

However, valid these assumptions for the first decade of the 5-year plans may be, the continued absence of concrete information from official sources makes it increasingly difficult to estimate percentage relationships for recent years, and to make projections therefrom for the future.

One possibility is that the percentages will continue to be high in the future, that is, until fundamental changes in economic and social conditions create a climate in which a certain proportion of women and older people who are now in the labor force will be inclined to leave. (Visitors to the Soviet Union seem to think that such a climate does not yet exist, and that with respect to women in particular, labor force participation rates in urban as well as in rural areas remain relatively high.)

Until this decline does take place, labor force participation rates can be expected to stay near the 80 percent of the population age 16 and over which follows from the above assumptions, modified slightly by changes in the composition of the population by age and sex.

The data for the Soviet Union reproduced in table 2, however, are actually drawn up on the assumption of a definite but modest decline in the percentage of the female population and of the young and old of both sexes in the labor force, beginning with 1955. The only real evidence for making such an assumption is highly indirect, consisting of the observation that preplan rates were exceptionally high by international standards, implying that they should very well come down sooner or later, and that the period beginning with 1955 is the first to reflect a certain amount of "normality" and "stability" in Soviet affairs, a necessary condition for the ultimate decline. Having passed through the exceptional period of the 1930's as well as the war and its aftermath, i.e., through the death of Stalin, it can be argued,

[10] J. G. Chapman, "Real Wages in the Soviet Union, 1928–52," The Review of Economics and Statistics, May 1954, pp. 134–156. This refers to changes in the purchasing power of money wages, and does not include changes in "socialized" wages.

Soviet labor force participation rates may very well now begin to resemble those of other industrialized countries.

When and if such a decline in labor force participation rates does take place, it will tend to remove one of the features distinguishing the Soviet labor force from that of other industrialized countries, namely, the high percentage of females. At the turn of the century, according to table 1, the share of the labor force comprising females in Imperial Russia (45 percent) was almost three times that of the United States (18 percent). In the intervening years, due partly to the substantially greater mortality of males than females in World Wars I and II and the period of the early 1930's, and also to the assumption of continued high participation rates through 1950, slightly more than one-half of the Soviet labor force in 1950 was comprised of females. Over the same half century, however, the labor force participation rates of females in the United States has increased, with the result that the U.S. percentage in 1950 was only about one-half that of the Soviet Union (compared to one-third in 1900). If the assumptions on which the population and labor force projections in tables 1 and 2 are based are correct, by 1975 the sex composition of the respective labor forces will be roughly similar.

The Level and Distribution of Skills and Experience

The need to develop requisite skills among the members of the labor force and to raise the general level of their experience, if the Soviet Union is to become a truly industrialized nation, has been recognized from the earliest days of the regime. The country began the process of industrialization with essentially the same dearth of skills and experience among the labor force as a whole as other underdeveloped countries, with the added fact that a number of the most experienced and qualified people had to be effectively eliminated from positions of responsibility for essentially political reasons.

On the eve of the first 5-year plan (1928), approximately 80 percent of the Soviet population was dependent on agricultural or other rural sources of income (see table 4, below), signifying in this case an almost total lack of experience, training or even familiarity with an industrial way of life. In the intervening years—through the vastly expanded educational system, the large-scale movement of the population to urban areas and to non-agricultural employment, the mechanization of a certain amount of farm work, and incessant indoctrination through the press and radio—the Soviet population, although still more than half in rural areas, has become essentially familiar with the requirements of an industrial way of life.[11]

The outstanding feature of this development, of course, is not that it has happened, because in broad outline it follows the pattern of every industrializing country, including the United States, but that it happened in such a short period of time. A significant aspect of the way it took place, moreover, is not the expansion of the system of formalized training, important though it is, but the more indirect and generalized procedures by which the labor force has become acclimated through what is really "on-the-job-training" in the most general sense of the term.

[11] W. W. Eason, "Are the Soviets Winning the Battle of Production," Committee for Economic Development, "Soviet Progress vs. American Enterprise" (New York: Doubleday & Co., 1958), p. 100.

This is dramatized early in the period by the sudden and marked increase in the number of wage and salary workers in state enterprises during calendar year 1931. Largely the result of reactions against collectivization and appearing as a migration of peasants to urban areas, this increase was well above planned rates.

It may be argued that if industrial enterprise managers had been economically prudent, payrolls would not have increased by such a large amount in 1 year (1931), and remained more or less unchanged for several years thereafter. The mass exodus to the cities in 1931 would seem necessarily to have led to unemployment under "normal" conditions.

On the other hand, it is possible to view the "hiding" of manpower in these years as an investment in training, or at least in "indoctrination." One of the big problems facing the Soviet leaders during the 1930's was the acclimatization of the peasant migrant to industrial life. In this sense his inclusion on the payrolls, rather than being left unemployed and forced to return to the countryside, may be viewed as a contribution tending to balance the negative effects in terms of per capita productivity.[12]

Without discussing the Soviet educational system in any detail, since it has been the object of considerable attention in recent years,[13] certain observations can be made about the problem of developing the skills and experience required by the Soviet economy in its present stage of development.

The key to the orientation of Soviet administrators to these problems may very well lie in the broad aims according to which the educational system is presently being reorganized. The direction of the discussion seems to be toward a system which will provide some combination of the following objectives: (1) a stepping up of the exposure of the broad mass of the younger elements of the population to concrete work situations, regardless of their future career objectives, in the hope that this will make them accordingly more sensitive to the rank and file problems of an industrialized society; and (2) the provision for the selection and training of those most qualified for high level technical, managerial, and research positions, having in mind that the program for these individuals requires a good deal of formalized training.

These two objectives represent two schools of thought in the Soviet Union at the present time, and the final "balance" in terms of emphasis and direction remains to be determined. In any event, the evidence does seem to point to greater emphasis than in the past, for the mass of youth, on receiving production line experience before they are admitted to higher education. As long as this program is not pushed to the point where it depletes or seriously delays the training of individuals whose ultimate careers—for example, in scientific research—will never place them in direct contact with problems of industrial production, it has some merit.

In the first place, for technological and other reasons, the Soviet economy has until recently been operating under the general conditions of a relative abundance of labor, as noted above, with a level of efficiency of labor utilization which is relatively low compared to the more industrialized countries. As part of the efforts to raise the effectiveness of labor utilization, the goal will be achieved more easily to the extent that the worker feels a certain dignity and status in his

---

[12] W. W. Eason, "Labor Force Materials for the Study of Unemployment in the Soviet Union," The Measurement and Behavior of Unemployment, a conference of the Universities-National Bureau Committee for Economic Research (Princeton: Princeton University Press, 1957), p. 415.

[13] For example, N. DeWitt, "Soviet Professional Manpower: Its Education, Training, and Supply" (Washington, D.C.: National Science Foundation, 1955); and A. G. Korol, "Soviet Education for Science and Technology" (New York: John Wiley & Sons, 1957).

position as a worker. The ideology of the Soviet state, it is true, centers on the ordinary worker; but the evidence seems to be that in the overriding need to develop individuals with the higher skills and techniques, an understandable glorification of the manager and engineer has set in. The complaint is made that youths frequently regard production-line work as something less than desirable, and individuals so engaged as of relatively low status.

In other countries and systems, the trade union, by taking the part of the worker against management or the state, can sometimes give the worker a certain sense of status and even power. In the Soviet state, if the same objective is to be achieved, the worker must first of all identify himself with the socialized framework and objectives of society, at the same time that he regards his individual work situation with what is essentially a feeling of satisfaction. If the reemphasis of the reorganization of the educational system along these lines succeeds in raising the dignity and worth of ordinary labor, a difficult objective under any conditions, it may very well reap intangible benefits in worker morale and efficiency.

A second (and probably secondary) effect of the reorganization would seem to be related to the underlying structure of the labor force in terms of age, as a reflection of the distribution in terms of skills and experience. For this purpose, the labor force may be divided into the following groups:

(1) The senior group in the labor force in the next decade from which, in addition to others, are drawn top managerial personnel, as well as technical and lower personnel with accumulated years of experience, is the group born anywhere from about 1900 to 1920. Some of these were old enough to have been subjected to the military hazards of World War I; some were born during the Civil War, when the birth rate was low; and almost all would have been subject to military service in World War II. For all of these reasons, this is necessarily a relatively small group.

(2) The middle group in the labor force in the next decade will be the one born between the early 1920's and World War II. For most of these years, birth rates were relatively high, and the majority of the people in this group were of an age to have escaped military service during World War II. These are the members of the labor force in the next decade who are "in transition" to positions of responsibility, and who are otherwise acquiring experience in all types of jobs. For the aforementioned demographic reasons, this will be a relatively large group.

(3) The younger group in the labor force in the next decade, those entering the labor force, will be persons born during the years of relatively low birth rate, and will therefore be of relatively small number in the total.[14]

By taking a higher percentage of students for engineering institutes and other specialized schools from those who are otherwise qualified but who have production-line experience, the effect will be, among others, to raise the average age of the students in these schools. A higher percentage of youths presently in secondary schools will enter production for several years before going on to higher training; and

[14] This is discussed in greater detail in W. W. Eason, "Population Growth and Economic Development in the U.S.S.R.," in the "1958 Proceedings of the Social Statistics Section of the American Statistical Association."

a higher percentage of the entrants to the institutes will come from the somewhat older persons already on the production line.

This means that the bulk of those entering training (in institutes) in the coming years will be drawn from the relatively large middle group mentioned above which has already entered the labor force. This will serve to redress any "imbalance" in the proportion of trained and untrained people which occurred when this relatively large group passed through the ages heretofore devoted to advanced training. It will also tend to maintain a similar "balance" in terms of formal skills and age structure between the middle groups and the relatively small younger group in the labor force. This is done, in effect, by not expanding the educational network to supply trained people from all age groups, but by forcing the persons in the younger groups on the average to delay training by a certain number of years, and in the meantime to supply the needs for ordinary labor from this source.

In short, one effect of the educational reform is to give additional opportunity to the people in the middle-age cohorts to raise their qualifications, and to bring the rate at which the advanced schools turn out people of given ages more into line with the rate at which these people are being supplied to the national economy.

In the longer run, as the level of technology and the complexity of industrial organization in the Soviet Union continues to rise, one can expect, in line with recent developments in the United States,[15] that more and more attention will be paid to the development of higher level technical and managerial manpower, and less to the problems of the ordinary worker, whose proportion in the labor force will decline. We cannot say what effect this will have on fundamental ideology with respect to "labor" in the Soviet Union; but it will certainly have an important effect on the orientation of the educational process and the preparation of human resources for the demands of industry at the highest levels of technique and organization.

THE DISTRIBUTION OF THE LABOR FORCE BY SELECTED CHARACTERISTICS OF THE DEMAND FOR LABOR

Labor mobility is a hallmark of the industrialization process. Labor is required to move from one job to another and from one industry to another. The time and seasonal pattern of work changes, as does the geographical location of economic activity.

The Soviet and U.S. labor force will be compared in this section according to the following major characteristics: the distribution by socioeconomic groups; the distribution by agricultural and nonagricultural occupations; and the hours of work.

The distribution of the labor force by socioeconomic groups

Thirty years of rapid industrialization under national economic planning have led to significant changes in the economic characteristics of the Soviet labor force. The expansion of industry has increased the nonagricultural labor force from 18 percent to more than 50 percent of the total labor force; the widening of the network of state enterprises has tripled the number of wage and salary workers; collectivization has altered the characteristics of the agricultural labor force; and private economic activity has been drastically curtailed.

[15] S. E. Hill and F. Harbison, "Manpower and Innovation in American Industry" (Princeton: Industrial relations section, Princeton University, 1959).

These developments, in turn, have been reflected in an increase in the urban population to three times the 1928 level, or from 18 to about 50 percent of the total population.

TABLE 3.—*The labor force, by socioeconomic groups, U.S.S.R., 1928, 1940, and 1955* [1]

Socioeconomic groups	1928	1940	1955	Percentage distribution		
				1928	1940	1955
	Thousands	*Thousands*	*Thousands*	*Percent*	*Percent*	*Percent*
Wage and salary workers	11,600	31,400	49,300	13.5	29.8	44.2
Co-op handicraftsmen	800	1,800	1,800	.9	1.7	1.6
Non-co-op handicraftsmen	1,700	2,200	500	2.0	2.1	.4
Collective farmers	1,500	44,700	45,000	1.7	42.5	40.3
Private farmers	67,400	10,800	200	78.3	10.3	.2
"Bourgeoisie"	1,400			1.6		
Employed labor force	84,400	90,900	96,800	98.0	86.3	86.7
Unemployed and transients	1,100			1.3		
Discrepancies in derivation	0	11,400	10,600	0	10.8	9.5
Civilian labor force	85,500	102,300	107,400	99.3	97.1	96.2
Military	600	3,000	4,200	.7	2.9	3.8
Total labor force	86,100	105,300	111,600	100.0	100.0	100.0

[1] Derived from sources and by methods set forth in Eason, op. cit., adjusted to conform to the preliminary results of the 1959 Soviet census.

Most of these changes are apparent in other countries undergoing industrialization, but several aspects of the Soviet case are unique. First, the change has been more rapid than in other countries. Second, the rate of change was irregular during the transitional phase of the early years of the plans, more, it would seem, from the pressure for speed and from the superimposition of the planning mechanism than from the requirements of industrialization itself. Third, certain unique relationships between the labor force and the work process were established, primarily in the case of collective farming. And, finally, there is the matter of forced labor, a condition of Soviet economic development which has attracted particular attention from non-Soviet analysts.

Data to illustrate these developments, for 1928, 1940, and 1955, are in table 3. The total labor force for 1940 and 1955 is estimated from the population and assumptions with respect to the percentage of the population in the labor force, as described above. (See also table 1.) The data by socio-economic groups are based on "establishment-type" statistics reported separately for each of the indicated groups. An elaborate estimating procedure had to be devised in an attempt to eliminate sources of double counting, etc. However, it will be seen that for 1940 and 1955, as well as for other years in the 1930's for which similar estimates have been made, there is a residual category, "discrepancies in derivation." The sum of the parts, in other words, is less than the whole.

The fact that this residual is consistently positive would suggest one or more of the following factors as an explanation: (1) understatement of reported labor force data (establishment statistics) on which the estimates are based; (2) overestimate of the percentage of the population in the total labor force; (3) nonreporting of labor force categories, notably forced labor; (4) assorted errors in estimation. Although there is some discussion in Soviet sources to support the possibility that reported labor force data involve understatement, especially with respect to the collective farm labor force, the discussion is too general to be translated into quantitative terms.

Aside from the real possibility that some if not a major share of the residual is due to the nonreporting of certain labor force categories, we may very well be facing here, in somewhat exaggerated form, the assorted weaknesses in noncensus sources of information on the population and labor force that cause Soviet statisticians and other social scientists to look forward to the publication of the results of the 1959 census. In any event, the existence of the residual contributes a special difficulty to any analysis of the distribution of the Soviet labor force by occupations or socioeconomic groups.

As far as the demand for labor is concerned, the expansion of the nonagricultural sector of the Soviet economy under the 5-year plans has appeared almost entirely as an increased demand for wage and salary workers. Selected data for wage and salary workers, in comparison with the United States, are reproduced in table 4. (The data in this table refer to nonagricultural as well as agricultural wage and salary workers, although in the case of each country the latter comprises a relatively small proportion.)

TABLE 4.—*The number of wage and salary workers, U.S.S.R. and United States, selected years, 1928–65* [1]

[In thousands]

	U.S.S.R.				United States				U.S.S.R. percent of United States (both sexes)
	Both sexes	Males	Females	Females, percent of both sexes	Both sexes	Males	Females	Females, percent of both sexes	
1928, year's average	11,599	8,477	3,122	26.9					
1940, January–March [2]	29,401	18,111	11,290	38.4	34,770	24,200	10,570	30.3	84.6
1942–45 [3]	18,400	8,600	9,800	53.0	40,180	26,680	13,500	33.6	45.8
1950, September	40,400	21,410	18,990	47.0	49,015	33,547	15,468	31.6	82.4
1958, year's average	52,400				53,000	34,600	18,400	34.7	99.9
1965, year's average [4]	64,000								

[1] Data for the U.S.S.R. are derived from sources and by methods set forth in Eason, op. cit.; and Pravda, Jan. 16, 1959, and Nov. 14, 1958. Data consistently include servants but exclude collective farm tractor drivers (estimated). Data for the United States are from selected issues of the Monthly Report on the Labor Force.

[2] U.S.S.R. data are January; U.S. data, March.

[3] U.S.S.R. data are 1942; U.S. data, beginning of 1945.

[4] According to 7-year plan.

The demand for wage and salary workers in the Soviet Union was satisfied during the 1930's partly by the supply of manpower already in the urban areas, consisting of both the unemployed persons and those in other categories of the urban labor force; partly by the migration of labor from rural to urban areas; and partly by drawing persons into the labor force. In sum total, rural-urban migration and the transformation of formerly rural communities into urban areas appear to have accounted for more than 80 percent of the increased labor supply of wage and salary workers in urban areas.[16]

At the same time, the population of working ages was increasing, although the average rate of increase during the intercensal period (1926–39) was less than projected on the basis of preplan survival ratios. The absolute increase in the adult population age 16 to 59

[16] S. I. Sul'kevich, "Territoria i naselenie S.S.S.R." (Moscow, 1940), p. 30.

between 1926 and 1939 was at a rate of 1.5 percent per year, or in total 16.5 million. This may be compared to the reported increase of 18.3 million wage and salary workers over the same period. With an allowance for a lower rate of labor force participation among females than males, the absolute increase in the population of prime working ages (16 to 59) represents an increase in the labor force equal to almost two-thirds of the reported increase in the number of wage and salary workers alone.

All things taken into account, the sources of labor supply seem adequate to account for the indicated overall rate of increase in wage and salary employment without serious dislocation in other sectors of the labor force. Even in the most recent period, deficits in the population of working ages caused by the war, and what might otherwise be mounting resistance to rural-urban migration at past rates, have tended to be compensated for by the increase of the population of working ages brought about by the influx of persons born during the years of relatively high birth rates in the late 1930's.

Within this framework of demand and supply factors, it is of interest to note that over the period from 1928 to the present, the number of female wage and salary workers has increased at a more rapid rate than the number of males. The result is that females now comprise about 50 percent of the total number of wage and salary workers, compared to 27 percent at the beginning of the plans; or, in other words, that the absolute increase in the number of females (20 million to 1955 [17]) has been greater than the increase in the number of males (17 million). The demographic factors outlined above, in particular the declining sex ratio, and the traditionally high labor force participation rates of the female population, undoubtedly have contributed to these changes.

Considering the period of almost 30 years between 1928 and 1955, the overall increase of 17 million male wage and salary workers is very little more than the 15 million increase in the number of males age 16 to 59 in the population; and the corresponding increase in the number of female wage and salary workers (20 million) is considerably less than the increase in the number of females age 16 to 59 (29 million). It thus appears that the demand for wage and salary workers, a "priority" sector from the standpoint of manpower allocation, has been more than met (according to the reported data) by the net increase in the population of working ages.

Over the next decade, on the other hand, and in particular with respect to the increase projected in the 7-year plan (1965), the number of wage and salary workers will probably increase at the expense of other sectors of the labor force, or through a modification of alternative nonlabor demands, such as formal education. For all of the implications of the reorganization of education discussed above, a reduction in the number of students is not contemplated.

Data on the number of wage and salary workers in the United States, in table 4, show that as of 1958 the number in the two countries is essentially equal, culminating an overall trend since 1928 in which the Soviet figure increased more rapidly than the United States. However, these figures are in a sense not analytically comparable, because in some instances occupations receiving wages and salaries

[17] Eason, op. cit., for further details on this and other parts of this discussion.

in the Soviet Union receive self-employment income in the United States.

The distribution of the population by dependency on agricultural and nonagricultural occupations

At the beginning of the 5-year plans, the total population of the Soviet Union was almost 50 percent larger than the population on comparable territory in 1897, but the proportion of the population dependent on agricultural occupations was essentially the same—78 percent compared to 75 percent. Once the plans were underway however, and particularly after collectivization had been achieved, the agricultural population declined, both absolutely and in proportion to the total. Trends in these categories are indicated for selected years in table 5, together with data on the U.S. population by farm and nonfarm residence.

The absolute decline set in after 1930, with the most perceptible downward movement taking place between 1931 and 1933, coincident with the period of rapid collectivization followed by the food shortage; and there was another decline between 1936 and 1938. The reason for the decline in the latter period is not clear, although it appears primarily in the collective farm category.[18]

[18] Id.

TABLE 5.—*The population dependent on agricultural and civilian nonagricultural occupations, reported categories, Imperial Russia and the U.S.S.R., 1897–1955; and the population by farm and nonfarm residence, U.S.A., 1910–50*[1]

	1897 [2]	1928	1940	1955
U.S.S.R.				
Population dependent on agricultural and civilian nonagricultural occupations, reported categories:	*Thousands*	*Thousands*	*Thousands*	*Thousands*
Agricultural	93,702	113,300	105,700	87,100
Nonagricultural	31,938	34,900	68,300	80,500
Total (reported categories)	125,640	148,200	174,000	167,600
Percentage distribution:	*Percent*	*Percent*	*Percent*	*Percent*
Agricultural	74.6	76.5	60.7	52.0
Nonagricultural	25.4	23.5	39.3	48.0
Total (reported categories)	100.0	100.0	100.0	100.0
Population dependent on agricultural occupations, percent of total population, all categories	74.6	74.8	53.7	44.1
Population dependent on agricultural occupations, percent of rural population	86.1	91.8	78.2	77.2

	1910	1920	1930	1940	1950
U.S.A.					
Population by farm and nonfarm residence:	*Thousands*	*Thousands*	*Thousands*	*Thousands*	*Thousands*
Farm	32,077	31,614	30,445	30,547	23,332
Nonfarm	59,895	74,096	92,330	101,122	127,366
Total	91,972	105,710	122,775	131,669	150,698
Percentage distribution:	*Percent*	*Percent*	*Percent*	*Percent*	*Percent*
Farm	34.9	29.9	24.8	23.2	15.5
Nonfarm	65.1	70.1	75.2	76.2	84.5
Total	100.0	100.0	100.0	100.0	100.0
Population by farm residence percent of rural population	64.2	61.3	56.6	53.4	37.8

[1] Data for the U.S.S.R. are derived from sources and by methods set forth in Eason, op. cit.

Data for the U.S.A are from U.S. Bureau of the Census, "Historical Statistics of the United States, 1789–1945" (Washington, D.C.: Government Printing Office, 1949), p. 29; and "Continuation to 1952 of Historical Statistics * * *" (Washington, D.C.: Government Printing Office, 1954), p. 3.

[2] Territory for 1897 is Imperial Russian.

By 1938, the population dependent on agricultural occupations was 61 percent of the total population dependent on occupations in all "reported" categories, and 54 percent of the total population. Essentially the same relations are seen to hold on the eve of World War II (1940), including annexed territories.

The reason for distinguishing between the population dependent on occupations in "reported" categories and the total population lies with the "residual" category which was discussed above. The presence of the residual means that the indicated relationships, as a measure of the distribution of the population between agricultural and nonagricultural occupations, must be taken as rough orders of magnitude. With this in mind, it may be pointed out that the data show the population dependent on agricultural occupations as of 1955 to include something more than half of the population dependent on occupations in "reported" categories, and 44 percent of the total population. The true figure would depend on what would in effect be the distribution of the "residual" category between its agricultural and nonagricultural components.

Speaking in orders of magnitude, however, the distribution of the population between agricultural and nonagricultural sources of livelihood thus appears to have changed more rapidly in the Soviet Union than in other countries undergoing industrialization. At the same time, there remains a relatively large population in agriculture compared to other industrial powers. The United States with only 15 percent of its population now living on farms is one extreme example.

The percentage of the rural population dependent on nonagricultural occupations—roughly equivalent to our "rural nonfarm population"—has also increased proportionately under the 5-year plans. In this respect, the Soviet Union is moving in the direction of other industrializing countries, but at a slower rate. The nonagricultural share of the rural population increased from 8 percent in 1928 to 21 percent in 1940. The data indicate that only about 24 percent of the rual population were dependent on nonagricultural occupations as late as 1955.

Comparison with U.S. data show an increase in the rural nonfarm population from 36 to 62 percent of the total rural population between 1910 and 1950. The much higher percentage for the United States is in all probability related to the greater incidence of service and retail merchandising activities in rural areas.

Hours of work

A program is presently underway in the Soviet Union to reduce the average workday to 7 hours (and in some cases 6), without reducing take-home pay. Although this is quite consistent with long-run goals to have part of rising real wages take the form of reduced hours of work, the question which is intriguiging is why, in view of the imminent decline in the rate of increase of the population of working ages, the Soviets picked this particular time to reduce hours and in effect further contract labor supply.

The answer would seem to be largely an administrative one. It is known that Soviet administrators are exerting considerable pressure to introduce into production the benefits of technological progress developed in research establishments. The technique of reducing hours while maintaining per-man productivity is viewed by them as an effective method for stimulating each and every enterprise director to move in this direction, at the same time that it provides a ready check on the success of the move.

The question still remains, of course, as to whether this does not aggravate the labor supply problem unduly. The answer is, undoubtedly, that it does. On the other hand, if we take into account the age structure of the labor force in terms of the three groups, above, and the fact that the rate of increase of the labor force in the future will never again be as high as in the past, this reduction of hours may not necessarily be ill-timed.

In the first place, to reduce hours at any time in the future will be to do so in the face of a slower rate of increase of the labor force than in the past. Furthermore, the rate of increase over the past 7 years or so has been unusually high. Taking this 7-year period together with the next 7 years, produces an average increase of about 1 million per year, or not below the figure for a number of years since 1928.

As the program is carried out over the next few years, the hours of labor reduced will be primarily those supplied by the relatively large middle group in the labor force. The effect would seem to be to change the balance between skilled and unskilled labor inputs that will appear as long-run labor force growth rates are maintained after the next decade. In short, given the desirability of reducing hours reasonably soon on other grounds, the demographic factor is not a particularly strong argument against doing it now.

EFFICIENCY OF THE LABOR FORCE

The implication of the declining rate of increase in the labor force, as already pointed out, is a decided pressure on Soviet planners and administrators to use manpower more effectively. In the past, the cost of using it more or less "wastefully" (by Western standards) may have been too small to warrant the effort required to develop a more enlightened manpower policy. From now on the cost of such waste should be much more apparent.

The evidence is that the Soviets may be thinking along the same lines. They have taken a number of steps in recent years which, judged by Western experience, could take them in the direction of increasing the effectiveness of their manpower—from enterprise management to the production worker.[19] If we characterize Soviet manpower policies in the past as embodying a combination of the "carrot" and the "stick," with considerable emphasis on the "stick," the recent evidence indicates a shift in the direction of the "carrot," although the change is not in all aspects of policy uniform.

In the main, direct controls over the labor force have been relaxed. Compared to the period beginning with 1940, when workers were not permitted to leave jobs without the permission of management, subject to criminal penalties, recent policy changes permit the workers to change jobs on short notice, and the scope of involuntary transfers has been reduced.

[19] Portions of the following discussion also appear in Eason, "Are the Soviets Winning the Battle of Production," loc. cit., pp. 98–106.

Except as a graduate of specialized training, the worker is now freer than he has been at any time since the 1930's to respond to wage and other considerations in seeking and changing the terms and conditions of his work. At the same time, this increased "mobility" of labor does not seem to have resulted in labor turnover as high as it was during the 1930's. Recent evidence on this subject is, however, very fragmentary. Turnover certainly remains a problem, but a larger share of labor "recruitment" appears to be through upward movement within a given enterprise, aided by an expanded system of training programs.

There have also been a number of recent policy changes designed to influence the worker in his relationship to a given job situation. On the one hand, there has been a relaxation of policies to discourage negative manifestations of labor toward the demands of the work. For example, punishment for absenteeism, heretofore treated as a criminal offense, is now left to management itself within its prerogatives to "discipline" its work force.

On the other hand, Soviet labor policy has moved in many respects to encourage the positive manifestations of application and effectiveness on the job. The first of these is in the crucial area of wage policy. Without at all rejecting the principle of differential wages adopted in the early 1930's, the movement in recent years has been to improve the wage structure. The pay of the lowest paid workers has been raised, differentials have been widened for certain important skills, greater uniformity in regional differentials has been introduced, the bonus system has been simplified, and base rates (for both piece and time workers) have been raised to a larger share of total earnings—all with a view to increasing the effectiveness of the worker on the job and thereby increasing the productivity of labor.

As part of the reorganization of the administration of the national economy which took place in 1957, labor is being called upon to play a greater role in the day-to-day decision making of the enterprise—without, however, fundamentally usurping the prerogatives of management. This job is to be done by having more and better attended production conferences and by strengthening the system of rewards for suggestions by workers toward improving the work process. The trade unions are supposed to help guide this program. Since the 1930's the unions have been predominantly an arm of the state in mobilizing the workers for production, but recent discussion also stresses their function in seeing to it that all phases of labor policy, as it affects both management and labor, are duly executed in the individual enterprise.

It should be noted that these are not in and of themselves new aspects of Soviet labor policy; rather that they seem to be receiving greater stress than in the past, within the framework of the discussion attending the reorganization of industry.

Finally, labor, as always, is called upon to work for the ultimate success of socialism and the building of communism, as much as for private and present gain. Although the use of a distant goal is open to question as a device for getting individuals to work (and sacrifice) every day at given jobs, it is probably true that the picture of the goal itself has been brought into focus both visually and figuratively by the presence of the earth satellites and rockets to the moon and beyond.[20]

[20] Questions of improving the efficiency of higher level manpower, although logically falling within this section, will not be dealt with, in view of the papers dealing exclusively with this subject.

By way of concluding comments, it should be stressed, first, that we cannot tell, nor do the Soviets know, whether these indicated policy modifications will produce the desired results, or what later changes will have to be made. It is true that there are many aspects of the Soviet system which are unique, and which many people feel are at variance with economic efficiency, let alone human welfare. On the other hand, the basic problems of industrialization and economic growth, and the kind of solutions required in the area of manpower resources, are substantially similar wherever they are found. Soviet leadership, especially since the death of Stalin, has shown increasing signs of recognizing this fact. It has also shown a greater willingness to integrate what is uniquely Soviet with what is required by efficient economic growth, to make a practical compromise.

Equally significant, certain basic characteristics of the Soviet scene have irrevocably changed. The Soviet Union has been transformed from an agricultural to an industrial society, with all that this implies for the readiness of the work force to respond to the requirements of modern economic life.

It would be difficult to make predictions about the effect of these fundamental changes on the utilization of manpower in the future. But the potential influence on the overall effectiveness of the Soviet economy is great enough that we cannot afford not to watch closely this particular area of their overall activity in the years to come.

INDUSTRY

THE STRUCTURE AND GROWTH OF SOVIET INDUSTRY: A COMPARISON WITH THE UNITED STATES

(By G. Warren Nutter, University of Virginia)

Introduction

Summaries are always treacherous, particularly when treating such a complex subject as the structure and growth of Soviet industry. In a brief report, one may present either a detailed picture of a narrow aspect of the topic or a bold sketch of the subject in the large. The latter approach seems most appropriate here, but it should not be undertaken or studied without an awareness of the importance of things left unsaid. Few topics of the day are more controversial than the question of Soviet economic growth. Scholars who have devoted their professional careers to this subject reach vastly different conclusions, on matters of both fact and interpretation. We are a long way from the scholarly ideal of agreement.

For this reason, it is as important to know how conclusions are reached as what they are. And there is the dilemma: full documentation, usually tedious and complex in this field, cannot be presented in a summary report. Nor can all the necessary qualifications be kept constantly before the reader. This paper represents an effort to compress voluminous materials and qualifications into a brief report, with all the unavoidable vices of a summary. It draws on preliminary findings of a broad study of Soviet economic growth sponsored during the last 5½ years by the National Bureau of Economic Research. Since the study has not yet been completed, the findings are subject to revision before the final report is published. That report will, of course, contain a documentation of the basic statistics. Meanwhile, as far as this symposium is concerned, we may hope that the basic points at which other specialists might disagree with the findings given here will be brought to light in their papers.

Any summary of Soviet industrial performance must start with a few words on the difficulties of appraising it. The student of the Soviet economy takes his data from the official Soviet press, and therein lie unusual troubles. Some scholars may find it hard to believe that Soviet statistics are really worse than others, because every specialist in no matter what field quickly becomes convinced, for rather good reasons, that no data could be as bad as those he is forced to work with. Why call the kettle black when it is probably no grayer than the pot?

Let us acknowledge at once that all statistics contain faults and errors. Let us also acknowledge that no government or other agency resists the temptation to stretch figures to its own account if it feels it can get away with it. Representative government, competitive scholarship, and free public discourse are the western institutions that have counteracted error and misrepresentation in statistics, imperfectly to be sure but at least to some degree.

The peculiar difficulties with Soviet statistics stem, in the first instance, from the system of authoritarian, centralized planning—from what has been called a command economy. Published statistics come from only one source: the state. There are no independent sources to restrain each other or to be used as checks against each other, except to the extent that related figures published by different state agencies might not be fully coordinated before publication. On the other side, the suppliers of data to the central authorities—the economic and administrative units—have a stake in the figures they report, since their performance is judged on the basis of them. The Soviet statistical authorities do not hide their concern over the misreporting that results from this feature of the economic system.

A second set of difficulties stems from the crusading nature of Soviet communism. Statistics are grist for the propaganda mill. Knowing the ideological views of Soviet leaders, one cannot expect them to dispense facts in a passive and detached manner.

For both broad reasons, Soviet statistics are selective and of varying reliability and ambiguity. The policy of selectivity has two rather opposing results as far as statistics on physical output are concerned. On the one hand, some areas of poor performance are shielded from view, being underrepresented in published data. On the other hand, some of the more rapidly expanding economic activities associated with the military sector are also not reported on. It is impossible to determine the net bias of the sample of published data: whether there is, on this count, a net over- or under-statement of growth.[1]

A few broad generalizations can be made about the reliability of the published statistics. In the first place, absolute output is probably overstated in the case of most industries, particularly for the years within the plan period, though the degree of overstatement cannot be determined. In the second place, growth in output is also probably overstated relative to a prerevoluitionary or an early Soviet base, but not necessarily over other parts of the Soviet period. Over some of the latter years growth may be overstated, over others understated, and over still others more or less accurately reported. This will vary from industry to industry and from one situation to another.

Whatever the faults of data on output of individual industries, they are more reliable than official aggregative measures, such as the official Soviet index of industrial production. Although the details underlying this index have not been made public, Western specialists are generally agreed that, from what they know about the construction and behavior of the index, it exaggerates industrial growth.

There are other factors in addition to the defects in basic statistics that make it difficult to construct meaningful measures of aggregate industrial production. Soviet prices generally do not reflect relative costs of production; the industrial structure has shifted radically over short periods of time; growth rates have differed widely from sector to sector; growth has been interrupted at critical points by major disturbances; and so on. Finally, quantitative growth has not been

[1] These brief comments apply to the condition of economic statistics since 1956. Between 1938 and 1956, statistics on physical output of individual industries were not published at all in the Soviet Union, with a few minor exceptions.

accompanied by the general improvement in quality that has characterized industrial development in most Western countries.

These considerations make it difficult to summarize Soviet industrial performance in terms of mere numbers. But summaries are useful and necessary, and they cannot be fully qualified at every point without turning them into the voluminous reports they are supposed to summarize. In the summary to follow, the necessary qualifications are intended to be implicit throughout—and they should be kept in mind to dull the edge of deceptively sharp figures.

TABLE 1.—*Indexes oj industrial production for Russia, Soviet Lnion, and Lnited States: benchmark years, 1870–1955*

[1913=100]

	Total output		Output per person engaged in industry [1]		Output per head of population	
	Russia or Soviet Union [2]	United States	Soviet Union	United States	Russia or Soviet Union	United States
1870	13	12			21	29
1875	17	14			25	30
1880	22	20			36	38
1885	28	23			36	39
1890	38	35			55	54
1895	52	39			59	56
1900	74	50			77	65
1905	72	74			69	91
1910	102	85			61	88
1913	118				99	100
1913	100	100	100	100	100	100
1920	20	125			20	113
1928	102	172	110	149	93	138
1933	150	119	85	139	123	91
1937	258	194	121	158	195	145
1940	265	213	117	169	178	156
1945	119	342			124	234
1950	384	365	138	215	252	232
1955	558	454	167	246	358	264

[1] Persons engaged measured in full-time equivalents.
[2] For 1913, 1st figure applies to tsarist territory; second, to interwar Soviet territory. Otherwise, current territory. Index covers civilian products only.

CHART 1

INDUSTRIAL PRODUCTION: Tsarist Russia, Soviet Union, and United States
1870 - 1955
(1913=100)

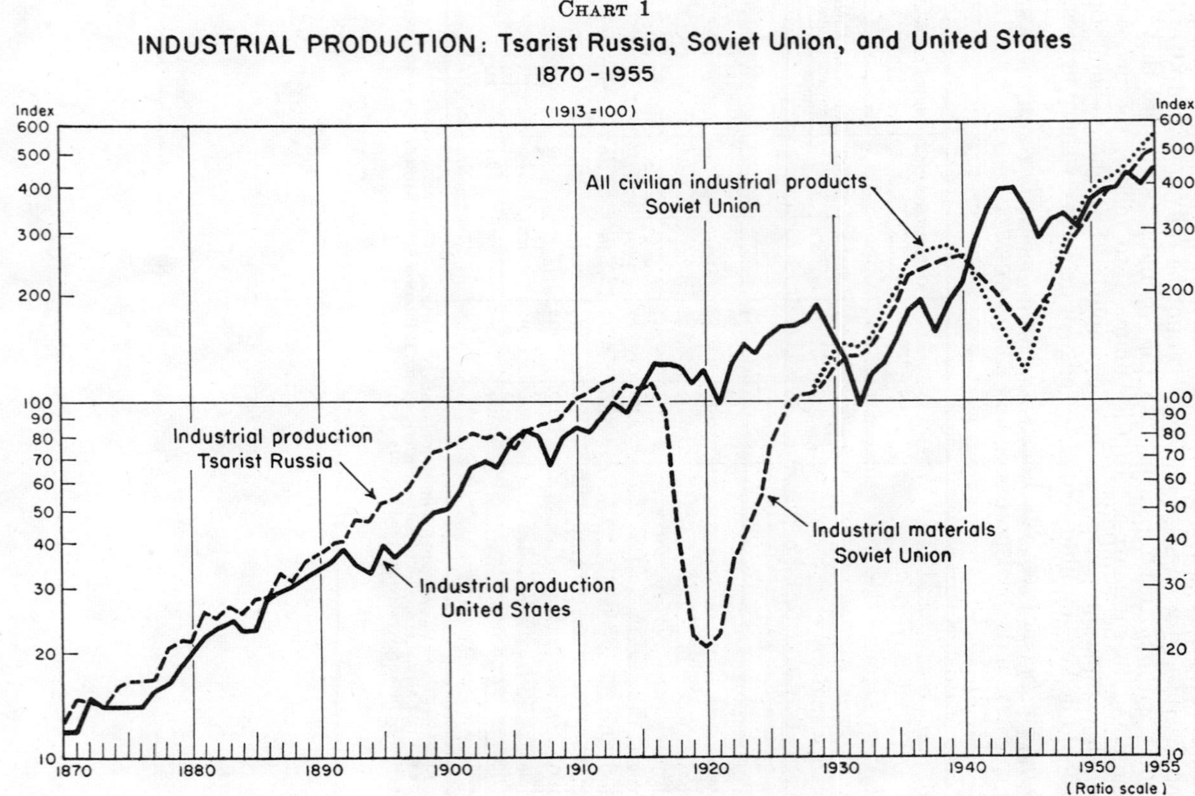

Soviet Industrial Growth

GROWTH IN OUTPUT

Soviet industrial output multiplied between five and six times over the period 1913–55. (See table and chart 1.) [2] Performance varied widely among sectors, with output multiplying 16 times in the case of machinery and equipment, 9 times in the case of intermediate industrial products, but only 3 times in the case of consumer goods. The average annual growth rate was 4.2 percent for industry as a whole, 6.8 percent for machinery and equipment, 5.5 percent for intermediate industrial products, and 2.6 percent for consumer goods (see table 2).

Some of this growth is attributable to the territorial expansion that took place during and after World War II. We have estimated that the acquired territories added about 11 percent to industrial output and, if we suppose that this relation would also have held true in 1955, the average annual growth rate for all industry over the Soviet period would have to be reduced from 4.2 to 3.9 percent to eliminate the effects of territorial expansion. The assumptions underlying such an adjustment are, of course, somewhat arbitrary.

The dispersal of growth trends (unadjusted for territorial expansion) may be seen more clearly by examining a finer breakdown of industries. For a sample of 70 industries, growth rates ranged from an average annual decline of 0.9 percent to an average annual increase of 16.8 percent; the middle half of these growth rates ranged between increases of 2.5 and 8.5 percent. The median was 5 percent, which is higher than the weighted average of 4.2 percent shown by the production index. Industries producing consumer goods dominate a distinct lower region of growth and are essentially confined to it, while other industries are concentrated about a higher region.

---

[2] For the purpose of this summary, aggregate Soviet output is measured by a comprehensive index based on moving Soviet weights. That index directly covers almost all categories of products except military end items and the more heterogeneous categories of machinery. Alternative indexes using different product coverages, weighting systems, and weight bases give results dispersed about those given by the comprehensive index with moving weights.

TABLE 2.—*Average annual growth rates for Soviet industry—Output, labor productivity, and per capita output for selected periods*

[Per cent]

Period	Industrial materials [1]	All civilian industrial products			
		Total	Intermediate products	Machinery[2]	Consumer goods
	Output				
1913-55 [1]	4.0	4.2	5.5	6.8	2.6
1913-28 [3]	.1	.1	.5	.4	−.2
1928-55	6.2	6.5	8.4	10.6	4.3
1928-40 [3]	8.0	8.3	11.9	15.7	4.8
1940-55	4.7	5.1	5.6	6.7	3.7
1928-37	9.6	10.9	15.0	26.3	5.5
1950-55	9.0	7.7	9.0	2.6	10.0
	Output per person engaged [4]				
1913-55	1.0	1.2	0.2	1.4	1.2
1913-28	.7	.7	1.4	−.2	.3
1928-55	1.3	1.6	2.7	2.3	1.9
1928-40	.2	.5	3.3	1.7	.9
1940-55	2.0	2.4	2.2	3.5	2.5
1928-37	.1	1.1	4.8	6.3	1.0
1950-55	5.4	3.9	5.7	−1.5	5.9
	Output per head of population				
1913-55	3.1	3.3	4.6	5.8	1.7
1913-28	−.5	−.5	−.1	−.2	−.8
1928-55	5.0	5.3	7.2	9.4	3.2
1928-40	5.6	5.9	9.4	13.1	2.4
1940-55	4.7	5.1	5.6	6.7	3.7
1928-37	8.6	9.9	14.0	25.2	4.6
1950-55	7.2	5.9	7.2	.9	8.2

[1] Output per person engaged derived by dividing index for industrial materials by index for all persons engaged in industry. That is, for purposes of this calculation. The index of industrial materials is taken to represent an index of total industrial production

[2] Output does not explicitly cover military end products while employment does. Hence growth in labor productivity is probably understated.

[3] Territorial gains may be approximately excluded from growth rates in the first 2 columns by subtracting the following percentage points: 1913-55, 0 3; 1928-55, 0.4; 1928-40, 0.9.

[4] Persons engaged measured in full-time equivalents.

The overall growth rate is lower for the Soviet period than for the last forty-odd years of the Tsarist period, when the growth rate was 5.3 percent a year according to our index (see table 2). Although the latter is based on a weak foundation of data and might have come out quite differently if better data had been available, one may allow for substantial relative overstatement of Tsarist growth, presuming all the error in that direction, and still conclude that it was faster than growth over the entire Soviet period. As to individual industries, higher growth rates in the one period are not systematically related with either higher or lower growth rates in the other. Here again, the sample is small, covering only 23 industries, and conclusions must therefore be tempered.

There has been a rather striking inverse relation between the rapidity of growth in an industry over the Soviet period and its "stage of development" at the beginning of the period. For a sample of 48 industries, those whose outputs were smallest relative to the United States in 1913 have shown a strong tendency to grow fastest. The tendency is even more pronounced when the plan period is considered by itself, the stage of development in this case being measured as of 1928 and the growth over 1928–55. A growth pattern of this sort is to be expected of any country undergoing rapidly industrialization, but in the Soviet case the evidence suggests it has been accentuated by planned design, an effort to "overcome and surpass the leading capitalist economies."

Growth has varied widely not only among industries, but also over different spans of time. The early years were marked by external and internal wars, so that measurable industrial output dropped by 80 percent between 1913 and 1920. By 1927 or 1928 industrial output had roughly recovered to its 1913 level in quantitative terms, though a general deterioration in the quality of industrial goods over this period meant that the recovery was less complete. Moreover, it was uneven even if no allowance is made for deterioration in quality: the 1913 level of output was not achieved in the case of consumer goods, while it was somewhat exceeded in the case of all other products.

With the institution of the first 5-year plan at the end of 1928, growth accelerated rapidly and generally except in the area of consumer goods. The acceleration continued through the second 5-year plan and extended into consumer goods. Against a background of political purges and partial wartime mobilization, the pace of industrial growth slackened in the succeeding 3 years of the short-lived third 5-year plan, and such growth as took place may be attributed to territorial expansion. The growth of output over 1937–40 is understated by our comprehensive index because it does not reflect the partial conversion of certain industries, principally chemicals and machinery, to military-type products. Output of industrial materials grew by 10 percent over this period, while output of all civilian products grew by only 3 percent. By the end of 1940, industrial output stood at about 2.6 times its level in 1913 and 1928; or, if territorial gains are excluded, at about 2.3 times its earlier level.

World War II brought with it a sharp decline in output—offset in large part by lend-lease shipments—and heavy losses in manpower and capital. Recovery was swift in the fourth 5-year plan, being aided by collection of reparations and other economic policies in Eastern Europe, so that the prewar level of industrial output was apparently regained by 1948 or 1949. Rapid growth was maintained through the fifth 5-year plan, where our study largely ends. Industrial output multiplied about 2.1 times between 1940 and 1955.

Over the plan period (1928–55) the average annual rate of growth was 6.5 percent for all industry (6.1 percent if territorial gains are excluded), 8.4 percent for intermediate industrial products, 10.6 percent for machinery, and 4.3 percent for consumer goods. The growth rate has tended to slow down or retard: for all industry, it was 8.3 percent a year over 1928–40 (7.4 percent if territorial gains are excluded) and 5.1 percent over 1940–55; or, if the war years are removed from consideration, it was 10.9 percent a year for 1928–37 and 7.7 percent for 1950–55. There is a similar retardation in growth for each of the categories of intermediate industrial products, machinery, and consumer goods.

As in other countries, retardation in growth has been general for individual industries, narrowly defined. The available evidence indicates that most industries experienced a slower growth over the Soviet period than over the late Tsarist period, and over the later

Soviet years than over the earlier ones. Moreover, most of the industries with retardation in growth from the Tsarist to the Soviet period also had retardation within the latter.

GROWTH IN OUTPUT AND EMPLOYMENT

The growth in industrial output has been accompanied by a rapid expansion of the industrial labor force. The number of persons engaged in Soviet industry, expressed in full-time equivalents, multiplied 3.3 times between 1913 and 1955. Thus, 60 percent of the growth in output may be attributed to expanded employment and 40 percent to increased labor productivity. Put another way, persons engaged increased at an average annual rate of 2.9 percent, while labor productivity—output per person engaged—increased at an average annual rate of only 1.2 percent. The growth in labor productivity ranged from 0.7 percent a year for construction materials to 4.3 percent a year for electricity.

Growth in labor productivity, as we have measured it, has fluctuated from period to period, but there has been an underlying trend toward acceleration. Employment apparently grew slower than output between 1913 and 1928, 1933 and 1937, 1940 and 1950, and 1950 and 1955; it apparently grew faster between 1928 and 1933 and between 1937 and 1940, both periods of radical structural change in industry. The decline in labor productivity over 1937–40 is overstated somewhat because growth in output is understated by our comprehensive output index. Chemicals and machinery are probably the major industries for which the decline is overstated. For industry as a whole, labor productivity would be shown as rising slightly if industrial materials were used to measure industrial output. The average annual growth rate in labor productivity rose from 0.7 percent for 1913–28 to 1.6 percent for 1928–55; from 0.5 percent for 1928–40 to 2.4 percent for 1940–55; and from 1.1 percent for 1928–37 to 3.9 percent for 1950–55 (see table 2).

GROWTH IN OUTPUT AND POPULATION

While industrial employment was multiplying 3.3 times between 1913 and 1955, population multiplied only 1.4 times. Expansion of the industrial labor force has been achieved, particularly in the earlier phase of industrialization, by drawing upon a large supply of underutilized labor, attached primarily to agriculture. It follows that growth in industrial output has been more rapid per head of population than per worker: 3.3 percent a year as compared with 1.2 percent.

Soviet demographic statistics are sketchy and subject to many doubts, so that it is particularly difficult to say anything with confidence about fluctuations in per capita output. According to Soviet data as modified and interpreted by Western scholars, population within Soviet boundaries grew at an average annual rate of 0.6 percent over 1913–28, 0.9 percent over 1928–37, 6.4 percent over 1937–40 (because of territorial expansion), minus 0.9 percent over 1940–50 (because of war and its aftermath), and 1.7 percent over 1950–55. Despite a rather erratic relationship between growth in population and industrial output over different spans of years, growth rates have tended to move in the same direction for both total and per capita output. Thus the average annual growth in per capita output rose from minus 0.5 percent over 1913–28 to 5.3 percent over 1928–55; within the plan periods, it fell from 5.9 percent over 1928–40 to 5.1 percent over 1950–55, or from 9.9 percent over 1928–37 to 5.9 percent over 1950–55 (see table 2). We therefore see a contrast between retarding growth in output per head of population and accelerating growth in output per worker.

Industrial Growth Compared: Soviet Union and United States

WHAT TO COMPARE

The Soviet record of industrial growth may be placed in perspective by comparing it with the record of other countries. This is not so easy as it might seem, not only because it is difficult to design relevant comparisons, but also because so little is known about the course of industrial development in most countries. The latter factor alone has forced us, with our limited time and resources, to concentrate on comparisons with the United States, a country with relatively abundant historical statistics. The United States is an obvious first choice for comparative study in any case, since it presents a striking contrast in economic system while being similar in size and resource endowment. But while comparative study reasonably starts with the United States, it should not end there, and we may hope that others will take up where we have left off.

Comparative study may help us in answering two quite different questions. First, we are interested in knowing, for a variety of reasons associated with the current state of world affairs, which country has shown the more rapid industrial growth over recent years, so that we may have some basis for intelligent guesses about relative growth over the very near future. Second, we are interested in knowing which country has been able to generate the more rapid industrial growth under conditions in which "physical" capacities for growth have been roughly equivalent. Our quest here is for a more fundamental test of the growth-generating efficiency of vastly different economic systems under comparable circumstances, a matter of concern for the longer view.

The first question is obviously easier to deal with than the second, because it requires only a description of the "facts" of growth in the two countries over the same span of years. Of course, the facts are in dispute, and the quantitative evidence of growth is more representative and reliable for the United States than for the Soviet Union. But this problem must always be faced—whether the issues at hand are analytical or purely descriptive. The essential point is that, in making comparisons of concurrent growth trends, we are primarily concerned with what is or has been happening, not with why it is or has been happening. Our attention is focused on trends likely to be carried forward over an immediate future by their own momentum, in the absence of revolutionary change in conditioning factors.

The second question involves a complex problem of analysis that by its nature defies definitive solution. We try to find historical periods in two countries in which important determinants of growth are the same in both cases, while the economic systems differ. To do this we need to know, first, what factors affect growth in what degrees; and second, what periods of history in the two countries are comparable.

Neither economic theory nor history blesses our task: theory is mute and history mischievous. At best, the periods chosen will be "comparable" only in some rather crude sense. Even so, the exercise is worth doing, as an early step in the successive approximations that mark the path to knowledge.

If industrial economies do undergo comparable stages of development in some meaningful sense, setting those American and Soviet periods side by side carries with it an important byproduct in addition to direct comparison of growth. It enables us to project Soviet developments into a context with which we are more familiar, and thereby to reason by analogy in directions where direct evidence is lacking. There are also great hazards in reasoning by analogy: but judiciously applied, it enriches our knowledge of the likely growth and present status of Soviet industry. Our vision of Soviet industrial growth is clarified by associating it with American developments bracketing the turn of the century, but at the same time the analogy must not be taken too far. The sets of industrial conditions in the two periods abound with anachronisms relative to each other.

CONTEMPORANEOUS GROWTH

Over the same spans of years, industrial output has generally grown faster in the Soviet Union than in the United States (see table 3 and chart 1). This seems to be an old story since it was apparently true of the Tsarist era as well: according to our indexes, Russian industry grew slightly faster than American industry over the period 1870–1913, the respective average annual rates being 5.3 and 5.1 percent. The differential is similar for the Soviet period as a whole: output grew over 1913–55 at an average annual rate of 3.9 percent in the Soviet Union, when adjusted to remove territorial gains, as compared with 3.7 percent in the United States. Growth has apparently been faster in the Soviet Union than in the United States for all major sectors of industry except foods, textiles, and related products (see chart 3).

Over the plan period Soviet growth in percentage terms has outdistanced American growth by a wider margin, making up for a differential in the other direction for the earlier years. American output grew at the same rate over both sets of years—namely, 3.7 percent a year—while the Soviet rate rose from 0.1 percent for the preplan years to 6.1 percent for the plan years, territorial gains excluded. In turn, relative performance has varied within the plan period itself. Over 1928–40, industrial output grew 7.4 percent a year in the Soviet Union as compared with only 1.8 percent in the United States, reflecting accelerated activity in the one case and depressed activity in the other. Over 1940–55, on the other hand, the average annual growth rate was similar in both countries: 5.1 percent in the Soviet Union and 5.2 percent in the United States.

Moving to the recent postwar years 1950–55, we find the Soviet growth rate of 7.7 percent a year exceeding the American rate of 4.5 percent by a significant margin. A discrepancy in favor of the Soviet Union has persisted through 1958, though the Soviet growth rate has tended to decline somewhat, as for as one can see from the defective published data. It is too early to say whether the decline is permanent or only temporary, whether this reflects a persistent retardation or a temporary fluctuation. It is also too early to say what is happening to the tempo of American industrial growth. In any case, the record for postwar years and for other peacetime years in the plan period suggests that Soviet industrial growth will continue to be more rapid than American growth over the near future.

The picture of comparative growth in output per head of population is much the same as what we have just sketched for total output (see table 3 and chart 2). But when we turn to output per unit of labor—or labor productivity—we find something quite different (see table 3 and chart 3). In all but one of the periods covered in our summary of comparative growth trends in output, labor productivity, as we have been able to measure it, grew faster in the United States than in the Soviet Union. This conclusion holds for output per person engaged in industry—the only extensive measure of labor productivity we have for the Soviet Union—and it probably holds for output per manhour, since average hours of work did not change significantly in the Soviet Union, at least between 1928 and 1955.

TABLE 3.—*Growth rates for industry in Tsarist Russia, Soviet Union, and United States: Output, labor productivity, and output per capita, selected concurrent periods*

[Percent]

	Average annual growth rate						
	Output		Output per unit of labor			Output per head of population	
	Russia or Soviet Union [1]	United States	Soviet Union per person engaged [2]	United States: Per person engaged [2]	United States: Per manhour	Russia or Soviet Union	United States
1870–1913	5.3	5.1	(3)	(3)	(3)	3.7	2.9
1913–55	[4] 3.9	3.7	1.2	2.2	2.7	3.3	2.4
1913–28	.1	3.7	.7	2.7	3.6	–.5	2.3
1928–55	[4] 6.1	3.7	1.6	1.9	2.2	5.3	2.5
1928–40	[4] 7.4	1.8	.5	1.1	2.4	5.9	1.0
1940–55	5.1	5.2	2.4	2.5	2.0	5.1	3.6
1928–37	10.9	1.3	1.1	.7	2.4	9.9	.5
1950–55	7.7	4.5	3.9	2.7	2.2	5.9	2.8

[1] For Soviet Union, measured by index for all civilian industrial products.
[2] Persons engaged measured in full-time equivalents.
[3] Not available.
[4] Adjusted to exclude territorial gains. (See table 2.)

CHART 2

INDUSTRIAL PRODUCTION PER HEAD OF POPULATION:
Tsarist Russia, Soviet Union, and United States, 1870-1955

(1913 = 100)

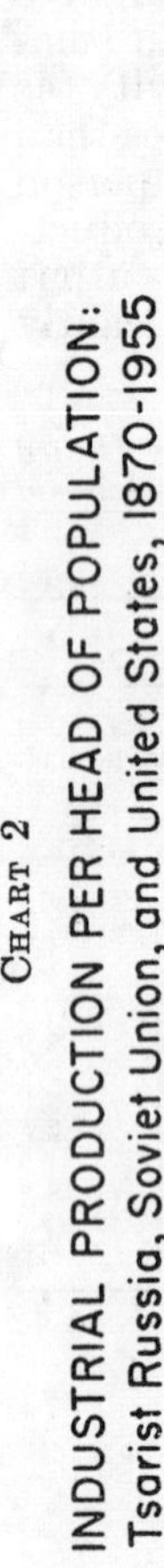

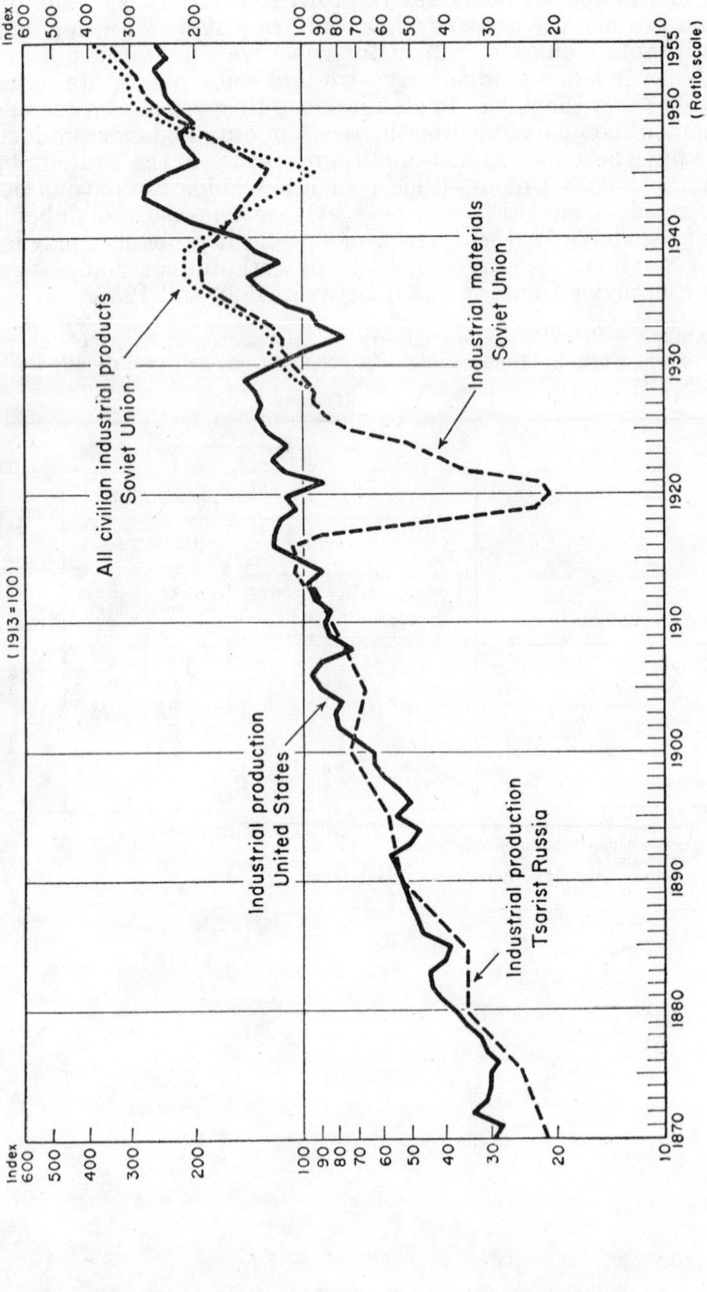

CHART 3

Indexes of Output, Employment, and Labor Productivity by Industrial Groups: Soviet Union, 1913-1955, and United States, 1909-1953

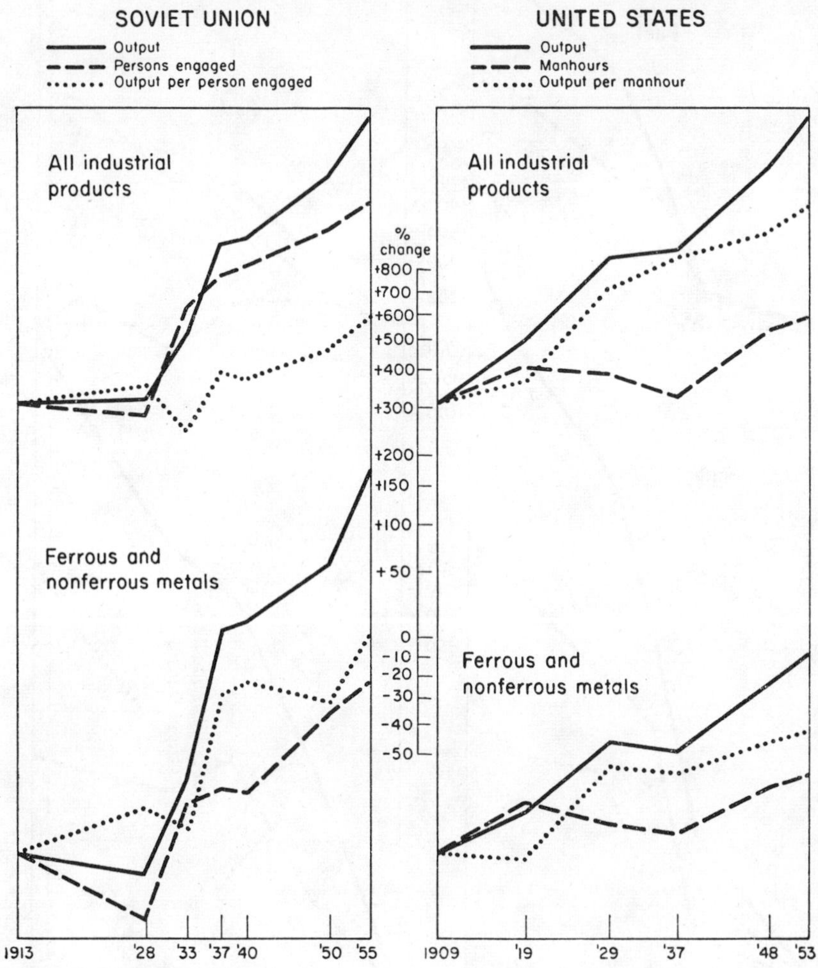

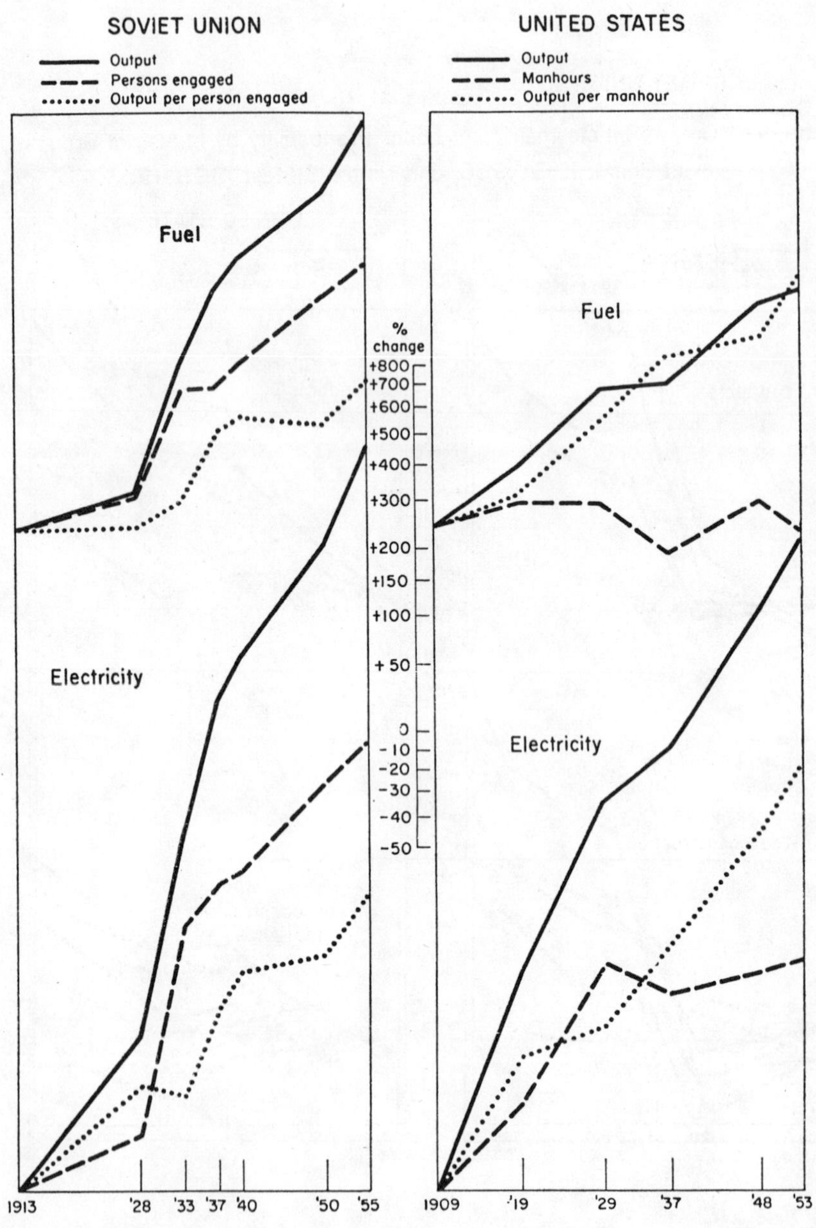
SOVIET UNION
Output
Persons engaged
Output per person engaged
UNITED STATES
Output
Manhours
Output per manhour
Fuel
Electricity
Fuel
Electricity
% change
+800
+700
+600
+500
+400
+300
+200
+150
+100
+ 50
0
-10
-20
-30
-40
-50
1913
'28
'33
'37
'40
'50
'55
1909
'19
'29
'37
'48
'53

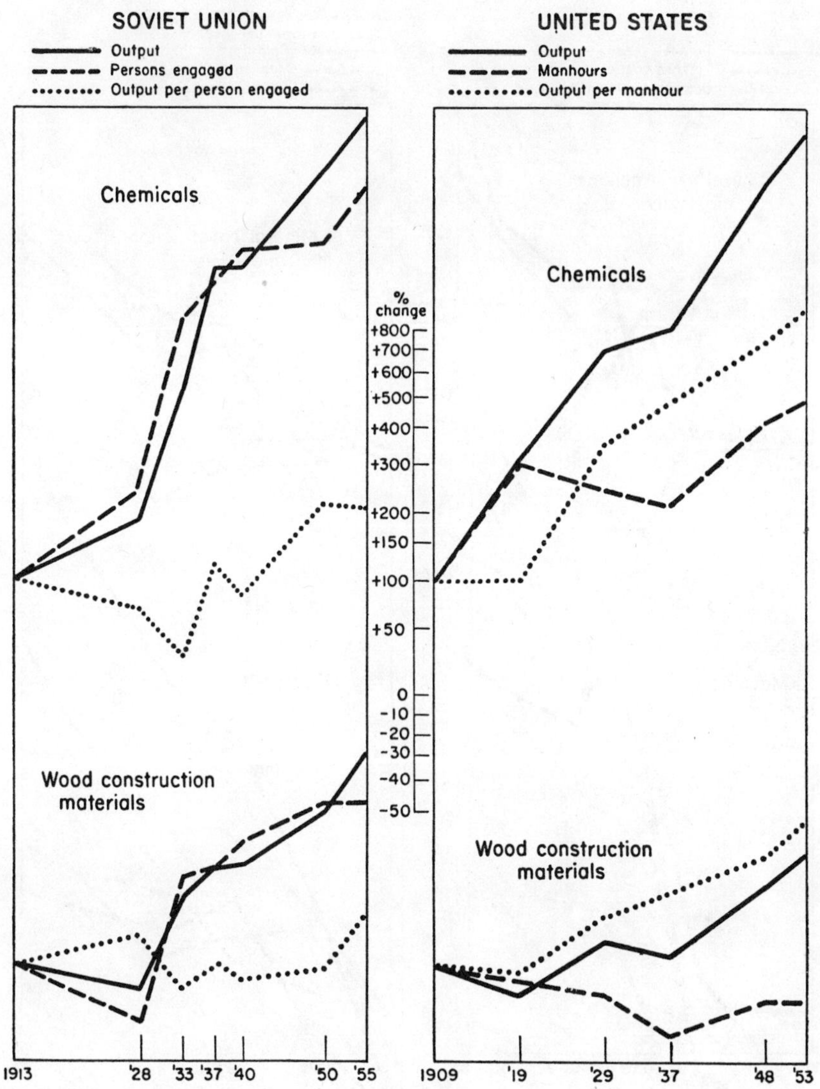
SOVIET UNION
Output
Persons engaged
Output per person engaged
Chemicals
Wood construction materials
1913
'28
'33
'37
'40
'50
'55
% change
+800
+700
+600
+500
+400
+300
+200
+150
+100
+50
0
-10
-20
-30
-40
-50
UNITED STATES
Output
Manhours
Output per manhour
Chemicals
Wood construction materials
1909
'19
'29
'37
'48
'53

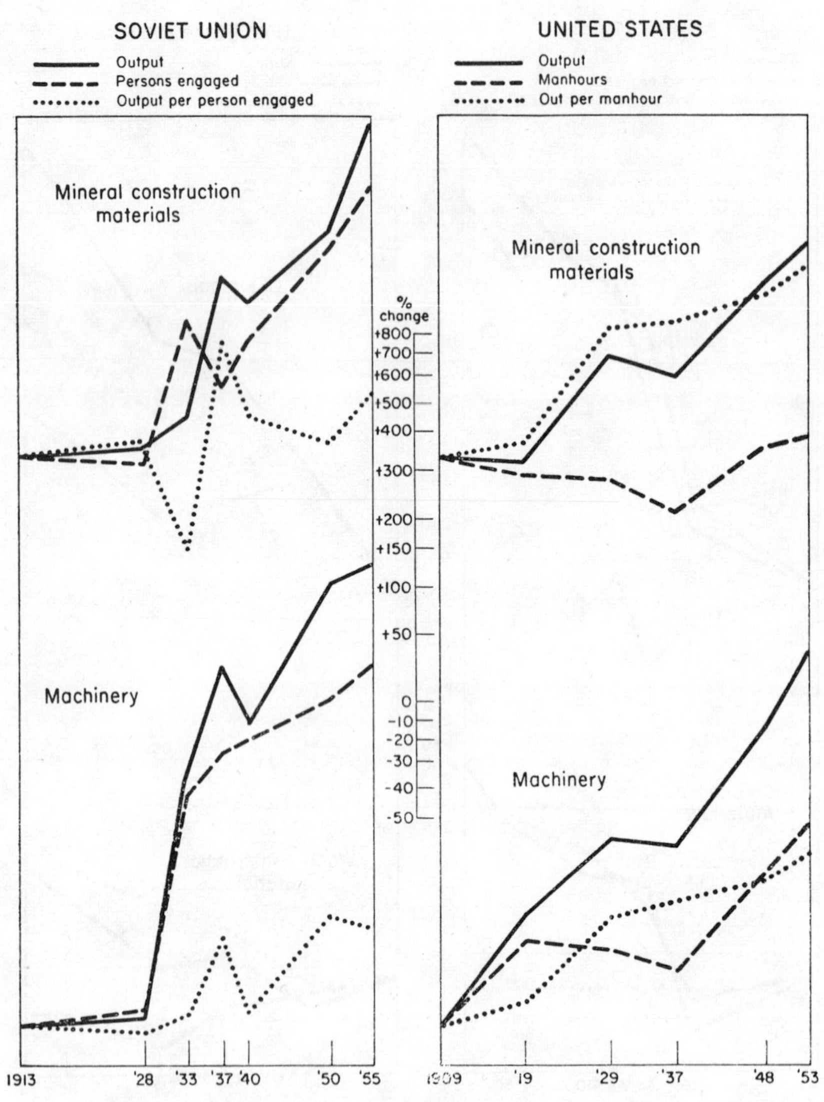

SOVIET UNION
Output
Persons engaged
Output per person engaged
Mineral construction materials
Machinery
1913
'28
'33
'37
'40
'50
'55
% change
+800
+700
+600
+500
+400
+300
+200
+150
+100
+50
0
-10
-20
-30
-40
-50
UNITED STATES
Output
Manhours
Out per manhour
Mineral construction materials
Machinery
1909
'19
'29
'37
'48
'53

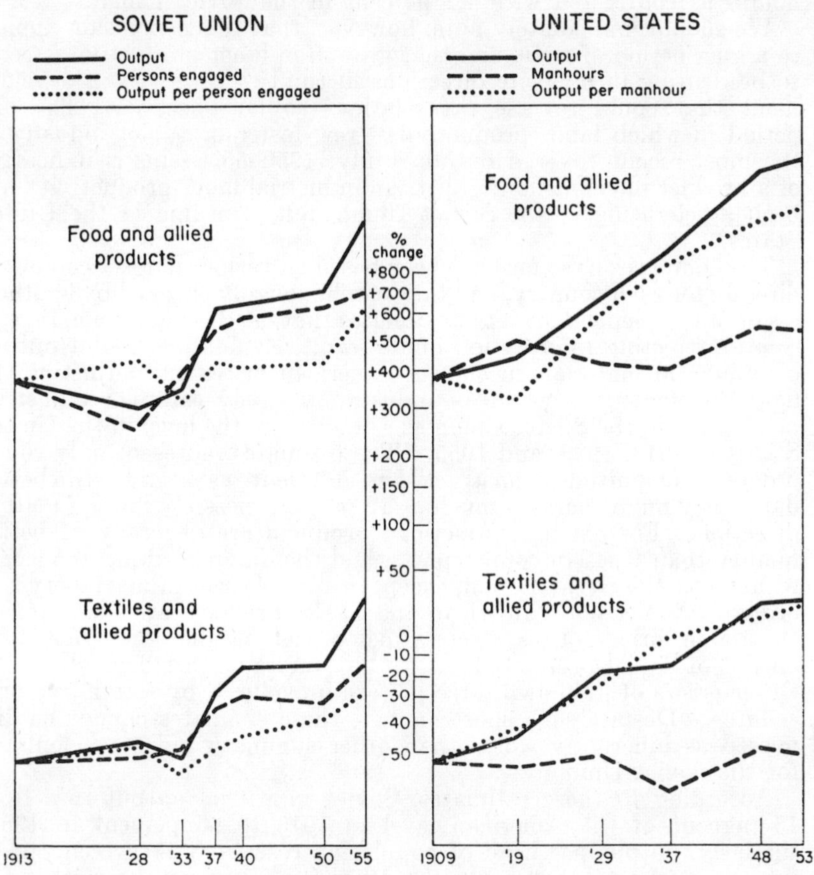
SOVIET UNION
Output
Persons engaged
Output per person engaged
Food and allied products
Textiles and allied products
1913
'28
'33
'37
'40
'50
'55
% change
+800
+700
+600
+500
+400
+300
+200
+150
+100
+50
0
-10
-20
-30
-40
-50
UNITED STATES
Output
Manhours
Output per manhour
Food and allied products
Textiles and allied products
1909
'19
'29
'37
'48
'53

In the United States, growth in industrial output has come mainly from improved labor productivity: Over 1913–55, output multiplied 4.5 times while employment multiplied only 1.8 times and man-hours only 1.5 times. In the Soviet Union, on the other hand, growth in output has come mainly from expanded employment, as we have seen. The contrast is sharp: Improved labor productivity accounted for 67 percent of the growth in output in the United States, but for only 40 percent in the Soviet Union. Labor productivity grew at 2.2 percent a year in the United States (2.7 percent based on man-hours) as contrasted with 1.2 percent in the Soviet Union.

We should immediately note, however, that this conclusion applies to a long period of time, and that growth in labor productivity seems to be drifting in opposite directions in the two countries, a development that could reverse the relations so far observed. The one period in which labor productivity grew faster in Soviet industry is the most recent covered by our study: 1950–55. This is indicative of a broader phenomenon: growth in industrial labor productivity has been accelerating in the Soviet Union, but retarding in the United States.

The comparisons so far have been based on various indexes computed directly for each country, and they can be roughly checked by another, essentially independent set of estimates that, at the same time, reveals some interesting information of its own. Evaluating Soviet output of industrial materials in current American prices and adjusting the figure to cover the whole of industry, we may estimate industrial production in the Soviet Union as a fraction of the level in the United States in 1913, 1928, and 1955. The estimates represent only rough orders of magnitude; constructed in different ways and with better data, they might vary as much as 10 percent, possibly more, in either direction. For example American products are generally of better quality than Russian counterparts, and the differential has tended to widen over the Soviet period, except in special cases of machinery and ordnance. Yet both American and Soviet products are evaluated at the same prices, thus overstating Soviet production. Similarly, output of Soviet products tends to be overstated in official statistics. Other errors of unknown direction are introduced by estimative procedures. Despite such shortcomings, these estimates cannot be dismissed as inherently worse than other summary indexes calculated for the Soviet Union.

According to these estimates, Soviet industrial output rose from 15 percent of the American level in 1913 to 23 percent in 1955; similarly, output per head of population rose from 11 percent to 19 percent. (See table 4.) On the other hand, output per worker fell from 25 percent to 21 percent, and output per man-hour from 23 percent to 18 percent. These findings are generally consistent with our more direct calculations, indicating that industrial output and output per capita grew faster in the Soviet Union than in the United States, while labor productivity grew slower.

At the same time, these estimates imply more rapid growth for Soviet industry than our direct indexes. In the case of total output, Soviet growth is indicated as 49 percent faster than American growth over 1913–55; in the case of per capita output, 77 percent faster. Hence, if we calculate Soviet growth indirectly on the basis of the American production index, Soviet output is indicated as multiplying

6.8 times (6.1 times excluding territorial gains) and per capita output, 4.6 times.[3] By direct calculations, the two multiples are 5.6 (5.0 excluding territorial gains) and 3.9, respectively. Put alternatively, output is shown as growing at 4.7 percent a year when calculated indirectly as compared with 4.2 percent when calculated directly; excluding territorial gains, the two rates are 4.4 percent and 3.9 percent. Similarly, growth in per capita output is 3.7 percent a year when calculated indirectly, but 3.3 percent when calculated directly; growth in output per worker, 1.7 percent when calculated indirectly, but1.2 percent when calculated directly.

TABLE 4.—*Relative value added and labor productivity of industry: Soviet Union as a percentage of United States, 1913, 1928, 1955*

	Soviet Union as a percentage of United States		
	1913	1928	1955
Value added of industry [1]	15.2	8.8	22.7
Persons engaged [2]	60.8	48.7	109.6
Man-hours	64.7	53.1	129.2
Value added per person engaged	25.0	18.1	20.7
Value added per manhour	23.4	16.6	17.6
Value added per head of population	10.8	7.0	19.1

[1] Evaluated in 1914 U.S. prices for 1913, 1929 U.S. prices for 1928, and 1954 U.S. prices for 1955.
[2] Measured in full-time equivalents.

We may pause here to note that our figures on the recent size of industry in the Soviet Union relative to the United States are rather lower than conventional Western estimates, which seem to place Soviet industrial output in 1955 at about 33 percent of the American level.[4] If there is no dispute over the relative size of Soviet industry in 1913, the conventional view implies that Soviet industrial output multiplied some 10 times between 1913 and 1955, which would mean a growth rate of 5.6 percent a year on the average, substantially higher than the rate of 4.2 percent found in our study.

The industrial distribution of employment (table 5) is the only information we have for comparing the changing structure of industry in the two countries. In both countries, the share of employment in the so-called heavy industries, particularly machinery and allied products, has been growing at the expense of the share in food processing and textiles and apparel. However, consumer durables account for a much larger fraction of machinery and equipment in the United States than in the Soviet Union. In the mid-1950's, the following major industrial groups accounted for a larger fraction of persons engaged in Soviet industry than in American industry: Fuel, wood construction products, mineral construction products, and food and allied products. The following groups accounted for a smaller frac-

[3] Our index of industrial production in the United States is 454 for 1955 with 1913=100; on a per capita basis, 264. (See table 1.) The Soviet indexes calculated indirectly are taken as 149 percent and 176 percent of the respective American indexes.

[4] See, e.g., "Soviet Economic Growth: A Comparison with the United States," Joint Economic Committee, Washington, 1957, p. 11.

tion: Ferrous and nonferrous metals, electricity, chemicals, machinery and allied products, and textiles and allied products.[5]

TABLE 5.—*Percentage distribution of persons engaged by major industrial groups: Soviet Union and United States, benchmark years* [1]

[Percent]

	Soviet Union [2]						United States [3]				
	1913	1927–28	1933	1937	1950	1955	1909	1929	1937	1948	1953
Ferrous and nonferrous metals	7.4	5.3	5.8	5.3	6.3	6.0	7.9	7.8	8.6	7.8	7.6
Fuel	5.5	7.6	7.3	6.3	8.0	8.0	10.2	9.1	8.4	6.8	5.3
Electricity	.3	.5	1.0	1.1	1.5	1.6	.9	2.9	2.8	2.2	2.2
Chemicals	1.2	1.9	2.8	3.0	2.8	3.3	3.2	4.9	5.0	5.8	5.9
Wood construction materials [4]	18.7	14.6	18.2	16.5	17.8	15.3	13.3	9.6	8.4	7.3	6.6
Mineral construction materials	4.0	4.2	5.3	3.0	5.1	6.2	6.5	4.6	4.2	4.5	4.2
Machinery and allied products	12.0	14.2	28.4	30.3	31.5	32.4	21.1	27.8	28.0	35.3	41.5
Machinery and equipment	(5.1)	(7.4)	(8.2)	------	[5] (16.1)	------	(8.0)	(17.5)	(17.7)	(22.9)	(27.6)
Metal products [6]	(5.4)	(5.2)	(4.3)	------	[5] (12.4)	------	(13.1)	(10.3)	(10.3)	(12.4)	(13.9)
Repair shops [7]	(1.5)	(1.6)	(15.9)	------	[5] (3.0)	------	([8])	([8])	([8])	([8])	([8])
Food and allied products	18.7	15.2	11.1	12.6	10.4	9.5	10.7	9.8	10.8	9.7	8.8
Textiles and allied products [9]	32.2	36.4	20.2	21.9	16.5	17.7	26.2	23.5	23.8	20.6	17.9
Total	100.0	99.9	100.1	100.0	99.9	100.0	100.0	100.0	100.0	100.0	------

[1] Omits printing and publishing industries. Persons engaged measured in full-time equivalents.
[2] Breakdown for 1937–55 applies to production workers only.
[3] Based on unpublished data of John W. Kendrick.
[4] For Soviet Union, includes paper and paper products.
[5] Broken down by percentage distribution implied by official Soviet data on gross production (Promyshlennost' SSSR (Industry of the U.S.S.R.), Moscow, 1957, p. 203).
[6] For the United States, includes ordnance in the narrow sense. Other military products are covered by machinery and equipment. For the Soviet Union, all military products are covered by machinery and equipment.
[7] Repair shops are not covered by U.S. industry. They cannot be eliminated from Soviet data from 1937 onward.
[8] Not applicable.
[9] For the Soviet Union, includes furniture from 1937 onward.

"COMPARABLE" GROWTH

Once industrialization has gotten underway in a country, the pace of industrial growth at any moment would seem to depend on the resource potential, the state of industrial arts, the prevailing level of industrial output (i.e., the extent to which potential is being utilized), and that catchall, the economic system. The process of economic growth is mysteriously complex and cannot be summarized in these brief comments. But this is not the place to discuss the manifold preconditions and environmental factors essential for sustained economic growth. We take it for granted that industrialization and the accompanying process of growth are a fact in the Soviet Union, just as they were, more incipiently, in Czarist Russia. We are, therefore, concerned here only with the more fundamental conditioning factors, making that growth faster or slower than it would otherwise be. As far as such things can be quantified, the larger the resource potential, the more advanced the technology, and the smaller the output, the more rapid the growth in output will be given the economic system. None of these factors can be clearly defined, but they can all be represented by certain more or less adequate indicators. Our immediate problem is to find indicators that will allow us to select periods in

[5] Employment in production of military products is included under machinery and equipment in the case of the Soviet Union and under both that category and metal products in the case of the United States. The relative importance of military production in the two countries has not been discussed in this paper because of the formidable difficulties in making estimates for the Soviet Union. By a very roundabout procedure, I have estimated that the value of Soviet military production (excluding atomic energy) in 1955 was about 42 billion rubles, or about $6 to $10 billion. The value of American production was around $13 billion in the same year ("Statistical Abstract of the United States, 1958," p. 242).

Soviet and American industrial history that are comparable except with respect to economic system.

What is a good indicator of resource potential? If we may judge from the general practice of comparing economies in per capita terms, it would seem that population is typically used as the indicator of resource potential. But it is often a poor indicator since populations grow in response to economic development and differently in different economies. Moreover and more importantly, population can grow from immigration as well as from natural increase. As a concrete example for the problem at hand, in the United States the expanding industrial labor force in the latter part of the 19th century was recruited in important measure from economically underutilized population in other countries, including Russia.[6] The expansion in the Soviet Union during the 20th century came, on the other hand, from the large internal pool of underutilized population. Hence, as compared with the Soviet Union, population understates the resource potential of the 19th century United States.

The resource potential of an economy is more adequately described by the volume of natural resources at its disposal, including climate and terrain. If this can be precisely and accurately measured, it remains to be done. In the meantime, we are perhaps justified in making the impressionistic judgment that the Soviet Union and the United States have roughly similar resource potentials. Both countries are rich in natural resources, though the endowments of specific resources obviously differ. Against the larger size of the Soviet Union must be offset the substantial climatic and topographical disadvantages—at least in the present state of civilization. Although in total area the Soviet Union is about 1½ times as large as the United States, in inhabitable area it is probably no larger at all. Other relevant things the same—like tastes, technology, population, economic system, and so on—we suppose that the two countries would be able to support roughly equivalent levels of industrial production on the basis of resource endowments.

This leads us to suppose further that, if the state of industrial arts and the aggregate level of industrial output were the same in the two countries, differences in the rate of growth of industrial output should be attributable to differences in economic systems. Unfortunately, we cannot standardize both level of output and state of technology simultaneously in the two countries. To find dates at which output was roughly equivalent, one must go back a number of years in American history. Thus, as we shall see, the level of Russian output in 1913 within the interwar Soviet territory was reached in the United States around 1885 or earlier. But the state of industrial arts—at least the available body of technology—was less advanced in the United States of 1885 than in the Russia of 1913: the same body of technical knowledge, if not skills, has been available to the two countries at roughly the same dates in history. Therefore, when we standardize the level of output from which growth starts—as we are about to do—any difference that we observe between growth rates in the two countries must be attributed to differences in both technology and economic system. While the effects of each cannot be fully iso-

[6] Foreign born accounted for about 18 percent of the net increase in total gainfully occupied population or labor force over 1870–1900 (see Simon Kuznets and Ernest Rubin, "Immigration and the Foreign Born," Occasional Paper 46, National Bureau of Economic Research, 1954, p. 46).

lated, we can at least say in whose favor the difference in technologies operates and thereby narrow the range of ignorance.

These remarks make the issues seem simpler than they are, because they presuppose that the periods to be compared represent normal times. This is, of course, not so for the Soviet Union, unless we view periodic disasters as a part of normal times there. Since the founding of the Soviet Union, no span of years longer than a decade has been free from major disturbances or recoveries from them. As we have emphasized before, we cannot possibly know which period has had a growth rate similar to what would be expected from a long stretch of normal years, and we must therefore choose several Soviet periods, representing differing circumstances, in making comparisons with American industrial growth.

Subject to the outlined qualifications, a Soviet period would have as its counterpart an American period whose terminal years had the same total industrial output, unadjusted for differences in population, as obtained in the Soviet Union in 1913 and 1955, or whatever years we might wish to choose. If industrial output is measured by weighted aggregates, the Soviet periods 1913–55 and 1928–55 are "comparable" with the American period 1877–1913; that is, for both countries industrial output started and ended at roughly the same levels within these periods, insofar as we are justified in making such broad intertemporal and international comparisons.[7] If output is measured by the median performance of a large group of individual industries, the Soviet periods are comparable to the American period 1885–1920. The dating of these periods implies that it took only 34 or 35 years in the United States to register the same growth as was accomplished over 42 years in the Soviet Union—or, if the depressed preplan years are ignored, over 27 years.

We must remind ourselves that these periods are comparable only with respect to two of the factors influencing rate of growth: resource potential and prevailing level of industrial output. They are not comparable with respect to the state of the industrial arts. The advantage—a substantial one—is in favor of the Soviet Union, since it has had the technology of the 20th century at its disposal in working out its industrialization. One can only dream about what difference it would have made to American industrial growth in the 19th century if it had proceeded under 20th century technology.

The choice of comparable stages of development in the industries of the Soviet Union and the United States is, therefore, unavoidably hazy and arbitrary to some degree. We shall summarize here the records of industrial growth in the Soviet Union and the United States over periods of equal length that are comparable in the sense that the beginning year in each case represents roughly the same level of output in the two countries.

We start with the longest period studied for the Soviet Union, 1913–55. The growth rate over this period—3.9 percent a year, excluding gains from territorial expansion—is slower than the rate for a comparable American period: 5.0 percent a year over 1877–1919 or 4.8 percent over 1885–1927 (see table 6). On a per capita basis, the Soviet growth rate is higher: 3.3 percent a year as compared with

[7] The American dates are derived as follows. Soviet industrial output was 15 percent of the American level in 1913. Looking back into American industrial history, we find that output in 1877 was also around 15 percent of the level of 1913. A similar procedure gives the American date 1913 as roughly equivalent, in level of output, to the Soviet date 1955.

3.0 percent. But we must recall the misleading nature of comparisons of per capita rates, in view of the fact that population growth overstates growth in resource potential in the United States as compared with the Soviet Union.[8] For lack of data in both countries, we cannot compare growth in labor productivity.

TABLE 6.—*Growth rates for industry in Soviet Union and United States: Output and output per capita, selected "comparable" periods* [1]

Period for Soviet Union	Average annual growth rate				Period for United States
	Output		Output per head of population		
	Soviet Union	United States	Soviet Union	United States	
1913-15	[2] 3.9	5.0	3.3	3.0	1877-1919.
		4.8		3.0	1885-1927.
1928-55	[2] 6.1	5.6	5.3	3.5	1877-1904.
		5.3		3.3	1885-1912.
1928-40	[2] 7.4	7.0	5.9	4.7	1877-1889.
		4.5		2.6	1885-1897.
		6.3		4.8	1939-51.
1950-55	7.7	8.0	5.9	5.9	1908-13.

[1] Periods are comparable for growth in output only, not output per capita. See text.
[2] Adjusted to exclude territorial gains.

If we turn to the plan period, 1928-55, we observe that the Soviet growth rate, again adjusted to exclude territorial gains, is higher than for a comparable American period: 6.1 percent a year as compared with 5.6 percent over 1877-1904 and 5.3 percent over 1885-1912. The difference in per capita rates is even larger in favor of the Soviet Union. We therefore do not observe comparable American periods in which the speed of industrial growth has matched that during the plan period in the Soviet Union.

For shorter spurts of growth, the Soviet performance also seems to have the edge, although not so clearly. The Soviet growth rate over 1928-40 is almost matched by the American rate over 1877-1889, but it exceeds by a wide margin the American rate over 1885-1897. In a sense, this period of Soviet growth may be likened to the 12 years in the United States following the great depression; in both cases, growth was beginning again after a decade of depression and stagnation. The Soviet rate is faster in this comparison as well: 7.4 percent a year as compared with 6.3 percent.

We conclude this summary of growth over comparable periods on an exceptional note: Soviet industrial growth over 1950-55 may have been a bit slower than American growth over 1908-13. The point of this is that it proves nothing. The experience of a 5-year period, plucked from history, carries no permanent message with it.

[8] If population were taken as a guide to industrial potential, we might identify as comparable "stages of development" those periods in which industrial output per head of population was the same in both countries. This procedure is not only difficult to justify for reasons just stated, but it is also impossible to apply. The Soviet level of industrial output per capita in 1955 corresponds roughly with the American level in 1887; the Soviet level in 1913 was lower than the American level in 1860, the earliest year for which aggregate industrial output can be calculated. Similar results are found by taking the median dates at which per capita output of a large group of industries were the same in both countries.

Some Tentative Observations

What can be said about Soviet industrial achievements? In the first place, they have been impressive. In terms of its ability to generate sheer growth in industrial output—the question of the structure of products and of how they are put to use being left aside—the Soviet system of centralized direction has proved itself to be more or less the peer of the market economy, as exemplified by the United States. This much seems beyond dispute even in the face of the questionable reliability of Soviet statistics.

Of course, the character of Soviet industrial growth has not been the same as in other Western economies. Enhancement of state power has been the primary objective, the consumer being treated essentially as a residual claimant. Investment goods and ordnance have been emphasized at the expense of consumer goods; and other important sectors of the economy—agriculture, construction, and consumer services—have been relatively neglected to help foster industrial expansion. At times, large groups of the population have been sacrificed or made to work in forced labor to promote internal economic policies. Leisure has shown little tendency to grow. This is all well known but deserves repetition to place Soviet industrial achievements in perspective. The character of industrial growth being so different from elsewhere in the West, there is a sense in which the two sets of achievements cannot be compared at all.

The last point should be underlined: The pattern of industrial growth observed in the Soviet Union would never be duplicated by a market economy. Sovereign consumers would not choose the paths of growth chosen by Soviet rulers. This raises the awkward question of whether a highly generalized measure of growth has much meaning even as an indicator of expansion in productive capacity available for whatever use it may be put to. It can be demonstrated that measures of economic growth, as they are conventionally made in the form of index numbers, depend in fact on the path of growth—on the uses to which productive capacity is put.[9] If we bowed to the stern dictates of logic, we would be able to compare Soviet and American industrial growth only if both economies served either consumer welfare or state power. But that is ruled out by the very difference in social order whose influence on growth we wish to assess. This dilemma can be mastered only by admitting it—by avoiding the delusion that there is some single-dimensioned, neutral measure of growth, equally meaningful for all types of economies.

The question of economic waste is a related matter and equally difficult to treat. Growth is measured in terms of things "produced," not in terms of things usefully consumed. In a market economy, the two magnitudes are similar but not at all identical: mistakes are made by both entrepreneurs and consumers, rendering some productive activity worthless. The same kinds of mistakes are made in the Soviet Union, probably on a larger scale since centralized planning is involved. In addition, because of the weak position of most buyers, substandard goods often pass for standard quality, goods are damaged and spoiled in transit beyond normal experience in a market economy, and so on. Although Soviet industry does not experience business

[9] See, e.g., my article "On Measuring Economic Growth," Journal of Political Economy, LXV, (February 1957), 51–63.

cycles as they are known in market economies, it is periodically faced with the need to reallocate resources on a large scale, and the accompanying waste that would appear in the form of temporarily unemployed resources in a market economy will appear, at least in part, in the form of unwanted accumulation of inventories. It is difficult enough to say something sensible about which type of economy has the more waste inherent in it. It is even more difficult to say what all this has to do with problems of measuring growth. Unless wastage has, in some meaningful sense, been growing at different rates in American and Soviet industry, there is nothing to be gained by taking account of this factor as far as comparing growth of industrial output is concerned.

These qualifications serve as warnings against careless comparisons of either the relative size or the relative growth of Soviet and American industry. In particular, broad aggregative measures of industrial output tell us nothing about capacities for specific tasks, such as waging war or promoting consumer welfare. While Soviet industrial output in 1955 may have been, in the aggregate, less than a quarter of the American level, production directly available for military purposes was undoubtedly a larger fraction, and production available for consumers a smaller one. Similarly, growth in the two areas has differed in the same way in the two countries.

It remains also to be noted that the quantitative achievements of Soviet industry have not been understated by Soviet authorities. The official Soviet index of industrial production embodies a myth that should be dispelled from the popular mind. On this matter, Western scholars speak as one, though they may disagree as to the gravity of the myth. The official Soviet index shows industrial output as multiplying 27 times between 1913 and 1955; the indexes presented here, based on official Soviet data on physical output and unit values and constructed according to conventional Western methods, show output as multiplying 5 to 6 times. If our indexes are taken as reasonably accurate, the official index contains a four- to five-fold exaggeration of growth over this period.

Somewhere in these generalizations and the mass of figures behind them lie lessons of history. The trick is to find them. The interesting lessons point to the future in one way or another, for the main purpose of history is as prolog: to help us to foresee what is likely to come if things continue developing as they have been; or, barring that—and it generally will be barred—at least to help us to understand why things are happening as they are.

My task is largely finished in providing the stuff from which the lessons will be drawn. But I cannot evade the responsibility for stating some opinions. And so I venture with great hesitation into the field of lesson drawing, leaving it quickly once my minimal obligation is fulfilled.

As one looks to the immediate future—the next 5 years, say—it seems reasonably certain that industrial growth will proceed more rapidly in the Soviet Union than in the United States, in the absence of radical institutional changes in either country. This conclusion does not seem to be in doubt even when all due allowance is made for the shortcomings of Soviet data. It is more doubtful that industrial growth in the Soviet Union will be faster than in rapidly expanding Western economies, such as Western Germany, France, and Japan.

Over the more distant future—the next generation, say—the outlook is veiled, even if we might suppose there would be no important changes in the economic systems of either West or East, a most improbable assumption. There is no definitive evidence that the Soviet economic system has been able to generate more rapid industrial growth over the long run than the traditional private enterprise system of the West. Despite the fact that the Soviet Union was able to inherit an advanced Western technology at little cost, industrial growth over the entire Soviet period has been less rapid than in the United States over the 40 years bracketing the turn of the century, a period more or less comparable in other important respects. It has also been less rapid than growth in the last half century of the Tsarist era, a less comparable period.

On the other hand, if Soviet performance is best illustrated by achievements over the plan period, the Soviet record of industrial growth appears more exceptional. Which period is more representative of longrun growth trends: 1913–55 or 1928–55? There are good arguments to be made for both, and inevitable differences of opinion will be finally resolved by the course of history alone—which suggests the virtue of avoiding a dogmatic position one way or another.

In any case, the future will not be a simple reflection of the past. Growth has not been a mechanical process in either the United States or the Soviet Union. The driving force within the American economy has been private initiative mobilized by the incentives inherent in a free society. The trend of the day is in the direction of choking off incentives. One foreboding economic symptom is the slackening speed at which resource productivity has been growing in American industry. Incentives are being strangled and nothing is being put in their place to drive the machinery of growth.

There is in fact only one thing to put in their place: the whiplash. The Soviet system has made clever use of both knout and honey, and the latter has been rapidly supplanting the former. If this evolution continues, the balance of economic growth will surely tip further in Russia's favor, since—fortunately, from the broader point of view—the West does not intend to take whip in hand.

INDUSTRIAL INVESTMENT IN THE U.S.S.R.

(By John P. Hardt, Corporation for Economic and Industrial Research, Inc., Washington, D.C.)

Introduction [1]

Tempo—the high rate of industrial growth—motivates Soviet economic society. Continuation of their rapid industrial growth makes increasingly credible the Soviet claims for overtaking U.S. levels of industrial production at some future date. How has the high Soviet rate of industrial growth—perhaps as much as three times the average for the United States—been maintained? Moreover, can Soviet industry continue to expand at as high a rate in the future? The answers to these vital questions are to be found, in large part, in an analysis of the Soviet investment policy. In short, our view is that the rate of Soviet industrial growth depends on the rate, pattern, and efficiency of industrial investment.

Sustainable rate of investment, to be sure, is a fundamental factor in determining the growth rate of any economy. The willingness of the Soviet regime to defer consumption in favor of investment is well known and not unique in economic development processes. A singular feature of the Soviet pattern of economic growth, however, has been the use to which available investment funds have been put. Industry, particularly certain producer-goods sectors of industry, has been favored in the overall investment pattern for Soviet growth. But the Soviets have not sought growth for its own sake. This industrial growth has been directed to fulfill strongly felt and reasonably definable needs. Primarily, the attainment of the maximum growth in certain preferred industrial sectors is sought in order to maximize national power, both political-military power and economic power on an expanding industrial base.

The Soviet method or formula for bringing about a maximum attainment of their primary aims has been to direct the investment outlays in a pattern leading to structural changes in the economy different from those which occurred in the United States and other western industrial countries. A reasonably clear outline of an investment allocation formula for attaining maximum growth in the preferred industrial sectors will be drawn for the Stalinist period by examining the 5-year plan period (1928–55). An analysis of this Stalinist formula for industrial investment is important to understand the relatively high rate of industrial growth that has been sustained in the Soviet Union, but failed to fit the situation after Stalin's death.

After the failure and revision of the sixth 5-year plan, the Stalinist formula was revised under Nikita Khrushchev's direction for the 7-year plan (1958–65). In the Khrushchev reformulation, pressing problems in energy and labor force utilization were recognized. The

[1] Special indebtedness is due to M. Gardner Clark of Cornell University and Leon Herman of the Library of Congress for useful comments in the preparation of this paper.

planned volume of capital investment was increased and the investment program was reorganized to improve efficiency in the management of construction. The initial revisions in the Stalinist formula, in turn, were tempered by a chorus of criticisms and suggested further revisions led by Academician Strumilin.

The primary test of the success of the revised Stalinist formula for industrial investment is: Will the rate of industrial growth be retarded in the new plan period ahead? Retardation may result if the rate of investment for the expansion of industrial capacity is reduced or if the marginal product of capital declines. The rate and effectiveness of industrial investment depends in large part on the success of the Khrushchev reformulation of the Stalinist formula for industrial investment. It is our view that serious retardation in industrial growth will not result from changes in their industrial investment policy in the current plan period.

Chapter 1. Maximum Industrial Growth

RATIONALE FOR GROWTH

The primary aim of Soviet industrial investment policy has been to maximize industrial growth. At the same time growth in industrial production or the tempo of industrialization has not been a Soviet end but a means. The end is power. More specifically, the establishment of heavy industry is a necessary power base for the attainment of political-military objectives.[2] At the same time the share of total goods and services available for expanding the industrial base is limited by the prior and increasing claims of political-military projects. These political, military projects represent present as contrasted with the future power accruing from growth in the industrial base. So even in attainment of power the choice of present power may limit the maximum increase in industrial growth so vital to the long-run power position.

POLITICAL-MILITARY POWER

In the total Soviet approach to international power struggles, the needs for expanding political-military power have a wide range. While development of missile-rocketry and atomic weapons projects have priority, so, too, do certain scientific-technical projects such as atomic icebreakers and accelerators. Likewise, certain foreign economic ventures may fit into this same priority area, in that they are deemed important in the international power struggle.

Significant as this area is, we have only carefully guarded releases on the nature of the projects. The Soviet criminal code not only prohibits disclosure of information on military projects but also on advanced scientific projects.[3] Moreover, whereas these political-military projects consume a large share of Soviet industrial production, they do not, for the most part, contribute to growth in industrial production levels.

---

[2] These Soviet power-oriented aims appear to be similar to the mercantilist aims of Peter the Great and Colbert. Indeed, it was not by chance that interest in Peter the Great had a renaissance under Joseph Stalin.

[3] The type of data that cannot be legally made public is indicated in the law of Apr. 28, 1956, in Ministerstvo Ustitsii RSFSR, Ugolovnoe kodeks RSFSR (Criminal Code of the RSFSR), Moscow: Gosurizdat, 1957.

A primary aim of the Soviet regime has been an expansion of this political-military base in some context of the world situation, currently their power position relative to that of the United States. The satisfaction of these expanding needs for political-military objectives is one overriding reason for the ever-increasing requirements for industrial production in the U.S.S.R.

INDUSTRIAL BASE

The construction of iron and steel complexes, the installation of machine tools in machine-building plants, the erection of electric power stations—in short the expansion of the industrial base—is the other basic reason for Soviet industrial growth. The U.S. levels of industrial production provide targets which give focus to this drive. The immediate aim is to overtake the United States in the important areas of industrial production in the shortest possible time period. Which industrial areas are preferred depends on an estimation of the future needs of political-military objectives and the continued expansion of the industrial base.

A CONTINUING SELLER'S MARKET

The full satisfaction of the primary aims, important secondary aims notwithstanding, has not been possible to date in the U.S.S.R On the one hand, the post-World War II revolution in military technology occasioned by the simultaneous demands of military-rocketry, atomic weapons, and the coming of the jet age in aircraft made fulfillment of immediate political-military needs at any time difficult. The notable Soviet efforts in military-rocketry and related fields have obviously made heavy claims on their industrial production for meeting these political-military requirements. On the other hand, expanding the industrial base to catch up with a growing U.S. industrial economy has required a large supply of industrial products.

Catching up in a political-military and economic context has been much more demanding on a relatively poor Soviet economy than staying ahead has been for the U.S. economy with our greater abundance and has placed Soviet industrial production in a continual seller's market. Meeting these insatiable demands on industrial production for political-military and industrial projects is the problem of Soviet economic growth. Their investment program, in turn, has been oriented to resolving this problem of expanding industrial supply needs.

CHAPTER 2. STALINIST INDUSTRIAL INVESTMENT FORMULA

INVESTMENT AND HIGH TEMPO INDUSTRIALIZATION

The Soviet launched a 5-year plan in December 1928. But they also set in motion an economic revolution, the second and perhaps more basic Russian revolution. The key feature of this economic revolution was the high tempo of industrialization. In order to maintain the high tempo of industrialization, the rate of investment was doubled.[4]

[4] The rate of net investment of 18.9 percent in 1927–28 was raised by the plan only to 25.1 and 28.2 percent in 1928–29 and 1929–30, respectively, but actually resulted in a rate for 1929–30 one-third over the original figure, or 37.5 percent. See F. D. Holzman, "The Burden of Soviet Taxation," American Economic Review, September 1953, p. 567.

The basic economic decisions in the Soviet Union have always been made by the top leaders of the Communist Party. The simplicity and priority of these primary aims and the basic approach to satisfying the demands in these areas have facilitated direct control by the top leadership. It is perhaps without historical precedent to find the top leadership of a country so directly involved in the economic decision-making process. Thus the use of the names of Stalin and Khrushchev to describe formulations of investment policy reflects their personal and direct participation in its determination.

Meeting the needs of construction projects for expanding the Soviet industrial base was a first-order problem during the 5-year-plan periods. The method of providing the necessary supply for construction of as much new capacity as possible for industrial production growth took on reasonably definable characteristics over the period during which the guiding hand of Joseph Stalin was most clearly felt (1928–55).[5] The share of current production made available for expanding the industrial base was large and the pattern of investment outlays employed took on many characteristics not common to Western industrializations.

THE RATE OF INVESTMENT FOR INDUSTRIAL GROWTH

This willingness of the Soviet people to accept low levels of consumption places an upper limit on the sustainable rate of investment. Soviet policy seems to have maintained consumption at levels where some small but noticeable increase in consumption per capita could be claimed. The Russian people are doubtless very sensitive, as most people elsewhere are, to reductions in their standard of living; whereas any increase even from a very low standard of living may provide considerable psychological gain. This policy of maintaining slowly rising consumption levels, especially in the cities, seems to be borne out in Soviet practice, with the exception of the first 5-year plan and the Second World War.

The rate of gross investment has been up to 30 percent of the estimated total Soviet gross national product. Although this rate of investment compares with circa 20 percent of the U.S. GNP devoted to investment, the absolute allotment to gross investment has been lower in the Soviet Union than the United States as a result of the much larger U.S. GNP.[6] Still it is the rate of investment not the absolute outlays which are crucial to the rate of industrial growth.

The total investment outlays resulting from the high Soviet investment rate do not alone account for the rapid industrial growth in the Soviet Union. Total investment funds, in turn, must be shared by projects which would expand the industrial base with outlays related to raising the standard of living and improving transportation facilities, as well as political-military projects.

Investment outlays related to the standard of living, i.e., investment in residential construction and commercial construction, have been minimized at least as much as direct consumption outlays, perhaps close to what is known as productive consumption—the consumption necessary to maintain production. Assuming, again, an official policy

[5] Although Stalin died in March 1953, the period through the end of the fifth 5-year plan in 1955 was mainly conditioned by his economic thinking.

[6] The current rates of investment are 30 percent and 17 to 20 percent of the gross national products in the U.S.S.R. and U.S.A., respectively. See Allen Dulles' speech in the New York Times of Apr. 9, 1959, p. 8.

of gradually rising levels of consumption, the Soviet faces a danger of awakening expectations which may lead, paradoxically, to lower satisfaction from higher living standards. For example, once some people have certain consumer durables (cars, refrigerators, television sets, etc.), many people within a given status group may be dissatisfied until they too have these attributes of a rising standard of living. Raising consumption levels, especially in the area of consumer durables, housing, etc., may lead to difficulty in sustaining the investment rate for industrial expansion.

Investment in transport facilities has carried a higher priority than raising the standard of living, but even the expansion of the favored railroad transport facilities, have been largely kept to a minimum during the Stalinist era. Expansion of highway, sea, and river transport facilities has been all but ignored.

Although of higher priority for investment outlays than for such purposes as transportation and housing, investment for growth in the industrial base reflected the generally higher priority given to political-military purposes. At the same time the disentangling of projects for political-military and those for industrial growth has been difficult.[7] Estimating the importance of such projects which are not conducive to industrial growth is very difficult from Soviet sources, but crucial to the rate of industrial growth. The choice of long run and short-run gains in military-economic power is bound up in this proposition.

STALIN'S INVESTMENT FORMULA FOR EXPANDING THE INDUSTRIAL BASE

Probably more than the rate of industrial investment has been the maximum expansion in industrial production capacity with the investment funds available.[8] The application of this formula during the Stalinist period may be summarized in the following directions or policies of the top leadership:

1. Emphasize leading sectors in setting the pattern of investment outlays for expanding the industrial base.
2. Choose processes among alternatives needed to establish the industrial outlays which minimize capital outlays relative to factor inputs, i.e., labor, fuel, etc.
3. Set up project lists for attaining construction goals which reflect optimal results from previously established pattern of outlays. This optimal tautness in investment planning implied minimum factor requirements and gestation periods for construction projects and maximum output per unit of new capacity.
4. Organize administration of investment to enforce a maximum incentive system on construction trusts to complete projects as planned.

1. The leading sector theme

The application of the leading sector theme has been embodied in the slogan, "Communism is Soviet political power plus electrification of the entire country." Of the structural changes which occurred in

[7] Figures on the machine-building output to defense industries for the period 1938–41 may be drawn from Bureau of Foreign Commerce, U.S. Department of Commerce, Basic Data on the Economy of the U.S.S.R., February 1956, Washington, D.C.

[8] A considerable debt is also due to the previous works in this field on Soviet investment. Cf. especially for discussion of "leading branches," Gregory Grossman, "Suggestions for a Theory of Soviet Investment Planning" in "Investment Criteria and Economic Growth," Cambridge, Mass.: Center for International Studies, 1955; Norman Kaplan, "Capital Formation and Allocation," A. Bergson (ed.) "Soviet Economic Growth, Considerations and Perspectives," Evanston, Ill.: Row, Peterson, & Co., 1953.

most Western industralization processes, i.e., the structural changes noted in the N.B.E.R. studies of the United States, the ones related to this slogan were singled out for special emphasis whereas other structural changes were, for the most part, deemphasized in the Soviet pattern.[9] In emphasizing the electrification route, electric power generating capacity was to be expanded as rapidly as possible to provide electric drive for industrial branches and industrial processes dependent on electricity and process heat. Preferred industrial branches in the allocation of increased output from the expanded capacity, in turn, were such industries as metallurgy (ferrous and nonferrous), machine-building, and chemicals. Output from these branches was important to the fulfillment of political-military needs and future growth in the industrial base. Expansion of the electric power industry and the machine-building industries, as the Soviets often note, is the "heart" of this leading sector process.

Structural changes common to other industrializations not stressed in the Soviet approach during the Stalinist period included the shift from solid to liquid fuel; the shift from using ferrous to nonferrous metals for a number of purposes, especially in construction; and the rise of service industries. This conscious emphasis on structural changes related to electrification and deemphasis of structural changes common to other industrializations is a cardinal feature of the leading sector approach.

The idea of stressing a leading sector in industrialization is akin to the Leninist theory of the avantgarde. The party as a small group of well disciplined revolutionary leaders was, in Lenin's view, to carry the populace through the revolution and on to eventual communism. Also in Lenin's view, electrification as the second plan of the party was to carry the economy toward the same goal. This economic plan of structural change, moreover, facilitated the participation of top leadership in economic planning. If close attention was paid to the leading sector—electrification—then the necessary high tempo of industrialization could be thought to be assured.

2. *Minimization of capital outlays*

In carrying out the structural change embodied in the electrification route, minimum capital outlay variants were generally chosen. Induction motors might not provide electric drive as efficiently as synchronous motors for industry, but capital outlays for given coefficients of electrification of industrial processes were less. Likewise, large rolling mills and machine cutting tools were installed in the steel industry but not the materials-handling auxiliary equipment to go with them.[10] This spreading of capital may not have economized on the inputs of labor and other factors, but it probably led to a greater expansion in the industrial base than otherwise possible with available capital.

Apparant violations of the criteria of capital minimization are: capital intensive projects such as hydroelectric station (e.g., the Dnieper project), and large-scale industrial installations modeled after some Western prototype (e.g., the Gorki auto factory). On the

[9] Scholars associated with the National Bureau of Economic Research such as F. C. Mills, George Stigler, and Solomon Fabricant have particularly dealt with important structural changes in the U.S. economy over the last half century.

[10] The relatively high percentage of work force in auxiliary activities in the Soviet as compared with U.S. metallurgical plants of 56 and 39 percent, respectively, was critically noted by S. Kheinman, Kommunist, No. 4, 1959, p. 23.

former, the relative capital intensity of hydro over comparable steam capacity may not have been as great as appeared. The relatively small inputs in weight of machines and equipment for steam capacity may not have accurately reflected the relative scarcity or opportunity costs relative to inputs such as cement and reinforcing rods for hydrostations. On the latter, reproduction of Western prototypes may have been the only option open to Soviet planners without the technical capability for adaption of Western techniques to Soviet conditions. Or, again, the decisions may not have been economically rational.

Capital minimization was generally consistent with the relative scarcity of capital, labor, and other factors. In cases where the capital was relatively less scarce, i.e., to coking coal in the blast furnaces of the iron and steel industry, the general line of capital minimization was modified. As a result, the blast-furnace operation of Magnitogorsk is reportedly among the most efficient in the world.[11] Likewise, what evidence we have indicates that the capital minimization policy was not carried over to the defense industries.[12]

An adjunct of the choice of minimal capital variants in the capital minimization policy was the stricture on replacement investment. Obsolesence did not actually come in for formal discussion in Soviet journals until after the death of Stalin. Replacement based on very low amortization charges was very small compared to new investment.

Finally, since the return on capital was probably higher in the developed regions of European Russia, the choices continually tended to favor the older industrial regions over the newer, Siberian areas.[13] The failure to shift eastward as planned may also have resulted from overambitious plans which were pared downward at the expense of Eastern projects.

3. Optimal tautness in construction planning

Having established the pattern of development of industrial capacity for a certain time period, e.g., the 5-year plan, project lists were drawn up in detail and production goals set. The policy was to make maximal estimates of the productive capability of projected capacity and minimal estimates on the time, materials, and labor required for constructing the new capacity. This tautness in construction planning resulted in establishment of ambitious construction project plans.[14] These plans were targets for the construction trusts or their administrative equivalents. The targets were for a series of specific definable projects, e.g., steam condensing electric power station of 100,000-kilowatt capacity with two turbogenerators and four boilers of definable technical characteristics, in, say, the city of Sverdlovsk. The tautness came in the supply plan and the time schedule set for the projects. The supply of materials, available construction equipment, and labor planned for the project was usually minimal; whereas, the construction time for the capacity expansion was short as judged by previous experience. The minimal supply plan and short construction times made the plan ambitious or taut, anticipating substantial improvement on past performance records.

---

[11] See "Interview With Carney," Business Week, Dec. 7, 1957, and American Iron and Steel Institute, "Steel in the Soviet Union," New York, 1959, pp. 138 ff.

[12] See a reference to an aircraft plant by N. Khrushchev's plenum speech, Pravda, July 3, 1959.

[13] Injunctions against further construction in the older industrial centers of European Russia have been honored largely by their violation.

[14] "Tautness" in Soviet economic planning is referred to in an interesting unpublished manuscript by H. Hunter, entitled "The Economics of Catching-Up."

Depending on the priority of the projects, the elaborate incentive mechanism of the Soviet society was placed behind the projects. In the 1930's for example, Soviet writers visited various projects and dramatized their accomplishments. Such novels as Gladkov's "Power," featuring the Dnieper hydroproject, were results of these literary efforts.

4. Administration of maximum incentives

The administration of maximum incentive for the completion of the construction plans involved methods similar to those well covered in the discussion by Professors Berliner and Granick of the day-to-day administration of the Soviet factory.[15] The response to the excessive pressure in construction probably also led to the development of an "underground" or conspiracy on the part of those at the operating level (e.g., the construction trust) to simulate plan fulfillment. The degree to which the incentive system was effectively applied to attain efficient use of scarce factors was related to the realism of the construction plans. As long as the plans were barely attainable the results of administrative pressure encouraged actual fulfillment. But to the extent the plans were not thought to be realistic at the operating levels, the temptation was probably to simulate success.

Chapter 3. Khrushchev's Revision of the Stalinist Investment Formula for the 7-Year Plan (1958–65)

THE THAW IN SOVIET INDUSTRIAL INVESTMENT POLICY

With the ascendancy of Nikita Khrushchev there has been a revision of the Stalinist investment formula. In preparation for the 7-year plan, policies which involved changes in the Stalinist formula were initiated. In part this reformulation was a response to the shortcomings of the sixth 5-year plan, and in part a result of an economic reappraisal reflecting among other things greater flexibility resulting from a larger gross national product, relative increase in supply of capital and improved planning techniques.

Each of the four basic elements of the Stalinist formula were revised or reformulated: The leading sector theme, capital minimization, tautness in construction planning, and the administration of a system of maximum incentives on the construction trusts. The initial modifications were, however, moderated by policy changes following a "debate in planning" which featured an argument by Academician Strumilin for a return to important elements of the Stalinist formula.

LESSONS DRAWN FROM THE SIXTH 5-YEAR PLAN FAILURE

As late as July 1955, relatively modest goals for Soviet industrial expansion were still in force as indicated by a party plenum speech by Nikolai Bulganin.[16] These modest goals were actually the long range targets set by Stalin in his election district speech in 1946. Less than 6 months later very ambitious goals for the sixth 5-year plan were set requiring drastically stepped-up plans for expansion in indus-

[15] On Soviet managerial administration of production, see J. Berliner, "Factory and Manager in the U.S.S.R.," Cambridge: Harvard, 1957; and D. Granick, "Management of the Industrial Firm in the U.S.S.R.," New York: Columbia, 1954.

[16] For Bulganin's party plenum speech see Pravda, July 17, 1955.

trial capacity. Whether these expansion plans were feasible under the best of circumstances is open to question. In any event, the domestic developments followed by international events in October 1956 in Poland and later in Hungary probably occasioned a material shift of construction goals away from fulfillment of domestic Soviet projects for expanding their industrial base. Not only were supplies from the European bloc countries probably not delivered as planned, but additional political-military projects must have exercised prior claims on scarce investment goods.

In this unfavorable context for fulfillment of the industrial investment plan, the lax administration of the construction projects was apparently responsible for further failures to fulfill plans. A multiplicity of projects were apparently started at the outset of the sixth 5-year plan as if the plan were realistic. Even if the construction plan had been attainable with available supply the international developments which intruded during the course of the year should have occasioned a reexamination of the project lists and a gradual scaling down of expansion plans. Apparently the "taking of stock" was delayed until December 1956, when the capital requirements were found to be not only inadequately supplied for 1956, but about 40 percent greater than the investment funds available for 1957, and even more excessive for the rest of the projected sixth 5-year plan.[17] By that late date in 1956 the scarce supply for the numerous projects was spread hopelessly thin, and no redirection of supply could bring about reasonable construction plan fulfillment. As a result of the plan failure, the years 1957 and 1958 were largely devoted to completion of the projects initiated in 1956 and preparing for the new plan period to begin in 1959.

The lessons drawn from the sixth 5-year plan failure were probably most directly related to the third and fourth elements in the Stalinist formula for industrial investment: the attainment of the optimal tautness in the investment plan, and the organization of the administration of construction to provide maximum incentives for project plan completion.

Even as originally conceived, the sixth 5-year plan for construction was probably too ambitious. The advantage of tautness in construction planning remains only as long as the plan can be represented to be realistic, and the sixth 5-year plan was not. Coupled with this overtautness was the loose administration of the plan. Not only the lack of central supervision but the poor utilization of existing supplies were singled out for criticism. An alternative explanation is that apparent looseness was a result of the power struggle in the councils of the top leadership. Projects related to the power struggle may have been added for their short-run political effect without regard for adequacy of supply.

KHRUSHCHEV'S MODIFICATION OF THE STALINIST FORMULA

Having raised the question of revision of the Stalinist formula as a result of the review of the sixth 5-year plan failure, many other questions could be and were raised in Soviet economic circles. This

[17] The failure of the sixth 5-year construction plan was well described by I. Kulyev. Investment funds would have to be increased by 70 billion rubles for 1957 and 371.5 billion rubles for 1957–60 above the original plans of 170 and 990 billion rubles for the 1957 and 1957–60 periods, respectively. I. A. Kulyev, "O dal' neishem sovershenstvovanii planirovania i rukovodstva narodnim khoziaistvom (Concerning the Improvement and Planning and Leadership of the National Economy)," Moscow: Znanie, 1957, p. 9.

fresh look led to many proposals for revisions not directly related to the sixth 5-year plan experience. The continued application of the leading sector theory and capital minimization themes came in for critiques, and further examination was made of the management of construction planning. This reexamination paralleled a general "thaw" in the Soviet body politic. What resulted in some cases was merely a matter of putting the old wine in new bottles, but in the area of industrial construction planning some significant changes resulted.

Although the Stalin formula was in the main preserved, the proposed changes noted below could be significant if fully carried out during the course of the 7-year plan:

1. The leading sector theme broadened to include the petroleum-natural gas route.

The primacy of the electrification route to industrial growth was to be shared by other structural changes, principally the shift from solid to liquid fuel in the energy balance.[18] The shift in the energy balance meant that additional energy needs for the 7-year plan in the European regions of the Soviet Union were to be largely met by increased consumption of petroleum products and natural gas; new electric power and cement capacity was to be operated on natural gas or petroleum; and much of the railroad mileage was to be dieselized or electrified. Correlated to this shift in the energy balance was the expansion of the petroleum refinery capacity and the related petrochemical industry. In short, the petroleum-natural gas route for industrial expansion was to become a leading sector comparable to the electrification route in Soviet industrial expansion. This might be considered an "Americanization" of the Soviet economic development, as the structural changes are to be more similar in the future to those which have occurred in the American economy than was the case during the Stalinist era.

2. Capital minimization tempered to improve economic efficiency

The emergence of the shift to higher quality fuel in the energy balance as a leading sector is related to the capital minimization policy. The use of petroleum and natural gas is more economically efficient than comparable operation with solid fuel, coal, or peat; i.e., in terms of inputs of fuel equivalents per unit of output and labor requirements in extraction per unit of fuel of standard heating capacity. The input savings are not only measured in heating capacity of the fuel required per unit of output but in the transport requirements to bring the fuel to the consumer. The latter is less clearly definable as it involves balancing investment alternatives such as rail transport against oil and natural gas pipeline installations. Continued industrial expansion on a solid fuel base would probably have required less direct capital outlay than a shift to petroleum and natural gas.

Likewise, the nature of the choices among processes have been modified toward the more capital intensive alternatives. In many cases automatic or controlled equipment is being preferred over simpler variants consuming less capital. Larger scale equipment with more advanced technical features such as high temperature steam boilers for electric power stations have been featured in the

[18] The shift to petroleum-natural gas from solid fuel sources (coal, wood, and peat) is indicated in appendix table 1 below.

7-year plan. These variants conserve inputs of energy and labor usually by the choice of more capital intensive alternatives.

Finally, obsolescence and replacement are not only openly discussed but actually constitute important parts of the 7-year plan. Much of the capacity available at the time of the revolution is now being renovated or replaced, as is some capacity installed during the Soviet era. All this more intensive use of capital is an important part of what the Soviets are referring to as "technològical progress."

3. Optimal tautness in the construction plans given increased attention

To say that the projects to be completed in the time schedule set, with materials available from the initial plans for the period 1958–65, was less taut or more realistic than before is not to say that there was any slack built into the plan. For the leading sectors related to the carrying out of the electrification route and the shift from solid fuel to petroleum and natural gas consumption, the goals are probably not unattainable. The downgrading of hydro as announced by Khrushchev at the Kuibyshev hydroelectric station dedication [19] was apparently intended to release investment goods from the electrification route to supply additional capital for other industrial expansion related to the petroleum-natural gas route.

Some of the goals in the new plan still appear to be very ambitious, especially those not related to primary goals; i.e., residential housing. The degree of tautness in construction is a useful clue for estimating not only the possible success of the certain types of construction plans but also for evaluating their priority. It is difficult, for example, to see how the plans for residential housing can be carried out within the supply plan norms announced.

4. Maximum incentives in the administration of industrial construction improved by industrial reorganization and introduction of mathematical techniques to economic planning

The reorganization of construction planning was largely instituted to make more effective the operation of the incentive system for project plan fulfillment and increase the efficiency of planning. As a result of the reorganization of 1957, about one-half of the annual construction activity was to be performed by enterprises under the direct authority of the Sovnarkhozy—the local economic councils.[20] Of the remaining half of the construction work, an appreciable part was to be directed after the reorganization from the republic ministry level.

Two advantages were expected to accrue from this integration of construction work at the local level: local supply could be used more efficiently whether locally or centrally obtained, and there would be a unification of the interest between those dependent on the completion of the project for production target and construction plan fulfillment. The latter, coincidence of the local interest in fulfillment of both the construction and production plans, is perhaps the most pursuasive logic for this aspect of the reorganization. The Oblast party secretary, the Sovnarkhozy chairman, the directors of large enterprises, and the foremen of construction trusts are to have a community of interest in the completion of the projects needed to expand production

[19] Infra.

[20] For excellent summarizes of the 1957 reorganiation, see M. C. Kaser, "Changes in Planning Methods During the Preparation of the Soviet 7-Year Plan," Soviet Studies, April 1959; Oleg Hoeffding, "The Soviet Industrial Reorganization of 1957," American Economic Review, May 1959, pp. 65–77.

levels on schedule. To the extent that the community of interest is real, the supplies available for construction projects are probably more efficiently employed. Many of the crucial sectors of the materials-supply plan are still centrally controlled, but efficient central control would not alone be sufficient to insure supply to even priority projects.

In addition to the reorganization of industrial construction, the use of new mathematical techniques and electronic computers was added to increase the precision and allow for rapid accommodation to changes in construction planning. Precision in construction planning, of course, greatly improves the operation of a system of incentives. The Central Planning Commission (Gosplan) started using input-output and other econometric techniques in 1956, and by 1959 mathematical applications employing electronic computers were being widely adopted in Soviet economic planning.[21]

A DEBATE IN SOVIET PLANNING

Although the revision or reformulation is largely made in the name of Khrushchev of principles held while Stalin was in power, clear distinctions between policies and leaders is very difficult to make. More often the decisions to change follow a stare decisis route; that is, the new policy is in line with Lenin, Stalin, and previous policy. Such protestations of continuity appear in Soviet sources in spite of the fact that in application fundamental changes were to result.

A rare opportunity for associating leadership with policy changes was a public planning policy discussion which took place in the interim between Khrushchev's enunciation of the "Thesis" for the 7-year plan and the publication of the "Control Figures" (November 1958–February 1959).[22] A detailed discussion of the arguments presented in this discussion are interesting not only because of the light thrown on the Khrushchev revision of the Stalinist formula but because of the unusual indication of divergent viewpoints and current flexibility within the Soviet planning structure. This controversy focused on the plan for construction of the huge Krasnoyarsk hydroelectric station in Siberia, but had broader implications. The published part of this controversy may provide us the basis for some reasonable speculation on the rationale for the revisions in the Stalinist investment formula and the current direction in Soviet investment policy. Also, we may make some provisional judgments on the position taken or the stake of various groups of Soviet officials in revisions of Soviet construction planning policy.

The specific question raised on the Krasnoyarsk project was this: Would further work on this project be deferred until at least 1966 or would it be actively included in the current 7-year plan? On the one hand, a decision was apparently made in August 1958, to postpone any additional work on this project until about 1968. In January 1959, the argument was strongly made that the station should be in opera-

[21] In this adoption of econometric techniques, the leading role of the top political leadership in planning is still maintained. For example, "In the economic area the leading role of the political economy and the auxiliary, subordinate role of mathematics is recognized." A. Voyarski, "Matematika dlia ekonomistov (Mathematics for Economists)," Moscow: Gosstatizdat, 1957, p. 10. The need for use of mathematical economics and electronic computers has been stressed by Academician Nemchinov. See Voprosi ekonomiki, No. 4, 1959.

[22] Sources for the debate include: Pravda's for Aug. 11, Dec. 4, 1958, and Jan. 18, Feb. 1, 3, 8, 1959. Also, Promyshlenno-ekonomicheskaya gazeta, Feb. 15, 1959, Gidro-tekhnicheskoe stroitel'stvo, No. 6, 1959, pp. 1 fff; and Lituraturnaya gazea, Dec. 2, 1958.

tion by 1963–64 and presumably at full power by the end of the 7-year plan.

The decision on Krasnoyarsk has implications for the following specific planning policies:

1. The continuation of electrification as the sole leading sector as indicated by the rate of electric power expansion thought to be needed to provide for maximum industrial growth in the economy.

2. The capital minimization policy, as shown by the relative preference of steam, hydro, and other type electric power stations to meet given electric power needs, with the related estimate of the time preference implied in "maximum industrial growth." Likewise the capital minimization implications of the relative preference of development in European and Siberian parts of the U.S.S.R.

A careful examination of the events reported in the Soviet press relative to the Krasnoyarsk project indicates the following types of Soviet officials were alined for and against the Krasnoyarsk project and were associated with related policy planning positions. For rapid development of the Krasnoyarsk hydroelectric station were found "planners" and central "project makers." Against, is harder to define, but appear to have been officials at the operating levels—local Sovnarkhozy chairmen and perhaps regional party secretaries. These latter officials were not so much against Krasnoyarsk as for the alternatives that would appear to be foregone for activating the Krasnoyarsk project. These alternatives are not very well spelled out, but we shall try to speculate about them. The general policy positions taken by those for Krasnoyarsk were not entirely clear on all points listed above. However, they seemed to favor hydro and electrification development in the previous proportions in order to insure maximum industrial growth at the expense of economic efficiency, if necessary. Other than the fact that Krasnoyarsk was in the eastern regions they would appear not to have a preference, unless as political-economic planners east Siberian development was thought of as a counterweight to Chinese industrial expansion.

Before the dedication of the Kuibyshev hydroelectric station by Nikita Khrushchev in August 1958, the 4-million-kilowatt Krasnoyarsk station on the Yenesei River in east Siberia was one of a number of stations which were to be built during the next planning period—the 7-year plan. Then, Khrushchev indicated that virtually all of the new hydro capacity, including the Krasnoyarsk project, was to be deferred for perhaps a decade. By the end of the 21st party congress in February 1959, this policy had been modified, and the question of the timing of the Krasnoyarsk project had been reopened.

Khrushchev set the new policy which not only downgraded the Krasnoyarsk project but the electrification route, at the dedication of the Kuibyshev hydroelectric station in the following manner:

> Given present conditions, the main thing is to win time, to reduce the construction time, and to obtain more electric power with the least expense. At the same time, from the viewpoint of the state, it is expedient to accept deliberately a certain rise in kilowatt-hour costs with a view to winning time and to obtain in a short span of time a maximum increase in the electric power output. This way of looking at the problem is due to the fact that we must in a short time invest more funds in the development of heavy industry, especially in the chemical industry, iron and steel and nonferrous metallurgy, and other branches. In this context we have to analyze the question as to how one could get more and quicker electric power in a given economic area with the same outlay. If we do

so, then we arrive at the conclusion that, at present, one has to arrest to some extent the development of the construction of some hydroelectric power stations in order to give priority for some years—maybe for 7 or 8 years—to the construction of thermal power stations.

Moreover, in the case of Krasnoyarsk, Khrushchev indicated in a later speech that even the operating costs of steam stations there were "almost equal" to those in the comparable hydro, presumably the Krasnoyarsk project.

As a result of Khrushchev's statement and the new policy on hydro stations, the work on Krasnoyarsk which had been started in 1955 was stopped and the inactivity was to last for "at least 10 years" according to a latter statement by Academician Strumilin. This new policy apparently held also for the smaller Saratov station to be built on the Volga. In fact, as the specific plans for electrification came out, it became clear that the hydrocapacity to be introduced in the 7-year plan was to be largely as a result of the completion of projects well underway. Of the 10 million kilowatts for 1959–65, 8 million would result from the completion of the Bratsk, Stalingrad, Votkinsk, Kreminchug, and Bukhtarma stations, which were all well underway by the time of the policy change. To carry through this hydroelectric program only 16 percent of the total investment in electric power was needed compared with 48 percent in the previous 7-year period—about 20 of the total 125–129 billion rubles for electric power.

With the policy of downgrading hydro in vogue, we can see who was for it. In the "Technical-Economic Bulletin" of the Krasnoyarsk Sovnarkhoz we find the deputy chairman of the Sovnarkhozy writing in apparent approval of this policy of steam station preference. In a later issue of the same bulletin another deputy chairman of the Krasnoyarsk Sovnarkhoz wrote about the development of the nonferrous metals industry and its power needs. The Nazorovsk steam station in Krasnoyarsk Oblast was to meet the primary power needs of the Krasnoyarsk economic region for the expanding nonferrous metal needs. This station was given priority as indicated by front page accounts in Pravda calling for operation by the second quarter of 1960; that is, the construction of a steam station in a year and one-half—half the average time for comparable stations previously installed—would seem to require considerable priority. The Nazorovsk and other steam projects were apparently under the control of the Sovnarkhozy. Much of the construction responsibility after the 1957 reorganization passed from the special construction trusts of the Ministry of Electric Power Station Construction to the individual Sovnarkhozy, in which the power of the Oblast party secretaries (obkom's) was primary. It may not be irrelevant to point out that it was from the vote of these "obkom's" that Khruschev carried the day against forces of Malenkov, Molotov, et. al., in June 1958.

But the policy decision announced by Khrushchev against continuing the Krasnoyarsk project was formally challenged by Academician Strumilin, the doyan of Soviet economists on December 2, 1958, as follows:

Why, in the thesis, is it planned to *begin* building several entirely different hydroelectric stations of local importance, and "freeze" the construction of the least expensive and most effective station, Krasnoyarsk, which has attained worldwide importance with its yearly production of 19 billion kilowatt-hours and a production cost for 1 kilowatt-hour of 0.5 kopeck. It is true, that the construction of the hydro station, which was started in 1955, will require an additional investment of 4 billion rubles, nonetheless there is no reason, having already started work on it in the current 7-year period, to lose the capital invested in noncompleted construction for a period of more than 10 years. It is possible, for the funds lacking for completion of this work under construction, to economize on expenditure anywhere possible, especially in raising the labor productivity on the construction itself, providing it is not stretched out for excessively long construction periods.

Strumilin's argument was thus not so much that the Krasnoyarsk project should be undertaken in place of the steam projects underway, but that it be added to the electrification program. His view was that that the rate of electrification in the 7-year plan was "too small" relative to the overall growth of industry. Specifically on this point Strumilin argued:

The law of development strongly demands the maintenance of the determined proportions in planning. For instance, in the production area, the electric power and machine building industries should grow faster than the other production branches in the interest of facilitating labor and increasing its effectiveness.

Strumilin's statement apparently encouraged the hydroelectric "project makers" in Moscow, as an article appeared immediately after the Strumilin comments in "Gidrotekhnicheskoe stroitel'stvo." The author reports that, on "reexamination", the operation and investment costs for the Krasnoyarsk station were lower than formerly held. Moreover, it appeared on further "reexamination" that the construction time advantage of steam over hydro was not quite what had been reported by Nikita Khrushchev.

A logical question to Strumilin's proposition that the Krasnoyarsk station should be built would have been, What would the additional 19 billion kilowatt-hours of electric power be used for in the relatively nonindustrial east Siberian region? A part of the answer, to that question was soon in coming—for aluminium from alumina clay in the southern part of the Krasnoyarsk region. A. Zubkov, the director of an institute at the All-Union Academy of Science in Moscow, reported on the large aluminium plant at Bratsk to be supplied from the new Bratsk hydroelectric station and called for a comparable plant at Krasnoyarsk.

Another member of the Gidroproekt in Moscow joined the debate 2 weeks later with an article entitled "For and Against" in discussion of A. Zubkov's article. In his discussion Mr. Gregorovich appears to be more for than against the Krasnoyarsk project.

If the electrification route was to be reinstated to something comparable to its former state as Strumilin et al. appeared to be arguing, would the additional projects be too ambitious in view of foreseeable materials-supply plan. Specifically, could the electric-power-equipment industry meet the stepped-up requirements? As if to answer this question, the lead article in the electric-power machinery journal of January 1959, pointed out that the original sixth 5-year plan goals for 1960 in electric-power-generating equipment would still be met. In short, the electric-power expansion plan in the sixth 5-year plan did not fail because of equipment shortages, nor would this be a bottleneck for the 7-year plan.

Finally, in early 1959, a plethora of articles appeared in Soviet journals restudying the Leninist principles for economic development, i.e. the electrification route as the leading sector. In these articles a continuing theme was that the 7-year plan would be the decisive step in the pattern of economic development set in motion by Lenin in December 1920, with the announcement of the GOELRO, the State electrification plan.[23]

AFTERMATH OF THE "DEBATE"

The problem in evaluating the consequences of the debate in planning which featured the Strumilin advocacy of the Krasnoyarsk project is that if the victors can be identified (i.e., Central planners, such as those associated with Gidroproekt in Moscow), then who were the vanquished? With limited investment funds, the addition of the Krasnoyarsk complex could not be made without an eventual downgrading of some other group of projects. Will, for example, the gasification of Moscow and other European cities be delayed? Or, will materials to residential housing projects be less than needed to carry out the tempo of construction projected? It may be that the downgrading of some projects to make way for the east Siberian hydroelectric complex has not been made yet or may be made only on an ad hoc, project-by-project basis.

In any event, the result of the additional projects resulting from the Krasnoyarsk decision is probably a considerable tightening in the construction material-supply plan. Form the point of the Soviets' own self-interest, a decision on downgrading projects should be made soon and probably on the basis of interrelationships of projects or the potential impact on industrial growth. For example, if petroleum extraction is expanded, so also should refining capacity, the building of diesel and other petroleum-consuming motors, and the productive processes to utilize these motors. Or putting it another way, if projects are to fail to meet construction schedules, their impact on industrial expansion would be minimized if those projects not be be completed, were not, in turn, to represent bottlenecks for the utilization of other new capacity from projects retaining sufficient priority to be completed. The projects downgraded should thus be made with the full utilization of all projects in view in order to maximize the effectiveness of new investment on industrial growth.

---

[23] Typical of many "postdebate" articles on the rightful position of electrification of the leading sector is an article entitled, "The Great Vital Power of the Leninist Idea for Planning the National Economy" in "Planovoe khoziaistvo," No. 4, 1959, pp. 1–8. The following are indicative of the type of points made therein:

"The current 7-year plan will be the decisive stage in the realization of the Lenin ideal of complete electrification of the country, the ideal which Lenin connected with the changeover of all branches of economy to the highest level of technical development."

"* * * He considered it obligatory to instill comparative calculations of the expenditure on restoration of transportation, industry, land-grants 'according to the old style' and on an electrification basis. 'Old style' restoration—describes Lenin—is a method of calculation, which requires:

A *million rubles*
or +B *work-days*
A *fuel*

For restoration on an electrification basis, it will require:

A−X *million rubles*
or +(B−Z) *work-days*
A−Y *fuel*

V. I. Lenin predicted yet another possibility—that for restoration on the basis of electrification it will require just as much capital, but with an effect so many times greater than the former."

CHAPTER 4. INVESTMENT FOR FUTURE INDUSTRIAL GROWTH

THE ECONOMIC POWER STRUGGLE

In the Soviet effort to overtake the United States in industrial production they must maintain a more rapid rate of industrial growth. Of course, it need not be as high a rate as it is now relative to that of the United States; that is, about 9 percent for Soviet industry compared with about 3 percent per annum for U.S. industry.[24] Although the time required to attain these levels depends on the comparative rates, there is considerable gain to the Soviets if progress is made in catching up.

Actually, the comparative growth of Soviet to U.S. industrial production levels is uneven. They are doing much better in industrial growth sectors and sectors oriented to political-military ends. Moreover, the image of success for the Soviet method of industrialization can be maintained if any progress is made in closing the gap. So only some substantial slowing down or retardation in the Soviet rate of industrial growth or acceleration of U.S. growth rate could have serious implications for Soviet leadership in their economic power struggle with the United States.

Yet from our examination of the Soviet investment policy, we do not find sufficient evidence to indicate material retardation in Soviet industrial growth in the near future. Retardation might result if the net rate of investment for expanding their industrial base were materially reduced or if the marginal efficiency of capital for new industrial investment projects were generally declining. These could result from changes in the volume of investment or the formula for utilizing capital funds.

INDUSTRIAL GROWTH—FOR WHAT PURPOSES?

The power motivation of Soviet industrial growth is important to anyone evaluating the comparative rates of growth and factors such as the investment policy which maintain the growth in the U.S.S.R. and the United States. If the U.S. rates were to be accelerated, we should ask: For what purposes is the industrial growth rate in the United States to be accelerated? Is this acceleration to meet strongly felt needs in the United States or to compete with the Soviets? On serious examination we may decide that we do not wish to change our priority scheme to approach the rate the Soviets find it necessary to maintain to meet their power-oriented aims.

RATE OF INDUSTRIAL INVESTMENT AND RETARDATION

The rate of investment for expanding the Soviet industrial base could be less in the current 7-year plan than in previous plan periods if the share of capital goods to either political-military or standard of living projects were stepped up. Although this does not appear to be their intention from the evidence available from the 7-year plan, changes could be made to result in these shifts.

---

[24] As noted by Herbert Levine on the comparative rates of industrial growth, "For example, if Soviet industry grows at an average annual rate of 9 percent and that of the United States at 3 percent (a very likely situation), then Soviet industrial output will equal ours in 14 years." "The New Leader," June 1, 1959, p. 12. This would presumably coincide with the Soviet 15-year plan projects for circa 1972.

The requirements for political-military projects might increase if there were either a considerable inflation in the cost of projects in the current plan or if new projects were added. Inflation in the cost of political-military projects on the frontier of military technology is probably as common in the U.S.S.R. as in the United States. However, this is not a new problem to the Soviets now midstream in the development of missile-rocketry, space vehicles, etc. New political-military projects might be expected to be added, if the international political climate were to worsen. Conversely, a reduction in the cold war preparations of the Soviet Union could mean a reduction of political-military undertakings from their project lists.[25]

Pressure for greater increases in the standard of living must be seriously considered. With greater cultural exchanges and the limited increase in consumer goods in the Soviet Union, the need to provide greater satisfaction may become persuasive on the Soviet regime. This is of particular interest at the moment in the area of consumer durables, especially those related to housing, household appliances and furnishings, and transportation. More, to be sure, is being done by the Soviets in these areas than in the past. But how long the Soviet citizen can be kept without autos and in cramped housing space with few of the conveniences common to Western homes is indeed conjectural. And it is this very deprivation that is an essential underpinning of the Khrushchevite and Stalinist formula for industrial investment. When these pressures for improved living standards will become effective is difficult to calculate. But when these pressures make themselves felt, we may expect a third revolution in the Soviet Union—this time not for political power or economic growth, as were the first two revolutions, but for consumer satisfaction.

DECLINE OF THE MARGINAL PRODUCT OF CAPITAL AND RETARDATION

Even assuming, as we do, that the rate of investment for industrial growth will remain stable at a high level, some retardation in industrial growth might result. Retardation could come from a reduction in the return in increased production from new projects or a decline in the expected rate of increase in marginal product of capital.

The Khrushchev modifications in the Stalinist formula for industrial investment might lead to a reduction in the marginal efficiency of capital if the resulting changes in the capital-labor ratio and administrative reforms were to lead to lower returns in industrial output for given capital outlays.

The modifications of both the leading sector and the capital minimization themes of the traditional Stalinist formulation for investment planning in the current 7-year plan will lead to a faster rate of growth in capital relative to labor. The broadening of the leading sector theme to include the petroleum-natural gas route with the electrification route as the basis of structural change in Soviet industry

[25] The relative importance of political-military industrial growth, and standard of living projects, may be generally drawn from the official distribution in appendix table 2 below. There are at least two problems which make these figures of limited use: (1) A separation of the outlays in the productive sectors to political-military and industrial growth projects is all but impossible; (2) the actual outlays to various sectors may be widely different from the planned figures in the table below.

In appraising changing developments, it would be well to watch closely the industrial press and the speeches of Premier Khrushchev. Evidence of changing priorities can be read with close attention to these primary sources. One very important source is, paradoxically, a completely negative indication—no mention of an industrial project or industrial planning policy may well mean that it has been downgraded.

will result in greater capital outlays. Likewise, automation, mechanization, and other attributes of the Soviet plan for technological change are basically saving of labor and other factor inputs.

It has been argued in Western economic writings that if the supply of capital grows faster than that of labor, then the marginal product of capital must in the long run be dragged down.[26] However, it has further been noted that this tendency for the marginal product of capital to decline can be offset by technical progress. In line with this view it appears most unlikely that a decline in the marginal product of capital will occur in Soviet industry as a result of their current policies leading to more capital intensity. The shift from solid fuel to natural gas and petroleum and the industrial automation and mechanization would appear to be areas in which increasing marginal returns to capital might be expected and is counted on in Soviet plans. Also, these areas are not only very labor saving but also conserve inputs in other currently scarce factors (in particular, fuel) Moreover, in each area emphasized in the current Soviet technical advances, some experience of United States or West European industry may be drawn on by the Soviets to gain the maximum return with minimum research effort.

The administrative changes in industrial investment planning under the Khrushchev aegis would seem to contribute (through the use of optimum tautness and maximum incentive in planning) to efficiency of capital utilization. The addition of mathematical techniques and electronic computers to planning, the horizontal integration of construction projects at the local or Sovnarkhozy level, the greater realism in the setting of targets, all added to the already effective total incentive system of the Soviet economy would seem to cumulatively increase efficiency in the utilization of investment funds. More projects may be added to make the industrail exapnsion plan too ambitious but a repeat of the overtautness of the sixth 5-year plan debacle seems unlikely.

Perhaps as important as the administrative changes made in construction planning is the evidence of willingness to continue to make changes. The new flexibility of the Khrushchev era makes possible public discussion of planning principles such as that led by Academician Strumilin and critiques of old methods with prescriptions for changes such as those recent outspoken articles of Academician Nemchinov, I. A. Kulyev, and S. Kheinman. This new flexibility suggests that the administrative innovations now in vogue may be publicly or privately reviewed and replaced if not successful.

---

[26] D. Hamburg, "Production Functions, Innovations, and Economic Growth," Journal of Political Economy, June, 1959, p. 244:

"A rising capital-labor ratio, resulting from a faster rate of growth of capital than of labor, need not necessarily and generally result in a declining marginal product of capital and a declining profit rate. * * * innovations are of course, needed to maintain profit rate, or at least to keep it from falling below a critical level."

Cf. Francis Seton, "Production Functions in Soviet Industry," American Economic Review, May 1959, pp. 12 ff.:

"Continuing high growth rates in postwar Soviet industry are no longer in the main the effects of labor influx and capital accumulation. * * * They seem to be predominately the reward of rapidly increasing efficiency (technological, administrative, and both) in utilizing these inputs at any given level—a progress whose present tempo still outweighs the retarding effects of diminishing returns (such as may be caused by the gradual depletion of the more readily available resources in a maturing economy)."

See also, Joseph S. Berliner, "Capital Formation and Productivity in the U.S.S.R.," Special Publication Series of the National Academy of Economics and Political Science, No. 14, June 1958.

SUMMING UP

Thus, our examination of the Soviet industrial investment policy indicates that it is the emphasis on policies related to the leading sector, capital minimization, optimal tautness, and maximal incentive themes which is the unique factor in Soviet industrialization, explaining in large part the effectiveness of capital outlays in maintaining the particularly high rates of growth in Soviet industry.

On balance, the revisions in the Stalinist formula made under Nikita Khrushchev would appear to increase rather than decrease the effectiveness of capital utilization for industrial expansion. Assuming no material reduction in the current rate of investment for industrial expansion, the rate of Soviet industrial growth may be expected to be maintained in the near future at or near its present high rate. Moreover, with no dramatic increase in the U.S. industrial growth rate, the Soviet levels will continue to draw significantly closer to equivalence with U.S. levels of industrial production.

APPENDIX TABLE I.—*Soviet production of primary energy, 1955, 1958, 1965*

	1955 [1]			1958 [2]			1965 [2]		
	Natural units (in megatons)	Conventional units (in megatons)	Fuel (percent)	Natural units (in megatons)	Conventional units (in megatons)	Fuel (percent)	Natural units (in megatons)	Conventional units (in megatons)	Fuel (percent)
Coal	391.0	324	64.8	496.0	348.1	59.0	496–609	430.0	43.0
Crude petroleum	70.8	112	22.4	113.0	153.4	26.0	230–240	335.0	33.5
Gas	[3] 9.0	12	2.4	30.0	29.5	5.0	150	175.0	17.5
Peat	51.0	22	4.4	51.5	25.4	4.3	71	29.0	2.9
Wood	[4] 224.0	27	5.4		29.5	5.0		24.0	2.4
Shale oil	10.8	3	.6	13.2	4.1	.7	21.5	7.0	.7
Hydro	[5] 23.1								
Total		500	100.0		590.0	100.0		1,000.0	100.0

[1] TsU, "Promyshlennost' SSSR" (Industry of the U.S.S.R.), Moscow: 1956, Passim.
[2] Planovoe khoziaistvo, No. 1, 1959, pp. 46–52; Ugol, No. 3, 1959, p. 3; Promyshlenno-ekonomicheskaya gazeta, Dec. 5, 1958.
[3] Billion cubic meters—natural gas, including 1.4 billion cubic meters of manufactured gas.
[4] Million cubic meters.
[5] Billion kilowatt-hours converted at 0.4 tons per thousand kilowatt-hours, but not included in the total.

APPENDIX TABLE II.—*Soviet investment in the 7-year plan, 1959–65* [1]

Economic sectors or industries	Planned outlays (billion rubles)	Percent of total
Productive sectors	1,517	77
Industry	1,252	65
Petroleum and natural gas	173	8
Electric power	129	6
Chemicals	105	5
Ferrous metallurgy	100	5
Light metallurgy	80	4
Coal	78	3
Timber	60	3
Other nonmilitary industry, especially machine building and nonferrous metallurgy (aluminum, copper, zinc, etc.) and direct military industry	627	31
Transportation	115	6
Agriculture	150	8
Unproductive sectors: Housing, municipal and trade facilities	380	19
Housing	300	15
Others	80	4
Cultural sectors: School, theaters, hospitals, etc	83	4
Total	1,970	100

[1] Pravda, Nov. 14, Dec. 28, 1958, and Jan. 15, and Feb. 8, 1959.

SOVIET-AMERICAN MANAGEMENT COMPARISONS [1]

(By David Granick, Carnegie Institute of Technology)

Introduction

Prospects for future industrial growth in both the American and Russian economies depend upon much more than the natural resources of the two countries, their labor skills, and the amount of capital invested in expansion. As important as anything else is the level of management skill and organization which is employed.

Both American and Russian industrial managements have displayed a high level of competence and ingenuity. American managers who have talked with Soviet executives have brought back highly complementary reports, and Russian respect for American managerial efficiency is well known. Both nations' managements have shown themselves capable of successful adjustment to rapid change in their environments, and both have shown an unusual regard for research and development and a willingness to make use of research findings.

Many of the problems of industrial management are similar, whether the industry is found in the United States or in the Soviet Union. Often the Soviet managerial solution is also similar to the American. Sometimes, it represents a different approach. Let us consider a number of different aspects of managerial environment and behavior in the two countries. These aspects, of course, are only a few among many which might have been chosen. In particular, management problems arising from central planning itself will be ignored. Such problems are of vital importance for Soviet-American comparisons, and the excuse for ignoring them is only that they are perhaps better known than the features which shall be treated below.

Education

In comparing industrial managers, it is possible to generalize as to distinctions in the backgrounds of men holding these positions in the Soviet Union and in the United States.

1. There is a considerably higher proportion of college graduates among Soviet than among American managers.
2. Of the college graduates, a much larger percentage of the Russians have engineering degrees.
3. Soviet college education provides a firmer factual base than does American, but a weaker analytic training.
4. At the same time, the total Russian tradition is more theoretic. The Soviet manager, after his school years, is more prone to do general reading than is the American manager.
5. The Soviet manager is much less likely than is the American to have received any formal training in human relations. On the other

[1] Much of the material in this paper will appear in my forthcoming book, "The Red Executive: A Study of the Organization Man in Russian Industry," to be published by Doubleday & Co. Any reference to this paper should identify these remarks with the book which is expected to be released in January 1960.

hand, because of his Young Communist League activities he will probably have had a good deal more practical experience in this during his years in school.

6. The Russian's first major practical experience in business is during his last college year, and thus it occurs while he is still under academic tutelage. This year serves as a strong bridge between college and the "real world." Such a bridge is generally missing in the American manager's experience.

7. Russian managers have an early, heavy dose of work directly in production. By and large, this is not true of American managers.

8. Early jobs held by Russian managers are most often those of minor executives. American managers are much more likely to begin with staff or other technical roles.

One deduction which we might draw from this national difference in educational and training background is that, since Russian top management is completely dominated by graduate engineers, Soviet industry should be even more receptive to new technological ideas than are American firms. This Russian receptivity is heavily reinforced by the fact that the early work experience of managers is in production, and that their first study of technology in the factory is under the guidance of professors who are professionally most concerned with what is novel. The quicker Russian absorption of new technological schemes should apply particularly to those schemes aimed at better performance in existing jobs.

This is not to suggest that we should necessarily expect Russian industry to be more inventive than American. But it is to say that technical innovations should spread faster throughout the Russian economy. While clearly other factors are important, the interests and training of top managers will be an important factor in determining this rate of adoption.

On the other hand, if we leave the field of technology and turn to other aspects of business, we would expect precisely the reverse pattern. The Russian engineer-type manager, whose first mistress was production, will tend to treat everything except technology as frosting on the cake. Changes in accounting, procurement, and marketing, and finance should all have tough sledding in gaining acceptance in Russian business.

Management Incentives

Managers comprise part of the high-income group of Soviet society, just as they do in the United States. A director of a successful Soviet factory with 1,000 workers would earn some five to six times as much as the average worker; the comparable American executive would be in roughly the same position relative to the American factory worker, although the American's absolute standard of living would, of course, be far superior to the Russian's. In terms of income inequality the relation between worker and manager in Russia and in the United States does not differ too greatly. Pretax, the American manager would be a bit ahead; but, then, his income tax rate is higher. In both countries, there is considerable financial incentive for reaching managerial status.

However, the pattern of managerial compensation is radically different in the two countries. In the United States, although there are dramatic exceptions, executives are compensated primarily by means of their salaries. One 1957 study of 50 companies showed that only half of them had executive bonus plans at all, and even in these firms the bonuses averaged barely 10 to 20 percent of the base salaries. In contrast, Soviet executives depend on bonuses for an average of one-fifth to one-third of their total income.

Such a system of payment places considerably greater pressure on Soviet than on American managers. Moreover, an American executive's bonus is generally awarded on the basis of a whole year's operations, and often has only a loose connection with the specific actions of this executive even over this time period. The Soviet manager's bonus, on the other hand, is paid monthly and is tied directly to the success of the production unit which he is directing; a bare miss of the production target may cut his monthly pay by as much as 30 to 50 percent.

Not only do methods of compensation place greater pressure for immediate results on the Soviet executive than on the American executive, but a similar effect is achieved by the extraordinary willingness to replace Soviet managers who cannot produce results quickly, and to promote those who can deliver the goods. In the 1930's, before the great political purges, no more than 1 to 15 percent of management personnel—at different levels of management and in different branches of industry—had held the same post for more than 5 years. During the single year 1956, one-fourth of all directors of coal pits in the major Ukrainian center of the Donbas were replaced. Considering a broader group of top personnel in the Soviet Union—those who in February 1956 were elected to membership of the Central Committee of the Soviet Union's Communist Party—some 42 percent of the total shifted to other full-time positions during the following 1¾ years.[2]

To sum up, we can see in both countries a strong financial incentive for the young ambitious man to strive for a management post. It is true that in the Soviet Union, unlike in the United States, he can reap equal financial rewards in an academic or research career. But once a man is launched on a management career, he is put under far greater pressure for immediate and continuing results in the Soviet Union than he would be in the United States. It is possible that this leads to greater managerial motivation and creativity in the Soviet Union than in the United States, although it is clear that management in both countries is a career accompanied by long hours and a high ulcer rate. But it is fairly certain that the Soviet incentive system forces managements to place more emphasis upon short-run considerations than they might otherwise do. This is because bonuses, promotions, and demotions all follow one another too quickly to allow any but the most secure or idealistic Soviet manager to give full weight to the long-run implications of his decisions.

Bureaucracy

Both in America and Russian industry, the proportion of staff to productive workers rose steadily during the prewar period. This is a tendency which was also noted in Great Britain. The number of

[2] This proportion is calculated on the basis of a sample of 117 out of the full 133 members. There is no particular reason to believe that this sample is biased. In any case, the range of possibilities lies between 37 and 49 percent of transfers for the entire Central Committee.

Americans performing white-collar functions in all factories and mines as a proportion of manual workers in these same institutions rose from 9 percent in 1899 to 15 percent by 1937. The proportion of white-collar personnel in Soviet industry and mining was still higher, and had reached 19 percent by 1940.

During the postwar period, however, this tendency continued in American industry while it was reversed in the Soviet Union. By 1954–56 the proportion had reached 26 percent in the United States, while it had fallen to 15 percent in the Soviet Union. Parkinson's law of self-generation of administrative and office personnel does not seem to have applied to Soviet industry of the postwar years.

A more interesting question is that of the proportion of white-collar to industrial personnel in all industry and mining, whether on the enterprise level or not. Here we must include all the higher administrative, applied research, marketing and procurement personnel in the central offices of our own large companies and in the regional and central headquarters of the Soviet Union. As is to be expected, our data on this question is less exact than when we limit ourselves to the enterprise level. But the available evidence seems to show that in 1937–40, the American proportion was only 16 percent compared to the Russian figure of 27 percent. By 1954–56, however, the pattern was reversed; the American proportion had risen to 29 percent, while the Russian had fallen to 20 percent.[3]

These figures seem highly significant in indicating that Soviet industry does not absorb in its bureaucratic functions a proportion of its work force which seems disproportionate by American standards. The reverse is the case if anything; although, of course, the proportion in either country would seem extraordinarily high by the standards of many West European countries. These data refer to Soviet industry before the reorganization of 1957, but this reorganization does not seem to have affected the picture particularly.

In short, whatever problems are created for Russian industry through the Soviet system of central planning—and certainly they are multitudinous—the creation of an enormous bureaucracy, gobbling up Soviet manpower, does not seem to be one of these difficulties. In this regard, the Soviet Union has made enormous managerial strides since the period of the 1930's.

---

[3] At least two questions about these statistics may occur to the reader. One is the question of whether these differences in proportions are a result of the changes and differences in industry mix in the two countries. I have made some calculations to test this issue, and the results were completely negative.

The second question is that of whether the results are not due simply to the large number of manual workers in Soviet industry and mining who are needed because of the low level of mechanization and efficiency. Now it is true that Soviet labor productivity is vastly lower than American in manual trades. But the same thing is true—and I would guess to even a greater extent—in white-collar occupations. The American revolution in office procedures and equipment has not get crossed en masse to the Soviet Union. There seems no obvious reason to think that the universally lower level of Russian labor productivity affects the proportions of white collar to manual workers.

CHART 1

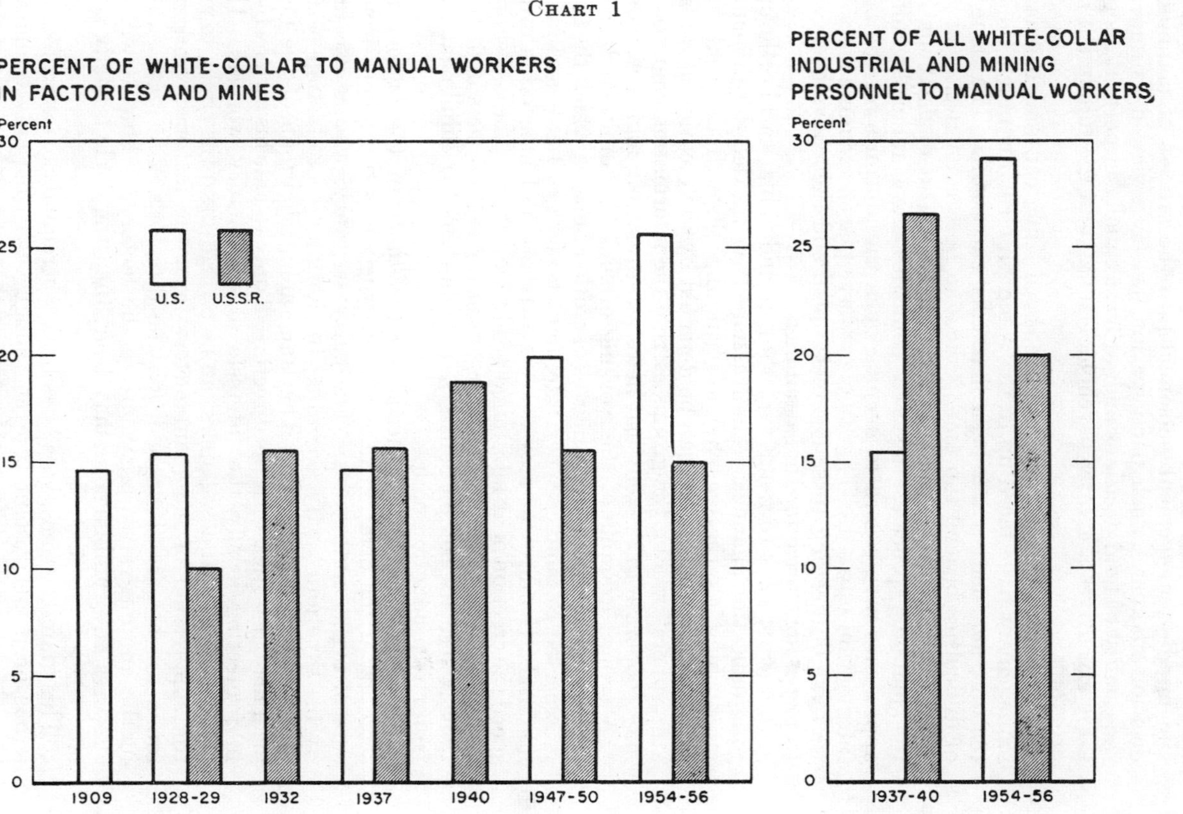
PERCENT OF WHITE-COLLAR TO MANUAL WORKERS
IN FACTORIES AND MINES
Percent
30
25
20
15
10
5
0
U.S.
U.S.S.R.
1909
1928-29
1932
1937
1940
1947-50
1954-56
PERCENT OF ALL WHITE-COLLAR
INDUSTRIAL AND MINING
PERSONNEL TO MANUAL WORKERS,
Percent
30
25
20
15
10
5
0
1937-40
1954-56

The Problem of "Communication Upward"

Administrative theory, and both American and Russian industry in practice, have long recognized the key importance of bringing lower and middle management personnel into the process of planning and decision making. Such participation has been viewed as improving the quality of final decisions and, at least equally important, as giving these executives a greater psychological stake in the fulfillment of the programs.

In this aspect of communication, both American and Russian top management have faced up to the same problem for much the same reasons, and neither has been markedly successful. The same sorts of difficulties bedevil top management in both countries.

Although this similarity exists in the treatment of participation in the planning process, the two countries have radically different approaches with regard to keeping open the pipelines for the flow of information upward. The Russians have placed far more stress than we have on keeping these channels open, and they have been willing to pay a high price for this attainment.

One problem is to make sure that no individual can bottle up the communication channel. The Russians have tackled this difficulty by establishing alternative channels running through different hands. This approach, however, can be defeated by the creation of a "family atmosphere" among the groups astride the information channels, who may cooperate to prevent bad news from reaching higher authorities.

A typical example of the working of such a "family circle" might be secrecy concerning the progress of worker housing which the factory is expected to build. Where the plant is short of funds and building materials, the director may delay construction of housing in order to speed the erection of an additional production shop. The new shop may seem to him to be far the more urgent of the two projects under conditions where its completion is a precondition for fulfillment of the factory's production plan.

However, the director needs the assistance of the factory party secretary if the delay in housing construction is to be kept from the ears of higher authorities. The party secretary, who is also judged by his superiors partly according to the plant's production performance, may well go along. The trade-union chairman of the factory local may also stick with the director—if only to hide his own feebleness in protecting locally the interests of the factory workers. If the editor of the town newspapers can be brought into the circle, to assure the suppression of indignant letters from the factory's workers, so much the better. If in addition the director's immediate superior, in the administrative organ above the factory, is himself willing to suppress any rumblings he may hear, then the circle is really a tight one.

This "family atmosphere" has been a perennial Soviet problem, and it has been met resolutely even though each time only temporarily. One device is to shift people around between jobs sufficiently frequently so as to prevent solid "rings" from being formed. A second, equally drastic approach, is constantly to reshuffle the organizations themselves. Both procedures have regularly been used in Soviet industry although, of course, they have not solely been directed toward the problem of communication.

In addition to the costs involved in keeping in flux both executive personnel and organizational charts, there is the morale cost of using an espionage system. This, too, is a price the Russians have been willing to pay. In fact, the secret police—in the form of "special sections"—has been openly used as an official organization with a recognized role in the factory.

A third cost which Russian administration has been willing to pay is that of sharply reducing the effectiveness of staff as advisers to middle management. Staff groups are specifically instructed to report to higher bodies. They act as a check on management, and thus have difficulty in also functioning as a support. The clearest case of this is in the controllership department, and Russian administrators have been quite clear as to the nature of their difficulties here. Although Russian administrators would naturally like to eat their cake and still have at least some of it left, they have been willing to pay the price required to maintain the flow of information.

Thus the maintenance of channels of information upward is a management goal which seemingly is given much greater relative weight in Soviet than in American industry. In the hierarchy of management goals, those of stability, management contentment, and successful fulfillment of staff functions stand higher on the American business ladder.

Conclusions as to the "Red Executive"

The Red executive has come far since the days of the Revolution. Today he is a college-educated engineer with a sound technical and administrative background, and he bears little resemblance to the flamboyant party director of the early days whose credentials were years in Tsarist prisons, escapes from exile, and oratory exercised in stirring the masses. But the present-day Red executive is also no throwback to the bourgeois plant manager of the later twenties and early thirties who, for all his education, was distrusted as an enemy of the Revolution and a potential saboteur. Today's executive combines sound training with the political assurance and power which permit him the freedom to make creative use of this training.

The Soviet manager may not live well when judged by the standards of his American counterpart, but he does quite satisfactorily compared to the ordinary Soviet citizen. He is given powerful monetary incentives to turn in a first-rate job. Yet never in his life will be have any certainty of tenure in his post. No civil-service rules or old school tie protect him; his superiors show a marked impatience with failure. This impatience, it is true, is now tempered more with commonsense than was the case in the past. No longer, as often occurred during the mid-1930's, do production lapses lead swiftly to charges of sabotage and to a forced-labor camp. Nevertheless, blunders can result in swift demotion. The executive ulcer rate is high.

The Russian manager is a man with power, but he is no independent decision maker. He is an organization man, filling a slot in an industrial bureaucracy which has lines reaching to the very heights of Soviet power. His production goals, his costs, and even his industrial research objectives are set for him. Moreover, he must establish and maintain successful contact with the members of other powerful bureaucracies—and in particular with that of the Communist Party.

46283—59—pt. 1——11

But if the manager's goals are established for him, their achievement is his personal responsibility. No excuse exists for failure. Often, the drive to meet quotas will force him into illegal activities; this cannot be helped. It is a basic part of his task to determine what is necessary in order to "succeed"; in this sense, the Red executive is very much an independent businessman.

The Soviet manager is oriented to production. Volume of output is the acid test of his work. Marketing is no problem; finance is a trivial concern. But the purchasing department is the rock on which the factory organization stands, for supply shortages lead to production shortages. A good procurement man is above price.

Although the situation is now in the process of change, raw materials and machinery are still the items of greatest scarcity to the Russian manager. It is these which are his bottlenecks. Labor, of course, is also a problem—but a labor-saving device is not nearly as valuable to him as one which saves materials or which permits more production to be gotten out of a machine. Thus, the Soviet manager tends to emphasize in his daily work different problems and different shortages than does the American company president or even the plant superintendent.

Well trained, well disciplined, politically conscious and active, the Red executive seems a figure permanently established in the seats of the mighty. There is no justification for picturing him as a man in conflict with the Communist Party official, the two uneasily sharing power for the moment. Rather, the industrial manager and the party secretary are old classmates, neighbors, and colleagues, seeing the world from the same perspective.

Neither the Red executive nor his party-official colleague is any longer the revolutionary of the 1920's to whom ideology was everything. Both are men well established in the second most powerful country in the world, with enormous personal stakes in world stability and in peace. When Marx in the "Communist Manifesto" appealed for world revolution, he addressed himself to the worker who had "nothing to lose but his chains." The Red executive and the party administrator have a great deal more to lose—and they know it well. Their attitude toward world revolution and other threats to peace must inevitably bear the imprint of this knowledge.

THE CENTRALIZED PLANNING OF SUPPLY IN SOVIET INDUSTRY*

(By Herbert S. Levine, Russian Research Center, Harvard University and University of Pennsylvania)

Introduction

Superficially, Soviet industrial supply methods do not appear to be much different from our own. A firm "buys" the input materials it requires, in most cases directly from the producer. Payment is made by transfers in bank accounts. Terms of the sale are stipulated in commercial contracts, and both buyer and seller are protected by the courts against violations, by the other party, of these contracts.

The similarities, however, end abruptly. First, the atmosphere in which the Soviet supply system operates is different from the one normally prevailing in the United States. The Soviet economy since its early days has been marked by a chronic sellers' market; i.e., the situation where demand is consistently pressing upon supply. This has been one of the major factors contributing toward the many negative characteristics of the supply system, which have been so well documented in both Russian and American writings. These writings center on the frequent inability of the system to satisfy the basic commandments of any supply system; namely, to get materials to consuming enterprises in the required quantity, of the required quality and at the required time, in the cheapest way possible. And they discuss what Soviet firms have had to do to counteract these deficiencies: padded orders, excess inventories, staffs of "expediters," vertical integration, etc.[1]

A second and more fundamental dissimilarity is the centralized nature of the planning and control of supply in the Soviet Union. The Soviet firm does not buy its major input materials on an open market where the ability to pay the price asked is the only requirement for acquisition of the material. Major materials in the Soviet Union are centrally allocated even though on the operating level of the firm; material transfers are accompanied by money payments. In order to acquire these major materials, a Soviet firm not only has to have the money, but it also has to have an authorization, in the form of a fund, from the government.[2]

---

*This is part of a study I am doing as a doctoral dissertation in the Department of Economics, Harvard University. I am happy to acknowledge my indebtedness to Prof. Abram Bergson for his advice and guidance, and the Russian Research Center and Ford Foundation for the assistance they have given me. I am also indebted to Profs. Alexander Gerschenkron, Robert Dorfman, and John M. Montias. I wish especially to thank the numerous Soviet economists who were kind and helpful to me on a trip I took to the Soviet Union during May and June 1959.

Note on Footnotes —Short titles are used throughout, author and date of publication. An alphabetical listing of sources is to be found at the end of the paper. All references to interviews in the Soviet Union are cited as: Personal interview with a Soviet economist.

[1] A good Russian source is "Gal'perin 57-1," Also any random sampling of Promyshlenno-Ekonomicheskaia Gazeta will pick up numerous examples of supply deficiencies. For American discussions see "Berliner 57," "Granick 57," and "Granick 59."

[2] In the American economy, also, something more than the mere ability to pay is sometimes required for the acquisition of certain materials. But we are here thinking of the capitalist process in its more generalized form, i.e. as an "ideal type," in the Weberian sense.

Many of the operating characteristics of the Soviet supply system have already been well described in the works of Professors Berliner and Granick.[3] In this paper I would like to focus on the planning of this supply system—the major element of dissimilarity between the Soviet and American supply systems. The planning of supply is differentiated from economic planning in general in that the fundamental question of the allocation of economic resources is not one of the primary problems. Supply planning begins from a set of given production targets, and its primary problem is achieve balance in the plan, i.e., to assure that if a certain number of tons of steel output is planned, then the necessary amounts of all the input materials into steel are also planned. It is this vitally important problem of achieving balance in the plan which will form the core of this paper: how is it done, how effectively is it done and what changes and improvements are in sight.

The operational plan in the Soviet Union is not the long-term plan, the 5- or 7-year plan, but the short-term plan, the annual plan. This paper will concentrate, therefore, on the problems of constructing the annual plan. The periods both before and after the recent reorganization of industrial administration will be covered. This is done because, first, as an aid in analyzing Soviet economic growth, both the present and the prereorganization systems are relevant; second, in order to understand and evaluate the reorganization, it is necessary to know what preceded it; and third, many of the essential features of the planning system have not changed, but they stand out more clearly in the prereorganization system than they do in the present system, which has by no means achieved any final form as yet. The coverage of the paper will be limited to the planning of supply within the industrial sector of the Soviet economy only.

The paper begins with a short description of the organizations involved in supply planning, as a sort of playbill to enable the reader to identify the performers. This is followed by a discussion of how the annual supply plan is constructed with special emphasis on the balancing methodology employed. Then comes a section on the major weaknesses of supply planning and the possibilities of correcting some of them through the use of modern mathematical methods and high-speed electronic computers. The paper ends with some brief conclusions. This is a lot of territory to cover within the delimited confines of this paper. As a result, many points have been brushed over quickly, often too quickly. For this, I apologize.

Those who are familiar with American handling of materials control problems during the war will see certain similarities in the description of Russian planning methods which follows.[4]

ORGANIZATIONS IN SUPPLY PLANNING

The basic impact of the reorganization of 1957 was to change the administration of Soviet industry from vertical, branch lines to horizontal, geographic lines. Prior to the reorganization, there were normally between 20 and 40 economic ministries (such as the Ministry of Ferrous Metallurgy), which administered firms throughout the country classified as being within a given sector.[5] Now almost all of

[3] See footnote No. 1.
[4] See "Novick 49."
[5] Actually the output of most ministries was fairly heterogeneous.

the ministries have been abolished and in their place there are more than 100 sovnarkhozy (councils of the national economy) each of which administers the firms lying within its economic-administrative region (a geographic area). The administration of the supply system has in a similar manner been changed from ministerial lines to regional lines.

At the top of the supply hierarchy, both before and after the reorganization, stands Gosplan S.S.S.R. (the State Planning Committee [6] of the Council of Ministers of the U.S.S.R.). This organization, since the end of World War II, has had a checkered career. At the end of the war, it was a "permanent commission" of the U.S.S.R. Council of People's Commissars (now Council of Ministers) responsible for the working out of long- and short-term plans, including the annual supply plan. Its primary mission, however, was not the initiating and formulating of major objectives, but the assuring of the feasibility and consistency of a plan, and the prevention and eradication of disproportions within the economy. Among its various departments, Gosplan had a set of branch departments and a set of summary departments (svodnye otdely) which were organized more or less parallel to the existing ministries. The former were concerned with the output and the latter with the distribution of the products which came under the planning jurisdiction of Gosplan. Soon after the war, control over supply planning was taken away from Gosplan, when in 1947, Gossnab (the State Committee of the U.S.S.R. Council of Ministers for the Supply of Materials to the National Economy) was formed. Gossnab took on the function of constructing the annual supply plan. In 1951, the planning of the distribution of consumers' goods was split off from Gossnab with the formation of Gosprodsnab (the State Committee of the U.S.S.R. Council of Ministers for the Supply of Food and Manufactured Consumer Goods). But in 1953, Gossnab and Gosprodsnab were put back into Gosplan and the top organizational level of supply planning returned to what it was 5 years earlier. However, this situation did not last very long. In 1955, not only supply planning was split off from Gosplan, but the entire function of short-term planning when a separate planning organ, Gosekonomkomissiia (the State Planning Commission of the U.S.S.R. Council of Ministers for the Current Planning of the National Economy) was formed. This arrangement lasted for 2 years. In 1957, under the reorganization of industrial management, current planning and, with it, supply planning were put back into Gosplan.

Even this short description of the repeated organizational changes at the top planning level is sufficient to give the flavor of the postwar developments. Change has been the rule rather than the exception.[7] There are several explanations for this, but one which is hard to avoid is that the political authorities have not been too happy with the organization of planning and within this of supply planning at the top level.

Before the reorganization, the hierarchy of supply planning below the top level ran as follows. Attached to the ministry, there was the glavsnab (main administration of supply) and the glavsbyt (main

[6] Gosplan keeps alternating between being a commission and a committee. At the end of the war it was a commission; in 1947 it became a committee; in 1955, a commission; and since 1957 it has again been a committee.

[7] This is also true at the ministerial level, where ministries were constantly being separated and consolidated.

administration of sales). In those cases where there were glavki (branch main administrations) between the ministry and a group of subordinate enterprises, each glavk had a supply department. Finally, at the lowest level, there was the supply department of the enterprise.

The reorganization led to a number of changes in the organizations involved in supply planning. The planning hierarchy is, of course, different. The various levels now are: Gosplan S.S.S.R., republican gosplan, sovnarkhoz, enterprise. At the top level, Gosplan acquired the former ministerial glavsbyty. Recently these were consolidated, reduced in number to between 10 and 14, and renamed, main administrations for interrepublican deliveries.[8] The gosplan of each union republic has increased in size and importance. The gosplan of the R.S.F.S.R. acquired the glavsnaby of the former ministries [9] and combined main administrations for supply and sales have been formed in every republican gosplan (one main administration for supply and sales for each broad category of product). Main supply and sales administrations have also been formed at the sovnarkhozy. In addition, the sovnarkhoz has a number of branch departments and each one of these branch departments has a supply section which is active and important in the planning of supply for the firms within that branch and subordinate to that sovnarkhoz. At the bottom level, remaining unchanged by the reorganization, are the supply departments of the individual enterprises.

II. Construction of the Supply Plan

THE SUPPLY PLAN AND WHAT IT COVERS

The planning of industrial supply is related more to short-term planning than to long term. There is no supply plan as such in the 5- or 7-year plan. But the annual plan for the development of the national economy contains, in addition to sections on targets for industrial output, agricultural output, capital construction, introduction of new technology, labor force, etc., a plan for the material-technical supply of the national economy. The main elements of this supply plan are (1) an introductory resolution of the U.S.S.R. Council of Ministers, which confirms the plan and contains its basic objectives, including some direct tasks to the individual ministries (now to the republics) for the economizing of materials; (2) material balances[10] compiled for all centrally allocated means of production; (3) distribution plans for each centrally allocated material, by user ministries (now by user republics); (4) norms for the input of materials, including fuels and electricity, in production and construction, and tasks for the lowering of these norms.[11]

The annual supply plan, confirmed by the U.S.S.R. Council of Ministers, does not cover the distribution of all materials used by industry, but only a selected group of them. Until recently, input materials were classified into three, sometimes four categories. First, there were the "funded" commodities. These were the commodities

---

[8] "Gal'perin 58," p. 52 and "Koldomasov 59," p. 57.

[9] "Gal'perin 58," p. 50. Thus, by preserving both the former glavsbyty and glavsnaby, a sharp break with the past was avoided and the transition from the old system to the new was made easier.

[10] Material balances are balance sheets of the sources and uses of an individual product (see below, pp. 19ff).

[11] "Lokshin 52," p. 65.

whose distribution was set in the state supply plan. The term "funded" meant they were products which could only be obtained if the consuming unit had a fund or an allotment for their acquisition. In other words, they were products centrally allotted by the Government. These included the most important producers' goods in the economy: ferrous and nonferrous metals, fuels, chemicals, etc. Also included were machinery and equipment, and in addition, the major materials used by the consumers' goods industries.[12] They were classified in varying degrees of specificity, but rarely as fine as an input material specification has to be at the level of actual use in production. For example, in 1946, there were 70 different classifications of "funded" rolled ferrous metal products, but the metallurgical industry produced several thousand different shapes, sizes, and qualities.[13] The number of "funded" commodities did not remain constant. It grew after the war, reaching a peak of 1,600 at the height of the centralization period just before the death of Stalin. In the early decentralization moves of 1953–54 they were reduced to about 800, and in 1958 they were reported to number 760.[14]

The second category was "centrally planned" commodities. The distribution of these goods was planned by the main administrations of sales of the producing ministries. They were either goods of lesser importance than the "funded" or they had a more restricted group of consumers. Also classified as "centrally planned" were those commodities whose distribution was planned by the republican gosplany.

The third category was "decentrally planned" commodities. The distribution of these was controlled by local governmental organs and by the local offices of the main administrations of sales of the producing ministries.

A fourth category was sometimes added: "decentralized and self procurement." This included those products a firm could procure by itself, such as sand, rocks, some types of lumber, etc.

After the reorganization, the classification into "funded" and "centrally planned" commodities lost much of its rationale. The main administrations of sales of the former ministries which distributed the "centrally planned" commodities were now part of Gosplan S.S.S.R. Therefore, Gosplan (or at least sections of it) was distributing both the 760 "funded" commodities and the approximately 5,000 "centrally planned" commodities. In addition, while the main administrations of sales at Gosplan were planning the distribution of "centrally planned" commodities, the republics were planning the output levels of these commodities.[15] The old classification system was clearly an anachronism. Soon the announcement came that "beginning in 1959, the notorious division of output into 'planned' and 'funded' will be abolished." [16]

Under the new classification system, Gosplan will plan the distribution of and issue fondy for the acquisition of those products which are the most important for the national economy, those which are in

[12] Classification as a "funded" commodity depended also on the degree of centralization of its production. In addition, I was told, in a personal interview with a Soviet economist, that the number of "funded" commodities in any 1 year was affected by how many Gosplan felt it could handle. For listings of "funded" and "nonfunded" commodities see "Shein 54," pp. 16–18, and "Demichev 57," pp. 29–32.

[13] "Kosiachenko 46," p. 14.

[14] "Lokshin 52," p. 76, "Glusker 54," p. 84, "Karpov 58," p. 18.

[15] "Gal'perin 58," p. 45.

[16] "Perov 58," p. 13. The use of the word "notorious" might reflect the Soviet proclivity for kicking fallen horses, but it also might be a reflection of some of the problems resulting from the classification system even before the reorganization, such as lack of coordination between the distribution of "funded" and "centrally planned" commodities.

the most serious short supply and those which are produced and used in several republics. These commodities include almost all of the former "funded" and some of the former "centrally planned" commodities. Estimates of the number to be planned by Gosplan vary from 800 to 1,500.[17]

The republics will plan the distribution of the commodities of lesser importance and those commodities produced either wholly or largely within one republic. The individual sovnarkhozy will distribute those commodities of least importance and those commodities which are produced wholly within a single sovnarkhoz.

Our major interest, in this paper, is the centralized planning of supply. Therefore, we will concentrate on the planning of the supply of those products which are under the jurisdiction of Gosplan S.S.S.R. and which appear in the annual state supply plan: formerly the "funded" commodities and presently those commodities in the first of the new three categories.

CHRONOLOGY OF PLAN CONSTRUCTION

In this section, we will outline the sequence of plan construction. The supply plan for the forthcoming year (the planned year) is constructed during the current year (the planning year). The process is roughly one wherein general instructions flow down the planning hierarchy followed by a counterflow of fill-in information and suggestions from the bottom. This is followed by coordination at the top and the issuance of a fairly detailed plan. In the final stage the plan flows down again and is put into the thorough detail necessary for operational purposes. The formal chronology which I have set out below is a generalized view of the process. In reality, the stages are not always clear cut and practice often varies from one industry to another. The prereorganization system is described first and then some of the changes introduced by the reorganization are discussed.[18]

The first stage of the planning process is a statistical analysis of the base period. This is finished in the first half of the planning year. It includes a thorough statistical investigation of the previous year (that is 2 years before the planned year), preliminary data on the first 6 months of the planning year and some estimated data for the second 6 months of the planning year. The purpose of this statistical work is primarily to aid in the construction of the control figures (stage two) by uncovering temporary "bottlenecks" which should be concentrated upon in the planned year and by uncovering possible supplementary sources of increased output.

The second stage is the drawing up of the control figures. These are preliminary notes on the forthcoming economic plan. They are a set of aggregate output targets for a dozen or so of the most important commodity groups. They also contain some major investment targets. Their purpose is to serve as guideposts to the lower economic units in the construction of the annual plan. The control figures are worked out in Gosplan by the industrial and the summary departments, use being made of material balances to attain equality

[17] "Gal'perin 58," p. 45, "Karpov 58," pp. 18-19. "Gal'perin 58," p. 45 gives a figure of 1,200 to 1,500; "Karpov 58," p. 19: 1,000. But I was told in a personal interview with a Soviet economist that Gosplan was still planning the distribution of only about 800 commodities.

[18] This chronology has been put together from many sources, including: "Braginskii 54," pp. 331-345; "Lokshin 52," p. 27-37; "Gal'perin 57-1," passim, especially pp. 17-20, 32-34; "P. Kh. Editorial 58"; "Gal'perin 58"; "Koldomasov 59"; and a number of personal interviews with Soviet economists.

between the supply and demand for each of the commodity groups covered. According to the Soviet literature, these preliminary targets are based first of all on the economic-political tasks set by the party and the government, which in turn are determined by "the given stage of Socialist construction." [19] They are also set in relation to the long-term plan then in force, relying heavily on the results of the statistical investigations carried out in the first stage. The control figures are worked out in June and early July, and are confirmed by the Council of Ministers.

The third stage is the key stage. It is the one in which the plan comes up the hierarchy, is coordinated on a national scale at the top, is confirmed by the government and becomes a law directing the operating units in the economy. Actually, this stage begins before the completion of the second stage. It appears that all the levels—ministries, glavki and enterprises—start to work on their plans prior to the publication of the control figures. Sometime in May, Gosplan sends out forms for the ordering of materials. These orders are called zaiavki. (See chart No. 1.) They contain data on materials required by the enterprise during the planned year, i.e., the year to come, and also data on materials used during the current year and the past year. The materials required are calculated by the "direct method": output targets are multiplied by a set of input norms (from this product, above-norm stocks are subtracted). Since work on the zaiavki begins before the release of the control figures, the enterprise puts together a set of tentative output targets, based on the enterprise's experience during the past year and the first part of the current year, and what directions it expects the forthcoming plan to take. Once the control figures are released (end of June–beginning of July) and are broken down by the ministry and the glavk, the enterprise has a clearer idea of what its production targets will be, and it is able to introduce the necessary corrections in the plan calculations it has been making.

In addition to output targets, in order to complete the zaiavki, the firm has to know how much of each input it will need per unit of output. This information is supplied by the input norms. The question, by whom and how these norms are set, is an extremely complicated one. For one thing, it depends upon the period. In some periods there were many norms inspected and confirmed by the highest planning organ. For example, in preparing the supply plan for 1949, Gossnab inspected more than 1,800 material input norms, and this grew as the drive toward centralization increased until for the 1952 plan it was above 7,500.[20] But then in the early decentralization moves of 1953–54, the ministries were given greatly increased power over norm setting and only the "most important norms" were to be inspected by the top planning organ.[21] The importance of the input material being normed, thus, is another contributing factor. The most important norms are established in the annual supply plan as obligatory direct tasks (adresnye zadaniia). These are set either as an average for a branch, or, in the case of the most important firms in the country, by specific firm and by specific item produced. In addition, the plan

[19] This is the phrase repeatedly used. In Western terms it means "planners' preferences." The planners look over the current stage of development and they (rather than the consumers) determine the major directions the economy will take in the coming year. (In this sense "planners" means the political leaders, rather than the people at Gosplan.)

[20] "Lokshin 52," p. 125.

[21] "Braginskii 54," p. 222.

Chart #1

ZAIAVKA

For (Group of Materials) needed by the enterprise in 1960

			1958			1959									Requirements in 1960						Sources covering 1960 needs						
							Fond		Delivered		Used					For maintenance		Temporary stocks						By Quarter			
Number	Designation of Materials	Unit of Measurement	Stocks on Jan. 1st"	Delivered	Used	Stocks on Jan. 1st	Confirmed	Including changes	Expected for year	Actual deliveries in first six months	Expected for year	Actually used in first six months	Actual stocks on July 1, 1959	Expected stocks on Jan. 1, 1960	For output sold	Total	For capital repairs	Quantity	In "days' needs"	TOTAL	Use of expected stocks	Mobilization of internal resources	Requested *fondy*	I	II	III	IV
1	2	3	4	5	6	7	8	9	10	11	12	13	14	15	16	17	18	19	20	21	22	23	24	25	26	27	28

This is a typical form of a *zaiavka*. It is illustrative of the documentation which constitutes the "paper pyramid" involved in centralized Soviet planning. (see *Grossman 55*, pp. 22-23) lists a number of targets for the general decrease in norms by industrial branch. The main mass of norms, however, are not listed in the plan, but are used for calculation purposes during the process of constructing the national economic plan. Some of these are confirmed directly at the enterprise and some at the glavk or ministry. Again there was much variation from year to year.[22]

The principle underlying the working out of input norms is that they must aid in the constant struggle to increase economic output by forcing the spread of technical progress and the economizing of material resources. To accomplish this, they must embody the achievements of the leading firms, but they must also be attainable by the average firm. The concept of an "average-progressive norm," which is a norm somewhere between the average and the best, was created to meet this need.[23] Norms are worked out originally by the firm and, depending upon the level at which they are confirmed, are inspected by technical bureaus up the bureaucratic line. As we will see below, norms are frequently changed by higher organs during the construction of the annual economic plan.

With its estimates of output targets and input norms, the enterprise fills out its zaiavki and sends these orders along with supporting documents up to the glavk. Thus begins what is in many ways a political process, something akin to our collective bargaining. The glavk checks the estimates and requests of the enterprise and tries to remove some of the slack the enterprise has put in. The "padding of orders" is one of the most common methods used by the Soviet firm to increase its chances of fulfilling its output plan, under the existing strains of tight plans and supply unreliability.[24] In its negotions with the glavk, the firm tries to defend the estimates and requests it has made. But since the glavk has administrative power over the firm, it can force its opinion to prevail (although a firm can appeal to the ministry).[25] The glavk then combines the zaiavki of the firms subordinate to it and sends the combined zaiavki up to the main administration of supply of the ministry. Here the bargaining process is repeated. The ministry then sends its aggregated plan and zaiavki up to Gosplan S.S.S.R. Usually this was to be done before September 1, or at the latest September 15.[26] The discussions which ensue between a ministry and the corresponding industrial department of Gosplan are a real analog of collective bargaining, for neither has administrative power over the other. In fact, there are at times unresolved disagreements which have to be settled by the Council of Ministers.[27]

22 In 1952, at the height of centralization there were 2,230 norms established by Gossnab and the ministries for the use of rolled ferrous metal products, which covered 69 percent of its total use in the economy, and 1,145 centrally established norms for the use of lumber products, which covered 97 percent of their use ("Shein 54," p. 113).

23 There are a number of different methods of calculating an average progressive norm. One is by the "analytical method." wherein the achievements of the leading firms are thoroughly analyzed and a realistic norm set as close to these achievements as possible. For more than 20 years this has been the only acceptable method and yet it would appear that in practice the more formal "statistical method" is still widely used. Under this method an average progressive norm is often just the average of all the above-average input relationships achieved in production. See, e.g., the December 1935 Plenum of the Central Committee of the Communist Party, "Direktivy II," pp. 485–6; "Shein 54," pp. 118–126; "Savkin 56," p. 67.

24 "Berliner 57," ch. VII, and passim.

25 The cutting away of fat is not carried to the limit because the plans of the glavki and of the ministries are (presumably) a summation of the plans of the enterprises, and thus their fulfillment depends upon the enterprise's ability to fulfill its own plan. (The appeal point is from a personal interview with a Soviet economist.)

26 Personal interview with a Soviet economist. "Braginskii 54," pp. 337–338 states that the ministries in 1952 were supposed to have their drafts up by Aug. 15.

27 "Strumilin 57," p. 39. It is also thought that the Central Committee of the Communist Party plays an important role in the settling of some of these disagreements.

During the period of September and early October, Gosplan is engaged in the crucial work of attempting to balance the supply and demand for each of the centrally allocated commodities. It does this by means of the material balances (this process will be discussed in some detail in the following section). Actually Gosplan, like the ministries and glavki, starts its work before the draft plans come up from below. In this way it has a forecast of what the material balances will be like when the ministries' plans do come up, and it is, therefore, prepared for the ensuing discussions. Gosplan sends a balanced draft of the plan to the Council of Ministers before the end of October.[28] The plan is discussed by the Council of Ministers and, if necessary, certain changes are made. The plan is then confirmed.

Stage 4, the final stage in the construction of the plan, is the bringing down of the plan to the enterprise and its transformation into detailed operational form. The final plan, the fondy for the centrally allocated commodities and the delivery orders for these commodities are sent to the ministries. The main administration of supply divides the fondy and the centrally established input norms among the subordinate glavki and the main administration of sales divides the delivery orders for the "funded" commodities produced by the ministry. The glavki in turn divide these among the enterprises.

A fund received by an enterprise entitles it to a certain amount of the "funded" commodity. But the "funded" commodity is defined in fairly gross terms and thus the enterprise must specify exactly what shape, grade, and size it requires. The firm constructs a complete, specified list of the materials it needs within the limits of the fondy allotted to it and sends this list up to the glavk. The glavk checks the lists it receives, combines them, and sends the combined, specified lists to the ministry.[29] There, the main administration of supply combines the lists it receives and sends the specified orders to the main administrations of sales of the appropriate producing ministries. This is to be done 1 to 1½ months before the beginning of the planned year.[30] The main administration of sales checks to see if the orders are within the limits of the fondy, and then it assigns specific orders to specific producing firms. Meanwhile, the aggregate delivery orders, which were sent down, have also been distributed to the glavki and the enterprises, so that the enterprises have already begun to work out their production and shipment schedules before receiving the specified orders from their main administration of sales.

As was the case with other stages, the fourth stage really begins before the end of the third. When Gosplan sends its draft of the plan to the Council of Ministers, it sends excerpts to each ministry so that the ministry can begin the arduous and labor-intensive job of specification and assignment of delivery orders. Then, when the plan is confirmed, the changes made by the Council of Ministers are incorporated by the ministries, glavki and enterprises into the work they have done up to that time.

---

[28] In 1952, Gosplan was to have this draft at the Council of Ministers by Oct. 10. "Braginskii 54," pp. 337–338.

[29] A census of inventories is taken in October, so that the glavk has a clearer idea of the stocks on hand at the enterprise and the expected stocks at the beginning of the planned year. It can take these into account in checking the specified orders of the enterprise.

[30] The specified orders cover only a 3-month period and thus the specification process is repeated before each quarter.

The planning process proper[31] concludes with the signing of contracts between producing units and consuming units, in which delivery schedules and other delivery details are stipulated.

Since the reorganization, the essential nature of the planning process has not changed, but some of its features have. The hierarchical line is now different: Gosplan S.S.S.R., republican gosplan, sovnarkhoz, enterprise.

The chronology also is somewhat different. Stage 2, the construction of the control figures, was omitted, but is now being reintroduced in altered form. Stage 3 now begins at the enterprise. No control figures containing output targets are issued, but rather each enterprise is to work out its own output targets on the basis of the yearly breakdowns of the 7-year plan. These yearly breakdowns have been worked out in much more detail and thus are more operational than were the yearly breakdowns of long-term plans in the past. As the middle and end years of the 7-year plan approach, the enterprise is expected to make corrections in these yearly breakdowns to take account of the accumulated divergences between experience and plan. The zaiavki are sent up to the sovnarkhoz, are reviewed, debated, and are combined and sent up to the republican gosplan. Here the bargaining process is repeated and then, for each centrally allocated product, the planned supply (including "imports" from other republics) and the planned demand (including "exports" to other republics) are balanced. For this purpose, regional material balances are used. A new procedure will be added starting in 1960. In order to give the gosplan of a union-republic some idea of how much of a given material it can expect to receive in the planned year, Gosplan S.S.S.R. will, at the beginning of June, issue a set of preliminary limits for the supply of somewhere between 50 to 200 of the most important input materials.[32] The gosplan of the republic is to send its output plan and zaiavki up to Gosplan by August 1. Gosplan then has until September 15 to work out a balanced all-union output and supply plan. The basic method is still the use of material balances. Fondy (now confirmed by Gosplan itself) are allocated to the republics; the republics distribute them among the sovnarkhozy; and the sovnarkhozy to the enterprises. The specified orders go up the line: sovnarkhoz, republican gosplan, Gosplan. This is supposed to be done 1½ to 2 months before the beginning of the planned year. In Gosplan S.S.S.R., the main administrations for interrepublican deliveries, which grew out of the main administrations of sales of the ministries, assign specified orders directly to individual producing enterprises. And the process again ends with the signing of delivery contracts between suppliers and users.

Summarizing the results of the reorganization, the following stand out as important new features of the process of supply planning: (1) the more detailed yearly subdivisions of the 7-year plan, which serve as a starting point for the planning process in place of the control figures which were formerly worked out each year by Gosplan; (2) the increased importance of the republican gosplany and of regional balancing; (3) also the increased importance of Gosplan S.S.S.R. with

[31] The other part of the planning process is the changing of the plan during the course of the year as the need for changes becomes apparent. Russian economists repeatedly claim this is an important part of the planning process, and indeed when one reads of the tremendous number of changes introduced during the year, it is hard to disagree. But a discussion of this falls outside of the restricted scope of this paper.

[32] Personal interview with a Soviet economist. See also Koldomasov 59, p. 60.

the addition to its staff of the former main administrations of sales of the ministries, now renamed, main administrations for inter-republican deliveries (this, however, may not be a permanent feature).

MATERIAL BALANCES

The key element in the planning of industrial supply is the material balance. Every Soviet writer on the subject pays homage to it:

> In the Socialist economy, the planned connection between the production and consumption of different types of products is guaranteed. Both the production and consumption of materials are determined by means of the material balances, which are an integral component of the plan for the supply of the national economy.
>
> By means of the material balances, the material needs of the national economy are determined, means for increasing the material resources of the economy are uncovered and the necessary proportionality in the growth of individual branches of the national economy in accordance with the demands of the law of the planned (proportional) development of the national economy is established.
>
> The material balances permit the planning organs to work out measures for the mobilization of production reserves, for the overcoming of "bottlenecks" in the development of individual branches and to uncover supplementary resources.[33]

A material balance is essentially a balance sheet of the supply and demand for a given product. At the Gosplan level a separate material balance is made out for each of the centrally allocated commodities (formerly the "funded" commodities.)[34] On the left side of the balance, are listed all the sources of the product and on the right side, its uses. (See chart No. 2.) Most of these categories are self-explanatory. On the sources side, the most important category is "Production." With most commodities it is often as high as 95 percent of the total supply. "Imports" is usually insignificant. "Other sources" is of varying importance. In some ferrous metals, for example, scrap metal ("other sources") is an important element of supply. "Stocks" includes only those at suppliers. This is done because they are the only stocks capable of being distributed.[35] Stocks at users (if they are above normed levels) are taken into account by being substracted from requirements when the zaiavki of an enterprise are made up.

The major categories on the distribution side are "production-operation needs" (which includes maintenance requirements) and "Construction." The "market fund" denotes that part of the output of the product which is distributed more or less without further processing to satisfy the consumption needs of the people. The two "reserves" are quite different from each other. The "state reserve" is a permanent one, built up as a protection against national disasters, natural or manmade. The "reserve of the Council of Ministers" is an operational reserve to be dispensed during the course of the years to firms which are overfulfilling their output targets and thus are in need of additional input materials, and to firms which did not get supplies which were allotted to them, because of supply failures.[36] The production categories on the sources and distribution sides, before the reorganization, were broken down by producing and consuming ministries.[37] They are now broken down by republics.

[33] Shein 54, p. 19.

[34] Material balances, in modified form, are also used by lower planning organs.

[35] Actually, the positive difference between stocks at suppliers at the beginning and end of the year is what comprises a source of distributable supply. A negative difference denotes an added demand for the product.

[36] The output targets of producers are set higher than the originally planned deliveries they have to make. This difference is what makes up the "reserves of the Council of Ministers." During the year the firms will receive orders telling them where to send this additional output. (Personal interview with a Soviet economist.)

[37] In most cases, there were a number of different ministries producing a given product.

Chart #2

MATERIAL BALANCE*

Product X

SOURCES	DISTRIBUTION
1. Production	1. Production-operation needs
a) By major producing Ministries (now by Republics)	a) By major user Ministries (now by Republics)
2. Imports	2. Construction
3. Other Sources	a) By major users
4. Stocks at suppliers, at beginning of period	3. Market Fund
a) By major supplier Ministries (now by Republics)	4. Export
	5. Increase of State Reserves
	6. Increase of Reserves of Council of Ministers
	7. Stocks at suppliers, at end of period
	a) By major supplier Ministries (now by Republics)

*This is a composite form. The categories often differ from product to product.

The material balances are used at two stages of Gosplan's work. First, they are used to assure consistency in the control figures (now the preliminary supply limits), and second, they are used in constructing the final draft of the annual economic plan. At the control figures stage, Gosplan uses its own estimates of sources and distribution, but in the final draft stage, the information which comes up from below is used. We will concentrate here on the final draft stage.

The crucial problem in material balance technology is how are the planned sources and distribution brought into balance when at first there is an imbalance? [38] Usually, the direction of an imbalance is that the demand for a product is greater than the originally planned supplies.[39] The procedure appears to be that the industrial departments of Gosplan (which are organized along product lines) work on the sources of each product, while the summary departments work on the distribution. The two work closely together in trying to achieve a balance, keeping each other constantly informed of the adjustments

[38] A subsidiary problem is: how is a change in the output target of one product reflected in the changes of other products?

[39] Personal interview with a Soviet economist. This can be logically deduced from the practice of padding orders by lower administrative organs.

each makes.[40] What steps do they take when it is found that the demand for a product is greater than the planned supply? [41]

The basic principle, it is claimed, is that a plan is not brought down to a "bottleneck," i.e., an output target of one branch is not reduced because of a "bottleneck" in the supply to it of a deficit commodity. This, one author states, would be the easiest way, but is sheer opportunism.[42]

What is done is that on the one hand the corresponding industrial department attempts to increase the supply of the deficit commodity. It sees if stocks at suppliers can be cut (further). Also, planned imports, in a few cases, may be increased. But the major effort is to increase current production. This is to be accomplished within the planned capacity, by better or more intensive use of equipment. Sometimes the planned introduction of new capacity may be speeded up so that more of the year is operated within the greater capacity.

At the same time that the industrial department is working on increasing the supply of the deficit commodity, the summary department is working on decreasing the demand for this commodity. The basic principle is to accomplish this without decreasing the output targets of the users of the deficit material. The method employed is to increase efficiency in the use of this material, to economize, to rationalize, to spread the advanced experience of the leading firms. In other words, pressure is applied to decrease (further) the input norms.[43] Another method is the substitution of nondeficit materials for the deficit. These are always described as "fully substitutable substitutes.[44] Throughout the balancing process, the priority principle is at work. Whenever possible, it is the sectors of secondary importance (usually the consumer oriented sectors) which have their allocations cut or are called upon to use substitutes. The emphasis is on guaranteeing the supply of the high priority sectors.

When a summary department makes changes which reduce the flow of the deficit commodity to other commodity sectors, it notifies the corresponding industrial departments. And when an industrial department increases the output of the deficit commodity in such a way as to call for an increase in required supplies, then it, in most cases, contacts the relevant summary departments.

To the extent that an imbalance is corrected by an increase in the output of a deficit commodity which is the type of increase that calls for an increase in the output of the materials used in its production, something similar to an iterative solution of the balancing problem might be envisaged. By an iterative solution, I mean one where the increase in the output of one commodity is followed by the increase in the output of all the inputs into that commodity, followed by the increase in the output of all the inputs into the inputs and so on down the line, all the time use being made of the set of input norms. Math-

---

[40] Personal interview with a Soviet economist.

[41] This is one of those clouded areas of administrative action, where a person would really have to be involved in the actual work before he could clearly analyze the method employed. The following "analysis" is based on personal interviews with Soviet economists and a number of written sources, including: *Zhukov 54*, pp. 103 ff.; *Braginskii 54*, pp. 292–294; *Strumilin 57*, pp. 54–56.

[42] *Strumilin 57*, p. 55. The phrase "deficit product" is used here to mean a product for which demand is greater than planned supply, during the process of plan construction.

[43] In a personal interview with a Soviet economist, the economist said that input norms could be decreased in two ways. One, he illustrated by tightening up his belt; the other was the method of increasing efficiency. He said they preferred to use the second method.

[44] It has also been suggested that the reserves of the Council of Ministers are originally set higher than required, so that, at the balancing stage, when the demand is greater than the supply, these reserves can be cut without any damage. But in a personal interview with a Soviet economist, it was strongly denied that such a method was used.

ematically, an infinite number of such steps will yield a perfectly consistent set of material balances.[45] But since the steps near the end become very small, the process may be stopped far short of infinity and an acceptably accurate solution derived.

It is frequently thought that the iterative approach is the basic method used by Soviet planners to achieve consistency in their plans. It do not think that this theory is correct. In order to see why, let us first look at the dimensions of the problem. How many steps, how many iterations would Gosplan have to perform in order to get a reasonably accurate approximation to a balanced plan? The number of iterations necessary, or in other words, the rate of convergence of the approximation procedure, depends on the structure of the economy—roughly speaking, on the degree of interrelatedness of the economy. The more interrelated an economy, the greater the number of iterations necessary. Unfortunately, data on the structure of the Soviet economy, in the detail necessary to give a precise answer to the question, are not available. But on the basis of *very crude* calculations, it might be said that somewhere between 6 and 13 iterations would be required.[46] It is inconceivable that Gosplan, under the conditions which prevailed, could have performed that number of iterations. First of all, Gosplan does not handle the problem in the formal way usually assumed in discussing iterative methods. It does not put together, into one list, all the imbalances which appear at the first

---

[45] This is so because, letting $[A]$=the matrix of input norms,

$$[I-A]^{-1}=[I+A+A^2+ \dots A^n] \text{ (where } n \rightarrow \infty)$$

The iterative procedure, discussed in the text, concerns the total effects (direct and indirect) of changes in total output levels rather than the calculation of a vector of total outputs starting from a given vector of final outputs. Formally, however, the two problems are similar; both involve the $[I-A]^{-1}$ matrix. This can be shown in the following way:

At the first attempted balancing of the material balances, a number of discrepancies between the originally planned supplies and demanded outputs appear (let us say they are all shortfalls):

Let,

$[A]$=matrix of input norms
X_s=vector of originally planned supplies
Y=vector of planned final outputs
X_d=vector of the calculated demands

Then,

$$[A]X_s+Y=X_d, \text{ where } X_d \geqq X_s \quad (1)$$

Now let,

ΔX=the unknown vector of changes in X_s necessary to get a consistent set of material balances.

Set,

$$[I-A]\Delta X=(X_d-X_s)$$

$$\Delta X=[I-A]^{-1}(X_d-X_s) \quad (2)$$

Add ΔX to X_s to get a new level of planned supplies and the plan will be balanced:

$$[A](X_s+\Delta X)+Y=(X_s+\Delta X) \quad (3)$$

(Proof of (3) is relatively simple, once it is seen that: $[A][I-A]^{-1}=[I-A]^{-1}-[I]$)

The iterative procedure discussed in this paper is the iterative approximation to $[I-A]^{-1}(X_d-X_s)$ from equation (2).

[46] The U.S. Bureau of Labor Statistics developed a method of approximating $[I-A]^{-1}[Y]$ through a series of iterations, followed by an extrapolation procedure. Using American data, they found that even with an extrapolation after the last iteration, in order to guarantee an acceptable level of precision, they would have to perform from 5-11 iterations ("Ritz 50," p. 4; "Evans 54," p. 78). The rate of convergence of $(I+A+A^2 \dots)$ depends upon the dominant characteristic root of [A], which is roughly related to the degree of interrelatedness of an economy ("Evans 54," p. 83). If the common assumption that the U.S. economy has a higher degree of interrelatedness than the Soviet economy is true, then it is possible that the rate of convergence of a Soviet matrix would be slightly faster than that of a U.S. matrix. Secondly, though Gosplan does not appear to use anything nearly as sophisticated as an extrapolation procedure, it most likely has developed some informal speed-up methods, such as increasing an output target more than the original shortfall called for. How much it does this and by how much it would speed up the convergence are hard to tell. Taking all these considerations into account, it would probably be safer to set the lower bound of the number of iterations required for a Soviet matrix somewhere toward the lower end of the number required for U.S. matrices by the BLS iteration and extrapolation method. Let us set it at 6.

The upper bound of 13 was calculated by means of an heroic adaptation of a method devised by Waugh. (See "Waugh 50.")

approximation, and then in an organized way apply the entire set of input norms to these imbalances. Rather, each product is handled by a separate section (indeed, by two separate sections), which keeps communicating its moves to the other sections. There does not appear to be any set order of communication such as first section A makes its changes, then section B, etc.; all sections work simultaneously.[47] Secondly, in the postwar period, Gosplan was trying to balance an extremely large number of material balances, ranging between the current 760 and a high of 1,600. The problem of working changes through that many different balances is a formidable one for any bureaucracy. Thirdly, all this was and is done without the aid of electronic computers. The method of material balances, in the form in which it exists, is not amenable to computer technology.

But we need not rely solely on deductive reasoning in this matter. In a recent book, the director of the Economic Research Institute of Gosplan stated, that it was rare for even three or four iterations to be performed in tracing the effects of a correction in an output target:

> Because of the great labor intensity of the calculation of changes in the material balances and the insufficiency of time for the completion of such work in practice sometimes only those balances which are linked by first order relationships are changed. As regards relationships of the second order, and especially of the third and fourth order, changes in the balances are made only in those cases where the changes are conspicuous (zametnyi).[48]

This statement points out the additional fact that Gosplan's calculation of indirect effects is not uniform; it is limited to "conspicuous" changes. Another facet of the nonuniform approach is that a change need not be passed on in the increased output even of all direct inputs, but can be balanced out by decreases on the demand side of any of these inputs. These nonuniformities in handling the problem make it difficult to "count iterations" or to see an iterative process clearly.

I believe that more important in Gosplan's balancing methodology than iteration procedures is the use of techniques which avoid second-round effects. This is certainly true when changes are made on the distribution side of the material balance of a deficit commodity. Pressure is put on users of the deficit commodity to economize its use by producing more efficiently. The supply of the deficit input material is cut without any change in the output target of the product which uses it. In this way the original rebalancing change does not reverberate through the entire system of material balances; it has no second-round effects. It is less clear to what extent avoidance of second-round effects is important in the making of changes on the sources side. When stocks are reduced, there are no second-round effects, and when imports are increased there are little if any second-round effects. But when a production target is increased in an effort to close a balance, is this always passed on to other sectors in increased orders for input materials? I have heard and read contradictory answers to this question.[49] I think the safest thing to say is that

---

[47] Personal interview with a Soviet economist.

[48] "Efimov 57," p. 107. If there are "n" centrally allocated commodities, then to calculate the direct inputs into a single output change, you need "n" multiplications (ignoring zeros). But to calculate the inputs into the inputs, you need "n^2" multiplications and for each succeeding iteration, you need "n^2" multiplications. Since $760^2=577,600$ and $1600^2=2,560,000$, it is no wonder that Gosplan, operating without electronic computers, has had to limit itself to only "conspicuous" relationships.

[49] For example, in a personal interview with a Soviet economist, it was said that the practice was to back up increased output targets with increased supplies. On the other hand, an economist in an extremely good dissertation, wrote that when trying to close a balance, the attempt is made to increase the output of a deficit product "by means of internal reserves of production, such as better use of equipment and materials * * *" ("Zhukov 54," p. 103).

usually increased supplies are ordered, but at times, increased output targets of the deficit commodity are to be met by more efficient production methods without additional supplies, thus avoiding second-round effects.[50]

If the analysis offered here is correct, then we are led to the following hypothesis about the balancing methodology used by Soviet planners. By relying heavily on balancing methods which avoid second-round effects, through pressure on input norms, Gosplan contributes to the further tightening of the plan. That is to say, the very planning methodology used by Gosplan (the material balances and the ways in which they are balanced) itself adds an additional tightening to the plan as the balances in the final draft are hammered out at the top planning level.

WEAKNESSES OF SUPPLY PLANNING

In this section, we will discuss the problems connected specifically with the planning of supply, not supply problems in general (see "Introduction"). First the major planning problems as they existed before the reorganization will be described, and then one or two of the possible effects of the reorganization will be indicated.

Unrealistic balances

The first question which arises is: How good are the balances worked out in the national economic plan? Are they realistic balances, or are they to some extent mere "paper balances"? From speaking with Soviet economists, one gets the impression that most economists are quite proud of their method of material balances despite some admitted shortcomings. I am sure their feelings were accurately represented by a Polish economist who told me: "The method of material balances is a primitive method, but it works." On the other hand, the Soviet economy is constantly beset by shortages. Are these shortages, these "imbalances," caused by faulty, unrealistic balancing of plans on the part of Gosplan, or are they caused by other factors operating in the Soviet economy? (See below.) A number of recent official pronouncements and analyses by Soviet economists lead one to believe that unrealistic balances are, at least, partly to blame. Khrushchev, at the 20th Party Congress, claimed that sometimes imbalances arise which are caused not only by failures to meet the established plans, but also by the fact that the plans themselves are deficient.[51] The resolution of the December 1956 Plenum of the Communist Party stated that the top planning organs do not base their plans on the "real possibilities" of supplying the required materials to meet the established output targets. This leads to "excess tightness in the fulfillment of plans." [52] In the book by the director of Gosplan's Economic Research Institute, mentioned earlier, he claims that the balancing methodology used, its lack of a sufficient number of full iterations, leads to the accumulation of "a number of errors in various parts of the plan, which under certain conditions manifest themselves, giving rise to certain imbalances and tensions in various material resources." [53]

---

[50] There are also cases where an imbalance results from improper planning of types of products. For example, there may be enough steel planned, but it is in the wrong assortment (even at Gosplan allocated categories). Correction of such imbalances does not involve many second-round effects.

[51] Cited in "Koldomasov 56," p. 32.

[52] "Direktivy IV," p. 670.

[53] "Efimov 57," p. 107.

Thus there is some evidence that at times the balances achieved by Gosplan do contain elements of "paper consistency." This results, in large measure, from Gosplan's inability, in the material balances method, to cover enough of the indirect effects of a change in an output target, and its consequent reliance on pressure methods, which although having positive aspects from the point of view of forcing economic growth, at times introduce unrealistic relationships in the balances.

Lateness

A major problem of planning concerns the frequent failure of the planning organs to complete the annual supply plan before the beginning of the planned year. The Soviet literature is full of complaints about final plans not coming down to the enterprise until January, February, or March, and sometimes even later. This failure to complete the plan on time is not too difficult to understand when one thinks of what a tremendously involved job it is for a bureaucracy first to work up a balanced supply plan for an entire economy in a great number of aggregated indicators and then for subordinate levels to disaggregate the plan into the necessary operational detail. This problem was made even more difficult by the discontinuous nature of the annual plans before the reorganization: "* * * the planning system that developed was such that the annual plans broke off at the end of the calendar year and therefore had to be drawn up every year from scratch, as it were." [54]

Some of the methods adopted by Soviet planners to cope with this time problem are of interest. One is what might be called the "correction principle." In order to speed up the planning process, planning organs usually begin their own work before receiving information from the previous planning stage. When they do receive the information, they then make the necessary corrections in their preliminary estimates.[55] As we have seen, work on the zaiavki began before Gosplan released the control figures and then when the control figures came out, the zaiavki were corrected. Also the specification process began before the confirmation of the plan by the Council of Ministers, and then the changes it made were incorporated by correcting the specified orders. A second speedup method sometimes used was to begin the construction of the zaiavki and the working out of the input norms not at the enterprise, but at the glavk or even the ministry.[56] A third method was the practice of issuing "advance fondy." In order to allow an enterprise to operate during the first quarter in the absence of a supply plan, it was allotted "advance fondy" usually in the amount of 23 to 25 percent of its previous year's total allotment.

Lack of coordination

There is often a lack of coordination between the supply plan of an enterprise and its output and financial plans.[57] This is partly a result of poor planning originally, but probably it is more a result of the constant changes introduced in plans both before and after they are confirmed. Changes are frequently made in one set of plans (say,

[54] "P. Kh. Editorial 58" (translated in the "Current Digest of the Soviet Press," X : 33, p. 11).
[55] This correction process is not limited to the period of the construction of the plan, but continues during the year, while the plan is in operation.
[56] "Savkin 56," p. 61, and a personal interview with a Soviet economist.
[57] For example, see "Turetskii 57," p. 108 and "Kalinin 58," pp. 43–44.

output) without the necessary changes being made in the other set (say, supply).

Specification

One of the weakest parts of the entire planning process is the stage wherein the plan is brought down to the level of the enterprise and is put into operational form—the stage where the aggregate allotments are turned into contracts for specific goods. Remember, the system was: The fondy were distributed by the ministry to the glavk and by the glavk to the enterprise. The enterprise worked up a list of specified requirements within the limits of the fondy. The specified orders came up the hierarchy of the user ministry and a combined specified order was sent to the main administration of sales of each corresponding producer ministry. This ministerial main administration of sales then sent out specified production and delivery orders to the producing firms. The weaknesses of this process lay primarily within three major categories: Excessive centralization, the administrative objectives of sales administrations, and the time factor.

(i) Excessive centralization: The sales administration of the ministry assigned detailed orders directly to the producing firms. The frequent enormity of this job is indicated by the fact that every year the metals main administration of sales issued about 500,000 specified production and delivery orders.[58] This excessive centralization frequently led to the lack of coordination between different plans mentioned in the previous section. Producing firms were often given delivery assignments greater than their planned outputs.[59] The rational geographic distribution of orders was not sufficiently studied, resulting in excessively long transportation hauls. Contract details which should have been set in negotiations between producer and consumer firms were actually set by the producing ministry sales administration and the consuming ministry supply administration.[60] This meant that the real needs of consuming firms and the real production capabilities and specialties of producing firms were often not adequately perceived. It also meant that the efforts to inculcate cost minimization at the enterprise level were weakened, because the enterprise was deprived of the power to decide what materials to use.

(ii) Administrative objectives of sales administration: The sales administrations were concerned with the problems of the producing units rather than with those of the consuming units. Their objective, in the last stage of plan construction, was to achieve an efficient loading of the productive capacities of the firms within their own ministry. As a result of this one-sided concern, consuming firms often ended up with an irrational array of suppliers. Frequently, a firm was to be supplied by a large number of suppliers rather than having its orders concentrated in a few. In fact, as specifications were made out for each quarter, suppliers sometimes were changed from one quarter to the next.[61] These factors gave rise to serious scheduling and coordination problems. Another weakness was that the sales administrations did not put enough pressure on producing firms to adapt their detailed output assortments to the specific needs of the consuming firms, thus leading to imbalances in the detailed supplies and demands.[62] The

58 "Gal'perin 57-1," p. 19.
59 Ibid.
60 Ibid., pp. 19–20.
61 "Kalinin 58," p. 45.
62 "Gal'perin 57," p. 85.

supply administrations of the consuming ministries were forced to accede to these imbalances because of their inferior power in the prevailing sellers' market. Finally, the aim of spreading technical progress was weakened because the sales administrations had little motivation to force the production if new and more economical (in use) types of materials.[63]

(iii) Time factors: A firm was supposed to make out its specified input requirements 2 to 3 months before the beginning of the planned year, at a time when it did not know its detailed output plan. This created a number of difficulties in matching specific inputs and outputs. Due to the nature and timing of their planning process, Russian planners were forced to compress the planning of essentially successive problems into one time period. This was one of the factors which led to the great number of revisions in the plan while it was in operation.

All that has been said, here, about the weaknesses of supply planning should not be understood to imply that they were the sole cause of the general unreliability of the supply system. For there are two other major causal factors. One is the overall practice of tight planning; the other is the poor operation of supply organs. The supply plan could be perfectly constructed, perfectly balanced, but if the overall economic plan were very tight (marginal stocks of materials, tight construction schedules, little slack anywhere), then a few failures to meet some individual targets would create significant supply difficulties throughout the system. Also, plans could be moderately slack and well constructed, but if the supply bureaucracy operated in an inefficient manner, then supply difficulties would result. All three factors are important causes of supply deficiencies.

One of the primary aims of the reorganization was to improve the operation of the supply system and, along with this, the planning of supply.[64] It is still too early to evaluate the effects of the reorganization on supply planning, but some comments can be made. The changed role of the long-term plan, with its more detailed, operational yearly subdivisions, will probably help to speed up the planning process and to provide needed continuity in the annual plans.[65] On the other hand, specification procedures do not seem to have improved at all.[66] And it is hard to judge what effects the reorganization will have on the vital problem of achieving balances in the plan—the prime function of the material balances method.

But a new possibility now looms on the horizon, one which might have a profound effect on this balancing methodology. It is the possibility of adapting modern mathematical methods and computer technology to the planning of the supply system.

MATHEMATICAL METHODS AND ELECTRONIC COMPUTERS

Limitations of space do not permit a full discussion of the possible use by Soviet planners of mathematical methods. But let me here

[63] Ibid.

[64] The prime concern of the reorganization in the supply field was with the deficiencies in the operation of the system, rather than, necessarily, with the planning of it. The major operational deficiencies, which resulted primarily from the absence of cross-ministerial coordination, according to Soviet sources, were retardation of specialization and subcontracting for components; supply mainly within ministerial channels and thus often irrationally long transportation hauls; failure to develop diversified firms producing a range of byproducts from the given inputs; and duplication of staffs and organizations.

[65] In a personal interview with a Soviet economist, I was told that the plans for 1958 and 1959 were late. But this was because they were unfamiliar with the new system, they said.

[66] See the strongly critical comments in "Gal'perin 58," pp. 50–52.

just briefly outline what the Russians are saying and what they are doing about the possible use of one of these methods.

Input-Output (I–O) is a mathematical method, which analyzes the interrelationships existing in an economy.[67] Its great advantage over the material balances method is that it puts the technical intersector relationships among economic sectors into one unified scheme and allows them to be expressed mathematically in a very convenient and useful form—useful in the sense that vast numbers of equations can easily be handled through the use of electronic computers.[68] Soviet planners, by means of I–O techniques and electronic computers, after they had put together a realistic set of input norms, could rapidly construct a completely balanced output and supply plan.

Since 1956, Russian economists have been discussing the possibilities of adapting I–O techniques to their balancing methodology. Perhaps the first question which comes to mind is why were they so late. Professor Leontief's first book on I–O was published in 1941 and serious work on I–O problems began in the West soon after World War II. Among the reasons for the Russians' delay, I think, one can include bureaucratic inertia and opposition, low level of the necessary mathematical skills among economists, and the relative unavailability to economists of computers until recent years. But as important as any of these, is the fact that the use of mathematical methods in economics was, up to a few years ago, considered to be anti-Marxist. However, now I–O (also linear programing) has been separated from other econometric methods, and is considered not to be "negated by the Marxist theory of political economy." [69] In addition, in an attempt to add further legitimacy, it is now claimed, but not proved, that since Professor Loentief was born and educated in Russia, his ideas were developed on the basis of early Russian experiments with national economic balances. Yet the charge of unorthodoxy is still a potent weapon, and the supporters of I–O, it would appear, still have to tread carefully.[70]

The Soviet discussion of I–O has both its negative and positive camps. Members of both camps almost always begin with the statement that I–O cannot be used for prediction purposes in the capitalist economy, because the capitalist economy is completely unpredictable. Although some do say that it could be used for more limited problems, such as mobilization. The rest of the criticisms are not too different from those one hears in the West: assumption of constant coefficients, no substitution, no restraints, staticness, exclusion of capital equipment. It is common for a critic to end his article with an admission that I–O can perhaps play a small, restricted role in Soviet economics.

[67] In the I–O method, the output of each sector is divided into flows to each other producing sector and also to final demands (consumption, investment, government, and foreign trade). Starting from the intersector flows, a set of direct input coefficients is derived (direct input of one product per unit output of another product). Then by solving a set of equations, the direct and indirect input coefficients per unit of final output are found. These tell us, for example, not only how much coal is directly required to produce one automotible for final use, but how much coal is needed for the steel which goes into the automobile and so on. Thus, the direct and indirect input coefficient of coal per automobile tells us that if we increase the output for final use of automobiles by one unit how much more coal will be required throughout the economy to support this change in output. In other words, with these total cost coefficients, if we have an estimate of final demand (be it forecast or plan), we can determine the total output of each sector required for the production of this final bill of goods. I–O makes use of electronic computers to solve, rapidly, large system of equations. Its development is associated with the name of Prof. Wassily Leontief of Harvard University.

[68] One weakness of the material balances is that they are similar to the rows of an I–O table, while the important technical relationships in an economy are to be found in the columns.

[69] "Nikitin 58," p. 103.

[70] It is a sobering irony that the U.S. Government's I–O program was discontinued in 1953 because of allegations that in some way it was a socialist scheme and a threat to private enterprise. (See Business Week, Aug. 29, 1953, p. 26.)

The supporters of I–O argue that it is a tool which could be used to utmost advantage in Soviet planning. It would assure a well-balanced plan. Through the use of total cost coefficients, the total effects of a change in any one output target could be calculated, and thus the necessary changes in all other outputs could be made.[71] And what is of extreme importance, all the required calculations could be done rapidly on electronic computers. One writer emphasized this point by showing that in the calculation of the total cost coefficients for a 44 sector I–O model (remember, at one point, Gasplan had to balance 1,600 "sectors") 2,500,000 arithmetic operations were necessary. Yet an electronic computer was able to complete this task within 8 hours.[72] Another advantage is that, after a balanced plan is derived, the calculation of the actual supply plan, i.e., the actual material flows from one sector to another, would be a simple matter—merely a multiplication of direct input coefficients times the levels of output of the corresponding products. Besides these basic points, supporters argue that changes during the operation of a short term or long term plan could more efficiently be made with the aid of total cost coefficients. The spreading of technical progress could be aided by using planned direct input coefficients rather than statistically derived ones as the basic data for I–O calculations. Under the new organization of industry, regional I–O balances could be made. On another level, I–O could be used for working out internally consistent prices. And finally, it could be used for some purely statistical purposes such as the calculation of certain economic proportions, comparisons of the labor and materials intensities of different products and certain statistical comparisons with the West.

If Russian planners were to adopt I–O methodology as it is practiced in the West, then among the many changes in planning techniques this would involve, there would be one of fundamental importance. This is the narrowing of the scope of politically determined basic plan goals from total outputs to final outputs (i.e., outputs for final uses: consumption, investment, etc.). In Western I–O practice, one starts with a given set of final demands and by means of a set of direct and indirect input coefficients, one solves for the levels of total outputs. Soviet planners, in the material balances method, start from a set of total output goals, which basically are determined by the political authorities in the society. That is the political authorities set targets, which include not only the amount of a product going to final uses, but also the amount, which is needed within the economy to produce other products.

Are Soviet economists advocating such a change? According to a number of leading economists, including the very highly placed Academician V. S. Nemchinov, they are not.[73] They intend to retain total outputs as the starting data for plan construction.[74] The primary use of I–O, according to these economists, will be to work out a number of different balanced variants of the plan. They say that

[71] Some articles point out that experiments have shown the total coefficients often to be many times larger than the direct. Thus, the ignoring of indirect effects leads to significant errors. (See "Tolkachev 58" and "Grebtsov 59," p. 61.)

[72] "Efimov 57," p. 11.

[73] Personal interview with Academician Nemchinov and other Soviet economists.

[74] The Soviet approach to the total output of steel and the total output of electricity as objectives in themselves is in part determined by the symbolic significance of these basic indexes as indicators of successful economic growth. But it is also a recognition of the fact that a high rate of growth of these basic industrial commodities is perhaps a safer assurance of economic growth than planning from a final bill of goods would be when foresight, knowledge, and techniques are still imperfect.

the material balances method enables them to work out only one balanced variant of the plan, but with I–O they will be able to work out many from which they will choose the "best." [75] In addition, they claim that the material balances approach will remain the dominant one and that I–O techniques will only be an auxiliary planning mechanism.

There are, however, a few Soviet economists who do favor planning from a set of final outputs:

> * * * the starting point of planning must be the final bill of goods [investment and consumption]. It is not sufficient to produce much steel or cement, lumber, or cotton. The aim is to produce a sufficient amount of machines, buildings, furniture, cloth, etc.[76]

Another possibility is a mixed model, where some total output targets and some final outputs are given, and the remaining total outputs and final outputs are derived by solving the set of equations.[77]

Only time will tell how far Russian planning will go into I–O techniques, but it does appear probable that in the beginning at least, its use will be restricted to the calculation of a number of plan variants and the use of total cost coefficients to calculate the total effects of any change in the plan.

As regards actual experimentation, there have been reports so far of four models worked out, including 9, 15, 17, and 44 order systems.[78] These are all pilot models. For a system to have any operational significance it would have to be of the order of 500–1,000 sectors. There is also an experiment now in progress on a regional I–O study involving a single economic region (the Mordovskoi region). This is based on the method used in a U.S. study of the state of Utah.[79]

The new Laboratory for the Use of Statistics and Mathematical Methods in Economics, headed by Academician Nemchinov and the famous mathematician, L. V. Kantorovich, and possessing a staff of about 20, is working on I–O problems, mainly on problems of adapting statistical data to computer use.[80] It is scheduled to operate, in the near future, at the computing center, which is being erected in Novosibirsk. In addition, there are people working on I–O in the Economic Research Institute of Gosplan and in the Institute for Electronic Control Machines of the Academy of Sciences.

Thus Soviet economists are beginning to take notice of I–O and the possibilities of applying it to problems of planning. I–O in the Soviet Union has come a far way from the days when it was almost taboo to discuss it or work on it. Yet, on the other hand, it has by

---

[75] Any vector X would be a feasible plan as long as no element of Y were negative, where $Y=[I-A]\ X$. One of the problems involved here is, of course, how do you choose the "best." But this is a problem of a different order. A choice out of many is still better than no choice at all.

[76] "Belkin 57," p. 144.

[77] See "Grebtsov 59," p. 62. I was told in Warsaw, that Polish planners are working on a combined model of this type.

[78] See "Grebtsov 59," "Tolkachev 58" and "Belkin 57."

[79] Personal interview with a Soviet economist. For a description of the Utah study see Moore and Petersen, "Regional Analysis: An Interindustry Model of Utah," Review of Economics and Statistics, November 1955.

[80] Personal interview with a Soviet economist. This is a major problem. There have been numerous complaints that Soviet statistics are not adequate for use in I–O work. The main criticism is that they do not clearly show the technical relationships between sectors. For example, see "Tolkachev, 58," "Grebtsov 59," p. 57, and "Nemchinov 59," pp. 33–34. Nemchinov's apparent suggestion that some I–O research be treated as classified work, in the same way as atomic energy and rocket research, has been interpreted as an attempt to gain access to detailed statistical data.

no means swept the field.[81] Much of the struggle still lies ahead. One bit of evidence of this is the extreme sensitivity, which supporters of I–O still retain, to questions of its origins and orthodoxy.

III. Conclusions

The general nature of Soviet supply planning can perhaps be best described as a combination of the central planning of aggregate categories with the successive setting of details down through the planning hierarchy and the application of constant pressure, from the center to tighten production methods and to economize materials. This is not a picture of finely calculated balances, but is a combination whose aim is to contribute to economic growth.

One of the important operating criteria in the Soviet economy is the priority principle. The possible negative effects on economic growth of imbalances in supply plans are lessened because there are low priority buffer sectors to absorb the shocks of these imbalances. The operation of the priority principle also lessens the negative effects of the interaction of imperfect supply planning, overall tight planning and a not overly efficient supply bureaucracy.

Even though overall tight planning prevails, it should not be thought that the Soviet economy is everywhere so taut that the slightest failure in any one place will cause the whole economy to burst. Some operational leeway does exist. There are usually some unemployed or underemployed labor and materials to be found, which can be pressed into service when the need arises. This leeway is, in large measure, a result of the "informal activities" of the Soviet firm.[82]

As an economy grows more developed, the number of interrelationships within it becomes larger. This intensifies the problems of supply planning. At the same time, however, the radical changes in the structure of the economy diminish, and thus supply relationships become more stable. This lessens the problems of supply planning. Yet it would appear that in recent years the increasing interrelationships have caused the Russians to become increasingly concerned with the deficiencies of their supply system.

One of the more promising means for counteracting these deficiencies is through the adoption of input-output techniques. The original flush of enthusiasm in the West for I–O may have diminished somewhat, and there are many perhaps who now feel that not too much should be expected of it. However, these criticisms apply to its use in the West. It should be kept in mind that under the type of economic organization that exists in the Soviet Union today, they have to plan their supply system. Thus, the appropriate question for them is not whether I–O is an ideal method, but whether it is better than the method Soviet planners use now—material balances. As far as assuring balance in the plan and speeding up the process of plan construction, there is no doubt of the superiority of I–O techniques. Yet the material balances method does have a significant organizational ad-

[81] In a personal interview with a Soviet economist, the economist complained that they could not get proper statistics for I–O work. When questioned on this, he said the data could be made available, but it would cost money to collect and process it and their problem now was to convince the higher-ups that I–O was a worthwhile project so that they could get the necessary budgetary allocations. He was told that this was a problem we could understand. See also the recent speech by L. V. Kantorovich in which he said, "The fear of mathematics has by no means been overcome" (Vestnik Akademii Nauk S.S.S.R., 1959:4, p. 61 and remarks by A. D. Kurskii, ibid., 1959:2, pp. 5–6).

[82] See "Berliner 57" and "Granick 59."

vantage. It allows for contact between planners and administrators and thus allows for the operation of certain pressure levers during the construction of the plan. What should perhaps be expected, therefore, is that the Russians will adopt I–O techniques in such a way as to combine it with these positive features of the material balances method.

If I–O techniques are adopted and thus the planning process speeded up, more time would be left for the troublesome specification stage. This would help, but an effective solution to the specification problem depends fundamentally on the creation of direct and stable relations between producers and users. It also depends on a diminution in the tightness of plans so as to lessen the degree of sellers' market and make the market power of buyers more equal to that of sellers.

This discussion has concentrated on centralized supply planning methods. It is theoretically possible, of course, for more decentralized methods to be used, ones that would give lower level units more freedom to make their own economic decisions. However, the efficacy of any meaningful decentralization would depend upon the significant improvement of the Soviet price system, which up to now has been incapable of playing an effective role in the Soviet industrial supply system.

Sources Used

Belkin 57: V. Belkin, "O primenenii elektronnykh vychislitel'nykh mashin v planirovanii i statistike narodnogo khoziaistva," Voprosy Ekonomiki, 1957 : 12.

Berliner 57: J. S. Berliner, "Factory and Manager in the U.S.S.R.," Cambridge, 1957.

Braginskii 54: B. I. Braginskii and N. S. Koval', "Organizatsiia planirovaniia narodnogo khoziaistva S.S.S.R." Moscow, 1954.

Demichev 57: G. M. Demichev, "Material'no-tekhnicheskoe snabzhenie na zheleznodorozhnom transporte," Moscow, 1957, (49 pp.).

Directivy: "Direktivy KPSS i sovetskogo pravitel'stva po khoziaistvennym voprosam, vols. I–IV," Moscow, 1957–58.

Efimov 57: A. N. Efimov, "Perestroika upravleniia promyshlennost'iu i stroitel'stvom v S.S.S.R., Moscow, 1957.

Evans 54: W. Duane Evans, "Input-output Computations," from T. Barna (editor), "The Structural Interdependence of the Economy," (Proceedings of an International Conference on Input-output Analysis, Varenna, 1954) New York, N.Y.

Gal'perin 57: N. Gal'perin, "Sovremennye zadachi organizatsii material'notekhmicheskogo snabzheniia proizvodstva," Voprosy Ekonomiki, 1957 : 4.

Gal'perin 58: "Sovershenstvovanie material'no-tekhnicheskogo snabzheniia i bor'ba protiv mestnicheskikh tendentsii," "Voprosy Ekonomiki, 1958 : 7.

Gal'perin 57–1: "Novoe v organizatsii material'no-tekhnicheskogo snabzheniia, Gospolitizdat," Moscow, 1957.

Glusker 54: B. Glusker, P. Krylov, "O sisteme pokzatelei narodnokhoziaistvennogo plana," Planovoe Khoziaistvo, 1954, No. 5.

Granick 57: D. Granick, "Organization and Technology in Soviet Metalworking: Some Conditioning Factors," American Economic Review, XLVII : 2 (May 1957).

Granick 59: "An Organizational Model of Soviet Industrial Planning," Journal of Political Economy, LXVII:2 (April 1959).

Grebtsov 59: G. Grebtsov, "K voprosu o razrabotke svodnogo material'nogo balansa," Planovoe Khoziaistvo, 1959 : 6.

Grossman 55: G. Grossman, "In the Land of Paper Pyramids," "Problems of Communism," IV: 4 (July–August 1955).

Kalinin 58: I. Kalinin, "Sovershenstvovat' organizatsiiu material'no-tekhnicheskogo snabzheniia v promyshlennosti" Kommunist, 1958 : 18 (December 1958).

Karpov 58: P. Karpov, "Organizatsiia i planirovanie material'no-tekhnicheskogo snabzheniia v novykh usloviiakh upreavleniia promyshlennost'iu i stroitel' stvom," Planovoe Khoziaistvo, 1958 : 7.

Koldomasov 56: Iu. Koldomasov, "Voprosy postroeniia material'nykh balansov v narodnokhoziaistvennom plane", Planovoe Khoziaistvo, 1956:4.
Koldomasov 59: -----, "Voprosy organizatsii i planirovaniia material'no-tekhnicheskogo snabzheniia," Planovoe Khoziaistvo, 1959:4.
Kosiachenko 46: G. Kosiachenko, "Preduprezhedenie disproportsii v narodnom khoziaistve—odna iz vazhneishikh zadach planirovaniia," Planovoe Khoziaistvo, 1946:4.
Lokshin 52: E. Iu. Lokshin, Planirovanie material'no-tekhnicheskogo snabzheniia narodnogo khoziaistva S.S.S.R., Moscow, 1952.
Nemchinov 59: V. S. Nemchinov, "Sovremennye problemy sovetskoi ekonomicheskoi nauki," Voprosy Ekonomiki, 1959:4.
Nikitin 58: S. Nikitin, "Ekonometrika v sovremennoi burzhuaznoi ekonomicheskoi nauke," Nauchnye doklady vysshei shkoly, ekonomicheskie nauki, 1958:2.
Novick 49: D. Novick, M. L. Anshen, W. C. Truppner, "Wartime Production Controls," New York, 1949.
Perov 58: G. V. Perov, "God raboty sovnarkhozov," Partiinaia zhizn', July 14, 1958.
Planovoe Khoziaistvo Editorial 58: "Planirovanie narodnogo khoziaistva—na uroven' vozrosshikh zadach," Planovoe Khoziaistvo, 1958:6.
Ritz 50: P. M. Ritz, Iterative Method for Applying a Bill of Goods to an Interindustry Matrix," Technical Memorandum No. 1, Bureau of Labor Statistics, July 6, 1950, Washington, D.C.
Savkin 56: A. Savkin, "Zadachi uluchsheniia material'no-tekhnicheskogo snabzheniia promyshlennosti," Planovoe Khoziaistvo, 1956:1.
Shein 54: P. A. Shein, "Material'no-tekhnicheskoe snabzhenie sotsialisticheskogo promyshlennogo predpriiatiia," Moscow, 1954.
Strumilin 57: S. G. Strumilin, "Planirovanie v. S.S.S.R.," Moscow, 1957.
Tolkachev 58: A. Tolkachev, "Elektronnye mashiny i voprosy planirovaniia," Promyshlenno-ekonomicheskaia gazeta, Mar. 19, 1958, p. 2.
Turetskii 57: I. Turetskii, "Ob uluchshenii snabzheniia predpriatii i material'nykh zapasakh promyshlennosti," Voprosy Ekonomiki, 1957:4.
Waugh 50: F. V. Waugh, "Inversion of the Leontief Matrix by Power Series," Econometrica, 18:2 (April 1950).
Zhukov 54: V. N. Zhukov, "Voprosy raspredeleniia sredstov proizvodstva v promyshlennosti S.S.S.R.," Kandidatskaia dissertatsiia, Institut Ekonomiki an S.S.S.R., Moscow, 1954. (Lenin Library, Moscow.)

TRANSPORTATION

SOME ASPECTS OF THE STRUCTURE AND GROWTH OF SOVIET TRANSPORTATION

(By Ernest W. Williams, Jr., Columbia University)

At the outset of this essay on certain phases of Soviet transportation development, it is well to put the reader on notice that I am not a specialist in Soviet economics nor a longstanding student of Soviet affairs. My work on Soviet transportation began in conjunction with the Soviet economy study of the National Bureau of Economic Research. It was rationalized upon the theory that one familiar with the American transportation scene by long study could contribute something to an understanding of Soviet transportation practice and could supply an interpretation of that practice in the light of our own experience. I was aided materially by the fact that Prof. Holland Hunter's excellent work was already in an advanced state, by the fact that James H. Blackman had made important contributions in the American literature, and by the further fact that I had the assistance for several years of George Nowak whose familiarity with the language and sources and whose great industry make it possible to explore a wide range of Soviet materials and to assemble additional statistical series. Although the work of others has doubtless influenced my interpretation of the available materials, I must accept full responsibility for that interpretation. Moreover, it should be noticed that the main body of my work on Soviet transportation was completed several years ago and that I have not had the resources to keep abreast of the most recent materials.

SOVIET TRANSPORTATION DEVELOPMENT UNUSUAL

In many respects the development of transportation in the U.S.S.R. is unparalleled. The present transportation system has certain characteristics, moreover, which set it apart from any other. In volume of traffic handled, stated in the usual quantititave measures, the Soviet transportation system is the largest of any in the world apart from that of the United States. Measured in this way it is and has been growing faster than our system and is performing a transport task of steadily increasing magnitude.

Perhaps the most noteworthy features in the departure of Soviet practice from that found elsewhere are to be seen in (*a*) the especially heavy reliance upon railroads for intercity movement of freight and passengers; (*b*) the intensity with which the railroad plant is worked; (*c*) the adjustment of railroad technology to overall resources within the economy and to the requirements of the general developmental policies; (*d*) the measures taken to control the volume and character of traffic in the effort to minimize transport outputs (and thus to minimize inputs in this industry, especially those of capital goods);

and (*e*) the limited investment in facilities, particularly in highways, which might provide scope for the development of transport operations in intercity movement other than those of the "common-carrier" system. Soviet transport development appears to have been severely controlled, especially through the capital budget. The cloth has been cut very fine at times in the effort to avoid committing more resources to the transportation system than were required to meet the needs of other sectors of the economy. The transportation system appears to have been under pressure almost continually during the Soviet period. Yet the evidence is slight that its performance has seriously hindered economic growth even during the widely advertised transportation crisis of the thirties.

There is, of course, in any economic system a close relationship between transportation development and the rate and character of economic growth. The measurement of the growth of freight traffic may serve, therefore, to provide a check upon the statistics which purport to record the progress of industrial and agricultural output. It was partly with this possibility in mind that the National Bureau included transportation among the subjects to be studied. Yet a direct relating of traffic data to production data would not serve the purpose fully. For Soviet freight traffic data have been under suspicion in the Western World along with the data on production. So great, indeed, is the reported traffic performance of the Soviet railways in comparison with the reported level of plant and equipment that a good deal of suspicion has attached to the traffic data. Hence an examination of the character of plant and equipment and of the operating and traffic practices is essential in order to reach a judgment about the credibility of the reported traffic. Such an examination is essential, in any event, to afford an understanding of the nature of the Soviet accomplishment in transportation.

SOVIET FREIGHT TRAFFIC COMPARED WITH THAT OF THE UNITED STATES

Tables 1 and 2 present, without the qualifications and explanations, the data on total intercity freight traffic in the United States and the U.S.S.R. as previously published.[1] It is not necessary here, to record the extent to which and the methods by which some of the components were estimated. Because of highly centralized control and a high degree of top-level Government interest in the development of the components of the transportation system and in their proper relationships one with another (given those general objectives of Soviet planning), the Soviets are somewhat better informed about some elements in their transportation system than we are about most of the unregulated portions of our system. Yet in both countries the most accurate and comprehensive data are those which refer to railroads and in both countries estimation from limited sample information is employed to approximate the volume of movement by highway.

Several things are noteworthy about the aggregate traffic data. First, the Soviet data as here shown include no ton mileage for motortrucks. Although truck transportation is increasing rapidly in the Soviet Union, the evidence indicates that it is almost exclusively confined to local urban cartage and rural feeder operations. The U.S. estimates for motor carrier ton mileage endeavor to exclude such

[1] National Bureau of Economic Research, Occasional Paper No. 65.

traffic and to approximate the intercity movement. No data are known to exist in the United States which reflect the ton mileage produced in local trucking operations of the type which the Soviets record. For comparability it is, therefore, necessary to exclude truck transportation from the Soviet intercity traffic composition.

Second, it will be apparent that intercity freight transportation in the Soviet Union is overwhelmingly performed by rail. In recent years the proportion by rail has approximated 90 percent. At no time in its history has the United States relied on rail transport to so great a degree and, at present, railroads account for only about 40 percent of our ton-miles.[2] Our trend has been steadily away from rail, both in the prewar period and again since the immediate postwar adjustment. By contrast the Soviets relied increasingly upon rail transport in the prewar period and, since 1946, railroads have handled an almost constant year-to-year share of the traffic.

It will be apparent that, except for the period of the wars, Soviet freight traffic has almost continually increased, although by no means at a constant rate. Sharp variations resulting fromc yclical movements in the economy to be absent from the record. Moreover the rate of growth of Soviet traffic exceeds that of any but very short periods in recorded U.S. transport history. As table 3 will show, the volume of Soviet freight traffic measured in ton-miles has been growing in relation to the U.S. volume and now exceeds one-half of the U.S. total. Soviet railroad-freight volume has exceeded that the United States in all recent years and annually registers a further gain. Moreover the Soviet railways handle a very heavy passenger traffic, both suburban and long distance.

Caution should be observed in comparing Soviet and U.S. railroad traffic data. For, although Soviet ton-miles are calculated on the short tariff distances whereas U.S. ton-miles reflect the actual routes of movement, Soviet tons originated from which ton-miles are derived are overstated, perhaps fairly substantially. There is, thus, an upward bias of unknown magnitude in the Soviet data. Moreover the ton-mile is a quantitative measure which enables transport volumes to be added and compared, but which abstracts entirely from the quality of the service. The American ton-mile product is undoubtedly of higher quality in respect of speed of delivery, variety of consignment sizes, variety of specialized equipment available, variety of intermediate and intransit services afforded, etc. Yet many of these services are of less importance in the U.S.S.R. than in the United States because of the lesser proportion of finished and consumer's goods in the traffic mix, the lack of competitive marketing and the disregard for consumer's desires in respect of the availability of merchandise. Indeed, a substantially lower standard of service that than with which we are familiar appears to fit Soviet needs reasonably well and no competitive impetus to the overdevelopment of service standards with the attendant higher unit costs exists.

[2] This varies from the percentage commonly published by the Interstate Commerce Commission and by the Association of American Railroads, since an estimate of coastwise and intercoastal water transport has been included.

SOVIET TRANSPORTATION AT THE CROSSROADS

Development of the Soviet transport system until approximately 1955 appears to have followed a pattern reasonably well adjusted to the needs of the Soviet industrialization effort, with its emphasis upon producers' goods and heavy industry. It appears to have been reasonably well adjusted, also, to the resource base of the U.S.S.R. While execution of policy was by no means perfect and official dissatisfaction was almost continually expressed, the achievement was a very substantial one. Put briefly and with undue simplification, Soviet policy concentrated upon the railroad as the prime long-distance hauler, but made sizable investments in water transportation where topography permitted in order to secure the benefit of the lower capital inputs in proportion to traffic capacity required by this form of transport (particularly, of course, an economy in the use of iron and steel). Motor transport came to be encouraged in the movement of freight for hauls of up to 10–15 miles length in recognition of its superior efficiency in these short hauls, but its use over longer hauls has been severely discouraged wherever more economical methods of transport are available. Pipeline construction on a significant scale is a very recent development. Prior to the development of interior sources of petroleum, water transport mixed well with the requirements for first-stage transportation of this commodity. Ultimate distribution was performed largely by rail, since the absence of concentrated demands because of the scant motor-vehicle population resulted in few flows of a volume sufficient to support large diameter pipe. Recently considerable pipeline construction has been taken in hand.

In railroad development care has been taken to keep the construction of new mileage at a minimum to support desired industrial and agricultural expansion. Little branch-line mileage has been laid down, other modes of transport being relied upon to assemble and distribute through railheads in the areas of newer development. Principal trunklines have been rebuilt to increase their capacity, this investment being concentrated where it is expected to achieve the most significant results. In consequence the Soviet railways handle today approximately one-third more freight traffic than our own with about one-half the line mileage.

Before the transition to diesel power got underway, the Soviet railways were worked entirely in steam except for limited electrified segments (generally on suburban lines having exceptional passenger volume and on main lines of difficult profile). Their steampower was of simple and rugged construction, with light axle loading and relatively limited tractive effort. Somewhat heavy in coal consumption, it was nevertheless relatively simple to build and to maintain. A high degree of standardization was achieved. Similarly car types were limited in number and heavy reliance was placed on versatile open-top cars for general service in order to permit maximum flexibility in use and to minimize empty-car mileage. Composite construction to conserve steel was common. Operating and traffic policies were, as will be noted below, adjusted in ways designed to insure maximum utilization of both plant and equipment. While administrative difficulties appear always to have been severe and while incentives have not always produced the desired results, nevertheless the performance of the system has been good and has shown fairly continual improvement.

All consideration of Soviet transportation data should allow, of course, for the fact that service standards have not been stimulated by competition or very much affected by the desires of shippers. Railroad performance is adjusted to secure the convenience and efficiency of the carrier. The contrasts in passenger service are sharp and obvious. Little attention has been paid until recently to improving the service for small shipments, a type of traffic generally discouraged because it makes a disproportionate drain upon the carriers' resources. The rail carload freight service appears, however, to be quite good. No data on individual car movements has come to our attention which would shed light upon the regularity and reliability of loaded car movement. Average car movement, considering the length of haul, is about as good as our own. Lower road speed appears to be offset by less loss of time in yards and terminals. The high concentration and density of the traffic, the absence of alternative routes, and the comparatively small trainload all result in very frequent freight-train movement over principal routes and in a reduction of yard delay. Special services of all kinds are, of course, at a minimum although they exist for the movement of perishables.

Under the present plan the railroad system is undergoing a rapid transformation. Electrification is being extended and dieselization is taking place rapidly. Although Soviet railway authorities had very early experience with diesel power, its earlier introduction on a significant scale appears to have been inhibited by concern about liquid-fuel supply and, perhaps also, by a limited level of skills in mechanical department forces. Whereas dieselization occurred in the United States primarily for the purpose of securing operating economy in the face of static or declining traffic, the Soviet railway authorities look upon dieselization as the least expensive way, in terms of material inputs, by which further to intensify the working of their rail system in the face of rapidly increasing traffic. In brief, many Soviet lines handle nearly a maximum of daily train movements at present, although capacity of lines is in some cases subject to signaling improvement. To increase capacity, therefore, an increase in trainload and in train speed is urgent. However, steampower would occasion an increase in axle load requiring heavier rail, deeper ballast section, and the strengthening or replacement of bridges. Diesel power, by contrast, can deliver much increased tractive effort at existing axle loadings and, because of high acceleration and good grade climbing characteristics, can increase speed over many segments of line while taking substantially heavier tonnages. Thus trainload and line capacity can be increased with a minimum of work on permanent way and with little additional running track construction. An all-diesel and electric system is an ultimate goal, but since steampower replacement must occur in the face of rapidly increasing traffic, steam locomotives will still be in use in sizable numbers some years hence. Dieselization, like electrification, is being undertaken first on selected segments where grade conditions, shortage of boiler water, or traffic congestion promise maximum relief through this means.

It can be argued with plausibility that, during the first three and one-half decades of transportation development under the Soviet regime, a policy was followed which, while it kept the railroads under continual pressure and risked transportation shortages and while it accepted technological obsolescence (measured by Western standards), made excellent sense in the face of conditions and requirements as interpreted by the Soviet Government. Thus we may postulate the following: (1) rapid industrialization with emphasis upon heavy industry was a prime objective, (2) the expansion of transportation plant would conflict with such an objective because of its large requirements for heavy machinery and heavy shapes and forms of iron and steel, (3) labor was abundant through most of the period and coal fuels were generally abundant, though not always of the best quality, (4) the level of mechanical and engineering skills was relatively low and could best be used with a relatively crude technology until the educational and training system could be sufficiently developed to fill the gap. Under these circumstances a policy for the use of relatively crude and uncomplicated equipment mass produced to a limited number of types and a policy of the most intense possible working of the physical plant made sense. Transport plant and equipment were to be held severely in check in order to make output available for industrial expansion, yet not so severely checked as to hamper such development. For the most part a rather delicate balance appears to have been achieved.

It is well to avoid judging Soviet transportation progress by the standards we are accustomed to apply to our own system functioning in a free enterprise economy. Such a way of appraisal may lead us into serious underestimation of the Soviet system. Instead we would do well to appraise Soviet transportation accomplishment in the light of its support of the objectives intended within the U.S.S.R. Efficiency as we define it is neither sought nor secured. But a strong effort is made to minimize critical inputs into transportation while accomplishing effectively the essential tasks. There is no competition among railroads and very little competition between railroads and other forms of transportation. The effort of the transport authorities is not to generate traffic, but to curb it wherever possible by eliminating long or unnecessary hauls and cross hauls. A minimum of service is tendered the shipper and he is required to adjust his operations to the convenience of the carrier rather than the other way round. In the process a remarkably even flow of traffic is secured, although at considerable expense in cost of inventory carrying and in goods shortages. It is not clear that these costs outside the transportation system are given adequate weight in determining transportation investment. It is clear, however, that needs are met sufficiently to avoid serious restraint upon an expanding economy, that a vast volume of traffic is handled with reasonable satisfaction to the industrial ministries and other users, and that indexes of efficiency in transport plant utilization tend to improve with some rapidity. What has been done effectively since reconstruction of the railroad system caught up with requirements about 1926 must be expected to continue to be done effectively.

SOVIET RAIL OPERATIONS

As Professor Hunter notes in his companion piece, Soviet basic resources, manufacturing capacity, and urban population are concentrated in a limited number of major centers. These are connected by a rail network which, except in the Donbas and related areas of older development, is surprisingly simple in its layout. Moreover a large part of the newer manufacturing and extractive capacity is in large enterprises possessed of their own plant railway facilities and delivering and receiving traffic from the railway system in large blocks. This phenomenon is probably proportionately more common than in the United States. Hence there tends to be a greater concentration in the origination and termination of tonnage.

Even in the pre-Soviet period railway construction was controlled and the development of competitive lines avoided. In the newer areas almost no branch-line network has been laid down, other forms of transport being used to deliver to and distribute from railhead. Thus the monolithic Soviet railroad administration has not only had complete control of the traffic, but its problem has been one primarily of handling long-haul carload business originating and terminating at a limited number of major points. That traffic has consisted of higher proportions of bulk commodities and lesser proportions of manufactures than is true in the United States. The proportion of light and bulky manufactured items, in particular, has been low. When there are no competitive routes, few alternate routes, a minimum of branch lines and little way freight work and where, moreover, the shipper has no control over the routing of his traffic, it is easy to effect prior classification and to minimize intermediate yard work. Great attention is paid to accomplishing this object.

The Soviet railway authorities are further assisted by the remarkable regularity with which traffic is tendered and by the effective pressure upon shippers to accept and unload traffic immediately the railway is prepared to place the cars. In the effort to secure maximum output from industrial plant, a good part of Soviet industry appears to work around the clock or, at least, to load and unload cars 24 hours a day and 7 days a week. Great emphasis is placed upon the "rythm" of traffic flows in the shippers' relations with the railway administration. And while local rail authorities sometimes make concessions to large plants, such practices are attended by considerable risk. In consequence Soviet car loadings show remarkable day-to-day regularity for those limited periods for which records are available to us.

When, during the thirties, data were published showing the seasonal pattern of traffic, it was apparent that the Soviet seasonal was much less marked than that of the United States and that in many years the secular trend virtually overcame the seasonal pattern. Recent evidence upon this point does not seem to be available, but continued rapid traffic growth implies a minimum of seasonal underutilization of plant. Instead of a decline in the winter months, a reduced rate of growth may be characteristic.

Given a highly concentrated and remarkably even flow of traffic, exceptionally high traffic densities may be obtained. The American railroad plant was, in large part, built ahead of the development of traffic and ended by being substantially overbuilt. The proliferation of light traffic branch lines and of duplicate main and secondary lines has always held the average traffic density to a comparatively low figure. Moreover, except during war, few American main lines of railroad have ever been worked to near their theoretical capacity. The requirements of a competitive commercial economy produce a bunching both of passenger and freight movements into limited portions of the day as a result of which congestion develops at particular times and places long before track capacity is being used near its theoretical capacity. And if the service is to meet shippers' requirements, bottlenecks must be removed by expansion of facilities even though the line is substantially unoccupied at other times of the day.

One would, therefore, expect to find Soviet average freight traffic density well above the comparable American figure. Prior to 1954 it appears unlikely that any segment of the Soviet system was handling a greater density than some of the busiest segments of the American system. Since that time it appears likely that our maximum both for single and double track may have been exceeded. But there is nothing improbable about the Soviet performance, given an understanding of the conditions under which their system is worked.

High traffic density and even flow of traffic over time create ideal conditions for intensive use of motive power. The Soviet locomotive-miles per locomotive-day are calculated upon a different basis than our own and, when adjusted to make them as nearly comparable as possible, do not depart so greatly from the performance upon some of our roads as to occasion any great suspicion of the Soviet data. In considerable part the low utilization of American power has resulted from the loss of time waiting for traffic and from the carrying in serviceable condition of sufficient power to cope with traffic peaks. Under Soviet conditions this factor is minimized in practice and, in any event, the statistics employed for calculating locomotive-miles per locomotive-day are designed to exclude all but currently active power.

The greatest disparity in plant utilization undoubtedly occurs in respect of freight cars. Reported Soviet freight car turnaround time has been reduced almost steadily since the wartime dislocation was overcome. In 1958 it was reported as 5.83 days. Car turnaround on the U.S. system approximates 15 days in most recent years and even under wartime pressures was not reduced much below 11 days. Yet the Soviet average haul is greater than our own. The figures for the two countries are not strictly comparable and car turnaround has not been subjected to the same intensive study in the United States as has characterized the whole Soviet period. The Soviet car stock is understated as a result of the methods underlying their car accounting. This understated figure for the car stock is further diminished by an active car concept which has no direct parallel in American practice. Hence the disparity is not quite so great as the bold figures would appear to indicate. But it does seem probable that Soviet car turnaround would not be in excess of one-half the U.S. turnaround if the two could be put on a fully comparable basis. While some of the difference is accounted for by the lesser time required in yards and terminals, most of the difference results from the expeditious loading and unloading of cars by shippers.

In 1958 in the U.S.S.R. 34 percent of the time of the average active car was sent in trains between terminals. Sixty-six percent of its time was spent in terminal handling and in the hands of shippers and receivers. The average active American car spends some 10 percent of its time in trains between terminals while 90 percent of its time is accounted for in terminals and in the hands of shippers and receivers. Since Soviet loading and unloading norms are adjusted to type and size of car and character of load and are expressed in hours, nerve exceeding 12 hours so far as we can determine, and since shippers are placed under very heavy pressures and subjected to continual close surveillance, the performance reported is in some measure understandable. Its actual achievement, particularly under winter conditions and with frozen bulk loads, remains somewhat of a mystery which would warrant further study.

A degree of inflation appears to characterize all Soviet operating averages. This arises in part from the strong incentive at the operating level to overreport whenever possible as an assistance in attaining norms or in affecting compensation when pay is related to certain performance factors. Originated tonnage is overstated because shippers frequently show higher billed weights than the weight actually loaded in cars in order to escape penalties for underloading. The system of car accounting is loose and appears to encourage understatement of cars on line. Other inaccuracies are no doubt encompassed in the data. Moreover concepts are changed from time to time so that statistics are not always comparable from year to year, nor are these changes always made clear in the literature which reports and analyzes performance. Although no quantitative measure of the overstatement of performance is possible, it is reasonably clear that if fully accurate data were capable of being secured the general picture of Soviet performance here presented would not be materially changed.

POSTWAR INTENSIFICATION OF RAILWAY OPERATIONS

Inasmuch as major technical change involving increased electrification and large-scale dieselization has only begun very recently, the intensification of Soviet rail operation in the present decade requires comment. Since 1950 line mileage has expanded approximately 10 percent while freight traffic, measured in ton-kilometers, has increased more than 50 percent. Meanwhile there has been continual growth in the passenger service and traffic as well as an improvement in the quality of the passenger train services. As Professor Hunter shows, these developments have been accompanied by a sharp decline in the unit cost of service which along with other indications, suggests that the system has not been overloaded or congested.

The steady increase in length of haul is, of course, favorable to increased efficiency in the railroad service since it tends to reduce the proportion of terminal work required within the ton-kilometer output as well as to contribute to improved train loading and road movement. Gross ton-kilometers per freight train hour, generally regarded as the best single index of line-haul efficiency, increased by 86 percent between 1950 and 1958. No small part of this improvement is attributable to the considerable strengthening of the locomotive fleet employed in road freight service. For, while the fleet has increased by only about 25 percent, its quality has vastly improved. The gross addition of 2,500 road freight locomotives largely of the heaviest types employed on Soviet railways, of which some 1,300 were electric and diesel having a greater haulage and utilization potential, cannot have failed to be one of the more significant factors. In addition, considerable upgrading of existing steampower seems to have been undertaken, particularly in the reduction of dynamic augment in small driving-wheel power and in increasing sustained steaming capacity at speed. The evidence also suggests improvement in signaling and yard facilities of a rather extensive character.

Technological development, although not revolutionary, must account for a considerable portion of the improvement in efficiency and will tend to set the stage, as respects companion facilities, for the transition toward diesel and electrical power called for by the present 7-year plan.

It is not insignificant that motor transport, as reported, has multiplied its ton-kilometer performance by 3.2 since 1950 without significant expansion of its length of haul. No small part of this increase of traffic must represent the diversion in industrial centers of extremely short-haul traffic from the railroad system. Such traffic makes grossly disproportionate demands upon railways' motive power and car stock and its diversion, without more, would result in substantial improvement of railway operating averages. By eliminating from the rail traffic composition much traffic which, even under the Soviet system of charges, was doubtless noncompensatory, it would also improve the financial position of the rail system.

CONCLUSION

The adjustment of the Soviet transportation system in reasonable accord with the broad Soviet development objectives has produced a transportation system vastly different from our own and a trend of development quite disparate from ours. The answers to the desirable relative roles of the several forms of transport which emerge under our regulatory and promotional system in servicing a free enterprise economy depart sharply in kind from those which emerge from the Soviet planning approach. The Soviet system nevertheless displays great strength and must be judged in the light of its capacity for meeting requirements as generated by Soviet economic policy.

TABLE I.—*U.S.S.R. freight traffic, selected years, 1913–57*

[Billion metric ton-kilometers]

Year	Rail	Inland waterway (powered)	Domestic maritime	Oil pipeline	Total	Rail as percent of total
1913	65.70	28.50	15.10	0.33	109.6	59.9
1920	14.40	(1)	(1)	(1)	(1)	(1)
1926	68.90	12.92	(1)	.39	(1)	(1)
1928	93.40	15.90	6.20	.70	116.2	80.4
1930	133.90	22.86	10.03	2.23	169.0	79.2
1932	169.30	24.90	13.85	2.86	210.9	80.2
1936	323.40	31.10	16.66	3.55	374.7	86.3
1937	354.80	33.10	17.00	3.60	408.5	86.9
1938	370.50	32.00	18.80	3.90	425.2	87.1
1939	391.70	34.60	23.00	4.20	453.5	86.4
1940	415.00	35.90	21.60	3.80	476.3	87.0
1945	314.00	18.60	10.10	2.70	345.4	90.8
1946	335.00	20.40	12.40	2.90	370.7	90.3
1947	350.90	24.40	14.70	4.30	394.3	89.0
1948	446.40	30.90	16.60	5.00	498.9	89.5
1949	523.70	37.20	19.60	5.60	586.1	89.3
1950	602.30	45.90	21.20	4.90	674.3	89.2
1951	677.30	51.50	22.90	5.50	757.2	89.4
1952	741.30	57.80	25.80	6.40	831.3	89.2
1953	798.00	58.90	28.00	7.60	892.5	89.4
1954	856.80	62.40	28.20	10.20	957.6	89.4
1955	970.90	67.40	(1)	14.70	1,081.2	89.8
1956	1,079.10	70.20	(1)	20.50	1,199.8	89.9
1957	1,209.00	76.00	(1)	26.40	1,346.4	89.8

Not available.

TABLE 2.—*U.S. intercity freight traffic, selected years, 1889–1956*

[Billion short ton-miles]

Year	Rail	Inland waterways	Coastwise and intercoastal	Motor truck	Pipeline	Total	Rail as Percent of total
1889	84.0	19.2	16.6	----------	----------	119.8	70.1
1920	456.2	78.0	59.0	----------	7.0	600.2	76.0
1926	490.8	93.0	158.0	5.0	19.0	765.8	64.1
1928	479.1	86.0	163.0	8.0	26.0	762.1	62.9
1930	423.2	78.0	160.0	12.0	33.0	706.2	59.9
1932	258.0	28.0	131.0	15.0	34.0	466.0	55.4
1936	375.3	86.0	192.0	28.0	40.2	721.5	52.0
1937	398.6	103.0	219.0	35.0	45.0	800.6	49.8
1938	320.2	60.0	202.0	40.0	42.5	664.7	48.2
1939	370.2	96.2	234.7	52.8	55.6	809.5	45.7
1940	411.8	118.1	243.4	62.0	59.3	894.6	46.0
1945	736.2	142.7	117.2	66.6	126.5	1,189.2	61.9
1946	642.7	124.0	229.7	81.7	95.1	1,173.2	54.7
1947	706.7	146.7	206.7	101.7	105.2	1,267.0	55.8
1948	688.7	161.8	210.5	115.5	119.6	1,296.1	53.1
1949	567.3	139.4	214.3	124.9	114.9	1,160.8	48.9
1950	628.5	163.3	233.0	170.2	129.2	1,324.2	47.5
1951	686.4	182.2	251.1	182.5	152.1	1,454.3	47.2
1952	651.4	168.4	248.1	184.1	157.5	1,409.5	46.2
1953	641.8	202.4	264.4	217.2	169.9	1,495.7	42.9
1954	577.5	173.7	270.2	214.6	179.2	1,415.2	40.8
1955	654.8	216.5	270.0	231.2	203.2	1,575.7	41.5
1956	680.2	220.0	(1)	253.8	230.0	1,664.0	[2] 40.9
1957	626.4	227.1	(1)	260.0	236.7	1,620.1	[2] 38.9

[1] Not available.
[2] Coastwise and intercoastal assumed at 270 billion in order to estimate total.

TABLE 3.—*United States and U.S.S.R. total freight traffic, selected years, 1889–1956*

[Billion short ton-miles]

Year	United States	U.S.S.R.	United States as a multiple of U.S.S.R.	Year	United States	U.S.S.R.	United States as a multiple of U.S.S.R.
1889	119.8	(1)	----------	1945	1,189.2	236.7	5.0
1913	(1)	73.5	----------	1946	1,173.2	254.2	4.6
1920	600.2	(1)	----------	1947	1,267.0	270.1	4.7
1926	765.8	60.4	12.7	1948	1,296.1	341.7	3.8
1928	762.1	79.6	9.6	1949	1,160.8	401.5	2.9
1930	706.2	115.8	6.1	1950	1,324.2	462.5	2.9
1932	466.0	144.6	3.2	1951	1,454.3	519.3	2.8
1936	721.5	256.7	2.8	1952	1,409.5	569.6	2.5
1937	800.6	279.7	2.8	1953	1,495.7	611.2	2.4
1938	664.7	291.3	2.3	1954	1,415.2	655.5	2.1
1939	809.5	310.6	2.6	1956	1,664.0	821.1	2.0
1940	894.6	326.7	2.7				

[1] Not available.

SOVIET TRANSPORTATION POLICIES—A CURRENT VIEW

(By Holland Hunter, Haverford College)

Introduction and Summary

It will be useful and accurate for this brief analysis to emphasize three broad questions confronting Soviet policymakers in the transportation field: (1) How much transportation capacity should be made available each year? (2) Which freight and passenger carriers should provide it? (3) How should these carriers be financed? The Soviet approach to each problem has been distinctively different from what we are used to.[1] As will be explained in more detail below, the Soviet answer to the first issue has been: Expand transportation capacity only to the minimum extent necessary for building national power. Reliance on railroads (partly unintended), has been their answer to the second issue. As regards the third, Soviet policy for financing transportation growth has gone through two stages. Up to 1953, the state provided capital grants and occasional operating subsidies like those for heavy industry. Since that time, shippers and passengers have paid user charges to the railroads that have covered all railroad operating and investment outlays, and also provided funds for capital expansion elsewhere.

The prospects for Soviet transportation between now and 1965 are examined in the closing section of this paper. Policy with respect to the provision of additional transportation capacity seems likely to remain stringent. Enough will be provided to avert bottlenecks—little more. As for the role of various carriers, it appears that pipelines will grow rapidly, and that long-distance passenger movement by air will continue its rapid expansion, but that in 1965 the railroads will still dominate the situation. The financial outlook is for continued railroad cost reductions reflecting improved technology. Expansion of highways and water transportation capacity will be expensive and may, therefore, be on a modest scale. In that case, the transportation sector can supply net funds for growth of the Soviet economy.

Major Policy Issues

Whether deliberately or through a composite of uncoordinated decisions, every economy must decide how much transportation capacity it should have, and how much its capacity should be expanded in the process of economic development. Traditionally, the Western policy has been to provide ample capacity, built ahead of traffic, as a powerful means of encouraging growth. Soviet policy has been different. In the 1920's, the Russians already had the basic skeleton of a transportation system. Consequently, the policy that evolved called for greatly intensifying the use made of exiting facilities, with expansion only

[1] For background, see my "Soviet Transportation Policy" (Cambridge: Harvard University Press, 1957), esp. chs. 3, 8, and 11.

where absolutely necessary. The policy went too far, and in the early 1930's there was a transportation crisis for some 3 years; but over the last three decades as a whole, the policy has paid off. It has therefore continued to this day, and is embodied in the current 7-year plan.

One consequence of this policy has been a low priority for development of good roads and of passenger cars to travel on them. Both in urban and intercity passenger transportation, Soviet policy has given almost complete sway to common carriers—trolleys, buses, and railroads. The contrast with the United States, where State financing of highways has been a major investment activity for 40 years, and where the private passenger car supports a considerable part of our economic activity, is profoundly striking. The scarcity of Soviet passenger cars is obscured for the foreign visitor by their prevalence, along with paved streets, in major cities, which is where he is likely to spend most of his time. Even in cities, however, trucks outnumber taxis and private automobiles, while back streets remain unpaved.

Thus one can discern a Soviet policy against lavish expansion of private passenger transportation. After the stormy internal migrations of the early 1930's, and except for the emergency wartime evacuation and reoccupation movements of the early 1940's, there presumably was little need to assign high priority to unhampered passenger travel. The public carriers were expanded sufficiently to handle the necessary urban commuting and long-distance official travel. But passenger-car production has remained infinitesimal by American standards: 1958 production was 122,000 units, and the 1965 plan evidently calls for some 200,000 to 225,000 units.

The policy of minimizing transportation capacity expansion, and maximizing the utilization of existing plant and equipment, has been facilitated by the geography of Soviet freight flows. Even with the deliberate attempt to develop new industrial districts, the bulk of the heavy freight traffic has moved between a handful of major centers. Trunklines joining them were strengthened enough to carry densities of traffic that have now gone beyond anything in American experience. It is clear that failure to provide an elaborate latticework of feeder lines like those of the West has not interfered with the growth of Soviet heavy industry. It was also made clear in World War II that the relatively sparse Soviet railroad network was not a decisive barrier to effective military operations.

A second major policy issue in every economy concerns the role of the various principal carriers. Western legislators have always faced difficult problems in deciding on the extent to which each should be promoted. Soviet policies seem curiously inverted. Heavy reliance is placed in practice on the railroads, while the regime and the railroads themselves call for the expansion of other means of transportation. This emphasis on railroad transportation reflects primarily the deficiencies of the other carriers. Internal waterway and coastal maritime shipping is badly handicapped both by long periods of freezing times and by a very awkward geographic layout in relation to the points generating traffic demands. Until very recently, the volume and geographic pattern of petroleum production and use have not seemed to justify replacement of rail and water carriers by petroleum pipelines. Intercity highway transportation by truck has scarcely begun to develop, lacking a highway system financed by consumers along Western lines.

In these circumstances, the authorities have regularly sought to shift increments of freight traffic from the heavily burdened railroads to these other carriers, but equally regularly the minor carriers have failed to meet their traffic targets, with railroads ending up by carrying more than was intended. It appears that exhortations to the minor carriers have not been accompanied by proportionate allocations of equipment, manpower, and scarce supplies. This may have been eminently sensible. A thoughtful Soviet transportation writer reported last year that "in the last two 5-year plan periods (1946–55), the relative capital investment per additional ton-kilometer of freight traffic has been, for river carriers, roughly 2 to 2.5 times as high as for railroads, and in sea transport it has been a little over three times as high."[2] The ratio for highway transportation would be even higher.

Soviet policy toward the major carriers has also been founded on belief in a "unified transportation system." The principle is one of avoiding duplication of facilities. All carriers are supposed to work together in a joint, smoothly functioning transportation process employing the inherent advantages of each carrier. In particular, wherever river or coastal maritime shipments can take the place of rail shipments during the ice-free season, the Government seeks to promote joint rail-water or rail-water-rail movements utilizing several components of the single, state-owned system. For various understandable reasons, however, the volume of joint shipments is small, partly because Soviet shippers suffer from what one railroad writer has ruefully called "hydrophobia."

Moreover, the various carriers are operated by separate organizations, and the ideal of coordinated service is marred in practice by unavoidable bureaucratic difficulties. The Ministry of Transportation is, in the scope of its responsibilities, the Ministry of Railroads. In addition to it, there are separate ministries for river and sea transportation (at times they have been combined at the top), while pipelines are operated by the oil industry and truck transportation is under decentralized administration through regional and local authorities. These various organizations have found, both locally and at the national level, that detailed coordination of their operations presents many difficulties. Scheduling, routing, billing, and similar functions are complicated by the division of responsibilities, and there is a steady stream of comment in the Soviet technical press on the resulting problems.

The objective of a unified transportation system has been sought under conditions of strong demand and limited supply, due to the first policy noted above. There is thus a fundamental contrast with recent Western experience. American shippers, for example, have typically been able to select from among several carriers, each with ample capacity to handle his business. The presence of duplicate facilities has strengthened the shipper's pressure for good service. in the U.S.S.R., on the other hand, the carriers, especially the railroads, have been in a position to dominate shippers. It is clear that the policy of having a "unified transportation system," without duplication of capacity, carries with it some dangers for the users of transportation facilities that should not be ignored.

A third major policy issue concerns the financing of transportation services and facilities expansion. Here the U.S.S.R. began by estab-

[2] IU. I. Koldomasov, in "Zheleznodorozhnyi Transport, 1958," No. 2, p. 22.

lishing freight and passenger rates that discriminated in favor of heavy industry and failed to cover all current and capital transportation outlays. Net grants were made from the central state budget for capital investments, and even (during the late 1940's), to cover operating deficits. In recent years, however, Soviet policy has shifted, in principle and to a considerable extent in practice, toward making each shipment cover its cost,[3] and toward a level of charges that more than covers the transportation sector's investment needs. This is evidently part of a broader policy change discussed elsewhere in these papers.

The new financial policy toward transportation has been made possible by remarkable railroad successes in reducing operating costs since 1949. Essentially, the explanation lies in full capacity operation enjoying great benefits from economies of scale. As unit costs have come down, freight rates have been reduced. At the same time, very substantial net income has accrued to the railroads and been syphoned off into the general state budget.

Since 1953, the railroads have contributed more to the central pool of investment funds than has been allocated to them for capital development. Thus railroad savings have been available for financing the growth of other carriers and other sectors of the economy. Between 1950 and 1958, railroad unit costs for freight and passenger traffic combined fell by some 36 percent; average unit revenue fell by some 24 percent, and the difference has reached a 1958 level of almost 20 billion rubles of net income from shipping operations, representing a profit rate of 40 percent over operating expenses.

Transportation Prospects to 1965

While there is considerable stability in the basic trends governing Soviet transportation development, one must be cautious in making detailed forecasts for the next 7 years. Readers should be aware that the following observations are based on fragmentary evidence and represent no more than preliminary judgments, subject to revision with emerging evidence. In sum, it seems likely that the transportation sector can continue to meet demands without creating a bottleneck, that railroads will continue to dominate the situation, and that the financial health of the transportation sector is unlikely to deteriorate.

The targets of the current 7-year plan make it clear that Soviet authorities intend to continue the drive for rapid industrial growth, with perhaps some slight slackening of growth rates compared to those of the preceding 5 or 10 years. Such continued expansion will obviously generate very large increments of additional freight traffic, and therefore require some additional transportation capacity to handle it. The plan makes provision for a substantial modernization and expansion program covering railroads and other carriers. On the basis of past performance, together with analysis of planned traffic and investment increments, the best prediction appears to be that the transportation sector will not hamper industrial growth in the next 7 years.

Readers of Soviet publicity know that grandiose plans for developing new industrial regions in the territory adjoining European Russia

[3] See the article on freight rates in the forthcoming "Economic Calculation and Organization in Eastern Europe," edited by Gregory Grossman.

on the east are now receiving great emphasis, as they have for many years. It is true that the percentage increases in minerals output and other production from the Urals, Kazakhstan, and parts of western Siberia have been remarkable, and that the absolute levels of activity here are no longer negligible. At the same time, older centers in European Russia have also continued to grow, and the net shift toward the east has been slow and modest. This has been significant for the transportation sector. It has been cheaper and easier to expand capacity to handle additional freight traffic increments among established centers than it has been to build capacity for the larger traffic increments associated with eastern industrial production. Part of the basis for the prediction above—that transportation bottlenecks will not develop—lies in a related judgment that the "eastward movement" will in fact not proceed as rapidly as the plan intends.

Tables 1 and 4 show the freight and passenger targets of the 7-year plan in relation to existing levels. It appears that no revolutionary changes are anticipated. The railroads' share of freight traffic is supposed to fall from 82 percent in 1958 to 73 percent in 1965, with the minor carriers raising their share from 18 to 27 percent. This structural change has been regularly programed in the 5-year plans but so far the Government has been unable to bring it about. The river and highway freight traffic targets are not especially ambitious in relation to the experience of the 1951–58 period, and thus appear attainable if resources for expansion are made available. The anticipated rise in maritime freight traffic probably reflects foreign trade plans—domestic and oversea traffic are combined in this series and the oversea component has been expanding rapidly since 1953 (notice the rising length of haul for sea traffic in table 3). In connection with the rapid growth of petroleum and natural gas production, pipeline transportation is expected to increase very rapidly.

On the passenger side, the rapid growth of long-distance air travel is expected to make domestic airlines a major factor in long-distance movement. Nevertheless, in these combined targets for local and long-distance passenger transportation, the railroads in 1965 are expected to handle 54 percent of the total, a structure that has not characterized American passenger transportation for half a century.

Soviet railroad financial policy in the coming period is predicated on a self-financed technological revolution that is expected to bring unit shipping costs down by some 21 percent, cover a large-scale reequipment program, supply several billion rubles of investment funds to the general state budget, and with all this, permit a very slight (2 percent) reduction in average unit revenue. The unit cost reduction of 21 percent in 7 years would be smaller than the 31 percent reduction achieved from 1951 to 1958. (See table 9). If the recent reductions represent exploitation of scale economies inherent in existing technology, the prospective additional cost reductions are expected to arise from the introduction of greatly improved technology.

In motive power, Soviet railroads are now launched on a changeover from steam to diesel-electric and electric locomotives, comparable to what was put through on American railroads some 10 years earlier. Table 6 shows, for example, that while less than 6 percent of Soviet freight traffic was handled by electric and diesel-electric traction in 1950, already by 1958 the share of these two advanced forms of locomotive power had risen to over 26 percent. Of the total number of locomotives in road freight service during 1958, amounting to almost 13,000, over 1,000 (8 percent of the total) were electric locomotives, and almost 900 (7 percent of the total) were diesel-electrics. Considering the network as a whole, there had already been an absolute fall in the mileage operated with steam traction from 111,000 kilometers in 1950 to 104,000 in 1958.

The 1965 targets call for use of diesel-electric traction on 52 percent of the network, and electric traction on another 22 percent, with steam traction remaining on only 25 percent of the road operated. The freight locomotive fleet in service is to drop by some 3,000 locomotives, to less than 10,000, divided roughly evenly among diesel-electrics (35 percent), steam (34 percent), and straight electrics (31 percent). Since the new forms will be concentrated on major routes, they are to account for a far more than proportionate share of the traffic, reducing the steam contribution to something like 13 percent of total freight ton-kilometers. The change will permit further gains in the weight and speed of freight trains, though table 7 indicates that the anticipated 43 percent rise in gross ton-kilometers per freight train-hour from 1958 to 1965, is smaller than the improvement of 61 percent achieved in the preceding 7 years.

In train movement, the basis of advance is to be further installation of automatic block signaling, centralized traffic control, and other communication devices familiar in American railroad practice. Between the end of 1950 and the end of 1958, the length of line equipped with automatic block signaling rose from 9,670 to 19,416 kilometers, while the proposed total by the end of 1965 is variously placed at from 37,500 to 40,000 kilometers.[4] In freight car management, large gains are expected from automation of classification yards, including use of electronic computers and television, comparable to what has been revolutionizing American classification yard practices in the last few years. It is clear from American experience and Soviet discussion that new equipment of these types pays for itself very quickly in reduced operating expenses. Hence there is nothing implausible about the logic of the Soviet financial program. If past experience is any guide to the future, the equipment will come into operation more slowly than planned, while the railroads will have to deal with a larger volume of freight traffic than the plan specifies. Progress is unlikely, therefore, to follow precisely the route laid out in advance. This is by no means equivalent to saying, however, that fatal difficulties will be encountered.

The feasibility of 1965 railroad performance targets is supported by inspection of the labor side of the picture. Table 5 shows that the number of operating workers on Soviet railroads has only risen by one-sixth since 1950, while the combined output of freight and passenger traffic has somewhat more than doubled. In the 7 years ending with 1958, it was necessary to add 232,000 railroad workers. For the next 7 years, the intention is to add only some 41,000. At a time when the war-induced shortfall of new entrants to the labor force will cause marked tightness, especially among skilled labor, this small claim of the railroads will unquestionably be helpful. Even if delays in the capital program make it necessary to add more labor than intended, a railroad need for twice or even three times as many new workers as the

[4] Estimates derived from data in "Vestnik Statistiki," 1959, No. 4, p. 96, and in "Zheleznodorozhnyi Transport," 1959, No. 3, p. 48.

plan specifies would still draw off less than half the number of workers taken by the railroads in 1952–58.

Thus in physical terms the 1965 railroad targets do not appear obviously unfeasible. The sketchy Soviet material so far available does not permit any detailed appraisal of financial prospects—assumptions as to price changes and so on are not explained—but the main outlines of the plan appear similary credible. What is not at all clear is the extent to which improvement programs for the minor carriers will be carried out. The net funds made available by the railroads might be fully swallowed up in river, sea, highway, and pipeline expansion programs if the Government so decided. In this case, the transportation sector would contribute no net funds for investment in other parts of the economy. On the other hand, if the ambitious language of the plan for expansion of these minor carriers is no more accompanied with proportionate investment allocations than has been true in the past, then the transportation sector as a whole can make a net contribution to pooled investment funds.

TABLE 1.—*Freight traffic, U.S.S.R., by carrier and year, 1949–58, and 1965 plan*

[Billions of metric ton-kilometers]

Year	Railroad	Sea	River	Road	Pipeline	Total [1]
1949	523.8	37.3	38.8	17.0	(4.5)	(621.6)
1950	602.3	39.7	45.9	20.1	4.9	713.1
1951	677.3	40.3	51.5	24.1	5.5	798.9
1952	741.3	44.3	57.8	27.6	6.4	877.6
1953	798.0	48.2	58.9	31.4	7.6	944.3
1954	856.8	56.6	62.4	37.5	10.2	1,023.8
1955	970.9	68.9	67.4	42.5	14.7	1,164.7
1956	1,079.1	82.4	70.2	48.5	20.5	1,301.0
1957	1,212.8	92.7	76.1	61.7	26.6	1,470.2
1958	1,302.0	106.3	85.2	67.6	33.8	1,595.2
1965 (plan)	[2] 1,850.0	235.0	140.0	130.0	187.0	2,542.0

[1] Includes an unidentified component of 0.2 billion ton-kilometers, 1949–53, and 0.3 billion (1954–58), which probably represents air freight traffic.
[2] Stated in the plan as a range, 1800–1850.

Sources: For 1949–56, TsSU, "Transport i Sviaz S.S.S.R." (1957), pp. 7, 32, 95, 116, 155, and 210, plus inserted 1949 estimates for pipeline and air. For 1957, 1958, and 1965 plan, Vestnik Statistiki, 1959, No. 4, p. 91, except that 0.3 billion of river traffic is here excluded to maintain comparable coverage.

TABLE 2.—*Freight shipments, U.S.S.R., by carrier and year, 1949–58, and 1965 plan*

[Millions of metric tons originated]

Year	Railroad	Sea	River	Road	Pipeline
1949	735.3	30.9	78.0	1,481.3	(13.2)
1950	834.3	33.7	91.5	1,859.2	15.3
1951	909.2	36.5	102.8	2,252.3	18.4
1952	997.0	41.2	109.8	2,652.8	23.2
1953	1,067.4	45.5	116.1	3,002.7	29.4
1954	1,131.4	48.5	128.2	3,305.9	39.7
1955	1,267.0	53.7	139.1	3,730.0	51.7
1956	1,371.0	57.7	146.8	4,200.9	65.3
1957	1,487.7	65.7	159.2	5,216.4	80.9
1958	1,605.0	74.9	178.3	----------	94.7
1965 (plan)	2,300.0	----------	----------	----------	----------

Sources: For 1949–56, TsSU, "Transport i sviaz' S.S.S.R." pp. 17, 32, 97, 116, 155, and 210, plus inserted estimate for 1949 pipeline shipments. For 1957, Vestnik Statistiki, 1958, No. 9, p. 85. The 1958 railroad figure is from Zhel. Trans., 1959, No. 2, p. 38; sea, river, and pipeline estimates derived from annual percent increases stated in CSA report. The 1965 railroad plan figure is from Zhel. Trans., 1958, No. 12, p. 5.

TABLE 3.—*Average lengths of haul, U.S.S.R., by carrier and year, 1949–58, and 1965 plan*

[Kilometers]

Year	Railroad	Sea	River	Road	Pipeline
1949	712	1,205	497	11.5	(340)
1950	722	1,179	502	10.8	320
1951	745	1,105	501	10.7	299
1952	744	1,075	527	10.4	276
1953	748	1,058	507	10.4	259
1954	757	1,168	486	11.4	257
1955	766	1,284	484	11.4	284
1956	787	1,429	479	11.5	314
1957	815	1,411	478	11.8	329
1958	811	1,419	478		357
1965 (plan)	804				

Sources: Quotients of ton-kilometer entries from table 1 over tons originated entries from table 2. The Official 1965 railroad target assumes accomplishment of the lower end of the ton-kilometer range specified (1800/2300=782.6), and is stated as 780 kilometers. (See B. P. Beshchev, Minister of Transportation, in Zhel. Trans., 1958, No. 12, p. 6.)

TABLE 4.—*Passenger traffic, U.S.S.R., by carrier and year, 1949–58, and 1965 plan*

[Billions of passenger-kilometers]

Year	Railroad	Bus	Air	River	Sea	Total
1949	81.3	(4.0)	(1.0)	2.5	1.1	89.9
1950	88.0	5.2	1.2	2.7	1.2	98.3
1951	98.5	6.5	1.5	2.9	1.2	110.6
1952	107.4	8.4	1.7	3.0	1.2	121.7
1953	118.3	10.5	2.1	3.3	1.5	135.7
1954	129.1	14.1	2.4	3.5	1.4	150.5
1955	141.4	20.9	2.8	3.6	1.5	170.2
1956	142.4	26.4	3.1	3.5	1.4	176.8
1957	153.4	33.7	4.5	3.8	1.4	196.8
1958	158.4		5.3			
1965 (plan)	192.0	125.0	30.0	5.0	2.0	354.0

Sources: For 1949–56, TsSU, "Transport i sviaz' S.S.S.R." (1957), pp. 12, 32, 95, and 116, plus inserted 1949 estimates for bus and air. For 1957, Vestnik Statistiki, 1958, No. 9, p. 85. The air traffic estimates are unidentified residuals between reported "all" traffic and the 4 explicit series. 1958 figures reflect percent increases stated in the CSA annual report. The 1965 targets are rough estimates based on stated percent increases over 1958.

TABLE 5.—*Operating labor force and labor productivity, U.S.S.R. railroads, by year, 1949–58, plus 1965 plan*

	Freight, ton-kilometers (1)	Passenger-kilometers (2)	Combined ton-kilometers (3)	Labor force (4)	Output per worker (5)
	Billions	*Billions*	*Billions*	*Thousands*	*Thousands*
1949	524	81	605	1,657	365.0
1950	602	88	690	1,712	403.0
1951	677	99	776	1,765	440.0
1952	741	108	849	1,866	455.0
1953	798	118	916	1,901	482.0
1954	857	129	986	1,968	501.0
1955	971	141	1,112	1,980	562.0
1956	1,079	143	1,222	1,980	617.0
1957	1,213	153	1,366	1,995	684.7
1958	1,302	158	1,460	1,997	731.1
1965 (plan)	1,850	192	2,042	2,038	1,002.0

Cols. (1) and (2): From tables 1 and 4 above.
Col. (3): Sum of cols. (1) and (2).
Col. (4): Covers operating workers only.
Col. (5): Col. (3) over col. (4).

Sources: 1949 from H. Hunter, "Soviet Transportation Policy," p. 383. 1950–56 from TsSU, "Transport i sviaz' S.S.S.R.," p. 64. 1957, 1958, and 1965 plan output-per-worker from Vestnik Statistiki, 1959, No. 4, p. 92. 1965 plan traffic from Zheleznodorozhnyi Transport, 1959, No. 2, p. 4. 1957, 1958, and 1965 plan labor force by division.

TABLE 6.—*Railroad motive power, U.S.S.R., 1950, 1955, 1958, and 1965 plan*

BREAKDOWN OF TOTAL ROAD OPERATED, BY TYPE OF TRACTION

[In kilometers, at end of year]

Year	Steam	Electric	Diesel-electric	Total
1950	110,800	3,000	3,100	116,900
1955	108,800	5,400	6,500	120,700
1958	104,400	9,500	11,100	125,000
1965 (plan)	34,000	30,000	70,000	134,000

Sources: Cols. 2 and 3 from Vestnik Statistiki, 1959, No. 4, pp. 92 and 96. Col. 4 from graph insert at p. 49, Zheleznodorozhnyi Transport, 1959, No. 2; col. 1 by subtraction.

BREAKDOWN OF LOCOMOTIVE FLEET IN ROAD FREIGHT SERVICE

[In physical units, annual average]

Year	Steam	Electric	Diesel-electric	Total
1950	10,000	240	250	10,490
1955	11,050	600	770	12,420
1958	11,030	1,020	870	12,920
1965 (plan)	3,345	3,075	3,510	9,930

Source: Derived from daily gross ton-kilometers per locomotive data give by P. G. Muratov, head of the MPS Locomotive Administration in Zhel. Trans., 1959, No. 2, p. 11, using the percentages below and net gross train weight ratios (actual for 1950 and 1955: assumed at 0.575 and 0.58 for 1958 and 1965 plan.

BREAKDOWN OF FREIGHT TRAFFIC CARRIED

[Percentage of total gross ton-kilometers, annual average]

Year	Steam	Electric	Diesel-electric	Total
1950	94.5	3.1	2.4	100.0
1955	85.9	8.3	5.8	100.0
1958	73.5	15.1	11.4	100.0
1965 (plan)	13.0	44.0	43.0	100.0

Sources: Vestnik Statistiki, 1959, No. 4, p. 92, and (for 1965 plan), Zhel. Trans., 1959, No. 2, graph insert at p. 48.

TABLE 7.—*Freight train performance, U.S.S.R. railroads, by year, 1950–58 plus 1965 plan*

Year	Gross ton-kilometers per freight train-hour	Average weight (metric tons)		Average speed (kilometers per hour)	
		Gross	Net	Excluding stops	Including stops
	(1)	(2)	(3)	(4)	(5)
1950	28,740	1,430	815	33.8	20.1
1951	32,520	1,478	839	34.5	22.0
1952	35,440	1,521	859	34.9	23.3
1953	37,110	1,579	894	35.0	23.5
1954	38,010	1,660	936	35.2	22.9
1955	43,420	1,758	1,002	37.1	24.7
1956	45,410	1,831	1,052	37.6	24.8
1957	48,130	1,880	1,100	37.8	25.6
1958	52,220	1,963			26.6
1965 (plan)	74,400	2,400			31.0

Sources: 1950–56 from TsSU, "Transport i sviaz' S.S.S.R.," pp. 52–61. Plan gross train weights from Zhel, 1957, 1958, and 1965. Trans., 1959, No. 1, p. 23, and No. 2, p. 39; 1957 and 1958 speed including stops from ibid., p. 40, and for 1965 plan from ibid., No. 1, p. 21; 1957 net train weight from T. S. Khachaturov, "Ekonomika Transporta" (1959), p. 289; 1957 speed excluding stops from TsSU, "S.S.S.R. v tsifrakh" 1958), p. 286. Col. 1 is the product of col. 2 times col. 5.

TABLE 8.—*Freight car performance, U.S.S.R. railroads, by year, 1950–58 plus 1965 plan*

Year	Average freight car trip				Average turnaround Time	Kilo-meters per day
	In kilometers			Percent empty		
	Loaded	Empty	Total			
1950	801	296	1,097	27.0	7.49	146.4
1951	826	308	1,134	27.2	7.13	159.0
1952	818	317	1,135	27.9	6.87	165.2
1953	825	316	1,141	27.7	6.64	171.8
1954	838	320	1,158	27.6	6.68	173.3
1955	844	328	1,172	28.0	6.23	188.2
1956	868	338	1,206	28.0	6.31	191.2
1957	896	366	1,262	29.0	6.12	206.4
1958	893	369	1,262	29.2	5.83	216.6
1965 (plan)					5.33	

Sources: 1950–56 from TsSU, "Transport i sviaz' S.S.S.R., p. 48, 1957 and 1958 from Zhel. "Trans.," 1959, No. 2, p. 40, 1965 turnaround target from ibid., p. 4.

TABLE 9.—*Selected financial performance indicators, U.S.S.R. railroads, by year, 1950–58 plus 1965 plan*

Year	Million rubles, current prices			Profits (percent) [1]	Unit revenue [2]	Unit cost [2]
	Operating revenues	Operating expenses	Net income			
1950	42,545	36,240	6,305	17.4	6.166	5.252
1951	46,635	37,915	8,720	23.0	6.010	4.876
1952		39,555				4.659
1953		40,845				4.459
1954	53,025	42,840	10,185	23.8	5.378	4.435
1955	58,125	43,725	14,400	32.9	5.226	3.932
1956	57,580	45,275	12,305	27.2	4.714	3.705
1957	64,230	47,540	16,690	35.1	(4.702)	3.480
1958	68,480	48,860	19,620	40.2	4.691	3.349
1965 (plan)	94,000	53,870	40,130	74.5	4.603	2.638

[1] Ratio of net income to operating expenses.
[2] Kopeks per "cumulated" ton-kilometer (sum of passenger-kilometers and tariff ton-kilometers).

Sources: 1951, 1958, and 1965 plan figures derived from data given by I. V. Ivliev, head of the MPS Financial Administration, in "Zhel. Trans.," 1959, No. 3, pp. 19–20. 1950 and 1954–56 unit costs from TsSU, "Transport i sviaz' S.S.S.R.," p. 24; 1952–53 from "Zhel. Trans.," 1956, No. 3, p. 32; and 1957 from "Vestnik Statistiki," 1959, No. 4, p. 92. 1950 and 1955 profits percent from Ivliev in "Voprosy Ekonomiki," 1956, No. 10, p. 40. 1945 and 1956 figures derived from unit freight and passenger revenues in S. K. Danilov, ed., "Ekonomika Transporta," 1956, p. 578, and 2d ed., 1957, p. 640. Other 1957 data derived from inserted estimate for unit revenue.

TABLE 10.—*Railroad freight traffic composition, U.S.S.R., 1950 and 1958, by major commodity group*

	Billions		Percent of total	
	1950	1958	1950	1958
Metric ton-kilometers:				
Coal and coke	178	350	29.6	26.9
Timber	72	184	12.0	14.1
Petroleum and products	52	154	8.6	11.8
Mineral building materials	47	110	7.8	8.5
Iron and steel	47	90	7.8	6.9
Grain and milled products	31	84	5.1	6.5
Ores	28	60	4.7	4.6
Other freight	147	270	24.4	20.7
Total	602	1,302	100.0	100.0
	Kilometer		Absolute rise	Percent rise
	1950	1958		
Average length of haul:				
Coal and coke	670	735	65	9.7
Timber	998	1,490	492	49.3
Petroleum and products	1,205	1,376	171	14.2
Mineral building materials	296	353	57	19.3
Iron and steel	1,095	1,025	−70	−6.4
Grain and milled products	795	1,152	357	44.9
Ores	574	554	−20	−3.5
Other freight	891	865	−26	−2.9
Total	722	810	88	12.2
	Millions		Percent of total	
	1950	1958	1950	1958
Metric tons originated:				
Coal and coke	266	476	31.9	29.7
Timber	72	124	8.6	7.7
Petroleum and products	43	112	5.2	7.0
Mineral building materials	158	312	18.9	19.4
Iron and steel	43	88	5.2	5.5
Grain and milled products	39	73	4.7	4.6
Ores	48	108	5.7	6.7
Other freight	165	312	19.8	19.4
Total	834	1,605	100.0	100.0

Sources: TsSU, "Transport i sviaz' S.S.S.R." (1957), pp. 34–38, and "Zhel. Trans.," 1959, No. 2, pp. 38–39, plus inserted estimates for 1958 mineral building materials ton-kilometers and iron-and-steel (including scrap) data.

AGRICULTURE

SOVIET AGRICULTURE: STRUCTURE AND GROWTH

(By D. Gale Johnson and Arcadius Kahan, University of Chicago)

During the past 3 years there has been a manyfold increase in the publication, and perhaps production, of official Soviet agricultural statistics. Many of these data were not available at the time of the preparation of the excellent publication, "Soviet Economic Growth: A Comparison With the United States," which was published by the Joint Economic Committee in 1957. The published data include detailed information on sown areas, on livestock numbers, on agricultural machinery and a large variety of miscellaneous information. In recent months long-term series have been published on the output of most major agricultural products, including, at long last, estimates that presume to reflect the actual harvest of grain for 1949 to date as well as for 1910–14 on present territory.

A. DATA PROBLEMS

Despite the very considerable increase in the volume of data available, it is not at all certain that our knowledge about and understanding of the agriculture of the Soviet Union have been significantly increased. Many of the data that have been released are of uncertain quality. Many other data that are vital to an understanding of the structure and growth of Soviet agriculture have not been made available. The pattern of release of agricultural data over the past several years has been consistent with the view that the selection of data to be made available is a part of a process designed to provide as favorable a picture as possible of developments in the Soviet Union. There are occasional exceptions to this, when the release of data is required to support an internal policy measure. But as a general rule, the agricultural data that have been made available have been timed to present a picture of achievement and progress. When the record is an unfavorable one, the data frequently have been withheld.

A brief résumé of the data that are still unavailable supports the view that statistics are used as a tool of the Communist state rather than as a means of providing a basis for analysis and understanding. While gross output data are available for most agricultural products, almost no information has been made available on the utilization of those products. How much of the milk is fed to calves? How much of the grain is available for human consumption? How many tons of potatoes are fed to livestock? Relatively few data are available on agricultural employment, apparently because the level of output per worker is so low compared to the United States and other western countries.

What of the quality of the data that are available? While generalization is not possible on the basis of present knowledge, brief comments concerning a few of the available series will indicate some of the difficulties involved in the use of these data.[1] The milk production estimates include the milk of goats, sheep, and other animals as well as cow milk.[2] The estimate of milk production apparently also includes the milk sucked by calves for recent years, though that does not seem to be the case for the period prior to 1940. Crude estimates indicate that the amount of milk sucked by calves may be as much as 6 or 7 million tons in recent years or more than 10 percent of total production. Separate estimates are not available for the amount of milk fed, by hand, to calves and this might amount to as much as 3 or 4 million more tons.

Furthermore, it is uncertain whether the estimate of total milk production is actual weight of milk produced or represents milk of standardzied butterfat content. The milk purchased from State farms is apparently paid for on the basis of milk of 3.2 percent fat content. If the average fat content is 3.8 percent, 5 million tons of milk may become almost 6 million tons in the reported data. And if the standardized fat content were changed or varied from period to period, the consistency of the series becomes very questionable. Finally, it is not at all clear that Soviet officials know the total output of milk with a reasonable degree of accuracy. Over half of the milk is produced by peasants and workers and employees. Several million different households are involved. Short of a carefully selected, large-scale sample with honest responses from the respondents, it is difficult to see how accurate estimates are possible. And such a sample does not exist.

The data on meat output, expressed both in slaughter and live weight, seem to provide a reasonably consistent series over time. At least comparisons with previously available data for the late twenties and the thirties indicate a consistent upward revision of the tonnage figures such as one would expect from the change in the concept of meat. One of the claims made for the American meatpacking industry has been that they make use of everything but the pig's squeal. The Soviet statisticians do the American industry one better; they weigh and count as meat everything but the pig's squeal. This is a slight exaggeration, but not by very much. The Soviet concept of meat includes offal products that are normally excluded in other nations, though there is little reason to believe that the Soviet utilization of offal products is much, if any, more extensive than elsewhere. The art of the sausage and bologna manufacture is well known throughout the world and the ability of the masters of that art to utilize any and every edible part of a slaughtered animal can hardly be questioned. Thus while the Soviet meat series may be internally consistent, the series cannot be compared to meat production or consumption figures for other nations.[3]

In the case of the grain production data, we are almost wholly in the dark concerning what concept of production is being used. Is it the weight of the grain as it comes from the combine? Or are adjustments made for loss of moisture and the trash and chaff included with the grain? Are postharvest losses excluded or included?

[1] More explicit comments appear as notes to some of the Appendix Tables.

[2] For an excellent discussion of the recent milk and meat statistics, see Nancy Nimitz, "Soviet Statistics of Meat and Milk Output: A Note on Their Comparability Over Time," RM-2326, the Rand Corp., 1959.

[3] The Soviet data on meat production should be discounted by at least 10 percent and perhaps as much as 20 percent to achieve comparability. See footnote C, table 12.

How accurately is the corn grain in the corn silage estimated? Khrushchev has accused previous holders of his office of deceiving the world about the level of Soviet grain production;[4] the level of production indicated by the recently released figures do not entirely persuade us that some degree of deceit is still not being practiced.

B. GROWTH OF AGRICULTURAL OUTPUT

Even if we ignore all questions of the accuracy of the available physical production data, there are a number of problems involved in the measurement of total agricultural output of the Soviet Union or any other country. One problem is that of the appropriate concept of output; another is that of the appropriate set of weights for aggregating the physical volume of the individual commodities to derive a single set of values or index numbers. In the particular case of the Soviet Union we have the difficulty arising out of the territorial expansion of the Soviet Union in 1939.

1. *Measures of agricultural output*

We have constructed two measures of total agricultural output. The first concept is that of gross agricultural farm output. In all reference to gross agricultural output we have used official Soviet data, when available, or have made estimates that we believe are consistent with the official estimating procedures and concepts.[5] Gross production figures are available for 11 groups of commodities. The data may be found in appendix table 3.

A legitimate objection to the concept of gross agricultural production, as a measure of total agricultural output, is that it involves duplication in the sense that a part of the output is required to produce the same or other agricultural products. The gross output of grain, for example, includes the grain that is used for seed and for feed for livestock as well as the amount that is available for direct human consumption, industrial use, export, or addition to stocks. For many reasons we are probably more interested in a concept of agricultural output that reflects the volume of production available for nonfarm use; in other words, we wish a concept which eliminates as much as possible the amount of double counting of agricultural output. In gross agricultural output, the grain that is used for feed is counted twice—first as a part of grain output and second as a part of livestock output. The concept that we have defined as net agricultural output is simply the gross agricultural output minus all farm uses of the various products. The farm uses are primarily feed and seed, though in some cases we have also subtracted a factor to represent waste.

We have used three different sets of price weights in the construction of the gross and net agricultural output indexes. The prices received by farmers in the 1926–27 production year are apparently those used by Soviet statisticians to measure agricultural output during the late twenties and the thirties. We have also used average prices received for 1925–29 in order to more fully reflect the under-

[4] Last December Khrushchev said: "Yet Malenkov, in defiance of the facts, declared before the Party Congress in 1952 that the country's gross grain harvest was 8 billion poods and that the grain problem had then, if you please, been solved once and for all. Malenkov acted dishonestly, manipulating by employing the data of the so-called biological yield. * * * In 1952, the best harvest year of the period. the collective and state farms harvested not 8 billion poods but only 5,600 million poods" (Pravda, Dec. 16, 1958).

[5] Our index of gross agricultural output is not directly comparable to the official Soviet index. The Soviet gross output index includes hay, straw, chaff, and manure as well as some minor commodities not included in our index because of lack of data.

lying conditions in the last years of peasant agriculture in the Soviet Union. The third set of price weights used is the official purchase prices announced in 1958.

2. Indexes of agricultural output.

As measures of the trend in agricultural output in the Soviet Union, it makes little difference which concept of output is used or which set of prices is used as weights. This is clear from inspection of the results presented in tables 1 and 2. The various indexes indicate that output in 1957 was approximately 64 to 67 percent greater than 1928.

TABLE 1.—*Indexes of gross agricultural output, Soviet Union* [1]

	1926–27 price weights (1926–29=100)	1926–27 price weights (1928=100)	1925–29 price weights (1928=100)	1958 price weights (1928=100)
1925	94.4	92.6		
1926	98.5	96.7		
1927	96.7	94.9		
1928	101.9	100.0	100.0	100.0
1929	102.9	101.0		
1930	106.2	104.2		
1931	94.1	92.4		
1932	83.2	81.7	80.3	79.3
1933	86 3	84.7		
1934	86.7	85.1		
1935	97.4	95.6		
1936	91.6	89.9		
1937	114.9	112.8	110.5	104.8
1938	100.4	98.5		
1940	122.5	120.3	120 3	118.0
1950	126.8	124.4	124.8	119.0
1951	115.2	113.1		
1952	131.1	128.6		
1953	131.0	128.6	128.8	125.7
1954	136.5	134.0	133.6	131.4
1955	154.6	151.8	149.9	148.2
1956	178.4	175.1	173.3	169.2
1957	170.4	167.2	167.3	166.8
1958 [2]	(195.6)	(192.0)		

[1] Indexes for each year are for the territory within the boundaries existing at the time; 1940 data refer to present territory. The prices used as weights in constructing the indexes are as follows (in rubles per ton, except as noted):

	1926–27	1925–29	1958
Grain	55.5	53.32	740
Potatoes	25.0	31.28	400
Vegetables	60.5	60.5	900
Sunflower seed	66.5	74.44	1,720
Sugar beets	11.6	12.08	235
Raw cotton	282.0	282.0	3,400
Flax fiber (scutched)	368.5	439.0	23,000
Wool (greasy weight)	1,079.0	1,126.8	
Wool, coarse			23,700
Wool, semicoarse			24,700
Wool, semifine			32,900
Wool, fine			41,000
Milk	59.8	68.5	1,150
Eggs (per 1,000)	30.47	32.864	600
Meat, dressed weight old concept	421.2	413.4	
Meat, dressed weight new concept	340.0		
Meat, live weight old concept	210.6		
Beef and veal live weight			6,190
Mutton, live weight			5,360
Pork			7,860
Poultry	725.0	772.5	
Hens and chickens			8,950
Ducks and geese			7,380

[2] A tentative estimate based on less complete data.

Sources: (1) Gossudarstvennaia Planovaia Komissia (Gosplan): Kontrolnye Tsifry Narodnogo Khoziaistva S.S.S.R. na 1929–30 god. Moscow 1930. pp. 581–583.

(2) V. K. Fedinin—Novaia Sistema Zagotovok Selskokhoziaistvennykh Produktovi Ekonomika Kolkhoznogo Proizvodstva. Moscow 1959. p. 12.

TABLE 2.—*Indexes of net agricultural output, Soviet Union* [1]

	1926–27 price weights (1926–29=100)	1926–27 price weights (1928=100)	1925–29 price weights (1928=100)	1958 price weights (1928=100)
1925	95.6	93.2		
1926	96.9	94.5		
1927	96.0	93.6		
1928	102.5	100.0	100.0	100.0
1929	104.7	102.1		
1930	110.2	107.5		
1931	97.1	94.8		
1932	83.6	81.6	79.6	77.3
1933	87.8	85.7		
1934	87.1	85.0		
1935	95.8	93.5		
1936	91.6	89.4		
1937	121.5	118.5	114.6	104.6
1938	103.3	100.8		
1940	123.9	120.3	120.5	115.1
1950	130.2	127.0	126.1	117.8
1951	122.4	119.4		
1952	132.6	129.3		
1953	134.4	131.1	130.1	125.2
1954	139.0	135.6	133.9	130.4
1955	156.1	152.3	149.0	146.1
1956	178.2	173.9	170.4	165.0
1957	170.5	166.3	165.7	164.1

[1] See appendix table 4.

However, one should not interpret all of the change in the index as a true increase in agricultural output. Some of the increase was the result of territorial change; on the basis of the available data it is not possible to determine with any precision the effect of territorial acquisition on the output index. As a rough estimate, if there had been no change in territory in the last three decades, the index of total agricultural output might have been 145 to 152 in 1957 instead of approximately 166. Put another way, approximately 12 to 14 percent of the net output on the present territory in 1940 was the output in the acquired territories.

A few comments may be pertinent concerning changes in the output indexes over time. There was a drastic fall in output following the collectivization of agriculture. Output in 1932 was about a fifth below that of 1928. While some of the decline was due to adverse weather, much of it was due to the resistance of the peasants, expressed in part through the slaughter of their livestock including over half of all the horses. Output gradually increased, reaching a peak in the favorable year weatherwise of 1937. Most of the increase in output between 1938 and 1940 was due to the acquisition of territory.

By 1950 the level of output was somewhat greater than in 1940, on the same territory. Output was relatively static through 1953. There was a small increase in 1954, but the gains in output through 1958 were very substantial indeed. At the present time it is not possible to determine how much of the recent increases in output have been due to favorable climatic developments. Of the 4 years, 1955 through 1958, one (1958) was an extremely favorable year, perhaps as far above average for the fifties as 1937 was for the thirties. Another year (1956) was also an exceptionally favorable one. In both 1955 and 1957 there were major areas of the Soviet Union that had adverse weather, but this is probably a normal or usual phenomenon and these 2 years were at least average in terms of the impact of climatic factors. It is probably true that a considerable fraction of the recent increase is the result of greater incentives, improved management and additional inputs, but at the present time it is not possible to indicate how large this fraction may be.

3. *Changes in output for major commodity groups*

The changes that have occurred in the output, both absolutely and relatively, of major commodity groups are of significance in indicating both the priorities of the planners and the productive possibilities that have existed. In table 3 we have divided total gross and net agricultural output into three broad groups. The first category includes the livestock products, for which the demand expands relatively rapidly as real income grows and which produce relatively few food nutrients per unit of land and labor. However, livestock do transform into food many agricultural products that cannot be directly consumed by the population—pasture, straw, chaff, certain byproducts of food preparation—and thus up to a certain level of output are not really competitive with the more economical sources of food. The second category is the major food crops and includes grain, potatoes, and vegetables. These crops provide a relatively high output of calories and other food nutrients per hectare of land and other inputs used in production. The third category includes the industrial crops.

The most striking change has been the rise in the level of output and the relative importance of the industrial crops in total output. The share in gross output has increased from less than 6 percent to almost 12 percent in recent years;[6] the output index increased from 100 in 1928 to 333 in 1957. This increase probably represents the priorities imposed by a policy of self-sufficiency. Recent levels of cotton output have been approximately five to six times the levels of the late twenties and have now reached approximately a half of the U.S. output which has been declining for the past three decades. The cotton area has more than doubled and yields have approximately doubled.

TABLE 3.—*Indexes of gross and net output of livestock products, technical crops, and food crops, Soviet Union* [1]

	Gross output			Net output		
	Livestock products	Food crops	Industrial crops	Livestock products	Food crops	Industrial crops
1928	100	100	100	100	100	100
1932	61	91	126	61	101	119
1937	71	131	218	71	161	213
1940 [2]	102	125	201	98	137	192
1950	107	124	240	100	140	240
1953	120	120	261	114	128	266
1954	127	125	267	120	131	266
1955	137	146	307	129	151	310
1956	149	176	342	142	183	343
1957	165	152	332	158	145	333

[1] 1926–27 prices used as weights; based on data in appendix tables 3 and 4.
[2] Present boundaries.

[6] The change in the share of net output has been 7.7 percent in 1928 to 15.5 percent in 1958.

4. *Importance of private producers*

Because of the basic differences in the relationship between the state and individual in the Soviet society from the relationships prevailing outside the Communist countries, it is pertinent to determine the relative shares of agricultural output produced by the private and socialized sectors in agriculture, as well as the relative shares of the prevailing institutions within the socialized sector, the collective farms (kolkhozy), the state farms (sovkhozy) and the auxiliary farms of various state institutions (podsobnyie khoziaistva). The distribution of gross output, valued in 1926–27 prices, is presented in the table below.

TABLE 4.—*Shares of producer groups in gross agricultural output*

[Percent]

Years	Collective farms	Socialized sector		Total social	Private sector
		Sovkhozy	Total State farms		
1940	51.7	5.9	7.0	57.7	42.3
1950	54.2	5.7	6.8	61.0	39.0
1953	57.7	6.6	7.8	65.5	34.5
1955	61.1	7.4	8.3	69.4	30.6
1956	59.2	10.0	10.8	70.0	30.0

The distribution of output among the various sectors in 1940 especially the large share of the private sector, is partially explained by the territorial expansion of the boundaries of the Soviet Union in 1939–40, and the private farms of the acquired territories were not yet absorbed by the socialized sector. During the year 1937 for example the distribution was much more similar to the one observed in 1953. The 1950 distribution reflects the wartime and postwar expansion of private output in potatoes and vegetables, as well as the incomplete collectivization of the new territories.

The overall trends, however, are indicated by the table and may be summarized as the slow decline of the share of private output relative to the socialized share and within the socialized sector, the growth of the share of the state farms (sovkhozy). The available data for 1957 and 1958 indicate a substantial rise in the output of the state farms, in part due to the conversion of collective farms into state farms. How far and how rapid this process is intended to go on, is of course anyone's guess.

With respect to the distribution of livestock output we have more detailed data which permit estimates of the relative shares of private and socialized sectors for several consecutive years.

TABLE 5.—*Shares of socialized and private sectors in gross output of livestock products*

[Percent]

Year	Socialized	Private	Year	Socialized	Private
1940	24.9	75.1	1954	38.8	61.2
1950	29.3	70.7	1955	41.6	58.4
1951	33.3	66.7	1956	42.6	57.4
1952	37.0	63.0	1957	44.6	55.4
1953	39.9	60.1			

There is little question that the Soviet authorities have decided to assure the socialized sector with a dominant position in the output of livestock products. Pressure is mounting upon all private producers—urban dwellers and state farm employees as well as collective farm members—to turn over their livestock to the collective and state farms. But by and large this policy is more subtle and cautious than similar policies in the past.

5. Comparisons of agricultural output, U.S.S.R. and United States

The data presented in table 6 provide measures of the changes in the absolute levels of gross output, as officially reported, for the 11 major agricultural commodities for the Soviet Union and data that permit rough comparisons with the output of 9 of the groups in the United States. The absolute level of output in the Soviet Union in 1955–58 exceeded that in the United States for potatoes, sugar, and wool. The Soviet output was substantially lower for grains, vegetables, cotton, meat, and eggs. While the gross output of milk was only 10 percent less than in the United States, we believe that the amount of milk remaining for human consumption was more than a fourth less than in the United States.[7]

Because of the change in territory of the Soviet Union it is more difficult to make meaningful statements concerning output growth since 1925–29. As noted above, Soviet agricultural output probably increased by about 12 to 14 percent in 1940 as a result of territorial expansion. If one attempts to adjust for this in a crude fashion, it is clear that the Soviet output growth was significantly greater than ours for potatoes, sugar, cotton, and wool. The increase in grain output was probably somewhat higher than in the United States, while the output growth of vegetables, meat, and eggs was less. The case of milk is uncertain, though Soviet output on comparable territory may have increased slightly more than in the United States

Between 1925–29 and 1955–58 the index of farm output for the United States increased by 58 percent.[8] This index is basically similar to the index of net agricultural output that we have calculated for the Soviet Union. Based on a tentative estimate of the index of net agricultural output for 1958, the increase for the Soviet Union between 1925–29 and 1955–58 was approximately 70 percent. This estimate is not adjusted for the change of territory. If one makes the extreme assumption that there would have been no change in output on the acquired territories if they had remained independent of the Soviet Union, one arrives at an increase for the period for the 1928 territory of approximately 55 percent.

While this increase in total agricultural output is no larger than that achieved in the United States during a period of time when we have been trying to restrict agricultural output, there is no question that the increase in output is a very substantial one. And output during 1958 was substantially above the average for 1955–58, though it may be noted that the same was true for the United States. In both cases climatic conditions undoubtedly were in part responsible for the favorable outcome.

[7] See table 13 for a presentation of a net milk output series for the two countries.
[8] U.S. Department of Agriculture, "Agricultural Outlook Charts, 1959," p. 64.

TABLE 6.—*Gross output of major agricultural commodities, Soviet Union and United States* [1]

[Million tons]

	Grain	Potatoes	Vegetables [2]	Sugar [3]	Seed cotton [4]
A. Soviet Union:					
1925-29	73.2	43.0	10.6	8.4	0.70
1950-54	84.1	72.8	10.5	22.0	3.85
1955-58	119.7	85.4	11.5	39.4	4.30
B. United States:					
1925-29	121.7	9.5	13.6	7.2	10.5
1950-54	140.7	10.1	19.0	14.2	9.7
1955-58	159.9	11.1	20.0	18.7	8.7
C. Ratio, Soviet Union to United States (percent):					
1925-29	60.1	452.6	77.9	116.7	16.7
1950-54	70.2	720.8	55.3	154.9	39.7
1955-58	74.8	769.3	57.5	210.7	49.4

	Flax-fiber	Sunflower seed	Wool	Milk	Meat (dressed weight)	Eggs [5] (billions)
A. Soviet Union:						
1925-29	0.30	1.97	0.17	30.0	4.69	10.3
1950-54	.21	2.06	.21	36.4	5.36	14.5
1955-58	.45	3.01	.28	51.1	7.04	21.0
B. United States:						
1925-29	---------	---------	.15	43.0	9.8	37.6
1950-54	---------	---------	.12	53.9	14.4	58.4
1955-58	---------	---------	.12	56.7	16.6	59.5
C. Ratio, Soviet Union to United States (percent):						
1925-29	---------	---------	113.3	69.8	47.8	27.4
1950-54	---------	---------	175.0	67.5	37.2	24.8
1955-58	---------	---------	233.3	90.1	42.4	35.3

[1] Sources: Soviet data, see appendix table 3. U.S. data: U.S. Department of Agriculture, Agricultural Statistics, 1957; "Livestock and Meat Statistics, 1957," Stat. Bul. No. 230; "Consumption of Food in the United States, 1909-52," Agriculture Handbook No. 26, supplements for 1954 and 1957; "The National Food Situation," July 1959, "Major Statistical Series of the U.S. Department of Agriculture," vol. 5, Agriculture Handbook No. 118; Crop Production, 1958 Annual Summary," Dec. 17, 1958.

[2] Vegetables for United States excludes melons of all types.

[3] Sugar output for United States is in terms of sugar beet equivalent. Sugar refined from cane sugar converted into sugar beets assuming 14 percent sugar content.

[4] Cotton output for United States converted to seed cotton by assuming lint to seed cotton ratio of 0.33

[5] Egg production for United States is farm production only.

6. Per capita availability of farm products

Our general discussion of changes in agricultural output in the Soviet Union may be concluded by presentation of certain estimates on per capita availability of various agricultural products. The data presented in table 7 do not purport to represent per capita consumption; the data are estimates of net output which include industrial use, exports and changes in stocks, as well as consumption by the Soviet population. Nor has any attempt been made to include imports, but imports have generally been of little significance. The estimates are admittedly subject to error.

The situation with respect to per capita availability in 1950–53 compared to 1926–29 implies little or no improvement. The availability of grain was approximately the same; potatoes, sugar, and cotton had increased substantially. There was a small improvement in the case of eggs, but there were fewer vegetables, less meat and milk, less wool and flax fiber, and less sunflower seed, the major source of vegetable oil for human consumption. Roughly speaking, the index of net agricultural output on a per capita basis was slightly lower in 1950–53 than in 1928.

The data indicate a clear improvement in recent years, especially in grain, sugar, sunflowers, milk, eggs and flax fiber. The change in per capita meat availability has been rather modest, but an improvement has occurred.[9]

TABLE 7.—*Per capita net output of major agricultural products, Soviet Union* [1]

[Kilograms per annum]

	1926–29	1931–34	1935–38	1940	1950–53	1954–57	1955–58
Grains	241.4	218.9	247.3	238.4	247.9	274.6	297.6
Potatoes	102.1	133.5	144.1	194.6	172.8	164.4	163.2
Vegetables	49.8	64.6	57.9	50.1	41.2	55.0	56.4
Sugar beets	52.0	51.7	104.6	90.5	118.0	151.5	187.5
Sunflower seeds	12.2	13.4	10.1	13.0	10.8	15.2	18.1
Milk	176.2	111.6	131.6	144.2	144.8	182.8	200.9
Meat	32.7	16.7	19.8	24.5	27.5	33.5	34.8
Eggs	64.2	25.7	41.6	58.9	68.0	89.7	95.1
Cotton	4.9	7.5	13.6	11.7	19.7	20.8	20.8
Wool	1.12	.4	.6	.81	1,06	1.25	1.34
Flax-fiber	1.86	2.38	2.33	1.82	1.18	1.87	2.09

[1] The population estimates used are as follows (in mllions): 1926–29, 150.6; 1931–34, 165.6; 1935–38, 169.3; 1940, 191.7; 1950–53, 186.9; 1954–57, 198.3; and 1955–58, 202.3.

C. CHANGES IN IMPUTS AND AVERAGE PRODUCTIVITY

The increase in Soviet agricultural output has been associated with a large increase in the sown area, a small increase in the total labor input, a marked increase in machinery and equipment, and a substantial increase in fertilizer. While it would be desirable to have a measure of the total quantity of inputs used in agriculture for various periods of time, satisfactory estimates are not yet available for all inputs. At this time, we can only indicate the change in some of the major inputs and estimate average productivity or yield. It should be noted that changes in average productivity of labor or yield of crops is not an indication of change in efficiency since the quantities of other inputs have increased much more rapidly than either labor or land.

1. Sown area

By 1925 the total sown area had reached the same level as 1913, for comparable territory. By 1931 the total sown area had increased from 104.3 million hectares to 136.3 million. There was some retrenchment in sown area during the next few years, but by 1938 the sown area was again approximately the same as in 1931. The sown area increased by approximately 14 to 15 million hectares as a consequence of territorial expansion. The 1950 sown area of 146.3 million hectares was somewhat below the 1940 area on comparable terri-

[9] The very great change in the proportion of urban population in the Soviet Union since the late twenties creates certain problems in the interpretation of the per capita data. According to food consumption studies made during the late twenties, there were substantial differences in the food consumption patterns of urban and rural residents. As a result, one cannot interpret an increase in the per capita availability of meat, for example, as meaning that the per capita consumption of urban residents is now greater than during the late twenties. If the per capita consumption of urban and rural residents for the late twenties is weighted by the current population distribution, the weighted per capita availability of meat meat in 1955–53 was lower than in 1926–29. However, in the case of certain other foods, rural consumption rates were greater than urban rates and the weighted availability increased more than the per capita availability. This was true of grains, for example. The consumption data for the twenties were taken from Gossudarstvennaia Planovaia Komissia (Gosplan) S.S.S.R.: "Piatiletnii Plan Narodno—Khoziaistvennogo Stroitelstva S.S.S.R," vol. I, p. 106. vol. II, pt. 2, p. 305. Moscow 1930, 3d ed.

tory. With the new lands program, which was inaugurated in 1954, the total sown area increased by 28 million hectares between 1953 and 1956 and has remained at roughly 195 million hectares in recent years.

While there is some cost in terms of alternative products foregone by increasing the sown area—the area of pastures and meadows is reduced—there can be no question that the expansion of the sown area has contributed to the increased output. If the increase due to the acquisition of territory is included, the sown area increased by 88 percent between 1925 and 1958.

There has been a significant expansion of irrigation since 1913. At that time approximately 4.0 million hectares was irrigated while in 1955 the irrigable area was 11.1 million hectares,[10] though apparently a significant fraction of this area is not being cropped currently.

2. Crop yields

Annual estimates of crop yields are presented in appendix table 5, based on official gross production data. In table 8 average yields for 4- or 5-year periods are presented. Notable increases in yields were achieved for cotton, sugar beets, and sunflowers, while the increases for grain, potatoes, and flax-fiber were approximately 20 percent or less. While we believe that the recent output data for grain are somewhat exaggerated, or at least may not be consistent with the earlier data, it should be noted that the eastward extension of the grain area would have resulted in a reduction in the average grain yields since the newer areas are intrinsically less productive than the areas sown to grain in earlier periods.

The increase in the yield of cotton is a striking one, but a major factor in the increase has been the virtual abandonment of the practice of growing cotton on unirrigated land in the Ukraine and the R.S.F.S.R. As late as 1952, about 35 percent of the cotton land was unirrigated, grown in climatically unsuited areas. The yield of cotton on irrigated land has probably increased by about a third since 1935–38.

TABLE 8.—*Crop yields, Soviet Russia, 1925–58* [1]

[Centners per hectare]

	Grain	Cotton	Sugar beets	Sunflower	Potatoes	Flax fiber
1925–29	7.91	8.82	132.0	6.24	79.3	2.08
1930–34	6.77	6.28	95.3	5.31	80.0	1.76
1935–38	7.07	11.40	147.3	5.50	78.5	1.90
1950–54	7.85	16.50	150.8	5.47	86.2	1.32
1955–58	9.49	20.24	185.6	9.31	90.9	2.53

[1] Obtained by dividing gross physical output (appendix table 3) by sown area (appendix table 1), except that flax-fiber output is our estimate of net physical output.

TABLE 9.—*Crop yields, United States, 1925–58* [1]

	Centners per hectare			Cotton (bales per hectare)	
	Grain	Sugar beets	Potatoes	All	Irrigated [2]
1925–29	13.9	244	76.4	0.84	
1950–54	17.0	347	169.2	1.47	
1955–58	20.6	378	193.2	2.08	4.9

[1] USDA, Agricultural Statistics, 1957, and Crop Production, 1958 Annual Summary (Dec. 17, 1958).
[2] Average yields for the States of New Mexico, Arizona, and California.

[10] Central Statistical Board of the U.S.S.R. Council of Ministers, "Forty Years of Soviet Power," (English translation), Moscow, 1958, p. 165.

The increase in sugar beet and sunflower yields have been significant ones. The very substantial increase in sunflower yields between 1950–54 and 1955–58 raises the possibility that climatic factors may have played a significant role in the higher yields, though increased application of fertilizer and manure, improved seeds and better cultural practices have undoubtedly been important as well. It may be noted that the sugar beet yield for 1937 of 183.7 centners per hectare was not exceeded in recent years except in 1957 and 1958. The latter 2 years were favorable growing years in the Ukraine, where over half of the sugar beets are grown.

3. Yield comparisons, Soviet Union and United States

A comparison of average yields for the United States and the Soviet Union for the period 1955–58 may be of interest, though such comparisons may be more indicative of climatic and soil conditions than of differences due to management or incentives.[11] The average grain yield was 20.6 centners per hectare in the United States or more than double the 9.5 centner yield in the Soviet Union. The average yield of cotton in the Soviet Union, essentially all grown on irrigated land, was almost 3 bales of lint cotton per hectare. The average for the United States as a whole was a little more than 2 bales per hectare. However, the average yield in New Mexico, Arizona, and California, where all of the cotton is irrigated, was 4.9 bales per hectare. The average yield of potatoes in the United States was 193 centners per hectare or more than double the 91 centners in the Soviet Union. The U.S. sugar beet yield was 37.8 tons per hectare compared to 18.6 tons. A large proportion of the U.S. sugar beet area is irrigated while probably only a relatively small proportion of the Soviet area is.

4. Labor employment

The measurement of the amount of labor used in Soviet agriculture is beset with many difficulties. Even if one had access to all of the data that exists in the Soviet Union, which we do not, it is probable that any estimates that one could make would still be subject to significant error. An indication of the possible hiatus in the estimates may be seen from the following estimates found in or derived from Soviet publications:

[Millions]

	1928 or 1929	1940	1950	1955	1956
Number of workers [1]	53.2	31.7			33.5
Labor power in man-years [2]	27.4	31.0	24.7	33.4	33.5

[1] Derived from "Forty Years of Soviet Power," Moscow, 1958. pp. 136–137 on the basis of relation between total horsepower in agriculture and horsepower per worker. Data for 1940 and 1956 are said to refer only to socialized sector, but this is probably not correct.

[2] Estimates made by S. Strumilin ("Some Problems of the Further Development of the Kolkhoz Regime," Problems of Economics, November 1958, p. 18. Originally published in Voprosy Ekonomiki, May 1958.) Strumilin's estimates include private peasants for 1940 and later, but does not include the labor input on household plots. (See "Planovoye Khoziaistva," 1957, No. 2, p. 48.)

The close correspondence between the estimates for 1940 and 1956 is probably no accident; the estimate of the horsepower per worker, as published in "Forty Years of Soviet Power," was apparently obtained by dividing total horsepower in agriculture by Strumilin's estimate of

[11] The yield data for the United States are from USDA, Agricultural Statistics, 1957, and Crop Production, 1958 Annual Summary (Dec. 17, 1958). Yield data are not available for sunflower seed or flax fiber.

labor power measured in man-years. The small difference for 1940 is apparently due to a rounding error.[12]

According to Strumilin's data, the total labor input in agriculture increased a minimum of 22 percent; the increase was presumably more than this since his data include all of agricultural output in 1928, but entirely ignores the 30 percent of the gross output produced in 1956 by the private sector. If we were to add our estimate of the labor input required in the private sector for 1956, assuming 265 days of work per year, of 4.8 million man-years to Strumilin's total,[13] an estimate of 38.3 million years is obtained. This would imply an increase of 40 percent in total labor input in Soviet agriculture between 1928 and 1956. While such a large increase does not appear consistent with other data, such as the changes in agricultural population or the number of farm households, it cannot be completely ignored as a possible upper limit to the increase in the labor input.

It is clear that the 53.2 million workers indicated for 1928 or 1929 is not consistent with the other figures in the same series, since the data for 1940 and 1956 represent some concept of full-time employment, while the figure for 1928 refers to some particular group that performed some farm work during the year or perhaps to the total number of workers in the agricultural population aged 15–59 with an adjustment for the lower productivity of females.

Our own estimates imply that there was an increase in labor inputs between 1926–29 and 1956 of 10 to 16 percent.[14] The estimates indicate that the postwar low level of employment was reached in 1953 and that the labor input increased by about 13 percent between 1953 and 1956. Such an increase was due to the new-lands program, the corn program, and the expansion of livestock output. The latter two endeavors were highly labor intensive under Soviet conditions.

There was undoubtedly a decline in the total number of persons employed in agriculture over the past three decades. This was made possible by the lengthening of the work year per person at work from perhaps 120 days to about 185–190 days. The increased participation was made possible by a reduction in the importance of cottage industry in rural areas and an encroachment upon the time of the housewife. We believe that a reasonable estimate of the decline in farm employment is from about 53 million in 1928 to about 42 million in 1956, excluding the employment of children and workers 60 years or older.

5. Labor productivity and requirements

If we compare the change in net agricultural output (index weighted by 1958 purchase prices) with the change in the labor input measured by man-years worked, we find that the average product of labor increased by 36 to 43 percent between 1928 and 1955–57. The increase in average product per worker was 100 percent, which is a substantial increase. In the United States the increase in average product per man-hour, for the same period, was 142 percent. Since the length of the work year declined in the United States, rather than increased as

[12] Strumilin gives the average as 3.53, while in "Forty Years" the average was rounded to 3.5. For 1956 the average given by Strumilin is 3.50, which is given as 3.5 in "Forty Years."

[13] See the forthcoming article by Arcadius Kahan, "Changes in Labor Inputs in Soviet Agriculture," to be published in the Journal of Political Economy, October 1959, for the derivation of this estimate.

[14] A. Kahan, ibid.

in the Soviet Union, the increase in average product per worker was 149 percent.[15]

In his speech before the December plenary session of the Party Central Committee, Khrushchev revealed the very large differences that existed between the amount of labor used to produce farm products in the U.S.S.R. and the United States. His data indicated that labor used per unit of output ranged from 160 percent of the U.S. level for cotton on state farms to 1,630 percent for production of hogs on collective farms.[16]

Two types of data on labor use by product are given. The first (table 10) is in terms of labor used per hectare. These data allow a comparison of labor use on the peasant farms for 1925–26 and on collective farms in 1937 and for 1954–55. These data indicate a very substantial decline in the use of labor for grain production following collectivization, though there was apparently no change between 1937 and 1954–55. The labor requirements for potatoes remained unchanged. The cotton data probably are not comparable because of the substantial increase in yield in the years just before 1956. The data for the other crops indicate a reduction in labor requirements of roughly 20 to 30 percent between 1937 and 1954–55.

The other table (table 11) presents somewhat more figures for 1956 and 1957 for the state farms than might seem to be appropriate. The reason for this is a remark made by Khrushchev in presenting the data for the United States:

> One may assume that the bourgeois statistics make the situation look better than it is.

TABLE 10.—*Labor used per hectare of land by peasants and collective farms, U.S.S.R.*

[Man-days]

	Peasants	Collective farms		
	1925–26 [1]	1937 [2]	1954–55 [2]	1956 [3]
Grain	20.8	10.6	10.0–12.0	
Potatoes	61.3	65.2	60.0–80.0	
Cotton	117.2	81.8		145.8
Flax		79.2	66.5	
Sunflower		13.4	10.6	
Sugar beets		131.8	89.6	

[1] See, Gosplan S.S.S.R., Perspektivnyi Plan Razvertyvania Narodnogo Khoziaistva S.S.R. na 1926/27–1930/31 gg. Edited by S. G. Strumilin, Moscow 1927, p. 15, and TsUNKhU Gosplana S.S.S.R., Sotsialisticheskoe Selskoe Khoziaistvo. Moscow-Leningrad, 1939, p. 47.

[2] See TsUNKhU Gosplana S.S.S.R., Proizvoditelnost' i Ispolzovanie Truda v Kolkhozakh vo Vtoroi Piatiletke. Edited by I. V. Sautin, Moscow, Leningrad, 1939, pp. IX, 12–16. Ekonomika Selskogo Khoziaistva #2, 1957. p. 96. Academia Nauk S.S.S.R., Voprosy Razmeschenia i Spetsializatsil Selskogo.

[3] Khlopkovodsvo, 1957, No. 11, p. 13. Khoziaistva, Moscow, 1957. pp. 65, 323.

[15] Based on U.S. Department of Agriculture, "Changes in Farm Production and Efficiency," Stat. Bull. No. 233, August 1958, pp. 6 and 27 and "Agricultural Statistics," 1957, p. 536.

[16] The data for the United States in table 10 are taken directly from Khrushchev's speech. We were not able to duplicate the result for cotton. The highest labor requirement obtained was 15.6 hours, while the requirement that seems most consistent with the Soviet data was 13.6 hours. For U.S. data, see USDA, "Agricultural Statistics," 1957, pp. 71, 139, and 589.

TABLE 11.—*Labor used per centner of output, U.S.S.R. and United States*

	State farms, U.S.S.R.						United States [3] 1956 (man-hours)
	Man-days		Man-hours				
	1956 [1]	1957 [2]	1956 [2]	1955 [2]	1954 [2]	1956–57 [3]	
Milk	1.76	14.5	14.0	15.9	15.6	9.9	4.7
Beef	10.0	64.0	76.0	79.0	82.0	52.0	7.9
Pork	8.0	57.6	65.9	73.4	73.0	43.0	6.3
Grain		2.9	2.0	3.5	3.6	1.8	1.0
Potatoes				8.0		4.2	1.0
Cotton	[4] 4.6					29.8	18.8
Sugar beets						2.1	.5

COLLECTIVE FARMS, U.S.S.R.

	1937 [5] (man-days)	1937 [6] (man-hours)	1956 [7] (man-days)	1956–57 [3] (man-hours)
Grain	(1.2–1.3)	(9–10)		7.3
Sunflower seed	1.97	16		
Potatoes	.67	5		5.1
Sugar beets	.73	6		3.1
Cotton	10.6	85		42.8
Flax	47.2	38		
Milk	4.6	37	2.9	14.7
Beef			21.0	112.0
Pork	23.6		20.0	103.0

[1] A.M. Brianskii, Voprosy Ekonomiki, 1957, No. 12, p. 118.
[2] I. Benediktov, Puti Snizhenia Sebestiomosti Produktsii Sovkhozov, Moscow, 1957 and "Sovkhoznoe Proizvodstvo," Nos. 6 and 8, 1958.
[3] N. Khrushchev, Pravda, Dec. 16, 1958.
[4] Figure is Uzbek S.S.R. only (V. Manyakhin, "Problems of Economics," November 1958, p. 29). Uzbek produces about ⅔ of the total U.S.S.R. cotton. If one assumes an 8-hour day, the total man-hours would be 36.8 hours.
[5] See footnote [2], table 10. Grain estimate based on man-days per hectare, assuming a yield of 8 centners per hectare.
[6] Based on man-day data, assuming 8-hour day.
[7] Voprosy Ekonomiki, No. 12, 1957, p. 118.

Regardless of what the situation may be with "bourgeois statistics," Khrushchev must have made some adjustment in the data for the state farms to "make the situation look better than it is." It is a little difficult to average 14.5 and 14.0 and obtain 9.9, the average labor used to produce milk for 1956–57, or to average 64 and 76 and obtain 52.0 as the labor used for beef. The man-hour data for the years 1956 and 1957 were published by I. Benediktov, formerly Minister of State Farms, who would hardly have any reason to exaggerate the amount of labor used. While the evidence is not quite as clear for the collective farms, since we have data only for 1 year and expressed in days rather than hours, it appears that Khrushchev found it necessary to make a few adjustments in the data to prevent the ratio of labor used on collective farms from reaching a level of 20 to 25, instead of 16, times the U.S. level.

6. Mechanization and power

There can be no question that there has been a very considerable degree of mechanization in Soviet agriculture during the past three decades. But two points need to be remembered. First, the animal draft power situation in Russia, either before the revolution or just prior to the collectivization drive, was a relatively favorable one. In 1916, before either the United States or Russia had any significant number of tractors, there were roughly 50 percent more horses in

Russia than in the United States, even though the cultivated area was some 10 to 20 percent less. The much larger relative number of horses was in part a consequence of the much greater number of farms, but nonetheless the draft power was available for the performance of all farm operations.

Second, a very large fraction of the investment in tractors and tractor-drawn equipment, perhaps all the investment made through 1940, was required to offset the decline in the number of horses and to replace the horse-drawn equipment. The number of horses declined from 32.6 million in 1929 to 14.9 million in 1934; there was an increase to 17.7 million in 1940 and a further increase in 1941 due to the acquisition of territory. Approximately half of the horses were lost during World War II. The postwar peak in the number of horses was 15.3 million, reached in 1953 and 1954.

While the substitution of tractor and other means of mechanical power for horses and oxen made possible labor savings, it is quite likely that crop output suffered as a result of the substitution until very recently. This may have occurred because there simply was not enough of the large and cumbersome tractors and combines to perform the farm operations in a timely manner.

Tentative results indicate that an index, in constant prices, of farm machinery, equipment, and workstock declined by almost a third between 1928 and 1933 and then increased to about the 1928 level by the late thirties. By 1950 the index was perhaps 5 percent below the 1928 level and by 1956 had reached a level approximately 50 to 55 percent above 1928.[17] This index has undoubtedly increased since 1956. Roughly speaking, there has been a similar long-term movement of the index of machinery and power and of net output. If mechanization had been primarily labor saving instead of primarily displacing animal power, the index of machinery and power should have increased much more rapidly than the index of output.[18]

D. AN ATTEMPT AT EXPLANATION OF LONG-RUN CHANGES IN OUTPUT

The previous two parts of this paper have developed our estimates of changes in output of agricultural products, of the quantities of the major inputs used, and of the changes in the average productivity or yield of labor and land. Comparisons of the changes in the average product per unit of land and labor in the United States and the U.S.S.R. indicate rather clearly that the organizational structure of Soviet agriculture has not resulted in any production miracles or especially outstanding increases in resource productivity. Nevertheless, output did increase enough to approximately maintain per capita output at the levels of the late twenties during the early fifties and to increase per capita output substantially since 1953.

In this part we shall be primarily concerned with the longer run factors that have contributed to the higher level of output. One way of explaining changes in output is to accurately measure changes in the total quantity of inputs used, including in quantity a measure of changes in quality, and to determine whatever changes in efficiency

[17] We have not made a comparison of the levels of mechanization in the Soviet Union and the United States since there has been little change from the relative quantitative position discussed in "Soviet Economic Growth: A Comparison With the United States" (1957, pp. 70–72). There has been, however, some qualitative improvement in the kinds and types of equipment. More row crop tractors are available and hydraulically operated, tractor mounted implements are now being produced in quantity. In general, the trend has been toward lighter and less cumbersome machinery and the adoption of labor-saving attachments.

[18] If animal draft is excluded from the index, the index increases from 100 in 1928 to about 450 in 1956.

of utilization of the inputs, if any, may have occurred. While our research studies are moving in this direction, at this stage a much more mechanical approach is required. The mechanical approach does permit us to identify some of the specific changes that have been associated with the increased output.

1. Decline in the number of horses

The two most important factors in the increase of agricultural output for human consumption have been the substitution of mechanical for animal power and the increase in the sown area. Since 1928 the decline in the feed required for horses alone has been enough to account for about 60 percent of the feed required to produce the additional livestock output of 1958 compared to 1928, including the estimated change in livestock inventories in 1958.[19] Since horses were heavy users of grain and other concentrates, the contribution to the increase in livestock output for human use may be somewhat greater than that indicated.

2. Increase in sown area

Between 1928 and 1958 the total sown area increased from 113 to about 195 million hectares or by 82 million hectares (73 percent). Approximately 14 to 15 million hectares of the increase was due to the acquisition of new territories, thus the increase in sown area due to the agricultural activities of the Soviet Union comes to 68 million hectares or 60 percent. Even if the yields of the sown crops had remained constant as the sown area was extended into the drier areas, as was the case, this does not mean that agricultural output would have increased in the same proportion as the change in sown area. If one assumed that all of the increase in sown area had been devoted to grain or feed crops and that the sole objective were to increase the feed supply, the increase in feed supply due to increasing the sown area by 62 million hectares might have been from 40 to 50 million tons of feed units. This may be compared to the 35-million-ton reduction in estimated feed requirements for horses between 1928 and 1958 and a total estimated feed requirement of about 200 million tons in 1958. Of course, a large fraction of the additional sown area was used to produce grain for human consumption and to increase the area of industrial crops. The total increase in feed used between 1928 and 1958, including that derived from pasture and assuming constant feed requirements, was about 20 million tons of feed units.

3. Increase in crop yields

A factor, which was relatively unimportant prior to 1955, has been increased crop yields per hectare. Grain yields in the 4-year period 1926–29 may have averaged about 7.9 centners per hectare; the average yield for 1949–53 was 7.7 centners. During 1955–58, if we accept the official production data, the average yield was about 9.5 centners. The shift in the location of grain production should have reduced yields by a little more than a half centner, implying a real increase in the grain yield of about 20 to 25 percent since the late twenties. In the case of cotton and sugar beets yield increases have been greater than for grains.

[19] See sec. E below for estimates of feed requirements.

4. Increases in labor intensive crops

A fourth factor has been the increase in the relative importance of the labor intensive industrial crops, especially cotton and sugar beets. These crops normally have a relatively high value per unit of land. With the very great amount of labor available and the great emphasis that has been placed upon autarchy, the expansion of the industrial crops was not an unexpected development. As noted earlier, the share of the industrial crops in net agricultural output increased from 7.7 percent in 1928 to 15.5 percent in 1957. The percentage of the total sown area for the industrial crops for which we have made estimates of output actually declined from 7.7 to 6.1 percent between 1928 and 1957.[20]

The following tabulation presents data on changes in sown area for the crops included in our estimates of output and changes in the value of gross output (in 1926–27 prices) of the same crops, total and average per hectare, for 1928 and 1955–57:

	1928	1955–57
Total:		
Area of included crops (million hectares)	107.6	149.7
Total output of included crops (billion rubles)	6.5	11.3
Output per hectare (rubles)	60.3	75.3
Index, output per hectare	100.0	124.9
Grain, potatoes; and vegetables:		
Area (million hectares)	99.9	137.9
Output (billion rubles)	5.9	9.3
Output per hectare (rubles)	58.8	67.3
Index, output per hectare	100.0	114.4
Industrial crops:		
Area (million hectares)	7.71	11.8
Output (billion rubles)	.61	1.99
Output per hectare (rubles)	79.1	168.6
Index, output per hectare	100.0	213.1

The output per hectare of the crops included increased 24.9 percent between 1928 and 1955–57.[21] The increase in output per hectare for grains, potatoes and vegetables was only 14.4 percent, while the increase for the industrial crops was 113.1 percent. While a considerable part of the increase in the output of industrial crops per hectare has been due to the increased importance of irrigation, it is nevertheless true that a significant part of the increase in total output of crops was due to the greater emphasis given to industrial crops which use a relatively small part of the total sown area.

5. Increase in livestock output per unit of feed

While there has been some increase in output of livestock products per unit of feed, it is very difficult to say how important this factor has been. Undoubtedly livestock are better housed today than they were during the thirties or in the period after the last war. Whether they are better housed than during the twenties is a moot point. But milk represents one instance in which the ratio of output to feed intake must have increased. For a cow that produces only 1,000 kilograms

[20] This statement may be somewhat misleading in the sense that a much larger fraction of the industrial crops was grown on irrigated land in 1957 than in 1928.

[21] A similar measure for the United States indicates an increase in crop yields per acre of 56.4 percent for the same years. See U.S. Department of Agriculture, Major Statistical Series of the U.S. Department of Agriculture, vol. 2, Agriculture Handbook No. 118, 1957, p. 50, and Crop Production, 1958 Annual Summary (Dec. 17, 1958), p. 49. The index of yields per harvested acre for 18 field crops was used. The estimates for the Soviet Union are based on official Soviet data, which we believe are somewhat too high for the grain crops for 1955–57.

of milk per year, at least three-fourths of the feed is required for maintenance. But if the milk yield increases to 1,500 kilograms, only two-thirds of the feed is required for maintenance. On the basis of the net production of milk that we have assumed, the feed requirements per kilogram of milk declined from somewhat more than 1.9 feed units in 1928 to less than 1.5 in 1958. There is little reason to believe that there has been much change in feeding efficiency for other livestock products, except for pork. The increase in the availability of feed grains in the last 2 or 3 years may have resulted in some reduction in the amount of feed required per centner of pork.

6. The corn program and the feed supply

A final factor must be commented upon because of the great importance that Khrushchev has attached to it, namely the corn program. In 1955 it was announced that the corn area was to be expanded to 28 million hectares by 1960. This represented an increase of about 24 million hectares. The maximum area thus far realized was 23.9 million hectares in 1956. In 1958 the total corn area was 19.7 million hectares, of which 4.4 million hectares was harvested as dry grain, 3.7 million hectares in the milk-wax stage, and 9.6 million hectares of silage.[22] The remaining 5.9 million hectares was harvested as green feed. The total grain equivalent of corn was reported as 16.2 million tons, indicating an average yield of 20 centners of corn grain per hectare. Since the gross yield of all other grains was only 10.8 centners per hectare, it would appear that the expansion of the corn area had indeed been a considerable success. But it should be remembered that corn is grown for grain in precisely the areas where other grains give yields substantially above the national average. Approximately three-fourths of all the corn harvested for grain is in three areas—the Ukraine, Moldavia, and the Kuban. Data are available that allow us to estimate the official absolute yields for corn and for all wheat in the Ukraine for 1950–55 and 1958. The unweighted average yields for this 7-year period were 14.7 centners for corn and 12.9 for wheat.[23] This is a difference of 11 percent. In 1958 the corn yield was about 30 percent greater than the wheat yield, but in 1953 and 1954 corn yielded slightly less than wheat. One obvious advantage of corn should be noted; namely, that its seed requirement is at least 1.25 centners per hectare less than for wheat, oats, barley, and rye. Thus even if the harvested yield of corn were the same as for wheat, the amount of grain available for feed would be greater in the case of corn.

The major net contribution that corn has made to the feed supply has not been the grain, but the silage and the green feed. And even here the contribution has not been so much the increase in total quantity of feed, as conventionally measured, but through improvement in the quality of the available feed and a change in the seasonal distribution of feed. The available data indicate that the vast majority of the cattle in the Soviet Union receive very little grain. In 1956 the average grain fed in the collective farms to all cattle (converted to a basis of an adult milk cow) was 180 kilograms; in the

[22] N. Khrushchev, Pravda, Dec. 21, 1958. The 9.6 million hectares of silage includes the 3.7 million hectares of corn harvested in the milk-wax stage.

[23] Estimated from data given in Pravda, May 12, 1959, "Ekonomika Selskogo Khoziaistva," No. 2, 1959, pp. 25, 28, and 29, and "Narodne Gospodarstvo Ukrainskoi R.S.R. Statistichnii Sbornik," Kiev, 1957 pp. 101 and 116.

United States approximately 775 kilograms were fed.[24] The roughage available in the Soviet Union while reasonably adequate in amount, is of very poor quality. Over half consists of materials other than hay, primarily straw and chaff. And most of the hay is what we would call wild hay, which is relatively low in protein and has a relatively low net energy value. Silage has represented a valuable addition to a feed ration of so little intrinsic merit. Morrison reports experiments that indicate that corn silage added to a ration roughly comparable to that described above resulted in an increase in butterfat production per cow of about 50 percent.[25]

The other value of corn is as a source of green feed during the middle and late summer months when the pastures provide relatively little feed. Available data on the distribution of milk deliveries indicate that the production of milk declined rapidly after the flush pasture feeding period of spring and early summer. Once the milk flow is reduced, increased feeding at a period later does little to regain the original flow. The availability of immature corn, fed directly from the field, has undoubtedly maintained the milk flow at a relatively high rate for a longer period than was the case in the past.

The corn silage yields, as estimated from production and area data, are hardly spectacular. The average annual yields for the years 1955 through 1958 did not exceed the following amounts (tons per hectare): 6.6, 7.5, 8.1, and 11.2. The yields may have been a quarter or more less than this, since the stalks and leaves from the corn harvested in the milk-wax stage is also put in silos. Most of the corn that is put in silos has apparently not ripened to the milk-wax stage, which results in a considerably lower feed value per ton than would be true of silage prepared in the United States.

E. OVERTAKE THE UNITED STATES IN THE PER CAPITA OUTPUT OF BUTTER, MILK, AND MEAT

1. The statement of the objective

A little more than 2 years ago Nikita Khrushchev announced a campaign to overtake the United States in the per capita output of butter, milk, and meat. The goal was announced in the following manner:

> The successes achieved in agriculture and the excellent prospects for its development permit us to set and accomplish a task which is of great importance for the state: to catch up with the United States in the near future in per capita production of meat, butter, and milk.[26]

In the case of milk and meat, he defined what was meant by the "near future":

> In 1957 we will already have as much butter or even a little more than the United States had in 1956. This means that we will have a total amount of butter that is equal to or greater than the amount produced in the United States. But because our population is bigger than that of the United States we will have to make an effort. In per capita production of milk we cannot only catch up with the United States but even surpass it as early as 1958.

[24] Soviet Union data from "Selskoe Khozyaistvo v S.S.S.R." p. 327. Data for United States from R. D. Jennings, "Consumption of Feed by Livestock, 1909-56," USDA, Prod. Res. Rept. No. 21, pp. 95, 97-98 and 64. U.S. data relate only to dairy cattle, including heifers and calves.

[25] F. B. Morrison, "Feeds and Feeding" (Ithaca, 1943), 20th ed., pp. 547-548.

[26] Pravda, May 24, 1957.

With respect to meat:

> * * * we can surpass the United States in per capita meat production by 1960. But it will not be a tragedy by any means if for some reason we are not able to surpass America in meat production by 1960. We can permit some postponement. It would not be bad if we accomplished this task in 1961.

This particular propaganda drive has a number of interesting aspects. First, in announcing the goal of overtaking the United States, Khrushchev revealed to the Russian population the very great disparity between the per capita outputs of livestock products in the two nations, especially in the case of meat. The following figures on annual per capita production for 1956 were given: meat, U.S.S.R., 32.3, and United States, 102.3 kilograms; milk, U.S.S.R., 245. and United States, 343 kilograms; and factory butter, U.S.S.R., 2.8, and United States, 3.8 kilograms.[27]

Second, despite Khrushchev's great confidence, neither the milk nor butter goals were achieved in 1958. The per capita output of factory butter in 1958 was 3.2 kilograms and total production per capita was 3.8 kilograms.[28] The per capita production of milk accepting the official figures was less than 280 kilograms or significantly less than the U.S. level.[29]

Third, in announcing the program Khrushchev indicated that he had disregarded the advice of the economists who had said that it would not be possible to surpass the United States in per capita livestock production before 1975. In a most sarcastic fashion, Khrushchev said:[30]

> In connection with the task before us I want to tell you about one fact. After talking to the collective farmers and the state farm and machine and tractor station officials and getting to know their pledges, the idea of catching up with the United States in the near future in per capita production of meat, milk, and butter arose, and I asked the economists to present estimates of when we could catch up to America in the production of these items.
>
> I shall tell you a secret. They handed me a signed paper, as Mikhlkov writes in his verse fable in Pravda of May 22 and stamped it with a seal. On that piece of paper was written: We can increase meat production by 220 percent and catch up with the United States in 1975. Excuse me, comrade economists, if I rub a little salt in your wounds.

The evidence available to this point indicates that the economists he so strongly ridiculed are much more likely to be correct than Khrushchev.

2. Khrushchev's admission of inability to achieve meat goal

Finally, in announcing the goals of the new 7-year plan (1959–65), it has been admitted that there is no chance of catching up with the United States in meat production by 1960 or 1961. The meat production goal for 1965 has been set at 16 million tons, substantially less than the 20 or 21 million tons required for the 1956 population of 200 million. This admission of failure has had no apparent repercussions, which is perhaps not altogether unexpected since the agricultural output goals of the 5-year plans or other agricultural programs have seldom been met in the past. Yet this failure, which is so typical in the

27 Pravda, May 24, 1957. If home production of butter is included, per capita production was 3.35 in the U.S.S.R. and 4.20 in the United States.

28 "Vestnik Statistiki," 1959, No. 3, p. 94.

29 Assuming a population of 206,500,000 for 1958 and total milk production of 57,800,000 tons. U.S. per capita production of milk declined 12 kilograms between 1956 and 1958. It may be noted that total and per capita production of butter has declined significantly during the past two decades. During 1935–39 per capita butter production was 7.7 kilograms. For U.S. data, see the National Food Situation, April 1959, pp. 4 and 22.

30 Pravda, May 24, 1957.

agricultural area, should warn observers that the announcement and achievement of an agricultural output goal are not quite the same thing.[31]

3. *Comparisons of livestock output and numbers, Soviet Union and United States*

Before attempting to evaluate the possibilities of the Soviet Union eventually overtaking the United States in per capita output of meat and milk, we shall present certain information on the long-run relation between the meat and milk output of the two nations. What many people forget, and what Khrushchev certainly fails to remind us, is that Russia, prior to the revolution was a major livestock-producing nation, second only to the United States. If output on comparable territory is used for comparison, the output of meat in 1958 for the Soviet Union was a smaller percentage of the 1958 United States meat output than in 1913. In 1913, on present territory, meat output in the Soviet Union was 58.1 percent of the United States level; in 1958, 48.0 percent. Actually the present level of Soviet output compared to ours is at a lower level than that achieved by the millions of peasant farms in 1928. It was not until 1952 that the absolute level of meat output reached the 1928 output.

With respect to milk output, we are somewhat less certain concerning the long-term relationship between the output of the two countries. In table 13, we have presented two milk series, one defined as gross output and the other as net milk output. Net milk output excludes all milk fed to calves that has been included in the gross output series. This involves a relatively minor adjustment for the United States, but a substantial adjustment for the Soviet Union. Roughly speaking it would appear that the Soviet Union, by 1958, had roughly regained the same position relative to the United States that existed in 1913.

In table 14 data are presented on the size of the livestock herds of the Soviet Union and the United States. In 1916 there were substantially more sheep and goats and horses in Russia than in the United States. There were considerably more hogs in the United States, but the disparity in cattle was relatively small. By 1959 the number of hogs in the Soviet Union had risen significantly relative to the United States and the same is true for the number of sheep and goats. The total number of cattle declined from 87 percent of the U.S. level in 1916 to 73 percent in 1959. It may be noted that the number of cows milked was probably greater in the Soviet Union on all three dates, since almost all their cows are milked while a large proportion of cows in the United States are of beef breeds and are not milked.

[31] Khrushchev, in discussing the 1959–65 plan goals, did feel it desirable to explain the reasons for the discrepancy between the 1965 meat goal and the overtake the United States objective. His explanation was as follows:

"Now to turn to our plans and potentialities for increasing meat production. In 1958 the Soviet Union produced 38 kilograms of meat per capita; in the United States the anticipated figure was approximately 194 kilograms. In order to overtake the United States in per capita meat production we must increase gross meat products to 20 million to 21 million tons. Our country now produces about 8 million tons and 16 million tons are scheduled for production in 1965.

"From this it is clear that the meat production assignments laid down by the control figures are below the level required to catch up with the United States in this commodity. But this by no means signifies that our country has no chance of raising meat production to 20 million to 21 million tons."

"Thus, while not raising the state's planned assignment to 20 million to 21 milliion tons of meat, which would strain the plan, we must at the same time not inhibit but encourage the initiative of the leading individuals who launched the movement to catch up with the United States in a short time in per capita output of meat and other livestock products" (Pravda, Dec. 16, 1959).

TABLE 12.—*Meat production, Soviet Union and United States, 1913–58, selected years* [1]

	Million metric tons, slaughter weight		Soviet Union-United States (percent)		Million metric tons, slaughter weight		Soviet Union United States (percent)
	Soviet Union [2]	United States [3]			Soviet Union [2]	United States [3]	
1913 [4]	4.05	8.50	47.6	1952	5.17	14.37	36.0
1913	4.94	8.50	58.1	1953	5.82	15.00	38.8
1928 [4]	4.90	9.94	49.3	1954	6.28	15.38	40.8
1940 [4]	3.88	11.40	34.0	1955	6.32	16.24	38.9
1940	4.70	11.40	41.2	1956	6.60	17.22	38.3
1950	4.87	13.61	35.8	1957	7.37	16.70	44.1
1951	4.67	13.79	33.9	1958	7.85	16.34	48.0

[1] Sources: Soviet Union, appendix table 2, United States, U.S. Department of Agriculture, Livestock and Meat Statistics, 1957, Statistical Bulletin No. 230, July 1958, p. 140; Supplement for 1954 to Consumption of Food in the United States, 1909–52, Agriculture Handbook No. 62, October 1955, pp. 67, 171–172, National Food Situation, April 1959, p. 22; Agricultural Statistics, 1957, pp. 500 and 509, and The Livestock and Meat Situation, May 1959, p. 36.

[2] Includes all animal fats and offal. This series of slaughter weight is not directly comparable to the series for the United States.

[3] Includes lard and edible offal, but does not include tallow. In 1956 the United States produced 1,480,000 tons of tallow and inedible greases. These fats are apparently included in the Soviet data. All poultry meats are on a ready-to-cook basis, with a dressing percentage of 75; poultry meat in Soviet calculations probably based on 90 percent yield. If Soviet definitions and conventions were followed for the United States for 1956, for example, the U.S. meat output would have been at least 19,140,000 tons and perhaps as much as 20,620,000 tons. The percentage increase would have been at least 11 percent and perhaps 20 percent. The smaller increase reflects only the difference in percentage yield of offal products, the larger increase reflects the difference in offal and the inclusion of tallow and greases in the U.S. data.

[4] Territory as of boundaries prior to Sept. 17, 1939 all other data for present territory.

TABLE 13.—*Milk production, Soviet Union and United States, 1913, 1928, 1940, 1950–58* [1]

	Gross output [2]			Net output [3]		
	Soviet Union	United States	Soviet Union-United States	Soviet Union	United States	Soviet Union-United States
	Million metric tons	*Million metric tons*	*Percent*	*Million metric tons*	*Million metric tons*	*Percent*
1913 [4]	24.8	30.7	80.8	21.4	29.4	72.8
1913	29.4	30.7	95.8	25.5	29.4	86.7
1928 [4]	31.0	43.5	71.3	27.0	42.2	64.0
1940 [4]	26.6	49.6	53.6	23.3	48.2	48.3
1940	33.6	49.6	67.7	27.6	48.2	57.3
1950	35.3	52.9	66.7	26.5	51.4	51.6
1951	36.2	52.0	69.2	27.3	50.4	54.2
1952	35.7	52.0	68.6	26.8	50.5	53.1
1953	36.5	54.5	67.0	27.6	53.0	52.1
1954	38.2	55.4	69.0	28.9	53.9	53.6
1955	43.0	55.8	77.1	33.3	54.3	61.3
1956	49.1	57.0	86.1	38.9	55.5	70.1
1957	54.8	57.1	95.8	43.9	55.6	79.0
1958	57.8	56.8	101.8	46.5	55.3	84.1

[1] Sources: Soviet Union: appendix tables 2, 3, and 4. United States: D. R. Jennings, "Consumption of Feed by Livestock, 1909–56"; U.S. Department of Agriculture, Prod. Res. Rept. No. 21, p. 77; and the National Food Situation, April 1959, p. 22.

[2] Reported total milk production; Soviet Union data apparently include an estimate of amount of milk sucked by calves; U.S. data do not.

[3] Net output data represents total milk production minus quantity of whole milk fed to calves. United States data for 1913 and 1957 and 1958 estimated by writers. For Soviet Union data, see appendix table 4 except that 1913 estimated on basis of cow numbers for 1916.

[4] Territory as of boundaries prior to Sept. 17, 1939; all other data for present territory.

TABLE 14.—*Livestock numbers, Soviet Union and United States, 1916, 1928, and 1959* [1]

[Millions of head]

	1916	1928	1959		1916	1928	1959
Soviet Union: [2]				United States:			
Cattle, all	58.4	66.8	70.8	Cattle, all	67.4	57.3	96.9
Cows	28.8	33.2	33.3	Cows, all	33.0	31.1	47.2
Hogs	23.0	27.7	48.5	Milk cows	21.2	22.2	21.6
Sheep and goats	96.3	114.6	[3] 138.6	Hogs	60.6	61.9	57.2
Horses	38.2	36.1	[4] 11.5	Sheep and goats	42.0	49.0	35.6
				Horses and mules	21.3	14.8	3.1

[1] Soviet Union data, see appendix table 2; U.S. data, U.S. Department of Agriculture, "Agricultural Statistics," 1957, pp. 388-389, 371-372, 403-404, 428-440, and "The Livestock and Meat Situation," March 1959, p. 5. Goat numbers estimated for 1959.

[2] All data refer to present territory.

[3] The number of sheep was 129,000,000; number of goats estimated to be 9,600,000. The number Jan. 1, 1958, was 9,900,000.

[4] The number of horses on Jan. 1, 1958, was 11,900,000; 1959 estimated.

NOTE.—Numbers are for Jan. 1 of each year.

4. *Feed requirements*

The major question concerning the feasibility of achieving either the objectives of the 1965 plan or of catching up with the United States in per capita production is that of the feed supply. While the labor inputs in livestock production are fantastically high compared to the United States, it is probably safe to assume that over a period of a decade that sufficient labor savings could be achieved to permit the production of the required output.

Data on the feed supply of the Soviet Union are extremely sketchy. While estimates for the late twenties have been published, no estimates covering all feed users for a more recent period have come to our attention. Khrushchev in his 1955 speech on livestock production provided estimates of the feed supply for 1953. However, these estimates were stated to pertain only to production in the socialized sector. While most of the feed is undoubtedly produced in the socialized sector, significant amounts of potatoes produced on private plots are apparently fed to livestock. While much of the feed for the private livestock owned by collective farm members and state farm workers come from the collective and state farms, we have little knowledge concerning the source of feed for the several million head of livestock owned by urban dwellers. One source was apparently the purchase of bread, but efforts have been made to stop such a use. Some of the relatively small amount of grain sold on the collective farm market is probably also used for privately owned livestock.

For present purposes, given the scanty and contradictory evidence on feed supplies, the most accurate indication of feed used may be estimates of the probable amount of feed required to produce the livestock output. At least this technique is accurate enough to give a reasonable indication of the magnitude of the necessary increase in feed availability if the Soviet Union is to overtake the United States in per capita production of meat and milk. The feed requirements used have been derived from Soviet sources. The results have been checked by the use of estimated feed requirements per unit of various kinds of livestock output in the United States. While there are differences for individual products, the total feed requirements are very similar. It is probable that the feed requirements used somewhat underestimate the actual feed consumed. The Soviet feed requirements have apparently been derived from experimental results and probably have not been duplicated under farm conditions.

The estimated feed requirements for specified years from 1928 through 1958 are of some interest since they indicate that until the past year there has been only a very small increase in the total feed supply. The increased output of livestock products for human consumption has primarily been due to the decline in the horse population. While the total feed requirements for 1928 and 1956 were almost identical, the amount required for livestock products increased from 122 to 158 million tons of feed units. There was an increase in feed of about 10 percent between 1956 and 1958. The 1958 feed supply was derived primarily from 1957 crop production; the feed supply available for 1959 is significantly greater than it was in 1958.

In estimating the feed requirements for the goal of overtaking the United States in per capita production, we have assumed a population of 230 million. At the current absolute rate of population increase, this level of population should be reached about 1964 or 1965. We have assumed the 1956 level of per capita consumption in the United States and in order to estimate total feed requirements, we have used the 1965 goal for egg production (37 billion eggs).[32]

The total feed requirements, including pasture, to overtake the United States amount to 385 million tons of feed units.[33] The estimated requirements for 1958 are 199 million tons. According to this method of estimation, it will require almost a doubling of the total feed supply from the 1958 level of utilization in order to reach the goal of overtaking the 1956 U.S. levels of per capita production of milk and meat.

TABLE 15.—*Estimated feed requirements, Soviet Union, selected years, 1928–58* [1]

	Other (million tons of charge feed units)					Horses	Total
	Hogs	Milk [2]	Livestock	Inventory	Total		
1928	13.1	59.1	49.9	0	122.1	57.8	179.9
1950	12.4	50.8	51.7	.7	115.6	22.9	138.5
1953	19.8	50.9	54.0	6.3	131.0	27.5	158.5
1956	23.3	61.8	60.6	12.6	158.3	23.4	181.7
1958	28.8	71.2	67.8	10.5	178.3	21.4	199.7

[1] Method of estimation: Hogs, live weight produced multiplied by 6.3 feed units per unit of production; milk, beginning of year number of cows multiplied by 1,460 feed units plus net milk production multiplied by 0.5 feed units; other meat than pork, live weight produced multiplied by 7.7 feed units per unit of production; eggs, number produced multiplied by 0.36 feed units; inventory change, live weight multiplied by 7 feed units per unit of output; horses beginning of year numbers multiplied by 1,800 feed units. Sources of feed requirements: V. S. Nemchinov, "Economic Problems of Livestock Development," Voprosy ekonomiki, 1955, No. 2, p. 18, for beef, pork, poultry, eggs and mutton and I. S. Popov, Kormovye normy i Kormovye Tablitsy, Moscow, 1955, 13th ed., pp. 6 and 21.

[2] Milk production includes milk production from all sources; milk output differs from gross output in appendix table 2, due to subtraction of 250 kilograms per calf for the years 1950–58.

[32] This goal implies a per capita production of about 160 eggs compared to 391 in the United States in 1956.

[33] We have assumed that the horse population would decline from about 11 million in 1958 to 6 million. An estimate made in a Soviet publication indicates that the goal of catching up with the United States would require over 500 million tons of feed units. Of this amount, 125 to 150 million tons would come from concentrates, 100 to 125 million tons from hay and other coarse fodder, 85 to 100 million tons from silage, potatoes and melons, and 185 to 200 million from pasture and green feed. See "Selskoe Khoziaistvo S.S.S.R.," Moscow, 1958, p. 154.

5. Possibilities of increasing feed supply

Can this additional amount of feed be produced? Obviously no one knows for certain, but the magnitude of the task is an enormous one. Several points may be made, which taken together indicate that the Soviet Union is likely to fall considerably short of producing the required amount of feed. First, despite the large geographic area of the Soviet Union, the pasture resources are quite limited. The pasture area in farms is estimated at 212,434,100 hectares.[34] Excluding the tundra, the Botanical Institute of the Academy of Science estimates that there are about 300 million hectares of pastureland with an average yield, converted into hay equivalent, of 4.3 centners per hectare.[35] According to these estimates the total feed units produced by the pastures does not exceed 65 million tons.[36] Consequently almost all of the increase in feed supply must come from other sources.

Second, the productivity of the land now in meadows or wild hay can probably be increased substantially. In 1956 the yield of meadows harvested on the collective farms was estimated at 0.28 tons of feed units per hectare or perhaps 0.8 tons of actual hay per acre.[37] The Botanical Institute implies a hay yield from meadows of 1.27 tons per hectare, but this is apparently a potential rather than an actual yield.[38] Accepting it as a potential yield, a doubling of meadow hay is implied. This is probably not unreasonable, since the yield of meadow hay is now apparently substantially below the level obtained by peasants in the late twenties.[39] But a doubling of output per hectare would not add more than 15 million tons of feed units.

Third, at least 80 percent of the increased feed supply must come from additional concentrates, potatoes, and the output from the sown fodder area. In 1956 the sown fodder area, excepting grain and potatoes, was about 42 million hectares. This includes the silage crops, including corn grown for silage, the hay from sown grasses and the sown area used for green feed. Unless the meadows are plowed up, the sown fodder area is unlikely to increase significantly in the next few years. It could do so only at the expense of the grain area and the 1965 plan apparently implies no reduction in the grain area. In 1956, a very good year climatically, the average yield of fodder crops per hectare was estimated to be 0.93 ton of feed units.[40] Even if this yield is increased by more than 50 percent, to 1.5 tons of feed units per hectare, the total contribution to the feed supply would be about 25 million tons.

The above estimates indicate that increased or more effective utilization of meadows plus a substantial increase in the yield of sown fodder crops, other than grains or potatoes, might result in an increased output of 40 million tons of feed units. This is a substantial increase (about 20 percent of the estimated feed use for 1958), but it falls far short of a required increase compared to 1958 of about 185 million

[34] Ibid., p. 120.

[35] See I. V. Larin, "Osnovnye Voprosy Sozdania Ustoichivoi Kormovoi Bazy v S.S.S.R.," Moscow, 1958, p. 5.

[36] Excluding tundra pasture. We have assumed a feed unit value of the hay equivalent derived from pasture of 0.5 centners of feed units per centner of hay. Our estimates of the relation between feed requirements and feed availability for a number of years (1928, 1953, 1956, 1958) indicate a residual of about 60 to 70 million tons of feed units that must have come from pasture plus the pasturing of growing crops and harvested fieldsplus other sources not accounted for. Since not all of the pasture area is now being fully utilized, the two sets of estimates seem to be roughly consistent.

[37] "Ekonomika Selskogo Khozyiaistva," 1958, No. 6, p. 73.

[38] Larin, ibid.

[39] N. Jasny, "The Socialized Agriculture of the U.S.S.R.," Stanford, 1949, p. 615. Meadow hay yields of 13.4 and 11.3 centners per hectare were reported for 1928 and 1929, respectively.

[40] "Ekonomika Selskogo Khozyiaistva," 1958, No. 6, p. 73.

tons. The additional amount of 145 million tons must come from additional feeding of concentrates and potatoes, primarily from grains. The 1965 plan goals call for feeding 85 to 90 million tons of concentrates (out of a gross grain harvest of 164 to 180 million tons) and approximately double the amount of potatoes fed in 1957. Compared to the last 3 or 4 years, these goals imply an increase in feed units of about 70 million tons or only a half of the additional amount required.

There is admittedly a great deal of conjecture and speculation in the above appraisal of the possibilities of the U.S.S.R. overtaking the United States in the per capita production of meat and milk.[41] But even when fairly startling increases in yields are assumed, there remains a considerable short fall in the available feed supply. On the basis of our interpretation of the possible situation over the next few years, Khrushchev's economists had a more adequate understanding of the potentialities of socialist agriculture than did Khrushchev.

F. PROGRESS DURING SIXTH 5-YEAR PLAN

There can be no question that the growth of agricultural output in the Soviet Union has been at a rather rapid rate in recent years. The increases in production that have been achieved, however, generally fall substantially short of the increases that would have been required for the period 1956–60 if the agricultural goals of the sixth 5-year plan were to be achieved. In the past, there has generally been little correspondence between agricultural goals and achievement for any of the plan periods and we also noted that it was quite clear that the goals of the catching up with the U.S. program have not and will not be met on schedule, if at all. Nevertheless, it is instructive to compare the performance of Soviet agriculture for the period 1956–58 with the performance that would have been required to meet the 1960 plan goals. In the table below, we have simply compared the annual increase in output that would have been required between 1955 and 1960 if the output goal were to be met. For example, the annual increase in meat output required was 1.27 million tons (6.35 million tons divided by 5 years). The actual annual increase during the 3 years, 1956, 1957, and 1958 over 1955 was 0.51 million tons or only 40 percent of the required rate of annual increase. In other words, the annual increase in output envisaged in the plan was 250 percent greater than that actually achieved.

[41] The Soviet Union can equal or exceed the United States per capita level of milk output, and may well do so within the next 5 years.

TABLE 16.—*Comparison of average annual increase in production of agricultural products, 1956–58, with increases required to achieve goals of 6th 5-year plan*

Product	Output [1]		1960 goal	Average annual increase		Percent actual of required
	1955	1958		1956–58	Plan period	
	Million metric tons					
Meat	6.32	7.9	12.7	0.51	1.27	40
Milk	43.2	57.8	84.2	4.86	8.20	59
Grain	107.0	139.4	180.0	10.7	14.6	73
Cotton	3.98	4.4	6.2	.17	.44	38
Potatoes	68.4	86.1	126.5	5.9	11.6	51
Sugar beets	30.7	54.1	47.2	7.8	5.3	147
Vegetables	13.0	14.3	28.3	.5	3.1	16
Wool	.26	.32	.47	.02	.04	52
	Billion units					
Eggs	18.0	23.5	46.7	1.8	5.7	31

[1] All output data are official gross output data without adjustment; the 1960 goals based on percentage increases given in Pravda, Feb. 26, 1956, except that the grain goal was specifically stated to be 180,000,000 tons.

The relative degree of attainment of the goals ranges from 16 to 147 percent. The first is for vegetables; the latter is for sugar beets. The relatively high degree of attainment for grain—73 percent—was undoubtedly due to the very favorable growing conditions in 1958. The 1957 output of grain, as officially reported, was slightly less than the 1955 output. It should be noted that if inventory change in the livestock herds is included, the actual increase in meat output was about 50 percent of the increase required to achieve the 1960 goal.

APPENDIX TABLE 1.—*Area sown to crops, 1913–59, selected years, Soviet Union* [1]

[Million hectares]

	1913		1925	1926	1927	1928	1929	1930	1931
	Present boundaries	Pre-1939 boundaries							
Total	118.2	105.0	104.3	110.3	112.4	113.0	118.0	127.2	136.3
Grain total	104.6	94.4	87.3	93.7	94.7	92.2	96.0	101.8	104.4
Spring wheat	24.7	24.3	17.0	20.4	20.6	21.6	23.2	23.7	25.6
Winter wheat	8.3	7.8	7.9	9.6	10.7	6.2	6.6	10.1	11.3
Rye	28.2	25.8	28.8	28.5	27.3	24.6	24.9	28.9	27.6
Millet, buckwehat, and legumes	7.3	7.2	10.9	10.1	8.6	10.8	10.8	10.1	11.5
Oats	19.1	16.9	12.8	15.3	17.9	17.2	18.9	17.9	17.5
Barley	13.3	11.5	6.5	7.4	6.9	7.3	8.1	7.4	6.9
Corn	2.2	1.4	3.4	3.0	4.5	4.5	3.5	3.7	4.0
Industrial total	4.9	4.55	7.17	6.66	7.29	8.62	8.84	9.56	14.08
Sunflower seed	.98	.97	3.10	2.59	2.83	3.90	3.62	3.39	4.57
Sugar beet	.68	.65	.53	.54	.66	.77	.77	1.04	1.39
Cotton	.69	.69	.59	.65	.80	.97	1.06	1.58	2.14
Flax for fiber	1.25	1.01	1.27	1.27	1.20	1.36	1.63	1.75	2.39

See footnotes at end of table, p. 230.

APPENDIX TABLE 1.—*Area sown to crops, 1913–59, selected years, Soviet Union* [1]—Continued

	1913		1925	1926	1927	1928	1929	1930	1931
	Present boundaries	Pre-1939 boundaries							
Total garden	5.1	3.82	-------	-------	-------	7.68	7.64	7.97	9.06
Potatoes	4.2	3.06	5.02	5.21	5.46	5.68	5.69	5.73	6.17
Vegetables	.6	.49	-------	-------	-------	.80	1.95	1.18	1.99
Melons	.3	.26	-------	-------	-------	1.21		1.06	.90
Grasses	3.3	2.05	-------	-------	-------	3.87	-------	-------	-------
Annual	.8	.60	.72	1.10	.91	1.16	1.47	2.02	3.28
Perennial	2.5	1.45	.85	1.05	1.78	2.40	3.15	3.94	4.13
Silage	-------	-------	-------	-------	-------	-------	-------	.17	.76

	1932	1933	1934	1935	1936	1937	1938	1940	1950
Total	134.4	129.7	131.5	132.8	133.8	135.3	136.9	150.4	146.3
Grain total	99.7	101.6	104.7	103.4	102.4	104.4	102.4	110.5	102.9
Spring wheat	22.7	22.4	24.4	24.6	25.9	27.1	26.9	26.0	26.0
Winter wheat	11.8	10.8	10.8	12.4	13.1	14.3	14.6	14.3	12.5
Rye	26.2	25.4	24.0	23.5	21.8	23.0	21.4	23.1	23.6
Millet, buckwheat, and legumes	11.5	13.1	13.1	10.5	9.5	9.2	8.5	10.4	8.8
Oats	15.4	16.7	18.0	18.3	18.1	17.6	17.9	20.2	16.2
Barley	6.8	6.9	8.1	8.3	8.6	8.6	8.5	11.3	8.6
Corn	3.7	4.0	3.7	3.2	3.1	2.8	2.6	3.6	4.8
Industrial total	14.88	11.98	10.72	10.64	10.83	11.15	10.96	11.8	12.23
Sunflower seed	5.31	3.90	3.50	3.31	3.18	3.25	3.14	3.54	3.59
Sugar beet	1.54	1.21	1.18	1.23	1.26	1.19	1.18	1.23	1.31
Cotton	2.17	2.05	1.94	1.95	2.03	2.09	2.08	2.08	2.32
Flax for fiber	2.51	2.39	2.11	2.11	2.15	2.13	1.88	2.10	1.90
Total garden	9.22	8.68	8.84	9.94	9.80	9.00	9.39	10.0	10.45
Potatoes	6.11	5.66	6.13	7.38	7.58	6.87	7.37	7.7	8.53
Vegetables	2.24	2.32	2.13	1.90	1.50	1.39	1.32	1.5	1.32
Melons	.87	.70	.58	.66	.72	.74	.70	.8	.60
Grasses:									
Annual	4.46	3.09	3.03	4.26	4.72	3.55	4.46	4.2	7.05
Perennial	3.79	2.88	2.86	2.91	4.53	5.56	8.23	12.1	11.19
Silage	1.66	.62	.59	-------	-------	.67	.64	.8	1.30

	1951	1952	1953	1954	1955	1956	1957	1958	1959
Total	153.0	155.76	157.2	166.1	185.8	194.7	193.7	195.6	196.0
Grain total	106.4	107.34	106.7	112.1	126.4	128.3	124.6	125.2	-------
Spring wheat	27.4	29.1	30.5	33.6	42.2	49.1	69.1	48.4	-------
Winter wheat	15.6	17.2	17.8	15.7	18.3	12.9		18.2	-------
Rye	23.9	22.8	20.3	20.5	19.1	18.4	18.2	17.7	-------
Millet, buckwheat, and legumes	7.7	7.6	8.3	10.1	11.9	10.4	8.0	-------	-------
Oats	17.4	16.6	15.3	15.9	14.8	15.1	14.1	14.7	-------
Barley	8.1	8.6	9.6	10.7	9.9	11.9	9.2	9.6	-------
Corn	4.1	3.9	3.5	4.3	9.1	9.3	5.8	8.1	-------
Industrial total	12.61	12.74	11.47	11.78	12.29	13.15	11.8	12.31	-------
Sunflower seed	3.61	3.67	3.90	4.03	4.24	4.51	3.46	3.94	-------
Sugar beet	1.39	1.46	1.57	1.60	1.76	2.01	2.11	2.50	-------
Cotton	2.72	2.83	1.88	2.20	2.20	2.07	2.09	2.15	-------
Flax for fiber	1.60	1.53	1.24	1.11	1.48	1.92	1.69	1.60	-------

See footnotes at end of table, p. 230.

APPENDIX TABLE 1.—*Area sown to crops, 1913–59, selected years, Soviet Union*[1]—Continued

	1951	1952	1953	1954	1955	1956	1957	1958	1959
	Present boundaries	Pre-1939 boundaries							
Total garden	10.30	10.05	10.26	10.98	11.44	11.58	11.9	11.6	-------
Potatoes	8.45	8.21	8.31	8.71	9.09	9.20	9.80	9.50	-------
Vegetables	1.28	1.27	1.32	1.49	1.51	1.59	-------	-------	-------
Melons	.57	.57	.63	.78	.84	.79	-------	-------	-------
Grasses:									
Annual	7.47	7.05	7.84	9.43	14.77	20.83	------- }	37.0	{ -------
Perennial	12.85	14.82	16.85	16.10	13.69	12.28	------- }		{ -------
Silage	1.82	2.09	2.31	3.86	5.69	7.10	-------	8.1	-------

[1] The figures for each year are for the territory within the boundaries existing at that time, unless otherwise noted. For sources, see notes for appendix tables 1, 2, and 3.

APPENDIX TABLE 2.—*Total livestock numbers, Soviet Union*[1]

[Million head]

Year	Cows	Cattle (including cows)	Hogs	Sheep	Goats	Sheep and goats	Horses
January:[1]							
1916[2]	28.8	58.4	23.0	89.7	6.6	96.3	38.2
1916[3]	24.9	51.7	17.3	82.5	6.2	88.7	34.2
1928[2]	33.2	66.8	27.7	104.2	10.4	114.6	36.1
1928[3]	29.2	60.1	22.0	97.3	9.7	107.0	32.1
1929	29.2	58.2	19.4	97.4	9.7	107.1	32.6
1930	28.5	50.6	14.2	85.5	7.8	93.3	31.0
1931	24.5	42.5	11.7	62.5	5.6	68.1	27.0
1932	22.3	38.3	10.9	43.8	3.8	47.6	21.7
1933	19.4	33.5	9.9	34.0	3.3	37.3	17.3
1934	19.0	33.5	11.5	32.9	3.6	36.5	15.4
1935	19.0	38.9	17.1	36.4	4.4	40.8	14.9
1936	20.0	46.0	25.9	43.8	6.1	49.9	15.5
1937	20.9	47.5	20.0	46.6	7.2	53.8	15.9
1938	22.7	50.9	25.7	57.3	9.3	66.6	16.2
1939	24.0	53.5	25.2	-------	-------	80.9	17.2
1940	22.8	47.8	22.5	66.6	10.1	76.7	17.7
1941	27.8	54.5	27.5	79.9	11.7	91.6	21.0
1945	21.6	44.2	8.8	57.9	12.3	70.2	9.9
1946	22.9	47.6	10.6	58.5	11.5	70.0	10.7
1947	23.0	47.0	8.7	57.7	11.6	69.3	10.9
1948	23.8	50.1	9.7	63.3	13.5	76.8	11.0
1949	24.2	54.8	15.2	70.4	15.2	85.6	11.8
1950	24.6	58.1	22.2	77.6	16.0	93.6	12.7
1951	24.3	57.1	24.4	82.6	16.4	99.0	13.8
1952	24.9	58.8	27.1	90.5	17.1	107.6	14.7
1953	24.3	56.6	28.5	94.3	15.6	109.9	15.3
1954	25.2	55.8	33.3	99.8	15.7	115.5	15.3
1955	26.4	56.7	30.7	98.9	14.0	112.9	14.2
1956	27.7	58.8	34.0	103.3	12.9	116.2	13.0
1957	29.0	61.4	40.8	108.2	11.6	119.8	12.4
1958	31.4	66.7	44.3	120.2	9.9	130.1	11.9
1959	33.3	70.8	48.5	129.6	-------	-------	-------

[1] The figures for each year are for the territory within the boundaries existing at that time, unless otherwise noted. Data from official sources; see notes for appendix tables 1, 2, and 3.
[2] Present boundaries.
[3] Boundaries prior to Sept. 17, 1939.

APPENDIX TABLE 3.—*Gross physical output for 11 major commodity groups, Soviet Union*[1]

	Grain	Potatoes	Vegetables	Sunflower seed	Sugar beets	Seed cotton
	Million tons	*Million tons*	*Million tons*	*Million tons*	*Million tons*	*Million tons*
1913[3]	----------	----------	----------	----------	----------	----------
1913[2]	----------	31.6	5.5	0.747	----------	----------
1925	72.7	38.6	12.7	2.230	9.070	0.567
1926	76.6	43.0	10.2	1.550	6.400	.550
1927	71.7	41.2	8.6	2.180	10.410	.720
1928	73.3	46.4	10.7	2.128	10.143	.821
1929	71.7	45.6	10.6	1.764	6.248	.864
1930	83.5	49.5	12.0	1.630	14.019	1.113
1931	66.0	44.8	14.6	2.506	12.052	1.290
1932	63.0	43.1	13.2	2.268	6.561	1.271
1933	67.1	49.2	16.5	2.354	8.989	1.315
1934	67.3	51.0	16.7	2.077	11.361	1.176
1935	69.3	69.7	19.8	1.850	16.200	1.729
1936	60.0	51.0	11.8	1.490	16.830	2.416
1937	91.9	65.6	15.5	2.080	21.860	2.576
1938	70.7	41.9	8.8	1.670	16.700	2.600
1939	----------	51.3	----------	----------	16.900	2.682
1940[3]	----------	----------	----------	----------	18.146	2.255
1940[2]	83.0	75.9	13.7	2.578	----------	2.255
1941	----------	----------	----------	----------	----------	2.478
1942	----------	----------	----------	----------	----------	1.329
1943	----------	----------	----------	----------	----------	.726
1944	----------	----------	----------	----------	----------	1.131
1945	----------	58.3	----------	----------	----------	1.161
1946	----------	----------	----------	----------	----------	1.666
1947	----------	----------	----------	----------	----------	1.703
1948	----------	----------	----------	----------	----------	2.206
1949	69.7	----------	10.4	----------	15.565	2.547
1950	81.4	88.6	9.3	1.798	20.841	3.584
1951	78.9	59.6	9.0	1.744	23.760	3.763
1952	92.0	68.4	11.0	2.211	22.276	3.799
1953	82.5	72.6	11.4	2.630	23.176	3.871
1954	85.7	74.8	12.0	1.905	19.847	4.229
1955	107.0	71.8	14.1	3.808	31.049	3.976
1956	127.6	96.0	14.3	3.947	32.488	4.458
1957	105.0	87.8	14.8	2.800	39.672	4.371
1958	139.4	86.1	14.3	4.500	54.144	4.400

See footnotes at end of table, p. 232.

APPENDIX TABLE 3.—*Gross physical output for 11 major commodity groups, Soviet Union*[1]—Continued

	Flax-fiber	Wool greasy weight	Milk	Meat live weight	Meat dressed weight	Eggs
	Million tons	*Million tons*	*Million tons*	*Million tons*	*Million tons*	*Billions*
1913 [3]	0.330	0.180	24.787	6,609	4.053	10.192
1913 [2]	.365	.192	29.430	7.933	4.954	11.919
1925	.300	.152	28.100	6.453	3.872	9.550
1926	.270	.164	30.500	7.183	4.310	10.470
1927	.240	.175	30.600	7.596	4.558	10.488
1928	.324	.182	30.978	8.047	4.900	10.770
1929	.361	.183	29.799	9.722	5.792	10.110
1930	.436	.141	26.955	7.835	4.301	8.000
1931	.553	.098	23.399	7.136	3.949	6.656
1932	.498	.069	20.558	4.949	2.762	4.432
1933	.548	.064	19.156	3.969	2.276	3.500
1934	.533	.065	20.800	3.463	2.049	4.200
1935	.550	.079	21.436	3.601	2.273	5.775
1936	.580	.099	23.507	5.910	3.749	7.449
1937	.570	.106	26.061	4.670	2.957	8.179
1938	.546	.137	28.955	6.933	4.457	10.475
1939	.500	.150	27.209	8.380	5.132	11.548
1940 [3]	----------	.151	26.623	6.260	3.880	10.228
1940 [2]	.565	.161	33.640	7.502	4.695	12.214
1941	----------	.161	25.495	7.044	4.087	9.261
1942	----------	.125	15.762	3.405	1.841	4.513
1943	----------	.100	16.391	3.288	1.767	3.460
1944	----------	.103	22.044	3.632	1.953	3.588
1945	----------	.111	26.428	4.690	2.559	4.883
1946	----------	.119	27.663	5.620	3.082	5.248
1947	----------	.125	30.204	4.536	2.508	4.917
1948	----------	.146	33.426	5.419	3.060	6.568
1949	.312	.163	34.898	6.361	3.751	9.120
1950	.255	.180	35.311	8.125	4.867	11.697
1951	.194	.192	36.154	7.557	4.671	13.252
1952	.212	.219	35.702	8.526	5.170	14.399
1953	.163	.235	36.475	9.394	5.822	16.059
1954	.218	.230	38.197	10.007	6.281	17.179
1955	.381	.256	43.009	10.215	6.322	18.481
1956	.521	.261	49.111	10.653	6.598	19.532
1957	.439	.289	54.750	11.633	7.374	22.269
1958	.443	.321	57.786	----------	7.851	23.451

[1] The figures for each year are for the territory within the boundaries existing at that time, unless otherwise noted. Data from official sources; see notes for appendix tables 1, 2, and 3.
[2] Present boundaries.
[3] Boundaries prior to Sept. 17, 1939.

SOURCES FOR APPENDIX TABLES 1, 2, AND 3

In compiling the table of the gross agricultural output reliance was placed primarily upon Soviet sources. The sources most frequently used were the following:

Gosudarstvennaia Planovaia Komissia (Gosplan) SSSR:
- Kontrolnye Tsifry Narodnogo Khoziaistva na 1925/26 god. Moscow 1926.
- Kontrolnye Tsifry Narodnogo Khoziaistva na 1926/27 god. Moscow 1927.
- Kontrolnye Tsifry Narodnogo Khoziaistva na 1928/29 god. Moscow 1929.
- Perspektivy Razvertyvania Narodnogo Khoziaistva SSSR na 1926/27–1930/31 gg. Moscow 1927.
- Piatiletnii Plan Razvitia Narodnogo Khoziaistva Soiuza SSR. Moscow 1930.
- Narodno–Khoziaistvennyi Plan na 1935 god. Moscow 1935.
- Narodno–Khoziaistvennyi Plan na 1936 god. Moscow 1936.

Narodnyi Komissariat Zemledelia SSSR i Narodnyi Komissariat Sovkhozov SSSR:
- Selskoe Khoziaistvo SSSR, 1935. Moscow 1936.

Tsentralnoe Statisticheskoe Upravlenie (TsSU) Gosplana SSSR:
- Slovar Spravochnik po Sotsialno Ekonomicheskoi Statistike. Moscow 1944.
- Statisticheskii Spravochnik SSSR na 1927 god. Moscow 1928.
- Statisticheskii Spravochnik SSSR na 1928 god. Moscow 1928.

Tsentralnoe Statisticheskoe Upravlenie (TsSU) Sovieta Ministrov SSSR:
- Chislennost' Skota v SSSR, Statisticheskii Sbornik. Moscow 1957.
- Narodnoe Khoziaistvo SSSR v 1956 godu. Moscow 1957.
- Posevnye Ploshchadi v SSSR. Statisticheskii Sbornik. Moscow 1957.
- Promyshlennost' SSSR. Statisticheskii Sbornik. Moscow 1957.
- Zhivotnovodstvo SSSR. Statisticheskii Sbornik. Moscow 1959.

Tsentralnoe Upravlenie Narodno-Khoziaistvennogo Ucheta (TsUNKhU) Gosplana SSSR:

Narodnoe Khoziaistvo SSSR, Statisticheskii Spravochnik 1932. Moscow 1932.

Posevnye Ploshchadi SSSR, 1913–1938 gg. Moscow-Leningrad 1939.

Proizvoditelnost' i Ispolzovanie Truda v Kolkhozakh vo Vtoroi Piatiletke. Moscow-Leningrad, 1939.

Sotsialisticheskoe Selskoe Khoziaistvo, Statisticheskii Sbornik. Moscow-Leningrad, 1939.

Sotsialisticheskoe Stroitelstvo SSSR, 1934. Moscow 1935.

Sotsialisticheskoe Stroitelstvo SSSR. Moscow 1936.

Sotsialisticheskoe Stroitelstvo Soiuza SSR (1933–38 gg.). Moscow-Leningrad 1939.

Zhivotnovodstvo SSSR za 1916–1938 gg. Moscow-Leningrad 1940.

Extremely helpful among the books published outside of the Soviet Union were the books by Naum Jasny, Vladimir Timoshenko, and Lazar Volin, as well as some of the RAND publications.

Grain.—In 1932, in connection with the report of the first 5-year plan completion, a half-hearted attempt to "adjust" the grain output figure was made (although the official shift toward a reporting of "biological yield" took place in 1933). This has necessitated an estimate of the "adjustment" and a correction in terms of gross output or barn yield of grain. The biological yield data reported for the period 1933–38, were adjusted downward according to the estimates of the Soviet economist M. Kubanin.

The output for 1940 had to be estimated in view of the lack of published data. Although the practice of reporting the biological yield was supposedly discontinued and ridiculed since 1953 and the 1950–58 grain yields are claimed to represent barn yield, there is sufficient evidence to question whether they accurately reflect the amount of dry grain in a suitable storage place. The grain estimate probably reflects the weight of grain at the combine, thus include waste and excess moisture. Nor are subsequent losses or waste accounted for. In the gross output table the official grain output figures for 1950–58 are accepted, however.

Vegetables.—The vegetable output data for the first half of the 1930's possibly include the output of food melons, without making it explicit.

Cotton.—The output of cotton is reported in the Soviet Union in terms of seed cotton or raw cotton rather than lint, as in other parts of the world. No attempt to convert the data to their lint content was made in view of the lack of available coefficients for each of the years. On the average the ratio of lint to seed cotton is about 0.3 to 0.33.

Wool.—The wool output is reported in terms of greasy weight. Apart from sheep wool, mohair and camel wool are included, as well as wool taken from hides.

Flax fiber.—Output is reported for the whole period until 1950 in terms of the biological yield; no attempt was made to adjust for it in the table of gross output. The reported flax fiber is on a scutched base.

Milk.—The milk series represents the output of milk of cows, goats, sheep, and mares. In view of the changed concept of milk output (the broadening of the reported output by making it more inclusive) an adjustment was made for the years 1925–27 output for which only cow milk data were available. Sometime during the 1950's (possibly in 1955) another innovation in reporting the gross output was introduced, namely an unknown volume of milk sucked by calves was included in the gross output. How far back the output figures were adjusted is not known. The data prior to 1940—and possibly the year 1940—seem not to be affected by this change in the "inclusiveness" of the milk concept.

Meat.—The gross output series of meat have a history of their own. Originally, during the 1920's gross output included the three principal types of meat (beef and veal, pork, and mutton) and separately poultry. Gradually the definition of meat became more inclusive. At first fat was included in the meat, next various kinds of offal, and finally all edible offal and meat of horses, camels, reindeers, etc. A recent Soviet source (TsSU–Zhivotnovodstvo SSSR. Moscow 1959) presents a recalculation of the meat output for the years 1928–57. Apart from the impact of the recalculation upon the index of meat output in various years when compared with previous data for the same years and their relative position to the base year, the general level of output was substantially increased in terms of both live and dressed weight. We have for the purpose of this presentation accepted the official data and adjusted upward the previous data for 1925–27.

APPENDIX TABLE 4.—*Net physical output for 11 major commodity groups, Soviet Union* [1]

	Grain	Potatoes	Vegetables	Sunflower seed	Sugar beets	Seed cotton
	Million tons	*Million tons*	*Million tons*	*Million tons*	*Million tons*	*Million tons*
1913 [3]						
1913 [2]			4.400			
1925	38.7	14.4	9.525	2.178	8.418	0.549
1926	38.2	14.5	7.650	1.493	6.132	.538
1927	34.9	13.7	6.450	2.100	9.771	.690
1928	36.9	16.7	8.037	2.056	9.367	.788
1929	35.7	16.6	7.968	1.696	6.038	.825
1930	48.4	23.6	8.400	1.538	13.238	1.073
1931	37.0	18.9	10.220	2.400	10.435	1.273
1932	35.5	18.4	9.240	2.190	6.117	1.216
1933	40.2	24.7	11.550	2.284	8.198	1.291
1934	38.9	26.4	11.690	2.010	9.509	1.172
1935	38.9	33.0	13.860	1.786	15.723	1.706
1936	31.6	17.8	8.260	1.425	15.810	2.340
1937	59.1	33.1	10.850	2.018	21.449	2.576
1938	37.9	13.6	6.160	1.600	16.350	2.590
1939					16.500	2.650
1940 [3]						
1940 [2]	45.7	37.3	10.305	2.500	17.357	2.237
1941						
1942						
1943						
1944						
1945						
1946						
1947						
1948						
1949						2.688
1950	46.3	44.3	7.475	1.726	19.822	3.539
1951	45.2	23.6	7.200	1.670	23.400	3.670
1952	49.6	30.4	8.800	2.133	22.100	3.700
1953	44.2	30.7	9.110	2.550	22.891	3.853
1954	45.9	29.5	9.600	1.820	19.522	4.122
1955	55.9	27.2	11.280	3.718	30.664	3.881
1956	67.8	37.7	11.440	3.850	31.451	4.332
1957	48.2	36.0	11.480	2.680	38.535	4.200
1958	68.9	31.1	11.440	4.370	51.037	(4.300)

See footnotes at end of table, p. 235.

APPENDIX TABLE 4.—*Net physical output for 11 major commodity groups, Soviet Union*[1]—Continued

	Flax fiber	Wool	Milk	Meat (dressed weight)	Eggs
	Million tons	*Million tons*	*Million tons*	*Million tons*	*Billions*
1913[3]	0.314	0.173		4.053	9.377
1913[2]	.347	.184		4.954	10.965
1925	.285	.146	24.517	3.872	8.786
1926	.257	.157	26.610	4.310	9.632
1927	.228	.168	26.595	4.558	9.649
1928	.308	.175	27.029	4.900	9.908
1929	.325	.176	25.904	5.792	9.301
1930	.349	.135	23.418	4.301	7.200
1931	.443	.094	20.416	3.949	5.990
1932	.376	.066	17.900	2.762	3.989
1933	.384	.061	16.708	2.276	3.150
1934	.373	.062	18.378	2.049	3.780
1935	.385	.076	18.950	2.273	5.198
1936	.406	.095	20.900	3.749	6.704
1937	.402	.102	23.281	2.957	7.361
1938	.382	.132	25.978	4.457	9.428
1939	.350	.144	24.225	5.132	10.393
1940[3]		.145	23.334	3.880	9.205
1940[2]	.349	.155	27.609	4.695	10.992
1941		.155	18.219	4.087	
1942		.120	10.866	1.841	
1943		.096	11.240	1.767	
1944		.099	15.567	1.953	
1945		.107	18.863	2.559	
1946		.114	19.860	3.082	
1947		.120	22.248	2.508	
1948		.140	25.266	3.060	
1949	.280	.157	26.602	3.751	
1950	.230	.173	26.509	4.867	10.820
1951	.175	.184	27.298	4.671	12.258
1952	.191	.210	26.846	5.170	13.319
1953	.154	.226	27.565	5.822	14.855
1954	.207	.221	28.909	6.281	15.891
1955	.362	.246	33.271	6.322	17.095
1956	.495	.251	38.905	6.598	18.067
1957	.417	.277	43.878	7.374	20.599
1958	.421	.308	46.482	7.851	21.692

[1] See attached notes for derivation of estimates. The figures for each year are for the territory within the boundaries existing at that time, unless otherwise noted. Territorial coverage for 1940 is uncertain, probably refers to boundaries prior to Sept. 17, 1939. Data from official sources; see notes for appendix tables 1, 2, and 3.
[2] Present boundaries.
[3] Boundaries prior to Sept. 17, 1939.

DERIVATION OF ESTIMATES OF NET AGRICULTURAL OUTPUT FOR APPENDIX TABLE 4

The estimates of net agricultural output, by commodities, are derived by deducting from gross physical output that part of output used in the process of production (seed, feed, eggs for hatching, milk for cow feeding, etc.), as well as some losses which are not recognized in the Soviet measurement of gross output. Given the nature of the available data (the last published Soviet estimates of the distribution of output for different uses are for 1928), our estimates are crude having been derived from scattered sources, but in general, we believe, they reflect approximately the appropriate order of magnitudes.

The net agricultural output for each of the accounted crops or livestock products reflects the volume of each year's available supply for human consumption, industrial processing, Government stockpiling and exports. No estimates of changes in the yearly carryover were attempted, since the size of stocks is a state secret in the Soviet Union.

Grain.—In order to account for the losses during the period 1932–38, an adjustment for the gross output figure was included in the table on gross output. For the years 1940, 1950–55, 1957, 1958 a loss of 7 percent was assumed and for 1956 a 10 percent loss seems to be a reasonable assumption in view of the Soviet admission of the existence of heavy losses during this particular year. In addition, for the years 1956–58, we have excluded from the gross output 2.7 million tons for 1956 and 2.4 and 6.2 million tons for 1957 and 1958, respectively, which represents the estimate of silage corn converted into a dry-grain figure. In our opinion, such an elimination of losses and corn in silage provides a greater degree of uniformty for the whole period. In any case, the corn in the islage is fed to livestock and should be deducted to arrive at net output. The seed requirements were estimated on the basis of an average seeding rate of 1.5 quintals per hectare of next year's reported sowing area.

The utilization of grain for feeding of livestock was estimated according to a combination of factors: availability of feed grain, feeding norms of the peasants households during the 1920's, and meat and milk output. As a check against the results estimates of food consumption, industrial use of grain and additions to the Government's stockpile for various years were computed. Nevertheless, the feed estimates do not pretend to be highly accurate, since the year-to-year carryover could be indicated only vaguely.

Potatoes.—For potatoes a uniform loss of 10 percent of the reported gross output was assumed, which by and large seems to constitute an underestimate for the following reasons: (1) We believe the gross output figure to be very crude in view of the large share of private output in the total, considering the Soviet procedures of estimating the private output to be inadequate to derive an estimate with a high degree of accuracy; (2) scattered sources reported heavy losses of potatoes during the harvest and postharvest period in the socia ized sector. The seeding rate was assumed to be 2 tons per hectare, which is below the collective farms' normative rate and was accepted on the assumption that the private producers make a more economical use of their seeding material. The seeding rate was multiplied by the next year's sown area to obtain the seed utilization out of each crop.

The feed utilization of potatoes was estimated on the basis of feeding norms prevailing in the peasant farms during the 1920's and by relating the feed to the meat output. Adjustment for certain years were made with respect to reasonable food use and with possible substitution of grain for feed.

Vegetables.—In order to arrive at an approximate estimate of actually available vegetables for the direct consumption by the population and for the processing industry, losses, waste, and spoilage were assumed to run about 25 percent of the reported gross output for the period 1925–29 and 1936–40. The estimated losses are 30 percent of the output for 1930–35 and 20 percent of gross output for 1950–58.

Sunflower seed.—The seeding rate of 20 kilograms per hectare of next year's sowing area was accepted for sunflower seed, which constitutes an unweighted average of various regional reported seeding rates. No attempt to arrive at a deduction for losses was made in view of the absence of data in this respect.

Sugar beets and cotton.—It was assumed that the officially reported marketed output for these two crops corresponds to the net output, since at least from 1928 the processing facilities were all in the possession of the State, and utilization in the household (especially in the case of cotton) was forbidden and heavy penalties imposed. An exception to our assumption might be the case of sugar beets in 1958, when some unspecified volume (negligible with respect to the total) was fed to livestock. But this is a possibility which has not been confirmed by official sources.

Flax fiber.—Deductions were applied to a series of gross output which was reported at least until 1950 in terms of a "biological crop" measurement. In fact, it was according to some official indication "very much biological." This made necessary the utilization of high deductions, which still may be on the low side. They are for the years 1925–28, 5 percent; for 1929, 10 percent; 1930–31, 20 percent; 1932, 25 percent; 1933–39, 30 percent; 1940, 38.2 percent (an officially used deduction for the year); for 1950–52, 10 percent; 1953, 57.5 percent.

Wool.—Since the reported gross wool output figure is given in terms of greasy wool, an estimated 4 percent of total output was assumed for waste, which for certain years may be an understatement.

Eggs.—The estimated percentage of eggs for hatching was assumed in the absence of yearly data pertaining to the size of the flock. For the 1920's, 8 percent; for the 1930's and 1940, 10 percent; and 7.5 percent for the 1950's.

Milk.—The deductions for milk pertain exclusively to estimated feeding of calves. For the period preceding 1940 the assumption was made that 150 kilograms of whole milk was fed per calf. For the period after 1940, 400 kilograms of milk per calf was assumed (since some time during the 1950's and estimate of milk supposedly sucked by calves was added to the gross output, and it is difficult to estimate how far back the output data were adjusted to include this "component"). For 1940 the average of 150 and 400 kilograms, or 275 kilograms was assumed; this is a purely arbitrary adjustment since three is some reason to believe that the 1940 output data on present territory is consistent with the older series for the 1930's. The yearly calf number was estimated as being 90 percent of the cow number for the 1920's, 85 percent for the 1930's and 1940, and 90 percent for the 1950's (the latest is an overestimate for the socialized sector, where the number of barren cows reported in various sources is still very large, but is probably offset by the lower percentage of barren cows in the private sector).

Meat.—Gross output series has been accepted as representing net output. Neither series includes changes in livestock inventories on farms, which have been substantial in recent years.

APPENDIX TABLE 5.—*Estimated annual yields of animal products and crops, Soviet Union* [1]

	Gross cow milk [2]	Net cow milk [2]	Gross sheep wool [4]	Net sheep wool [4]	Live pork weight [5]	Dead pork weight [5]
	Kilograms per cow	*Kilograms per cow*	*Kilograms per sheep*	*Kilograms per sheep*	*Kilograms per hog*	*Kilograms per hog*
1928	1,042	907	1.87	1.80	100	77
1929	1,017	882	1.88	1.80	115	88
1930	1,003	868	1.65	1.58	92	60
1931	925	797	1.57	1.51	110	68
1932	944	817	1.58	1.51	107	67
1933	1,000	873	1.88	1.81	87	56
1934	1,037	910	1.98	1.90	67	45
1935	1,069	942	2.17	2.08	62	45
1936	1,116	986	2.26	2.17	99	74
1937	1,195	1,068	2.27	2.18	65	50
1938	1,236	1,108	2.39	2.29	97	74
1939	1,163	1,035	2.15	2.06	90	69
1940	1,145	1,010				
1940	1,180	[3] 946	2.27	2.18	67	52
1945	1,139	799	1.92	1.84	88	58
1946	1,154	814	2.03	1.95	105	72
1947	1,235	895	2.17	2.08	71	50
1948	1,330	990	2.31	2.21	74	54
1949	1,356	1,016	2.32	2.22	70	53
1950	1,365	1,005	2.32	2.23	84	63
1951	1,381	1,021	2.32	2.23	87	65
1952	1,373	1,013	2.42	2.32	89	65
1953	1,385	1,025	2.49	2.39	101	75
1954	1,403	1,043	2.30	2.21	115	85
1955	1,521	1,161	2.58	2.48	108	78
1956	1,674	1,314	2.53	2.43	99	71
1957	1,775	1,406	2.67	2.56	108	79
1958			2.67	2.56		

	Gross flax fiber	Net flax fiber	Gross grain	Gross potatoes	Gross sugar beets	Gross seed cotton	Gross sunflower
	Centners per hectare	*Centners per hectare*	*Centners per hectare*	*Centners per hectare*	*Centners per hectare*	*Centners per hectare*	*Centners per hectare*
1925	2.4	2.2	8.30	76.9	171.1	9.61	7.19
1926	2.1	2.0	8.20	82.5	118.5	8.46	5.98
1927	2.0	1.9	7.63	75.5	157.7	9.00	7.70
1928	2.4	2.3	7.95	81.7	131.7	8.90	5.46
1929	2.2	2.0	7.47	80.1	81.1	8.15	4.87
1930	2.5	2.0	8.20	86.4	115.4	7.04	4.81
1931	2.3	1.9	6.32	72.6	105.0	6.03	5.48
1932	2.0	1.5	6.32	70.5	85.7	5.86	4.27
1933	2.3	1.6	6.60	87.0	74.3	6.41	6.04
1934	2.5	1.8	6.43	83.2	96.3	6.06	5.93
1935	2.6	1.8	6.70	94.4	131.7	8.87	5.58
1936	2.7	1.9	5.88	67.3	133.3	11.90	4.69
1937	2.7	1.9	8.80	95.5	183.7	12.32	6.40
1938	2.9	2.0	6.90	56.8	140.5	12.50	5.32
1940	2.7	1.7	7.51	99.8	153.8	10.84	7.28
1950	1.3	1.2	7.91	103.9	159.0	15.45	5.01
1951	1.2	1.1	7.42	70.5	170.9	13.83	4.83
1952	1.4	1.2	8.57	83.3	152.6	13.42	6.02
1953	1.3	1.2	7.73	87.3	147.6	20.59	6.74
1954	2.0	1.9	7.64	85.9	124.0	19.22	4.73
1955	2.6	2.4	8.46	78.9	176.4	18.07	8.98
1956	2.7	2.6	9.95	104.4	161.6	21.54	8.75
1957			8.43	89.6	188.0	20.91	8.09
1958	2.8	2.6	11.13	90.6	216.6	20.46	11.42

[1] Based on output data in appendix tables 3 and 4 and sown area (appendix table 1) or livestock numbers (appendix table 2).

[2] Average of cow numbers for beginning and end of year, except beginning year numbers for 1940 on prewar territory and end of year numbers for 1940 on postwar territory.

[3] An alternative estimate, based on 150 kilograms of milk per calf, is 1,052 kilograms.

[4] Sheep numbers for beginning of year.

[5] Average of hog numbers for beginning and end of year used.

SOVIET AGRICULTURAL PRICES AND COSTS

(By Nancy Nimitz, Rand Corp., Santa Monica, Calif.)

INTRODUCTION

The argument of this paper is that the disparity between prices and costs has been the chief constraint on Soviet agricultural performance, that price increases over the last 5 years have almost eliminated this disparity, and that improved incentives and attendant institutional changes have much increased Soviet agricultural potential. I am concerned mainly with collective farms, since they are the majority producers, and with the prices paid for sales to the state (procurement prices), since such sales account for the bulk of collective marketings. My specific aims are to show the trends in average procurement prices received by collective farms, to compare these prices with costs, and to indicate the impact of recent price trends on farm income. In treating the period 1928–50 I borrow heavily from Jerzy F. Karcz's very thorough, pioneering study of agricultural prices.[1]

To equate agricultural prices with procurement prices is admittedly a simplification, when up to one-third of total collective farm money income has come from sales to the population on the collective farm market and to farm members and other farms in off-market transactions. I choose to disregard these sales for reasons involving both principle and expedience. Quantitatively market sales are of dwindling importance compared with deliveries to the state, and their price level (at least in urban sales) has been comparatively stable since 1950. Their impact on collective income is less significant than aggregate data would suggest, since a large part of the income is received by the minority of farms located close to large cities. Their main impact is on the income of individual collective farmers, who account for 85 percent or more of urban market sales.[2] So long as individual farming and marketing activities compete with the collective farm for the labor of the colletive farmer, market sales have, of course, a contingent interest. But even in this connection they are not a decisive factor, since individual farming is subject to direct controls which preclude its expansion. Finally, published data on market and other sales at uncontrolled prices do not permit us to form reliable estimates of their influence on the prices realized by collective farms.

In view of these facts it seems preferable to concentrate exclusively on procurement prices, recognizing that neglect of market sales results in understatement of the average prices received for some products. Efforts will be made later to estimate the degree of understatement.

Procurement price data are abundant. Absolute cost figures for collective farms are not; therefore the cost yardstick generally used is of necessity state farm costs. These tend for a number of reasons to

[1] Soviet Agricultural Marketings and Prices, 1928–54, Rand Corp., Research Memorandum RM–1930, July 2, 1957.

[2] According to Sov. torg., 1956 No. 11, p. 9: "The share of collective farms in total sales on collective farm markets . . . was 14.8 percent in 1940, 13.4 percent in 1950, and a little more than 9 percent in 1955." The share of farms varies from product to product; it tends to be higher for grain, vegetables, and milk (cf. 40 let sovetskoi torgovli, M., 1957, p. 129).

be lower than collective farm costs, which means that their use in price/cost comparisons aimed at measuring hypothetical net income of collective farms exaggerates profits and understates losses. On the other hand, state farm cost data have the merit of being unequivocally real: calculations for each farm are based upon complete and appropriate accounting records, and average cost statistics are calculated from figures reported by every farm. By contrast, the collective farm average cost data published so far (July 1959) are obtained from a sample of farms, and are derived from records not originally intended to yield information on commercial costs of production.[3] The concept of cost underlying these sample data appears to be proper, in that it includes most true commercial costs. But the values imputed to labor inputs and machine-tractor station operation may not be entirely appropriate.

To the degree that lower state farm costs reflect higher levels of investment and superior organization of production—that is, acquired as distinguished from locational advantages—they have the additional interest of being indicators of feasible costs under Soviet conditions. As such, they have served Soviet planners as a standard in determining present procurement price levels.[4]

While state farm costs are central to the present study, state farm prices are (like collective farm market prices) of merely peripheral interest. For one thing, they are in effect elastic: when prices do not cover costs, the difference is made up by operating subsidies from the budget. Investment in state farms is largely budget financed. Thus price by itself does not constitute an absolute constraint upon the level of state farm production. In any case, state farms are minority producers and are destined to remain so in the foreseeable future.[5]

It is collective farm production which must expand if agriculture output goals are to be met. And here price is crucial, because collective farms do not receive subsidies from the state.[6] That is their raison d'etre (ideological considerations aside): price does not have to cover real costs of production, because losses will be borne by the collective farmer, the nominal owner of, and residual claimant to, collective output. He receives for his labor not a fixed wage but what is left after farms have met the various rigid claims on gross farm income—material production costs, money taxes, and the prescribed allocation to investment. To the extent that the farmer's earnings fall below the real value of his labor, he pays a tax in kind to the state.

The tax in kind collected through low procurement prices has been, since collectivization, the major tax levied upon agricultural pro-

[3] Most collective farms calculated costs of production for the first time in their annual accounts covering the year 1958 (Silin in Vestnik statistiki, 1958 No. 12, p. 54).

[4] "State farms are supposed to be examples of efficient farming, disseminators of better methods of production, and models for collective farms in the effort to raise labor productivity * * *. Therefore the cost of production on state farms must be, to a certain extent, a criterion for procurement prices on collective farms * * *. This is the more necessary because collective farms have not in the past calculated costs of production, while all state farms have done so." (Moiseev in Vop. ekon., 1958 No. 7, p. 17. See also D. I. Iakushkin, Novaia sistema zagotovok sel'skokhoziaistvennykh produktov, M., 1958, pp. 27-28.)

[5] Their planned share in gross agricultural output in 1958 was 16.4 percent (Kuzmin in Pravda, Dec. 20, 1957). Their planned shares in state procurements of grain, meat, milk, and wool in 1965 (as given by Krushchev in ibid., Dec. 16, 1958) are close to their actual shares in 1958.

[6] Collectives producing certain raw material crops (cotton, sugar beet, flax fiber) have been subsidized in the sense that they have bought producer's goods at privileged prices and have sold their output to the state on exceptionally favorable terms. But these concessions were at the expense of producers of food products.

ducers as such.[7] Insofar as deliveries to the state are compulsory, such a tax is impossible to evade. If not invisible, it is at least not easily recognized as a tax, or readily measured. It is understandable, therefore, why the Russians resorted to it when the tax burden became, with industrialization, extremely heavy. But if the tax in kind served industrialization, it also distorted the procurement price structure in ways which had unfavorable consequences in almost every area of collective farm production.

To illustrate the extent to which agricultural policy has been compromised by price (tax) policy, it is useful to mention some of these consequences here, briefly and categorically (with the understanding that they remain to be demonstrated and qualified):

(1) Because low procurement prices provided little inducement to deliver to the state, economic incentives were perforce supplanted by direct controls. This led on the one hand to excessively centralized, detailed, and dogmatic planning, and on the other, to the degradation of machine-tractor stations (the local instruments of control) into agencies concerned more with guaranteeing the flow of deliveries than with using machinery efficiently.

(2) Because it was expedient to concentrate the tax in kind in products where procurement price did not provide the only incentive to produce, the burden fell most heavily on basic food products (consumed in part by farmers) as distinguished from raw material crops (most of which are delivered to the state). The disparity between relative prices and relative costs was in increasing contradiction with output requirements.

(3) The system of multiple procurement prices (low for compulsory or planned deliveries, higher for above-quota or unplanned deliveries) which assured the receipt of the tax in kind also distributed the burden inefficiently. Less productive farms, unable to make above-quota deliveries, paid a higher rate of tax. In other words, average price tended to vary inversely with cost, with the result that backwardness was perpetuated.

(4) As long as average procurement prices were low, reference to real costs was politically inexpedient. Accordingly, collective farms did not calculate their costs of production (until 1958), nor did the state bother (until 1955) to investigate the level and structure of average costs.[8] Consequently, central planning decisions involving regional specialization, the direction of agricultural investment, choices between alternative technologies, the structure of procurement prices, and so on, were made without benefit of cost criteria. Similarly, the only costs considered in decisions affecting organization of production at the level of the individual farm were outlays on materials: labor had no price, and machine operations were inflexibly allocated from above. It is impossible to estimate the waste which this deliberate disregard of real costs entailed, but some examples come to mind: the attempt to grow cotton on unirrigated land in the south of

[7] The direct money taxes upon collective farm income and upon farmers' individual plots have not been important sources of budget revenue. Their main function has been to provide a mechanism for encouraging or discouraging (through differential rates of tax) types of economic activity not entirely amenable to direct regulation; in addition, they foster the illusion that such explicit taxes are the only bite on agriculture

As buyers of manufactured goods at retail prices, collective farms and farmers have also paid, like the urban population, substantial indirect money taxes. These constitute a tax on agriculture only insofar as they affect producer's goods (machinery, oil products, tools, building materials, and so on), or result from prices higher in rural than in urban areas.

[8] It is true that calculation of collective farm costs of production posed methodological and conceptual problems. But the solutions discovered in 1955 were accessible in 1933.

European Russia, the neglect of on-farm mechanization, the insistence on a system of crop rotation not suitable to large areas of the U.S.S.R., and a distribution of price incentives that resulted in unnecessarily high incomes for a minority of farms and disablingly low incomes for the majority. All of these policies have since been repudiated or criticized. If adequate cost data had been available, their disadvantages would have been more obvious.

(5) The tax in kind fell more heavily upon collective than upon private farming. Though farmers as individuals also made compulsory deliveries to the state of livestock products and potatoes from their private plots, they sold as much or more to the population at high market prices. Hence the average prices realized in private farming were considerably above those realized by collectives, and income from the private plot exceeded earnings from collective labor. This meant that the structure of material incentives was at odds with the ideological objective of strengthening socialized as opposed to private agriculture.

Under these circumstances it does not seem very surprising that collective output of basic food products lagged, that disparities in income among farms were very great, that collective farm managers found it just as expedient to use 50 men for a job as 5, and that the 50 men put out as little effort as possible.

Since this investigation is focused on the procurement prices received by collective farms, it is desirable to begin by establishing the importance of collectives in agricultural production, and of procurement in collective marketings (sec. I). Section II summarized price trends from 1928 to 1950. Section III describes the methods and results of the first studies made of collective farm costs in the fifties. Section IV outlines price trends from 1950 to 1958, and section V discusses some of the effects of recent price trends on income and institutional arrangements.

Common sources are abbreviated throughout; the code of abbreviations follows the text.

I. THE PATTERN OF OUTPUT AND MARKETINGS. PROCUREMENT PRICES AND AVERAGE REALIZED PRICES

Table 1 shows that collective farms have been the principal producers of grain and raw material crops ever since 1932. They still account for less than half of outputs of potatoes, vegetables, meat, milk, and eggs (when the private sector predominates). But they are the main suppliers to the state of all products except eggs, and their importance in procurements of livestock products may increase further as the share of the private sector declines.[9] So far as meat, milk, and wool are concerned, collective farms are now the main source not only of procurement but of all marketed output, as the following figures indicate:[10]

[9] Compulsory deliveries from the private sector were abolished effective Jan. 1, 1958 (Pravda, July 5, 1957). So long as the farmer's right to purchase manufactured goods in rural retail stores is contingent upon his sales of farm products to consumer cooperatives, he will continue to make some deliveries, even though other marketing channels are also open to him. It is clear, however, that increasing pressure will be brought upon state farm workers, and ultimately collective farmers, to sell their livestock to the socialized sector.

[10] 1956 from Dostizheniia 1957, p. 182; 1957 from SSSR v tsifrakh, p. 221. The decline in 1957 in the collective share in meat and wool marketings is due to the conversion of about 5,000 collective farms into state farms.

Share of collective farms in marketed output

[Percent of total]

	1956	1957
Meat (carcass weight)	54	50
Milk	61	61
Wool	73	62

TABLE 1.—*Share of collective farms in U.S.S.R. output and procurement of selected products, 1932–56* [1]

[Percent of total]

Product	1932		1940		1950		1956	
	Output	Procurement	Output	Procurement	Output	Procurement	Output	Procurement
Food products:								
Grain	67	74	X	(89)	86	91	79	72
Potatoes	X	49	33	61	23	58	29	55
Vegetables	X	100	44	92	45	82	43	75
Meat [2]	[3] 23	11	20	43	22	[4] 52	34	64
Milk [5]	16	39	17	50	19	42	36	66
Eggs	X	X	4	4	9	31	9	33
Raw materials:								
Sugar beet	68	69	90	90	97	97	98	98
Raw cotton	80	96	94	94	96	96	95	95
Flax fiber	64	63	X	84	X	X	99	100
Wool [6]	23	46	49	58	66	69	65	72

[1] The letter "X" means not available.

[2] Output data not otherwise specified refer to carcass weight including offal. Procurement data not otherwise specified refer to liver accounting weight. Data for 1932 refer to the 3 major meats and poultry; data for later years include minor meats (rabbit, horse, etc.).

[3] Carcass weight excluding offal.

[4] Live natural weight.

[5] Including milk products converted to milk. Data for 1932 refer to cow's milk only, while those for later years include goat and sheep milk.

[6] Output in natural weight, procurement in accounting weight.

Sources:
1940–56 computed from appendix tables 1 and 2.
1932 output: Grain, sugar beet, raw cotton, flax fiber: SKH 1935, p. 214. Meat, milk, wool: Computed from absolute figures for total output (SSKh 1939, p. 73) and collective farm output (KVSP 1939, p. 105).
1932 Procurement: Grain: Computed from absolute figures in SKh 1935, p. 216. All other products: Computed from absolute figures in Vest. stat., 1957, No. 6, pp. 78–79.

Table 2 presents comparable data for the private sector. It will be seen that the significance of the private sector (so far as food supply to the nonagricultural population is concerned) is much less than its share in output might suggest. This is of course because it markets a relatively small proportion of what it produces (table 3). Table 3 also shows that something like half of private sector marketings of meat and milk occur through channels other than procurement, that is, at market prices. The proportion of potatoes and eggs sold at market prices is probably not lower, and with vegetables it must be on the order of 80 to 90 percent.

The question of the importance of market sales in total marketings by collective farms is somewhat harder to answer, because of both gaps in data and the inappropriateness of available data for our purpose. Our interest is in the extent to which the average prices realized by collective farms are affected by sales other than procurement. Hence we are concerned with all transactions which influence average price, whether they are regarded as market output in Soviet statistical practice or not. The scope of published data on market output in physical terms has changed over time, and has never been entirely clear.[11] It appears, however, that at least the data for 1940 and later years exclude off-market sales between farms and farmers (vnutriderevenskii oborot), which are of interest in the present connection because they occur, like market sales, at uncontrolled prices which are presumably higher than procurement prices. On the other hand, market output data include some nonmonetary transactions by collective farms (payments in kind to hired labor; allocations of food products to collective dining halls, nurseries, and the like).[12]

TABLE 2.—*Share of the private sector in U.S.S.R. output, marketings, and procurement of selected products, 1940, 1956* [1]

[Percent of total]

Product	1940		1956		
	Output	Procurement	Output	Marketings	Procurement
Potatoes	65	37	67	X	41
Vegetables	47	2	42	X	5
Meat [2]	72	39	55	28	19
Milk [3]	78	34	57	23	16
Eggs	94	92	87	X	49

[1] The letter "X" means not available.
[2] Output and marketings data refer to carcass weight including offal. Procurement data refer to live accounting weight.
[3] Cow, goat, and sheep milk and milk products.

Sources: Output and procurement computed from appendix tables 1 and 2. Marketings from Dostizheniia 1957, p. 182.

TABLE 3.—*Share of marketings and procurement in gross private sector output of selected products, 1940, 1956* [1]

[Percent of gross output]

Product	1940		1956	
	Marketings	Procurement	Marketings	Procurement
Potatoes	X	6	X	6
Vegetables	X	1	X	3
Meat [2]	X	15	30	15
Milk [3]	21	8	17	10
Eggs	X	22	X	9

[1] The letter "X" means not available.
[2] The marketings figure refers to carcass weight, procurement data to live weight.
[3] Cow, goat, and sheep milk and milk products.

Sources: Marketings computed from appendix table 1, Dostizheniia 1957, pp. 154, 182, and SKh 1958, p. 364. The calculation for meat involves the conversion of U.S.S.R. market output in 1956 from live to carcass weight. The ratio of carcass to live weight is assumed to be 62 percent, as in total output (cf. Zhivotnovodstvo 1959, p. 157).
Procurement computed from appendix tables 1 and 2. The calculation for meat involves the conversion of private sector meat output from carcass to live weight. The ratios of carcass to live weight are estimated as 62 percent in 1940 and 65 percent in 1956. These estimates are based on the structure of private sector output by type of meat (as deduced from Zhivotnovodstvo 1959, pp. 159–162) and the following ratios for individual types of meat (percent): Beef, 55; pork, 75; mutton, 50; poultry, 90 (cf. RM–2326, p. 13).

[11] For an exhaustive discussion of this problem, see Karcz, RM–1930, appendix C.
[12] Cf. RM–2101, pp. 52–53.

TABLE 4.—*Share of marketings and procurement in gross collective farm output of of selected products, 1932–56* [1]

[Percent of gross output]

Product	1932		1940		1950		1956	
	Marketings	Procurement	Marketings	Procurement	Marketings	Procurement	Marketings	Procurement
Food products:								
Grain	X	27	X	43.0	X	44	X	39
Potatoes	X	X	X	21.0	X	X	20	18
Vegetables	X	X	X	46.0	X	40	X	46
Meat [2]	37	13	[3] 80.0	56.0	X	57	93	75
Milk [4]	30	23	65.0	58.0	59	52	71	66
Eggs	X	X	X	20.0	X	58	X	61
Raw materials:								
Sugar beet	X	94	97.0	97.0	95	95	97	97
Raw cotton	X	95	99.8	99.8	99	99	97	97
Flax fiber	X	57	X	77.0	X	74	X	83
Wool [5]	72	X	X	88.0	79	79	96	96

[1] The letter "X" means not available.
[2] Marketings data refer to carcass weight, procurement data to live weight.
[3] 1937.
[4] Including milk products converted to milk. Data for 1932 refer to cow's milk only, while those for later years include goat and sheep milk.
[5] Natural weight.

Sources to above table:
Marketings:
Meat: 1932, 1940 (1937), KVSP 1939, p. 105; 1956, Dostizheniia 1957, pp. 154, 182 (see sources to table 3 for conversion of U.S.S.R. market output of meat from live to carcass weight) and appendix table 1.
Milk: 1932, KVSP 1939, p. 105; 1940, 1950, SKh 1958, p. 364; 1956, Dostizheniia 1957, pp. 154, 182, and appendix table 1.
Sugar beet, raw cotton: Identical with procurement at least from 1940 on (cf. Vest. stat., 1957, No. 6 and Dostizheniia 1957, p. 154).
Wool: Identical with procurement from 1950 on (cf. RM-1178, p. 13). 1956 from Dostizheniia 1957, pp. 154, 182, and appendix table 1.
Procurement:
Computed directly from appendix tables 1 and 2, with the following exceptions.
All products in 1932: See sources to 1932 data in table 1.
Grain: 1940, SSEP 1958, p. 118.
Meat: 1940, 1950, ibid. The calculation for 1956 involves the conversion of collective farm meat output from carcass to live weight. The ratio of carcass to live weight is estimated as 60 percent; it is based on the structure of collective output by type of meat and ratios for individual types. (See sources to table 3 for source and individual ratios).
Wool: 1940, 1950 from SSEP 1958, p. 118; 1956 natural weight identical with marketings. (See above).

These limitations must be borne in mind in interpreting table 4, which gives the share of marketings and procurement in gross collective farm output. The data for raw materials are not significantly affected, but in the case of food products not all the difference between marketings and procurement represents market sales, nor do the figures for total marketings include all sales.

Table 4 shows that procurement accounts for all of nearly all collective marketings of raw materials.[13] Taken at their face value, the meat and milk data indicate that the proportion of marketings other than procurement has declined in the case of meat from roughly two-thirds to one-fifth, and in the case of milk from about one-fourth to less than one-tenth.

With regard to grain: data on the allocation of collective farm grain harvests in the late thirties indicate that the proportion of market sales in all marketings for which farms received a price (i.e., compulsory deliveries, above-quota purchases, and market sales) was something less than (percent): 1937, 28; 1938, 25; 1939, 22.[14]

[13] An exception is sunflower seed (a technical crop not considered here), procurement of which accounts for about 80 percent of marketings (compare Dostizheniia, p. 154, and Vest. stat., 1957, No. 6, p. 78).
[14] Computed from percentage distributions of A. Arina, reproduced in Naum Jasny, The Socialized Agriculture of the U.S.S.R., Stanford, Calif., 1947, p. 738. The source lumps above-quota purchases (a form of procurement) with market sales, so that the percentages given in the text above include both.

So far we have considered only quantity data. Clues may also be obtained from value data, specifically, from information on collective farm money income by origin. Table 5 shows that market and other sales at uncontrolled prices have accounted for up to 38 percent of total collective income from agricultural sales. Figures on collective income from grain crops in 1955 and 1956 show that sales other than procurement accounted for 20 to 30 percent of the total value of sales:

[Billion rubles]

	1955	1956
Total income from grain crops [1]	8.6	12.1
Estimated income from grain procurement [2]	6.8	8.4

[1] ESKh, 1957, No. 7, p. 33.
[2] 1955 from RM-2101, p. 186 (sum of payments for compulsory deliveries and above-quota purchases); 1956 from appendix table 5.

Aggregate data may be misleading so far as the majority of farms is concerned. For example, the relative importance of market sales in a densely populated agricultural area such as the Ukraine is considerably higher than for the U.S.S.R. as a whole. In 1950 and 1954, when income from market sales accounted for 31 and 21 percent, respectively, of U.S.S.R. collective income from sales, the corresponding figures for Ukrainian collectives were 42 and 30 percent.[15] Within comparatively homogeneous regions, such as a single oblast (province), collective farm income in districts with easy access to major urban centers is several times average income in remoter districts;[16] a large part of this disparity must be due to differences in the proportion of market sales in total marketings. It is clear, therefore, that the influence of market sales on average price is quite uneven.

TABLE 5.—*Distribution by origin of collective farm money income, 1935–56*

[Billion rubles, unless otherwise specified]

	1935	1940	1950	1952	1954	1956
Sales to procurement agencies	5.25	10.4	21.3	24.5	46.5	74.7
Sales at market prices [1]	1.89	6.1	9.4	14.7	12.4	13.9
Other income [2]	1.74	4.2	3.5	3.6	4.4	6.0
Total	8.88	20.7	34.2	42.8	63.3	94.6
Sales at market prices as a percentage of total sales	26	37	31	38	21	16

[1] Sales on the urban and rural collective farm market, and off-market sales to other farms and to farm members.
[2] Earnings of subsidiary enterprises (mills, shops, etc.); earnings from services; interest on bank deposits.

Sources:
1935: Nesmii in PKh, 1938, No. 9, p. 95.
1940: Total and "other" income given or implied in NK 1956, p. 140. Market sales from RM-2101, p. 47. Procurement sales derived as a residual.
1950–54: RM-2101, p. 44.
1956: Total from S.S.S.R. v tsifrakh, p. 200. Market and procurement sales from ESKh, 1957, No. 7, p. 32. "Other" income derived as a residual.

[15] Computed from Statistichne upravlinnia Ukrains'koi R.S.R., Narodne gospodarstvo Ukrains'koi R.S.R., Kiev, 1957, pp. 283, 298.
[16] Cf. Moskovskoe oblastnoe statisticheskoe upravlenie, Narodnoe khoziaistvo Moskovskoi oblasti, M., 1958, pp. 129–130; Statisticheskoe upravlenie Leningradskoi oblasti, Narodnoe khoziaistvo Leningradskoi oblasti, M., 1957, pp. 72–78; and any atlas which shows railways and highways in these oblasts.

Still, average realized prices provide some idea of the extent to which we do violence to reality in neglecting market sales of food products in this paper. Fairly good estimates can be made of the average prices realized by collective farms in 1937 for four products; they are compared below with average procurement prices:

Prices received by collective farms in 1937 for urban marketings

	Rubles per ton		Percent, col. 2÷col. 1
	Average realized price	Procurement price	
	(1)	(2)	(3)
Grain	137	88	64
Potatoes	120	53	44
Milk	357	240	67
Meat (live weight)	1, 194	950	80

Sources: Col. 1 computed from quantities and prices estimated by Karcz in RM–1930, pp. 333–337. The meat price includes market sales of livestock on the hoof, col. 2 from table 6 in sec. II below.

The average realized prices refer to urban marketings only; if rural sales were taken into account, the prices in column 1 would be higher, and the ratios in column 3 lower.

Estimates of average realized prices can be made for three products in 1956; the calculations are shown below:

Prices received by collective farms in 1956

	Quantity (millions of tons)	Price (rubles per ton)	Value (billions of rubles)
	(1)	(2)	(3)
Grain:			
Procurement [1]	15. 9	530	8. 43
Market sales	[2] 1. 5	[3] 2, 500	[4] 3. 7
Total sales	17. 4	695	[5] 12. 1
Meat (live weight):			
Procurement [1]	2. 37	3, 640	8. 63
Market sales	[6] . 8	[3] 9, 000	7. 20
Total sales	3. 2	4, 950	15. 83
Milk:			
Procurement [1]	10. 371	970	10. 06
Market sales	[7] . 9	[3] 2, 400	2. 16
Total sales	11. 3	1, 080	12. 22

[1] See appendix table 5. The quantity data are net of deliveries for which farms received no price (return of seed loans, payments in kind to MTS).

[2] Col. 3÷col. 2.

[3] Based on the prices realized in commission sales in 1956, as derived from quantity and value data in Vest. stat., 1958, No. 8, p. 84. The derived price of flour, food grains, groats, and legumes (3,285 rubles per ton) was adjusted downward to 2,500 rubles per ton to eliminate the value of milling and to allow for the presumably higher share in sales by collective farms of the lower priced feed grains. The carcass meat price (14,645 rubles per ton) was adjusted to live weight assuming a carcass to live weight ratio of 60 percent. The milk price refers to whole milk.

[4] Difference between total collective farm income from grain crops and income from procurement.

[5] ESKh, 1957, No. 7, p. 33.

[6] Difference between estimated total marketings of 3.5 million tons live weight and total procurement of 2.7 million tons including deliveries for which farms received no price (appendix table 2). The estimate of total marketings is derived from a carcass weight estimate of 2.1 million tons (cf. table 4 and appendix table 1), assuming a ratio of carcass to live weight of 60 percent (cf. sources to table 4).

[7] Difference between total marketings of 12.4 million tons (cf. table 4 and appendix table 1) and total procurement including deliveries for which farms received no price (appendix table 2).

The ratio of procurement price to average realized price is (percent): grain, 76; meat, 74; milk, 90. In this calculation the average realized price of grain presumably includes rural marketings.

To summarize: disregard of market sales involves a considerable understatement of the average prices for food products realized by collective farms. The understatement evidently diminishes over time, being on the order of perhaps 50 percent in 1937 and 25 percent in 1956. There are grounds for suspecting that a great many farms without access to urban markets received prices closer to the level of procurement prices than to average realized prices. But it is clear that index numbers of procurement prices (to be presented in secs. II and IV) are not representative of average prices. Comment on the divergence between trends in procurement and average realized prices will be made as the index numbers are presented.

II. PROCUREMENT PRICES, 1928–50

Before examining price trends, it may be useful to review briefly the procurement arrangements affecting the level, formation, and significance of prices.[17]

Virtually all procurement in 1928 came from independent peasants. Raw material crops were obtained on the basis of contracts concluded between procurement agencies and groups of farmers who agreed in advance to deliver specified amounts of product at specified prices. The contract system (which involved a large measure of compulsion) was beginning to be applied to food products as well; however, the bulk of these were still obtained in a more or less unorganized fashion from individual farmers offering produce on the market or at procurement collection points.

The system of procurement associated with collectivized agriculture was introduced in late 1932 and 1933 (by which time collectivization embraced two-thirds of all peasant households and four-fifths of the sown area), and remained essentially unchanged through 1957. Its characteristic features were: a defined minimum obligation to deliver, multiple prices, and the extension of payments or benefits not reflected in procurement prices.

With most technical crops the obligation was defined, as in earlier years, by a contract which specified the area to be sown and the quantity of produce to be delivered per hectare. In the case of cotton and sugar beet the quantity was the whole crop; in no case was delivery wholly or even primarily voluntary. Planned deliveries per hectare were paid for at base prices uniform (for a given quality within a given price zone) for all farms. A farm's above-plan deliveries were, from 1935 on, paid for at premium prices anywhere from 50 to 300 percent above the base price. Generally speaking, the larger the quantity per hectare which a farm contracted to deliver, the higher the premium price for above-plan deliveries. Unlike food producers, farms delivering technical crops received part of their payment in advance. They were also guaranteed the opportunity to buy stipulated amounts (in proportion to their total deliveries) of certain consumer's good, some at prices on the order of 50 percent below regular retail prices.[18]

---

[17] Cf. I. M. Slatin, Gosudarstvennye zagotovki sel'skokhoziaistvennyh produktov v S.S.S.R., M., 1956; M. M. Lifits, ed., Ekonomika sovetskoi torgovli, M., 1950, ch. 6; M.I. Moiseev, Ekonomicheskie osnovy gosudarstvennykh zagotovok sel'skokhoziaistvennykh produktov, M., 1955; L. N. Bakhovkina, Gosudarstvennye zakupki sek'skokhoziaistvennykh produktov, M., 1955.

[18] Cf. Moiseev in SSKh, 1954, No. 3, p. 58.

Cotton farms bought seed and mineral fertilizers at privileged prices, while sugar beet farms received free seed.[19] The value of benefits not expressed in procurement prices for technical crops was considerable. Data on receipts for sugar beet in the years 1933–35 indicate that the value of natural payments (beet pulp, sirup, seeds, fertilizers, pesticides) received by farms was equivalent to about 25 percent of the cash payments.[20]

A source in the midfifties estimated that total benefits (most of which were received by technical crop producers) were equivalent to 10–12 percent of the total bill for state procurement from the collective sector.[21] The discount on wheat purchases by flax farms alone in the years 1955–56 amounted to about 2 billion rubles, equivalent to 17 percent of cash payments for flax in these years.[22]

Compulsory deliveries of basic food products and wool were determined by regionally differentiated quotas. From 1933 to 1940 the quotas were based on a farm's sown area and numbers of livestock. Thereafter, they were proportional to the amount of land a farm held: arable land, in the case of crops, or total agricultural land (arable, meadow, pasture, orchard), in the case of livestock products. At no time were the quotas dependent upon output: the state could count on fixed amounts of compulsory deliveries, at low prices, in good years and bad. After a farm discharged its quota obligation, and also its obligation to make payments in kind for MTS services, any marketable surplus could be sold to procurement agencies at higher, above-quota prices. These were still far below market prices, but since above-quota deliveries entitled farms to buy (at regular retail prices) scarce producers' goods which were otherwise unobtainable, they were made even by farms with access to collective farm markets.[23] Above-quota deliveries were abandoned at the beginning of World War II and remained negligible until 1953. Compulsory deliveries, on the other hand, increased both as a result of higher quotas for all farms and (from 1947 to 1953) violation of the principle of equal quotas: farms with a visible surplus were required to make whatever deliveries were needed to meet local procurement plans.[24]

One fact about multiple pricing as it affected both food products and technical crops is worth emphasizing. The lowest price applied to the basic or inescapable obligation and the higher to exceptional or voluntary deliveries. Such a system may offer long-term incentives to increase yield and deliveries,[25] but it also results in annual fluctuations in average price which tend to be inversely related to cost (in bad years when unit costs are higher, average price is lower), and in any given year it penalizes the low yield producer.[26]

Procurement prices in 1928 were rather close to average realized prices; the ratio of the former to the latter was as follows (percent): grain, 87; potatoes, 59; meat, 107; milk, 77; eggs, 94; sugar beets, 84; raw cotton, 100; flax fiber, 94.[27] In the case of raw material crops, this was because the state was virtually the only buyer. It was the domi-

---

[19] Izvestiia, July 1, 1958, p. 2, par. 15.

[20] Narodnyi komissariet pishchevoi promyshlennosti, Glavsakhara, Otchet a rabote sakharnoi promyshlennosti za 1933–35 gg., M., 1936, p. 38.

[21] Popova in SSKh, 1955, No. 6, p. 40.

[22] Zagorodneva in Vest. Mosk. Univ., 1958, No. 3, pp. 47, 50.

[23] Peter Uranov, "Some Aspects of Soviet Price Policy," New York, 1952, pp. 59–60.

[24] Cf. RM–1178, pp. 9–10.

[25] Whether it actually does so depends on the feasibility of rewarded performance, on the relation of the basic price to cost, and on the differential between basic and premium prices.

[26] Examples are given in sec. IV.

[27] Computed from the absolute prices in Karcz, RM–1930, pp. 340, 345.

nant buyer of food products, but the comparative lack of compulsion to deliver meant that procurement prices were influenced by the market prices paid by private traders and the population.

Trends after 1928 have been summarized by Moiseev as follows: [28]

> [Compulsory delivery] prices for grain, potatoes, vegetables, meat, and a few other food products remained unchanged from 1928–29 until 1953, though prices of manufactured goods were increased after the war. Clearly, this signified a marked change in the terms of trade for food products, as a result of which the real payment received by collective farms declined.
>
> Technical crops fared better. Contract and premium prices for cotton, flax, hemp, sugar beet, and other technical crops were raised substantially several times. As a result, changes in technical crop prices approximately matched changes in retail prices for manufactured goods * * *. But even in technical crop production the situation varied from crop to crop.

Moiseev is not entirely accurate. Compulsory delivery prices for grain, potatoes, and meat unquestionably increased somewhat in the thirties. And they are not in any case the whole story, since average price was influenced by above-quota deliveries. Nor is it true that prices of manufactured goods increased only after the war, as he appears to suggest in speaking of food products. In fact they increased (as he tacitly recognizes in speaking of raw material crops) several times; i.e., throughout the period from 1928 to 1948. Still, Moiseev's statement appears to be broadly correct in the light of the estimates to follow.

Table 6 shows for seven products the procurement prices paid to all producers in 1928 and to collective farms in 1937 and 1950. Prices for 1928 were derived by Karcz from reports of average prices actually paid or planned by centralized procurement organizations; they appear to be highly reliable.

Prices of food products in 1937 and 1950 are averages of compulsory delivery and above-quota prices (as estimated by Karcz), weighted by the proportions of each in collective farm deliveries.[29] Since Karcz's prices refer to deliveries by both collective farms and the private sector, some error may be involved in this procedure, but it can hardly be significant except in the case of meat, where differences in assortment and weight of animals are likely. Karcz's price estimates appear to be quite reliable except in the case of meat (where special difficulties were encountered). The estimates of compulsory and above-quota deliveries by which I weigh his 1937 prices are reliable for grain, meat, and milk, but dubious for potatoes. The 1950 weights are also dubious, but the resulting error in average price could be important only in the case of meat, where the differential between above-quota and compulsory delivery prices was 10 to 1. Because of the generally lower reliability of the meat prices and weights, Karcz's prices (which refer to major meats only) are accepted as the price of all meat.[30]

---

[28] Vop. ekon., 1958, No. 7, pp. 20–21. Gaponenko confirms this résumé (PKh, 1958, No. 11, p. 33), adding with respect to technical crops: "The level of average prices was adequate, but it was [strongly] influenced by premiums; the base price even for technical crops remained low." According to Terent'ev (Vop. ekon., 1958, No. 3, p. 59), "Compulsory delivery prices for important [food] products remained approximately at the level of 1928 market prices until 1955. Over this period wholesale and retail prices for many manufactured foods were substantially increased." His terminal date is misleading: compulsory delivery prices for livestock products, potatoes, and vegetables increased in 1953; grain, in 1955.

[29] The prices estimated by Karcz for grain, meat, and milk in 1952 are attributed here to 1950, as no change in prices is known to have occurred between these 2 years. Karcz's estimate of the compulsory delivery price of potatoes in 1952 includes a "new premium" of 5 percent for punctual delivery; I assume that this was not paid in 1950.

[30] Major meats (cattle, hogs, sheep, and goats) accounted for 94 percent of total carcass meat output in 1937 and 92 percent in 1950 (cf. Zhivotnovodstvo 1959, p. 159). Their share in collective farm output was probably higher (cf. ibid., p. 160).

TABLE 6.—*Average procurement prices received by collective farms for selected products, 1928, 1937, 1950* [1]

	Rubles per ton			Price relatives, 1928=100	
	1928	1937	1950	1937	1950
Food products:					
Grain	61.0	88	91	144	149
Potatoes	22.0	53	40	241	182
Meat (live weight)	235.0	950	700	404	298
Milk [2]	58.0	240	300	414	517
Raw materials:					
Sugar beet	10.3	44	110	427	1,068
Raw cotton	282.0	1,570	3,600	557	1,277
Flax fiber	450.0	1,050	4,423	233	983

[1] Data for 1938 refer to the average procurement prices received by all producers (independent peasants, state farms, and the few collective farms then in existence).
[2] Including milk products converted to milk equivalent.

Sources: 1928: Karcz, RM-1930, p. 345. 1937: Appendix table 3. 1950: Appendix table 4.

Prices of technical crops in 1937 and 1950 are weighted averages of base and premium prices; they exclude the value of discounts and other benefits. Estimates for 1937 are Karcz', as is the cotton price attributed here to 1950; they appear to be quite reliable. The flax price in 1950 is the reported average, the sugar beet price is my adjustment of Karcz' estimate for 1952.

Prices for 1928 and 1937 refer not to a constant grade of product but to the average product marketed in those years. This is true also of the flax price in 1950; other prices for this year in effect assume no change in quality from 1937.

Products in table 6 accounted in 1937 for an estimated 6.5 billion rubles of collective farm sales to procurement agencies, or something like 75 to 80 percent of the total.[31] In 1950 they accounted for an estimated 15.2 billion rubles, or 71 percent of the total.[32] Whether they are representative of the trends for all products is moot; probably food products are better represented than technical crops.

The price relatives in table 6 are weighted by the values of collective farm sales of these products to state procurement agencies in 1937 to obtain the price index numbers in table 7. In view of the doubts attached to some price estimates and to the representativeness of products included, a high degree of reliability cannot be claimed for these numbers, but they probably indicate the orders of magnitude involved. Two interesting facts emerge: (1) between 1928 and 1950 raw material prices increased more than tenfold, while food product prices increased less than threefold; (2) prices of food products were more or less constant from 1937 to 1950.

As was indicated at the end of section I, the average prices realized by collective farms for food products in 1937 (taking all sales at market prices into account) may have been double procurement prices, so that a fivefold increase in average realized prices of food products over the period 1928–37 is possible. This would be about the same as the increase in raw material procurement prices (table 7). A rough equality probably persisted to 1940 (there were no major pro-

[31] Cf. appendix table 3. Total collective farm sales to procurement agencies in 1937 are not known. All agricultural sales amounted to 12 billion rubles (KVSP 1939, p. 115); if the share of sales to procurement agencies was 66 percent, as in 1936 (Nesmii in PKh, 1938, No. 9, p. 95), total sales to procurement agencies were about 8 billion rubles.
[32] Cf. table 5 and appendix table 4.

curement price changes, and market sales flourished). Between 1940 and 1950, however, the situation changed radically: procurement prices for raw materials doubled, while average realized prices for food products (disregarding the war years) declined. According to Moiseev: [33]

Even after the war, state above-quota purchases of grain were not resumed, and above-quota purchases of other products were sharply curtailed. On the other hand, compulsory delivery quotas for grain and other products were again increased in these years, while the principle of equal quotas * * * was violated. The increase in compulsory deliveries, together with the decline in total output resulting from the war, led to a reduction in quantities of products sold on the collective farm market.

This was reflected in the trend in average realized prices * * * The curtailment in state above-quota purchases and the reduction in market sales somewhat reduced the average realized prices for grair, potatoes, vegetables, meat, milk, and other food products, since almost all marketed output was delivered at compulsory delivery prices.

TABLE 7.—*Index numbers of procurement prices received by collected farms, 1928, 1937, 1950* [1]

[1928=100]

Product group	1928	1937	1950
Food products	100	274	274
Raw materials	100	510	1, 218
All products	100	420	858

[1] Index numbers for 1928 refer to the prices received by all producers.

Sources: Computed from the price relatives in table 6 and the 1937 value weights in appendix table 3.

To appreciate what these movements meant in terms of real receipts, we need, of course, measures of the prices paid by collective farms for goods. Some notion of the nature of the goods involved may be formed from data on the composition of money outlays on production and investment (in both of the examples below, the data exclude any remuneration to collective farm members). In 1937 production expenses were distributed as follows (percent): [34]

Current repair of buildings and tools	8. 8
Purchase of small tools	9. 5
Purchase of mineral fertilizers	8. 2
Purchase of pesticides	1. 8
Purchase of fuel and lubricants	9. 4
Purchase of materials for subsidiary enterprises (shops, mills, etc.)	5. 8
Purchase of seed	7. 3
Purchase of feed	12. 3
Cash payments to MTS	11. 0
Wages of hired specialists	4. 7
Miscellaneous	21. 2
Total	100. 0

[33] Vop. ekon., 1958, No. 7, p. 20.
[34] KVSP 1939, p. 138.

In 1950 the distribution of money investment was as follows (billion rubles):[35]

Purchase of materials; payment of hired construction labor	2. 097
Purchase of machinery, motors, power equipment, large tools	2. 304
Irrigation and land improvement	. 227
Purchase of livestock	3. 235
Orchard and timber plantings	. 249
Capital repair of buildings and machinery	1. 215
(Miscellaneous)	(. 220)
Total	9. 547

Farms undoubtedly purchased agricultural commodities such as seed, feed, and livestock from state enterprises (procurement agencies, state farms) as well as from other collective farms and individual farmers. To the extent that purchases were made from the collective and private sector, they probably occurred at an approximation of rural collective farm market prices. Fertilizer was sold to cotton farms at a special discount;[36] other farms paid the wholesale price.[37] All other manufactured commodities—tools, machinery, spare parts, fuel and lubricants, building materials—were bought by collective farms at retail prices: that is, at prices involving a substantial markup over wholesale prices.[38]

Unfortunately, there is little or no information about movements of rural market prices, wholesale fertilizer prices, and the retail prices paid by collective farms for industrial producer's goods. Nor is it self-evident that available price indicators (table 8) provide good analogs. For example, market price trends differ somewhat between different aggregates of cities;[39] differences between urban and rural areas might be much larger. Janet Chapman's index numbers of official retail prices of all manufactured goods (row 2a of table 8 refer almost entirely to consumer's goods. A building materials group is included (shown separately in row 2b) but the group may not be very well represented. The relation of the retail prices paid by collective farms to the wholesale prices shown in rows 3 and 4 is unknown; very possible it fluctuated over time.[40]

[35] Golev in Fin. S.S.S.R., 1956, No. 2, p. 58.
[36] Cf. Izvestiia, July 1, 1958, p. 2, par. 15.
[37] Terent'ev in Vop. ekon., 1958, No. 3, p. 60.
[38] Ibid. See also E. I. Iakushkin, Novaia sistema zagotovok sel'skokhoziaistvennykh produktov, M., 1958, p. 35.
[39] Compare data for 251 cities and 71 large cities in ST 1956, pp. 182–183.
[40] Between 1928 and 1937, when the average increase in wholesale brick prices was 35 percent, the increase in retail brick prices in Moscow was 118 percent (cf. Chapman, Review of Economics and Statistics, vol. 36 (May 1954), p. 154.)

TABLE 8.—*Indicators of prices paid by collective farms for agricultural and manufactured goods, 1928–52*

	1928	1937	1940	1948	1950	1952
1. Urban market prices:						
(a) Grain, 1928=100	[1] 100	1,428				
(b) Livestock, 1928=100	[2] 100	[3] 1,136				
(c) All products, 1937=100		100	200			
(d) All products, 1940=100			100		104	
2. Official retail prices, Moscow (1937 weights), 1928=100:						
(a) All manufactured goods	100	461		1,291		1,000
(b) Building materials	100	258		650		539
3. Wholesale prices of selected industrial goods (1937 weights), 1928=100:						
(a) Miscellaneous metal articles (wire, nails, screws, bolts, etc.)	100	150			360	
(b) Selected lumber and wood products	100	175			580	
(c) Bricks	100	135			726	
(d) Cement	100	154			319	
4. Wholesale prices of selected petroleum products, 1928=100:						
(a) Gasoline, 2d grade	100	350			315	
(b) Kerosene	100	648			608	
(c) Motor oils	100	214			319	

1 Average realized price.
2 Average realized price of meat, live weight.
3 Market price of livestock sold on the hoof.

Sources:
Rows 1 (a), (b): Computed from absolute prices in Karcz, RM–1930, pp. 245, 296, 340.
Row 1(c): Crude estimate derived from known increase in total value of market sales between 1937 and 1940 (63 percent) and an estimated decline in volume of sales of 16 percent. The latter is derived from Karcz's estimates of prices of grain, potatoes, meat, and milk in 1937, and estimates of quantities sold in 1937 and 1940.
Row 1(d): "ST 1956," p. 182.
Rows 2 (a), (b), Janet Chapman in "Review of Economics and Statistics," vol. 36 (May 1954), p. 141.
Rows 3 (a). (b), (c), (d): Abram Bergson et al., "Basic Industrial Prices in the U.S.S.R, 1928–1950," Rand Corp., Research Memorandum RM–1522, Aug. 1, 1955, pp. 20, 23, 25.
Rows 4 (a), (b), (c): N. Nimitz, "Prices of Refined Petroleum Products in the U.S.S.R, 1928–50," Rand Corp., RM–1497, May 26, 1955, p. 11.

Thus no very firm conclusions can be drawn from table 8. It does suggest, however, that the rise between 1928 and 1937 in prices paid for agricultural commodities was rather large. If rural prices rose only half as much as urban prices, a fivefold or sixfold increase is indicated. The increase in prices of manufactured goods bought by farms was perhaps closer to row 2(*b*) than to row 2(*a*): that is, about threefold. Between 1937 and 1950 prices of agricultural commodities could have doubled while prices of manufactured goods increased somewhere between twofold and threefold. Taking agricultural and manufactured goods together, the increase over 1928 in all prices paid by collective farms was perhaps fourfold to fivefold by 1937 and eightfold to tenfold by 1950.

Obviously these are very crude estimates. For what they are worth, they suggest (in connection with the trends in average realized prices discussed earlier) that the average price of raw material crops did keep pace between 1928 and 1950 with the prices of goods purchased by farms. Prices of food products may have kept pace to 1937; thereafter average realized prices declined while prices paid by farms roughly doubled; in other words, real receipts fell by something like one-half.

Another clue to the trend in costs is provided, for the period 1937–50, by data on state farm costs. Table 9 compares these costs with the prices received by collective farms for three products in 1937 and 1950. In columns 1 and 4, the lower figures for grain and milk are average procurement prices. The upper figures, which are double the lower, are intended to represent the probable maximum average realized price (including market sales); the estimates for 1950 are clearly on the generous side. In the case of cotton, the average procurement price is identical with the average realized price. The costs in columns (2) and (5) may be lower than collective farm costs similarly defined; they are not likely to be higher.[41]

TABLE 9.—*Comparison of prices received by collective farms for grain, milk, and raw cotton with state farm costs, 1937, 1950*

Product	1937			1950		
	Collective farm price (1)	State farm cost (2)	Col. 1 ÷ col. 2 (3)	Collective farm price (4)	State farm cost (5)	Col. 4 ÷ col. 5 (6)
	Rubles	*Ton*	*Percent*	*Rubles*	*Ton*	*Percent*
Grain	88–176	190	46–93	91–182	508	18–36
Milk	240–480	432	56–111	300–600	1,298	23–46
Raw cotton	1,570	[1] 1,087	144	3,600	1,826	197

[1] Planned cost in 1938.

Sources:
Cols. 1, 4: Lower figures (average procurement prices) from table 6. Upper figures (national average realized prices) are double procurement prices.
Col. 2: Karcz, RM–1930, p. 51.
Col. 5: From table 12.

Table 9 suggests that procurement price covered something like half of grain and milk costs in 1937 and one-fifth in 1950. In 1937 the difference may have been made up by market sales; in 1950 even average realized prices were less than half of cost. Cotton price exceeded cost by a wide margin in 1937 and an even wider one in 1950 (and it will be recalled that cotton producers also received significant benefits not reflected in price). It might be noted that all these ratios exaggerate the extent to which income covered costs, since approximately one-quarter of total collective farm money income in both 1937 and 1950 went to payments to the state (in the form of taxes, fees, loan repayments, etc.) and to investment funds;[42] these payments were compulsory, and took priority over other demands on income. Material production costs also had to be met. The collapsible element in cost was wages, i.e., the payment for labor of collective farm members.

Trends in collective farm output and yields over the period 1928–50 clearly show the relevance of price and cost movements to agricultural performance. In the single case where the state was unmistakably willing to pay prices which covered collective farm costs (cotton), yields increased markedly both before and after the war. Sugar beet yields also increased markedly, though most of the increase was achieved by 1940. In the case of food products, yields increased very little. It would clearly be rash to conclude that price policy alone restrained yield increases for food products, or that any prices would have elicited the rapid and massive increases associated with cotton and sugar beet (where production technology was initially extremely backward). It is also quite clear, however, that price policy was not calculated to encourage food production.

[41] In the 1950's state farm costs were generally below collective farm costs, as will be shown in sec. III.
[42] Cf. "KVSP 1939," p. 108; RM–2101, pp. 35, 211.

III. COLLECTIVE FARM COSTS OF PRODUCTION

Given the trends summarized in section II, it is understandable that the Government was not anxious to invite comparison between costs and procurement prices. It is not surprising, therefore, that collective farms did not calculate their costs of production, and that estimates of costs were not published. It is a little surprising that estimates were not even made: real costs were apparently ignored from the late twenties until 1953, and the notion was widely accepted that the concept of cost was not applicable to collective farms. Commenting on this "pernicious misconception", an editorial in the journal of the Institute of Economics noted that [43]

> * * * Neither the Institute of Economics * * * nor any agricultural institute conducted research even to establish a methodology of investigating cost, as an economic category, in collective farms * * *
>
> Because of failure to study calculation of production outlays and costs of collective farm output, there is no solid theoretical basis for studying the important problem of price formation in agriculture.

The program of agricultural reform announced in 1953 placed great emphasis on economic incentives to produce, thus indicating at least obliquely a concern with real costs. By 1955 the need for cost data as a guide to price policy was generally acknowledged, and the problems of defining and calculating collective farm costs began to be widely discussed in general economic and agricultural journals. Two orders of difficulties emerged. One involved basic data: The accounts kept by collective farms and MTS were simply not set up to show accurately the expenditures of labor, machine operations, materials, etc., on individual products. Depreciation as an accounting category did not exist. Labor inputs were measured not in man-days but in labor-days, a complex unit of effort which could vary in significance from one product to another, from one farm to another, and from one year to the next.[44] Second, conceptual difficulties arose particularly in in valuing machine operations and labor inputs. From the point of view of the individual farm, the cost of machine operations was represented by payments in kind for MTS services; it was extremely difficult to place a meaningful value on these payments, given the multiplicity and artificiality of agricultural prices. For purposes of national economic planning, on the other hand, it was desirable to value MTS services at actual operating costs. Similarly, from the point of view of the individual farm, the cost of labor was represented by actual payments for labor-days. But since payments varied widely from one farm to another, and fluctuated from year to year, valuation at actual earnings made interfarm and intertemporal comparisons impossible. In farms with high earnings per labor-day, costs would appear higher than in backward farms where labor inputs were greater but earnings lower.[45] For purposes of comparison, then, some fixed, notional value had to be assigned to labor inputs.

A great variety of solutions was proposed by individual discussants. Many are of interest as examples of cultural lag—that is, as evidence of persistent confusion about the nature of cost and the purposes of calculating it. We need bother, however, only with the essential features of the methods underlying published average cost figures.

---

[43] Vop. ekon., 1955 No. 5, p. 4. See also: Terent'ev, SKP 1957, pp. 5, 11, 17; SSKh, 1955 No. 3, p. 123.
[44] Makarov in Vop. ekon., 1956 No. 9, pp. 120-121.
[45] For an example, see Vest. stat., 1958 No. 12, p. 50.

Most of the figures available so far are found in a single book by M. L. Terent'ev, which presents the results of average cost calculations for individual regions and the U.S.S.R. as a whole over the years 1953-55.[46] The calculations were made by the Planning and Economic Administration of the Ministry of Agriculture, with the immediate purpose of establishing the basis for price revisions. Basic data were derived from annual accounts and primary bookkeeping records in a farm sample of undisclosed size. The method of calculation includes two variants (which differ only in their treatment of MTS operations).

The main features of Terent'ev's method are as follows. Labor-day inputs are valued at the average daily wage of seasonal state farm workers: that is, at about 9 rubles per labor-day (with slight zonal variations).[47] Purchased materials and services are valued at actual purchase prices; materials and services originating on farm are valued at a farm's own cost of production.[48] The depreciation charge on farm capital is estimated on the basis of the norms prescribed for various types of assets on state farms.[49] In what might be called the national planning variant, MTS services are valued at operating costs to the state: these include actual outlays on fuel and lubricants, current and capital repair of machinery, wages of MTS administration, and that part of the wages of production (tractor brigade) workers which is guaranteed by the state. They notably exclude a depreciation charge for replacement of MTS capital, which means that they considerably understate the real cost of machine operations.[50] In what may be called the farm planning variant, the cost of MTS operations is equated with payments in kind for MTS services. These are valued at the farm's own cost of production, which is calculated by dividing the aggregate cost of the farm's own inputs (seed, fertilizer, live draft power, labor, and so on) by total output net of payments in kind.[51]

The values placed on MTS services by these two variants did not differ significantly for the U.S.S.R. as a whole. They did differ in individual regions. This was because regional rates for MTS services did not reflect only, or even primarily, the levels of MTS operating costs; they were also an instrument for extracting differential rent. Generally speaking, rates were high on good land where MTS costs were low, and vice versa.[52]

The method of calculating cost which was used by the Institute of Agricultural Economics (VNIIESKh) was essentially the same as Terent'ev's national planning variant: labor was valued at an approximation of state farm wage rates, and MTS operations were valued at actual operating costs.[53] The method underlying absolute data for 1956 cited by Silin in the journal of the Central Statistical Administration is not specified;[54] however, an earlier article by the same author recommended valuing labor at state farm wage rates, and

[46] Sebestoimost' kolkhoznoi produktsii, M., 1957 (SKP 1957).
[47] Ibid., pp. 23-26, 80, 94.
[48] Ibid., p. 65.
[49] Ibid., pp. 74-75.
[50] Ibid., p. 95; Vest. stat., 1957 No. 2, pp. 29-34; ibid., 1957 No. 3, p. 36.
[51] SKP 1957, pp. 29-35.
[52] Ibid., pp. 156, 164-165; Turetskii in Vest. stat., 1956 No. 6, p. 29.
[53] SSKh, 1956 No. 4, pp. 24-41.
[54] Vest. stat., 1958 No. 3, p. 17.

MTS operations either at actual cost or at the value of payments in kind at above-quota prices.[55]

Minor differences certainly existed between the methods described above, but their results may have been broadly comparable. On this presumption, data from various sources are treated as comparable in deriving estimates of collective farm costs in absolute terms to be presented below.

The studies of collective farm costs made between 1955 and 1957 established two facts which called for basic changes not only in prices but also in agricultural institutions. The first was the large variation in costs between regions (table 10). In the light of these variations, existing regional price differentials were quite inadequate, while the exaction of quota deliveries from some regions (grain from Belorussia, potatoes from central Asia) made little sense.[56] On the positive side, the regional data indicated the possibility of significant reduction in average costs through improved specialization.

[55] Ibid., 1957 No. 3, pp. 29–37.
[56] Kartashov in Izvestiia, Mar. 11, 1959, p. 2.

TABLE 10.—*Regional variations in cost of production on collective farms, 1953–55*

[U.S.S.R. average=100]

Region	Grain	Potatoes	Vegetables and cucurbits	Sugar beet	Sunflower	Cotton	Fiber flax	Beef	Pork	Milk	Wool	Eggs
RSFSR	100	102	106	111	101		88	112	122	109	127	99
North	276	137	128				112	152	136	128	271	159
Northwest	229	145	122				98	140	134	113	243	105
Central nonblack soil	195	91	106	220			93	167	175	133	239	157
Central black soil	98	98	102	111	106			129	158	116	148	107
Volga	100	116	101	329	146			102	114	105	125	114
North Caucasus	69	155	90	64	81			91	93	93	105	65
Urals	95	118	137	171	210			117	122	114	153	118
West Siberia	70	92	144	205	222			87	90	86	112	97
East Siberia	76	115	156	549	280			88	88	94	103	145
Far East	78	240	148	156	487			106	114	100	165	134
Belorussian S.S.R.	274	94	130	271			107	156	133	137	160	195
Ukrainian S.S.R.	87	93	89	95	105	144		94	76	92	95	98
Moldavian S.S.R.	89	283	91	90	109	563		80	67	82	70	101
Kazakh S.S.R.	72	230	131	115	195	108		65	84	73	68	160
Uzbek S.S.R.	153	233	93			101		90	34	97	39	122
Turkmen S.S.R.	158	879	130			116		66		76	30	103
Tadzhik S.S.R.	194	277	109			98		88		90	62	131
Kirgiz S.S.R.	105	236	153	103		121		95	100	93	75	119
Azerbaidzhan S.S.R.	133	200	108			75		153	58	124	93	129
Georgian S.S.R.	154	209	149	92	217			138	143	127	83	183
Armenian S.S.R.	165	147	76	133		87		69	78	70	76	120
Lithuanian S.S.R.	265	93	202	175			76	95	105	90	112	87
Latvian S.S.R.	193	72	125	140			109	70	59	62	125	80
Estonian S.S.R.	208	72	88	244			82	81	58	70	165	84

Source: SKP 1957, pp. 232–233.

The second fact which emerged was that costs on collective farms (table 11) were typically a good deal higher than on state farms (table 12). According to Volosenkov, average collective farm costs for basic products over the years 1953–55 exceeded state farm costs by one-tenth to one-third; with a few products the difference was "somewhat larger." [57] According to tables 11 and 12, costs compared as follows:

Average costs of production on collective and state farms, 1953–56

[Rubles per ton]

	(1) State farms	(2) Collective farms	(3) Column 2 as percent of column 1
Grain	390	690	177
Potatoes	[1] 495	350	71
Vegetables	[1] 525	[2] 480	91
Milk	1, 200	1, 570	131
Sugar beet	[3] 150	160	107
Raw cotton	[3] 1, 685	2, 000	119

[1] 1954–57.
[2] 1953–55.
[3] 1955–56.

TABLE 11.—*Average costs of production on collective farms, 1953–56* [1]

[Rubles per ton]

Product	1953	1956	1953–56
Food products:			
Grain	660	[2] 560	690
Potatoes	X	260	350
Vegetables	X	X	[3] 480
Pork (live weight increment)	X	12, 010	X
Milk	1, 530	1, 300	1, 570
Raw materials:			
Sugar beet	X	150	160
Raw cotton	2, 180	1, 920	2. 000
Flax fiber	7, 780	6, 145	6, 800
Sunflower seed	X	X	455

[1] The sign "X" means not available.
[2] Specified as excluding corn.
[3] 1953–55.

Sources:
1953: Flax fiber: Computed from absolute and percentage reduction in costs between 1953 and 1955 (SKP), 1957, pp. 186–188). Other products: Given 1956 figures, computed from percentage reduction in costs between 1953 and 1956 (Tereat'ev in Vop. ekon., 1958, No. 3, p. 61).
1956: Flax fiber: Given 1953 figure, computed from percentage reduction in costs between 1953 and 1956 (ibid.). Other products: Silin in Vest. stat., 1958, No. 3, p. 17.
1953–1956: Flax fiber: Unweighted average of costs in each of the 4 years. 1954, 1955 computed from SKP, 1957, pp. 186–188. Vegetables: Estimate based on the range in absolute costs given by Tulupnikov (ESKh, 957, No. 3, p. 45) and the percentage range in SKP, 1957, pp. 172-173. All other products: Given the estimate for cotton, computed from the percentage ratios given by Tereatlev in Vop. ekon., 1958, No. 3, p. 65. Cotton costs in 1954 and 1955 are believed to have been below 1953, since yield increased (NK, 1956, p. 107) while labor inputs per centner or per hectare decreased (Kalatov and Ul'dzhabaev in Izvestia, Feb. 19, 1958). The estimate of 2,000 rubles is rule of thumb.

[57] SSKh, 1956, No. 8, p. 64.

TABLE 12.—*Average costs of production on state farms, 1950–60 plan*[1]

[Rubles per ton; eggs, rubles per 1,000]

Products	1950	1953	1954	1955	1956	1957	1960 plan[2]
Food products:							
Grain	508	382	399	458	325	(3)	300
Potatoes	417	(3)	464	544	479	485	(2)
Vegetables	494	(3)	538	487	543	532	(3)
Meat (live weight)	(3)	(3)	(3)	(3)	8,080	(3)	(3)
Pork	15,085	9,994	9,983	9,770	9,858	9,434	7,420
Mutton	(3)	4,430	(3)	4,250	(3)	3,820	(3)
Beef	6,513	6,640	6,558	6,599	7,008	5,976	5,670
Poultry	(3)	(3)	(3)	(3)	13,904	13,028	(3)
Milk	1,298	1,176	1,171	1,175	1,276	1,162	880
Eggs	872	653	645	583	562	539	(3)
Raw materials:							
Sugar beet	(3)	(3)	(3)	143	160	(3)	(3)
Raw cotton	1,826	(3)	(3)	1,792	1,582	(3)	(3)
Wool	17,085	16,379	17,988	15,758	18,461	(3)	14,750

[1] Ministry of State Farms through 1956; thereafter, state farms under the Ministry of Agriculture.
[2] As of January 1956.
[3] Not available.

Sources:
Grain: 1950, 1954–56: PSS 1957, p. 58. 1953: I. A. Benediktov, Sovkhozy nashei strany, M., 1957, p. 66. 1960 plan: Computed from planned reduction from 1955 level (SSKh, 1956 No. 5, p. 25).
Potatoes: 1950, 1954–55: PSS 1957, p. 59. 1956–57: ESKh, 1958 No. 5, p. 39.
Vegetables: 1950, 1954–56: PSS 1957, p. 59. 1957: ESKh, 1958 No. 5, p. 34.
Meat (all kinds): 1956: Khrushchev in Pravda, Jan 25, 1958.
Pork: 1950, 1954–56: PSS 1957, p. 65. 1953: Vop. ekon., 1958 No. 1, p. 34. 1957: Sov. proiz., 1958 No. 6, p. 11. 1960 plan: Computed from planned reduction from 1955 level (SSKh, 1956 No. 5, p. 25).
Mutton: 1953, 1955, 1957: Zhiv., 1958 No. 8, p. 9.
Beef: 1950, 1954–56: PSS 1957, p. 60. 1953: Vop. ekon., 1958 No. 1, p. 34. 1957: Sov. proiz., 1958 No. 6, p. 11. 1960 plan: Computed from planned reduction from 1955 level (SSKh, 1956 No. 5, p. 25).
Poultry: 1956–1957: Zhiv., 1958 No. 8, p. 4.
Milk: 1950, 1954–56: PSS 1957, p. 70. 1953: Vop. ekon., 1958 No. 1, p. 34. 1957: Sov proiz., 1958 No. 6, p. 11. 1960 plan: Computed from planned reduction from 1955 level (SSKh, 1956 No. 5, p. 25).
Eggs: 1950, 1954–56: PSS 1957, p. 77. 1953: Vop. ekon., 1958 No. 1, p. 34. 1957: Sov. proiz., 1958 No. 6, p. 11.
Sugar beet: 1955: Khrushchev in Pravda, Mar. 10, 1957, p. 2. The year to which the figure refers is not specified. It is inferred to be 1955, since the cotton figure given in the same source is almost identical with the known 1955 cost. 1956: Khrushchev in Pravda, Jan. 25, 1958.
Raw cotton: 1950, 1955: PSS 1957, p. 6. 1956: Ibid., p. 16.
Wool: 1950, 1954–56: Ibid., p. 75. 1953: Vop. ekon., 1958 No. 1, p. 34. 1960 plan: Computed from planned reduction from 1955 level (SSKh, 1956 No. 5, p. 25).

Lower state farm costs reflected, in part, preferential treatment: they were generally better supplied with capital; they purchased producer's goods at wholesale instead of retail prices; and in the case of grain they enjoyed advantages of location and scale.[58] As Turetskii noted, however, costs on collectives were significantly higher even in regions where collective and state farms were equally supplied with capital;[59] cotton production is a good example. In other words, collective production was intrinsically less efficient.

Labor costs were particularly high. According to Tulupnikov, they accounted for about 50 percent of total collective farm costs of production over the years 1953–55.[60] Data for some individual products are shown below:

[58] In the case of potatoes and vegetables, the level of mechanization was low on all farms, while scale favored collectives.
[59] Sov. torg., 1958 No. 6, p. 14.
[60] ESKh, 1957 No. 3, p. 46.

Share of labor in costs of production on collective and state farms

[Percent]

	Collective farms (1955)	State farms (1956)
Grain	45.0	23.5
Beef	32.3	20.7
Pork	36.9	18.4
Milk	49.0	27.0

Sources: Collective farm data from SKP 1957, pp. 153, 203, 207, 215. State farm data from PSS 1957, pp. 58, 60, 66, 71; the figure for grain is an unweighted average of the figures for winter grains (23.3 percent) and spring grains (23.8 percent).

According to figures cited by Khrushchev on man-hours expended per centner of output in 1956–57, the ratios of collective farm labor inputs to those on state farms were: grain, 4.2; potatoes, 1.2; sugar beets, 1.5; raw cotton, 1.4; milk, 1.5; beef (life weight increase), 2.2; pork (live weight increase), 2.4.[61]

The comparatively high level of collective farm costs in general and labor in particular was doubtless suspected even before cost investigations were made. But the scale of the difference between collective and state farm costs must have jolted policymakers who were ready to concede in principle that prices should cover cost, but who were equally aware that "The state cannot raise prices indefinitely." [62]

Reasons for high costs on collective farms were fairly obvious. Farm managers lacked incentive to reduce labor costs, since penalties and rewards depended only on output, and labor had no fixed price. They lacked a measure of real cost to serve as a criterion for organizing production more efficiently. Finally, their control over total costs of production was incomplete so long as machine operations were performed by MTS.

To correct these conditions within the framework of the existing collective farm system was next to impossible. However, many features of the system were obsolete and expendable if the state was willing to raise prices somewhat, thereby reducing the need for coercion and cost concealment. The price increases which paved the way for institutional changes are described in the next section.

IV. PROCUREMENT PRICES, 1950–58

Dates of price changes between 1950 and 1958 are tabulated below. It will be noted that three major revisions occurred: in 1953, 1956, and 1958. They may be regarded as successive approximations, based on increasing knowledge of the level and structure of collective farm costs and an increasing readiness to pay prices which covered costs.

[61] Pravda, Dec. 16, 1958, p. 6. Khrushchev's man-hour data for state farms are below figures published earlier (Sov. proiz., 1958 No. 6, p. 11; ibid., 1958 No. 8, pp. 7–9; PSS 1957, p. 78), and it appears that they have been adjusted downward to make them comparable with data for the United States. Presumably the same adjustment was made to the collective farm data, so that the ratios shown above are correct for actual U.S.S.R. inputs.

[62] Tulupnikov in ESKh, 1957 No. 3, p. 38.

Changes in procurement prices of selected products, 1950–58 [1]

	1952	1953	1955	1956	1958
Food products:					
Grain	-------	(2)	(3)	-------	(4)
Potatoes	-------	(5)	-------	(6)	(4)
Vegetables	-------	(5)	-------	(6)	(7)
Meat	-------	(8)	-------	-------	(4)
Milk	-------	(8)	-------	-------	(4)
Eggs	-------	(8)	-------	-------	(4)
Raw materials:					
Sugar beet	-------	-------	-------	(9)	(4)
Raw cotton	-------	-------	-------	(10)	(4)
Flax fiber	(2)	-------	-------	-------	(4)
Wool	-------	(8)	-------	(11)	(4)

[1] Increase in base prices reported in Vop. ekon., 1954, No. 4, p. 60.
[2] Increase in above-quoted prices reported in Spravochnaia kniga brigadira polevodcheskoi brigady, 2d ed., M., 1955, p. 304. See also RM–1552, p. 23.
[3] S. A. Ilin, Gosudarstvennye zagotovki zerna v SSSR, M., 1957, pp. 41–42.
[4] Izvestiia, July 1, 1956.
[5] Pravda, Sept. 29, 1953.
[6] Pravda, Feb. 2, 1956.
[7] Unpublished decree of the Soviet of Ministers, No. 583, May 30, 1958, as reported in ibid.
[8] Ibid., Sept. 26, 1953.
[9] Ibid., June 7, 1956.
[10] Unpublished decree of Aug. 11, 1956, reported in SKP 1957, p. 193.
[11] Pravda, June 21, 1956.

1953–55

The first round of price increases in 1953 bore the stamp of improvisation and compromise. In some measure this may have been due to hasty preparation: most of the program was presumably planned between Stalin's death in March and the Supreme Soviet session in August at which Malenkov announced forthcoming price changes. It is also likely that party leaders differed or were undecided about the extent to which state resources should be committed to increasing agricultural incentives. And it is certain that they had only a general idea of the extent to which incentives were being denied or misapplied, since real collective farm costs had not yet been investigated. Hence the 1953 adjustments were necessarily rule of thumb.

The price increases reported in agricultural decrees were in some cases very substantial, as the following data indicate:

1953 procurement prices as percent of 1952

	Compulsory delivery	Above quota
Meat	[1] >550	[1] 130
Milk	[1] 200	[1] 150
Potatoes	[1] 250	[2] 100
Vegetables	[1] 125–140	[2] 100–170
Eggs	[3] 100	[2] 115
Wool (average price)	[4] 115	

[1] Khrushchev in Pravda, Sept. 15, 1953.
[2] Deduced from Moscow oblast data in SSKh, 1953 No. 10, p. 38.
[3] Karcz, RM–1930, p. 431.
[4] Notes to app. table 4.

However, even the new above-quota prices for meat and milk were still considerably below state farm costs of production,[63] let alone collective farm costs, and the effect of price changes on livestock production was less than expected; 1954 procurement plans for meat and milk were not met until 1956.

[63] Compare tables 12 and 13 (1956 meat and milk prices are unchanged from 1953).

A partial and unpublicized revision of grain prices also occurred in 1953. Compulsory delivery prices remained at the old level (which covered about 15 percent of average collective farm costs), but above-quota prices were raised to more than 10 times the compulsory delivery price. The measure suggests indecision or compromise between two points of view: the conviction that average grain prices had to rise, and a reluctance to make an irrevocable change in the minimum price of a product of such crucial importance. At the new prices, the average farm which made two-thirds of its grain sales in the form of above-quota deliveries broke even. The planned proportion was in fact rather close to two-thirds in 1954 (which proves a real intent to raise grain incentives), but the actual composition of deliveries diverged widely from plan in individual regions. In the Ukraine and Volga, which suffered a severe drought, average price must have been close to the compulsory delivery price. On the other hand, average price in the Kazakh SSR and west Siberia, which had bumper harvests, was probably more than incentive considerations required. By 1955 the inequity and inefficiency of extreme differentials was dimly recognized; compulsory delivery prices were increased 2.5 times while the above-quota price was reduced, so that the new differential was a little over 3 to 1.[64] Even a 3 to 1 differential, however, was sufficient to produce in 1956 (when the pattern of drought in the Ukraine and bumper yields in the Kazakh SSR was repeated) the anomalies shown below:

Collective farm grain prices and ccsts in 1956

	USSR	Ukraine	Kazakh SSR
Average price	[1] 530	[2] 295	[2] 610
Average cost	[3] 560	[4] 610	[4] 280

[1] Table 13.
[2] Computed from relationship to average U.S.S.R. price given in PKh, 1958 No. 11, pp. 40-41.
[3] Table 11.
[4] Computed from relationship to average U.S.S.R. cost given in Vest. stat., 1958 No. 3, p. 19.

Differences in yield within a region, due to varying efficiencies, produced the same effect: price tended to be highest where cost was lowest. The data tabulated below refer to a single district in Stalingrad oblast in 1956, where grain delivery quotas (per unit of land) were identical for all farms. At actual realized prices, the more efficient farms in group I showed large profits while the less efficient in group III showed losses. If a single price (equal to the average price realized by all farms) had been in effect, profits would still have varied with efficiency, but less drastically.[65]

[64] See sources to table 13.
[65] ESKh, 1958, No. 4, p. 51.

Group	Number of farms	Actual average realized price (r/t)	Cost (r/t)	Profit per ton	
				At actual realized price	If sold at average price realized by all farms
I	9	633	422	211	95
II	6	475	451	24	66
III	6	303	466	−163	51
All farms	21	517	440	77	77

1956

The price revisions of 1956 represent the initial response to the cost investigations which began in 1955. Although they affected only five of the product groups with which we are concerned, they were of prime significance for two reasons.

First, they were avowedly intended to result in average procurement prices which more than covered cost. According to Terent'ev: [66]

The * * * procurement prices established in 1956 for sugar beet * * *, potatoes, and vegetables were based on the principle that [the average procurement price] received by collective farms in average conditions should not only fully cover production expenses and [money] payments to the state, but should also provide a surplus for accumulation.

Similarly, Tulupnikov noted that in 1956: [67]

* * * Prices for flax, cotton, potatoes, vegetables, sugar beet, and sunflower seed covered average U.S.S.R. production expenses of collective farms * * *, and provided for essential accumulation and for payment of [money] taxes and insurance. Prices for these products allowed for payments to collective farm labor at rates not less than the average U.S.S.R. rates for seasonal state farm workers (8.8 rubles per labor-day).

The same could not be said for either grain or livestock products, where average price was still below cost (let alone cost plus taxes plus accumulation). But the overt acknowledgement of the principle that average price should more than cover the cost, not only of technical crops but also of some food products, was a new departure.

Second, the 1956 price revisions constituted an experiment with a new hypothesis: that basic or compulsory delivery prices should approach cost, and that the differential between basic and higher incentive prices should be moderate—not 4 to 1 (as used to be possible with technical crops), or even 2 or 3 to 1 (as was still the case with grain and livestock products), but something like 1.5 to 1. Thus, sugar beet base prices were raised roughly fourfold, while the maximum premium price was reduced from 400 to 150 percent of base. Cotton base prices were raised something like 50 percent; a reduction in premium prices obviously occurred, though its scale is not known. As a result of these changes, the share of premiums in average U.S.S.R. prices of sugar beet and cotton dropped from one-third or one-quarter to one-tenth or less (see table 13). Similarly, the compulsory delivery prices of potatoes and vegetables were raised substantially, and the gap between compulsory and above-quota prices reduced.

The new structure of prices was calculated to benefit particularly the low-yield producer, and thus to promote yield increases on those

[66] SKP 1957, p. 9.
[67] ESKh, 1957, No. 3, p. 38.

farms where effort and efficiency were held down by low income.[68] Whether it actually did so cannot be determined from available yield data. But it is reasonable to infer from the subsequent course of events (the emergence of a single price system in 1958) that the net effect of reduced differentials on average yield was favorable, or at least acceptable in view of the other advantages inherent in reduced differentials (predictability of average price, stability of farm income and wages, etc.).

TABLE 13. *Procurement prices received by collective farms for selected products in 1956*

	Average	Compulsory delivery	Above-quota delivery	Contract base	Contract premium
Food products:					
Grain	530	235	800	—	—
Potatoes	410	330	530	—	—
Vegetables	540	425	615	—	—
Meat	3,640	2,000	5,100	—	—
Beef and mutton, average	X	1,500	4,100	—	—
Pork, meat grade	X	3,200	7,000	—	—
Milk	970	550	1,200	—	—
Eggs	250	200	500	—	—
Raw materials:					
Sugar beet	240	—	—	215	25
Raw cotton	3,680	—	—	3,450	230
Flax fiber	14,488	—	—	5,562	8,926
Wool	25,810	X	X	—	—

NOTE.—The sign "—" means not applicable. The sign "X" means not available.

Sources:

Grain: Average price given by Khrushchev in Pravda, January 25, 1958. The above-quota delivery price is from S. A. Il in, Gosudarstvennye zagotovki zerna v S.S.S.R., M., 1957, pp. 41–42. It is specified as an average for the U.S.S.R. as a whole, and is evidently intended to be used as an accounting price in procurement organizations.

Given the average above-quota price. the average compulsory delivery price is estimated from price differentials in zone I (which includes the major grain-surplus areas). Available zone I prices, from travel notes by visitors to the U.S.S.R., are as follows (rubles/ton):

	Compulsory delivery	Above-quota
Soft wheat	250	850
Barley, oats	150	650
Millet	150	600

The ratio of above-quota to compulsory delivery prices ranges from 3.4 to 1 for wheat to 4.3 to 1 for barley and oats. On the assumptions that the smaller ratio is more typical for food grains, and that food grains account for the bulk of procurement, the ratio of the average above-quota price (800 rubles per ton) to the average compulsory delivery price is taken to be 3.4 to 1, which yields an estimate of 235 rubles per ton for compulsory deliveries.

Potatoes: The compulsory and above-quota prices shown are those introduced in 1956 for the late crop in the major producing zone (Pravda, Feb. 2, 1956). The estimated average assumes that the shares of compulsory and above-quota deliveries were 60 and 40 percent respectively.

Vegetables: The prices introduced in 1956 for the six basic vegetables are as follows (Pravda, Feb. 2, 1956) (rubles per ton):

	Compulsory deliveries	Above-quota deliveries
Cabbages	250	380
Cucumbers	650	800
Tomatoes	700	900
Beets	300	500
Carrots	450	700
Onions	900	1,800

[68] High-yield producers of potatoes, vegetables, and sugar beet also benefited, though to a smaller degree. In the case of cotton, the exceptional producer received a lower price than before for above-plan deliveries, and possibly a lower average price.

Their shares in compulsory and above-quota deliveries are estimated as (percent): cabbages, 55; cucumbers, 15; tomatoes, 15; beets, 5; carrots, 5; onions, 5. The percentage weights are freehand estimates oriented on areas sown to each vegetable on collective farms in 1956 (cf. Posevnye ploshchadi SSSR, v. 2, pp. 205 ff.) and yields planned for collective farms in 1954 (Pravda, Sept. 29, 1953).

The estimated average price assumes that the shares of compulsory and above-quota deliveries were respectively 40 and 60 percent.

Meat: Average price given by Khrushchev in ibid, Jan. 25, 1958. The compulsory and above-quota prices are those estimated by Karcz, RM–1930, pp. 426–427.

Milk: Average price given by Khrushchev, Pravda, Jan. 28, 1958. Compulsory delivery and above-quota prices estimated by Karcz, RM–1930, pp. 418–419.

Eggs: The prices shown for compulsory and above-quota deliveries are from ibid., pp. 431–432. The estimated average price assumes that the shares of compulsory and above-quota deliveries were 85 and 15 percent respectively.

Sugar Beet: Average price given by Khrushchev in Pravda, Jan. 25, 1958.

In 1956 base prices were raised to the levels shown below; premiums for deliveries above plan were reduced to 50 percent (Pravda, June 7, 1956):

	Rubles per ton
Ukrainian (except western oblasts), Kazakh, Kirgiz, Georgian, and Armenian republics; Krasnodar krai; central black-soil oblasts	210
Moldavian SSR, western Ukraine	230
Nonblack soil regions of European USSR	250
Urals, Volga, Siberia	320

On the basis of a regional distribution of sugar beet procurement in 1956 (Compare Vest. stat., 1957 No. 6, p. 84), the shares of the four zones in total deliveries are estimated at 89, 7, 2 and 2 percent respectively, which yields the rounded estimate of 215 rubles per ton for the average contract base price. Given an average realized price of 240 rubles per ton, this implies average premiums of 25 rubles per ton.

Raw Cotton: Khrushchev in Izvestiia, June 21, 1958.

Flax fiber: Vest. Mosk. univ., 1958 No. 3, p. 52.

Wool: Khrushchev in Pravda, Jan. 25, 1958.

1958

The decision early in 1958 to transfer tractors and tractor-drawn implements from machine-tractor stations to collective farms provided the occasion for the third round of price revisions. Henceforth farms would directly bear the cost of operating machinery (instead of making payments in kind for MTS operations). They would also directly bear the burden of replacing and expanding machinery stocks (instead of financing such investment indirectly through the tax in kind). Both changes dictated an overall increase in procurement prices. The general constraint upon the increase, as stated by Khrushchev, was that the total cost to the state of deliveries from collective farms should not increase under the new arrangements.[69] that is, that the new procurement bill should not exceed the former bill for paid deliveries plus MTS operating outlays plus MTS investment.

The outstanding feature of the 1958 price revision is that it abolishes multiple pricing. The new single prices are supposed to be both "stable" and "flexible," meaning that they are expected to remain basically unchanged for some time, but that annual adjustments up or down may be made in abnormally bad or good years. Thus price will tend to vary directly with cost, instead of inversely, as under the multiple price system. This does not imply the intent to maintain a constant relationship between price and average cost, but only to moderate the impact of pronounced fluctuations in yield. The principle of adjustment may be, quite simply, that the planned bill for total procurement shall not be exceeded: in other words, the flexible P may be the result of dividing a fixed V by a fluctuating Q. (This was evidently the basis for the downward adjustment in the average grain price in 1958.)

Soviet comment on the 1958 prices makes much of the fact that they are calculated to encourage rational regional specialization. If so, this represents an innovation second in significance only to single pricing. Up to 1958 regional differences received only token recognition. Quotas, MTS rates, and prices varied somewhat from region

[69] Pravdr, Jan. 25, 1958, p. 3.

to region, but the general principle was that every farm (regardless of its natural advantages or disadvantages) should deliver some grain, potatoes, vegetables, meat, and milk. The logic behind this policy is indicated in Kartashov's statement that—

> When prices for vegetables didn't cover production costs, the state was compelled to establish equal procurement plans for every farm.[70]

In 1958 quotas for grain and potatoes were abolished over wide regions where other products could be produced to better advantage; local authorities in all regions were empowered to exempt individual districts or farms from inappropriate quotas.[71] Little is known about regional price differentials, but the general principle underlying them may be something like this: price tends to be highest in high cost regions, but the margin of profit is highest in low cost regions. Thus the new average grain price in the central nonblack soil zone (where average cost over the years 1956–57 was 1,180 rubles per ton) is 800 rubles; the average price in the north Caucasus (where average cost was 370 rubles per ton) is 600 rubles.[72] Since grain quotas in the central nonblack soil zone are now small if not zero, grain deliveries will be made (voluntarily) only by the more efficient producers to whom the zonal price yields some profit. Zonal price in the north Caucasus is intended to provide even the less efficient producer with a profit and hence with the means of improving technology and yields.

The expectation is that eventually, after output has expanded in naturally favorable areas, the U.S.S.R. will be able to do without production from high cost regions, and procurement prices can be reduced. In Khrushchev's words: [73]

> At present, while state requirements for a number of products are not fully met, we are forced to procure from all regions, and to buy products even where the price is not advantageous to the state. But this is temporary. Conditions have now been established for a rapid improvement in collective production.
>
> Consequently, the quantity of products produced will also increase from year to year. The time is not far away when we shall not only fully satisfy the nation's requirements for all products but also have a reserve. We shall then have substantial surpluses of agricultural products.
>
> Naturally, in our Soviet land with its planned economy, overproduction and its consequence—crisis—cannot exist. But conditions for buying agricultural products will alter. Collective farms will themselves offer their surpluses to the state (as happens even now with a few products in some districts). The state will be able to buy grain, meat, and other products in the regions where they are cheaper, because their cost is lower.

The image of the Soviet Union escaping crises of agricultural overproduction only because it is a planned economy is a novel one; even the optimistic Khrushchev may not take it very seriously. His expectation of substantial cost reductions from regional specialization is, however, quite reasonable.

The 1958 prices are purported to cover average costs of production, and to provide for accumulation.[74] "Average cost" probably means feasible cost in the near future in regions from which quota deliveries of a product are required. It should be lower than average U.S.S.R. collective farm costs in the past for two reasons. First: as was indicated above, quota deliveries have been abolished or greatly re-

---

[70] Izvestiia, Mar. 11, 1958, p. 2.
[71] Ibid.
[72] Vest. stat., 1958, No. 12, p. 52.
[73] Izvestiia, Mar. 28, 1958.
[74] It is noteworthy that some Soviet economists proposed basing prices not on average cost, but on cost on marginal land. See M. M. Sokilov in Vest. Mosk. Univ., 1958, No. 4, pp. 34–36.

duced in exceptionally high cost areas. Second: cost reductions are certainly anticipated from transfer of MTS machinery to farms.

Table 14 compares 1958 prices with average collective and state farm costs over the years 1953–56. It will be seen that crop prices cover cost more or less generously; probably the wool price does also. The prices for beef, pork, and milk are below even state farm costs. The reason for this may be that further increase in meat and milk prices would require increasing state retail prices, a move the state is extremely reluctant to make.

TABLE 14.—*Procurement prices introduced for selected products in 1958, compared with average costs of production, 1953–56* [1]

Rubles per ton; eggs, rubles per 1,000]

	Procurement price	Costs of production		Price as percent of cost on—	
		Collective farms	State farms	Collective farms	State farms
	(1)	(2)	(3)	(4)	(5)
Food products:					
Grain	[2] 740	690	390	107	190
Potatoes	400	350	[3] 495	114	81
Vegetables	500	[4] 480	[3] 525	104	95
Meat (live weight)	6, 600				
Beef, average	6, 190	X	6, 700	X	92
Mutton, average	5, 360	X	[5] 4, 165	X	129
Pork, meat grade	7, 860	X	9, 900	X	79
Poultry	8, 165	X	[6] 13, 465	X	61
Milk	1, 150	1, 570	1, 200	73	96
Eggs	600	X	610	X	98
Raw materials:					
Sugar beet	235	160	[7] 150	147	157
Raw cotton	3, 400	2, 000	[7] 1, 685	170	202
Flax fiber	11, 000	6, 800	X	162	X
Wool	30, 500	X	17, 145	X	178

[1] The sign X means not available.
[2] This is the price for an average year. The actual grain price in 1958 (a bumper year when procurement was considerably above plan) was 630 rubles per ton (Khrushchev in Pravda, Dec. 16, 1958).
[3] 1954–57.
[4] 1953–55.
[5] 1953, 1955, 1957.
[6] 1956–57.
[7] 1955–56.

Sources: With the exceptions noted below the prices are taken directly from *Izvestiia*, July 1, 1958, p. 2. They are specified as U.S.S.R. average prices for a normal year.

Vegetables: The average price is assumed to be slightly below the average price realized in 1956 (as in the case of potatoes). The estimate of 500 rubles per ton is roughly confirmed by the reported average price of 490 rubles per ton for a farm in Moscow oblast (Ministerstvo vysshego obrazovaniia S.S.R.R, *Edkonomicheskie nauki*, 1959, No. 1, p. 69.

All meat: Average of prices shown for individual types of meat, weighted by their relative importance in collective farm output in live weight in 1957 (as estimated from carcass weight data in *Zhivotnovodstvo 1959* pp. 161–162).

Poultry: Unweighted average of the prices for fowl and chickens (8,950 rubles per ton and ducks and geese, (7,380 rubles per ton, as given in *Izvestiia*, July 1, 1958, p. 2.

Flax fiber: The price shown in *ibid.* for a single grade of flax fiber provides no basis for estimating the average price of fiber equivalent, since a large part of flax deliveries are in the form of unprocessed or partly processed stalks. There is a strong presumption that the avaerge price of fiber equivalent declined (*Vest. Mosk. Univ.*, 1958, No. 3, p. 53), but the extent of the decline is conjectural. It is assumed here that the ratio of the 1958 price to 1956 cost (as shown in table 11) was the same for flax fiber as for cotton, i.e., 177 percent.

Wool: The estimate is a weighted average, rounded to the nearest hundred rubles, of the prices given for 4 grades:

Grade	Price, (rubles per ton)	Weight (percent)
Fine	41,000	26
Semifine	32,900	22
Semicoarse	24,700	27
Coarse	23,700	25

The weights represent the estimated proportions of each type of wool in collective farm output in 1958. The actual proportions in 1953 and 1956 were as follows (percent):

Grade	1953	1956
Fine	12	20
Semifine	17	20
Semicoarse	30	29
Coarse	41	31

(Cf. notes to appendix table 4. The 1956 distribution is computed from the same source given there for 1953.) A rather marked improvement in quality between 1956 and 1958 is inferred from the change in the distribution of total U.S.S.R. procurement (as shown in Zhiv., 1959, No. 6, p. 10).

The trend in average procurement prices, 1950–58

The average prices received by collective farms in 1950, 1956, and 1958 are shown in table 15. Comment on the derivation and reliability of most of the 1950 prices was made in section II. The three additional products included here are vegetables, eggs, and wool. The estimate for vegetables is a weighted average of the compulsory delivery prices for six individual vegetables; the individual prices are fairly good, but the quantity weights are rule of thumb, so that an error of 25 percent is possible. The egg price is a weighted average of the compulsory and above-quota delivery prices estimated by Karcz, and is fairly reliable. The wool price is a backward projection of a reliable estimate for 1953; it takes into account the intervening change in prices but not changes in grade, and is subject therefore to an error on the order of 15 percent.

The 1956 prices (with the exception of potatoes, vegetables, and eggs) are reported averages, and appear to be completely reliable. The three estimated prices are subject to weighting errors which may reach 20 percent.

The 1958 prices (except vegetables, meat, flax fiber, and wool) are the reported U.S.S.R. average prices introduced in 1958 for a normal year. Estimates for meat and wool are subject to a weighting error of 10 percent. Estimates for vegetables and flax fiber are based largely on the known trend in analogous products; the margin of error is on the order of 20 percent.

TABLE 15.—*Average procurement prices received by collective farms for selected products, 1950, 1956, 1958.*

	Rubles per ton [1]			Price relatives 1950=100	
	1950	1956	1958	1956	1958
Food products:					
Grain	91	530	740	582	813
Potatoes	40	410	400	1,025	1,000
Vegetables	150	540	500	360	333
Meat (live weight)	700	3,640	6,600	520	943
Milk	300	970	1,150	323	383
Eggs	204	250	600	123	294
Raw materials:					
Sugar beet	110	240	235	218	214
Raw cotton	3,600	3,680	3,400	102	94
Flax fiber	4,423	14,488	11,000	328	249
Raw wool	12,000	25,810	30,500	215	254

[1] Eggs: rubles per 1,000.

Sources: Appendix table 4, tables 13 and 14.

The products in table 15 accounted in 1950 for an estimated 16.7 billion rubles of collective farm sales to the state, or 78 percent of the total.[75] The comparable figures for 1956 are 60.9 billion rubles, or 82 percent of the total.[76] The principal omitted food productis fruit; omitted raw materials include oilseeds, tobacco, tea, and other minor technical crops. In 1956 such omitted technical crops accounted for an estimated 9 billion rubles of collective farm sales to procurement agencies, while the value of omitted food products was something less than 5 billion rubles.[77] It is evident, therefore, that food products are better represented in table 15 than raw material products.

The price relatives in table 15 are weighted by the value of collective farm sales to procurement agencies in 1956 to obtain the price index numbers in table 16. Within each category (food, raw materials) the weights are sales of the individual products represented. In obtaining the index number for prices of all products, the index number for raw materials was weighted by the value of sales of represented products plus minor (omitted) raw material crops. Little is known about the price movements of the latter, but they are presumed to be closer to the trend for raw materials than to the trend for food products.

TABLE 16.—*Index numbers of average procurement prices received by collective farms, 1950, 1956, 1958*

(1950=100)

Product group	1950	1956	1958
Food products	100	485	689
Raw materials	100	187	172
All products	100	316	396

Sources: Computed from the price relatives in table 15 and the 1937 value weights in appendix table 5.

[75] Cf. appendix table 4 and table 5.
[76] Ibid and appendix., table 5.
[77] Ibid.

Table 16 presents a picture of price trends which is more or less the reverse of table 7. Between 1928 and 1950 food product prices lagged; between 1950 and 1958 they set the pace, increasing about sevenfold. In the earlier period, food prices were stable from 1937 to 1950 while raw material prices continued to climb; between 1950 and 1958 it is raw material prices which hit a ceiling, and even decline somewhat.

The increase in procurement prices for food products was undoubtedly much greater than the increase in average realized prices, taking market sales into account. If market sales accounted for 50 percent of average realized prices in 1950 and about 20 percent in 1958, the increase in average realized prices for food products was somewhere between fourfold and fivefold.

As in the earlier period, the trend from 1950 to 1958 in prices paid by collective farms for agricultural commodities and manufactured producer's goods cannot be estimated reliably in quantitative terms. However, it is quite plain that the general movement was downward. If rural market prices moved like urban market prices, they declined slightly.[78] If the retail prices paid by farms (through 1957) for manufactured producer's goods moved anything like manufactured consumer's goods prices, they declined.[79] A decline is certain in 1958, with the decision to sell collective farms machinery, oil products (except gasoline), metals, and hardware at wholesale prices.[80] Thus the price trends in table 16 understate the increase in real payments for deliveries to the state.

V. RESULTS

The impact on income of recent trends (from 1953 to 1958) is the principal concern here. However, one fact which emerged from the review of earlier trends in section II is worth emphasizing: this is the pronounced decline between 1940 and the early fifties in the real payments received by collective farms producing food products. We tend to regard forced collectivization in the early thirties as the period of maximum demoralization of Soviet agriculture. So far as overt violence and acute suffering are concerned, this is probably true. But the big deterioration in economic incentives for the majority of farms came later.

On the eve of the price reforms described in section IV, the structure of relative prices strongly favored raw materials, and above all, cotton: in 1950 the three main cotton-growing republics (Uzbek, Turkmen, and Tadzhik S.S.R.'s) with 3 percent of all collective farm sown area and 4 percent of the on-hand households received 30 per-

[78] NK 1956, p. 237.

[79] Ibid., p. 232.

[80] Izvestiia, July 1, 1958. The decision was associated with increases in the wholesale prices of many agricultural machines (compare the 1958 prices in Sovetskaia Estoniia, Aug. 9, 1958, p. 2, with the 1956 prices in Spravochnik tsen na stroitel'nye materialy i oborudovanie, M., 1956, vol. 2, pp. 884, 903, 908, and vol. 3, pp. 160–167). It appears, from two pieces of evidence, that the increases were required to bring machinery prices in line with costs. First, it was announced that acquisition of improved types of machinery by collective farms was to be encouraged by introducing new models at prices intended to cover costs in the second year of mass production plus a profit of 3 percent (Izvestiia, July 1, 1958); this suggests an intent to sell machinery to farms as cheaply as possible. Second, Makarova has indicated that prices for many machines sold MTS and state farms before MTS reorganization were below cost (Vop. ekon., 1958 No. 6, p. 101).

cent of collective farm money income. Wide variations in income existed not only between regions but also within regions: for this multiple pricing was partly responsible. Earnings for collective labor were low compared with income from private agriculture: in 1952 total cash distributions for labor-days were about one-fourth of private sector cash income from market sales alone. Cash payments for collective labor were not only small but unpredictable and deferred on most farms to the end of the year: from April to December many farmers worked for little or nothing. The bulk of the payment for collective labor—about three-quarters in 1952—was in kind (grain, potatoes, vegetables, rough feed).

Between 1952 and 1958 collective farm money income increased threefold. The rise was due entirely to increase in receipts from sales to procurement agencies, and largely to the rise in the level of procurement prices. Because price increases were concentrated in food products, their impact on income of the majority of producers was greater than aggregate U.S.S.R. data suggest: while Uzbek-Turkmen-Tadzkik income increased by 40 percent between 1950 and 1956 (the last year for which complete income data by republics are available), the income of all other republics rose by 250 percent.[81]

Increase in income was accompanied by significant changes in the structure of money outlays. Production expenses (row 9 in table 17) increased less rapidly than total income, despite the transfer of MTS machinery to farms; accordingly, the share of production expenses in total outlays declined from 30 percent in 1952 to 25 percent in 1958. The share of deductions to the investment fund (row 8) nominally increased from 17 to 22 percent; defined in comparable terms, however, this category increased at about the same rate as income.[82] The lion's share of increased income went to payments for collective labor. Taking into account payments from investment funds in 1958, total labor-day payments rose from 12.4 to about 52 billion rubles, or from 29 to 40 percent of total money outlays.

[81] Income data by republics from Ia. I. Golev, "Sel'skokhoziaistvennyi kredit v SSSR," M., 1958, p. 75.

[82] The range of expenditures made from investment funds was enlarged in 1956 to include payments for labor-days worked in construction (formerly made from the regular labor-day fund) and repayments of long-term loans (formerly made from current income). Net of these two types of expenditures, allocations to investment in 1958 were close to the 1952 level of 17 percent.

TABLE 17.—*Collective farm money outlays from current income, 1952–58*

[Billion rubles]

	1952	1956	1957	1958
1. Total money income	42.8	94.6 / [1] 87.4	95.2	>130.0
2. Administrative expenses	.5	.9	1.0	1.0
3. Cultural fund	.9	1.4	2.0	2.0
4. Payments to the state	8.0	11.0	11.0	17.0
5. Long-term loan repayments [2]	2.0	1.0	----------	----------
6. Income tax	4.2	7.5	8.0	13.0
7. Insurance and fees	2.0	3.0	3.0	4.0
8. Investment fund	7.4	16.7	16.8	28.5
9. Production expenses [3]	13.0	23.5	22.0	32.0
10. Payments to members	13.0	42.0	42.0	50.0
11. Labor-day payments [4]	12.4	40.6	41.0	48.0
12. Fixed cash payments	1.0	1.0	1.0	2.0

[1] Excluding collectives converted to state farms in 1957.
[2] Paid after 1956 from funds allocated to investment.
[3] I.e., outlays on purchased materials and hired labor, and money payments for MTS services.
[4] Figures for 1956 and later years exclude labor-day payments from funds allocated to investment. Such payments amounted to 1.6 billion rubles in 1956, and are estimated to have amounted to 3 and 4 billion rubles in 1957 and 1958 respectively (see sources to row 11).

Sources:

Row 1: 1952, 1956 from table 5. 1956 excluding collectives converted to state farms in 1957 from ESkh, 1958 No. 3, p. 15. 1957 from "SSSR v tsifrakh," p. 200. 1958 from Pravda, Jan. 16, 1959.

Row 2: Estimated as 1.2 percent of total income in 1952, and 1 percent thereafter. The maximum prescribed in the model artel charter is 2 percent.

Row 3: 1956 from ESKh, 1957 No. 7, p. 37. Other estimates are arbitrary.

Row 4: Sum of subitems.

Row 5: Estimates oriented on the known amount of repayments in 1955, 2.3 billion rubles (Fin. SSSR, 1956 No. 2, p. 14). In March 1956 farms were authorized to repay long-term loans from funds allocated to investment (Pravda, Mar. 10, 1956); actual repayments from this source amounted to almost 2 billion rubles in 1956 (Garbuzov in FISS 1957, p. 171). Accordingly, loan repayments from current income are presumed to have dropped to 1 billion rubles in 1956 and to have been zero thereafter.

Row 6: 1952, 1956 from ibid., p. 66. 1957 assumed to have remained at the level of 1956 (like total money income). 1958 said to be slightly below the 1959 plan figure of 13.3 billion rubles (Pravda, Dec. 24, 1958).

Row 7: Estimates which assume that insurance premiums account for the bulk of this outlay categorv, and that premiums are at least equal to indemnities received by farms (which amounted to 1.6 billion rubles in 1950 and 2.2 billion rubles in 1956: FISS 1957, p. 356).

Row 8: 1952 given by Khruschchev in Pravda, Jan. 25, 1958. 1956 from FISS 1957, p. 167. 1957 from ESKh, 1958 No. 3, p. 15. 1958 from Fin. SSSR, 1959 No. 2, p. 13.

Row 9: 1956 from Vestnik Akademii nauk SSSR, 1958 No. 6, p. 19. The same source predicted that production expenses in 1958 would be approximately 25 billion rubles; the figure is rejected as impossibly low (it evidently excludes outlays on tractor operations). Estimates for years other than 1956 are derived as a residual.

Row 10: Sum of subitems.

Row 11: 1952 given by Khrushchev in Pravda, Jan. 25, 1958; his figure for 1956 (42.2 billion rubles) is inclusive of about 1.6 billion rubles paid for construction labor-days from funds allocated to investment (FISS 1957, p. 171); accordingly, payments from the general labor-day fund are estimated as 40.6 billion rubles. The average payment per labor-day in 1957 is estimated as 4.00 rubles (i.e., "almost 3 times 1952": Matskevich in Komm., 1958 No. 12, p. 25) and total labor-days at about 11 billion (slightly below the 1956 level). Of the 44 billion rubles of estimated total payments, 3 are assumed to have been paid from investment funds. Total payments in 1958 are estimated at 8 billion rubles over 1957, or about 52 billion rubles. The increase represents mainly payments to machine operators, part of whose earnings as MTS workers were formerly paid by the state. Of the 52 billion rubles of estimated total payments, 4 are assumed to have been paid from investment funds.

The change in the level and structure of procurement prices resulted in a notable improvement not only in the size but also in the regularity and predictability of payments for collective labor. Higher prices for livestock products (which are delivered throughout the year) increased collective farm receipts in spring and summer months. In addition, procurement agencies began to pay advances on deliveries of food crops as well as raw material crops. Higher prices in general meant that farms began to build up cash reserves against seasons of low income. Consequently, most farms by 1958 were able to pay quarterly or monthly advances for labor-days worked. A minority had shifted to wages—that is, full monthly payments at fixed rates for specific tasks or norms of production. Thus they abandoned accounting in labor-days (the only purpose of which is to divide up a fluctuating product). The introduction of single prices in 1958, by contributing to stability of farm receipts from year to year, will probably accelerate the trend toward payment of wages. The significance of this trend for labor productivity can hardly be overestimated. Under a wage system using piece rates, the relation between individual effort and reward is direct and certain. When payments are shares in an uncertain total, the individual incentive to intensify effort is negligible.

While money payments for collective labor increased fourfold between 1952 and 1958, the volume of payments in kind increased little if at all. Therefore, the share of cash in total payments rose (according to Soviet statements) to 48 percent in 1954, about 50 percent in 1956, and 56 percent in 1957.[83] The trend is toward payment entirely in cash, with farm members then buying from the farm only the amounts of produce needed to supply their own consumption requirements. This will simplify cost accounting, and also curtail the volume of market sales by the private sector (which divert significant amounts of labor from collective production).

On farms of more than average efficiency, price increases have resulted in "excess profits" which, if fully distributed to members, would result in labor-day payments higher than state farm wages. Such farms have been urged to invest in cultural and social construction—hospitals, schools, nurseries, homes for the aged, bakeries, restaurants, and so on—as an alternative to higher cash payments to members. Investment in urban amenities is probably welcomed by farmers, and recognized as the kind of improvement in living standards which income from private agricultural activities cannot buy.

Income from private farming rose much less rapidly than payments for collective labor. The rise in the value of sales to procurement agencies (row 3 of table 18) was largely offset by the decline in market sales (row 4), so that gross money income from sales increased between 1952 and 1958 by not more than 10 percent. By 1958 cash payments for collective labor had overtaken gross income from private sales.

[83] Fin. SSSR, 1959 No. 2, p. 12; Vop. ekon., 1959 No. 2, p. 113; ibid., 1959 No. 3, p. 11. Unfortunately none of these sources specified the prices at which income in kind is valued. There is some presumption that it is an approximation of retail prices, and that the statements refer to prices of the current year, but this cannot be proven.

TABLE 18.—*Indicators of peasant income, 1950–58*

	1950	1952	1955	1956	1957	1958
1. Total money incomes of collective farmers (presumably at current prices), 1950=100	100	114	145	163		
Of which (not exhaustive):						
2. From collective farms	100	135	255	339		
3. From sales to procurement agencies	100	95	145	220		
4. From market sales	100	114	103	91		
Total labor-day earnings, in money and kind, at constant prices:						
5. 1950=100	100		>180			
6. Billion rubles (1952 prices?)		47.5			83.8	94
7. Money		12.4			52	61
8. Kind (retail prices?)		35.1			32	33
9. Money and kind income from collective and private farming, per worker, at constant prices (presumably net of taxes), 1950=100	100		150	168	176	

Sources:
Rows 1 to 4: Garbuzov in FISS 1957, p. 172.
Row 5: Pravda, Apr. 25, 1956, p. 2.
Row 6: 1952 and 1957 given by Khrushchev in ibid., Dec. 16, 1958, p. 5. The figures are specified as being in constant prices. If normal Soviet practice is being followed, this means base year prices (cf. S. P. Partigul, Statistika material'nogo i kul'turnogo urovnia naroda, M., 1956, p. 55). 1958 labor-day payments in money and kind were almost double 1952 (Gatovskii in Vop. ekon., 1959 No. 3, p. 11).
Row 7: Money payments for labor-days at current prices were (bil. r.): 1952, 12.4; 1957, 44; 1958, 52 (table 17, sources to row 11). The level of prices in 1957-58 (1952=100) is estimated as 85 (cf. NK 1956, p. 232).
Row 8: Residual. Assuming that grain accounts for the bulk of payments in kind, and that grain payments in 1952 were about 17 to 18 million tons, the value derived above for 1952 implies an average grain price of close to 2,000 rubles per ton. This suggests that kind income must be valued at some approximation of retail prices.
Row 9: 1955, 1956 from NK 1956, p. 42; 1957 from PKh, 1958 No. 5, p. 17.

Besides greatly improving the size, structure, and stability of farm income, price reforms since 1953 have made possible two major institutional changes which promise cost reductions. One is the sale of MTS machinery to collective farms. After abandoning the pretense that farms could produce at a loss and make it up by volume the state had no reason to preserve an instrument designed primarily for extortion. Historically, and perhaps incorrigibly, MTS were wasteful proprietors of machinery. Apart from performance, their very existence fostered pervasive waste, since it complicated the introduction of cost accounting on collective farms and confused responsibility for managing production.

Cost accounting is the other major change made possible by price increases. By providing farm management with a criterion of efficiency hitherto lacking, it removes the last important handicap on collective production.

Cost reduction on collective farms will not follow automatically from these two innovations. But they are certainly indispensable conditions for it.

Code of Sources Cited in Abbreviated Form

Dostizheniia 1957	TsSU, Dostizheniia sovetskoi vlasti za sorok let v tsifrakh, M., 1957.
ESKh	Ekonomika sel'skogo khoziaistva (journal of the Ministry of Agriculture).
Fin. SSSR	Finansy SSSR (journal of the Ministry of Finance).
FISS	Finansy i sotsialisticheskoe stroitel'stvo, M., 1957.
Komm	Kommunist (journal of the Central Committee of the Communist Party).
KVSP 1939	TsUNKhU, Kolkhozy vo vtoroi stalinskoi piatiletke, M., 1939.
Moiseev 1955	M. I. Moiseev, Ekonomicheskie osnovy gosudarstvennykh zagotovok sel'skokhoziaistvennykh produktov, M., 1955.
NK 1956	TsSU, Narodnoe khoziaistvo SSSR v 1956 godu, M., 1957.
PKh	Planovoe khoziaistvo (journal of the State Planning Commission).
PSS 1957	I. A. Benediktov, Puti snizheniia sebestoimosti produktsii sovkhozov, M., 1957.
RM–1178	N. Nimitz, The New Soviet Agricultural Decrees, The Rand Corporation, Research Memorandum RM–1178, January 13, 1954.
RM–1552	N. Nimitz, Soviet Agriculture Since the September 1953 Reforms, the Rand Corporation, Research Memorandum RM–1552, September 15, 1955.
RM–1930	Jerzy F. Karcz, Soviet Agricultural Marketings and Prices, 1928–1954, The Rand Corporation, Research Memorandum RM–1930, July 2, 1957.
RM–2101	O. Hoeffding and N. Nimitz, Soviet National Income and Product, 1949–1955, The Rand Corporation, Research Memorandum RM–2101, April 6, 1959.
RM–2326	N. Nimitz, Soviet Statistics of Meat and Milk Output: A Note on Their Comparability Over Time, The Rand Corporation, Research Memorandum RM–2326, February 6, 1959.
SKh 1935	Narodnyi komissariat zemledeliia, Sel'skoe khoziaistvo SSSR; ezhegodnik, 1935, M., 1936.
SKh 1958	Sel'skoe khoziaistvo SSSR, M., 1958.
SKP 1957	M. L. Terent'ev, Sebestoimost' kilkhoznoi produktsii, M., 1957.
Sov. proiz	Sovkhoznoe proizvodstvo (journal of the Ministry of Agriculture).
SSEP 1958	Akademiia obshchestvennykh nauk, Kafedra politicheskoi ekonomii, Sbornik statei po ekonomicheskim voprosam (vypusk tretii), M., 1958.
SSKh	Sotsialisticheskoe sel'skoe khoziaistvo (journal of the Ministry of Agriculture).
SSKh 1939	TsUNKhU, Sotsialisticheskoe sel'skoe khoziaistvo Soiuza SSR, M., 1939.
SSSR v tsifrakh	TsSU, SSSR v tsifrakh, M., 1958.
ST 1956	TsSU, Sovetskaia torgovlia, M., 1956.
Vest. Mosk. univ	Vestnik Moskovskogo universiteta: seriia ekonomiki, filosofii, prava (journal of Moscow University).
Vest. stat	Vestnik statistiki (journal of the Central Statistical Administration).
Vop. ekon	Voprosy ekonomiki (journal of the Institute of Economics in the Academy of Sciences).
Zhiv	Zhivotnovodstvo (journal of the Ministry of Agriculture).
Zhivotnovodstvo 1959	TsSU, Zhovotnovodstvo SSSR, M., 1959.

APPENDIX TABLE 1.—*Outputs of selected products, distributed by type of producer, 1940, 1950, 1956*

[Million tons; eggs, billion units]

Product	1940	1950	1956
Grain	X	81	127
Collective farms	X	70	101
State farms	7	8	24
Private sector	X	3	2
Potatoes	75.9	88.6	96.0
Collective farms	25.2	20.2	28.2
State farms	1.5	3.2	3.9
Private sector	49.2	65.2	63.9
Vegetables	13.7	9.3	14.3
Collective farms	6.0	4.2	6.2
State farms	1.2	1.0	2.1
Private sector	6.5	4.1	6.0
Meat (carcass weight)	4,695	4,867	6,598
Collective farms	.918	1.082	2.261
State and institutional farms	.419	.516	.695
Private sector	3,358	3,269	3,642
Milk	33.640	35.311	49.111
Collective farms	5.591	6.796	17.497
State and institutional farms	1.965	2.067	3.799
Private sector	26.084	26.448	27.815
Eggs	12.214	11.697	19.532
Collective farms	.501	1.012	1.769
State farms	.201	.282	.785
Private sector	11.512	10.403	16.978
Sugar beet	18.0	20.8	32.6
Collective farms	16.2	20.2	31.7
State farms	.7	.6	.8
Private sector	1.1	(1)	(1)
Raw cotton	2.25	3.58	4.46
Collective farms	2.12	3.4	4.23
State farms	.13	.2	.23
Flax fiber	.349	.255	.521
Collective farms	X	X	.516
State farms	X	X	.004
Private sector	X	X	.002
Wool	.161	.180	.261
Collective farms	.079	.119	.169
State and institutional farms	.019	.022	.036
Private sector	.063	.039	.056

[1] Zero or negligible.

NOTE.—The sign "X" means not available.

Sources:

GRAIN

Total: 1950, 1956: Given 1953 (Vest. stat., 1959, No. 1, p. 20), computed from index in NK 1956, p. 107.
Collective farms: 1950, 1956: Residual.
State and institutional farms: 1940, 1950: Given 1956, computed from indexes in SKh 1958, p. 63, 75. 1956: Average yield estimated as 10 c/h (the average for the Ministry of State farms: PSS 1957, p. 57); total sown area was 24.2 mil. h. (NK 1956, p. 147).
Private sector: 1950: Average yield estimated as 8 c/h (U.S.S.R. average); sown area was 3.58 mil. h. (NK 1956, p. 114). 1956: Average yield estimated as 10 c/h; sown area was 1.66 mil. h. (ibid).

POTATOES

Total: 1940–56: SKh 1958, pp. 73, 259.
Collective farms: 1940: Ibid., p. 37. 1950: Residual. 1956: Ibid., p. 75.
State and institutional farms: 1940, 1950: Computed from index in ibid., p. 63. 1956: Ibid., p. 75.
Private sector: 1940, 1956: Residual. 1950: I.e., 73.6 percent, share not accounted for by collective and state farms (ibid., p. 260).

VEGETABLES

Total: 1940: Computed given share of collective farms and state institutions (ibid., p. 270). 1950, 1956: Ibid., pp. 73, 272.
Collective farms: 1940, 1956: Ibid., p. 37. 1950: Ibid., p. 273.
State and institutional farms: 1940, 1950: Computed from index in ibid., p. 63. 1956: Ibid., p. 75.
Private sector: 1940–56: Residual.

MEAT

All producers: Zhivotnovodstvo 1959, p. 161.

MILK

All producers: Ibid., p. 163.

EGGS

All producers: Ibid., p. 169.

SUGAR BEET

Total: 1940–56: SKh 1958, p. 223.
Collective farms: 1940, 1956: Ibid., p. 37. 1950: Estimated from procurement (app. table 2).
State farms: 1940, 1950: Estimated from procurement. 1956: I.e., 2.5 percent of U.S.S.R. total (SKh 1958, p. 80).
Private sector: 1940–50: Estimated from procurement. 1956: SKh 1958, p. 80.

RAW COTTON

Total: 1940–56: Ibid., p. 232.
Collective farms: 1940, 1956: Ibid., p. 37. 1950: Estimated from procurement.
State farms: 1940, 1950: Estimated from procurement. 1956: I.e., 5.2 percent of U.S.S.R. total (SKh 1958, p. 80).

FLAX FIBER

Total: 1940: A. M. Korneev, "Tekstil'naia promyshlennost' S.S.S.R. i puti ee razvitiia," M., 1957, p. 127. 1950: Ibid., p. 226. 1956: SKh 1958, p. 73.
Collective farms: 1956: Ibid., p. 75.
State farms: 1956: Ibid., p. 80.
Private sector: 1956: Residual.

WOOL

All producers: Zhivotnovodstvo 1959, p. 165.

APPENDIX TABLE 2.—*Procurements of selected products, distributed by type of producer, 1940, 1950, 1956*

[Million tons, eggs, billion units]

Product	1940	1950	1956
Grain	36	33	54.1
Collective farms	32.0	30	38.8
State farms	[1] 3.674	X	15.3
Private sector	.5	X	
Potatoes	8.457	6.906	9.222
Collective farms	5.161	4.0	5.043
State farms	.138	X	.381
Private sector	3.158	X	3.798
Vegetables	2.970	2.043	3.782
Collective farms	2.730	1.68	2.822
State farms	.168	X	.767
Private sector	.072	X	.193
Meat (live accounting weight)	2.040	2.122	4.246
Collective farms	.881	1.22	2.727
State and institutional farms	.354	X	.695
Private sector	.805	X	.824
Milk	6.453	8.479	17.337
Collective farms	3.245	3.53	11.521
State and institutional farms	1.013	X	4.974
Private sector	2.195	X	2.842
Eggs	2.697	1.911	3.272
Collective farms	.100	.587	1.071
State farms	.085	X	.597
Private sector	2.494	X	1.604
Sugar beet	17.357	19.822	31.494
Collective farms	15.691	19.234	30.732
State farms	.654	.588	.762
Private sector	1.012		
Raw cotton	2.237	3.539	4.332
Collective farms	2.106	3.388	4.106
State farms	.131	1.51	.226
Flax fiber	.245	.174	.427
Collective farms	.206	.165	.427
State farms		X	.001
Private sector	.039	X	
Wool (accounting weight)	.120	.136	.246
Collective farms	.069	[2] .094	.178
State farms	.022	X	.041
Private sector	.029	X	.027

[1] Accounting weight.
[2] Natural weight.

Sources:

GRAIN

Total: 1940: Sum of subitems. 1950: Given estimate of 38 million tons for 1955, computed from reported increase between 1955 and 1950 (Pravda, Apr. 25, 1956). 1955 estimated from figure for 1953 (Dostizheniia 1957, p. 156) and annual increases reported in plan fulfillment reports. 1956: Dostizheniia 1957, p. 156.
Collective farms: 1940: Karcz estimate, RM-1930, p. 365. 1950: I.e., 44 percent of collective farm output (SSEP 1958, p. 118.) 1956: Khrushchev in Izvestiia, Mar. 1, 1958.
State farms: 1940, 1956: S.S.S.R. v tsifrakh, p. 191.

POTATOES

All producers, with the exception noted below: Vest. stat., 1957, No. 6, pp. 78–79.
Collective farms in 1950: I.e., 20 percent of collective farm output (SSEP 1958, p. 118).

VEGETABLES

All producers, with the exception noted below: Vest. stat., 1957, No. 6, pp. 78–79.
Collective farms in 1950: I.e., 40 percent of collective farm output (SSEP 1958, p. 118).

MEAT

All producers, with the exception noted below: Vest. stat., 1957, No. 6, pp. 78–79.
Collective farms in 1950: I.e., 57 percent of collective farm output, presumably in live weight (SSEP 1958, p. 118). Carcass weight output (shown in appendix table 1) estimated to be equivalent to 2.2 million tons live weight.

MILK

All producers, with the exception noted below: Vest. stat., 1957, No. 6, pp. 78–79.
Collective farms in 1950: I.e., 52 percent of collective farm output (SSEP 1958, p. 118).

EGGS

All producers, with the exception noted below: Vest. stat., 1957, No. 6, pp. 78–79.
Collective farms in 1950: I.e., 58 percent of collective farm output (SSEP 1958, p. 118).

SUGAR BEET

All producers, with the exceptions noted below: Vest. stat., 1957, No. 6, pp. 78–79.
Collective farms in 1950: Residual.
State farms in 1950: SKh 1958, p. 64.
Private sector in 1950: Assumed zero.

RAW COTTON

All producers, with the exceptions noted below: Vest. stat., 1957, No. 6, pp. 78–79.
Collective farms in 1950: Residual.
State farms in 1950: SKh 1958, p. 64.

FLAX FIBER

All producers, with the exception noted below: Vest. stat., 1957, No. 6, pp. 78–79.
Collective farms in 1950: From appendix table 4.

WOOL

All producers, with the exception noted below: Ibid.
Collective farms in 1950: I.e., 79 percent of collective farm output (SSEP 1958, p. 118).

APPENDIX TABLE 3.—*Quantities, prices, and values of sales by collective farms to procurement agencies, selected products, 1937*

	Quantity (million tons)	Price (rubles per ton)	Value (billion rubles)
Food products			2.47
Grain:			
Compulsory deliveries	10.17	80	
Above-quota deliveries	2.95	115	
Total	13.12	88	1.15
Potatoes:			
Compulsory deliveries	2.8	40	
Above-quota deliveries	.6	110	
Total	3.4	53	.18
Meat (live weight):			
Compulsory deliveries	.338	400	
Above-quota deliveries	.229	1,750	
Total	.567	950	.54
Milk:			
Compulsory deliveries	1.919	165	
Above-quota deliveries	.605	465	
Total	2.524	240	.60
Raw materials			4.02
Sugar beet: Contract deliveries	16.741	44	.74
Raw cotton: Contract deliveries	1.9115	1,570	3.00
Flax fiber: Contract deliveries	.2648	1,050	.28
Total accounted for			6.49

Sources: Quantities:
Grain: Karcz, RM–1930, p. 199.
Potatoes: Rule of thumb estimates. Total U.S.S.R. procurement was 7.021 million tons (Vest. stat., 1957 No. 6, p. 78) of which state farms accounted for not more than 0.1 million tons (ibid., p. 79), leaving 6.9 million tons for deliveries by collective farms and the private sector. Total above-quota deliveries were 1.2 million tons (Karcz, RM–1930, p. 211), payments in kind to MTS are arbitrarily estimated as 0.3

million tons, leaving 5.4 million tons for total compulsory deliveries. Collective farms are assumed to have accounted for half of total compulsory and above-quota deliveries (or slightly more than their share in joint collective-private sown area).
Meat: Karcz, RM-1930, p. 336.
Milk: Ibid., p. 335.
Sugar beet: Ibid., p. 203.
Raw cotton: Ibid., p. 257.
Flax fiber: Ibid., p. 207.
Prices of compulsory, above-quota, and contract deliveries:
Grain: Ibid., p. 236.
Potatoes: Ibid., p. 270.
Meat: Ibid., p. 284.
Milk: Ibid., p. 277.
Sugar beet: Ibid., p. 253.
Raw cotton: Ibid., pp. 257-258.
Flax fiber: Ibid., p. 268.

APPENDIX TABLE 4.—*Quantities, prices, and values of sales by collective farms to procurement agencies, selected products, 1950*

	Quantity (million tons)	Price (rubles per ton)	Value (billion rubles)
Food products			3.22
Grain:			
Compulsory deliveries	8.7	90	
Above-quota deliveries	.3	125	
Total	9.0	91	.82
Potatoes:			
Compulsory deliveries	3.5	40	
Above-quota deliveries	(1)		
Total	3.5	40	.14
Vegetables:			
Compulsory deliveries	1.68	150	
Above-quota deliveries	(1)		
Total	1.68	150	.25
Meat:			
Compulsory deliveries	1.1	400	
Above-quota deliveries	.1	4,000	
Total	1.2	700	.84
Milk:			
Compulsory deliveries	3.3	270	
Above-quota deliveries	.2	800	
Total	3.5	300	1.05
Eggs:			
Compulsory deliveries	.570	200	
Above-quota deliveries	.017	435	
Total	.587	204	.12
Raw materials			13.49
Sugar beet: Contract deliveries	14.7	110	1.62
Raw cotton: Contract deliveries	2.78	3,600	10.01
Flax fiber: Contract deliveries	.165	4,423	.73
Wool: Compulsory and above-quota deliveries	.094	12,000	1.13
Total accounted for			16.71

[1] Zero or negligible.

Sources: Quantities:
Grain: Total deliveries including those for which farms received no price amounted to 30 million tons (appendix table 2). MTS payments are estimated to have amounted to about 18 million tons, and return of seed loans and payment of the milling tax in kind to about 3 million tons, leaving a million tons for paid deliveries. Above-quota deliveries are known to have been very small (see text, sec. II); a token allowance of 0.3 million tons is arbitrarily made, and the residual is attributed to compulsory deliveries.
Potatoes: Total deliveries including MTS payments amounted to 4 million tons (appendix table 2). MTS payments are estimated at about 0.5 million tons. Above-quota sales to state procurement agencies are known to have been zero (Moiseev 1955, p. 117).
Vegetables: Total deliveries from appendix table 2. MTS payments and above-quota sales to state procurement agencies are known to have been zero (ibid., p. 118).
Meat: Total deliveries from appendix table 2. The distribution is arbitrary.

Milk: Total deliveries from appendix table 2. The distribution is based on indications that the share of above-quota deliveries was very small (Moiseev 1955, p. 118).
Eggs: Total deliveries from appendix table 2. The distribution is arbitrary.
Sugar beet: Total deliveries including MTS payments amounted to 19.2 million tons (appendix table 2). Payments in kind are estimated to have accounted for about one-quarter of this total, or 4.5 million tons.
Raw cotton: Total deliveries including MTS payments amounted to 3.39 million tons (appendix table 2). MTS payments are estimated to have accounted for about one-fifth of this total, or 0.60 million tons.
Flax fiber: Computed by dividing the total value of deliveries (0.728 billion rubles: Vest. Mosk. Univ., 1958, No. 3, p. 50) by the average price.
Wool: Total deliveries from appendix table 2.
Prices:
Grain: Karcz, RM-1930, p. 363 (1952 prices believed unchanged from 1950).
Potatoes: Karcz's compulsory delivery price for 1952 (ibid., p. 408) reflects a "new" premium of 5 percent for punctual delivery, not known to apply in 1950; it is excluded here.
Vegetables: Rule of thumb estimate based on compulsory delivery prices of major vegetables in Moscow oblast in 1952, as given in RM-1552, p. 156. The prices are (rubles per ton): cabbages, 100; carrots, 112; beets, 82; tomatoes, 175; cucumbers, 247; onions, 750.
Meat: Karcz, RM-1930, p. 422.
Milk: Ibid., p. 413.
Eggs: Ibid, pp. 431-432.
Sugar beet: Karcz's estimate for 1952 is 95 rubles per ton (ibid., p. 386). The average realized price in 1951 was about 130 rubles per ton (SSKh, 1956, No. 8, pp. 65-66). Most of the difference between the Karcz and SSKh figures is believed to be due to the higher share of premiums in 1951, when yield was 11 percent over 1952 (NK 1956, p. 108). Yield in 1950 was below 1951 and above 1952; accordingly, the intermediate price of 110 rubles per ton is estimated.
Raw cotton: Karcz's estimate for 1952 is 3,600 rubles per ton, of which 2,400 represents the average base price and 1,200 the premium (RM-1930, pp. 397-398). In 1950 the average quality of deliveries may have been slightly lower (which would make for a lower base price) but yield was about 15 percent higher (which would make for a larger premium). On balance, the price of 3,600 rubles per ton appears to be reasonably appropriate for 1950 as well as 1952.
Flax fiber: Vest. Mosk. Univ., 1958 No. 3, p. 52.
Wool: The estimate is derived from the average price in 1953 (computed below as 14,000 rubles per ton) and information that the average price increase in 1953 was 2,000 rubles per ton (Komm., 1953 No. 15, p. 35).
The 1953 estimate is a weighted average, rounded to the nearest 100 rubles, of prices for four grades:

Grade	Price (rubles per ton)	Weight (percent)
Fine	24, 410	12
Semifine	16, 510	17
Semicoarse	13, 130	30
Coarse	10, 850	41

The prices are from Zhiv., 1959 No. 6, p. 10. They evidently represent the actual average price paid for compulsory and above-quota deliveries of each grade; this may be deduced by comparing the 1956 prices given in this source with the compulsory delivery and above-quota prices prevailing in 1956 (Pravda, June 21, 1956).
The weights represent the proportions of each type of wool in collective farm output of sheep wool in 1953, as computed by subtracting state farm output of each grade (as given in Zhiv., 1957 No. 10, p. 35) from joint state and collective farm output of each grade of sheep wool (Zhivotnovodstvo 1959, p. 168).

APPENDIX TABLE 5.—*Derivation of value of sales by collective farms to procurement agencies, 1956*

	Quantity sold (million tons)	Average price (rubles per ton)	Value (billions of rubles)
Food products			30.29
Grain	15.9	530	8.43
Potatoes	3.58	410	1.47
Vegetables	2.65	540	1.43
Meat	2.37	3,640	8.63
Milk	10.37	970	10.06
Eggs	[1] 1.071	[2] 250	0.27
Raw materials			39.61
Sugar beet	26.7	240	6.41
Raw cotton	3.75	3,680	13.80
Flax fiber	0.426	14,488	6.16
Wool	[3] 0.163	25,810	4.21
Minor raw materials			9.03
Total accounted for			69.90
Unaccounted for			4.8
Total sales			74.7

[1] Billion units.
[2] Rubles per 1,000.
[3] Natural weight.

Sources: Quantities:
Grain: Total collective farm deliveries amounted to 38.8 million tons (appendix table 2) of which compulsory and above-quota deliveries accounted for 17.2 and 23.9 percent, respectively (ESKL, 1957 No. 2, p. 34).
Potatoes: Total collective farm deliveries amounted to 5.043 million tons (appendix table 2), of which MTS payments accounted for an estimated 1.462 million tons (i.e., 29 percent: cf. Benediktov in Izvestiia, Dec. 27, 1957, p. 2), leaving 3.58 million tons for paid deliveries.
Vegetables: Total collective farm deliveries amounted to 2.822 million tons (appendix table 2), of which MTS payments accounted for an estimated 0.169 million tons (or 6 percent), leaving 2.65 million tons for paid deliveries.
Meat: Total collective farm deliveries amounted to 2.727 million tons (appendix table 2), of which MTS payments accounted for an estimated 0.355 million tons (i.e., 13 percent: cf. Benediktov in Komm., 1957 No. 8, p. 53), leaving 2.372 million tons for paid deliveries.
Milk: Total collective farm deliveries amounted to 11.521 million tons (appendix table 2), of which MTS payments accounted for an estimated 1.15 million tons (i.e., 10 percent: cf. Benediktov in Komm., 1957 No. 8, p. 53), leaving 10.37 million tons for paid deliveries.
Eggs: Equivalent to total collective farm deliveries.
Sugat beet: Total collective farm deliveries amounted to 30.7 million tons (appendix table 2), of which MTS payments are estimated to have amounted to 4 million tons (or 13 percent), leaving 26.7 million tons for contract deliveries.
Raw cotton: Total collective farm deliveries amounted to 4.11 million tons (appendix table 2), of which MTS payments are estimated to have amounted to 0.36 million tons (about 9 percent), leaving 3.75 million tons for contract deliveries.
Flax fiber: Equivalent to total collective farm deliveries. Data on total payments for flax fiber and the average price per ton in 1956 imply a figure for paid deliveries which is identical with total deliveries (Vest. Mosk. univ., 1958 No. 3, pp. 52, 54).
Wool: Equivalent to total marketings by collective farms. The latter are computed as 73 percent of total U.S.S.R. marketings of 0.223 million tons (Dostizheniia 1957, pp. 154, 182).
Prices: From table 13.
Values: Minor raw material crops: Estimated as the difference between collective farm income from all technical crops (35.4 billion rubles: ESKh, 1957 No. 7, p. 33) and income from the three technical crops ncluded in this table (beet, cotton, and flax, which together accounted for 26.37 billion rubles).
Total sales: From table 5.

AGRICULTURAL POLICY OF THE SOVIET UNION

(By Lazar Volin, Foreign Agricultural Service, U.S. Department of Agriculture)

Summary and Conclusions

1. Agricultural policy has been a prominent question in the Soviet Union as it was in Czarist Russia. It has emerged at every critical juncture in the history of the country. The recent transition from the Stalin to the Khrushchev regime has been no exception.

Agriculture, with close to half the people depending upon it for a livelihood, continues to be a more important sector of Soviet national economy than it is in the more industrialized countries of the West—and this despite the industrial growth of the Soviet Union.

2. The Soviet Union, notwithstanding its huge crop acreage, has been bedeviled by agricultural underdevelopment, by the failure of its agriculture to meet increasing food and fiber requirements of a growing population that is becoming increasingly urbanized. Therefore, the principal objective of the Soviet Government has been expansion of agricultural production. A sharp upsurge in farm products output has become, for political and physical reasons, extremely urgent for the post-Stalin regime, which cannot afford to proceed at Stalin's pedestrian pace. Hence the flood of official reports, speeches, and decrees spotlighting the agricultural problem. This preoccupation of the Soviet Government with increased production sharply contrasts with the concern of the United States with farm surpluses and farm relief.

3. Climate is more of a limiting factor in agricultural production in the Soviet Union than in the United States. More important is the fact that other basic and closely related objectives of Soviet policy clashed with expansion of production, namely: the centrally controlled collectivization, ruthlessly forced in the 1930's on the small peasant family farming, which emerged victorious after the revolution, and (b) the acquisition by the Soviet state at a low cost to itself of large quantities of farm products, which left little incentive to the collectivized peasantry to work as diligently on the large collective farms as on their own little kitchen garden plots.

4. Solely from the standpoint of production, central direction and planning of collective agriculture permit the marshaling of all available resources to achieve a specific goal on a large scale. This has resulted both in improvements and in costly mistakes—and both often made with little regard to economy and efficiency. The impossibility of public criticism of a policy once it has been officially adopted and, often, inadequate critical discussion before it is adopted—coupled with reliance on pseudoscience of the Lysenko type, which promises spectacular "pie in the sky" results—make prevention or correction of such mistakes more difficult.

5. An early example of improvement was the consolidation into large fields, adopted for power farming, of the numerous noncontiguous

strips. These strips, into which small holdings were formerly divided, meant waste of land (for boundaries) and of labor. The plowing up and adding to the crop area of 90 million acres of virgin land within a period of 4 years (1954–57) is a more recent accomplishment; and it is a significant accomplishment even though much of this land must be considered marginal or even submarginal from a climatic standpoint.

Among the examples of costly mistakes committed by central authorities are: The great loss of livestock during the initial all-out collectivization drive; the indiscriminate adoption of many farm practices such as the universal use of perennial grasses in crop rotation without regard to regional differences; the equally indiscriminate adoption of certain types of farm equipment such as large tractors; the shift of crops into areas climatically or otherwise unsuitable for their production, such as the abortive extension of cotton growing from the irrigated regions of Soviet central Asia and Transcaucasia into the more northern dry farming regions of the Ukraine and north Caucasus; or the present extension of corn cultivation into regions in which it is either too cold or too dry for a successful corn culture. Yet another manifestation of large scale policy errors is the persistent "giantism" which, despite recognition of mistakes committed in the early 1930's, led to the creation again in the 1950's of huge unwieldy farm units through widespread mergers of collectives and growth of state farms.

6. The efforts of the Khrushchev regime to remedy weakness on the agricultural front is being done without deviation from the basic principles of agrarian collectivism. In fact, the grip of state and party rule over collective agriculture has been tightened, although a shift of authority from Moscow to the republics, provinces (oblasts), and districts (raions) and some decentralization of the rigid, highly centralized planning of Stalin's days has taken place. However, decentralization is not permitted to interfere with national goals which are deemed of critical importance, such as the expansion of corn growing to bolster the lagging feed supply, the expansion of the crop acreage on the virgin lands east of the Volga and the Urals and the campaign to overtake the United States in per capita production of dairy products and meat.

7. The most important reform of the institutional structure of collective farming during the post-Stalin period was the liquidation of machine tractor stations and sale of the machines to the collective farms. This move, stanchly opposed by Stalin during his lifetime, was made by the Khrushchev administration primarily to eliminate virtual dual management of collective farm operations or, as Khrushchev put it, the existence of "two bosses on the land."

8. The reform, undertaken to increase farm efficiency, tends to enhance the position of collectives, considerably enlarged by mergers, in the Soviet agrarian institutional scheme. Nevertheless, the rapid expansion of state farming which now accounts for more than a fourth of the crop area instead of 12 percent in 1953, may point to the eventual takeover of collectives. State farms had already absorbed many collectives and ideologically they have always been considered a superior type of economic organization, though this is at present officially minimized. How long the coexistence of two organizational types of Soviet agriculture will continue may depend largely upon

whether the Soviet Government extends to collective farms the regular wage system now prevailing on state farms—a system which is similar to that in Soviet factories. The peasants or collective farms are residual sharers in the income after the state secures its share and current production expenses and capital outlays are met.

9. Although there has been no decollectivization recently in the Soviet Union such as took place, for instance, in Poland and Yugoslavia, limited concessions were made to peasants within the framework of Soviet agrarian collectivism. There was tax relief for the small allotment holdings of the peasants' and workers' families which plays such an important part in their income and in the national food supply, especially in animal products. Because this small "acre and a cow" type of farming competes with the collective farm economy for the labor and loyalty of the peasants, as well as for ideological reasons, the Stalin regime came to look upon it with a jaundiced eye and behaved accordingly. But the attitude of Stalin's successors, after the initial spurt of liberalism, also has been ambivalent—now relaxed, now restricted.

10. In general, Soviet policy toward peasants has always consisted of a combination of force, indoctrination, and economic incentives but the proportion varied from time to time. During the Stalin regime force predominated. After Stalin, Soviet policy shifted to a greater emphasis on economic incentives. The very low prices paid by the Government for the farm products which the collectives had to deliver were raised considerably. The whole system of deliveries was reorganized and simplified. Larger incomes of collectives as a result of higher prices and larger output permitted increased and often more regular distribution to peasants. But the stimulating effect of increased agricultural prices is to some extent lost when there is only a limited supply of consumer goods for farmers to buy because of the imbalance in Soviet industrialization. For the underemphasis on production of consumers goods has not been sufficiently redressed.

In any event, the visiting team of U.S. Department of Agriculture economists pointed out in its report.[1]

> The system of collective and state-operated farms is not likely to provide production incentives for farm people that are equal to the incentives on family farms in this country. In other words, it may be difficult to substitute for the "magic of ownership which turns sand into gold." Also, the struggles incidental to establishment of collective farming may have left scars that will impede development of adequate production incentives.

11. The lagging capital investment in agriculture and inputs of agricultural machinery, commercial fertilizers and construction were increased. But capital investment is still inadequate to make possible an effective use of labor and land. Measures were also taken to increase or retain skilled labor on farms and to bring agricultural specialists nearer to grass roots. However, the problem of finding suitable managers for the large collective farms apparently has not been solved to the satisfaction of the government despite the large number trained and graduated from the agricultural colleges and vocational schools. Low labor productivity in agriculture, especially compared with the United States, has been giving considerable concern to the government which seems to lay increasing stress on cost

[1] "Economic Aspects of Soviet Agriculture. Report of a Technical Study Group," p. 54, Agricultural Research Service, U.S. Department of Agriculture, 1959.

reduction, economy of operation and greater incentive for individual effort in both work performance and management.

12. The changes in agricultural policy which have taken place during the post-Stalin period have had, for the most part, a beneficial effect on production. But some aspects, such as the persistent predilection for farm giantism and corn expansion on so large a scale, seem questionable. In the long run, even the program of expansion on the new lands in the eastern regions may prove unsound under the climatic conditions prevailing in those areas. During recent years, however, acreage expansion has been a highly important, if not the most important factor next to the weather in the rapid expansion of production. However, recent Soviet figures on grain, meat and milk outputs seem overoptimistic. Further progress in increasing farm output may be expected. But, inasmuch as the government plan (1959–65) relies primarily on improvement of yields rather than on increased crop acreage to achieve its targets of large farm output, the progress may be at a slower rate. For experience indicates that the Soviet system of centrally planned collective agriculture has been generally more successful in increasing acreage than in improvement of yields and most successful in extracting large quantities of farm products which the Soviet State requires.

Introduction

The problem of agricultural policy has long been in the foreground as a vital national issue in Soviet as in Czarist Russia. Following official revelation of weaknesses in Soviet agriculture after Stalin's death in 1953, agricultural policy aiming to remedy them has become the subject of many official decrees, lengthy reports, and speeches of Soviet leaders and officials. Prime Minister N. S. Khrushchev seldom fails to touch on agriculture in his numerous speeches and has made it one of his main preoccupations. The rapid industrial growth that began at the end of the past century and that was accelerated during the last 30 years, has not appreciably diminished the prominent role of agricultural policy. Even though the Soviet Union has lost its predominently agrarian character, close to half of the population still depends on agriculture for a livelihood. The expanding food and fiber needs of the growing population and the strains and stresses of agrarian collectivization have combined to keep agriculture in the public eye.

Chapter 1. Contrasting Objectives of Agricultural Policy in the Soviet Union and the United States

Agricultural policy, to be sure, has been a major problem in the United States as in Russia. But there the similarity ends. Actually the root causes and objectives of the agricultural problems and policies of the United States and the Soviet Union are diametrically opposite.

The United States, because of rapid technological development, has been steadily preoccupied with the problem of farm surpluses and excess capacity in agriculture, except during World War II and the years immediately thereafter, when maximum farm output was essential. Control of farm surpluses and other aspects of farm relief, therefore, have been the principal concern of U.S. policy.

The Soviet Union, on the other hand, has long been bedeviled by agricultural underproduction and agrarian overpopulation. Accordingly, not farm relief, but a rapid expansion of agricultural production in the face of considerable climatic obstacles,[2] to feed and clothe growing numbers and a reduction of the agricultural population has been the central objective of Soviet policy. In pursuit of that objective, considerable emphasis has been laid on modern technological development in Soviet agriculture, particularly on mechanization of farming, for which the United States has served as a model. Tractors and combines, for instance, were largely imported from the United States in the early 1930's until new Soviet factories could be built with the help of American engineering skill. However, expansion of agricultural production in the Soviet Union has been firmly bound up with another and, as it often proved, conflicting objective; namely, an all-embracing state control of agriculture. That led to the forced collectivization in the 1930's of small peasant farming, the horrors of which are only too well known.

In the collectivization process, the economic welfare of the Soviet farm population was sacrificed and subordinated to the ideological and economic objectives of the ruling Communist Party. Among these, a rapid and lopsided industrialization with an overriding emphasis on heavy industry acquired the highest priority. For Stalin was set on building socialism in a country where, ironically, it could not have been expected to develop according to the strict Marxian tenets, precisely because Russia was not an advanced industrial country. Accordingly, agriculture was forced to make a heavy contribution of farm products, little being given in return by the government to the collectivized peasantry. And, of course, the overpopulated and often starving Russian villages supplied in the 1930's most of the large labor force required by industrial expansion and inefficient factories. But a part of this increased manpower was labor of liquidated "kulaks" (the more prosperous small peasant farmers) and others forced off the land. The "colonial" role of agriculture was practically acknowledged by Stalin, when he said 30 years ago that agriculture provides the Soviet state, bent on industrialization, with "something like a tribute."[3] This idea strongly colored the Kremlin's attitude toward agriculture for many years, especially during the Stalin era.

In the United States, by way of contrast, agricultural policy has been aimed at protecting the independent family farm enterprise, based on private ownership of land and capital, from the adverse effects of depression, surpluses, and other economic maladjustments. This has been done through programs for "stabilizing, supporting, and protecting farm income and prices" [4] for reducing farm costs, and conserving soil resources. While there has been considerable divergence of opinion about the effectiveness and desirability of some of these programs, nevertheless, there has been widespread public agreement concerning the desirability of maintaining and improving the standard of living of the farm people and of protecting it and the family farm enterprise as far as possible, against the vicissitudes of the elements and sweeping economic changes.

[2] Harris, Chauncy D., "Soviet Agricultural Resources Reappraised," Journal of Farm Economics, 38: pp. 262-4, 1956; Volin, Lazar, "A Survey of Soviet Russian Agriculture." U.S. Department of Agriculture Monograph 5, pp. 5-9, 1951.

[3] J. V. Stalin's Collected Works (Russian) vol. 12, pp. 49-51.

[4] Sec. 2, Charter, Commodity Credit Corporation, 1933.

Another striking operational difference between agricultural policies of the Soviet Union and most non-Communist countries, including the United States, pertains to foreign trade. It is the field in which Government intervention on behalf of agriculture had early come on the scene and become especially active with the onset of the great depression. Tariffs, import quotas, and other forms of import restrictions to protect domestic producers from excessive imports and export subsidies and other export aids to help dispose of surpluses have become common practices of an active agricultural policy. (We are not concerned here with the merits or desirabilit of many of these devices, but merely with the hard facts of their existence.) In the Soviet Union, however, all foreign trading operations, exports as well as imports, are in the hands of the Government, which exercises a complete monopoly of foreign trade. There is no need, consequently, for the various restrictive and promotional devices employed in foreign trade policies of other nations. Those in authority decide how much and when and where to export or import farm products.

Chapter 2. Collective and State Farms

In aiming at the expansion of agricultural production and, at the same time, at the establishment of a tight state control, Soviet agricultural policy was in a large measure devoted to making Russian agriculture conform to the Marxist-Leninist-Stalinist image. The transformation usually meant loss of efficiency, which became a problem in itself. It is still a problem of the Kremlin.

It was to the small family peasant farming that the weight of this collectivization policy was applied—and it was a crushing weight. Remember that small family peasant farming in Russia was important even before the revolution, when two-thirds of the private farmland in European Russia was owned by peasants who also leased a considerable proportion of the remainder. After the revolution and division of the larger land properties, small peasant farming became preponderant in the Soviet Union. (The collective sector, which came into being early in the Soviet regime, was insignificant.) Agriculture largely retained its individualistic character for a longer period than other branches of Soviet economic life, thanks to Lenin's new economic policy, or NEP, which replaced the regime of war communism in 1921. But toward the end of the 1920's this breathing spell came to an end, and it was the turn of agriculture to be ruthlessly collectivized. Thus the historic Russian trend toward small peasant agriculture, which began with the emancipation of peasants from serfdom in March 1861, was reversed by Soviet policy.

In developing agriculture along new collectivist lines, the Communist rulers were guided by the Marxist orthodox doctrine of the absolute superiority of large-scale production in agriculture as in industry. Lenin added to this doctrine the enthusiasm for that American invention, the tractor, as a vehicle for collectivist transformation of small peasant agriculture. As far back as 1918 he thought that if the Russian peasants were given 100,000 tractors and supplies needed to operate them, they would plump for communism, which he recognized was a mere fantasy in those days.[5] Stalin com-

[5] Lenin's Works, vol. 29, ed. 4, p. 190.

bined this ideological heritage with his notion of "building socialism in one country" through vigorous industrialization at the expense, initially at any rate, of agriculture. Resistance of peasants to such squeezing tactics of the Soviet state was only an additional argument from the Communist standpoint for speedy collectivization. For it is much easier, as experience proved, to make government-controlled collectives deliver grain and other required produce to the state at low fixed prices than to force a small individual farmer to do so. The latter is likely, under such conditions, to produce less, to consume more, in short to become more self-sufficient and turn away from commercial production.

This tough Soviet agrarian policy, which began in the late 1920's, was softened somewhat from time to time by concessions to the peasants in order to win their cooperation. Nevertheless, there has never been any tampering with the basic principles of agrarian collectivism. Except for a brief period at the very beginning of the collectivization campaign in 1930, there has been no move toward decollectivization in the Soviet Union—not even after Stalin's death as in other countries of the Soviet bloc, notably in Poland. It is, therefore, symptomatic that Khrushchev recently selected Poland as the place to make a speech extolling agrarian collectivism.

Two collectivist types of farm enterprise have emerged in the Soviet Union. One is the collective farm proper, commonly known as kolkhoz or artel (plural kolkhozy). The other type is the state farm or sovkhoz (plural sovkhozy). These units have often been described and only a few words need to be said here. The state farms are owned outright and managed by the state and are usually larger in size and more specialized than collective farms. The collective farm represents in theory a self-governing producer's cooperative consisting of the pooled holdings of the formerly independent small peasant farmers. The self-governing character of the collectives, however, has become a fiction. They are in reality subject to tight state control and their formally elected managers are actually selected and removed at will by Communist authorities.

What principally distinguishes the two kinds of farms is the position of the workers. On state farms, workers are paid wages as in Soviet factories. On collective farms, the rank and file members, both men and women, work in the fields and in livestock centers under the direction of managers and supervisors just as they do on state farms. But, as a rule, they are not paid wages. They are residual sharers in in the income of the collectives, after the state secures its share and provision is made for current production expenses and capital outlays. Thus, the workers have neither the certainty of income from their work on collective farms, which other Soviet workers possess, nor the control of farm operations exercised by independent farmers, (although, like the latter, collective farmers must bear the risks of weather, pests, and plant and animal diseases). Collective farmers are not covered by the national social security system as farmers are in the United States. Collectives are supposed to have their own individual pension funds.

The payments to collective farmers vary with their skill and the amount of work performed. The greater the skill required, the larger the remuneration. A cumbersome system of payment has developed, based on so-called workday units, in which the performance of specified tasks or norms is measured and which serve as a basis for distribution at the end of the year of cash, grain, and other products. These are prorated to the total number of "workday" units earned per year by membership, so that each "workday" unit is credited with the same amount of cash, grain, etc. But the number of "workday" units and consequently the earnings of individual workers vary.

The uncertainly, the irregularity, the long waiting and confusion engendered by this complicated system has led recently to efforts to simplify it and make payments more regularly, by means of so-called advances. There is also a tendency to substitute cash payments for the multiple distribution of various types of produce and cash, and dispense with the workday units. If was found that, in addition to its cumbersomeness, the workday system does not encourage reduction of labor expenditures and costs, since the greater the number of workdays earned by an individual or a group of workers the greater the payments.

To a considerable extent, the improvement in the methods of payment however depends upon the improved economic position and the larger incomes of collectives. As was stated by the official report on the fulfillment of the economic plan for the first half of 1959: "As a result of increased cash receipts from the sale of agricultural products to the state, the number of collectives making money advances to their members increased considerably * * *"

To complete the picture of a collective farm, it must be pointed out that the peasant families have continued to live in their rather primitive dwellings, grouped in farm villages as they did before collectivization. Even those peasant families in the western regions of the U.S.S.R, who lived on separate farmsteads (so-called khutors) similar to those in the United States, were, for the most part, forced by the Soviet Government to move into villages. Thus, collective farms, just as state farms, are essentially units of production. Consumption is of peripheral importance, and is left to the peasant household, except for the maintenance of such public welfare and educational institutions, as clubhouses, hospitals, schools, etc. It is true that Khrushchev has urged increased concentration by collectives on various forms of public consumption rather than continue augmenting the earnings of their members. He stressed especially such institutions as canteens, children's nurseries, school dormitories, etc., which tend to release woman labor that could be used in farm production. While some progress along these lines may be anticipated, for the present, there is no question, of any basic changes in the fundamental character of collective farms.

There is a question, however, whether the coexistence of collective and state farms, so unlike in many respects, will continue, or whether collectives will be supplanted by state farms. For, ideologically, the state farm has always been considered a superior type of economic organization, or in Soviet parlance, a higher type of "Socialist property" than the so-called kolkhoz-cooperative property; though recently this theoretical distinction has been officially deemphasized. According to official slogans, state farms were supposed to serve as a model for the less advanced collective farming and, by inference, at any rate, could be considered the future Communist ideal goal of the institutional structure of Soviet agriculture. There was a wide gap, however, between theory and practice. State farming expanded considerably in the early 1930's when many giant farms were created, and then came a reversal. The unsatisfactory production results led to official condemnation of the giantism, subdivision of the huge units was ordered, and deflation of the state farm sector took place through transfer of land to the collective farm sector. In 1940 less than 10 percent of the total sown area was in state farms.

The limited role of state farming continued until the beginning of the Khrushchev program of expansion on uncultivated land beyond the Volga and Urals in 1954. In this area large mechanized state farms already were well established and, when the decision was again made to increase the grain area, several hundred new state farms were organized and many of the existing ones were enlarged. In the process, however, there was also a considerable absorption of collective farms. For instance, in the Kazakh Republic, where much of the expansion of the sown area on the so-called new lands took place, 833 collectives were merged into 188 state farms in 1957.[6]

Conversion of collectives into state farms, however, was not confined to the "new lands" regions of the eastern U.S.S.R., but spread to a number of other regions; among these were, for instance, the irrigated cotton-growing regions in Soviet Central Asia and areas in the former war zone, where collective farming disintegrated during the occupation and remained weak despite postwar rehabilitation. The need of new capital investment by the state has been, apparently, an important criterion in determining whether to convert collectives into state farms. As a result of the process of expansion on new lands and absorption of collectives, the share of state farms increased from 12 percent of the sown area in 1953, to more than one-fourth of the expanded acreage in 1957.

Another recent development also indicates greater reliance by the Soviet Government on state farms. It is the designation of a number of state farms, first near Moscow and subsequently near other large cities to specialize in growing cheaply potatoes and vegetables so as to lower their cost to the city consumer. Should this experiment prove successful it would operate to the disadvantage of those collectives which derive an important share of their income from selling potatoes and vegetables at high prices on the free market in the cities.

There are also other reasons why the revived dynamism of the state farming sector may portend a serious threat to collective farming. One is the considerably increased size of collective farms as a result of mergers and their acquisition of farm machinery from machine-tractor stations to be discussed in other sections. This further diminishes the difference between the two types of farming. Second is the revelation, by Khrushchev himself, of considerably lower labor productivity in collectives than on state farms (table 5).

Khrushchev's figures show that both state and collective farms in the U.S.S.R. have much higher labor requirements per unit of product than U.S. farms, but collective farms, have the highest of all, exceeding considerably even the state farm. Assuming similarity in the method of collecting these statistics on collective and state farms, some of the variations may be accounted for by differences in geographical location, in the quality of the labor force (age and sex distribution) in capital equipment or perhaps in some other aspect

[6] Kazakhstanskaya Pravda, Dec. 14, 1957.

of a sampling process. It is possible, too, that the system of regular wage payments on state farms, for which the authorities are responsible, as compared with the sharing principle in collectives, tends to induce a greater economy of labor on state farms. Since the Government is not responsible for the payment of labor in collectives, it could tolerate this inefficiency, so long as it was not required to raise the fixed low prices for farm products and there was an abundance of manpower in the villages. But the latter condition no longer prevails since the war. Also the Government raised agricultural prices during recent years. However, it aims at lowering such prices eventually in order to reduce the consumers' cost of living. If collectives are not to be economically injured by lower prices, increased efficiency and greater labor productivity is essential. Awareness of this need, and consciousness of a growing relative shortage of manpower, probably explains Khrushchev's emphasis on increased labor productivity even to the point of publishing comparisons with the United States, which are highly unfavorable to Soviet agriculture.

Chapter 3. Farm Giantism

Farm giantism has become a distinctive trait of Soviet agricultural organization. The cult of bigness, a feature of Soviet policy, has its ideological roots, as was pointed out earlier in the orthodox Marxist doctrine of economic concentration, which stresses the similarity, as far as large-scale methods of production are concerned, between agriculture and manufacturing. This doctrine, which makes no distinction between the large and the optimum size of an enterprise, was further reinforced by the unbounded enthusiasm of Lenin and his disciples for farm mechanization, modeled on the American pattern. It was one of the motivating forces in the collectivization of small peasant agriculture and establishment of huge state farms.

As already indicated, this cult of bigness miscarried in the case of huge state farms in the early 1930's and corrective steps were taken. As for collective farms, it was also found, in the mid-1930's, that a number of units in the southern and eastern regions were too large for efficiency and subdivision was not uncommon.[7] On the other hand, a "voluntary" merger of the usually small collective farms in the northern and north central regions was "recommended" by the decree of December 19, 1925, "Concerning the Economic and Organizational Strengthening of the Kolkhozy of the Non-Black Soil Area." In some regions then, before the war the average size of the collective farms was increasing, in other regions it was decreasing. In the country as a whole, however, the number of collective farms was slowly decreasing (after it reached a peak of 245,400 in 1935) to about 237,000 in 1940.

After collectivization in the annexed western regions after the war, the number of collectives in the U.S.S.R. increased to 252,000 at the beginning of 1950. In that year, however, a far-reaching change in the number and size of the collectives began. A mass campaign for merger and enlargment of farms was inaugurated, which resembled in its speed and relentlessness, and in the revival of gigantomania, the original mass collectivization drive of the early 1930's. This time, however, the pressure was exerted not on individual peasant farmers to join a collective, but on kolkhozy to merge "voluntarily" into super-

[7] Sautin, I. V., ed., Kolkhozy vo Btoroi Stalinskoi Pyatiletke, p. V, 1939.

collectives. The merger drive which Stalin initiated in 1950, was spearheaded by no other person than N. S. Khrushchev, then one of Stalin's lieutenants, who was just transferred from the Ukraine to Moscow. Khrushchev remains a dedicated believer in mergers on the ground of efficiency and economy, such as reduction of administrative expenses, etc. A decree of the Council of Ministers of the U.S.S.R. of June 7, 1950, No. 2427, which was not published at the time in the daily Soviet press or in other sources available to western students of Soviet affairs, gave a formal blessing to the merger drive, which was then already in full swing.[8]

The mergers, ostensibly undertaken to increase farm efficiency, were not confined to small collectives or to specific geographic areas. Already—large collectives were also merged and the drive extended to regions with most diverse national and economic conditions. Collectives with a large expanse of level farm land were merged with those whose terrain was criss-crossed by marshes, lakes, bushland and forests and, consequently, had small fields. Neither sparsely nor densly settled regions escaped the merger drive. Several collectives, whose members lived in one village, were merged with collectives whose members lived in several scattered villages. In such cases, the peasants who became members of the new enlarged collectives continued, for the most part, to live in their separate villages which were connected, as a rule, by very poor roads, which often become no more than mud tracks in the early spring and fall. However, Khrushchev's idea of speedy resettlement of villages into so-called agrotowns proposed by him in the spring of 1951, was quickly jettisoned by the Kremlin and has never been revived in its original form, even after its author came into power.

The irrationality of at least some farm mergers in the northern part of the country was acknowledged by an official report dealing with the Vologda Province.[9]

> In a number of districts the enlargement of the collective farms was made without taking into account the natural economic and other peculiarities * * *. Many collectives consist of 25 to 30 and more inhabited points which are not only separated from each other by 5 to 7 kilometers, but often are also cut off by natural obstacles—lakes and rivers.

Even Khrushchev cautiously hinted in June 1955 at the desirability of breaking up some large units resulting from recent farm amalgamation in the Baltic Republics.

After only 1 year of the merger drive, the number of collectives decreased by more than one-half, from 252,000 at the beginning of 1950 to 121,000 at the end of that year. By the end of 1953, there were only a little more than 91,000 collectives.[10] Since 1954, a new factor—the absorption of collectives by state farms mentioned above enters the picture. However, since the total figure of collectives absorbed by state farms has not been released, it is impossible to segregate the effects of such absorption from that of the mergers of farms into larger collectives. The liquidation of machine-tractor stations as machine operating units in 1958, which will be discussed later, probably also contributed to the mergers. It is significant that as late as the fall of 1958, Khrushchev urged the "model" collective in his native village, Kalinovka, with a tillable area of 3,200 acres, to

[8] Direktivy KPSS i Sovetskogo Pravitel'stva po Khozyaistvennym voprosam V. 4, pp. 726–727, 1958.
[9] Partiinaya Zhizn', No. 6, 1957, p. 50.
[10] "Norodnoye Khozyaistvo SSSR v 1956 Godu," p. 139, Moscow, 1957.

merge with a neighboring collective, as he did not consider it sufficiently large.[11] At any rate, as a result of the two processes, mergers of collectives and their absorption by state farms, the total number of collective farms decreased to about 60,000 by July 1959 [12] or to less than one-fourth of the number at the beginning of the present decade.

The merger process resulted, of course, in a considerable enlargement of collectives. In terms of sown area per farm, the average size of the collective increased nearly 3½ times, compared with the prewar period, and the average number of families per farm trebled. Collectives, however, vary considerably in size from region to region. Thus, in 1956, in the northwestern region of European Russia, for instance, 64 percent of all collectives had a sown area of 500 hectares and under (1,236 acres and under); whereas, in northern Caucasus, 23 percent of collectives and in western Siberia, only 5 percent had acreages that large. On the other hand, no farms of more than 5,000 hectares (12,355 acres) were in the northwestern region, but more than one-third of the collectives in northern Caucasus, and nearly one-fourth in western Siberia had acreages of 5,000 hectares and over.

The large size of Soviet farms is particularly striking in comparison with U.S. units. Although farm size in the United States in recent years has been trending upward, paralleling the growth in farm efficiency, yet only slightly over 2 percent of commercial farms in 1954 (not all the farms enumerated by the census, which includes a number of smaller units) had 500 acres or more of cropland harvested; many others had much less.

Yet collective farms despite their enlargement continue to be much smaller than state farms. The latter also have become enlarged and in 1957 had on the average an area of more than 20,000 acres under crops per farm as compared with about 2,800 acres in 1940. While a considerable number of new state farms were organized in recent years, some of the smaller farms were merged and others were transferred to various institutions or liquidated and a few were subdivided. The net result was first, a decrease in the number of state farms from 4,988 at the beginning of 1951 to 4,742 at the beginning of 1953, and subsequently an upward trend, which brought the number of farms to 5,905 at the beginning of 1958.[13]

The huge size of collective and state farms has made it necessary to decentralize operations into more manageable units. The workers in collectives are organized into brigades, consisting of 40 to 60 workers, headed by a brigadier or a foreman. Each brigade is assigned to a unit of cropland or to a livestock center. Still smaller units, called zveno or squads are formed and these workers cultivate the more intensive crops such as sugar beets and cotton. State farms also are subdivided into branches (otdelenie), each of which is a farm unit by itself.

The team of U.S. Department of Agriculture economists which visited the Soviet Union in the summer of 1958, states in its report that they—

> inquired about the availability of studies analyzing the relation between the size of the farm unit and its efficiency, with a view to determining the optimum size in

[11] Sel'skoe Khozyaistvo, Oct. 21, 1953.

[12] Report of the Central Statistical Administration of the Council of Ministers of the U.S.S.R. on the "Fulfillment of the State Plan of Economic Development for the first half of 1959," Pravda and Izvestia July 14, 1959.

[13] "Narodnoye Khozyaistvo SSSR v 1956 Godu," p. 145; "SSSR v Tsifrakh, Statisticheskii Sbornik," p. 190.

different regions. We were told that such information was not available at the present time, although apparently some studies of this type are under way. We gained the impression that in striving for bigness, per se, farm efficiency was actually neglected. Even with brigade subdivisions, much time is consumed in going to and from places of work. Although Soviet agricultural authorities stress increasing efficiencies associated with larger sizes of operations in discussing desirable sizes of farms, their thinking is in terms of very large units by U.S. standards. They did state, however, that some of their largest farms, up to 150,000 hectares (about 375,000 acres), are considered to be too large. The present sizes probably are influenced by the greater ease of centralized management and control than by economics associated with size of operation. Large farms means fewer units of contact for state direction of planning and operation; also fewer managers will be needed to translate the overall plans into specific operations.[14]

In addition to the fact that it facilitates central control over collective farming, the Soviet predilection for farm giantism may perhaps be also explained by its tendency to widen the gulf between the rank and file peasant membership and the management of the big collective, now mostly in the hands of outsiders. This gap is useful in the context of Soviet rule for it tends to enhance the driving power of management over labor.

Chapter 4. Machine-Tractor Stations: Their Rise and Fall

The merger process was also extended to another type of farm unit, which was the handiwork of Soviet policy—the state machine-tractor stations or MTS. These were the special units into which tractors, combines, and other large machinery operating on collective farms were grouped, together with facilities for repairing machinery and operating and supervising personnel. For a long time, in fact, the collectives were not allowed to own such machinery. While originally the idea of MTS was associated with the advantages of pooling power and machinery for joint cultivation by small peasant farmers, too poor to own tractors individually, it was adopted since the early stages of collectivization as an important instrument of state ascendancy and control over collective agriculture.

It should be borne in mind that the very fact of a catastrophic reduction in the number of horses early in the collectivization greatly enhanced the importance of the tractor, which was thrown, so to speak, into the breach on the draft power front. It can, in fact, be truly said that the tractor in the Soviet Union did not displace the horse, as in the United States, but replaced it in an emergency. Thus, he who controlled the tractor—the new source of farm power—controlled agriculture. This helps to explain why the Soviet Government, which was anxious to extend a tight control over the amorphous structure of the peasant collective farming, was clinging to the possession of tractors and other farm machinery. Since MTS were paid for their services to the collectives in kind, they have also become significant revenue producers (in terms of farm products) to the state.

There was at first no change in the pivotal role of the MTS after Stalin. On the contrary, one of the first steps of the post-Stalin regime in the agrarian sphere was, in various ways, to still further enhance the supervisory powers and the importance of the MTS, as, for instance, by transferring collective farm personnel, seasonally employed by MTS, to their permanent staff. However, the advantage of pooling tractors and machinery in a central unit, like MTS, was offset, some-

[14] "Economic Aspects of Soviet Agriculture," pp. 12–13.

times seriously, by dual management of farm operations by the managers of the MTS and of the collectives. Khrushchev described this situation as having "two bosses on the land." There was often a conflict of interest between the management of the MTS and the collective. The former was interested primarily in performing those operations, like plowing, which brought the greatest financial returns, often at the expense of other necessary operations, like mowing hay. There were cases when plowing done by the MTS was superfluous or even harmful. Difficulties also often developed regarding the timeliness of MTS farm operations, which is so important in agriculture, especially in Russian agriculture with its short season. It was complained, on the other hand, that collectives tended to rely too much on the MTS, for even for the simplest type of work, such as carting feedstuff for livestock, which could have been done by farm horses.

The decreased number and the increased size of the collectives, as a result of the merger campaign, made the existence of separate MTS seem less essential even from the Soviet point of view. There were anomalous cases where one MTS serviced a single collective farm. At any rate, an abrupt about-face by the regime ended this dichotomy in the collective farm system. On January 22, 1958, following some limited public discussion, Khrushchev proposed that MTS were to sell most of the machinery, except highly specialized equipment to collective farms and, thus, be divested of the vital farm operating functions. They were to be converted into mere service and supply centers, so-called repair-technical stations or RTS. This radical reform was formally approved by the Supreme Soviet of U.S.S.R. on March 31, 1958, and was rapidly carried out. By July 1959, 94 percent of collectives bought farm machinery from the MTS on cash or credit. The magnitude of this transaction can be gaged from the fact that by July 1, 1959, there were purchased 512,000 tractors, 221,000 grain combines, and a large quantity of other machinery. In addition, collectives purchased also 100,000 new tractors, more than 25,000 grain combines and other new machinery. The total cost of the machinery purchased was 21.7 billion rubles, of which 17.2 billion rubles is the cost of the machinery acquired from the MTS. These expenditures may be compared with a total cash income of all collectives of around 95 billion rubles in 1956 and 1957 and a record of 130 billion in 1958.[15]

The liquidation or, as it is officially termed, reorganization of MTS encountered, judging from what Khrushchev said, some ideological opposition within the Communist ranks. It was apparently based on objection to the downgrading of what was regarded by the official Communist line as a higher type of property—the "state" property of the MTS to the lower level of so-called cooperative-kolkhoz property. It may be surmised that this opposition found support or was inspired by Stalin's adamant stand against liquidation of MTS, which was proposed during his lifetime by some economists. Khrushchev tried to meet this ideological opposition by arguments, which minimized the distinction formerly made by Soviet theoreticians between the two types of property. But in the main, in abandoning Stalin's legacy regarding MTS, Khrushchev was guided, to judge from his own utterances, less by ideological than by pragmatic considerations.

[15] Pravda, July 14, 1959.

First of all, reorganization of MTS eliminated dual farm management. Second, considerable strengthening of the party apparatus in the countryside during the past 5 years made it feasible to dispense with the control function of the MTS. Third, the importance of MTS had diminished as an instrument of state acquisition of farm products, Fourth, the leadership calculated that increased prices and incomes and anticipated economies from more efficient management made it possible for the collectives to afford to purchase, maintain, and operate the MTS machinery. Indeed, its purchase may be also desirable from the Soviet point of view as a proper channel for investment of part of their increased income by collectives. For otherwise, the opportunity for productive capital investment by collectives is restricted if acquisition of machinery is barred, as it largely had been heretofore. The alternative to capital investment is, of course, a further increase of peasant earnings. But if this is not to be inflationary, it would necessitate a considerably faster pace for the Soviet consumers' goods industry and more efficient distribution of such goods in rural areas. There are, therefore, some implications in the sale of machinery by MTS to collectives of deflationary or disinflationary character.

While the transition which the virtual merging of MTS with collectives involved seemed to be rapid, the very considerable readjustment necessary was not always smooth, and it posed new problems. Among the various problems of adjustment, are those of adequate repair facilities and relations with the repair-technical stations, of supplying farms adequately with proper machinery, and especially with spare parts. A case for instance, was reported in the Soviet press when, because of the impossibility of finding a wheel for a tractor, a new tractor had to be purchased.[16] Repair technical stations were accused of selling defective machinery to collectives and not being helpful with repairs.[17] But the elimination of "two bosses on the land" should make it possible to pinpoint managerial responsibility. This should, in the long run, contribute to farm efficiency, though the problem of finding suitable managers of collectives has, apparently, also not been solved.

Chapter 5. Household Allotment Farming

While the dichotomy of the MTS and the collective farms was eliminated by Khrushchev's 1958 reform, another dichotomy remains; namely, the coexistence side by side of the large collective farm enterorise and the small household allotment farming (priusadebnoe khozyaistvo). The collectivist Leviathan has not swallowed as yet the individualist dwarf.

At first, a few words about the nature of the allotment farming. Peasant households in collectives as well as workers' families on state farms and some others are allotted small plots of land on which they grow potatoes, vegetables, sunflower seed, and other crops. These plots are allotted to a whole family and not to an individual member of the collective. This seems to be a survival of the old Russian institution of family property, though the plot, of course, is not legally owned by the peasant family; it is merely set aside for the family's

[16] Sel'skoe Khozyaistvo, Aug. 9, 1959.
[17] Sel'skoe Khozyaistvo, July 18 and Aug. 7, 1959.

use at the discretion of the collective. Furthermore, all adult members of the household must do a certain amount of labor on collective farms or work in state enterprises to obtain the household allotment. The peasant households are also permitted to own a small number of livestock and an unlimited number of poultry. They can sell their produce direct to the consumers on the free, so-called kolkhoz market in the cities, but they cannot use middlemen.

Household allotment farms accounted for only 3 percent of the sown area in 1956 but for a much larger proportion of the livestock population, including almost half of all the cows. Such allotments were originally conceived as a subsistence, "an acre and a cow" farming, merely auxiliary to the collectives' farm economy at a time when they were not considered strong enough to take care fully of their members' needs. As so often happens, "the tail began to wag the dog". The household allotments not only helped greatly to feed the collectivized peasant population, but they frequently became the chief, or the only, sources of the peasants' cash earnings through sale at higher prices (not the low government fixed prices) on the free kolkhoz market.

How important the free market was as a source of peasants' cash earnings during the Stalin era can be gathered from the fact that, for some years, at any rate, the volume of sales on the kolkhoz market, mostly by members of the collectives, exceeded total cash income of collectives. This "acre and a cow" farming, however, is important, not only for the economic welfare and morale of the peasants, but also for the food supply, of the nonfarm population, especially the supply of livestock products—products sold not only through the kolkhoz market, but also through government controlled outlets. Even in 1957, when the share of allotment holdings in state acquisitions of agricultural products was considerably less than formerly, they accounted for 19 percent of meat deliveries, 16 percent of milk and 11 percent of wool.[18]

Yet the household allotment became a thorn in the Kremlin's side, since it competed with the collective farm economy for the labor and loyalty of the peasants. The official view, therefore, has been that, as the collective farming becomes stronger and better able to satisfy the needs of its members and of the nation, the importance of household allotment farming should decline and eventually wither away. But, like the Soviet doctrine of the withering of the state—it is still in the future. Accordingly, the Soviet policy toward this kind of farming has been ambivalent, now restrictive, now relaxed—then again restrictive.

As during a short period in the mid-1930's under Stalin, so in 1953 after the late dictator, the "thaw" in agrarian policy began with a more encouraging or tolerant attitude toward allotment holdings. The cumbersome money tax on allotment holdings was simplified and taxes reduced in the fall of 1953. Acquisition of cows by peasant households was facilitated. Compulsory deliveries of farm products to the government were first reduced and since January 1958 were entirely abandoned.

This new liberal phase again did not last long. In 1956, legislation was passed ostensibly for the purpose of permitting collectives to set up their charters without modeling them on the general model char-

[18] Pravda, July 5, 1957. (Decree on abolition of compulsory deliveries by allotment holdings.)

ter of 1935. The really consequential provisions of this law was to enable each collective to set its own minimum of labor, the size of the household allotments and the number of privately owned livestock. This was accompanied by a declaration favoring, indirectly but not prescribing a reduction of the size of the plots. Subsequently there had been cases of reduction of plots, some apparently for purposes of equalization of such holdings between different families. But this has not assumed so far a mass character.

However, the government attitude toward private ownership of livestock, the most valuable component of household allotment farming, has become more restrictive in recent years, as was foreshadowed by Khrushchev in 1953 at the outset of the new post-Stalin course of agrarian policy. Khrushchev has been advocating during the last few years the sale of cattle by members to the collectives. He "recommended" to the peasants of his native Kalinovka to sell their cows to the model kolkhoz, and the "recommendation" was acted upon. But such liquidation is to be gradual with no definite time limit placed, depending upon when collectives are ready for the transition. Steps taken by authorities in some districts to hasten the process by pressuring the peasants were strongly rebuked. A much sterner attitude, however, has been adopted by the government toward private ownership of livestock by workers on state farms and by nonfarm population which is marked for elimination.

To sum up: household allotment farming is again being deflated. But, so deeply rooted is it in the rural fabric of the U.S.S.R., that it would be premature to conclude that its doom is near at hand.

Chapter 6. Government Procurements of Farm Products

Acquisition of farm products by the state is a fundamental problem of Soviet economics and politics. It runs like a red thread throughout the whole of Soviet history. It was at the root of both Lenin's new economic policy of 1921 and of Stalin's rural collectivization a decade later. It helped to kindle bitter intraparty strife in the 1920's and was a basic presupposition of the industrialization program under the 5-year plans. It is through government procurements and prices paid for them that economic incentives and disincentives to the farmers largely operate.

The procurement system, however, was characterized, with respect to the same commodity, by a considerable diversity of methods or types of delivery and by a corresponding multiplicity of prices. Basic to all were the compulsory delivery quotas, calculated as so much grain, potatoes, meat, etc., per unit of tillable or total land. The lowest fixed price was usually paid for this type of procurement. Next, there was the so-called contracting method used for industrial and intensive crops like cotton, sugar beets, etc. Though essentially similar to compulsory deliveries, this method involved a graduated price scale, depending upon the quantities delivered, and also provided an opportunity for the farmers to buy some commodities at concession prices. Then there were the extra-or-above-quota purchases by the state for which considerably higher prices were paid after 1953 than for the compulsory deliveries. In recent years the extra-quota purchases became increasingly important while lower priced compulsory deliveries declined. Finally, there were payments in kind for the work of machine-tractor stations, which, of course, are now being eliminated with the dissolution of the MTS.

The reform of 1958 unified the different types of procurements into a single system of state purchases. Compulsory deliveries as such were nominally abolished, but the new system retains quotas per unit of land which collectives are supposed to meet. Instead of multiple prices, single prices are now fixed by the state for each commodity within a region. Although price stability is one of the aims of the reform, provision is made for raising or lowering of prices to cope with sharp fluctuations in output, thus, some recognition is given to the law of supply and demand. Another important change is the abolition of the variable premium prices for larger deliveries used for some crops like cotton, under the so-called contract system, on a considerable scale. A sample study of three groups of cotton growing collectives in 1956 showed that the differential in the average price per unit of cotton between the highest and the lowest was 40 percent and between the highest and the middle group 20 percent.[19]

These changes simplified the cumbersome procurement and price system. There can exist now only two prices for a commodity in each locality, a government price and a free market price if a commodity is traded on the limited private market. This is still a far cry from a rational price system, the lack of which, as many western economists pointed out, greatly handicaps economic calculations and planning decisions in the Soviet Union. But the reform takes at least a small step towards such a goal.

The abolition of premium price payments, no doubt, hits collectives growing such crops as cotton, sugar beets, hemp, and others which received preferential price treatment. So much was openly admitted by Khrushchev, who contended that the more productive collectives should obtain higher income, not from price differentials but by lowering of production costs and increasing output. In any event the average prices paid by the state to such collectives will be lower and so will probably the gross money income. This may have an adverse effect upon the output of certain crops in these usually more productive farms, which may or may not be compensated by increased production of other farms. In general, the new prices appear to have been tailored to benefit the average or less prosperous collective farms. The guiding principle was stated by Khrushchev in 1958 as follows: "Although the total expenditures of the state for the purchase of agricultural products will remain approximately at the same level as last year, they will be distributed more fairly among the collective farms, thanks to the new prices."[20] Khrushchev indicated further that the total procuring expenditures include also the expenses formerly incurred by the state for the machine-tractor stations which are now borne by the collectives themselves.

As a matter of fact, the stated objective of Soviet price policy in the years to come is that of achieving lower prices, concomitant with a reduction of the production costs. This brings up a new important facet of the procuring policy, namely the projected concentration of procurements in areas of most economical production, instead of requiring every region from the Baltic to the Pacific and from the Arctic to the Black Sea to deliver identical products like grain, for

[19] Khrushchev's speech, Pravda, June 21, 1958.
[20] Ibid.

instance. This move is linked with what appears to be now more than a mere academic concern (as it had long been) with regional agricultural specialization. And regional specialization is to be based on production cost studies. This cost consciousness is itself a new phenomenon in the management of Soviet agriculture, heretofore preoccupied almost exclusively with fulfillment of physical targets. Khrushchev himself reflected the new cost consciousness when he said in his December 15, 1958 report: "It is impossible to carry on farming without a thorough analysis of the cost of commodities being produced, and without control by means of the ruble." [21]

Chapter 7. Economic Incentives and Farm Labor

Soviet policy in the agrarian as in other fields has always been a combination of coercion, indoctrination, and economic incentives. However, the proportions vary from time to time. There has been, for example, a special emphasis on economic incentives whenever a critical or difficult agricultural situation arose and appeasement of the peasantry was considered essential. It is only necessary to recall Lenin's celebrated NEP in 1921, which supplanted the harsh regime of war communism, with its requisitions of peasants' produce. Again, in the mid-1930's, Stalin relaxed his iron grip somewhat to secure a recovery of agriculture from the ravages of the initial collectivization drive.

But relaxation always was a short-lived luxury. Khrushchev himself showed in his famous "secret" de-Stalinization speech at the 20th Communist Party Congress, in February 1956, how harsh and unrealistic Stalin's policy toward the peasantry became in its latter stage. For instance, he proposed raising taxes on collective farms and their members by 40 billion rubles, when they received, in 1952, for instance, altogether only 26 billion rubles for the large quantity of products acquired by the state. This helps to explain the unsatisfactory agricultural production situation, particularly in the livestock sector, which Stalin's heirs inherited.

The contrast between agriculture and industry was especially glaring. According to Khrushchev, agricultural production in 1952 was only 10 percent higher than in 1940, when industrial production was more than twice as high.[22] Even the 10-percent increase may have been optimistic. During the Stalin era crop production estimates, especially the important grain figures, were inflated by the use of the so-called biological estimates which grossly exaggerated the picture. These were estimates of crops standing in the field prior to the harvest, which did not reflect the officially admitted large harvesting losses and, in general, lent themselves to manipulation. They were not comparable with crop figures for other countries, or, indeed, with Russian figures prior to the 1930's. Such a statistical malpractice brought down, after Stalin's death, even the official Soviet wrath. Malenkov, for instance, declared in August 1953 that: "it should not be forgotten that our country, our collective farms can prosper with a crop gathered in the barn and not with a crop standing in the field".[23] Khrushchev in December 1958, spoke even more harshly about biological estimates, which he called eyewash

[21] Pravda, Dec. 16, 1958.
[22] Ibid., Sept. 15, 1953.
[23] Ibid., Aug. 9, 1953.

(ochkovtiratel'stvo), accusing Malenkov himself of indulging in their use during Stalin's lifetime.[24] Incidentally, the U.S. Department of Agriculture and other agencies of the U.S. Government, as well as a number of other Western specialists, were long critical of these inflated biological figures and stressed the need of considerable downward adjustment if they were to be used at all.[25]

When it came to livestock figures, even Soviet official figures showed that cattle numbers at the beginning of 1953 were considerably below the precollectivization figures in 1928. No secret was made of the fact that livestock was greatly underfed. This, notwithstanding, the much publicized official policy to increase the output of livestock products and improve the monotonous starchy diet of the Russian people.

To remedy the difficult agricultural situation and increase production of food and feed, Stalin's heirs once more put in the forefront of their blueprint of agricultural policy, in 1953, increased economic incentives to stimulate the interest and cooperation of the peasants in expansion of production. Thus, with Stalin's exit, the big stick was again to be accompanied by a somewhat larger carrot.

Turning to the question of implementation, of economic incentives programs, it should be borne in mind that the collective farm system of payment for labor, described in an earlier section, was designed precisely to provide economic incentives to producers. For this reason equality of income, usually associated with socialism, has been rejected by the Communist rulers of Russia. They do not consider it applicable to the present economic stage of development of the U.S.S.R., which they call Socialist, as distinguished from a future, full-fledged Communist society. On the contrary, variation in earnings among members of collectives to provide incentives to workers has always been encouraged. In fact, the very method of payment, based on workday units, is patterned on a kind of incentive piecework wage. Attempts of collectives to introduce some sort of a uniform daily wage in terms of workday units has always been strongly disapproved by the authorities.

That is also why rural communes, in which not only production but also consumption is socialized on egalitarian lines, have been proscribed by the Soviets. There were, to be sure, some communes organized in the U.S.S.R. in the 1920's and during the initial collectivization drive in 1930, but they were converted to the present artel form of collective farming. It is significant, in view of the recent Red Chinese experiment with communes, that Khrushchev attacked this type of agrarian collectivism in his speech in a Polish collective in July 1959.[26]

Although the principle of economic incentives was thus recognized during the Stalin era, incentives failed to produce desired results because incomes of the collectives were very low, largely due to the low fixed prices paid by the Government, as admitted later by Khrushchev,[27] for the heavy quotas of grain and many other farm products which they were obligated to deliver. This resulted in very small earnings of the peasants from their labor on many collective farms.

[24] Ibid., Dec. 16, 1958.
[25] Jasny, Naum, The Socialized Agriculture of the U.S.S.R., pp. 659 and 728; Volin, Lazar, "Agricultural Statistics in Soviet Russia: Their Usability and Reliability," American Statistician VII, pp. 8–12, 1953.
[26] Pravda July 21, 1959.
[27] Ibid., June 21, 1958.

The effect was to make peasants less willing and less efficient workers and to encourage them to concentrate on their household allotment farming.

It is true that the delivery quotas of farm products were legally fixed quantities, which were not supposed to be increased, in order that the farmers should be interested in maximizing output. In practice, however, increased output often led to increased exactions. If some collectives in a district could not meet their quotas, other farms, which had already delivered theirs, were frequently called upon to supply additional quantities so that the plan for the district should be completed. Khrushchev called this pruning of the more prosperous or efficient collectives.[28] The disincentive effect of such exactions on the peasantry needs no elaborations and was reflected in the unsatisfactory agricultural situation during the Stalin regime described above.

The post-Stalin leadership adopted a policy of substantially raising the very low prices paid by the Government for farm products. Thus, in 1953 prices of livestock and poultry products were increased more than 5½ times; milk and butter 2 times; potatoes by 2½ times; and vegetables, on the average, by 25 to 40 percent. Prices of grain and other products also were raised later. As a result of the increased prices and larger quantities acquired, the payments of the Government to collective farms and small household allotment holders more than trebled between 1952 and 1957. See table 8. The total cash income of collectives more than doubled between 1952 and 1956–57, increasing from 43 billion to 95 billion rubles. This in turn made possible cash payments to peasants in many collectives in which such distribution had formerly been negligible. The cash payments, in fact, more than trebled between 1952 and 1956, increasing from 12 billion to 42 billion rubles.[29]

Yet, even the greatly increased volume of cash distributed in 1956 represents only an average cash income of something over 2,100 rubles per peasant family on the collective farms, a sum roughly equivalent to about $200 at a realistic rate of exchange. In 1952 the average was as little as 623 rubles, equivalent, with higher prices, to less than $60 per peasant household. Moreover, since distribution of cash in some areas of intense crop production (such as cotton, sugar beets, etc.) are considerably above the average rate, many peasant families in the less prosperous collectives received much less than the average. However, it is well to remember that cash distribution by collectives is not the only major source of peasants' money income. As was pointed out earlier, the anomaly persists of the small household allotments, playing not just the theoretically assigned minor role of a mere subsistence-farming appendage, but actually rivaling and often outstripping collective economy as a significant source of peasants' income. In this connection, as was pointed out earlier, sales on the free market in the cities are very important. However, receipts from private sales have become smaller in recent years and they no longer overshadow cash income from collective farms; though the situation varies widely from region to region and from farm to farm.

---

[28] Ibid., Sept. 15, 1953.

[29] Khrushchev's speech in Minsk, Pravda, Jan. 25, 1958, for figures of payments to collective farm members. S.S.S.R. v. Tsifrakh, p. 200 for total cash income of collectives.

Much less information is available concerning what is still the most important component of peasants' income from the collective farms—payments in kind. Without such information it is impossible to adequately assess the changed economic position of the peasantry. However, since in-kind payments are mostly in grain, and there were several large harvests in recent years, it can be assumed that more grain was distributed.

What of the effect of the post-Stalin policies of increased economic incentives on labor input? While helpful statistics on this point are by no means abundant, we do have some clue, however imperfect, from the reported total number of workday units earned annually by peasants in collectives. Between 1952 and 1956 the total number of workday units increased by 26 percent.[30] Incidentally, the figure for 1952 was still below prewar, but in 1956 it was 19 percent above. This improvement reflects both a larger number of workers and a greater contribution per worker. The latter is shown roughly by the claimed increase of the average number of workday units per able-bodied worker—from 295 in 1953 to 335 in 1957, or 14 percent.[31] The increased contribution per worker, however, does not signify anything like a corresponding rise in the efficiency of labor. For workday units do not measure uniformly labor input in different collectives. Moreover, Soviet sources often criticize the so-called waste of workdays, meaning simply the wasteful, inefficient employment of farm labor. Attention has already been called to Khrushchev's striking statistical comparison between labor requirements per unit of product in the United States and the U.S.S.R., thus confirming first-hand observations of western specialists regarding low labor productivity in Soviet agriculture.

Raising of labor productivity in agriculture has been a major concern of Khrushchev's administration. Considerable attention in this connection has been given to improved training of farm labor through the establishment of short-term courses and of special schools. Drives were also organized to return to the farms skilled workers who migrated to cities and to bring farm specialists closer to grassroots.

In 1954, a drive began to recruit several hundred thousand young men and women for agricultural development in the eastern virgin lands region. Since then, each summer additional thousands have been sent to those areas on temporary assignments. Their services, however, have not always been effectively utilized. There have been also many stories in the Soviet press of hardship suffered by the newcomers in those regions due to the housing shortages and other causes. Finally there must be mentioned the annual or perennial mobilizations of students and other city dwellers to assist in harvesting crops. However, Khrushchev, for some time, has been highly critical of this practice and called for its elimination.[32]

Chapter 8. Capital Investment in Agriculture; Fertilizer Program

Agricultural production in the Soviet Union has been handicapped by a shortage of capital, as well as by climatic obstacles, and inefficient

[30] Narodnoe Khozyaistvo v 1956 Godu, p. 140.
[31] S.S.S.R. v Tsifrak, p. 198.
[32] Pravda, Dec. 16, 1958.

labor and management under the regimented system of a highly centralized agrarian collectivism.

For a long time agriculture served as an important source of capital accumulation for financing the Soviet industrial program. Reference has already been made to Stalin's statement in the late 1920's that agriculture contributed "something like a tribute" to the Soviet state. In addition, Russian agriculture suffered heavy capital losses during the all-out collectivization in the 1930's; as Jasny puts it: [33]

Instead of increasing by one-third, as planned, the investment in means of production in agriculture declined by considerably more, perhaps as much as one-half, during the first plan period, chiefly by livestock destruction in the collectivization drive. This decline was not fully made up until 1938.

During the post-Stalin period, however, belated recognition has been given to the capital needs of agriculture itself. Government capital investment in agriculture in 1956 was officially estimated (in July 1, 1955, prices) at 21 billion rubles, compared with a total of 63 billion during the preceding 5 years, and 25 billion during 1946–50.[34] The collectives also were spurred to increase their own capital accumulation out of increased income. Their officially estimated capital investments more than doubled between 1952 and 1957, increasing from less than 10 billion to more than 23 billion rubles.[35] The so-called indivisible funds, representing the capital assets of collectives, were estimated at 63 billion rubles at the end of 1952 and at 102 billion at the end of 1957, a rise of more than 60 percent.[36] Parenthetically, it may be noted that sizable collective farm investments acted as a brake on the rise of the peasant earnings. In addition to using their own resources for capital investment, there were also available to collectives increased long-term state credits in recent years. Whatever the faults or biases the above figures may have they are believed to be indicative of the trend.

Despite the marked improvement of the capital position of Russian agriculture during the post-Stalin era, the investment is still inadequate to use land and labor effectively. From this inadequacy stems, for instance, the imbalance in mechanization. Some operations, such as cutting the grain, are highly mechanized, while others, such as cleaning and drying of grain, are still to a large extent carried out inefficiently by hand labor.

Again Khrushchev stated in his June 29, 1959, speech that shortage of tractors hampered fall plowing in the new lands regions and consequently increased the load of fieldwork during the short spring season and affected adversely crop yields. As a matter of fact, Soviet farms have fewer tractors than the United States, even though the latter has a crop area of about 150 million acres less than the Soviet Union. At the beginning of 1957 there were 892,000 tractors on farms in the Soviet Union[37] compared with 4,975,000 in the United States.

Another example of a shortage of capital investment in agriculture is the paucity of irrigation development in the extensive subhumid zone plagued by frequent devastating droughts and low crop yields. It is doubtless because of the need of considerable capital investment that Stalin's large program of irrigation in the subhumid regions of

[33] Socialized Agriculture of the U.S.S.R., p. 61.
[34] Forty Years of Soviet Power in Facts and Figures, p. 193.
[35] Narodnoe Khozyaistvo v 1956 Godu, p. 173; S.S.S.R. v Tsifrakh, p. 254.
[36] Narodnoe Khozyaistvo S.S.S.R. v 1956 Godu, p. 140; S.S.S.R. v Tsifrakh, p. 198.
[37] Narodnoe Khozyaistvo S.S.S.R. v 1956 Godu, p. 155.

the European U.S.S.R. was deflated by his successors, though it would have paid off in stable and higher yields.

Still another type of deficiency in capital investment in Soviet agriculture is a qualitative one. It is characterized by wastefulness and decreased economic, and sometimes even physical, effectiveness of some forms of capital investment. There has been, for instance, a tendency in some collectives to build far too elaborate and costly shelters for livestock—so-called cow palaces. Then there were the tractors, produced uniformly much larger in size than needed in many regions. But this particular "gigantomania" is being corrected at present.

The utilization of capital equipment has also been often inefficient. The Soviet press, for instance, has been complaining year in year out about the idleness of tractors during the busy season because of poor repair work, shortage of spare parts, etc.

A field in which considerable investment of capital would be beneficial to agriculture is highways. As the report of the economists of the U.S. Department of Agriculture points out:[38]

> The lack of all-weather roads in much of the country no doubt explains in part the separation of cream for butter producton on most farms rather than the marketing of whole milk. The inadequate transportation system also probably hinders the development of such agricultural crops as fruits and vegetables. The relatively few trucks and automobiles (631,000 trucks and very few automobiles on farms in 1957, compared with nearly 3 million trucks and over 4 million automobiles on U.S. farms) makes for cultural as well as economic isolation for the rural villages and their inhabitants.

A new government program, which, if successful, is destined to have a significant effect on Soviet agricultural production is that of greatly stepped up output of commercial fertilizer. The importance of this program is accentuated by the fact that, following a large expansion of crop acreage during the years 1954–57, the new 7-year plan, 1959–65, relies for the achievement of its high farm output targets primarily on an increase of per acre yields. Certainly increased use of commercial fertilizer, especially in the humid regions, would contribute to this objective.

The gross supply of commercial fertilizer available to Soviet agriculture increased between 1953 and 1957 by nearly 60 percent.[39] But, on a plant nutrient basis of 2.7 million short tons, the 1957 supply was still only 40 percent of fertilizer consumption in the United States. Actually, commercial fertilizer in the Soviet Union so far has been used only in the growing of the most valuable crops, like cotton and sugar beets.

The 1957–59 plan calls for nearly trebling of the fertilizer supply. Whether this high goal will be achieved or not, it is reasonable to expect that a considerable increase of commercial fertilizer supply will take place during the next few years.

There is, however, great room for improvement in the handling, quality, and application of fertilizers. The Soviet press has been replete with complaints about the failure of collective farms to move fertilizer from warehouses. Even worse is the practice of dumping fertilizer in the open, near the railroad station, and allowing it to

[38] Economic Aspects of Soviet Agriculture, p. 32.
[39] S.S.S.R. v Tsifrakh, p. 182.

deteriorate. The U.S. soil and water use exchange group, which visited the Soviet Union in the summer of 1958 comments in its report:

The physical quality of mineral fertilizers in the U.S.S.R. is poor by our standards. The use of unmixed goods results in high expenditures of time on farms in handling, mixing, and application.

Fertilizer-application methods generally are crude, and there seems to be a lack of precision fertilizer-application machinery. On the other hand, airplanes are used extensively for broadcasting solid fertilizers, and the anhydrous ammonia applicators appear to be comparable to ours.

Decisions supplant extension education in obtaining widespread adoption of fertilizer practices on farms. This insures rapid adoption of practices but magnifies errors of judgment and prolongs poor practices that otherwise would soon be discontinued.

It should also be borne in mind that, while the use of commercial fertilizer has been increasing, Soviet authorities were seriously concerned in recent years about a decline, or inadequate use, of manure in the northern and central regions of the U.S.S.R. with their podzolic soils. The very low yields of grains and other crops in the podzolic soil area was attributed largely to the unsatisfactory manure situation.

Chapter 9. Planning and Management

Not only in the case of state farms, machine-tractor stations, and repair-technical stations, but also with respect to collective peasant agriculture, the Soviet Government has largely taken over the function of planning and management, which formerly devolved on decisions of numerous independent farmers. The Government now makes many decisions on crops to be planted and livestock raised; assembling of seed; sowing and harvesting practices; supply and use of farm machinery; manure, and commercial fertilizer; crop rotation; capital investment; proper care of livestock; provision of adequate fodder; and other details of farming with which the Government formerly did not concern itself directly.

During the Stalin era, agricultural planning and direction were highly centralized. Plans and targets for many details of farm operations were laid down for different regions in Moscow and on their basis goals were established by local authorities for each collective farm. By 1955, however, the Kremlin finally became convinced that detailed rigid planning of agriculture from the top stifled initiative on the farm and was detrimental to efficiency. Khrushchev and other Soviet spokesmen now severely criticized the old planning methods. One practice particularly, aroused their ire; namely the widespread adoption of a crop rotations scheme in which perennial grasses played an important part. This crop rotation was recommended primarily as a soil improving practice, by a soil scientist named Williams who came to exercise a great deal of influence with the Communist Party leadership during the Stalin regime. It was adopted, not only in humid regions for which it was suitable and where it had been, in fact, long practiced, but also in subhumid regions where it only aggravated the difficult animal feed supply problem by displacement of other forage crops.

This incident highlights a striking peculiarity of Soviet agricultural policymaking and planning—the wholesale introduction by decree of innovations. It makes possible such accomplishments as expansion of the crop acreage in the course of 4 years by 90 million acres and rapid consolidation of the numerous noncontiguous strips of land into large fields adopted for modern power farming. But such planning from above also often leads to costly mistakes; sometimes, because the practice or measure introduced is based on unsound or obsolete principles and often, because of indiscriminate, general application of practices, suitable under certain conditions, but not under others. Since open criticism of principles is taboo in the U.S.S.R., once a certain line of policy is officially laid down, it often takes considerable time before such mistakes are corrected by an official reversal. Such was the case with crop rotation. A more recent example of indiscriminate application is the so-called double stage or windrowing method of grain harvesting, taken over from North America, which speeds the cutting of grain. It is very useful in regions with a short harvest season, like Siberia, often characterized at such times by inclement weather. But in the U.S.S.R. again all regions are urged to adopt this practice; those in which it is essential and those in which it is not necessary.

A good example of pushing a practice, which in the United States is considered largely obsolete, is checkrowing of crops. And for an illustration of the introduction of unsound pseudoscientific practices we must turn to the activity of the notorious opponent of Mendelian genetics and, for a time, under Stalin, a virtual dictator of Soviet biological and agricultural sciences, Lysenko. Although Lysenko's influence on research in biological and agricultural sciences declined considerably after Stalin's death, his star apparently is rising again. The Soviet Botanical Journal, which had vigorously criticized Lysenko and his methods, was curbed and had to change its tone.[40]

Khrushchev's dissatisfaction with highly centralized agricultural planning led to a move toward its decentralization. The decree of March 9, 1955, assigned responsibility for detailed production planning of crops and livestock to collective farms themselves. Central planning was to be confined to the setting of the delivery quotas for farm products and the volume of work to be performed by the MTS. With the liquidation of the latter, this task now also devolves on the collectives. However, the 1955 decree has given to local authorities (including then the MTS) certain responsibilities in farm planning supervision with the result that these agencies often usurped the planning functions of collectives.

National goals, or drives, like the corn growing drive or the campaign to "overtake the United States in per capita milk and meat output" often result also in intervention by authorities with collectives. It is inconceivable, for instance, that a collective in a cotton growing region could shift to raising other crops at the expense of cotton. Again a collective would probably have to give a very good reason for not growing corn (maize) in view of the strong advocacy of that crop by Khrushchev. In planning its livestock production the management of a collective is expected to set high targets of output per 100 hectares of land. For milk and all meat it is tillable land, meadows and pastures; but for pork a special target must be set per 100 hectares of tillable land only. The goal for the output of eggs is per 100 hectares of the sown area of all grain.

---

[40] Among some of the recent evidence of Lysenko's "comeback" is the appearance in Pravda of Dec. 14, 1958, of an unsigned lengthy article entitled "Concerning the Agrobiological Science and the False Position of the Botanical Journal," criticizing the Soviet and Western critics of Lysenko * * *. Subsequently considerable prominence was given to the attack of Lysenko himself on the Biological Department of the Academy of Science at the meeting of the Central Committee of the Communist Party (Pravda, Dec. 18, 1958).

It should also be remembered that for most agricultural products there exist two sets of prices: those fixed by the Government at which it buys farm products, and the usually higher free market prices. (Cotton is an example of a commodity for which there is no free market price since the whole output has to be sold to the Government.) Thus the managers of collectives are confronted by a multiciplity of yardsticks and pressures which makes proper planning difficult.

The pivotal role of the collective farm manager (chairman) and his assistants in the success of collectives, or lack of it, has been long recognized by the Soviet Government. The importance of the managerial function has been enhanced with the enlargement of the farm enterprise. But finding efficient and reliable managers poses a problem which the regime, apparently, has not been able to solve to its satisfaction, despite several campaigns to shift qualified and reliable party personnel and specialists from the cities to the farms, and notwithstanding the large number of agricultural specialists trained by colleges and vocational schools. In his speech at a meeting of the central committee of the Communist Party on June 29, 1959, Khrushchev again complained that party organs in a number of places, despite their large personnel—

cannot select good chairmen [managers] for the backward collectives. The result is as the proverb has it: "With 7 nurses in attendance—the child still manages to lose an eye." And what does it mean to select a good chairman of a collective, good brigadiers [foremen]? It means success of the enterprise * * *. Why is it that collective and state farms do not organize their work as well as factory personnel? Because some collectives have been headed by poor chairmen for long stretches at a time; some have brought as many as three collectives to ruin and are looking toward a fourth * * *. And the party organizations put up but a weak fight against such an evil * * *.

On the other side, there had been complaints of frequent turnover and irresponsible removal of managers of collective farms. The managerial problem apparently continues to be a serious one.

Chapter 10. The Battle for Grain; Wheat and Corn

Special Government programs, aiming at increasing the output of important commodities, have been characteristic of Soviet agricultural policy, both during the Stalin and post-Stalin periods. Such programs consist, as a rule, of a varying combination of increased economic incentives, higher targets for supply to collective and state farms of machinery, fertilizer, etc., and direct orders to local authorities and to collective and state farms, prescribing production targets and improvements in farm practices and management. Two of such programs, initiated by Khrushchev, have been of far-reaching significance; namely, the expansion of small-grain production, principally of wheat, and an increase in corngrowing. Together they constitute the latest phase in the "battle for grain" which the Soviet regime has waged throughout its history.

The importance of grain in the Russian economy cannot be exaggerated. It predominates in the caloric intake of the population, which is growing at the rate of over 3 million a year. Increasing quantities of grain are also needed as livestock feed, to assure the large increases in output of dairy products and meat called for by the Government.

Grain production during the postwar period, however, failed to keep pace with increased requirements. During the Stalin era this was obscured from public view, as was pointed out earlier, by the misleading huge "biological" estimates of the crops standing in the fields and not stored in the barn. A considerably larger production, of course, was desired by the Stalin administration (of which Khrushchev was an important member). It was one of the goals of the last Stalin 5-year plan, 1950–55. The total grain area, however, during the years 1951–53 of 263 to 265 million acres was below the prewar area of 273 million acres (1940), though the wheat acreage was above prewar and trending upward. Thus the steeply increased grain production target for 1955 was to be accomplished predominantly through increased yields per acre. The increase was expected to result from a combination of measures for a putative improvement of agricultural technique, such as soil-improving rotation with perennial grasses mentioned above, tree shelterbelts, irrigation of 15 million acres in the subhumid regions of European U.S.S.R., the whole array known as the great Stalin plan for reconstruction of nature.

The post-Stalin administration largely abandoned, or deflated, the great Stalin plan for reconstruction of nature, some aspects of which, like the universal crop-rotation scheme with grasses, appeared questionable, while others, like the irrigation program, were considered too costly. Under Khrushchev's leadership, the Kremlin returned to the traditional Russian pattern of increasing agricultural production extensively by expanding acreage. To pursue this the Soviet Government turned eastward, where there were still considerable tracts of long uncultivated, or virgin, lands.

Acreage extension, paralleling settlement of these eastern regions—which are to Russia what the West was to the United States in the last century—has been proceeding since the 1890's. But never before has the extension occurred at so rapid a rate. In the 3 years, 1954–56, 90 million acres were plowed up with the aid of tractor power and added to the Soviet crop area, mainly the spring wheat area. This acreage is almost equal to the combined arable land of France, Western Germany, and the United Kingdom—an achievement which should not be underestimated. However, most of this new acreage is in a zone of unfavorable climatic conditions. It is characterized by severe winters, a short growing season accompanied all too often by devastating droughts, and frequently a rainy and cold harvesting season. It is, therefore, a zone of hazardous agriculture, suited mainly to spring crops and characterized by sharply fluctuating yields. This is shown by data for Kazakhstan, one of the main areas where the new development took place. (See table 9.)

Even with low average yields, the multiplier of the large additional acreage is bound to result in a substantial increase of production, though one may be skeptical whether it is low-cost production as the Soviets claim. Since the eastern regions are relatively sparsely settled there is proportionately more grain available in good years above local requirements than in the older, more densely populated regions. This factor, and the prevalence of large state farms, facilitates the task of Government collections. Again, the extension of the acreage in the east provides a kind of insurance against mediocre crops in other regions of the country, as illustrated by the situation in 1959, when a considerable part of the new lands area was not affected by a drought or affected less seriously than most of the other important agricultural regions.

On the other side of the ledger is the fact of further considerable extension of Soviet agriculture into the precarious climatic zone of marginal or submarginal land. It is well recognized in Soviet agricultural circles that, in order to prevent dust bowl conditions and disastrous crop failures, a part of the acreage in these new land regions, perhaps a fifth or more should be annually rotated as summer fallow, a practice which has been little followed so far. To replace this acreage, additional new land must be brought under cultivation if the cropped acreage is to be maintained. Thus the maintenance of the acreage at its present level presents a problem. But so long as the huge wheat acreage is maintained, with correspondingly large harvests, especially in years of good weather, Soviet wheat exports pose the threat of increased competition on the world markets.[41]

The program for corn expansion is aimed directly at remedying the shortage of feed, which had been largely responsible for the weakness of the Soviet livestock sector. Khrushchev saw in corn a panacea for the unsatisfactory feed situation and he began to push strongly for a huge expansion of the corn acreage. In this he was admittedly influenced by the example of successful cultivation of corn as a major fodder crop in the United States.

Prior to 1955, corn acreage in the Soviet Union was small, varying between 9 and 12 million acres. By contrast there were planted 20 to 26 million acres of barley and 38 to 40 million acres of oats. Yields of corn per acre were about 14 to 17 bushels, or less than half of those in the United States. Climatic conditions in the Soviet Union do not favor corn growing beyond a limited southern area. In the rest of the country it is either too cold or too dry for successful corn culture. Nevertheless, the Khrushchev program in 1955 set a goal of not less than 70 million acres under corn by 1960, or nearly a sevenfold increase compared with 1954.[42] It was realized that this would involve considerable extension of corn cultivation into regions where the growing season was too short for the grain to mature. Consequently, a much larger proportion of corn was to be used as silage in the Soviet Union than in the United States.

This crash program was undertaken in the face of climatic obstacles and without adequate preparation, without proper varieties, machinery, fertilizer, and significant incentives to the farmers. It met only with limited success. It is true that the corn acreage increased from less than 11 million acres in 1954 to 59 million in 1956. But this was, so far, the high water mark and during the 2 succeeding years less than 50 million acres were planted to corn. This is still a fivefold increase and corn is now grown in many regions where it had not been known before. But Khrushchev himself was scornful of the results in 1958, a generally good crop year, with respect to more than half of this acreage from which corn was either harvested for

[41] For further discussion of this program, see: Volin, Lazar, "The New Battle for Grain in Soviet Russia," Foreign Agriculture, November 1954, pp. 194–199; Harris, Chauncey D., "Soviet Agricultural Resources Reappraised," Journal of Farm Economics, 38, pp. 258–273; W. A. D. Jackson, "The Virgin and Idle Lands of Western Siberia and Northern Kazakhstan: A Geographical Appraisal," Geographical Review, 46, pp. 1–19, 1956.

[42] Direktivy KPSS i Sovetskogo Pravitel'stva po Khozyaistvennym voprosam, vol. 4, p. 335.

silage before the ears were formed (30 percent of acreage) or was reported as having been used for green forage (29 percent of acreage). The latter is a euphemism, according to Khrushchev, for "the lost corn crop." Yet Khrushchev's enthusiasm for corn as "the queen of the fields" has remained unabated, despite some cautionary remarks, which he makes from time to time. Incidentally, he strongly recommended corngrowing to Polish farmers during his visit to Poland in the summer of 1959. However, the excessive concentration on corn has probably increased the Soviet feed supply to a lesser degree than it might have been with a more balanced program.

TABLE 1.—*Area sown to crops in selected years, Soviet Union* [1]

[Million acres]

Crop	1940 [2]	1945 [2]	1950	1951	1952	1953	1954	1955	1956	1957	1958 [3]
Wheat:											
Winter	35.34	22.24	30.89	38.55	42.50	43.98	38.79	45.22	31.88	------	------
Spring	64.25	39.29	64.25	67.71	71.91	75.37	83.03	104.28	121.33	------	------
Total	99.59	61.53	95.14	106.26	114.41	119.35	121.82	149.50	153.21	170.75	165.06
Rye, winter	57.08	50.16	58.32	59.06	56.34	50.16	50.66	47.20	45.47	44.73	43.74
Corn grown [4] for grain	8.9	10.38	11.86	10.13	9.64	8.65	10.63	22.49	22.98	14.33	20.02
Other [5]	------	------	------	------	------	------	------	21.74	36.08	30.89	28.66
Total	8.9	10.38	11.86	10.13	9.64	8.65	10.63	44.23	59.06	45.22	48.68
Barley	27.92	25.70	21.25	20.02	21.25	23.72	26.44	24.46	29.40	22.73	23.72
Oats	49.91	35.58	40.03	43.0	41.02	37.81	39.29	36.57	37.31	34.59	36.32
Rice	.49	.49	.25	.25	.25	.25	.25	.25	.25	------	------
Buckwheat	4.94	4.45	7.41	6.67	6.18	6.42	6.92	6.92	6.67	------	------
Millet	14.83	14.58	9.39	8.15	8.65	10.13	13.59	19.03	15.81	------	------
Grain legumes	5.93	3.71	4.94	4.20	3.95	3.95	4.45	3.46	3.21	------	------
Other grain	3.46	4.20	5.68	5.19	3.56	3.21	2.97	2.47	2.72	------	------
Total grain	273.05	210.78	254.27	262.93	265.25	263.65	277.02	[6] 312.35	[6] 317.03	[6] 307.89	[6] 309.37
Potatoes	19.03	20.51	21.25	20.76	20.26	20.51	21.50	22.49	22.73	24.22	23.47
Vegetables	5.68	5.68	4.69	4.69	4.69	4.94	5.68	5.68	5.93	3.71	3.71
Sugar beets	3.04	2.05	3.24	3.43	3.61	3.88	3.95	4.35	4.97	5.21	6.23
Sunflowers	8.75	7.24	8.87	8.92	9.07	9.64	9.96	10.48	11.14	8.55	9.74
Cotton	5.14	2.99	5.73	6.72	6.99	4.65	5.44	5.44	5.11	5.16	5.29
Flax for fiber	5.19	2.47	4.69	3.95	3.78	3.06	2.74	3.66	4.74	4.18	3.95
Flax for seed	.86	.47	.89	.82	.94	1.14	1.09	1.04	1.16		
Hemp	1.48	.69	1.38	1.41	1.33	1.26	1.43	1.46	1.53	1.14	.99
Tobacco	.25	.20	.25	.25	.27	.27	.30	.27	.27	------	------
Makhorka	.27	.27	.27	.27	.27	.27	.25	.22	.20	------	------
Forage crops [7]	44.73	25.20	51.15	58.56	63.33	70.92	77.10	66.47	66.96	112.18	114.00
Other crops	4.18	2.64	4.82	5.36	5.09	4.25	4.00	3.48	3.24	------	------
Total crops	371.65	281.19	361.50	378.07	384.88	388.44	410.46	459.13	481.09	478.63	483.08

[1] Data from official sources. Exclusive of winterkilled grain not resown in the spring.
[2] Figures for territory within the boundaries existing in that year.
[3] Preliminary.
[4] Includes some immature corn grown for silage and converted to dry-grain equivalent.
[5] Included with grain until 1955.
[6] Excludes corn not grown for grain.
[7] Includes some corn grown for silage and green fodder.

TABLE 2.—*Acreage and production of selected crops, United States and the Soviet Union, 1958*

Crop	United States		U.S.S.R.	
	Acreage	Production	Acreage	Production
	Million acres	*Million bushels*	*Million acres*	*Million bushels*
Wheat	53.6	1,462.0	165.0	2,300.0
Rye	1.8	32.0	43.5	650.0
Barley	14.9	470.0	23.5	440.0
Oats	31.8	1,422.0	36.0	890.0
Corn	73.5	3,800.0	[1] 20.1	[2] 600.0
Grain sorghum	16.8	615.0	(3)	(3)
Soybeans	23.8	574.0	(3)	(3)
		Million bales		*Million bales*
Cotton	11.8	11.5	5.3	6.9
		Million short tons		*Million short tons*
Sugar beets	0.9	15.2	5.9	46.0
Sunflower seed	(3)	(3)	9.7	5.0
		Million hundred-weight		*Million hundred-weight*
Potatoes	1.5	266.0	23.5	1,898.0

[1] In addition nearly 29,000,000 acres of corn harvested for silage and fodder.
[2] Including some corn harvested in the milky stage for silage.
[3] Not available. USDA estimates and official figures.

TABLE 3.—*Livestock numbers in the United States and Soviet Union, selected years*

[In millions]

Year January	All cattle		Hogs		Sheep	
	United States	U.S.S.R.[1]	United States	U.S.S.R.[1]	United States	U.S.S.R.
1928	57.3	66.8	61.9	27.7	45.3	----------
1953	94.2	56.6	51.8	28.5	31.9	94.3
1958	93.4	66.8	51.0	44.3	31.3	120.2
1959	96.9	70.8	57.2	48.5	32.6	129.6

[1] Figures for the territory within present boundaries. Official sources.

TABLE 4.—*Livestock numbers in the Soviet Union by kinds of farms, Jan. 1, 1958*

[Million head]

Item	Collective farms	State farms	Other	Total
All cattle	29.2	8.0	29.5	66.7
Cows	10.7	2.8	17.9	31.4
Hogs	20.0	9.0	15.3	44.3
Sheep	70.0	24.0	26.1	120.1

Official sources.

TABLE 5.—*Labor requirements for crops and livestock products in the United States and the Soviet Union*

Item	U.S.S.R.[2] (Man-hours per centner)			Percent U.S.S.R. is of U.S.A.	
	U.S.A.[1]	State farms	Collective farms	State farms	Collective farms
Grain	1.0	1.8	7.3	180	730
Potatoes	1.0	4.2	5.1	420	510
Sugar beets	.5	2.1	3.1	420	620
Seed cotton	18.8	29.8	42.8	159	228
Milk	4.7	9.9	14.7	211	313
Cattle, liveweight gain	7.9	52.0	112.0	658	1,418
Hogs, liveweight gain	6.3	43.0	103.0	683	1,635

[1] In 1956.
[2] Average for 1956–57.

Source: Khrushchev's report of Dec. 15, 1958.

TABLE 6.—*Percentage distribution of collective farms by sown area, Soviet Union and selected regions, 1956* [1]

Sown area	All U.S.S.R.	North-western	Northern Caucasus	Western Siberia
500 hectares (1,236 acres) and under	17.8	64.2	22.6	5.4
501 to 1,000 hectares (1,238 to 2,471 acres)	24.7	25.9	6.7	5.8
1,001 to 2,000 hectares (2,473 to 4,942 acres)	29.0	9.3	7.5	17.9
2,001 to 5,000 hectares (4,944 to 12,355 acres)	22.5	.6	28.3	46.5
Over 5,000 hectares (12,355 acres)	6.0	----------	34.9	24.4
Total	100.0	100.0	100.0	100.0

[1] Source: Narodnoe Khoziaistvo SSSR v 1956 Godu, p. 143.

TABLE 7.—*Percentage distribution of collective farms by number of households, U.S.S.R. and selected regions, 1956* [1]

Number of households	All U.S.S.R.	North-western	Northern Caucasus	Western Siberia
100 and under	19.0	61.6	9.2	17.3
101 to 200	34.3	33.2	24.4	44.4
201 to 300	20.7	4.4	20.6	25.0
301 to 500	17.6	.7	18.9	12.3
Over 500	8.4	.1	26.9	1.0
Total	100.0	100.0	100.0	100.0

[1] Source: Narodnoe Khoziaistvo SSSR v 1956 Godu, p. 142.

TABLE 8.—*Government payments to collective farms and individuals for farm products acquired, selected years* [1]

Year:	*Billion rubles*
1952	31.3
1953	41.4
1955	64.0
1956	88.5
1957	96.7

[1] Including payments by government controlled cooperatives.

Source: SSSR v Tsifrakh, p. 187.

TABLE 9.—*Yields of all grains in Kazakhstan, selected years*

	Centners per hectare [1]	Bushels of 60 pounds per hectare
1954	9.1	13.5
1955	2.9	4.3
1956	10.6	15.8
1957	4.6	6.8
1958	(2)	(2)

[1] 1 centner= 1/10th of a metric ton or 220.46 pounds.
[2] Reported as more than 9 centners, or more than 13.4 bushels.

Source: Plenum Tsentral'nogo Komiteta Kommunisticheskoi Partii Sovetskogo Soiuza 15–19 dekabrya 1959. Stenograficheskii otchet, p. 101.

LEVELS OF LIVING AND INCENTIVES IN THE SOVIET AND UNITED STATES ECONOMIES

LEVELS OF LIVING, WAGES AND PRICES IN THE SOVIET AND UNITED STATES ECONOMIES

(By Lynn Turgeon, Hofstra College)

INTRODUCTION

In the study of Soviet economic growth prepared for the Joint Economic Committee in 1957, a rather thorough evaluation was made of Soviet and United States levels of living in 1955, as well as changes in consumption between 1928 and 1955.[1] Since I find myself in general agreement with these earlier findings, I shall concentrate my attention on developments in Soviet levels of living since 1955, including projected changes in the current 7-year plan.

As the earlier report makes clear, the measurement and evaluation of international levels of living is a complex and difficult task, particularly when the consumption patterns of the nations involved differ significantly. It seems equally clear that recent and projected developments in the Soviet economy have tended to accentuate rather than reduce these methodological difficulties.

Generally speaking, the area of communal consumption—principally the free health and educational services, as well as the partially subsidized consumption of housing—seems to be expanding at a faster rate than the sector producing goods and services with price tags that more or less ration their supply. Direct taxes are being reduced and transfer payments (pensions and grants) are being liberalized. As a consequence, ordinary measures of real wage changes taking account of only the movements in price and money wage levels tend to understate the real improvement in Soviet levels of living.

To the degree that similar developments are not forthcoming in the United States, comparisons of price and wage levels in the two countries are also tilted in our favor. In an attempt to circumvent some of these difficulties, the major portion of this report will consist of an exercise designed to give greater meaning to Soviet prices relative to our own.

Finally, some consideration will be made of the potentialities for improving the Soviet level of living as well as the possibility that the Russians might achieve something comparable to our way of living.

RECENT AND PROJECTED DEVELOPMENTS IN SOVIET LEVELS OF LIVING

Each year a potential develops for raising levels of living in the Soviet Union. The two principal factors most directly responsible for this potential are the increase in the labor force employed in food processing and so-called light industries generally, and, coupled with

[1] Legislative Reference Service of the Library of Congress, "Soviet Economic Growth: A Comparison With the United States," U.S. Government Printing Office, Washington, 1957, pp. 107-123.

this, the increase in output per worker in these branches. Indirectly, levels of living also depend on the ability of Soviet agriculture and other industries to supply the food processing and light industrial sectors with the capital plant and equipment, raw materials, fuel and power required. In addition, a number of relatively minor factors may also influence levels of living in the Soviet Union: Changes in the available produce on the collective farm markets; the impact of Soviet foreign trade on domestic supplies of consumer goods; and Government policies with regard to inventory accumulation or stockpiling of consumer goods.

Some recent, though incomplete, data on changes in the labor force and output per worker in industry generally, as well as in food processing and light industries, are presented in table I.[2] If we discount for a certain amount of possible unrepresentativeness in the Soviet labor force data divulged, as well as some possible upward bias in the Soviet labor productivity claims,[3] we might reasonably expect an average annual increase in the labor force of between 2 and 3 percent and a 4 to 5 percent increase in labor productivity in these sectors producing consumer goods. This would suggest that the potential average annual increment in the output of goods available for Soviet consumers might be expected to run roughly from 6 to 8 percent. All of these estimates are slightly below the rates of expansion for Soviet industry generally.

Taking population growth into account, it would seem that the potential per capita increase in consumption might be running around 5 percent annually. In recent years, there may have been a tendency for Soviet collective farmers to raise their much lower levels of living at a somewhat faster rate than urban inhabitants. As a consequence, urban consumption levels may be rising by slightly less than 5 percent annually.

TABLE I.—*Series reflecting changes in levels of living in the U.S.S.R., 1955–65* [1]

Series	Year						
	1955	1956	1957	1958	1959	1960 plan [2]	1965 plan [3]
(1)	(2)	(3)	(4)	(5)	(6)	(7)	(8)
1. Labor productivity (as percent of previous or indicated year):							
(*a*) All industry	108	107	106.5	106	108	150	145–150
(*b*) Light industries	[4] 106	([5])	104	106	105	[6] 135	([5])
(*c*) Food processing	[4] 105	([5])	106	103	111	([5])	([5])
2. Labor force:							
(*a*) Workers and employees in industrial labor force by end of year (millions)	47.9	50.0	52.1	53.5	55.3	55.0	+66
(*b*) As percent of previous or indicated year	102.4	104.4	104.2	102.7	103.4	114.8	123.4
(*c*) Workers in light industries (millions)	([5])	[7] 2.349	[7] 2.425	([5])	([5])	([5])	([5])
(*d*) As percent of previous or indicated year	([5])	([5])	103.2	([5])	([5])	[6] 117.0	([5])

See footnotes at end of table, p. 321.

[2] During plan V (1951–55), in contrast to more recent years, expansion in light industries was apparently somewhat greater than it was in food processing. In 1950, workers in light industry constituted 15.9 percent of the labor force, while by 1955, they had risen to 17 percent. Workers in food processing fell from 10 to 9.1 percent of the total during the same period. According to official Soviet labor productivity claims, output per worker in both light industries and in food processing in 1955 was 36 percent above the 1950 level. See Tsentral'noe statisticheskoe upravlenie pri sovete ministrov S.S.S.R., Promyshlennost' S.S.S.R.—statisticheskii sbornik (Industry of the U.S.S.R.—Statistical Handbook), Gosstatizdat, Moscow, 1957, pp. 24, 27.

[3] At present, this latter bias is thought to be less important than in earlier periods, since 1955 rather than 1926–27 "constant ruble" prices are now being employed in output valuations.

TABLE I.—*Series reflecting changes in levels of living in the U.S.S.R., 1955–65* [1]—Con.

Series	Year						
	1955	1956	1957	1958	1959	1960 plan [2]	1965 plan [3]
(1)	(2)	(3)	(4)	(5)	(6)	(7)	(8)
2. Labor:							
(e) Workers in food processing (millions)	(5)	[7] 1.563	[7] 1.641	(5)	(5)	(5)	(5)
(f) As percent of previous or indicated year	(5)	(5)	105.0	(5)	(5)	(5)	(5)
3. Savings:							
(a) Total savings, bank deposits (billion rubles)	[8] 53.7	63.7	80.6	+87	94.0	(5)	(5)
(b) Increase in bank deposits (billion rubles)	5	10	16.8	7	7	(5)	(5)
4. Transfer payments and communal consumption:							
(a) Pensions (billion rubles)	[9] 30.1	36.5	57.9	[10] 62.9	[10] 67.5	(5)	(5)
(b) Total transfer payments and communal consumption (billion rubles)	[11] 154	169	[11] 202	[11] 215	232.0	210.0	345
(c) As percent of previous or indicated year	105	110	119	106	108	136	160
5. Average workweek (hours)	[12] 47.2	[2] 47	[12] 45	[12] 44	(5)	[12] 42	−40
6. Money wages (as percentage of previous or indicated year)	[13] 101.2	103	[13] 104	[13] 104	(5)	(5)	126
7. Real income (as percentage of previous or indicated year)	[13] 103	[13] 103.6	[13] 107	[13] 105	(5)	130	140
8. State and cooperative trade:							
(a) Total sales (billion rubles)	502	547	[11] 617.3	[11] 668.5	727	750	[11] 1,030
(b) As percentage of previous or indicated year	104	109	113	108	109	15	157–162
9. Housing:							
(a) Total construction excluding collective farm housing (million square meters)	35	36	48	68	77	205	650–660
(b) As percent of previous year	108	103	133	142	113	-------	-------

Notes to table I:

[1] Unless otherwise indicated, the data for the following years are obtained from the following sources:

1955: Pravda, Jan. 31, 1956.

1956: Pravda, Jan. 31, 1957.

1957: Pravda, Jan. 28, 1958.

1958: Pravda, Jan. 16, 1959; Pravda, July 24, 1958. The labor productivity claims for light industries and food processing refer to the first 6 months of the year compared with the first 6 months of 1957.

1959: Pravda, July 14, 1959. Data are estimated on basis of achievement in the first 6 months of the year compared with the first 6 months of 1958.

1960 (plan): Direktivy XX S"ezda KPSS po shestomu piatiletnemu planu razvitiia narodnogo khoziaistva S.S.S.R. na 1956-60 gody (Directives of the 20th Congress of the Communist Party of the Soviet Union on the 6th 5-Year Plan for the Development of the National Economy of the U.S.S.R. from 1956 to 1960), Izdatel'stvo Pravda, Moscow. 1956.

1965 (plan): "Control Figures for the Economic Development of the U.S.S.R., 1959–65," Foreign Languages Publishing House, Moscow, 1958.

[2] 1955=100.

[3] 1958=100.

[4] Tsentral'noe statisticheskoe upravlenie pri sovete ministrov S.S.S.R., "Promyshlennost' S.S.S.R.—statisticheskii sbornik" (Industry of the U.S.S.R., Statistical Handbook, Gosstatizdat, Moscow, 1957, p. 27.

[5] Not available.

[6] Editorial, "Proizvoditel' nost' truda v shestoi piariletke" (Labor Productivity in plan VI), "Legkaia Promyshlennost'," No. 7, 1956, p. 1. The increase in the labor force is estimated from the planned increase in output and in labor productivity.

[7] Tsentral'noe statisticheskoe upravelenie pri sovete ministrov S.S.S.R., "S.S.S.R. v tsifrakh—statisticheskii sbornik" (The U.S.S.R. in Figures—Statistical Handbook), Gosstatizdat, Moscow, 1958, p. 59.

[8] Tsentral'noe statisticheskoe upravlenie pri sovete ministrov S.S.S.R., Narodnoe khoziaistvo S.S.S.R. v 1956 godu—statisticheskii ezhegodnik (National Economy of the U.S.S.R. in 1956—Statistical Yearbook), Gosstatizdat, Moscow, 1957, p. 282.

[9] V. Lavrov, "The Soviet Budget," Foreign Languages Publishing House, Moscow, 1959, p. 47.

[10] Pravda, Dec. 23, 1958, p. 3.

[11] Vestnik Statistiki, No. 5, 1959, p. 90.

[12] United Nations, "World Economic Survey, 1957, New York," 1958, p. 129; "Economic Survey of Europe in 1958," Geneva, 1959, ch. I, pp. 6, 11. Although the increases for 1955, 1957, and 1958 are presented as increases in real wages, they are believed to refer to increases in real income.

[13] S. Figurnov, "Formy povysheniia real'noi zarabotnoi platy v S.S.S.R." (Forms of Real Wage Increases in the U.S.S.R.), "Sotsialisticheskii Trud," No. 5, 1959, p. 52.

Between 1947 and 1954 the Soviet Government pursued a somewhat unorthodox policy with respect to distributing the annual gains to consumers. The average annual increase in money wages amounted to a little over 2 percent per annum,[4] but substantial additional benefits were being provided to all consumers as a result of annual price reductions of considerable magnitude. By the time of the last of these annual price cuts in April 1954, the Russians claimed that the price index for all consumer goods stood at 43, taking the fourth quarter of 1947 as a base of 100. The corresponding food price index was 38; the index for other than food items stood at 53.

Since 1955 there seems to have been a definite change in the previous policy of passing on the gains to all consumers indiscriminately via the massive price cuts. Instead, selective corrections of existing wage and income inequities have been effected. The price level has been virtually stable, although a slight increase of about 2 percent in the consumer price index may have occurred in 1958 as the Government tood steps to reduce alcoholism and the black marketing of automobiles, which were being sold in Government outlets at prices which failed to ration effectively the existing relatively small supply.[5]

This does not mean that there have been no further price reductions since 1954, but rather that the cuts have been insignificant with respect to their effect on the general price level. In 1956 there were price reductions on clothing and other items for children, some fabrics, aluminum kitchenware, radios and radio equipment. In 1957 price reductions were made on medicines, watches, canned fish, fruits and vegetables, food concentrates, fat, pork, poultry, and smoked goods. Gains to consumers resulting from these reductions were said to be over 5 billion rubles.[6] More recently, on July 1, 1959, reductions of about 15 to 20 percent affected the prices of watches, bicycles, radios, cameras, nylons, wines, and children's toys. The Consumer savings involved were said to amount to over 6 billion rubles annually.[7]

Some idea of the relative magnitude of the price reductions which have occurred since 1954 can be obtained by comparing the above claimed savings to consumers with the savings announced in connection with the earlier massive price reductions. The previous aggregate annual savings to consumers supposedly ranged from a low of 20 billion rubles in 1954 to a high of 80 billion rubles in 1950.[8] The 20 billion rubles saving for consumers in 1954 corresponded with a 4 percent reduction in the general price level; the 80 billion rubles saving in 1950 coincided with nearly a 20-percent cut in retail prices.

The increases in money wages since 1955 have been somewhat greater than those taking place between 1948 and 1955. Although the average increase was 1.6 percent from 1951 to 1953, it averaged 3.6 percent from 1956 to 1958.[9] Part of the increase in average wages

[4] Between 1947 and 1954 average wages of workers and employees in industry grew by 22 percent; for the entire national economy, the increase was 20 percent. See S. Figurnov, "Formy povyshenila real'noi zarabotnoi platy v S.S.S.R." (Forms of Real Wage Increases in the U.S.S.R.), "Sotsialisticheskii Trud, No. 5, 1959, p. 52.

[5] See United Nations, "Economic Survey of Europe in 1958," Geneva, 1959, ch. I, p. 14. The losses to Soviet consumers as a result of the substantial increase in the prices of automobiles and motorcycles at the beginning of 1958 are difficult to estimate because the price hike may have resulted partly in a trasnfer of windfall gains from the hands of speculators into the Government treasury. Also, there were some concomitant price increases on machine-woven rugs, vodka and wines, as well as some price reductions on some models or types of TV sets, cameras, bread, jam, fish, and children's wear. See S. Figurnov, op. cit., p. 53.

[6] Pravda, Jan. 2, 1958, p. 1.

[7] Ibid., July 1, 1959, p. 2.

[8] A. G. Zverev, "Voprosy natsional'nogo dokhoda i finansy S.S.S.R." (Problems of National Income and Finance in the U.S.S.R.), Gosfinizdat, Moscow, 1958, pp. 214–215.

in 1957 occurred as a result of minimum wage legislation which raised the statutory minimum wage from 110 to 300 rubles per month and supposedly added 8 billion rubles to consumer incomes. The revision of the wage structure in a number of industries beginning in 1956 has also meant that average wages in these sectors have increased rather sharply.[10] In revising wage structures, it has apparently been much simpler as well as more palatable to raise wages selectively than it has been to lower some wages and raise others.

The great improvement in old age pensions meant approximately a doubling of pensions of all types between 1955 and 1958. At present about 5 billion rubles is being added to disposable income annually from this source. The elimination of the taxlike compulsory bond purchases in 1958 also gave many consumers the equivalent of 2 to 4 weeks of additional pay annually. It is claimed that the increase in the minimum wages, the improvement in old age pensions, and the elimination of the compulsory bond sales were giving Soviet consumers in 1958 over 60 billion rubles more disposable income than they received in 1955.[11]

Transfer payments of all types and expenditures for communal consumption have been expanding at an especially rapid rate. Judging by the data in table I, this is one of the few targets of the discarded plan VI which will be overfulfilled by a considerable margin.

There seems to have been some acceleration of the Government's housing program in the past few years. During the last 3 years, more housing has been built than during the entire 5 years of plan V.[12] But despite the fact that the original 1960 target for housing construction seems likely to be overfulfilled by a substantial margin, housing undoubtedly still remains as the single weakest aspect of the Soviet level of living.

Not all of the increases in money income have been realized in current increases in consumption. Net additions to savings bank deposits are currently running around 7 billion rubles annually. But it is interesting to note in this connection that the planned increase of 13 billion rubles in 1958 was underfulfilled by a large margin, an increase of only 7 billion rubles having been realized. This can be compared with an increase of around 17 billion rubles in 1957. Quite possibly there is some connection between this lower rate of voluntary saving and the Government's announcement that no further massive price cuts can be expected in the coming 7 years. The substantial increase in old-age pensions may have also tended to reduce the propensity to save.

Increases in personal savings may also reflect the nonavailability of desired consumer goods. For this reason, great caution must be

---

[9] S. Figurnov, op. cit., p. 52.

[10] In this connection, see Nauchno-issledovatel'skii institut truda gosudarstvennogo komitet soveta ministrov. S.S.S.R. po voprosam truda i zarabotnoi platy, Iz opyta perekhoda promyshlennykh predpriiatii na semi- i shestichasovoi rabochii, den' v 1956–58 gg. (From the Experience of the Transition of Industrial Enterprises to a 7- and 6-hour working day in 1956–58), Gospolitizdat, Moscow, 1959, pp. 23, 45, 63, 78, 93–94, and 105. The increases in average wages associated with the transition in chemicals, coal, ferrous metallurgy, and machine-building have ranged from 6 to 25 percent.

[11] See Khrushchev's speech at the anniversary session of the Ukraine Republic's Supreme Soviet in Pravda, Dec. 25, 1957. (Translated in Current Digest of the Soviet Press, vol. IX, No. 52, Feb. 5, 1958, p. 12.) In addition, some minor taxes designed to encourage marriage and childbearing were greatly reduced in 1958, which supposedly gave bachelor women and small families 6 billion rubles in extra disposable income.

[12] A total of 156 million square meters were built compared with 151.7 million square meters during plan V. See Tsentral'noe statisticheskoe upravlenie pri sovete ministrov S.S.S.R., "S.S.S.R. v tsifrakh (The U.S.S.R. in Figures)," Gosstatizdat, Moscow, 1958, p. 447. Although the quality of the recent housing constructed is very poor, this has also been true since the inception of planning, and there is apparently no recent qualitative deterioration involved.

exercised in interpreting movements in money wages and the price level as measures of real wage changes. The Soviet Government only imperfectly reflects equilibrium prices for consumer goods in their official price decrees. For example, it seems fairly clear that the 1954 consumer price reductions were too great, considering the available supplies of consumer goods. As a consequence, forced savings probably took place and personal savings accounts rose by 10 billion rubles. The following year, although the increase in average wages was only a little over 1 percent and the official consumer price level was stable, real wages probably rose to a greater extent due to the fact that a greater percentage of the money wage increase was realizable in current consumption. Consequently, the rise in savings accounts in 1955 amounted to only 5 billion rubles.

As near as one can judge, the current 7-year plan calls for something like a continuation of the policies of the past several years. Money wage increases are to be confined largely to the lower income groups, minimum monthly wages being scheduled to rise to between 400 and 450 rubles between now and 1962 and to between 500 and 600 rubles by 1965. Pensioners will also receive greater benefits, with the minimum monthly payment rising from the present 300 rubles to between 450 and 500 rubles by 1966.

Since wages on the average are to rise by only 26 percent during the 7-year period, and the wages of those in the lowest income brackets will rise by 70 to 80 percent, it seems evident that the wage increases for those in the upper income groups will be extremely modest. To compensate somewhat for the lack of increase in money wages at the medium and especially the upper income levels, the plan is to eliminate income taxes. Some price reductions in public catering establishments will also probably benefit, principally those in medium and upper income groups. The recent introduction of installment credit on items selling at prices exceeding 400 rubles will probably also tend to benefit more proportionately than those in medium and upper income brackets. Since real wages are scheduled to rise by approximately one-third on the average, some additional selective price reductions designed to reduce excess inventory accumulations may be planned along the same lines as those occurring since 1955.[13]

In addition, some of the potential for improving levels of living is being taken in the form of increased leisure. Two hours were lopped off the statutory workweek in 1956, and a number of industries have already been converted from a 46- to a 42-hour week.[14] Some difficulty may be experienced when the food and light industries convert to this shortened workweek, as they are scheduled to do by 1960. Although there has usually been an increase in man-hour productivity associated with the reduction of the workweek in the industries already affected, the rate of increase in man-year productivity has fallen substantially. This means that at the time when this reduction in the workweek takes place in the light and food processing industries, the improvement in living levels will depend heavily on any increase in the labor force in these sectors. Further reductions in the statutory minimum workweek are scheduled for the sixties, ones which, in the absence of any reduction in our workweek, are supposed to give

[13] Real incomes, including pensions and grants, will supposedly rise by 40 percent between 1958 and 1965.
[14] Coal miners are exceptional in that they are only required to work a 36-hour week at the present time

Soviet workers more voluntary leisure than any other workers in the world.

It seems clear that amny of the changes which are taking place, as well as those which are planned to improve the lot of the Soviet citizens, are not designed to affect materially the relationship between Soviet average wages and retail price levels. In general, the price level is apparently to be more or less stabilized; average wages are to be increased modestly; direct taxes are to be cut and perhaps eliminated; communal consumption and transfer payments will be systematically increased; and the statutory workweek is to be shortened. As a result of these new policies, international comparisons of wage and price levels involving the Soviet economy tend to become less meaningful.

INTERNATIONAL LEVEL OF LIVING COMPARISONS

The relationship between wage and price levels is clearly an appropriate object for study in a number of comparisons of relative well-being. In measuring real wage changes within any economy, for example, we must measure the relative changes in these two levels over a specified time period. If there has been no drastic change in the number of dependents per wage earner, the measure of real wage changes should ordinarily give us some indication of the change in the level of living. Likewise, a study of the relationship between wage and price levels in two economies as similar as those of the United States and Canada would also seem to produce meaningful results. But what happens when we attempt to compare price and wage levels for economies where the institutional differences are very considerable?

It is entirely conceivable that two economies might provide virtually identical levels of living, yet in one case the gap between the price and wage levels might be very great, while in the other the gap would necessarily be much smaller. The first of our hypothetical economies might have the following characteristics: a very high proportion of wage earners per household; heavy reliance on indirect or excise taxation; subsidization of the housing and transportation sectors; virtually free medical and dental services; and, in general, provisions for a smaller range of commodities from which consumers satisfy their other requirements. In the second hypothetical economy there might be higher dependency ratios; greater reliance on direct or income taxes; rental and transportation charges which include some substantial net income for property owners; price tags attached to the services of doctors and dentists; and a much larger range of commodities from which to choose.

With one exception—the number of breadwinners per family—Western European economies correspond more closely to the first model, while our own economy resembles the latter. The economy of the Soviet Union, as well as the economies of countries within the Soviet bloc, in addition to having all of the above institutional characteristics of many Western European economies, also has a very high proportion of households with more than one wage earner.

Most Western studies of comparative real wages or levels of living in the United States and the Soviet Union have been confined largely to a measurement of the relationship between wage and price levels in the two countries. We might first review briefly some typical approaches to the problem.

46283—59——22

In the pioneer studies of our Bureau of Labor Statistics,[15] ruble and dollar prices for various consumer goods produced in the two economies were divided by the average hourly wage to obtain the working time required to enable the purchase of a unit of the same product in the two countries. As a hypothetical example of this type of calculation, we might assume that the average hourly wage in the two countries is 2 dollars and 4 rubles, respectively. With a loaf of bread selling for 20 cents in the United States and 80 kopeks in the Soviet Union, the working time required to buy a loaf of bread would be 6 minutes in the United States and 12 minutes in the Soviet Union.

Attempts have been made more recently to compute average ruble-dollar ratios for the principal commodities and services entering into American and Russian budgets.[16] Although the most ambitious of these calculations was undertaken primarily to provide "deflators" for various components of Soviet national income, tentative comparisons were made of relative real wages in the two countries. In this type of study, the Soviet retail prices expressed in rubles are divided by the dollar prices for the same unit of consumer good or service. The individual ruble-dollar ratios are then weighted in accordance with the relative importance of the different goods and services in either an American or Russian budget in a given year, resulting in an average ruble-dollar ratio with respect to consumer goods and services generally.[17] The ratio obtained is used to convert the average monthly ruble wage in the Soviet Union into a dollar-equivalent wage, which is then compared with our own average wage.

Presumably one could also reverse the above procedure by computing a ruble-dollar ratio for the average monthly industrial wages in the two countries (roughly 800 rubles and 320 dollars), and then proceed to convert the ruble prices of Soviet consumer goods and services into dollar-equivalent prices at this roughly 2.5:1 ratio.

The above-mentioned Western studies simply measure the relationship between the wage and price levels in the two countries, and not only tend to give an inflated picture of the height of Russian prices but also, to some extent, magnify the size of the gap between the levels of living in the United States and the U.S.S.R. Furthermore, these procedures which have ordinarily been employed extensively in the past will probably to an increasing degree tend to exaggerate the relative height of Russian prices as well as the gap between the two levels of living to an even greater extent in the future, as the Soviet area of communal consumption expands relative to our own.

---

[15] See, for example, Edmund Nash, "Purchasing Power of Soviet Workers, 1953," Monthly Labor Review, July 1953, pp. 705–708. Cf., also, the earlier studies of Irving B. Kravis in ibid., November 1949, and February 1951.

[16] See Norman M. Kaplan and Eleanor S. Wainstein, "A Comparison of Soviet and American Retail Prices in 1950," Journal of Political Economy, December 1956, pp. 470–491; also, "A Note on Ruble-Dollar Comparisons," ibid., December 1957. See also a similar rube-pound sterling ratio computed by Alec Nove, "The Purchasing Power of the Soviet Ruble," Bulletin of the Oxford University Institute of Statistics, vol. 20, No. 2, 1958. To the extent that British institutions resemble to a greater extent those of the U.S.S.R., ruble-pound sterling ratios would seem to be more meaningful than those of Kaplan and Wainstein.

[17] Transportation and housing are included in the Kaplan-Wainstein computations. Although mention is made of such factors as the number of workers per family, taxation, and free health services, no precise evaluation is made of their impact on real wages or levels of living in the two countries.

A RUBLE-DOLLAR RATIO OF DISPOSABLE INCOME FOR FOOD, CLOTHING, DURABLE CONSUMER GOODS, PERSONAL CARE, AND RECREATION

The following calculations will focus on the relationship between disposable income and price levels rather than wage and price levels in the United States and the Soviet Union. A ruble-dollar ratio will be calculated for family disposable income available for the purchase of food, clothing, durable consumer goods, personal care, and recreation.[18] In other words, I believe that the meaningfulness of relative retail prices for Soviet and United States consumer goods and services can be ascertained more correctly in terms of the rubles and dollars available for these expenditures in the respective household budgets in the two economies.

In making such a comparison, we are handicapped to some extent by the relative lack of current Soviet budget data, but fortunately information is now available on budgeting in Eastern European households where the institutions affecting consumer expenditure patterns are virtually identical with those in the Soviet Union.[19]

Conceivably it might have sufficed to make this computation of family disposable income solely with respect to some sort of "average" worker or employee in the two countries. However, the computation of average family income in the Soviet Union is somewhat controversial, for reasons which will become evident presently. As a result, an additional ruble-dollar ratio for family disposable income will also be calculated with respect to subsistence workers at what we might label the "poverty level" in the two countries.

Gross family income

As a result of some comparatively recent Soviet legislation, roughly 8 million inhabitants of the Soviet Union, whose basic wages were formerly less than 300 rubles per month, had their basic wages raised to at least this legal minimum.[20] Some fairly recent labor legislation in the United States has established a minimum wage of $1 per hour for workers in industries engaged in interstate commerce.[21] On a yearly basis, this would amount to a little over $2,000. But it is well known that considerable numbers of American urban inhabitants, particularly among the nonwhite segment living in Southern States, still do not average even this minimum pay. We therefore take $2,000 as the annual subsistence wage for principal wage earners in the United States.

We assume that some chief breadwinners are included among the roughly 8 million Soviet workers whose earnings are near the subsistence basic wage. However, it seems fairly certain that no average family of four could subsist on these meager earnings. Supplementary

[18] In making my estimates of U.S. budgetary expenditures, I have relied very heavily on the advice of Prof. Doris Pullman, School of Home Economics, College of Agriculture, University of Wisconsin.

[19] See United Nations, "Economic Survey of Europe in 1958," Geneva, 1959, ch. IV.

[20] See Pravda, September 9, 1956, p. 1. The minimum wage now ranges from 300 to 350 rubles per month (in rural areas, it is as low as 270 rubles per month). The wages of these workers and employees were supposedly increased by one-third and the total cost of this increase to the Government budget in 1957 was put at about 8 billion rubles. It can be estimated that the wage increase amounted to about 1,000 rubles per subsistence worker per annum. The percentage of the labor force living at or near this subsistence level is surprisingly high. Occupations of those whose earnings are near this minimum amount might be the following: guards, maintenance personnel, firemen, messengers, domestic servants, street sweepers, and possibly some students on stipends. In addition to receiving the minimum wage, some of these individuals undoubtedly also share in bonuses distributed by the enterprise to which they are attached.

[21] It should be emphasized that the present calculation excludes those employed in agriculture. Levels of living for these persons in both countries are believed to be considerably lower than they are for urbanites. Rural inhabitants, of course, constitute a considerably lower percentage of our total population than they do in the Soviet Union.

earnings, therefore, either in the form of additional breadwinners or welfare payments from Soviet trade unions, would be required. Likewise, it seems doubtful that any U.S. urban family of four could subsist for any length of time on the assumed minimum for the principal wage earner.

In the Soviet Union, where women constitute about 45 percent of all workers and employees, and where a rather extensive system of preschool child care prevails, it seems certain that at least another member of the family would be working on a full-time basis.[22] Assuming that the additional worker also received the minimum basic wage, the subsistence level gross family income would be approximately 600 rubles per month.

In the United States, where less than one-third of the labor force are women, and where inexpensive preschool child care is to a great extent unavailable, it seems unlikely that a second full-time worker could possibly be maintained for long at the subsistence level. Instead, it is assumed that a second wage earner on the average brings in one-half of a full-time subsistence wage, as a result of part-time housework, sewing, paper routes, etc. In other words, gross family income at the margin in the United States is estimated to be $3,000 per annum, or $250 per month, compared with 600 rubles per month earned by the Soviet counterpart.[23]

The average monthly wage for urban workers and employees in the U.S.S.R. is taken to be 800 rubles.[24] Although this estimate is somewhat higher than the figure usually accepted for average wages, it should be borne in mind that rural workers are excluded, while higher paid engineers and professionals are included in this calculation. As was the case for subsistence workers, it is believed that a second full-time breadwinner would more often than not be essential for the Soviet family.

According to the findings of a recent Soviet budget study, in 1956 there were only 0.86 dependents per each worker, pensioner, or stipend recipient.[25] Between 1930 and 1935 the number of dependents per worker fell from 2.05 to 1.59 or a reduction of 22 percent; at the same time, the number of workers per family rose from 1.32 to 1.47 or by 11 percent.[26] We assume a continuation of the same inverse relationship between these variables; that is, a 1 percent increase in workers per family for each 2 percent decline in the number of dependents per worker or pensioner. Thus a 59 percent reduction in the number of dependents per worker or pensioner since 1935 would entail roughly a 30 percent increase in the number of wage earners per family. Our very tentative conclusion is that there were approximately 1.7 workers per Soviet family in 1956.[27]

[22] At present roughly 5 million children are accommodated in kindergartens, nurseries, and children's homes.

[23] We are aware that a fair number of urban families earn incomes of less than $3,000 in some years, but feel that welfare payments, dissaving, or gifts would bring total gross disposable income for all but a statistically insignificant minority up to this assumed subsistence level. In New York City, for example, one-sixth of the families on home relief in 1959 had a fully employed family head. A similar reservation would also be in order with respect to the assumed Soviet subsistence family income.

[24] See Leon M. Herman, "The Seven-Year Haul," Problems of Communism, volume VIII, No. 2, March-April 1959. Average workers' wages are scheduled to rise from 785 to 990 rubles per month between 1958 and 1965.

[25] Tsentral'noe statisticheskoe upravlenie pri sovete ministrov SSSR, Narodnoe khoziaistvo SSSR v 1956 godu—statisticheskii ezhegodnik (National Economy of the U.S.S.R. in 1956—statistical yearbook, Gosstatizdat), Moscow, 1957, p. 218.

[26] Tsentral'noe upravlenie narodno-khoziaistvennogo ucheta gosplana SSSR, Trud v SSSR-statisticheskii spravochnik (Labor in the U.S.S.R.—statistical handbook), Moscow, 1936, p. 342.

[27] In Czechoslovakia, where women constitute about 42 percent of the labor force, there were about 1.5 persons employed per household in 1956. See Statisticky obzor, No. 11, 1958, p. 503. The social and economic pressure driving women into the labor force in Czechoslovakia has probably been less due to generally higher Czech levels of living.

Because of lower skill composition, women's wages are on the average below those of men in the Soviet Union. But the average wage figure given above includes payments to both men and women. It is assumed that the typical principal wage earner on the average would earn more than 800 rubles per month; that his wife would earn less than this amount; but that their combined earnings would amount to roughly 1,400 rubles monthly.

For the average worker or employee family in the United States, a median yearly income of $5,200 was reported for nonfarm families in 1957.[28] It is possible that there may have been some decline in 1958 associated with the recession of that year, but our current median urban family income is taken to be roughly $5,200. No assumption concerning how this income was obtained need be made, but in many cases, additional income from supplementary wage earners is undoubtedly included. Gross family monthly income is thus taken to be 1,400 rubles in the Soviet Union and $435 in the United States at the level of the average worker or employee.

We now proceed to subtract from these gross family incomes some comparatively inflexible deductions and expenditures in the two budgets at both the subsistence and average income levels. These deductions and expenditures are summarized in table II.

Taxes

Our first deduction from gross family income will be direct taxes; that is, taxes other than those included in the retail prices of consumer goods. Some State and city sales taxes are levied in the United States, but principally we shall be considering income taxes withheld from pay envelopes in both countries. For the United States, we must also deduct social security taxes; in the Soviet Union, such deductions are paid out of enterprise funds as a cost of production.

TABLE II.—*Estimate of family disposable income available for food, clothing, durable consumer goods, personal care, and recreation in the United States and the U.S.S.R., 1958* [1]

	United States		U.S.S.R.	
	Subsistence family (dollars per month)	Average family (dollars per month)	Subsistence family (rubles per month)	Average family (rubles per month)
Gross family income before taxes	250	435	600	1,400
Family income after taxes	235	380	600	1,315
Less following expenditures for items other than food, clothing, durable consumer goods, personal care, and recreation:				
Shelter and household operations	70	100	40	100
Medical, dental, and child care	15	20	5	15
Transportation expenses	25	50	30	40
Insurance, contributions, savings, etc	10	30	5	40
Total deductions	120	200	80	195
Family disposable income remaining for food, clothing, durable consumer goods, personal care and recreation expenditures	115	180	520	1,120
Ruble-dollar ratio	1	1	4.5	6.2

[1] Estimates are explained in some detail in the text.

[28] Bureau of Census, U.S. Department of Commerce, Current Population Reports—Consumer Income Series, P-60, No. 30, December 1958.

At the subsistence level, no income taxes have been levied in the Soviet Union since January 1, 1957. The U.S. subsistence family with two children would pay roughly $140 per annum in Federal income and FICA (social security) taxes. This sum is increased to $180 per annum to take account of various sales and State income taxes. After these deductions, monthly family income after taxes in the two countries amounts to 600 rubles and $235 at this poverty level.

In the case of average workers or employees in the U.S.S.R., the income of each member is taxed separately at slightly progressive rates resulting in deductions of approximately 50 rubles monthly on the average wage. For the average family with 1.7 wage earners, we deduct 85 rubles for Soviet income taxes, leaving monthly family income after taxes of 1,315 rubles. The average U.S. family would pay almost $600 per annum in Federal income and social security taxes. When sales and State income taxes are considered, total taxes might amount to $55 monthly, leaving a net monthly family disposable income of $380.

Shelter and household operations

Rent is ordinarily based on the income of the principal wage earner in the Soviet Union, and along with heat, electricity, and other utilities, accounts on the average for no more than 4 to 5 percent of the family budget.[29] At the subsistence level, these expenditures would amount to certainly no more than 25 rubles, while at the average income level, they might amount to 70 rubles monthly. There are probably great variations in the quality of housing obtainable for the same rent, but on the average, available shelter is considerably less adequate in the Soviet Union than it is in the United States. At the subsistence level, however, the difference may not be too great, particularly if one considers the quantity and quality of nonwhite and/or recent immigrant subsistence workers' housing in our large cities.

Shelter in the United States, in addition to being much more plentiful, is also more expensive. Rental income in the United States, unlike the U.S.S.R., considerably exceeds the expenses connected with the maintenance, repairs, taxation, and depreciation of the property. The Soviet Government, which is the landlord in most instances, makes no net income or rent on housing; that is, the rent charged is only designed to cover the upkeep of the state property. Judging by the accounts of the upkeep on Soviet housing, rent collections are probably inadequate for even these limited purposes. At our subsistence level, rent, including fuel, is assumed to account for about 20 percent of gross disposable income or about $50 monthly. The average family, on the other hand, is assumed to spend roughly 16 percent of its disposable income for rent, which would amount to about $70 monthly.

These U.S. estimates of shelter expenditures exclude gas, water, and light, as well as a rather large number of other miscellaneous items, all of which we might lump together and classify as "household operations." In the U.S.S.R., electrical appliances are far less prevalent, and consequently such things as repairs are probably relatively unimportant as compared with our family expenditures. Telephones, paper supplies, laundry, and drycleaning expenditures would also

[29] A. G. Zverev, op. cit., p. 152.

undoubtedly be of much less relative importance in Soviet budgets, especially at the level of the average worker or employee.

In the United States, these expenditures for household operations constitute roughly 8 percent of all outlays at both income levels, while in Soviet families, they probably do not run more than 2 percent of gross disposable income. At the Soviet subsistence level, these items are assumed to account for 15 rubles monthly; at the average level, 30 rubles are deducted. In the United States, $20 and $30 are deducted respectively at subsistence and average family income levels. Our remaining disposable incomes are now 560 and 1,215 rubles and $165 and $280.

Medical, dental, and child care

Although medical and dental services are provided free of charge to all Soviet workers and employees, drugs must still be paid for by outpatients. In addition, nominal charges for all but the indigent are made for child care by the nurseries. Some doctors evidently engage in private practice in addition to their employment by the Government health system, and these expenditures might figure in the outlays of Soviet citizens in upper income brackets. But in both subsistence and average budgets, it hardly seems likely that more than 1 percent of gross family income would be spent here. It is assumed that 5 and 15 rubles monthly would suffice for our subsistence and average Soviet families, respectively.

In the United States, medical, dental, and drug expenses (including medical insurance) are probably larger percentagewise at the subsistence level than they are at higher income levels, despite the existence of inexpensive clinics and some unpaid-for medical service. At the subsistence level, it is assumed that about 6 percent of income is spent for these items, while at the average income level, only about 5 percent is so allocated.[30] In absolute terms, $15 and $20 would be spent by subsistence and average families monthly. After these deductions, 555 and 1,200 rubles remain to be spent by Soviet families, while $150 and $260 are left for the U.S. counterparts.

Transportation

Workers and employees generally are believed to live in the same area as the factory or enterprise in which they work in the Soviet Union. A good deal of worker and employee housing is built and maintained by the factory and located in its environs. Nevertheless, it is assumed that one member of both families in the U.S.S.R. used public transportation at the rate of 50 kopeks per ride, or a ruble daily. In addition, some expenses connected with the operation of bicycles or motorcycles might figure in the transportation outlays at the level of the average Soviet family. We deduct 30 rubles from the gross family income at the subsistence level and 40 rubles at the level of the average family.

Transportation is much more important in the budget of U.S. citizens, even at the subsistence level where ownership of a "beat-up jalopy" might even be possible. Ten percent of gross family income of the subsistence family, or about $25 monthly, is deducted; at the average income level, 13 percent, or $50, is assumed. Remaining disposable income amounts to 525 and 1,160 rubles, $125 and $210 respectively.

[30] See U.S. Department of Labor, "How American Buying Habits Change," U.S. Government Printing Office, Washington, 1959, p. 167.

Insurance, contributions, savings, and other miscellaneous

Although life insurance is now being sold in increasing amounts in the Soviet Union, it is believed that persons in upper income brackets must be the principal purchasers. In the United States, personal insurance (mostly industrial life insurance) expenditures might amount to around $5 monthly at the subsistence level. At the level of the average family, $20 is deducted for life insurance.

Religious and other contributions including tipping are undoubtedly more significant in the budgets of Americans than they are for Russians. Trade union dues may figure in the budgets in both countries. In the Soviet Union, 1 percent of gross monthly wages is payable in initiation fees plus 50 kopecks per 100 rubles of monthly income. In the United States, union dues might average $3 to $4 monthly.

Personal savings may be of some minor consequence at average income levels in both countries. Some voluntary bond purchases may be taking place at average income levels in the two countries, but these outlays are probably not too representative of budgets at this level. Some savings may be taking place in personal savings accounts. In the Soviet Union, it is claimed that there are about 40 million depositors. Much of this saving may be taking place in anticipation of purchases of expensive durable consumer goods. In the United States, in contrast to the Soviet Union, some purchases of common stocks might be possible at average income levels, but here again these purchases are probably not too representative of family budgets at this level.

At most, it is believed that these various items could not account for more than 5 rubles monthly at the Russian subsistence level. But for the average family, as much as 40 rubles might be so allocated monthly. In the U.S. subsistence family, $10 is allocated for these items; at the average level, $30 is assumed.

Food, clothing, durable consumer goods, personal care and recreation

The balance of disposable income available for these purposes comes to 520 and 1,120 rubles for the two Soviet families; for the American counterparts, income available for these purchases amounts to $115 and $180. In other words, while U.S. families have already disposed of over 50 percent of their initial money earnings, the Russian family units have only been required to part with 15 to 20 percent of theirs.

In the case of the U.S. families, how realistic are the calculated residual amounts? We know that food and drink accounts for about 40 percent of income at subsistence levels which would amount to roughly $95 monthly for a family of four. Less than 10 percent of subsistence family income or about $20 would then be left for clothing, consumer durables, and other miscellaneous personal expenses. It is clear that hand-me-downs would have to be the principal source of apparel and consumer durables at this level.

For the average family in the United States, food and drink would constitute about 30 percent of all income or about $115 to $120 monthly. Clothing could easily comprise a further 10 percent of all expenditures or about $40 monthly. We would then have $20 to $25 monthly remaining for personal care and recreation, or a little over 5 percent of the initial family income. It seems fairly certain that the calculated disposable income for these items is not unreasonable in view of what we know about current U.S. budgets.[31]

Such data as are available for Soviet and Eastern European budgets are presented in table III. The data indicate that food and drink must account for about 50 percent of all expenditures in Soviet budgets. Although the scattered budgetary data published for Soviet families indicate that something less than 50 percent of all income is expended for food, beverages, tobacco, and housing, these surveys are believed to cover especially favored workers employed in industries where wages and salaries are above the national average. The Soviet level of living is probably somewhere between that of Czechoslovakia and Poland, which would imply food, beverage, and tobacco expenditures of somewhere between 48 and 54 percent of the family income; that is, approximately 700 rubles monthly. For the subsistence family at least 65 percent of all income would be allocated for food or approximately 400 rubles monthly.[32] At above-average income levels, food and drink expenditures undoubtedly absorb at least 1,000 rubles monthly.[33]

Clothing expenditures are undoubtedly very important for Soviet workers and employees, partly because of the climatic conditions, but also because of the general lack of personal clothing inventories. In 1956, total sales of clothing, including shoes, were equal to about 45 percent of the total sales of food in state and cooperative outlets.[34]

TABLE III.—*Composition of personal expenditures of workers in Eastern Europe and the Soviet Union, selected years (as percent of total)*

Country	Year	Food	Food, beverages, and tobacco	Rent, heat, and light	Clothing, including footwear	Household equipment	Transportation
(1)	(2)	(3)	(4)	(5)	(6)	(7)	(8)
Bulgaria [1]	1957	40.4	44.2	4.2	15.6	4.3	2.6
Czechoslovakia [1]	1957	44.1	48.5	4.3	10.6	5.7	1.9
Eastern Germany [1]	1955	42.0	49.8	8.9	16.7	3.4	2.3
Hungary [1]	1957	(2)	48.5	7.3	17.9	7.7	(2)
Poland [1]	1957	49.2	54.1	3.9	19.5	3.9	1.1
Rumania [1]	1956	42.2	46.9	(2)	17.1	(2)	2.1
Eastern Europe [3]	1956–57	(2)	(4)	6–9	13–24	(2)	(2)
U.S.S.R. [5]	1956	(2)	46.3–49.4	(2)	(2)	(2)	(2)

1 United Nations, Economic Survey of Europe in 1958, Geneva, 1959, ch. IV, p. 18. The budgetary data for Hungary cover workers and employees. The data for Poland cover workers in coal mining, metallurgy, engineering, and textiles only.

2 Not available.

3 Voprosy Ekonomiki, No. 11, 1958, p. 127. The percentages for rent, heat, and light also include expenditures for furniture.

4 About 50.

5 Nauchno-issledovatel'skii institut truda gosudarstvennogo komiteta soveta ministrov S.S.S.R. po voprosam truda i zarabotnoi platy, Voprosy truda v S.S.S.R. (Problems of Labor in the U.S.S.R.), Gospolitizdat, Moscow, 1958, p. 393. Percentages include housing expenditures and cover workers in machine building, oil extraction, and textiles.

31 Ibid., p. 232. Estimated 1956 expenditures for these items are about the same for food and clothing and somewhat higher for personal care and recreation.

32 United Nations, op. cit., ch. IV, p. 22. In Poland, workers in the lowest income group spent 64.9 percent of their income for food and beverages.

33 One recent traveler in the Soviet Union reports that a family with considerably above average income was spending 32 rubles daily for food.

34 Tsentral'noe statisticheskoe upravlenie pri sovete ministrov S.S.S.R., Narodnoe khoziaistvo S.S.S.R. v 1956 godu—statisticheskii ezhegodnik (National Economy of the U.S.S.R. in 1956—Statistical Yearbook), Gosstatizdat, Moscow, 1957, p. 229.

Assuming that 10 percent of total food purchases were made on the collective farm markets, we can estimate that about 20 percent of total family income went for clothing, or about 275 rubles monthly at the average income level. At the subsistence level, a somewhat lower percentage might go for clothing or about 100 rubles monthly.

The average Soviet family would then have about 150 rubles remaining monthly for expenditures on durable consumer goods, personal care, or recreation.[35] Personal care and recreation services are priced fairly reasonably, so consumption of these items would probably be rather liberal. But the Soviet subsistence family would have virtually nothing left for such expenditures.

MEANINGFULNESS OF SOVIET RETAIL PRICES

Our findings indicate that for every dollar that the U.S. subsistence family has available for food, clothing, consumer durables, personal care, and recreation, the Soviet counterpart has about 4½ rubles; for every dollar the average American family has, the average Soviet family has around 6.2 rubles. One thing seems certain: inequality or the gap between subsistence and average income levels as far as the purchases of these day-to-day items is greater in the Soviet Union than it is in the United States. The average Soviet family's net disposable income for these purposes is about 2.1 times that of the subsistence family; the average American family's disposable income is only 1.6 times that of the family at the poverty level. On the other hand, the consumption of housing, medical and dental services, and transportation is more egalitarian in the Soviet Union than it is in the United States.

The meaningfulness of Russian prices for food, clothing, consumer durables, personal care, and recreation is now calculable at both income levels using the indicated ruble-dollar ratios of disposable income for these purposes: 4.5:1 for families at the subsistence level and 6.2:1 at the average income level. Obviously, the dollar-equivalent prices will be considerably lower than they would be were we to use the 2.5:1 conversion rate implicit in the calculations of Kaplan and Wainstein.

The conversion of ruble prices for representative goods and services into dollar-equivalent prices is presented in table IV. The resulting dollar-equivalent prices for different goods and services at each of the two income levels can then be compared with current prices prevailing in our markets giving U.S. families at subsistence and average income levels some idea of both the absolute and relative prices a person in their relative income position would face were he instead a Soviet citizen.[36]

It seems clear from the dollar-equivalent prices in columns (3) and (4) of table IV that the prices of practically all consumer goods and services are higher for Russians than they are for Americans. Except for rye bread, all food items are more expensive for Russian subsistence families. Potatoes, salt fish, and cabbage are only slightly higher

[35] Additional sources of income for purchasing durable consumer goods would come out of past savings referred to above.

[36] Occupational wage differentials might be somewhat different in the two economies. In both countries engineering and technical personnel would be paid above average, while unskilled workers would be found near the subsistence margin. Coal miners on the average are among the better paying industries in both economies.

and these items would undoubtedly constitute an important component of diets at this level. Fortunately, the noon meals at the factory are relatively inexpensive. A three-course meal can be obtained for the equivalent of a little over a dollar at this poverty level. Children also receive substantial meals in their nurseries.

TABLE IV.—*Conversion of Soviet prices for food, clothing, consumer durables, personal care, and recreation to dollar-equivalent prices at average and subsistence family income levels, 1958* [1]

Commodity (1)	Official Soviet price (rubles per kilogram unless otherwise indicated for food) (2)	Dollar-equivalent price, subsistence family level (dollar per pound or indicated unit) Soviet price÷4.5 (3)	Dollar-equivalent price, average family level (dollar per pound or indicated unit) Soviet price÷6.2 (4)
Food:			
Chicken	16.50	1.63	1.21
Beef (stewing)	12.00	1.20	.88
Mutton (moderate quality)	13.00	1.30	.95
Pork	19.50	1.95	1.42
Frankfurter sausage	16.50	1.63	1.21
Average fish	11.00	1.18	.80
Coarse salt fish	4.00	.40	.29
Butter	28.00	2.82	2.04
Margarine	14.00	1.41	1.02
Milk (liter or quart)	2.20	.46	.32
Eggs (10)	7.50	1.67	1.21
Sugar	10.00	1.01	.73
Ice cream cone	1.90	.42	.30
Tea	70.00	7.05	5.12
Rye bread	1.24	.12	.09
White bread	2.35	.24	.17
Potatoes	1.00	.10	.07
Cabbage	1.50– 2.00	.15– .20	.11– .15
Carrots	3.50	.35	.26
Onions	3.00– 4.00	.30– .40	.22– .29
Oranges	15.00– 20.00	1.51– 2.02	1.09– 1.46
Lemons (each)	3.50	.77	.56
Strawberries	15.00	1.51	1.09
Apples	20.00	2.02	1.46
Prunes	17.90	1.80	1.30
Cucumbers (each)	3.00	.66	.49
Beer (small bottle)	3.00– 3.50	.66– .77	.49– .56
Coffee	40.00	4.03	2.92
Cigarettes (box of 25)	2.20	.49	.36
Champagne (bottle)	30.00	6.67	4.89
Noon meal at work	5.00– 6.00	1.11– 1.33	.80– .96
Clothing:			
Cheap cotton print (meter)	6.50	1.44	1.04
Wool-mixture blanket	100.00+	22.00	16.00
Silk dress fabric (meter)	110.00– 125.00	24.00– 28.00	17.00– 21.00
Rayon-crepe fabric (meter)	57.00– 62.00	13.00– 14.00	9.00– 10.00
Cotton print dress	200.00	44.00	33.00
Wool dress	475.00	106.00	76.00
Man's overcoat	720.00	160.00	116.00
Man's all-wool suit	2,000.00	444.00	326.00
Man's wool mixture suit	700.00	156.00	112.00
Poplin shirt	50.00	11.00	8.00
Man's felt hat	69.00	15.00	11.00
Man's fur hat	63.00– 300.00	14.00– 67.00	10.00– 49.00
Wool sox	11.00	2.44	1.74
Kapron (nylon) hose	14.00– 30.00	3.11– 6.67	2.28– 4.89
Shoes (adequate)	200.00	44.00	33.00
Boy's leather shoes	85.00	19.00	14.00
Canvas shoes	27.00	6.00	4.35
Felt boots	140.00	31.00	23.00
Durable consumer goods:			
Aluminum frying pan	7.50– 8.50	1.67– 1.89	1.21– 1.30
Fountain pen	17.50	3.89	2.83

See footnotes at end of table, p. 336.

TABLE IV.—*Conversion of Soviet prices for food, clothing, consumer durables, personal care, and recreation to dollar-equivalent prices at average and subsistence family income levels, 1958* [1]—Continued

Commodity (1)	Official Soviet price (rubles per kilogram unless otherwise indicated for food) (2)	Dollar-equivalent price, subsistence family level (dollar per pound or indicated unit) Soviet price÷4.5 (3)	Dollar-equivalent price, average family level (dollar per pound or indicated unit) Soviet price÷6.2 (4)
Durable consumer goods—Continued			
Bicycle	450.00– 600.00	100.00– 133.00	73.00– 97.00
Motorcycle	4,200.00	933.00	674.00
Radio receiver (good)	400.00	89.00	64.00
Pobeda or Volga auto	30,000.00	6,667.00	4,890 00
Washing machine	2,250.00	500.00	369.00
TV (14 inch)	2,400.00	533.00	381.00
Record player	250.00– 300.00	55.00– 67.00	40.00– 49.00
Refrigerator (Zil)	2,000.00	444.00	326.00
Vacuum cleaner	425.00	94.00	68.00
Alarm clock	30.00– 50.00	7.00– 11.00	5.00– 8.00
Popular wristwatch	500.00	111.00	80.00
Family divan	1,300.00	289.00	207.00
Hi-fi radio	2,100.00	467.00	337.00
Pillows	35.00	7.78	5.65
Personal care:			
Toilet soap (bar)	2.20	.49	.36
Real leather handbag	140.00	31.00	23.00
Lipstick	4.50– 6.00	1.00– 1.33	.73– .97
Haircut	.90– 1.50	.20– .33	.15– .25
Shoeshine	1.00	.22	.16
Recreation:			
Film (roll)	5.80	1.29	.93
Football	35.00	7.78	5.65
Balalaika	40.00	8.90	6.42
Accordion	300.00–1,000.00	67.00– 222.00	49.00– 161.00
Record (12-inch long play)	7.90	1.76	1.27
Gasoline (gallon)	3.00	.67	.49
Newspaper	.20	.04	.03
Movie admission	3.00– 5.00	.67– 1.11	.49– .80
Theater seats	5.00– 25.00	1.11– 5.56	.80– 4.00
Postage (domestic)	.60	.13	10.00

[1] All dollar-equivalent prices above $10 have been rounded to nearest dollar.

At the average family income level, the Soviet citizens are faced with a set of food prices which most Americans would consider to be high but within reason. At this income level, only the prices of pork, butter, sugar, fresh fruits and vegetables, and imported products (coffee, tea, lemons, and oranges) appear to be outlandish by our standards. The price of tea appears to be particularly high, but fortunately Russians have always preferred weak tea. By a process of substituting beef or fish for pork, margarine for butter, cabbage and carrots for other fresh fruits and vegetables, the average Soviet family—particularly the workers and students who eat their noon meal in the factory or school restaurant or cafeteria—probably eat reasonably well by American standards.

Clothing is relatively much more expensive than food, even for the average Soviet family. Furthermore, styles are very passé, again by our standards. The only bright note here is found in children's apparel which sometimes sells below cost.[37] Consumer durables are not as expensive as might be imagined. Since in most cases the established prices ration a fairly limited supply (at least compared to United States per capita supplies), it seems obvious that not a

[37] There seems to be some possibility that children's apparel may be among the first items to be distributed according to Communist principles, that is, according to need.

great deal of family disposable income remains after purchases of the more essential food and clothing.

Although no effort will be made to establish the level of living in Soviet upper income groups, the relative prices and other information given above provide us with clues as to the nature of conspicuous consumption in the Soviet Union. The Soviet family with above-average income probably pampers himself with pork, butter, imported foods, eating out in restaurants, a more stylish and diversified wardrobe, including perhaps imported fabrics, and a few extra consumer durables. At very high income levels, wives may even give up their jobs unless social pressure is too great. In addition, domestic servants, private medical attention, voluntary saving, and insurance might enter into their budgetary expenditures. For the elite, automobiles, travel abroad, and country homes become attainable.

Some mention should be made of the qualitative differences in the consumer goods sold in the two countries. In the United States, we most frequently have a situation which can perhaps be best described as a buyers' market, where sellers are ever searching for potential buyers; in the Soviet Union, the reverse situation prevails chronically. There is a sellers' market with potential buyers chasing frequently unavailable commodities. As a result, despite some long-run improvement in the quality of Soviet consumer goods, our products and retail services are undoubtedly generally superior qualitywise. The range of commodities, grades, and models from which Soviet consumers are able to select is also much narrower than is the case in the United States. To some extent, this is counterbalanced by the fact that many more consumer durables are purchased on time in the United States, so that a rather substantial interest charge should be added to some of our prices. Finally, a considerable amount of food must be purchased on the collective farm markets in the U.S.S.R., where prices are ordinarily considerably higher, especially in winter when food supplies are short.

A COMPARISON OF CONSUMPTION IN THE UNITED STATES AND SOVIET ECONOMIES

It is somewhat easier to gage the meaningfulness of retail prices in the Soviet Union than it is to estimate Soviet consumption relative to our own. Since the earlier report prepared for the Joint Economic Committee compared per capita availability, consumption, or stocks of various consumer goods in the two countries, I shall suggest a somewhat different approach to the problem.

The industrial labor forces of the two countries are of approximately the same overall magnitude. Actually, the Soviet industrial labor force may be slightly larger than ours. Consequently, the relative number of workers engaged in light industry (principally textiles, apparel, and footwear) and in food processing will also indicate approximately the absolute numbers of workers employed in these sectors in the two countries. According to a very detailed analysis of the labor forces of the two countries, about the same percentage of workers are engaged in food processing in both countries, while a slightly greater percentage of Soviet workers is engaged in light industry as compared with the corresponding U.S. sectors.[38]

[38] A. David Redding, "Nonagricultural Employment in the U.S.S.R., 1928–55," unpublished Ph. D. dissertation, Columbia University, New York, 1958, pp. 162, 165, and 166.

Very roughly speaking then, the relative output per worker in the two economies will give us the relative output of these two sectors in the two countries. A recent Soviet study of comparative labor productivity in a good many sectors of both Soviet and United States industry has produced results which appear to be fairly consistent with the earlier findings of Galenson, and must therefore be taken seriously.[39] According to these Soviet claims, labor productivity in the U.S.S.R. as a percentage of the United States ranged from 17.1 percent in the production of margarine to 147.4 percent in bakery products, with an average level of labor productivity in food processing and light industry of between 50 and 65 percent of our own. According to these calculations, Soviet output per worker relative to our own is higher in the food processing and light industries, particularly the former than it is in industry as a whole. This phenomenon is explained primarily by the fact that many U.S. consumer goods sectors are less concentrated as well as more backward technologically as compared with our heavy industry.

If we assume only the lower limit of the Soviet claims, it would seem that very roughly speaking the output of their light and food processing industries could hardly be much more than roughly half of our own. Still to be considered is the fact that the Russians have 30 million extra people to feed and clothe. On the other hand, a much larger percentage of the Soviet population—those living in rural areas and growing much of their own food—do not rely on state industry for a great deal of their food. Also the Soviet Union seems to be a net importer of consumer goods, while we tend to have an export surplus in this respect.[40] Taking all of these modifying factors into account, as a first approximation, we might estimate that Soviet per capita consumption of food might be slightly more than half of our own. On the other hand, Soviet per capita consumption of clothing might be somewhat less than half of our own. But the big advantage that American consumers have over their Soviet counterparts must surely be found in the area of durable consumer goods and services.

CAN THE SOVIETS ACHIEVE THE U.S. LEVEL OF LIVING?

In terms of food and clothing, the Soviets stand the best chance of overtaking our level of living. As consumers, we tend to have reached something of a plateau with respect to our per capita consumption of food.[41] As our incomes rise, we also tend to be increasing our purchases of durable consumer goods and services generally rather than clothing. More specifically, to a great extent, we tend to have substituted the automobile and travel for additional food and clothing. The ability of the Russians to close the gap with respect to food and clothing will therefore depend primarily on their own ability to augment the labor force employed in these branches as well as their success in increasing labor productivity in these sectors.[42]

[39] A. Kats, "Proizvoditel'nost' truda v SSSR i v kapitalisticheskikh stranakh" (Labor Productivity in the U.S.S.R. and in Capitalist Countries), Sotsialisticheskii Trud, No. 1, 1959, pp. 42–55. (For a translation of this article, see the Current Digest of the Soviet Press, vol. XI, No. 32, 1959, pp. 3–8.) Cf., also, A. Aganbegian, "Dognat' i peregnat' SSHA po urovniu proizvoditel'nosti truda" (To Catch Up With and Surpass the United States in the Level of Labor Productivity), ibid., No. 4, 1959, pp. 11–22, especially p. 15.

[40] In 1956, when imports and exports virtually balanced for the Soviet Union, 24.6 percent of all exports could be classified as consumer goods compared with 27.7 percent of all imports which could be so classified.

[41] According to the U.S. Department of Agriculture, Agricultural Statistics, U.S. Government Printing Office, 1958, p. 688, the index of per capita food consumption in the United States in 1956 was still slightly below the 1946 level and only 13 percent above the 1928 level.

[42] This assumes that there is no massive import program for consumer goods.

Until 1964 at least, there will undoubtedly be certain difficulties with respect to increasing the labor force employed in these branches due primarily to the lowering of the Soviet birthrate during World War II. By scraping the bottom of the barrel, they may be able to get more work from students, older persons, and housewives than they are currently, but the prospects for a greatly expanded labor force in food processing and light industries remain rather dim, at least until the latter half of the sixties. As far as increasing labor productivity is concerned, there seems to be no increase in the relative planned investments in light and food processing industries during the coming 7 years, although the absolute amounts invested will approximately double. Some improvement in the rate of increase in output per worker may possibly be expected since diminishing returns are probably less significant in light and food processing industries than they are in the extractive industries.[43] Even a below normal rate of growth due to the labor shortage would undoubtedly mean a closing of the gap with respect to the consumption of some food products or apparel; as a result, Soviet per capita consumption of a few items—fish, woolen fabrics, butter, etc.—may equal or even exceed ours by 1965.

For the period after 1965, there are a number of important variables which could potentially affect any closing of the gap in levels of living and which make predictions at this point seem especially hazardous. Nevertheless, we might mention a number of factors which may or may not affect the achievement of something approaching our level of living by the Soviets.

By the latter half of the sixties, the normal yearly influx of new, young workers into the Soviet labor force should be resumed. Presumably at least a proportionate share of this manpower would be available for the light and food processing industries. If there should be any shift in the pattern of investment favoring light and food processing industries after 1965, the growth in the labor force employed in these sectors might even be greater than the gains for industry as a whole. Any increase in the proportion of total capital investment allocated to consumer goods industries would also presumably show up in a more rapid increase in labor productivity in these sectors.

Any reduction or elimination of Soviet occupation forces in Eastern Germany, Poland, and Hungary would also release additional labor, part of which would possibly find its way into the consumer goods sectors. Reduction in domestic defense requirements might also have a similar beneficial impact on levels of living in the U.S.S.R.

On the other hand, any extension of the Soviet sphere of influence or program of economic assistance to the underdeveloped areas of the world would tend to retard the closing of the gap in levels of living. In this connection, it has also been made clear by Premier Khrushchev that all members of the Soviet bloc will approach communism or their version of the "affluent society" at approximately the same time.[44] As a result, the rise in levels of living in Czechoslovakia and the Soviet Union will be retarded to the extent that workers and employees in

[43] As mentioned above, the reduction in the statutory workweek to 42 hours will further interfere with the ability of the Soviets to increase annual output per worker.

[44] See Pravda, Jan. 28, 1959. (Translated in the Current Digest of the Soviet Press. Mar. 11, 1959, p. 13.)

these economies are required to assist underdeveloped areas in the Soviet bloc in their industrialization and development programs.

It also seems reasonably clear that lack of effective demand should never be a retarding factor in raising the Soviet level of living, as it sometimes is in our own economy. Up until the present, the principal problem of Soviet planners has been one of restraining effective demand, and, as we have already noted, a permanent sellers market prevails. Furthermore, the Soviet Government, through its control over prices and the relationship between prices and costs, can virtually guarantee a continuation of these operating conditions if it so chooses.

A COMPARISON OF INCENTIVES IN THE ECONOMIC SYSTEMS OF THE UNITED STATES AND SOVIET RUSSIA

(By Benjamin A. Javits, president, United Shareholders of America, New York, N.Y.)

Before beginning the analysis of incentives in the United States and Russia, it must be understood that the basic differences in the ideologies of the two countries make strict parallel comparison unfeasible. It is analogous to comparing an orange to an apple or, better still, using the symbolic caricatures of the two powers, an eagle to a bear. Both subjects have features alike and dissimilar. To put a specific label on many of the categories to be used would invite a discussion of semantics. Therefore, certain latitude must be permitted the writer in definitions and examples in the ensuing discussion.

It is taken for granted that others in these hearings will point out the vast differences between the economic systems of the United States and the Soviet Union. However, I should like to submit a definition of the capitalistic system as presented by John Chamberlain in his book "The Roots of Capitalism":

> The test of an economic system lies in the choice it offers, the alternatives that are open to the people living under it. When the choices are limited by coercion of one sort or another, the system must fall short of meeting the test in greater or less degree. The virtue of a free system—i.e., competitive capitalism—is that it allows energy to flow uncoerced into a thousand-and-one different forms, expanding goods, services, and jobs in myriad, unpredictable ways. Every day, under such a system, a consumer's plebiscite (the phrase is von Mise's) is held, the vote being counted in whatever money unit is the handiest. With his votes the consumer directs production, forcing or luring energy, brains, and capital to obey his will.

Perhaps this is placing the conclusion before the discussion, but it is the writer's belief that the above description points out the ultimate ends of free capitalism, while the means can be judged in the light of the incentives toward those ends.

A human being is not a machine that can be turned off and on at will. He has certain basic desires and needs, and the system to which these will be put to benefit must utilize them with a plan of initiatives, both contrived and evolutionary. The primary drive of the human being is security. To achieve this security the individual must have the money to pay for the commodities and services that this condition requires. In the capitalistic system, either planned or free, this remuneration is earned through work. It is simple economics that the greater the degree of money that is needed (for people have many and varied goals of security) the greater the effort and skill must be put forward. In the United States, where a free and competitive economy flourishes, the employer must vie in the labor market for his employees, offering what has been called "a fair day's pay for a fair day's work." The level of remuneration is governed by minimum-wage standards, both Federal and State, and the degree of skill required. In most parts of the country, the existence of unions plays an important part in the amount of compensation. The employer will offer to labor a variety of fringe benefits, both economic and social. He will point to the prospects for advancement and permanency.

As the labor market reacts to the law of supply and demand, he will often find it necessary to bid for this employees and raise his standards of compensation during times of labor stringency, either in the particular region in which his enterprise is located, or in the specific field of endeavor dictated by job analysis. In extremely rare cases does political affiliation or Government interference have any bearing on either the wage scale or the job requirement. He may offer to train or educate his employee if the latter's particular skills are not suitable at the time of hiring. In the Soviet Union, the Government sets the wage scale and the job requirements. These are carried out by the various regional councils established by decentralization, and instituted by Khrushchev in the latest 7-year plan. In Russia, the base pay incentive is used for the purposes of production goals rather than for competitive reasons. Under the new plan, wages are being increased commensurate with long-scarce consumer products. The importance of this is pointed out in the following excerpts from the official resolution of the 21st Congress of the Communist Party of the Soviet Union:

> Provision is made for increased wages and, in particular, a substantial increase for low- and medium-paid sections of workers and office employees.
>
> The law of development of Soviet society is a continuous improvement in the people's living standards on the basis of the development of social production and the rising of labor productivity.
>
> There will be a plentiful supply for the Soviet people of high-quality and beautifully designed clothing and footwear. The people's housing conditions will be fundamentally improved by the implementation of a wide-scale housing program in towns, worker's settlements, and country districts. The production of furniture and household goods will be considerably expanded.
>
> The real income of factory and office workers per worker will rise on an average by 40 percent as a result of the increase in wages, pensions, and grants alongside the further price reductions in public catering. * * *

While wage and fringe benefit incentives are utilized by U.S. corporations for the direct purpose of profiting individual enterprise, in the Soviet Union the state benefits to its own personal profit, both in an economic sense and in their determination for advancing communism. As one of the panelists in a later hearing, Mr. Harry Schwartz of the New York Times, so ably stated it to the National Industrial Conference Board this year:

> We have to think of economic growth for them as being a kind of religious good, not something one does for material gain or profit * * *

In the United States, the fact that a high level of production and income aids the Government is almost unnoticed. The feeling of an American citizen for his country is as ingrained a part of his person as his belief in God or love of his family. For our purposes it cannot be used as an authentic contrived incentive. In Russia, on the other hand, it is uppermost in the formation and execution of the system. I shall dwell on further aspects of this later on.

In the Soviet system, wages are, for the most part, based on a piecework basis.

[The wages] are paid in accordance with a tariff system, which helps to fix wages depending on the conditions of labor and the qualification of the worker concerned, the importance of the branch of industry and enterprise and its geographical location.

The tariff system consists of three related elements: rates of tariff, which determine the level of payment per hour or day, tariff scales, which determine the correlation in payment for labor in a given branch of industry between workers of different qualifications (grades), and tariff qualification tables, which help to assign workers and work to different grades (in accordance with the complexity of the work). From "The Land of Soviets," Moscow 1957.

These wages are fixed for the required output planned for the specific job. As the worker exceeds his quota, the incentive system sets up a rising scale to compensate him for increased production. For the laborer who raises his output from 1 to 10 percent, the commensurate increase in the piece rate is 100 percent; over the 10 percent level of production, his base remuneration becomes 200 percent.

In a recent article for The Wall Street Journal, titled "Ivan's Incentives," Edmund K. Faltermayer points out the increasing importance of this wage system in referring to an interview with a Soviet toolmaker.

[His] incentive is far from ideological. Simply put, it's plain hard cash, plus a desire for self-betterment. If he consistently doubles his quota, his monthly take-home pay will reach 1,500 rubles (equivalent to about $150) instead of his regular wage of 850 rubles (Aug. 13, 1959).

Mr. Faltermayer goes on to say that "cash * * * by the use of the capitalistic piecework system is * * * what makes the wheels go round in Russia * * *" While this may, on the surface, tend to conflict with my earlier reference to the "religious" aspect of Soviet incentives, it actually points out an increasing use of this capitalistic tool rather than a diminution of the "fatherland" philosophy.

In the United States, the wage scale is more on a salary system, with piecework prominent in only a few major industries. As I have mentioned, a variety of factors other than the state accounts for the degree of cash compensation.

Another major incentive in use in both economies is the bonus. In many cases the bonus will make up the larger amount of a Russian worker's annual wages. As in the United States, it is paid out of profits. In the sense of the Soviet system, the profit is gaged by its reflection in the Government income figures. In the United States, of course, corporate profit dictates the size of the bonus. There is more of a tendency in the Russian incentives to reward an individual on a performance basis; in other words, he can assess his potential income and work toward it. In the United States, among both factory and executive employees, the amount of the annual bonus is generally a "surprise" to its recipient. It is based upon the overall profit of the corporation as well as the individual's contribution toward it.

Up to this point, we have mainly discussed the incentive system as it applies to the rough description of the working class. The managerial class of industry in both countries presents another broad phase of this subject.

In the United States, the salary increase along with the bonus, has become one of the main institutions of business. Corporations will raid one another's staff, enticing them with various incentives both financial and of the status variety. Foremen, department heads, junior executives, vice presidents, and operating executives are rewarded for individual and group effort. If the rewards do not justify their claims they will look elsewhere to offer their services, generally to a competitor. The supply-demand factor is very strong in this sector. In the Soviet Union, wages are paid and bonuses are offered under the following procedure:

Heads of enterprises, technical personnel and employees [non piecework] are paid monthly salaries fixed by the Government and which depend on the conditions and volume of work, the importance of enterprise, the complexity of the technological processes, and the qualification of the worker concerned and his length of service.

Furthermore, technical personnel and employees [salaried] of industrial enterprises receive bonuses when their enterprise fulfills or overfulfills its output plan. "The Land of Soviets," 1957. [Brackets author's.]

Recently, the incentive of competition, although not akin to that found in the United States, has cropped up in Russia. Should one auto company, says Volga, have a better quality and sales performance than Moskovitch, the former will receive a kickback in the form of a bonus for personnel from the state. Generally, management will take the lion's share of this. It stands to reason, however, that under the state control of the Russian economic system, changes will be instituted in the Moskovitch section to bring them up to par with their "competition."

One of the greatest forms of Soviet incentive is to be found in the almost lavish rewards held out to technical people. A great stress is laid upon the advancement of scientists, engineers, and physicians in the U.S.S.R. Education in this country is considered almost holy in practice. Great sums of money are poured into the educational system. Academic accomplishment is one of the outstanding efforts of the Soviet Government. High wages and impressive fringe benefits are paid to promising technical people. The incentive here is contrived not alone for the security drive, but also to the status or recognition desire. In the United States, this incentive is not nearly so profound. One might point to certain tax allowances permitted industry for research and development expenditures, but this is about as far as a national effort can be detected. Scientists and technicians are generally not well paid here, and their status symbol is not outstanding. Outside of the physician (and even here we have a problem of quantity) there is very little done in the way of outstanding reward. American educators are constantly pleading for plant and classroom laboratories to meet this Soviet challenge.

An interesting statement concerning his country's attitude toward science is made by Botanist I. Michurin:

★★★ The Communist Party and the working class have provided me with all the facilities, with all an experimenter can wish for. The dream of my life is coming true.

I don't think that we have to look any further than our newspapers for the proof that great incentives to scientists by the Soviet system have been successful.

Earlier I referred to a "religious" incentive in the Soviet system. This has taken many years to accomplish but it now functions as an integral and vital part of their economy. The Communist Party has rewarded duty to Government with wages and status. Party functionaries are alongside of industrial and technical management. Their wages and bonuses are dispensed according to their success in the ideological branch of the Soviet effort. In addition, great feats of nonproductive (in a profit sense) accomplishment are rewarded as victories for the Communist system. For example, we have the scientists who developed and launched the sputniks and the moon rocket. They are given the best available fruits of Russian society, both financial and symbolic.

One of the highest honors that can be given a productive enterprise is the "Premier's Banner," an award of achievement highly treasured by its recipients. It is reminiscent of the World War II days when the Army-Navy E was a goal of the American corporation. In today's economy, there is nothing in the United States comparable to this.

I have made reference to a status or recognition symbol. This is more or less of an intangible as it relates to both societies on a comparison basis. The United States is virtually deluged with the status symbol; we can almost expect a new one by the day. Yet here, the incentive is built into the economy. The auto, the second auto, the boat, the television set, the color television set, the country club, the better country club—take your pick. The reward is to a degree set out by industry, but an individual generally creates his incentive on a social basis and carries it out as a result of his earning power. It can be put, and rather roughly at that, that status in the United States must be bought; that it has a price tag. In Russia, however, the status incentive is one of accomplishment and service to the state. The automobile, for example, is given to all executive and managerial personnel. And, ludicrous as it may seem, an individual awarded such a status may not refuse it. If he or she does, it is almost considered a crime against the state. The country club equivalent is found in the factory that has constantly exceeded its quota. The state will build recreational facilities for such outstanding effort.

A joint status and money incentive shared by the people of both nations is the expense account. This is a surprising demonstration of a capitalistic practice at work in the Soviet Union. A recent order was issued by the Government of the Soviet Union entitled "The Introduction of Order and the Abolition of High Living on the Expense Account." According to Mr. Faltermayer's report, "* * * despite recent crackdowns, abuses of this type seem to be chronic."

At this point, I believe that it should be evident that the Soviet reliance on the status initiative to so great an extent is due to the lack of consumer goods available to the wage earners. This also explains quite a bit of the "religious" category. Since Mr. Khrushchev succeeded in his battle to increase concentration on these consumer goods, the accent of incentive has been more on wages. How this continues depends to a great extent on the success of this capitalistic venture.

As far as the advancement reward is concerned, it would be unrealistic to present here the achievements of the American worker. The "rags to riches" or "Horatio Alger" story is universal and legend in this country. Let us simply say that the "opportunity for all" and the road for advancement have been witnessed by the world. Our ancestors came here for these goals, and the jury has come in a long time ago with their verdict.

In the Soviet, the incentive of advance has been difficult. There is a vast middle class, or working class—call it what you may. There simply is not enough leeway for the average Russian worker to advance. Of course, a few do get through, but the degree of affluence in Russia is minuscule to that found here. Political implications play an important part in the Russian scheme, so that a common denominator is almost impossible to apply. There exists at the top a small strata filled by the families of government luminaries and top managerial and technical personnel. The arts contribute their share as well.

There is one incentive that is paradoxical insofar as it shows a relaxation of state incentive on the one hand by the Soviet, and a continued experimentation on the other hand by the United States. It refers to the highly publicized incentive to agriculture offered by the United States at its expense for the private gain of the farmer. It guarantees certain prices to farmers based on their own costs in the amount of crop to be produced. Members of both major parties will probably agree that this has been a great failure. It narrows the free market in agriculture considerably and has become a great burden for both the Government and the taxpayer.

In the Soviet Union, the collectives have been guaranteed certain prices for their crop based upon the level of production. The determination of these prices has been increasingly left to the leaders of the collectives to decide. As in piecework, the greater the effort, the greater the reward. This area of Soviet economy is about the only one in which a free market can be found. After having sold the required crop to the Government, the members of the collectives are permitted to market the excess to the public on a supply-and-demand basis. For all practical purposes, the farm group is out of the matrix of Soviet economics. The U.S.S.R. has, of necessity, reversed its whole governmental relationship to the farmers by giving the collectives their own way almost completely.

The following incentive is of particular importance to me in my position as president of the United Shareholders of America. It was as head of this organization that I visited the Soviet Union just recently. The great American incentive of capital investment by the individual is simply unheard of in Russia. The Soviet may say that the wealth belongs to the state, and the state belongs to the people, but if any nation in the world wishes to look at a true "people's capitalism" they can look only to those nations under the free capitalistic system—and specifically to the United States. Regardless of what position he holds, the American can invest his savings in whatever direction his interests may dictate. A machine-tool maker can invest in his own shop, or, if he so desires, he may buy shares in Chicago Pneumatic Tool Co. The auto worker on a Ford assemly line may decide to set up his own repair shop, or, if he wishes, he may become an investor and part owner of his own employer through the purchase of stock. He may participate in a broader form of American industry by purchasing shares in a mutual fund, or else he may subscribe to the monthly investment plan of the New York Stock Exchange.

The Government of the United States offers tax advantages to industry to expand through capital investment. Rapid depreciation, interest cost deduction, and depletion and amortization are all incentives toward this objective. These are opportunities built in through years of toil, defended by life, nurtured through depression, which must never be vitiated if we are to continue our rights of self-determination. United Shareholders are dedicated to the preservation and broadening of this system in America. We urge that our allies and friends among nations institute private investment through all the means at their disposal. Only through this system will the aims and progress and freedom be gained.

In summation, the incentive systems of the subject countries, while alike in many instances, aim toward different philosophies. In Russia, we see that control of many by a few is the ultimate goal. Coercion, rather than freedom, is the underlying instrument of growth. Wages, security, recognition—all are given by the state for the state. In the United States, the reqards are geared to the individual for the individual. Perhaps we have been too lax in our feelings toward nationalism and freedom in certain instances. If that be the case, then these hearings should alert the Government as the servants of the people toward action through legislation, to insure our freedoms to our children and the future generations.

I should like to acknowledge the research contribution of Mr. Robert B. Ritter. In addition, the utilization of the following printed matter: The Wall Street Journal articles by Edmund K. Faltermayer; the New York Times articles by Harry Schwartz; the National Industrial Conference Board Studies on U.S.S.R., "The Roots of Capitalism" by John Chamberlain; "The Land of Soviets" (Moscow, 1957); "The Official Resolution of the 21st Congress of the Communist Party of the Soviet Union."

MANAGERIAL INCENTIVES AND DECISIONMAKING: A COMPARISON OF THE UNITED STATES AND THE SOVIET UNION

(By Joseph S. Berliner, Syracuse University)

Summary

The rewards in income and prestige in the United States and Soviet economies are such that a larger proportion of the best young people in the U.S.S.R. turn to careers in heavy industry, science, and higher education, whereas in the United States a larger proportion of the best talent flows into such fields as heavy or light (consumer goods) industry, finance, commerce and trade, law, medicine, etc. Higher education, particularly technical, is more of a prerequisite for the attainment of a top business career in the Soviet Union than in the United States.

The principal managerial incentive in Soviet industry is the bonus paid for overfulfillment of plan targets. The incentive system is successful in the sense that it elicits a high level of managerial effort and performance. But it has the unintended consequence of causing managers to engage in a wide variety of practices that are contrary to the interests of the state. Managers systematically conceal their true production capacity from the planners, produce unplanned types of products, and falsify the volume and quality of production. In the procurement of materials and supplies they tend to order larger quantities than they need, hoard scarce materials, and employ unauthorized special agents who use influence and gifts to ease management's procurement problems. The incentive system causes managers to shy away from innovations that upset the smooth working of the firm.

Since American managers operate in a different economic environment, their problems and therefore their practices differ from those of Soviet managers. But in those aspects of economic life in which the U.S. economy approximates the operating conditions of the Soviet economy, American managers develop forms of behavior similar to those of Soviet managers. The separation of management and ownership characteristic of the modern corporation leads to conflicts of interest between managers and stockholder-owners, and management's pursuit of its own interest leads to activities similar to those of the Soviet manager striving to defend his interests against those of the owner-state. The spread of legislation constricting the freedom of operation of the American firm leads to the evasion of laws and regulations characteristic of the Soviet economy, though on a larger scale there. Finally, under wartime conditions the burgeoning of Government controls and the dominant role of the Government as customer alters the operating conditions of the U.S. economy in such ways that it closely approximates some of the normal operating conditions of the Soviet economy. The change is accompanied by black-market operations, hoarding, quality deterioration, and the use of influence, practices which are normal in the peacetime Soviet economy.

Chapter 1. Managerial Incentives and Recruitment

The most important decision a manager has to make is made before he ever becomes a manager; namely, the decision to prepare for a managerial career. The factors influencing this decision are of vital importance for our industrial society. Imagine the consequences if no one aspired to become a manager, or if young people chose management only as a last resort, or if other careers were so attractive that management got only the last pickings of each year's crop of youngsters. It might therefore be appropriate to begin with some reflections on the incentives that the United States and the U.S.S.R. offer their young people to choose a managerial career rather than some other.

The factors motivating young people to choose one or another occupation are probably not vastly different in the two countries. Family tradition is often decisive; many a youngster chooses a career simply because he wishes to be like his father (or mother). Special talents such as those of the artist, or early conceived deep interests, like the boy who must be a scientist, account for the career choices of some others. But most teenagers have no clear idea of what they would like to be. It is with respect to these youths that it is most interesting to speculate upon the incentive-pulls that the two systems offer for the choice of one career or another.

EDUCATION AND CAREER CHOICE

The role of higher education in career choice is different in the two nations. Higher education is very much more of a prerequisite for the prestigeful and high income occupations in the U.S.S.R. than in the United States. To be sure, the person with a high school education or less has an increasingly difficult time entering the managerial ladder of the large American corporation. But in such fields as trade, commerce, construction and in small business in general, the opportunities are still vast for a financially successful career. College, and education in general, is not of decisive importance. And the brute fact is that a college diploma can always be obtained somewhere in the United States, with very little effort or ability, by just about anyone who can pay the tuition and write a semiliterate paragraph. Those who don't aspire to a managerial position or who fail to make the grade can, as workingmen, nevertheless enjoy a standard of living that is the the envy of the world. The point is that the young American who is not inclined toward academic work need not feel that he is out of the competition for our society's best rewards.

This is not true in the U.S.S.R. A number of conversations with young Soviet people have convinced me that to be "worker" is something devoutly to be shunned by most young people who have reached the high school level. There are at least two reasons for this attitude, which seems so anomalous in a "worker's state." The first is the enormously high prestige that Russian (and European) culture has always placed upon the "intelligent," the learned man, the man who works with his mind instead of his hands. The Soviet regime has striven hard to make manual labor respectable, and it undoubtedly has succeeded in endowing the worker with a social position relatively much higher than before the revolution. But the young person who has reached the educational level at which he can choose between being a worker or an "intelligent" would, other things being equal, choose the latter without question.

Other things are not equal, however. In particular, the income possibilities of a worker are far smaller than those of a college graduate, and this is the second reason for the desperate, and sometimes pathetic, drive for a higher education. Of course, a person must have reached the high school level before he can even begin to think about choosing between the career of a worker or an "intelligent." The steady annual expansion in the high school population has had the effect of presenting ever-increasing numbers of young people with the choice, and few of them would freely choose to be workers. If the expansion of the school population had continued, giving more and more young people the opportunity to avoid being workers, it would have raised serious problems for the recruitment of the labor force. The radical reform of the educational system by Khrushchev was undoubtedly motivated, in part, by the wish to avoid that problem.

Thus, the undesirability of a career as a worker has intensified the desire for higher education. Add to this the fact that there is no private enterprise, no small business in which a man could pull himself out of a worker's status and reach a position of prestige and income comparable to the self-made American businessman. I do not wish to state that the door is completely closed. By dint of hard work, ability, and certain other qualities, a Soviet citizen without the college diploma can from time to time rise to an important position in some economic hierarchy. But his chances are about as good as those of an equivalent person in a progressive American corporation. And the young person evaluating the importance of higher education understands this.

Finally, the Russian teenager who decides he has to get a college diploma has very few easy ways out. He can't buy his way into college, as the American student can if he has the money. There are no private colleges that can set whatever standards they wish. To be sure there are instances of bribery or influence, but they are certainly the exception. If the Soviet student wants a college diploma very badly, he has to work hard to gain admission and to be graduated. The very intensity of the drive for education, and the competition of many applicants for the limited number of admissions, permits the high schools and colleges to maintain high standards of performance. Moreover the colleges are financially independent of student tuitions: not only are there no tuitions but most of the students earn stipends. The consequence is that the typical Soviet student works harder and has to meet higher standards of performance than the typical American student. The standards are different in the two countries, of course, because of differences in the philosophy of education. But there is no doubt that study is a much more serious business for the young Soviet student than for the American.

One final note on education and incentives. The quality of the managerial (and technical) manpower of a nation depends on the proportion of the population comprising the pool from which the managers are drawn. That is, if half the population were for some reason excluded from the pool, the quality of the managers would be lower than if the whole population comprised the pool. Both nations suffer in this respect from the fact that rural educational facilities are poorer than urban, which reduces the pool of the potential college group. Since the Soviet rural population is larger percentagewise than that of the United States, and since their rural educational facilities are probably relatively worse than ours, they suffer more than we from this loss. But there are other ways in which our pool is curtailed more than the Soviet. First is the fact that the private cost of education keeps a substantial portion of our talented young people in the lower income groups out of college. I admit that this fact puzzles me. With our network of free State universities and with a fairly abundant scholarship program, I don't fully understand why any competent student who really desired it could not get a college education. It is my impression, however, that systematic studies generally show that we are losing an unfortunate number of young people to higher education for financial reasons. If this is so, we are worse off than the Soviets in this respect, for their education is absolutely free, and most students of any merit earn stipends besides. Lower income young Soviet people may nevertheless be unable to go off to college if the family needs their earnings. A young Soviet women told me, in reply to my question, that this was why she never went on to college. She is not a very good illustration of my point, however, for she went on to say that she really wasn't very smart anyhow.

The second group that is largely lost from America's pool of potential managerial manpower is the Negro and some other racial minorities. It may well be that the proportion of college graduates among some of the Soviet national minorities is smaller than for the Slavic nationalities; I have seen no data on this. But I would doubt that their loss from racial discrimination is as large as ours.

The third and largest group lost from our pool comprises exactly half our population—the female half. Sex discrimination certainly exists in the Soviet economy, probably more in management than in science and technology. But undoubtedly the female population enlarges the pool of technical and managerial manpower much more in the U.S.S.R. than in the United States. The difference in the role of women in the two countries must, I think enter into the balance I am trying to strike, but it is not a subject on which I would recommend that your committee consider writing corrective legislation. For one thing it is not perfectly clear which way sex discrimination works in the United States. Women discriminate against working about as much as jobs discriminate against women.

Let me summarize briefly this discussion of the relationship of education to career choice. Education, and particularly higher education, is more important in the U.S.S.R. than in the United States as the gateway to a prestigeful and highly remunerative career. Competition is keener for higher education, the cost of education to the individual is less, and the standards of admission and performance are higher in the U.S.S.R. Both nations lose part of the potential pool of managerial talent, the U.S.S.R. because of its large rural population, the United States because of financial burdens and racial and sex discrimination.

COMPETITION AMONG CAREERS

How does a managerial career compare with the attractiveness of other careers in the two nations? The young American not dedicated to some particular field, but motivated by a roughly equal desire for prestige and money, might select some field such as law, medicine, business, or engineering. He would decidedly not go into education or science. An equivalent young Soviet person would make a somewhat different choice. He would certainly not select law, which has been assigned a most humble role in Soviet society. Nor would he select medicine, for while the prestige is high, the income is low. On the other hand, higher education or science would be an excellent choice. The very title of "Professor" or "Scientific worker" would assure him one of the highest places of honor in the society. And an outstanding career in either of those fields would assure him an income ranking in the upper 10 percent or perhaps even 5 percent (data are hard to come by) of the population. The difference in the economic and social position of the scientist and teacher in the two countries is of fundamental importance in the matter of career recruitment.

The American who decides to choose a career in the business world has a much wider range of choice than his Soviet counterpart. A great variety of fields offer roughly equivalent rewards in prestige and incomes: advertising, accounting, finance, commerce, trade, sales, light manufacturing, heavy industry. Of all these fields, it is only the latter that would exert a great pull on the young Soviet person. For 40 years the Government and party have hammered home the central role of heavy industry, children are instilled with an admiration of technology, and heavy industry has been endowed with an aura of glamour that exceeds even our American fascination with technology. The ideological cards are stacked, in varying degree, against all other branches of the economy. In keeping with the ideology, the prestige and income possibilities in heavy industry are decidedly greater than in the other branches.

Not only will the student be attracted to heavy industry, but he is likely to choose engineering as his path of entry into whatever branch of heavy industry he selects. He would be attracted to engineering for the educational reasons discussed above. Engineering is, moreover, the most direct line of approach to a managerial career.

The Soviet engineering graduate will find his first job opportunities rather different from those of his American counterpart. If he is at the top of his class, the best offers will come from the research institutes, with top starting salaries and opportunities for graduate work. The poorer students will find lower paying jobs in industry. In the United States the situation is quite the reverse. The most successful students will be snapped up by recruiters from the large corporations, with the best starting salary offers. Some of the top students will, to be sure, spurn the attractive job offers and go on to further graduate work, but I suspect that many of those who go immediately into graduate work are the men who didn't get the good job offers. To be sure, many of the top American students who join the corporations are put immediately into research and development, but as many of them will be working on new passenger car or dishwasher design as will be working on electronic development and automation technique. The Soviet researcher is more likely to be working on the latter than the former.

The young Soviet engineer who goes into industry starts at the bottom of the managerial ladder, as chief of a production shop, or the design or maintenance departments of the enterprise. As new job opportunities develop, he faces the choice of continuing in direct production or taking one of the staff jobs in the enterprise, such as the planning department. If he stays in production proper, his career path may lead to chief engineer of an enterprise or to one of the higher economic agencies. If he moves into staff work, his career may lead to the directorship of an enterprise or of one of the higher organs. Either career leads to the pinnacle of Soviet management.

The paths that are least likely to lead to top management are finance or sales. I would guess the proportion of top management in the United States who started in such fields as finance and sales is much larger than in the U.S.S.R. There are no "colleges of business administration" in the Soviet Union. The ambitious youngster who wants to work for the top of the Soviet business world studies engineering, not personnel and marketing.

Summarizing, industry in the United States has to compete with a wide variety of other branches of economic activity for its share of the best potential managerial talent. In the U.S.S.R. the values and the rewards are concentrated in relatively fewer fields, and industry is far more attractive than most others. Science and higher education, which scarcely compete with industry in the United States, is a strong competitor of industry in the U.S.S.R. Among the various branches of industry, in the United States the light and consumer goods industries compete very effectively for both managerial and engineering talent. In the U.S.S.R. light and consumer goods industries are much less attractive than heavy industry. And finally the nature of industrial recruitment is such that technical education is much more important as part of the training of a would-be manager in the U.S.S.R. than in the United States.

My conclusion is that heavy industry, science and higher education attract, by and large, a better and more competent crop of young people in the U.S.S.R. than in the United States. Moreover, the competition for education is keener in the U.S.S.R., so that they get a more rigorously trained (trained in different ways, to be sure) corps of managerial, engineering, scientific and university personnel. On the other hand, such branches of the economy as sales, advertising, finance, trade and commerce, light industry, and law attract a much more competent group of people in the United States than in the U.S.S.R. Most of the outstanding people in these fields in the United States would, if they were Soviet citizens, have enjoyed successful careers in heavy industry, science, technology, or higher education. There is, after all, nothing startling in this conclusion. It is but another way of saying that each society gets what it pays for.

Chapter 2. Managerial Incentives and Decisionmaking

MATERIAL INCENTIVES

The incentives that attract people into management are not necessarily the same incentives that motivate managers to do their jobs and do them well. What are the goals of the manager? What are the considerations that impel him to make one decision rather than the other?

The moving force of our economic system is the pursuit of private gain. The worker chooses the higher paying job, the businessman accepts the more profitable contract, the investor buys the higher interest security. The usual exceptions must of course be made; the laws must be obeyed, public opinion may sometimes require that one decision be made rather than another, people make wrong decisions, a short-run loss may be accepted for a longer term gain. But by and large—"other things being equal," as the economist likes to say—it is private gain that determines economic decision.

The Soviets have at various times experimented with other forms of incentive, for it did not at first seem quite appropriate that a Socialist economy should stress private gain. But practicality won out over dogma, and private gain has for the last 25 years been the keystone of the managerial incentive system. To be sure, we still find references to various social incentives such as Communist enthusiasm. But we are also reminded that while enthusiasm is well and good, communism, as Lenin used to say, must be built "not directly on enthusiasm but with the aid of enthusiasm born out the great revolution; [communism must be built] on private interest, on personal incentive, on businesslike accounting." [1] Moreover, the incentive of private gain will be with us for a long time. According to the eminent labor economist E. Manevich, it will not disappear until the day of general overabundance arrives, until the differences between country and city are eliminated, and until the differences between mental and manual labor vanish.[2] We are safe in saying that for the next several decades at least, private gain will be the central economic inventive in both economic systems.

The form that material incentives take is of some importance. For the American businessman it is clearly profit. If you ask why did he take on this contract rather than that, why did he order this machine rather than that, why did he ship by truck rather than train, the answer would normally be, "because it's cheaper that way," or what comes to the same thing, "because he would make more money that way."

For the private businessman managing his own business, profit is clearly the guide to his actions. But most American business is not managed in this way. The men who actually run the firm are salaried managers, hired by the stockholders' representative body, the board of directors. The profit of the business does not belong to the manager but to the stockholder-owners. The fact is that the private interest of the manager need not necessarily coincide with that of the stockholder. In order to bring the manager's private interest into closer coincidence with that of the owners, most corporations have instituted some kind of bonus system, on the assumption that if the

[1] Voprosy ekonomiki, 1958, No. 6, p. 74.
[2] Voprosy ekonomiki, 1959, No. 1, p. 35.

manager has a direct stake in the profit of the enterprise, his decisions are more likely to be those that will earn more profit.

In fashioning an incentive system for its managers, the Soviet Government faced a problem similar to that of the American corporation. For all Soviet enterprises are run by salaried managers. If the Soviet manager's income consisted solely of his salary, it was conceivable that his private interest would not coincide at all points with the interest of the Government. Accordingly a considerable variety of supplementary bonuses are available to the managerial staff. The bonuses are designed to motivate managers to make those decisions that the Government considers to be in its own interest.

The amount of income earned in the form of bonuses is substantial. In 1947, the last year for which detailed data are available to me, the managerial personnel of the iron and steel industry earned bonuses averaging 51.4 percent of their basic income. In the food industry at the low end, the percentage was 21 percent.[3] Since these are averages, many individual managers earned considerably more than this. Bonuses of this magnitude must be a potent incentive indeed.

But incentive for what? This is surely the crucial question. For we can readily imagine an incentive which was extremely successful in motivating action, but action of an undesirable kind. The test of an incentive is therefore not only its motivating power, but the extent to which it leads to the desired kind of decision.

Before proceeding to the relationship of incentives to decision making, let me clarify the sense in which I use the term incentive. By incentive I mean that consideration which explains why one decision was made rather than another. If a young person decides to find employment in the electrical machinery industry rather than in the furniture industry, the difference in basic salaries in the two industries may well have been the decisive consideration. In this case salary is the effective incentive. But once in the job, the salary does not vary according to whether one operating decision is made rather than another. When the manager decides to put one order into production ahead of another, or to substitute one material for another, it is not his salary he is thinking about. It is usually the size of the month's bonus that will depend on the decision taken. It is in this sense that the bonus is the principal incentive in the operational decisions of the Soviet enterprise.

PRODUCTION DECISIONS

Two generations ago people debated the question of whether a Socialist economy could possibly work. History removed that question from the agenda. The last generation changed the question to whether the Soviet economy could work at all efficiently. That question has also been answered. These hearings would not otherwise be taking place. My discussion takes for granted that the Soviet economy is reasonably efficient, and that the question at issue is how efficient.

There is little doubt that the system of managerial incentives, broadly viewed, has created a corps of managers dedicated to their

[3] Documentation and further discussion of this chapter's argument may be found in the author's "Factory and Manager in the U.S.S.R." (Harvard University Press, 1957).

work and responsive to the production demands made upon them. Like their American counterparts, they are deeply involved in their work, they worry about production quotas, they demand results from their labor force. As hired managers, they are aware that if their performance is not satisfactory, there are always other persons spoiling for a chance at their jobs. I have no way of knowing whether the intensity of managerial life is greater in the U.S.S.R. than in the United States; in both countries there are variations from industry to industry. But there are two reasons why industrial life probably proceeds at a faster tempo in the U.S.S.R. than here. The first is that the absence of free trade unions makes it difficult for workers to resist pressure for intense operation. The second is that industry is under constant exhortation from Government and party for ever-increasing levels of production.

But the question as indicated above is not whether management is motivated to work hard. It is rather whether the incentive system motivates them to do what the state wishes them to do; whether, in other words, they get as much mileage out of their effort as they might get.

One of the most interesting conclusions of the study of Soviet managerial incentives is that the bonus system is directly responsible for motivating management to make a variety of decisions contrary to the intent and the interests of the state. The decisions to be described go far back in the history of the Soviet economy, and have resisted countless efforts by the Government to eliminate them. Most of them have survived the great organizational changes in industrial organization of the past several years. They are clearly deeply rooted in the soil of Soviet economic organization.

First, consider the matter of the reporting of information. In a planned economy it is vital that the central planners have as accurate information as possible about the productive capacity of enterprises. The bonus system, however, acts as a prevailing motivation for managers to understate their real production capacity. The reason is that the most important of the bonuses available to managers depends on the extent to which the production target of the enterprise is overfulfilled. If the manager honestly reports his full production capacity, and if for some reason something goes wrong in the course of the month, then he and his staff will lose that month's bonus. It is safer therefore to report a smaller capacity than really exists, in order that the production target will be kept low enough to allow for emergencies. The Russians call this "insurance" or "security." The consequence is that the planners can never be sure that their plans are based on accurate figures. The Government is aware of the problem: "This is fully understandable," writes a Soviet economist, "because the lower the plan, the greater the opportunity to fulfill and overfulfill it * * *." [4]

Because the higher state agencies cannot trust management's reporting of its productive capacity, various techniques have been fashioned for setting targets high enough to force the firms to operate as close as possible to capacity. One of these techniques is the arbitrary increase of targets over last year's production. As a prominent state planning commission economist put it, "they take as the base magnitude the level of production achieved during the pre-

[4] Voprosy ekonomiki, 1959, No. 3, p. 61, 67.

ceding period and raise it by some percentage or other."[5] Sometimes this technique helps flush out the manager's "hidden reserves," but in other cases the arbitrary increase in targets leads to impossibly high tasks. Indeed, the spirit of planning is reflected in the systematic use of high targets as a device for keeping managers working at as fast a tempo as possible. In the past targets have been set so high (deliberately, one suspects) that one-third of all enterprises failed to fulfill their annual plans. There is some evidence that in the last year or two this policy of deliberate overplanning has been modified, and we are told that in the first half of 1958 only 19 percent of all enterprises failed to fulfill their plans.[6] This still represents one out of five enterprises, and indicates that the high level of plan targets remains a dominant fact of life for the Soviet manager. The intense pace of plant operation has its distinct advantage from the state's point of view: it elicits from management a high level of effort that might not be forthcoming if the plans were set at a more modest level. But the price paid by the state is the manager's effort to defend his enterprise by concealing his full capacity.

When the target has been set, the manager's bonus depends on the success with which he fulfills it. Most of the firm's production does indeed follow the lines laid down in the plan. But when the end of the month rolls around and, as often happens, production is far short of meeting the month's target, then managers turn to a host of time-tested techniques of meeting—or seeming to meet—the targets. In certain types of production, such as metals, the target is expressed in tons; in such cases the manager might order his shops to curtail the production of relatively lightweight products (special and quality metals) and to throw more men and materials into the production of the heavier products.[7] In textile production we read that the practice of setting targets in "running meters" (that is, in measures of length, without regard to width) causes managers to overproduce narrow-width cloth and underproduce broad width.[8] In firms with a considerable variety of products, the production targets are expressed in value units—so many millions of rubles of production. In such cases managers tend to overproduce those products that have high fixed prices (all prices are fixed): they may deliberately use more expensive materials in order to drive up the value of production.[9] These are some of an endless variety of ways in which managers "violate the planned assortment of production"—to use the official expression of disapproval.

How widespread are these practices? We really don't know. From time to time individual managers are publicly excoriated for such practices, and figures are published to show how widely the planned assortment of production had been departed from. But these may well be extreme cases, and it would be unwise to generalize from them. Occasionally, however, the results of special studies are published, and they give us some idea of the magnitude of the problem. The State planning commission recently released the results of a survey of the production practices of 63 enterprises. Of the total production by these enterprises in excess of the plan targets,

[5] Voprosy ekonomiki, 1957, No. 4, p. 70.
[6] Planovoe khoziaistvo, 1958, No. 10, p. 5.
[7] Voprosy ekonomiki, 1958, No. 7. p. 51.
[8] Voprosy ekonomiki, 1959, No. 6, p. 19.
[9] Voprosy ekonomiki, 1958, No. 6, p. 129.

only 43 percent consisted of the basic products normally produced by them; 26.5 percent consisted of "products not included in the plan when it was originally confirmed," 20 percent consisted of "other production," and 7 percent consisted not of finished products but of an increase in semifabricated parts and good-in-process.[10] While these data are not precisely in the form in which we would want them, they do provide a good indication of managers' tendency to produce those products that are best from their own enterprises' point of view, rather than those products that the State would most wish to have produced.

Two other consequences of the bonus system (and the pressure of high targets) should be noted. One is the simple falsification of reported production. "Thus, for example," we read in a Soviet article, "if the plan is fulfilled 99 percent, the managerial and engineering personnel receive no bonus. But if the enterprise fulfills the plan 100 percent, they receive bonuses of from 15 to 37 percent of their salary." [11] Quite a lot of money hinges on that last percentage of production, and it is no wonder that management may succumb to the temptation to "fudge" the report a bit in order to earn the bonus. Again, the techniques of covering up for falsely reported production are myriad. To cite only one, production is "borrowed" from next month. That is, production that is expected to occur next month is reported as having been produced this mouth. If things go well next month, the "borrowed" output is "repaid"; if not the manager may get into trouble.

More serious than falsification, however, is the deterioration of the quality of production. The poor quality of much of Soviet consumer goods production is well known. In other types of production the danger of detection is greater, and quality standards are less readily violated. But the explanation of management's tendency to shave on quality is the same: the high production targets are so often not attainable, and the manager wants to keep his job. Much of the quality shaving is of a kind that is not easily detected: fewer stitches in the garment, fewer screws in the piece, greener lumber in the building, more impurities in the metal. But if the pressure is keen enough, more extreme forms of quality deterioration will be adopted.

Summarizing, the bonus system is an effective device for eliciting a high level of managerial effort, but in the context of excessively high production targets, it induces management to make certain types of decisions that are contrary to the intent of the State. The production of unplanned products, the concealment of production capacity, the falsification of reports and the deterioration of quality are the unintended consequences of the system of managerial incentives.

PROCUREMENT DECISIONS

The high level of production targets is but half the problem facing the Soviet manager. The other half is the perpetual shortage of materials and supplies. In order to get the greatest possible production from the available stocks of materials and supplies, the State employs a variety of devices to minimize the use of materials in production and inventory. Undoubtedly these devices have served to

[10] Planovoe khoziaistvo, 1958, No. 10, pp. 5–6. The study deals only with that portion of the firm's production in excess of their planned targets.

[11] Voprosy ekonomiki, 1959, No. 3, p. 67.

control wasteful use of resources, and they have also helped channel the flow of resources in the direction most desired by the State. But they have been self-defeating to some extent for they have forced managers to make certain kinds of decisions which frustrate the intent of the State.

The core of the matter is that managers simply don't trust the planning system to provide them with the supplies and materials they need in the right quantity and quality, and at the right time. The recent decentralization of industrial organization may have improved matters somewhat, but the evidence we have indicates that supply problems are still the most troublesome feature of managerial life. Moreover, the reasons are similar to those we used to read about before decentralization. For all important materials the manager must still obtain an allocation order from his home office (usually the Council of the National Economy of his district), which must in turn get the allocation order from the republican or all-union planning commission.

Thus, we still read of the "existing complicated system of obtaining allocation orders, under which every enterprise must submit detailed requisitions to Moscow a long time before the new planning quarter is to begin." [12] Because plans are not always finally set at the time the planning period is to begin, enterprises sometimes start with "advance allocations," that is, temporary allotments of resources designed to keep them operating until the final allocation orders are available.[13] Decentralization of the economy was supposed to have made it easier for neighboring enterprises to sell to each other without having to go through Moscow. But central purchasing agencies still exist, and agencies anywhere must find something to do. Thus the Chief Purchasing and Marketing Administration located in the republic capitals (Moscow, for example) still insist on being the middleman in purchase and sale contracts between enterprises, even when the latter are located in the same outlying city (such as Sverdlovsk).[14] Perhaps even more serious than the complex supply planning system is the large percentage of enterprise that regularly fail to fulfill their plans, or fulfill them by producing the wrong products or substandard products. Since the production of these enterprises constitute the planned supplies of other enterprises, the supplies of the latter are delayed or simply not available. Perhaps enough has been said to explain why "managers of enterprises did not have confidence in the possibility of getting their materials on time and having them delivered to the factory by the supply depot's trucks." [15]

What does the manager do to make sure he gets his supplies? Just as he "secures" his production plan by attempting to conceal the existence of some production capacity, so he "secures" the flow of supplies in various ways. He overorders, in the hope that if he doesn't get all he ordered, he may at least get as much as he needs. He also orders excessively large amounts of some supplies in order to be able to buy directly from the producer, instead of having to go through the maze of jobbing depots. A survey of 15 Moscow enterprises showed a 10.4 percent overordering of metals for just this reason.[16] Sometimes management's boldest efforts to obtain supplies

[12] Planovoe khoziaistvo, 1959, No. 4, p. 58.
[13] Ibid., p. 65.
[14] Voprosy ekonomiki, 1959, No. 5, p. 75.
[15] Planovoe khoziaistvo, 1959, No. 5, p. 85.
[16] Planovoe khoziaistvo, 1959, No. 5, p. 84

are unsuccessful: "* * * over 300,000 construction workers undergo work stoppages daily because of the absence of materials at the workplace." [17] In other cases their padded requisitions are accepted and they receive more than they need of some materials. The consequence is the piling up of hoards of supplies of all kinds, one of the most enduring problems of Soviet industrial organization. The Government has waged a longstanding war against hoarding. One of the weapons by which it attempts to hold hoarding within bounds is through the use of quotas of working capital; that is, for its annual production program the enterprise is allowed to keep on hand at any one time no more than so many tons of coal, so many board feet of lumber, so many rubles worth of inventory. These quotas must be negotiated between enterprise and government, and the enterprise's interest demands that they be set as high as possible. The mutual attempt at outguessing the other leads to a familiar bureaucratic game: "* * * enterprises try to 'justify' and obtain as large quotas of working capital as possible. The financial agencies, aware of this, strive on the other hand to reduce the quotas of working capital." [18] This kind of planning is hardly calculated to lead to the establishment of the optimal quotas. It is more likely that some quotas will be too large and some too small.

The most interesting of the techniques used by managers to "secure" their supply of materials is the employment of special supply expediters called tolkachi, or "pushers." The table of organization does not provide for this occupation, yet so great is the need that firms manage somehow to employ these people. The chief job of the expediter is to make sure that his enterprise gets the materials it needs and when it needs them. Accordingly he spends most of his time on the road, visiting his enterprise's suppliers, handing out little gifts here and there to assure that his orders are well-handled,[19] picking up supplies of one kind or another that his firm may be able to use or trade for other goods. Much of their activity is associated with the black market, that is, obtaining materials for which no allocation order has been issued. This may be done either by wrangling an allocation order out of a reluctant government official by one means or another, or persuading an approachable enterprise official to sell him the things he needs without an allocation order.

Some tolkachi take up permanent residence in the city in which the chief suppliers are located, and only occasionally return to their home firms for consultations. To keep the record clean, they are carried on the books as "senior buyer," or "supply agent." If they are known to be particularly adept at their jobs, they may be asked by other firms to represent them. Nothing is known of their incomes, but there is no doubt that they earn many times their base pay. And they fully earn it, both because of the vital nature of their work, and because the risks they take make them vulnerable to prosecution.

How widespread is the use of these expediters? Again, we catch only occasional hints of their prevalence. The most recent outburst against them reports that the number of tolkachi who annually visit the typical large enterprise runs into the thousands of rubles.

[17] Voprosy ekonomiki, 1957, No. 8, p. 50.
[18] Voprosy ekonomiki, 1958, No. 7, p. 120.
[19] The gifts are not always very little. An expediter sent out recently to get tires for his trucking firm, was given 62,000 rubles in cash for the trip. He spent 42,000 rubles for gifts. He is now in prison. *Izvestiia*, Apr. 4, 1959, p. 2.

These, however, are only the reported expenses. More often than not their expenses are not reported as such but are concealed under such rubics as "exchange of technical information," or "contract negotiations." Our latest informant, who is a senior investigator for the state control commission of the U.S.S.R., is of the opinion that despite continued official criticisms of the use of expediters, their number has actually been increasing. One of the reasons he adduces is interesting. In 1956, along with a wave of measures designed to give more freedom to plant managers, an order was issued relieving managers of the need to report in detail on all minor expenditures. Travel expenditures were among the items exempted. The measure had the unintended effect of encouraging the increased use of expediters.[20]

The economic effect of the use of expediters is difficult to assess. There is no doubt that they are of vital importance to individual enterprises, but from the national point of view much of their activity involves merely the transfer to one fortunate enterprise of resources that otherwise would have gone to another. Since the higher priority enterprises have less need for expediters, the chances are that the net effect of their activity is to cause more resources to flow to lower priority enterprises at the expense of higher priority ones. On the credit side, however, their wide knowledge of sources of supply, of who has what to sell, is of some importance, and they do arrange for the movement of supplies that otherwise would have lain idle in one plant while another had need for it. In short the expediter possesses a certain kind of knowledge that may be as important to economic organization as the knowledge of the engineer or the machinist. The planning system is able to direct the bulk of the nation's resources with reasonable effectiveness, but substantial quantities of materials and equipment elude the main stream of planning. How to get these resources back into the system is a problem that has exercised Soviet economists for a long time.[21]

In summary, the incentives that motivate managers to strive for the fulfillment of their production targets are the same incentives that motivate them to evade the regulations of the planning system. Because of the tightness of the supply system, which is deliberately engineered by the state, managers are compelled to defend their enterprises' position by overordering supplies, by hoarding materials and equipment, and by employing expediters whose function it is to keep the enterprise supplied with materials at all costs, legal or otherwise. The very planning system that serves to channel most of the nation's resources in directions desired by the state, serves also to misdirect a substantial volume of resources toward uses that are contrary to the wishes of the state.

INVESTMENT DECISIONS

If one were to ask what feature of the Soviet economic system accounts most of all for the rapid rate of growth, the answer would undoubtedly be the high rate of capital formation. The question at issue is whether it is as high as it might be, other things being equal. An

[20] Izvestiia, Apr. 4, 1959, p. 2.

[21] Recently there have been numerous suggestions that enterprises and economic region publish catalogs of the commodities they produce and the surplus materials and equipment they would like to sell. The expediters are rather like walking catalogs. Planovoe khoziaistvo, 1959, No. 4, pp. 64, 96.

examination of the system of managerial incentives will provide part, though by no means all, of the answer to this central question.

Management has a direct interest in obtaining new capital. It adds to productive capacity, and it is good for the record to show steady increases in production. Moreover fixed capital is provided to the enterprise as a free grant by the state, with no interest charge. The problem, therefore, has not been one of inducing management to accept more machines; it has rather been one of dissuading management from ordering too many machines. Far back in Soviet economic history one can find expressions of the problem similar to that recently uttered by Khrushchev in connection with the dissolution of the agricultural machine-tractor stations:

> The machine-tractor stations accept any machine whether they need it or not. They don't grow flax, but they take flax-growing equipment. They don't grow cabbage, but they take cabbage-planting machines. Consequently many machines are not used for years and hundreds of millions of rubles worth of state resources are frozen.[22]

The reason enterprises accept any piece of equipment they can get their hands on is similar to that discussed above in connection with materials hoarding. One can never tell when he may need just that kind of machine and not be able to obtain it. If one has a chance to get it now, order it by all means. It may come in handy some day for trading in return for something one might be able to use more readily. And above all, there is no charge for holding the equipment; there is no interest payment, and if the machine is not used there is no depreciation charge either. Hence there is everything to gain and nothing to lose by holding on to as much machinery and equipment as one can obtain.

How to induce managers to take a less cavalier view of capital has been a longstanding concern of economists. They look with some nostalgia at the effectiveness of the profit motive under capitalism in this respect. An eminent Soviet economist put it this way recently:

> In order to increase his profit as much as possible, the capitalist strives to use his equipment to the fullest extent possible, and in no case will he buy a machine that he doesn't need at the moment, since every surplus machine slows down the turnover of his capital and reduces his profit. For the same reason he strives to keep his inventories down to the very minimum and to market his finished products as quickly as possible.[23]

Recent economic literature contains a number of suggestions of ways in which Soviet managers might be induced to order only that amount of capital needed for production purposes. One of the more interesting is a proposal advanced by the author quoted above. He suggests that profit be calculated not as a ratio to total production cost (as has always been done), but as a ratio to value of invested capital. In this way the enterprise with too much idle capital will show a lower rate of profit, and profit is one of the principal indicators of overall performance. The suggestion is interesting because it proposes that return on capital be used as a criterion of performance, a rather "bourgeois" notion. It should not, however, be thought that the proposal envisages reliance on the "profit motive" as we know it. Profit is an important indicator of the efficiency of plant operation, but the firm does not "own" its profit, although it shares in the profit

[22] Planovoe khoziaistvo, 1958, No. 7, p. 121.
[23] Ibid., p. 122.

in a minor way. As a personal incentive, profit is relatively unimportant in Soviet industry, certainly by comparison with the bonus.

If the incentive system motivates managers to overorder and hoard equipment, the situation is quite the reverse with respect to technological innovation. Concern over managerial resistance to innovation is of long standing, but it has come to the fore in recent years in connection with increased emphasis on automation and modernization of plant and equipment. The reasons for managers' tendency to drag their feet in introducing new products or production techniques are well understood by Soviet economists:

> The explanation is, first of all, that the introduction of new technology involves certain risks and requires a considerable expenditure of time; secondly, after new technology has been introduced, more difficult plan targets are set and consequently there is less opportunity for fulfilling them and receiving bonuses.[24]

When a manager has a well-running plant, when the workers have learned their jobs and have become experienced in using the existing equipment, he is reluctant to upset the cart by trying something new. A new production line means trouble. Production bugs have to be eliminated, workers have to be retrained, time is lost, and spoilage is high. The chances are that plans will be underfulfilled and the precious bonuses lost, particularly in view of the tendency for plan targets to be raised to the rated capacity of the new equipment. It is courting disaster to try new things. If the old machines are wearing out, it is safer to repair or even rebuild them rather than introduce the more complicated new models. Outlays on the rebuilding of old machines often exceed the price of a new modern machine.[25]

There is another reason why managers shy away from innovation. Even if the potential gains from new technology are great, it usually takes a number of years before they are realized. But it is Soviet policy to shift managers around from plant to plant every few years. Therefore managers have a strictly short-run point of view. Why take on all the headaches of introducing a new line when one is not likely to be around to enjoy whatever benefits may eventually accrue? Capital investment policy is by its very nature a matter of long-term planning, and therefore does not commend itself to the short-run horizon of management.

How does the state combat managerial resistance to innovation? One technique is direct pressure. Pressure exerted on and by their own superiors explains much of the innovation that does occur. Enterprise managers may drag their feet for a long time, but when the direct order comes down that the new automatic line must be installed in the next 6 months, it is eventually acted upon. Pressure is also exerted through the Communist Party; if the party officials in the enterprise are under direct orders from Moscow that automation must be accelerated, they are in a position to force the manager to move faster than he otherwise might. Such pressures are important, although it must be noted in passing that both the manager's bosses and the local party people often try to shield the enterprise from such pressures. They are as dependent for their careers upon successful plan fulfillment as are the plant managers themselves.

Direct orders from above are one way of getting management to innovate. But innovation would proceed more rapidly if managers

[24] Voprosy ekonomiki, 1959, No. 1, pp. 44, 45.
[25] Voprosy eKonomiki, 1957, No. 4, p. 69.

could be made to wish to innovate, instead of waiting until they are forced into it The literature of the past few years is full of suggestions on how this can be accomplished. It is suggested, for example, that attractively high prices be set on new machines, in order to stimulate the producers of those machines to put them into production more rapidly.[26] While this measures might ease the financial strain on the innovating firm, it will not remove the risk that the production plan may be sacrificed. And production is much more vital to the success of the enterprise than finance.

More to the point are the suggestions that the bonus system be employed as an incentive for innovation. Soviet economists seem to have enormous confidence in bonuses as a device for getting management to wish to do what the State wishes them to do. But how to adapt the bonus system to this purpose is more difficult. In the course of years a variety of special bonuses have been introduced for one purpose or another, in addition to the major bonus that comes from fulfillment of the production plan. There are special bonuses available for economizing certain critical materials, for reducing the volume of goods in process, for conserving fuel, for increasing labor productivity, for keeping the plant clean, for reducing the volume of spoilage, for operating the plant without stoppages, for winning Socialist competitions, and many others.[27]

This dilution of the bonus system may actually weaken its power as an incentive. If the special bonuses are small, they will not be very effective. If they are large they may detract effort from what is, after all, the main objective of the state: fulfillment of the production plan. For it is interesting to note the evidence that the relative size of the bonus for this or that special purpose often determines the manager's decision to concentrate on this or that objective. There are two types of innovation: relatively small measures such as organizational improvements or inexpensive alterations, and the more dramatic large-scale changes in production techniques. The former are included in the overall enterprise plan each year, under the name of the plan or organizational and technical measures (Orgtekhplan). It happens that there are certain bonuses available for the design and introduction of the large-scale innovations, but none for the fulfillment of the Orgtekhplan. The consequence is that research and managerial personnel concentrate on the large items, and pay little attention to the small ones, even though the latter could result in great savings with relatively little cost and effort.[28] Thus the very potency of the bonus as an incentive militates against its use for too many special purposes which may compete with each other.

To conclude this discussion, the unreliability of the supply system and the absence of a charge for the use of capital motivates management to order more fixed capital than they need and to hoard machines and equipment. This tendency deflects a certain amount of currently produced capital goods from being put directly into production in their best uses. On the other hand, the incentive system discourages management from taking the risks associate with innovation. Direct orders from above lead to a substantial volume of

[26] Voprosy ekonomiki, 1959, No. 6, p. 16.

[27] Voprosy ekonomiki, 1959, No. 3, p. 66. Not all these types of bonus are available to the director himself, but they are available to different groups of managerial personnel.

[28] Voprosy ekonomiki, 1958, No. 2, p. 136.

innovation, and in many cases management may consider certain forms of innovation to be to their interest. The provision of special bonuses for innovation, if they were large enough to compete with the production plan bonus, might help provide an incentive for innovation, and much of the current discussion in the Soviet Union seems to point to this as the next phase.

Chapter 3. Some Comparative Observations

The preceding chapter has shown that Soviet managers are motivated to make a variety of decisions that are contrary to the interest of the state. Since the state's interest is paramount in the Soviet scheme of things, we may properly conclude that the incentive and decision making system is "relatively inefficient," or "less than perfectly efficient." Let me caution the reader once more against inferring from this that Soviet managers do not do a good iob. They do. There is no doubt that their system works well. If I have chosen to concentrate on the "pathology" of Soviet management, the purpose was not to create the impression of ineffectiveness, but to illuminate the gap that every economy shows between the actual and the ideal.

A comparison of Soviet and American management will help drive the point home. No one doubts that American management does a good job. But it would be fatuous to allege that it operates with perfect efficiency. An exploration of the inevitable gap between the actual and the ideal in the case of American management will help to place the corresponding gap in the U.S.S.R. in proper perspective.

A comparison of Soviet and American management is difficult for a curious reason; namely, we don't know enough about the more intimate aspects of American managerial practice. A moment's thought will make the reason clear. The American firm is a private enterprise in the full sense of the word. Its internal affairs are no one's business but its own. No one has the right to pry except with special cause. To be sure, the laws of the land have, over the years, required enterprises to disclose more and more of their private affairs to public and governmental perusal. But large sectors of the enterprise's internal operations are protected from the eyes of curious outsiders.

One of the most striking differences in the conduct of American and Soviet management is precisely in this matter of privacy. The Soviet enterprise is a public enterprise in the fullest sense of the word. It has no right to conceal its operations from any officially recognized agent of the state. And a great range of such agents have been deliberately endowed by the state with the obligation of keeping close watch on management and disclosing any irregularities or sources of inefficiency that come to their attention. These agents include the "home office" of the firm (the regional economic council, or formerly the ministry), the state bank, the local governmental body, the central government's State Control Commission, the Finance Department (the tax collector), the local Communist Party boss and his staff, the party secretary of the enterprise itself, and indeed just about anyone in the enterprise who enjoys the extracurricular activity of attending meetings to discuss the affairs of the enterprise (the aktiv).

If we can imagine an American business executive suddenly placed in charge of a Soviet firm, it is this public character of the enterprise which above all would drive him to distraction. It means that any government official can at any time demand to examine any aspect of the firm's operations he wishes to, that at any time he can be called on the carpet by the local party boss to explain a charge made by an irate customer, that any member of his staff (perhaps bucking for his job) can write a letter to Pravda exposing him for having made an irregular deal on some supplies, that any scatterbrained worker who wants to "get his picture in the papers" can rise at a public meeting that the director is obliged to attend, and compel the director to explain why he hasn't yet installed the new assembly line. The point is that the results of this authorized prying often finds its way into the published Soviet economic and political literature, which gives us an insight into the more intimate operations of the Soviet firm that we cannot have in the case of the American firm. But in view of this committee's expressed interest in comparisons of the United States and Soviet economies, I have attempted certain comparisons below which appear to be highly suggestive.

MANAGERS AND OWNERS

The original form of modern business organization was the small firm in which the owner was also the manager. The owner-manager was responsible to no one but himself for his business decisions, and his interest as manager could not conflict with his interest as owner. The development of the modern giant corporation, however, had led to that separation of management and ownership first elaborated in the work of Berle and Means.[29] Under the new conditions the private interests of the hired managers (and the controlling group) need no longer coincide at all points with the interests of the stockholder-owners. This is precisely the relationship between the hired Soviet manager and the owner-state.

Berle and Means concluded from their study that "the controlling group, even if they own a large block of stock, can serve their own pockets better by profiting at the expense of the company than by making profits for it." [30] This is precisely what Soviet managers do when they produce unplanned commodities that are advantageous to their firms but not to the State, when they overorder and hoard commodities, and when they resist innovation. Because of the differences between the two economic systems, we should expect that the precise forms that the owner-manager conflict takes would be different in the U.S.S.R. and the United States. In the United States they are to be found in such decisions as the awarding of subcontracts, the accounting of profit in such way as to benefit the claims of the controlling group, the awarding of bonuses and other benefits to management, and in dividend payment policy. As in the Soviet enterprise, the accountant is of crucial importance in handling the books of the enterprise in such way as make the best possible case for the manager; it is he, for example, who figures out the best way to distract the state's attention from the large expenditures on talkachi.

[29] Berle, Adolph A., Jr., and Gardiner C. Means, "The Modern Corporation and Private Property" (New York: Macmillan) 1945.
[30] Ibid., p. 122.

The accounting techniques are, of course, different in the United States; they involve "the charging or the failure to deduct depreciation; charging to capital expenses which properly should be charged against income account; including nonrecurrent profits as income though their real place is in surplus; and the creation of 'hidden reserves.' " [31]

A major difference between the Soviet firm and the American firm is that in the last analysis profit remains the criterion of managerial performance in the latter, whereas the Soviet manager is evaluated by a number of criteria that are sometimes mutually exclusive. Both systems have attempted to bring managerial interests into harmony with owner interests by some sort of profit-sharing system. In the Soviet case, it is clear that profit plays a very minor role, compared with bonuses, as a managerial incentive. In the United States the manager shares directly in profit to a very limited extent, and often follows other goals in his decisions. "The executive not infrequently tends to look upon the stockholders as outsiders whose complaints and demand for dividends are necessary evils * * *" concluded one American student of management.[32] In like fashion the Soviet manager often begins to feel like the "boss" and resents the intrusion into "his" affairs of the state, which after all is the owner. I have described above some of the ways in which the Soviet manager promotes the interest of "his" enterprise by means contrary to the interests of the owner-state. In the American corporation the forms are somewhat different. "* * * profits are reinvested in the business for the sake of bigness and to protect the company, and the interests of the stockholders may be given second place to the business leader's conception of what is best for the firm itself." Executives manifest a "general unwillingness to liquidate unsuccessful enterprises" and thus put themselves out of jobs, however consistent liquidation might be with the interests of the stockholders.[33] The dramatic growth of corporate self-financing in recent years has strengthened the power of management to expand their own enterprises without having to go through the "test of the marketplace" for capital.

It was observed earlier that the desire for "security" and for what the Russians call a "quiet life" motivates a wide variety of managerial decisions such as concealing production capacity and resisting technological innovation that might rock the boat. Students of American management have also noted the change from the adventurous business tycoons of earlier days to a more professionalized managerial climate in which "greater emphasis is placed on education, training, and a scientific approach, and less on rugged, venturesome, and frequently heedless individualism. The desire for security seems to have increased, and the concomitant of a growing emphasis on security is a diminishing desire for adventure for its own sake." [34] There is indeed a remarkable parallel to this development in the change in the character of Soviet managers. There would have been a great affinity between the industrial empire builders of 19th century America and the Soviet directors of the first two decades of the Soviet regime.

---

[31] Ibid., pp. 202-203, 335.
[32] Gordon, Robert A., "Business Leadership in the Large Corporation" (Washington: Brookings) 1945 p. 309.
[33] Ibid., p. 309.
[34] Ibid., p. 311.

Those directors were often men of little education who came out of the romantic conflict of revolution, who dreamed great dreams of building an industrial nation and who created an ethos of bold plans and adventurous undertakings. The old Commissar of Heavy Industry, Sergei Ordzhonikidze, would have understood the spirit of the ironmonger, Andrew Carnegie, and the man who built the great ZIL automotive works (now named after him) had the drives and the dreams of the bicycle mechanic Henry Ford.

Time, and Stalin's purges, removed most of those oldtimers and their place has now been taken by Soviet-educated young men born not of revolution but of bureaucracy. Organizations seem to develop "organization men" types, whether the organization happen to be communist or capitalist. An American reporter visiting with a group of Communist intellectuals reports that one of them had badgered him with questions about David Reisman's book, "The Lonely Crowd." "The Communist had read Reisman's book and had been fascinated by it—not, he said, because of its application to life in the United States but because of what he maintained was its extraordinary relevance to the present conditions of life in the Soviet Union." [35] It is not, on reflection, very surprising that the job of running an industrial bureaucracy should place a common stamp on men of otherwise different backgrounds. The same would probably apply to the running of a large city or a large university.

MANAGERS AND THE LAWS

We have found that the Soviet manager is often compelled to evade regulations or even break laws. Part of the explanation is simply that there are so many laws. If a Chicago manufacturer fails to ship an order to a New York firm, and ships it instead to another Chicago firm, he has nothing to fear but the ire of the New York firm. But if a Kiev manufacturer fails to ship an order to a Moscow firm and ships it instead to another Kiev firm, he has injured a state enterprise and is subject to administrative action, a fine, or even criminal prosecution. If an American firm sells a substandard generator, he may lose money or his business. But if a Soviet firm sells a substandard generator, the director may go to prison. Thus, even if Soviet managers acted exactly as American managers do, we should expect to find more illegal or evasive activity in the Soviet Union than in the United States.

With the growing complexity of our society, more and more legislation is enacted to protect the public from potential abuses. With the growth of such legislation, managers find their activities more and more circumscribed by laws and regulations. The Soviet manager apparently treats such legislation rather lightly when it conflicts with the interests of his firm (and his career and pocketbook). How does American management react when confronted by a spreading web of restrictive legislation?

It is not easy to find out very much about American managerial practice in this respect. Unlike the Soviet press, which throws its pages open to reports of the irregular activities of managers in order to warn others, the American press is likely to shy away from this kind

[35] The New Yorker, April 6, 1955, p. 52.

of reporting. Moreover the private nature of American business keeps this sort of activity from coming to light as easily as it might in Soviet industry. Nor is it the sort of thing that businessmen are inclined to talk about very readily. If it is true that a businessman would more readily be interviewed on his private sex life than on his private business activity, then we should require the late Dr. Kinsey to help provide the answers to the extent of unlawful or quasi-lawful business activity.

Prof. E. H. Sutherland, the eminent American criminologist and sociologist, made a bold attempt to investigate the phenomenon he refers to as "white collar crime." His study is based on the decisions of a limited number of courts and administrative commissions against the 70 largest industrial-type corporations in the country. In the period 1935 to 1944 these 70 corporations were convicted 585 times for such practices as restraint of trade, misrepresentation in advertising, patent and copyright infringements, unfair labor practices, granting of rebates, and a few others.[36] The average was 8.5 convictions per corporation. These data provide some idea of the extensiveness of such practices but they clearly understate the magnitude for a variety of technical reasons. Sutherland's conclusion is that "a great deal of scattered and unorganized material indicates that white collar crimes are very prevalent." [37]

The point I wish to make is that when American management finds itself in a position approximating that of Soviet management they tend to react in ways similar to those of their Soviet counterparts. Sutherland's unique study notes many aspects of American managerial practice that are astonishingly similar to those one might find in the literature on Soviet management. "These crimes are not discreet and inadvertent violations of technical regulations. They are deliberate and have a relatively consistent unity."[38] It is in precisely this way that the Soviet manager deliberately misappropriates earmarked funds or decides to shave on the quality of production. There is evidence that the Soviet manager, aware of the fact that "everybody does it" and that the investigating agencies have restricted budgets, counts on the law of averages (and his own superior shrewdness) to get away with it. So a member of Federal Trade Commission wrote that "about the only thing that keeps a businessman off the wrong end of a Federal indictment or administrative agency's complaint is the fact that, under the hit-or-miss methods of prosecution, the law of averages hasn't made him a partner to a suit," and "Samuel Insull is reported to have remarked during his trial that he had only done what all other businessmen were doing."[39]

Similarities in managerial practice are paralleled by similarities in attitude to such violations, and toward the administrative agencies enforcing the laws and regulations. The Soviet manager does not think it is "wrong" to use influence to obtain materials unlawfully, or to fudge his reports to the Government. Success is the important thing, and if you are successful you can get away with all sorts of violations. There is evidence that the Soviet manager feels contemptuous of government planners and of party hacks who try to tell him how to run his business but who themselves had "never met a payroll."

---

[36] Sutherland, Edwin H., "White Collar Crime," (New York: Dryden) 1949, p. 26.
[37] Ibid., p. 10.
[38] Ibid., p. 217.
[39] Ibid., p. 218.

Sutherland's picture of American management's attitudes contains strains of the same kind.

The businessman who violates the laws which are designed to regulate business does not customarily lose status among his business associates. Although a few members of the industry may think less of him, others admire him * * *. Businessmen customarily regard government personnel as politicians and bureaucrats, and the persons authorized to investigate business practices as "snoopers." [40]

In the first chapter of this paper, it was pointed out that a managerial career carries a great deal of prestige in the Soviet Union and attracts a large number of the better students. These youngsters have been raised in Soviet schools and have absorbed the incessant propaganda of the Communist regime. Many of them enter industry as green novices fresh from school, filled with high ideals about building the socialist fatherland and working for the common welfare. One wonders about the process by which the naive, idealistic young Komsomol member is transformed into the hard-headed manager who knows all the angles for survival in the Soviet business world. Numerous incidents such as the following provide a key to the answer. A young Soviet chemist had been assigned to the quality control department of his enterprise. He was quite pleased with himself when his test showed that a sample of production, which had previously been declared acceptable by his laboratory chief, turned out to contain an excess of phosphorus. He reported the "error" and expected to get a bonus for it. Instead, his boss obtained a new sample, gave it to an outside chemist for analysis, and submitted a report showing that the batch of production was acceptable after all. The young chemist protested, was transferred to another shop, and was finally fired on trumped-up charges.[41]

What happens to such young people? Some never quite get the point and remain ordinary engineers in the plants. Others learn to adapt themselves after a few buffetings and when they decide to play the game according to the real ground-rules, begin to rise in the managerial hierarchy.

It is interesting to note that Sutherland's interviews with American businessmen turned up accounts rather similar to that narrated above. His explanation of the process by which the naive American youngster is initiated into the business of selling used cars, settling insurance claims, covering up irregularities in clients' accounts—indeed, toning down the results of chemical analysis—helps explain the process of transformation of the young Komsomol member:

In many cases he is ordered by the manager to do things which he regards as unethical or illegal, while in other cases he learns from others who have the same rank as his own how they make a success. He learns specific techniques of violating the law, together with definitions of situations in which those techniques may be used. Also he developes a general ideology. This ideology grows in part out of the specific practices and is in the nature of generalization from concrete experiences, but in part it is transmitted as a generalization by phrases such as "we are not in business for our health," "business is business," and "no business was ever built on the beatitudes." These generalizations * * * assist the neophyte in business to accept the illegal practices and provide rationalizations for them.[42]

Summarizing, the economic world in which the Soviet manager operates compels him to engage in a variety of illegal or evasive practices. Since the Soviet business world is enmeshed in a much greater

[40] Ibid., p. 220.
[41] Mashinostroenie, Feb. 17, 1939, p. 3.
[42] Ibid., p. 240.

web of laws and regulations than the American, the Soviet manager finds his interest in conflict with the laws and regulations more often than his American counterpart. But when American managers' interests conflict with the laws, they too are prepared to take the chance of violating them. Both American and Soviet managers justify their actions by an attitude of contempt for governmental controls and investigating personnel, and by a hardheaded view that "business is business" and "everybody does it." Young people in both systems who wish to achieve managerial prominence have to learn to play the game according to the rules, or disqualify themselves from the tough competition for the top.

MANAGERS AND OVERFULL EMPLOYMENT

Many of the peculiarities of Soviet management spring from the fact that the economic system works under conditions of perpetual overfull employment. By "overfull" employment I mean a condition in which there are not merely as many jobs as employables (as under full employment), but the demand for labor far exceeds the available supply. The same applies to other factors of production: materials, equipment, and commodities in general are demanded in far greater volume than the current rates of production. The ability of the Soviet Government to maintain, through the planning system, a condition of permanent overfull employment is one of the greatest economic assets of the regime. We err when we interpret evidence of shortages in the Soviet economy as signs of economic weakness; they are rather indications that the economic engine is racing with the throttle wide open.

But just as an engine does not work at its maximum efficiency when it is working at its maximum capacity, so the Soviet economy pays a certain price for the advantages of overfull employment. It is the perpetual shortages of supplies that account in large measure for the losses due to overordering and hoarding. The hunger for goods by both firms and consumers encourages the deterioration of quality The "sea of ink" associated with materials allocations, price fixing, priorities, and all the rigamarole of a controlled economy nurtures the spread of the tolkach and the use of influence for personal gain.

The normally functioning American economy does not confront our managers with this kind of problem. Hoarding makes no sense when materials are in adequate supply. Competition and consumer resistance force the quality of production up to standard. The role of influence is narrowly circumscribed when the bureaucratic machinery of Government controls is removed. The biggest problem of American managers under normal conditions is marketing, not purchasing. The energy spent by the Soviet firm on obtaining materials is spent by the American firm on selling and advertising.

Thus, the major differences between the practice of American and Soviet management are to be ascribed to the differences in the economic environment. The interesting question is, How do American managers behave when placed in an environment that approximates that of the Soviet manager? The obvious test case is war. During World War II the national emergency forced us into a state of overfull employment. Along with this came the total immersion of Government into economic life, with a great burgeoning of materials allocation, price fixing, cost-plus contracting, and a prevailing shortage of supplies.

It is interesting to note that the rate of growth of production during the war rose to levels rivaling the current rates of Soviet economic growth. The implication of this fact is important; it means that there is no magic in the Soviet economic system. Our economy could grow as rapidly as the Soviet economy does if our people would consent to being pushed around as totally as the Soviet people are.

But like the Soviet economy, we paid for our high rate of production in various forms of waste. One of the first consequences of the introduction of materials controls was the rise of the black market. The only full-scale study of the black market, to my knowledge, confirmed what many people felt to be the case at the time:

> During the war at least a million cases of black market violations were dealt with by the Government. Illegal profits ran into billions of dollars. Business interests and Government vied with one another in estimating the seriousness of the black market; business estimates, curiously, often being higher than those of the Government. Such extensive conniving in the black market in illegal prices and rationed commodities took place among so many businessmen, ordinary criminals, and even the average citizen that serious questions might be raised as to the moral fiber of the American people.[43]

To understand the position of the Soviet manager, we must realize that the American black market flourished at a time when the Nation was fighting for its life and public indignation acted as a restraint. But if the economic controls that led to violations could not be justified by a national emergency, they would be thought of as just irritating obstacles, as so many hurdles that the resourceful manager must overcome as part of the risks of the game. There is good evidence that the Soviet manager takes just this amoral attitude toward economic controls, and it is therefore quite understandable that the evasion of controls would be more widespread.

The high quality of American production in normal times is a byword in international markets. But the effect of the economy of shortages was similar to that in the Soviet economy. One of the techniques used by Soviet managers is to represent lower quality merchandise as of higher quality, and to sell it at the higher price. In the United States during the war—

> upgrading was one of the most difficult violations to detect, particularly where no professional investigator was available who could appraise the grade or where there were no State or Federal grades stamped on the commodity.[44]

The reports of Government investigators read like some of the indignant letters of complaint we read in the Soviet press; men's shorts made of cheesecloth, water-resistant baby's pants which permit a third of glass of water to leak through after one laundering—

> if you pick up a board by both ends without breaking it in the middle, it's No. 1 Select—

testified an American businessman.[45]

One of the features of Soviet managerial life which helps protect the manager is the feeling of "mutual support" among various officials whose fortunes depend on the success of the enterprise. The Communist Party secretary doesn't report the manipulations of a success-

---

[43] Clinard, Marshall B. "*The Black Market*" (New York: Rinehart), 1952, vii.
[44] Ibid., p. 224.
[45] Ibid., p. 45.

ful director because the party benefits from the success of the enterprise; the people in the "home office" (the Ministry or the Council of the National Economy) are reluctant to fire a director who violates the laws in order to get the materials his plant needs, for while the next director may be more lawabiding, he may not succeed in fulfilling his plan. This tendency to maintain a solid front against authority is a source of great irritation to the Government, which periodically inveighs against it but has not been able to eradicate it. A similar sense of common front prevailed among groups of businessmen.

> Nothing better illustrates the degree of organization and consensus among businessmen then their reluctance to testify against each other * * *. Some businessmen felt that the trade would disapprove of behavior that might undermine the solid front against the Government as well as interfere with supplies.[46]

One of the major differences in the position of management in the two countries is the nature of the penalty for failure. Under ordinary conditions the unsuccessful manager loses his job. But the Soviet manager faces many more situations in which the action necessary to get the job done carries with it the threat of criminal action. Indeed, whenever the Soviet Government has found some managerial practice too damaging to its interests and too intractable to the normal sanctions, it has turned to the criminal courts. Immediately after the death of Stalin the punishment for economic transgressions was relaxed, but the new regime has not been able to continue operating without the courts. One of the severest economic problems following the decentralization of industry was the tendency toward "localism": that is, each economic region tended to favor the plants in its "own" region, and would discriminate against plants in other regions. When all exhortation failed, the Government had to turn to the law. Today, a manager who fails to honor the orders of plants outside his own region is subject to "administrative action, fines, or even criminal punishment." [47]

Financial penalties, such as fines, have rarely proved successful as restraints on Soviet managerial behavior. American managers seem to have reacted the same way to the fines imposed for black-market violations. "They don't hurt anybody." "It just comes out of profits, like a tax." "They make so much money on the black market they can afford to pay steep fines." But imprisonment was another matter. "Jail is the only way; nobody wants to go to jail." "A jail sentence is dishonorable; it jeopardizes the reputation."[48] This would not be quite the same in the case of the Soviet manager. At least during Stalin's lifetime some of the best people served their time in jail, and it definitely did not destroy their reputation among their neighbors; although the neighbors might be wary of associating with them. One has the impression that large numbers of Soviet managers feel the chances are fair that some day they will do their stretch, hopefully for a minor transgression.

The wartime economy of shortages injects the government into business life not only as an agency of control but also as the largest customer of many firms. In the Soviet case we have noted the importance of the tolkach, the expediter, the peddler of influence. We might note in passing that the economic system of Nazi Germany, in

---

[46] Ibid., pp. 306–307.
[47] "Planovoe khoziaistvo," 1958, No. 7, p. 14.
[48] Ibid., p. 244.

which government had also assumed a dominant role, also gave rise to this chap. The Germans called him the "contact man." As described by an American student of the German economy:

To influence the powerful agencies of control, however, he [the German businessman] has good use for what might suitably be called a private relations department. Under the Nazi system of control of business by an absolute government, the contact man, or graft, or both, take the place of the public relations executive.

The contact man is primarily a political figure. His job is to pull wires. He knows the influential members of the all-pervading Nazi Party in a position to bring pressure successfully to bear upon the men in charge of controlling agencies. * * * Two types of contact man are known to be used: one is an independent agent whom the businessman hires, or attempts to hire, whenever necessary; the other is carried on the payroll of the business in a more or less permanent capacity.[49]

The words might well have been written about the Soviet economy. In that sector of the U.S. economy in which Government plays a dominant role as customer, the symbols of the mink coat or Dixon-Yates, depending upon one's political persuasion, come to mind. "Washington," wrote Senator Paul Douglas, "is indeed full of lawyers and 'representatives' whose primary commodity is 'influence'."[50] The techniques of the American influence-peddler differ little from those of his colleagues in the Soviet or Nazi economy. Gifts and quid pro quo favors are standard among Soviet tolkachi. Another way in which Soviet enterprises manage to exert influence is to have one of "their" men placed in other organizations that can be of use, rather like the unusually high employability in industry of retired military personnel. During the war the problem was particularly acute because of our Government's desperate need for skilled managerial personnel, many of whom were on loan from corporations with which the Government placed contracts. But the use of influence is not confined to Government-business relations, as Senator Douglas pointed out in his critical defense of the ethics of Government personnel:

As a matter of fact, the abuses which have been exposed and properly denounced in the field of Government are quite widespread practices in private business. Thus the "padding" of expense accounts is so common that they are often referred to as "swindle sheets." Purchasing agents and buyers frequently exact toll from those who seek to sell to them, and their Christmas presents and other perquisites appreciably increase their income. Business managers and directors think nothing of awarding contracts, insurance, and underwriting privileges on the basis of friendship and relationship rather than the quality and prices of the goods and services supplied. All this is taken as a matter of course in private business, although it obviously increases costs and intercepts gains which should go to stockholders and consumers.[51]

While gifts, payoffs, and bribery play their role in the Soviet scheme of things, the subtler and much more pervasive technique of influence is known as "blat". To have good blat with someone means that one has an "in"; one can always count on him for a favor because of friendship or family ties or some other relationship of confidence. Blat may be used to obtain everything from a new apartment to a carload of coal. The prominent British observer, Edward Crankshaw, has called blat the most significant word in contemporary

[49] Hamburger, L. "How Nazi Germany Has Controlled Business" (Washington: Brookings), 1943, pp. 94–95.

[50] Douglas, Paul H. "Ethics in Government" (Cambridge: Harvard Press), 1952, p. 56.

[51] Ibid., p. 25.

Russia.[52] The way in which the American equivalent of blat is cultivated is described in one final quotation from Senator Douglas:

> Today the corruption of public officials by private interests takes a more subtle form. The enticer does not generally pay money directly to the public representative. He tries instead by a series of favors to put the public official under such feeling of personal obligation that the latter gradually loses his sense of mission to the public and comes to feel that his first loyalties are to his private benefactors and patrons. What happens is a gradual shifting of a man's loyalties from the community to those who have been doing him favors. His final decisions are, therefore, made in response to private friendships and loyalties rather than to the public good.[53]

Summarizing, many of the differences between Soviet and United States managerial behavior spring from differences in the economic climate in which they operate. The stress on quality and appearance, the drive for innovation and technological development, and the interest in cost reduction reflect the force of competition and the buyer's market. Such similarities as have been observed in managerial behavior, spring from features of the economic environment that are common to the two systems, such as large-scale organization and the intrusion of Government into the economy. Under wartime conditions our economy takes on more of the features of normal Soviet economic life, and the consequence is that our managers adopt more of the normal practices of Soviet management.

[52] New York Times Magazine, June 3, 1951, p. 35.
[53] Douglas, p. 44.

○

COMPARISONS OF THE UNITED STATES AND SOVIET ECONOMIES

Papers Submitted by Panelists Appearing Before the Subcommittee on Economic Statistics

---

JOINT ECONOMIC COMMITTEE
CONGRESS OF THE UNITED STATES

PART II

Printed for the use of the Joint Economic Committee

JOINT ECONOMIC COMMITTEE

(Created pursuant to sec. 5(a) of Public Law 304, 79th Cong.)

PAUL H. DOUGLAS, Illinois, *Chairman*
WRIGHT PATMAN, Texas, *Vice Chairman*

SENATE	HOUSE OF REPRESENTATIVES
JOHN SPARKMAN, Alabama	RICHARD BOLLING, Missouri
J. W. FULBRIGHT, Arkansas	HALE BOGGS, Louisiana
JOSEPH C. O'MAHONEY, Wyoming	HENRY S. REUSS, Wisconsin
JOHN F. KENNEDY, Massachusetts	FRANK M. COFFIN, Maine
PRESCOTT BUSH, Connecticut	THOMAS B. CURTIS, Missouri
JOHN MARSHALL BUTLER, Maryland	CLARENCE E. KILBURN, New York
JACOB K. JAVITS, New York	WILLIAM B. WIDNALL, New Jersey

RODERICK H. RILEY, *Executive Director*
JOHN W. LEHMAN, *Clerk*

SUBCOMMITTEE ON ECONOMIC STATISTICS

RICHARD BOLLING, Missouri, *Chairman*

JOHN SPARKMAN, Alabama	HALE BOGGS, Louisiana
J. W. FULBRIGHT, Arkansas	FRANK M. COFFIN, Maine
PRESCOTT BUSH, Connecticut	THOMAS B. CURTIS, Missouri
JACOB K. JAVITS, New York	

JOHN W. LEHMAN, *Economist*
JAMES W. KNOWLES, *Economist*

LETTERS OF TRANSMITTAL

OCTOBER 19, 1959.

Hon. PAUL H. DOUGLAS,
Chairman, Joint Economic Committee,
U.S. Senate, Washington, D.C.

DEAR SENATOR DOUGLAS: Transmitted herewith is part II of a series of papers submitted by the panelists invited to appear before the Subcommittee on Economic Statistics in connection with the subcommittee's current study of "Comparisons of the United States and Soviet Economies." Additional papers were released October 2 in part I. Part III, to be issued in November, will present papers in summary and conclusion.

This study is being conducted in accordance with instructions from the full committee as announced in the Joint Economic Committee's report on the 1959 Economic Report of the President. The study grows out of previous work of the Joint Economic Committee during the 83d and 85th Congresses.

It should be recognized, as was stated in the earlier studies, that the problems of making comparisons between any two national economies are exceedingly complex and even more so when those economies are at different stages of development and have different policy objectives. Such limitations are carefully set forth in the papers of the opening panel and will be further assessed by the panelists preparing the summary and conclusions.

The papers are presented in advance of the subcommittee's hearings in accordance with the Joint Economic Committee's usual practice in order to provide members of the subcommittee and the participating panelists an opportunity to examine thoroughly the analyses and findings in preparation for the discussions at the hearings.

RICHARD BOLLING,
Chairman, Subcommittee on Economic Statistics.

OCTOBER 15, 1959.

Hon. RICHARD BOLLING,
Chairman, Subcommittee on Economic Statistics,
House of Representatives, Washington, D.C.

DEAR REPRESENTATIVE BOLLING: Transmitted herewith is part II of the series of papers submitted by the panelists invited to appear before the Subcommittee on Economic Statistics at the hearings to be held November 16–20. The papers are arranged by panel topics in the order in which they are scheduled for discussion at the hearings. Part I, containing the papers of panelists appearing in the earlier part of the hearings dealt with the subjects of "Problems of Soviet-United States comparisions," "Population and Labor Force," "Industry," "Transportation," "Agriculture," and "Levels of Living and

Incentives in the Soviet and United States Economies." Part III, containing the papers on summary and policy implications, will be submitted in early November.

The papers are presented as submitted by the panelists, without deletions.

JOHN W. LEHMAN,
Economist, Subcommittee on Economic Statistics.

CONTENTS

NATIONAL INCOME AND PRODUCT

FOREIGN ECONOMIC ACTIVITIES

EVALUATION OF THE RUSSIAN ECONOMIC THREAT BY PRIVATE POLICYMAKERS

LIST OF CONTRIBUTORS

Part I

Part II

COMPARISONS OF THE UNITED STATES AND SOVIET ECONOMIES

NATIONAL INCOME AND PRODUCT

A COMPARISON OF SOVIET AND UNITED STATES NATIONAL PRODUCT[1]

(By Morris Bornstein, University of Michigan)

INTRODUCTION

The purpose of this paper is to make selected comparisons of the structure, size, and growth of the national products of the U.S.S.R. and the United States.

Of all the respects in which the economies of these two countries may be compared, national product comparisons probably provide the broadest, most comprehensive view, because they embrace, for each country, the net output of all goods and services produced during the specified period. Furthermore, because national product data are obtained from detailed national accounts studies, they not only provide summary measures of total output but also furnish much information regarding the structure of the economy. Thus, the pattern of resource allocation may be illustrated by analysis of the distribution of national product by its major end-use components, such as consumption, investment, defense, and government administration. Likewise, the pattern of resource allocation may be analyzed in terms of the relative importance of the different sectors in which national income, generated in producing national product, originates, such as industry, agriculture, services and trade. Finally, these end-use and sector-of-origin breakdowns, together with other data, make possible international comparisons of relative size and estimates of growth trends.

However, because national product comparisons involve the aggregation of quite different items by value weights, the results obtained are very sensitive to the weighting systems employed. The usual weighting problems of intertemporal and interspatial comparisons are intensified in a Soviet-United States comparison because of uncertainties about the meaning of Soviet prices. Hence, it is desirable to consider national product comparisons in conjuncture with other comparisons which are less susceptible to weighting problems, such as selected physical output comparisons and labor force comparisons.

At the same time, it should be recognized that while national product provides a convenient measure of overall economic capability, this

[1] The author wishes to thank Janet Riddle, Florence Roof, and Harold Demsetz for their suggestions about various aspects of this paper.

measure is not the most significant one for various economic, military, scientific, and political questions. For example, although Soviet national product may be only half the size of U.S. national product (by one measurement), the U.S.S.R. may, as a result of the particular composition and application of this smaller product, match or surpass the United States in military strength or in selected scientific programs. Thus, the usefulness of national product comparisons depends on the question at issue. For some questions, other measures are undoubtedly superior.

The national product comparisons in this paper concentrate on the period since 1950 because this period appears to be more representative of the conditions of economic competition between the two countries which may be anticipated in the future than would a longer historical period, such as that from 1913 or 1928 to the present. These longer periods span conditions of world war, the first rapid spurt of the Soviet industrialization drive, and a severe depression in the United States. In contrast, the period since 1950 has been more characteristic of likely future conditions in both countries. By 1950, the U.S.S.R. had largely recovered from the effects of World War II, while the United States had completed its reconversion from the war. In the conditions of internationl tension prevailing since 1950, both countries have endeavored to maintain a strong, up-to-date military posture while continuing to develop their civilian economies. So long as the international situation continues to be one of "cold war" and "competitive coexistence," analysis of the period since 1950 will be more useful for an appraisal of probable future trends and relationships than would reference to a longer period of significantly different political and economic conditions. Study of these longer, earlier periods does, of course, provide valuable insight into the dynamics of national product and is thus useful for an understanding of more recent developments and probable future trends. Some comparisons of Soviet and United States national product characteristics and trends before 1950 are available in various earlier studies.[2] For this reason, as well as for the reasons indicated above, attention will be focused on relationships and developments in Soviet and United States national product since 1950, with only limited reference to earlier periods.

The following sections of this paper are concerned, respectively, with (1) an analysis of the structure of Soviet and United States national product and income in 1955, (2) a comparison of their relative size in 1955, and (3) an estimate of trends in their gorwth since 1950. In each section, conceptual and statistical problems hampering such national product comparisons are discussed, and the approximate character of the estimates is stressed. Nevertheless, I believe the results provide a fairly reliable indication of the orders of magnitude involved.

---

[2] For national product comparisons for the period from 1928 to 1955, see Library of Congress, Legislative Reference Service, "Soviet Economic Growth: A Comparison With the United States," a study prepared for the Subcommittee on Foreign Economic Policy of the Joint Economic Committee, 85th Cong., 1st sess., Washington, Government Printing Office, 1957, ch. VI. References to other studies are given in this source.

STRUCTURE OF NATIONAL PRODUCT

In this section the structures of Soviet and United States national product are compared, first by analyzing the shares in the total product of each country of the principal end-use components, and second by analyzing the shares in the total national income of each country of the major sectors of origion in which income is generated. In both instances, reference is to each country's national product or income expressed in its own currency—rubles for the U.S.S.R. and dollars for the United States—with the resulting comparisons being only comparisons of the percentage shares of the specified uses or sectors in each country's total product or income. No comparison is made, at this point, of the relative size of the two economies. Rather only their resource allocation patterns are compared, without reference to the quantity of output produced in the two countries.

Before turning to these calculations, however, a few words are necessary regarding the serious conceptual and statistical problems encountered in such comparisons. Although these difficulties are not, in my judgment, so severe as to invalidate the basic conclusions to be drawn from such comparisons, they do qualify the precision which may be attributed to these figures, particularly the estimates for the U.S.S.R.

Two major conceptual problems are involved in such comparisons. First, output or productive activity in the two countries must be classified in comparable categories, which in some cases proves difficult because of the differences between the two countries in economic and political organization and objectives. Second, because of the different roles in the two countries of indirect taxes and subsidies, it is desirable to compare their economic structures not only in terms of established prices[3] but also in terms of adjusted prices, which allow for this difference and which, therefore, permit a somewhat more accurate comparison of real resource allocation.

The ability to make fairly precise comparisons of the structures of Soviet and United States national product is further hampered by a lack of necessary statistical data, chiefly for the U.S.S.R. The necessary basic national accounts are not published by the Soviet Government but must instead be compiled by a laborious and ingenious assembly of scattered Soviet data, supplemented by many estimates of varying precision. Likewise, Soviet data are lacking for many of the adjustments of basic accounts information which are needed to secure comparability with the figures for the United States. In contrast, most of the data needed for the U.S. side of such comparisons is readily available, primarily from the publications of the Department of Commerce. As a result, it ordinarily proves necessary to rearrange and adjust U.S. figures to match the categories used for the U.S.S.R., the opposite usually being impossible.

National product by end use

Table 1 shows the distribution of gross national product in the U.S.S.R. and United States in 1955 in terms of four end-use or

[3] The term "established prices" is used in this paper in preference to "market prices" in recognition of the fact that Soviet prices, with the exception of collective farm market prices, are determined by administrative decree rather than by market forces.

purpose categories: Consumption, investment, defense, and government administration.[4]

The consumption category in table 1 includes both household expenditures on goods and services (including income-in-kind) and government current (i.e., noncapital) expenditures on health and education. This coverage is necessary to provide comparability, because in the U.S.S.R. virtually all outlays on health and education are made by the government, whereas in the United States a significant share of expenditures for these purposes is made by households.

TABLE 1.—*Gross national product by end use in the U.S.S.R. and the United States, at established prices and at adjusted prices, 1955* [1]

End use	U.S.S.R.[2]				United States			
	At established prices		At adjusted prices		At established prices		At adjusted prices	
	Billion rubles	Percent of total	Billion rubles	Percent of total	Billion dollars	Percent of total	Billion dollars	Percent of total
Consumption	840.8	65.4	566.4	58.9	269.7	67.8	240.1	66.3
Investment	263.5	20.5	241.8	25.2	77.2	19.4	73.5	20.3
Defense	144.6	11.2	125.2	13.0	38.4	9.7	36.9	10.2
Government administration	36.9	2.9	27.6	2.9	12.1	3.1	11.7	3.2
Gross national product	1,285.8	100.0	961.0	100.0	397.5	100.0	362.2	100.0

[1] Gross national product (GNP) at adjusted prices=GNP at established prices−indirect taxes+subsidies. Components may not add to totals, because of rounding.

[2] Figures for the U.S.S.R. are for gross domestic product, exclusive of the net effect of transactions with foreign countries, rather than for GNP strictly defined, because of the lack of balance of payments information for the U.S.S.R. and even of merchandise trade data valued at internal prices. Published merchandise trade figures in rubles are expressed, essentially, at world market prices converted to rubles at the official exchange rate. This "valuta" or "foreign trade ruble" valuation differs from the value of these goods at their internal prices, which for most items exceeds their foreign trade ruble valuation. The effect of this omission on total product and its end-use distribution, however, is slight, because only net foreign sales or purchases of goods and services would be included in the calculation of GNP, and this net figure is undoubtedly a small fraction of Soviet GNP, much less than 1 percent. For data pertinent to this point, see A. Nove and Alfred Zauberman, "A Dollar Valuation of Soviet National Income," Soviet Studies, vol. X, No. 2, October 1958, pp. 146–150. Similarly, for the United States, the difference between GNP and gross domestic product is insignificant.

SOURCES AND DERIVATION

U.S.S.R.—Morris Bornstein, "Soviet National Accounts for 1955," unpublished manuscript.

United States, established prices.—GNP data in Department of Commerce, Office of Business Economics, U.S. Income and Output, Washington, Government Printing Office, 1958, p. 119, were reclassified into the four categories shown in the table on the basis of information in that study and in other sources.

Consumption includes personal consumption expenditures plus current expenditures on health and education by Federal, State, and local governments. The latter represent purchases of goods and services

[4] Figures for the United States are derived from data of the Department of Commerce and other U.S. Government agencies, as explained in notes to the table. Figures for the U.S.S.R. are from an unpublished manuscript of the author, "Soviet National Accounts for 1955." This study follows the general approach of the pioneering studies of national accounts for the U.S.S.R. by Bergson, Heymann, and Hoeffding (Abram Bergson, "Soviet National Income and Product in 1937," New York, Columbia University Press, 1953; Abram Bergson and Hans Heymann, Jr., "Soviet National Income and Product, 1940–48," New York, Columbia University Press, 1954; and Oleg Hoeffding, "Soviet National Income and Product in 1928," New York, Columbia University Press, 1954). The results of the author's study correspond closely to those in two other recent studies of Soviet national accounts for 1955, one by the Economic Commission for Europe (ECE) ("An Estimate of the National Accounts of the Soviet Union for 1955, "Economic Bulletin for Europe, vol. 9, No. 1, May 1957, pp. 89–107), and one by Hoeffding and Nimitz (O. Hoeffding and N. Nimitz, "Soviet National Income and Product, 1949–55," RM–2101, Santa Monica, Calif., the Rand Corp., 1959). For the same aspects of Soviet national accounts in 1955, the results of these three studies differ relatively little, with the differences in results being fairly readily explained by conceptual differences, differences in data available at the time the studies were completed, and differences in estimating procedures. The major differences are those of coverage. The ECE study does not contain end-use or origin breakdowns or an adjustment of established prices for indirect taxes and subsidies. The Hoeffding-Nimitz study contains an end-use breakdown in established prices but not one in adjusted prices; it also lacks an origin breakdown. In the present writer's study, from which data for the U.S.S.R. in tables 1 and 2 are drawn, end-use and origin breakdowns and a price adjustment are included.

exclusive of investment in construction and equipment and were estimated from data in ibid., pp. 175 and 190.

Investment includes gross private domestic investment (ibid., p. 119); new public construction exclusive of military facilities (Economic Report of the President, January 1959, Washington, Government Printing Office, 1959, p. 176); an estimate of governmental purchases of producers' durables for non-defense purposes (based on data in Department of Commerce, Bureau of the Census, Summary of Governmental Finances in 1955, Washington, 1956, pp. 29–30); stockpiling and defense production expansion (U.S. Income and Output, p. 175); and net exports of goods and services (ibid., p. 182).

Defense includes expenditures on the military services, foreign military assistance, and atomic energy development. It excludes stockpiling and defense production expansion and expenditures on civil defense and selective service (ibid., p. 175).

Government administration includes government purchases of goods and services (ibid.) less expenditures for national defense, nonmilitary public construction, nondefense equipment purchases, and current expenditures on health and education; and plus civil defense and selective service expenditures.

United States, adjust'd prices.—The distribution by end use of indirect business taxes was estimated by analyzing their composition and assigning to consumption Federal and State excise taxes on liquor and tobacco and most other Federal excise taxes, which are levied primarily on consumers' goods. Approximately half of all property taxes were estimated to be on residential property and therefore falling on consumption. The remaining indirect taxes were distributed among the end uses in the same proportion as the shares of the end uses in total GNP at established prices.

Both business transfer payments and subsidies were assigned to consumption. The statistical discrepancy was assigned to investment, in accordance with Department of Commerce practice (ibid., p. 116).

For both countries, the investment category comprises gross investment in construction and equipment and changes in inventories, including stockpiling and investment in defense production facilities, but excluding direct military construction and military equipment purchases. The U.S. figure includes net foreign investment, which is excluded from the figure for the U.S.S.R. for lack of data.

The defense category includes for the United States, and is believed to include for the U.S.S.R., the following: Pay, subsistence, and other current operational expenditures of the armed forces, military construction and equipment expenditures, military research and development expenditures, and atomic energy expenditures. For both countries, it excludes military pensions, which are considered transfer payments and accordingly excluded from gross national product. The figures for the U.S.S.R. include militarized internal security forces, such as border troops, for which there is no U.S. counterpart. The figures for the United States include, while those for the U.S.S.R. probably exclude, foreign military assistance and the cost of maintaining forces abroad. Soviet defense expenditures would, therefore, be understated relative to those of the United States. However, it should be noted that much of the cost of maintaining Soviet troops in Eastern Europe has been borne by the respective satellite countries, which have thus provided an offsetting form of reverse military assistance to the U.S.S.R.

The government administration category for both countries is essentially a residual of current government expenditures on goods and services not included in the other three categories. The figures for the U.S.S.R. exclude the cost of administering state-owned enterprises, as these overhead costs of enterprise management are included in product prices and appear, as in the U.S. figures, in the figures for the end uses to which these products correspond. However, the figures for the U.S.S.R. include expenditures of the Communist Party, which serves as a key arm of government administration and control in the U.S.S.R., and expenditures on nonmilitarized internal security activities, some of which have no counterpart in the United States.

Because the figures for the U.S.S.R. are derived from a national accounts study which (like all such studies for the U.S.S.R.) involves many estimates of varying reliability, they should be regarded as estimates intended to provide a fairly reliable, but by no means fully precise, indication of the pattern of resource allocation in the U.S.S.R. The consumption and investment figures may be considered to have a relatively high degree of reliability, because a substantial amount of data is available on these activities. On the other hand, the defense figure is necessarily more tenuous because of the need to make estimates for many items regarding which the Soviet Government discloses little or no information. The Government administration figure, being a residual of uncertain coverage, also is less reliable than the figures for consumption and investment, but its small size makes its deficiencies much less serious than in the case of the defense category.

In table 1, the distribution of Soviet and United States national product in 1955 among these four end-use categories is shown both at established prices and at adjusted prices. A comparison at established prices, however, does not adequately indicate the difference between Soviet and United States resource allocation patterns. A somewhat more accurate contrast is shown at adjusted prices, which attempt to exclude indirect taxes (which, although part of established prices, are not payments to factors of production) and to include subsidies (which are payments to factors of production not included in established prices). The resulting adjusted prices, intended to approach more closely a factor cost basis of valuation, depict more faithfully the distribution of resources among these end uses in the two countries.[5]

The effect of the adjustment is slight for the United States, where both indirect taxes and subsidies are of minor importance in the gross national product at established prices. For the U.S.S.R., however, the effect of the adjustment is striking, because indirect taxes account for over one-fourth of the gross national product at established prices and because they fall principally on the consumption end use, as a result of the heavy reliance of the Soviet budget on the turnover tax, an excise constituting about half of the value of state and cooperative retail sales. Subsidies, which were modest in 1955, also fell more heavily on consumption than on the other end uses in 1955, although this was not true in some earlier years, for example, 1948.[6] As a result of the importance and differential impact of indirect taxes, the share of consumption is much higher and the shares of investment and defense are significantly lower at established prices than at adjusted prices.

A comparison of resource allocation patterns at adjusted prices (cols. 4 and 8 of table 1) shows that in 1955 the U.S.S.R., in comparison with the United States, devoted a significantly greater share of its productive resources to investment (25 versus 20 percent) and defense (13 versus 10 percent) and a significantly smaller share to consumption (59 versus 66 percent). About the same share of resources went for general government administration in both countries.

---

[5] These adjustments follow the method developed in Bergson's "adjusted factor cost" approach; see Bergson, op. cit., ch. 4, and app. E. and Bergson and Heymann, op. cit., ch. III and app. D. Although these adjustments constitute only an approximation to a depiction of factor allocation in the U.S.S.R. because of many problems connected with the valuation of the services of land, capital, and enterprise in the Soviet setting, I believe they represent an improvement over the unadjusted established prices. For discussion of these problems, see the references just cited and also Peter Wiles, "Are Adjusted Rubles Rational?" Soviet Studies, vol. VII, No. 2, October 1955, pp. 143–160: Franklyn D. Holzman, "The Adjusted Factor Cost Method of Valuing National Income: Comment," Soviet Studies, vol. VIII. No. 1, July 1956, pp. 32–36; and ECE, op. cit., p. 94.

[6] See Bergson and Heymann, loc. cit.

National income by sector of origin

An alternative view of the difference in resource allocation patterns in the U.S.S.R. and the United States in 1955 is given in table 2. This table shows the distribution by sector of origin of factor incomes generated in the production of total national output in each country. The figures for the U.S.S.R., and the United States are, however, not strictly comparable, because of a difference in the national income concepts used for the two countries, which arises from the difficulties of valuing the return to property factors in the U.S.S.R.[7] A serious shortcoming of the calculation for the U.S.S.R. is the inadequate allowance for land rent and the consequent substantial understatement of the contribution of agriculture to Soviet national income. As a result, the percentage figures for the U.S.S.R. in table 2 understate the share of agriculture, and overstate the shares of the other sectors, in total Soviet national income.

With this caution in mind, one can nevertheless draw certain conclusions from table 2 regarding differences in the use of resources in the two countries in 1955. The most striking conclusion is the much greater share of total resources engaged in agriculture in the U.S.S.R. This conclusion is confirmed by the much greater share of the agricultural labor force in the total labor force in the U.S.S.R., as compared with the United States, and reflects the inefficiency of Soviet agriculture relative to U.S. agriculture. Another prominent difference between the two countries concerns the share in national income of services and trade. The much larger share in the United States reflects the orientation of the U.S. economy toward the satisfaction of household demand for goods and services. In the U.S.S.R., on the other hand, consumer services and retail trade facilities have been sacrificed in favor of investment and defense production. Finally, in 1955, the U.S.S.R. devoted a somewhat smaller share of its resources to industry and construction and to transportation and communications than did the United States.

TABLE 2.—*National income by sector of origin in the U.S.S.R. and the United States, 1955* [1]

Sector	U.S.S.R.[2]		United States [3]	
	Billion rubles	Percent of total	Billion dollars	Percent of total
Industry and construction	332.0	36.6	134.5	40.7
Agriculture	245.7	27.1	15.2	4.6
Transportation and communications	45.5	5.0	21.2	6.5
Services and trade	283.3	31.3	159.2	48.2
National income	906.5	100.0	330.2	100.0

[1] Components may not add to totals, because of rounding.
[2] National income includes wages, salaries, and other cash household income, income in kind, contributions for social insurance, and profits.
[3] National income includes wages and salaries and supplements to wages and salaries, proprietors' income of unincorporated businesses, rental income of persons, corporate profits, and net interest.

Sources: U.S.S.R.-Bornstein, "Soviet National Accounts for 1955." U.S. Department of Commerce, "U.S. Income and Output." p. 131.

[7] The calculation for the U.S.S.R. essentially follows the approach of Bergson, op. cit., app. C. Although the profits component in the present national income calculation for the U.S.S.R. contains some elements of rent and interest on capital, it clearly does not represent them adequately, either in total magnitude or in distribution by sector.

COMPARATIVE SIZE OF NATIONAL PRODUCT

In order to compare the size of Soviet and U.S. national product, the national product figures calculated in native currencies must be expressed in a common currency, either dollars or rubles. In essence, the task is to price Soviet output at U.S. dollar prices and/or to price U.S. output at Soviet ruble prices. In practice, this is done by using international price deflators to convert the Soviet national product figures in rubles to dollars, and/or to convert the U.S. national product figures in dollars to rubles.

Foreign exchange rates are unsuitable as price deflators for such comparisons because they fail, for a number of well-known reasons, to measure the internal purchasing power of currencies, even in the case of market economies whose structure and pricing practices are broadly similar.[8] Because the official Soviet exchange rate is arbitrary and not intended to measure the relationship between foreign and domestic prices, it is particularly inappropriate for international comparisons of national product.

For a comparison of the size of Soviet and United States national products, it is necessary instead to use international price deflators which measure the internal purchasing power equivalents of the ruble and the dollar in purchasing the goods and services composing national product. The first step in obtaining these deflators is to derive ruble-dollar (or dollar-ruble) price ratios for individual products by comparing their internal prices in the U.S.S.R. and the United States. Then the ruble-dollar price ratios for individual items are aggregated into ruble-dollar ratios for categories of national product, such as consumption and investment. For this aggregation, it is possible to use as a basis for weighting individual items either their relative importance in Soviet national product or their relative importance in U.S. national product. In the former case, the aggregate ratios are said to be Soviet weighted; in the latter, United States weighted.

Table 3 presents the results of an effort to compare the size of Soviet and U.S. national product in 1955 by this method. It compares the national products both in rubles and in dollars. The ruble figures for the U.S.S.R. were taken from table 1, while the ruble figures for the United States were obtained by converting the dollar figures for the United States in table 1 to rubles by appropriate ruble-dollar ratios. Similarly, the dollar figures for the United States are from table 1, while the dollar figures for the U.S.S.R. were obtained by converting the ruble figures for the U.S.S.R. in table 1 into dollars by appropriate dollar-ruble ratios. In both cases, the comparisons involve the established price figures, rather than the adjusted price figures, in table 1 because their purpose is to compare the output of goods and services entering national product in the two countries, rather than the quantities of factor inputs devoted to the production of national product in the two countries. In the figures taken directly from table 1, output is valued at established prices in each country. Where ruble-dollar (or dollar-ruble) ratios have been applied to figures in table 1 to obtain those in table 3, these ratios were constructed

[8] See Milton Gilbert and Irving B. Kravis, "An International Comparison of National Products and the Purchasing Power of Currencies," Paris, Organization for European Economic Cooperation (OEEC), 1954, pp. 14–17; and Milton Gilbert and Associates, "Comparative National Products and Price Levels," Paris, OEEC, 1958, pp. 29–33.

by comparing established ruble and dollar prices for individual items and aggregating the results by using established price weights.[9]

Table 3.—*Comparison of gross national product of the U.S.S.R. and the United States, at established prices, in rubles and dollars, 1955* [1]

End use	Ruble comparison			Dollar comparison			Geometric average of ruble and dollar comparisons
	U.S.S.R. (billion rubles)	United States (billion rubles)	U.S.S.R. as percent of United States	U.S.S.R. (billion dollars)	United States (billion dollars)	U.S.S.R. as percent of United States	U.S.S.R. as percent of United States
Consumption	840.8	4,045.5	20.8	105.1	269.7	39.0	28.5
Investment	263.5	540.4	48.8	52.7	77.2	68.3	57.7
Defense	144.6	192.0	75.3	36.2	38.4	94.3	84.3
Government administration	36.9	24.2	152.5	18.4	12.1	152.1	152.3
Gross national product	1,285.8	4,802.1	26.8	212.4	397.5	53.4	37.8

[1] Components may not add to totals, because of rounding.

SOURCES AND DERIVATION

Ruble figures for U.S.S.R. and dollar figures for United States are from table 1.

Ruble figures for United States were obtained by multiplying dollar figures for United States in table 1 by a U.S.-weighted ruble-dollar ratio for each end use, computed as

$$\frac{\sum\left(\frac{Ps}{Pu}\cdot PuQu\right)}{\sum PuQu},$$

and dollar figures for the U.S.S.R. were obtained by multiplying ruble figures for the U.S.S.R. in table 1 by a Soviet-weighted dollar-ruble ratio for each end use, computed as

$$\frac{\sum\left(\frac{Pu}{Ps}\cdot PsQs\right)}{\sum PsQs},$$

where Ps and Pu represent Soviet and U.S. prices, respectively, and Qs and Qu represent Soviet and U.S. quantities, respectively.

The ruble total for the United States and the dollar total for the U.S.S.R. are the sum of their respective components.

Ruble-dollar ratios for consumption of 15 rubles per dollar with U.S. weights and 8 rubles per dollar with Soviet weights were estimated as follows. Aggregate ruble-dollar ratios in 1954 prices for household consumption of food products, nonfood consumers' goods, and services are available with 1950 U.S. weights in Norman M. Kaplan and Eleanor S. Wainstein, A comparison of Soviet and American Retail Prices in 1950, RM-1692-1, Santa Monica, Calif., The Rand Corp., 1956, p. 28, and with 1954 Soviet weights in idem, An Addendum to Previous U.S.S.R.-United States Retail Price Comparisons, RM-1906, Santa Monica, Calif., The Rand Corp., 1957, p. 3. The pertinent Soviet prices did not change from 1954 to 1955, according to Tsentral'noe Statisticheskoe Upravlenie, Sovetskaia torgovlia (Soviet Trade), Moscow, Gosstatizdat, 1956' p. 132. The ratios were adjusted, however, for U.S. price changes from 1954 to 1955, from data in Department of Commerce, U.S. Income and Output, p. 228. Two further calculations were made to take account of items in the consumption end use not covered by the Kaplan-Wainstein studies. First, their ruble-dollar ratios for food products, which consider for the U.S.S.R. only prices of state and cooperative retail outlet, were adjusted to take into account information regarding the higher prices prevailing on the collective farm market in the U.S.S.R. in TsSU, op. cit., pp. 133–134; and data on the relative importance of the former and latter marketing channels in total Soviet food purchases, in TsSU, Narodnoe khoziaistvo SSSR v 1956 godu (National Economy of the U.S.S.R. in 1956), Moscow, Gosstatizdat, 1957, p. 228. Second, ruble-dollar ratios for health and education expenditures in the consumption end use were estimated. Ruble-dollar ratios for the wage component of these outlays were estimated from data on Soviet health and education wages in Bornstein, Soviet National Accounts for 1955, and from data on U.S. health and education

[9] Thus, in this comparison no adjustment was made for indirect taxes and subsidies in either the national product figures or the ruble-dollar ratios. For a comparison of inputs, factor costs should be used both for value of product and for the construction of ruble-dollar ratios. To obtain such factor cost ruble-dollar ratios, individual established ruble and dollar prices should be adjusted to exclude indirect taxes and include subsidies. Cf. Gilbert and Kravis, op. cit., pp. 91–92. Although rough adjustments of this type can be made for the U.S.S.R. for broad categories of national product, as was done in connection with table 1, data are lacking for similar adjustments of individual ruble prices.

incomes in Department of Health, Education, and Welfare, Public Health Service, Health Manpower Chart Book, Public Health Service publication No. 511, Washington, 1957, pp. 11, 13, 57; Department of Commerce, Office of Business Economics, National Income, Washington, Government Printing Office, 1954, p. 201; Survey of Current Business, July 1957, pp. 19–21; and Journal of the American Dental Association, December 1956, p. 719. In addition to wage outlays, health and education expenditures in the consumption end use include outlays for materials inputs, such as supplies, food, heat, and electricity. In the absence of data on the specific composition of these materials inputs, the ruble-dollar ratios for household consumption of food products, nonfood consumers' goods, and services were used for health and education materials inputs. Finally, the ratios for the various components of the consumption end use were combined into aggregate U.S.-weighted and Soviet-weighted ratios for the category.

For the investment end-use category, very rough ruble-dollar ratios of 7 rubles per dollar with U.S. weights and 5 rubles per dollar with Soviet weights were estimated as follows. For producers' durables, a U.S.-weighted ratio of 6 rubles per dollar and a Soviet-weighted ratio of 4 rubles per dollar were taken, on the basis of the estimates of Abraham S. Becker, Prices of Producers' Durables in the United States and the USSR in 1955, Santa Monica, Calif., The Rand Corp., 1959, RM-2432, pp. 47–48. In the absence of a comparable ruble-dollar ratio study for construction, it was more or less arbitrarily estimated that the construction ratios would approximate 8 rubles per dollar with U.S. weights and 6 rubles per dollar with Soviet weights, on the basis of scattered evidence, such as a comparison of thermal electric plant construction in the U.S.S.R. and the United States (Soviet data in Elektricheskii Stantsii, No. 11, 1956, pp. 26–28; No. 2, 1958, pp. 46–53; No. 3, 1958, pp. 39–44; and U.S. data in Tennessee Valley Authority, Engineering Data, TVA Steam Plants, technical monograph No. 55, vol. 2, ch. 1, p. 8, and ch. 6, pp. 10–18). Because of the lack of data on the composition of inventories and because of the relatively small share of inventories in total investment in both countries, no effort was made to estimate ratios for this component of investment. The aggregate ratios for the investment end-use category therefore were obtained by combining the producers' durables and construction ratios according to each country's weights.

For the defense end use, rough aggregate ratios of 5 rubles per dollar with U.S. weights and 4 rubles per dollar with Soviet weights were obtained as follows. A ratio for military pay was calculated by comparing average annual Soviet military pay, in Bornstein, op. cit., with similar data for the United States, in Department of Commerce, Bureau of the Census, "Statistical Abstract of the United States, 1957," Washington, Government Printing Office, 1958, p. 241. Ratios for subsistence were estimated by adjusting downward the household consumption ratios, to take into account the greater relative importance in the military subsistence "basket" of items, such as food products, with lower ruble-dollar ratios. For the remaining components of this end use, such as procurement, operations, and research and development expenditures, the ratios for producers' durables were used, on the assumptions that weapons, with inputs rather similar to those of producers' durables, would have similar ratios and that higher ratios for some of the other items would be offset by lower ratios for others. Aggregate ratios were then derived with each country's weights.

For the Government administration end use, a ratio of 2 rubles per dollar was obtained by comparing the average wage of production and office employees in the U.S.S.R. (in Bornstein, op. cit.) with the average wage of Federal, State, and local government employees, excluding those in State and local education, in the United States (from data in "Survey of Current Business," July 1957, pp. 20–21). This ratio was used both to convert Soviet ruble figures to dollars and to convert U.S. dollar figures to rubles, in the absence of data from which to derive adequate weighted ratios based on each country's weights.

In examining the results shown in table 3, it should be remembered that they are offered only as approximate indications of the relative size of the two national products and their major end-use components. All of the problems and qualifications mentioned in connection with the derivation of the established price figures in table 1 of course apply also to table 3. In addition, the precision of the results in table 3 is limited by the rough character of the ruble-dollar ratio conversions, stemming from the problems encountered in obtaining price data, in matching Soviet and U.S. goods and services, and in deriving satisfactory weights.[10]

In the comparison of gross national product and its chief end-use components in table 3, the size of the U.S.S.R. relative to the United States differs considerably depending on whether the comparison is made in rubles (i.e., at Soviet prices) or in dollars (i.e., at U.S. prices). This difference is simply a manifestation of the fundamental index number problem encountered in both intertemporal and international comparisons and arising from the existence of alternative but equally appropriate weighting systems, corresponding to the Paasche and Laspeyres formulae.[11] Even the extent of the disparity

[10] The methodology and problems involved in ruble-dollar ratio calculations are discussed in Norman M. Kaplan and William L. White, "A Comparison of 1950 Wholesale Prices in Soviet and American Industry," RM-1443, Santa Monica, Calif., the Rand Corp., 1955; Norman M. Kaplan and Eleanor S. Wainstein, "A Comparison of Soviet and American Retail Prices in 1950," RM-1692-1, Santa Monica, Calif., the Rand Corp., 1956; and Abraham S. Becker, "Prices of Producers' Durables in the United States and the U.S.S.R. in 1955," Santa Monica, Calif., the Rand Corp., 1959, RM-2432. For an extensive discussion of the construction of similar price deflators for Western Europe and the United States, see Gilbert and Kravis, op. cit., and Gilbert & Associates, on cit.

[11] Likewise, there are two sets of answers for the relative purchasing power of the ruble and the dollar in regard to national product, depending on whether the price relationships between the two countries are weighted by the relative quantities of goods and services in Soviet or in U.S. national product.

in results, attributable to differences in the two price structures, is not unexpected. A substantial, although not so great, spread was also found, as a result of differences in price structures, in a comparison of the national products of various Western European countries with that of the United States at their own prices and at U.S. prices.[12]

Likewise, it is not surprising that, for national product as a whole and for its components (except for Government administration),[13] the U.S.S.R. is smaller relative to the United States in the ruble comparison than in the dollar comparison. The explanation lies basically in a negative correlation between the relative prices and relative quantities; that is, goods which have lower relative prices tend to be produced in greater relative quantities in a country. Thus, goods and services with lower relative prices in the United States are, on the average, those which are relatively more abundant in the United States, as compared with the U.S.S.R.; an analogous situation prevails in the U.S.S.R. Consequently, when the two national products are valued at U.S. prices, a greater price weight is given to goods which are relatively more heavily produced in the U.S.S.R. than if Soviet prices are used. Similarly, when the two national products are valued at Soviet prices, a greater weight is given to items which are relatively more heavily produced in the United States, than if U.S. prices are used.[14] When one country's output structure is priced at the other country's price structure, the effect is to apply relatively high prices to relatively large quantities and relatively low prices to relatively small quantities. Thus, the comparison is more favorable to a country when the other country's prices are used for both.[15]

The existence of such a substantial disparity between the results of the ruble and dollar comparisons makes it inadvisable to use either one alone to depict the relative size of the two national products. Preferably, both comparisons should be used. However, because it is sometimes considered cumbersome to deal with two sets of compari-

---

[12] Gilbert & Associates, op. cit., pp. 97–106.

[13] Where separate U.S.-weighted and Soviet-weighted ratios were not used; see notes to table 3.

[14] See in this connection the results of Kaplan and Wainstein, op. cit., pp. 30–31, for the U.S.S.R. relative to the United States; and Gilbert and Kravis, op. cit., pp. 51–59, and Gilbert & Associates, op. cit., pp. 23–24, for several Western European countries relative to the United States.

[15] A quite different matter is involved when a calculation is made of the shares of the various end uses in a country's national product expressed in another country's currency. The results are likely to differ from the shares in a native currency calculation because of differences in the ratios at which the various end uses are converted from the native to the foreign currency (see notes to table 3). Thus, these shares of the several end uses in Soviet gross national product expressed in dollars in table 3 differ from their shares in Soviet gross national product expressed in rubles in the same table (and also from their shares in Soviet gross national product at adjusted rubles prices in table 1). The usual purpose of calculating the shares of end uses in total product is to measure resource allocation patterns in terms of the country's own price structure (at established or adjusted prices), as in table 1. The economic meaning of a calculation of end-use shares in terms of a foreign price structure is not clear. Under certain assumptions, however, the results may be of interest. For example, if U. S. prices were considered more "rational" (i.e., more indicative of scarcity relationships) for the U.S.S.R. than Soviet prices, then the shares of the end uses in Soviet gross national product in dollars would be regarded as more accurately reflecting their true relative importance. This is essentially the position of Colin Clark and Julius Wyler; see Clark, "The Conditions of Economic Progress," 2d ed., London, Macmillan, 1951, ch. IV, and 3d ed., London, Macmillan, 1957, ch. IV; and Wyler, "The National Income of Soviet Russia," Social Research, vol. 13, No. 4, December 1946, pp. 501–518, and "Die Schätzungen des sowjetrussischen Volkseinkommen," Schweizerische Zeitschrift für Volkswirtschaft und Statistik (Zurich), vol. 87, Nos. 5–6, 1951, pp. 1–35. While a dollar valuation of Soviet national product is of course of interest, and in fact necessary, for a comparison of the size of Soviet and United States national products, it is by no means clear that it provides a more reliable basis, than some (adjusted) ruble valuation, for measuring the resource allocation pattern at a given time or the real growth over time of Soviet national product. See Bergson, op. cit., pp. 53–54, and Abram Bergson, "National Income of the Soviet Union," Report No. A-5, Washington, Council for Economic and Industry Research, Inc., 1954, pp. 23–24.

sons, resort is sometimes made to an average of the results produced by the two sets of weights, such as the geometric averages in table 3. Such averages are convenient for various practical purposes, but it should be recognized that they have no unambiguous economic meaning. Where averages alone are presented, they may conceal a significant difference in results, corresponding to substantially different price structures, as in the case of Soviet-United States comparisons. Although the use of averages is often convenient for the sake of simplicity or brevity, a more precise discussion involves reference to both of the original comparisons.

The results in table 3 indicate that in 1955 Soviet gross national product was about one-fourth the U.S. level at Soviet ruble prices and about one-half the U.S. level at U.S. dollar prices. The geometric average of the ruble and dollar comparisons is about two-fifths. The relative size of the two economies (whether compared at Soviet or U.S. prices) differs, however, in regard to the several end-use components of national product.

Aggregate Soviet consumption was about one-fifth of the U.S. level at Soviet prices and about two-fifths at U.S. prices. If allowance is made for the 20 percent difference in population—about 200 million in the U.S.S.R. and 165 million in the United States in 1955—the respective per capita figures are even lower, approximately one-sixth and one-third. Such comparisons for consumption as a whole, however, conceal different relationships between the two countries regarding the various components of consumption, such as food, clothing, durable consumers' goods, etc. For example, Soviet per capita consumption levels are significantly closer to those of the United States in regard to food and basic types of clothing than they are in regard to durable consumers' goods, housing, and personal services.

In the case of investment, Soviet product was substantially larger relative to U.S. product than in the case of consumption; it was about half of the U.S. level at Soviet prices and about two-thirds at U.S. prices. The spread between the ruble and dollar results is not so great as for consumption, indicating less difference in the Soviet and U.S. price structures for investment goods than for consumption goods. As in the case of consumption, however, the aggregate nature of the investment comparison obscures important differences in the relationship between the two countries in regard to different types of investment. Because of the emphasis of the Soviet regime on economic growth, a much larger share of investment is devoted to industry, and a much smaller share to housing and consumer services, in the U.S.S.R. than in the United States. As a result, in 1955 Soviet investment in manufacturing, mining, and public utilities was larger, and Soviet investment in housing was smaller, relative to the U.S. level than the relationship for aggregate investment shown in table 3.

According to table 3, Soviet defense outlays in 1955 were about three-fourths of the U.S. level at Soviet prices and almost equal at U.S. prices. However, because of the especially crude nature of both the initial national accounts estimate for Soviet defense expenditures and the ruble-dollar ratios for this end use, it seems prudent to allow for some understatement of the Soviet level both in rubles and in dollars and to consider Soviet defense outlays as approximately equal to those of the United States. Even if aggregate Soviet and U.S.

outlays for defense are considered equal, however, it does not follow that the size, equipment, or effectiveness of the two military establishments is equal, for a number of reasons.

As in the case of the consumption and investment comparisons, the composition of the defense aggregate must be considered. Although total defense outlays may be equal in the two countries, the same relationship of equality obviously does not apply to all components of defense. The relationship of the two countries certainly differs in regard to troop strength and the various types of missiles, aircraft, ships, and other weapons. In a military contest, Soviet or U.S. superiority in one or more of these component categories of defense could be decisive, despite an accompanying inferiority in other categories. Other cautions must also be kept in mind in appraising national product comparisons of defense. For example, although Soviet and U.S. soldiers are, in this type of comparison, priced at the same pay rates, their productivity (i.e., combat effectiveness) may in fact not be the same. Also, because Soviet soldiers live more modestly than U.S. soldiers, Soviet subsistence outlays per man are less than U.S. outlays. Yet it should not be concluded from such a comparison that the effectiveness of Soviet soldiers is correspondingly below that of their U.S. counterparts. Instead, the U.S.S.R. may in fact support an equally effective soldier at less real cost in terms of resources devoted to his subsistence.

Comparisons of the relative size of the defense components of national product thus do not provide a sufficiently reliable index of the military strength of the two countries. For such an appraisal, other comparisons—of manpower, training, equipment, weapons technology, etcetera—are indispensable. The national product comparison does, however, furnish some corroborative evidence of the relative magnitude of the military programs of the two countries. The conclusion indicated by table 3, of an approximately equivalent military program in the two countries, seems consistent with other information on this question.

Little need be said about Government administration, the residual category in table 3. Outlays for the administrative apparatus concerned with planning, administration, and control in the U.S.S.R. far exceeded Government administration outlays in the United States, where some of the planning and control functions of the U.S.S.R. have no counterpart.

The general conclusions suggested by table 3 may now be summarized briefly in terms of the geometric average results. Although in 1955 the U.S.S.R. had a national product less than half that of the United States, the U.S.S.R. had an approximately equal defense effort and a level of investment about three-fifths that of the United States. In contrast, per capita consumption in the U.S.S.R. was only about one-fourth that in the United States. This performance reflects the desire of the Soviet regime for a strong and advanced military posture and a rapid rate of growth, and its willingness to pursue these objectives at the expense of the consumption level of the population.

GROWTH OF NATIONAL PRODUCT

In order to compare trends in the growth of national product in the U.S.S.R. and the United States, it is desirable to have for both countries data on national product and its components in constant prices for a series of years. Such data are published for the United States by the Department of Commerce, but comparable data are lacking for the U.S.S.R. Although national product accounts for the U.S.S.R. in current prices are now available for a number of years,[16] they have as yet not been deflated by appropriate price indexes to obtain a constant-price series.

In the absence of such a series, an effort was made for this paper to estimate the growth of Soviet national product from 1950 to 1958 by a sector-of-origin approach. Estimates of the growth of output in the principal sectors of the economy were combined into an aggregate index on the basis of the relative importance of the sectors in national product in 1955. This calculation must be regarded as very rough, because of the difficulties involved in establishing proper sector weights, the use of gross output rather than net output indicators, and the estimates necessary to obtain the indicators used.[17]

In table 4, these results are compared with an index for the United States derived from Department of Commerce data. In table 5, growth trends of Soviet and U.S. national product are shown in terms of average annual rates of growth, derived from table 4. In order to stress the approximate nature of the calculations for the U.S.S.R., the Soviet growth rates in table 5 are shown as ranges, within which the growth rates implicit in the estimated index in table 4 fall.

TABLE 4.—*Indexes of gross national product in the U.S.S.R. and the United States, selected years, 1950–58*

	U.S.S.R [1]	United States [2]
1950	100	100
1955	137	124
1958	170	125

[1] Index of gross national product (GNP) at factor cost. GNP at factor cost=GNP at established prices—indirect taxes + subsidies.
[2] Index of GNP at market prices.

SOURCES AND DERIVATION

U.S.S.R.: The index was constructed by aggregating sector indexes according to their weights in Soviet GNP at factor cost in 1955. The resulting index is shown in the table with 1950 as a base.

The sector weights were obtained by adding estimates of sector depreciation charges to figures for national income by sector of origin in Bornstein, op. cit., summarized in table 2. These charges were estimated by sector from data on amortization rates and capital stock and on the share of amortization charges in total production costs, in various Soviet sources.

For industry, the gross output index of Shimkin (Demetri B. Shimkin and Frederick A. Leedy, "Soviet Industrial Growth," Automotive Industries, vol. 18, No. 1, Jan. 1, 1958, p. 51) was used in preference to the Nutter index of all industrial output (G. Warren Nutter, "Industrial Growth in the Soviet Union," American Economic Review, vol. 48, No. 2, May 1958, p. 402) because the former includes and the latter excludes as estimate for military end items, which are an important component of Soviet industrial production. Although Shimkin uses 1934 value-added weights, based on Hodgman's work, these weights apparently do not yield much different results from 1955 price weights (see Joseph S. Berliner, "Capital Formation and Productivity in the U.S.S.R.," in The Economy of the U.S.S.R., National Academy of Economics and Political Science, Special Publications Series, No. 14, Washington, 1958, p. 6). The Shimkin index was

[16] See references in footnote 4.

[17] The construction of the index is discussed in the notes to table 4. The index is for gross national product at factor cost, rather than gross national product at established prices, because only an estimate for depreciation charges was added to the sector figures for national income to obtain sector weights, inasmuch as it was not possible to allocate indirect taxes and subsidies by sector of origin. If it is assumed that the sector weights in gross national product at established prices do not differ greatly from the respective sector weights in gross national product at factor cost, and that the net output indexes are similar to the gross output indexes, then the index for gross national product at established prices will not vary greatly from the present index for gross national product at factor cost. These assumptions do not appear implausible for the short period covered by this calculation.

extended from 1956 to 1958 on the basis of the results for 1956–58 of the official Soviet index and the relationship of the official Soviet index for 1950–56 and the Shimkin index for 1950–56.

For construction, the index used was based on the official Soviet series for state construction work (Vestnik statistiki, No. 4, 1959, p. 93) adjusted slightly to take into account collective farm construction.

The index used for agriculture is the index of Soviet agricultural output net of farm uses (such as seed and feed) based on 1958 prices prepared by Prof. D. Gale Johnson and Mr. Arcadius Kahan. This and alternative indexes prepared by them are presented in their contribution to the present Joint Economic Committee study. They kindly furnished me their results before publication.

For transportation, an index was constructed by weighting ton-kilometer data for the several types of transportation (in Vestnik statistiki, No. 4, 1959, p. 91) by their respective contributions to national income in 1955 (in Bornstein, op. cit.).

The trade index is a composite of a wage bill index, based on employment in state and cooperative trade, and a profits index, based on deflated state and cooperative retail sales. The former was estimated from data in TsSU, Sovetskaia torgovlia, pp. 113–114; TsSU, Narodnoe khoziaistvo SSSR v 1956 godu, pp. 204–205; and TsSU, SSSR v tsifrakh ("The U.S.S.R. in Figures"), Moscow, Gosstatizdat, 1958, p. 313. The latter was estimated from data in TsSU, Narodnoe khoziaistvo SSSR v 1956 godu, pp. 232–233; Sovetskaia torgovlia (magazine), No. 3, 1958, p. 4; Vestnik statistiki, No. 9, 1958, p. 88; and Pravda, Jan. 16, 1959.

For the services sector, indexes of employment were used for health and education (from data in TsSU, Narodnoe khoziaistvo SSSR v 1956 godu, pp. 204–205, and TsSU, SSSR v tsifrakh, p. 313), and a rough estimate of trends in armed forces manpower (based on scattered estimates of Western observers, such as Hanson W. Baldwin, "The Great Arms Race," New York, Praeger, 1958, pp. 37–38) was used for military services.

United States: Index calculated from series for GNP in 1954 dollars in Survey of Current Business, July 1959, pp. 6–7.

TABLE 5.—*Average annual rates of growth of gross national product in the U.S.S.R. and the United States, 1950–58*

	U.S.S.R.	United States
1950–55	6–7	4.3
1955–58	7–8	.5
1950–58	6.5–7.5	2.9

SOURCES AND DERIVATION

U.S.S.R.: Estimated on the basis of table 4, as explained in text.

United States: Computed from original figures, for the terminal years indicated, in the source cited for table 4.

The general conclusion indicated by the comparisons in these tables is striking. Even if allowance is made for the possibility of some overstatement of the Soviet growth rate, it is clear that Soviet national product has grown much more rapidly than U.S. national product in the periods indicated. Comparative growth trends shown for the 1955–58 period are particularly favorable to the U.S.S.R. and unfavorable to the United States, because in 1958 Soviet gross national product was exceptionally high as a result of an extraordinary harvest, while U.S. gross national product showed the full effects of the recent recession in business activity. The comparison for the 1950–55 period probably shows growth rates more representative of a high level of activity in both countries. The comparison for the 1950–58 period, on the other hand, understates the longer term U.S. growth rate somewhat, because it includes the recent recession but not the subsequent recovery from it. A rate of 3 to 4 percent is thus more representative of U.S. national product since 1950. Taking these various factors and qualifications into account, it nevertheless appears that since 1950 Soviet national product has been growing at approximately twice the U.S. rate—at an average annual rate of over 6 percent as compared with a rate of over 3 percent for the United States. These rates apparently represent a continuation of differential trends observed in the growth of Soviet and U.S. national product in the last three decades. A growth rate of 5 to 7 percent has been estimated for the U.S.S.R. during the "more normal" years of this period by various authors,[18] while the U.S. long-term growth rate since 1929 has been between 3 and 4 percent.[19]

As a result of its more rapid growth, Soviet national product has been increasing in size relative to U.S. national product. By combining the figures in table 4 with those in table 3, it is possible to derive an estimate of the change in the relative sizes of Soviet and U.S. national product from 1950 to 1958. In a ruble comparison, Soviet gross national product increased from about one-fifth the U.S. level in 1950 to about one-third in 1958. In a dollar comparison, it rose from a little less than half the U.S. level in 1950 to almost two-thirds in 1958. In terms of the geometric average of the two types of comparisons, Soviet gross national product grew from about one-third the U.S. level in 1950 to a little less than half the U.S. level in 1958. Inasmuch as Soviet gross national product was exceptionally high and U.S. gross national product was depressed in 1958, a 1958 comparison is particularly favorable to the U.S.S.R., as noted above. However, the increase in the relative size of Soviet national product compared to U.S. national product basically reflects the more rapid growth of the Soviet economy.

The reasons for the rapid growth of Soviet national product since 1950 have been analyzed in detail elsewhere and need only be summarized briefly here, as a basis for an estimate of future growth trends.[20] Primary among the factors responsible are the rate and composition of Soviet investment. Not only have the rates of Soviet gross and net investment been high, but, moreover, Soviet investment has been directed mainly toward heavy industry rather than toward consumers' goods industry, agriculture, housing, and consumer services.

Another factor of importance was the rapid growth of the nonagricultural labor force, chiefly from population increase, with little transfer from agriculture (in contrast to the prewar industrialization period and the postwar reconstruction period). In addition, there was continuing technological progress, in part through the adoption of Western technological progress and in part from Soviet technological achievements. Also significant was the increase in agricultural output after Stalin's death, as a result of the expansion of the crop area by more than 20 percent, greater investment in agriculture, and greater incentives to the peasants. Finally, explicit recognition should be given to the willingness of the Soviet leadership to restrain Soviet consumption levels in order to pursue the dual objectives of a rapid rate of growth and a strong military posture. In pursuit of these objectives, the Soviet leaders have used fully (though perhaps not always most efficiently) the resources at their disposal, maintaining a very high and steady rate of utilization of labor and capital, without the

---

[18] Estimates for the U.S.S.R. for 1928–37 and 1948–50 are examined in Gregory Grossman, "National Income," in Abram Bergson (editor) Soviet Economic Growth, Evanston, Ill., Row, Peterson, 1953, pp. 5–11.

[19] Survey of Current Business, July 1959, pp. 6–7.

[20] For a discussion of the factors responsible for past growth, as well as those influencing the future rate of growth, see, Bergson, "Soviet Economic Growth"; Library of Congress, Legislative Reference Service, op. cit.; Gregory Grossman, "Soviet Economy and Soviet World Power," ch. 2 in Columbia University, American Assembly, "International Stability and Progress," New York, 1957; and Grossman's statement in World Economic Growth and Competition, hearings before the Subcommittee on Foreign Economic Policy of the Joint Economic Committee, 84th Cong., 2d sess., Washington, Government Printing Office, 1957, pp. 29–33.

interruptions to production which occur in a market economy such as the United States as a result of business recessions and labor disputes.

It is difficult to estimate with precision what future trends in Soviet national product will be, even for comparatively short periods, such as 5 or 10 years. However, some idea of the probable trend of Soviet national product may be obtained by examining a number of factors in the economy which would tend to depress the rate of growth of national product in the future and, on the other hand, some which would tend to maintain or perhaps even accelerate it.

One set of retarding factors affects investment. The Khrushchev programs to improve the lot of the Soviet consumer by increasing per capita supplies of food and clothing and per capita housing space imply, if not a reduction in the overall rate of investment, a change in its composition which would reduce the share going to the producers' goods industries and increase the shares of agriculture, light industry, and housing. Although investment in the latter increases the output of goods and services, it does not, like investment in the former, provide the means for producing still more investment goods. In addition, as the age of the Soviet capital stock increases, a greater share of gross investment will probably be devoted to replacement of worn out and obsolescent facilities, leaving a smaller share for net investment. Also, investment costs associated with the exploitation of raw materials are likely to increase as it becomes necessary to use lowergrade or less accessible mineral deposits.

In addition, it does not appear likely that the nonagricultural labor force will grow as rapidly in the next few years as in the period since 1950. Annual increments to the labor force will drop sharply in the next 5 years, when the effects of the low birth rates during and shortly after World War II will be felt. In view of the continued emphasis of the Soviet regime on the expansion of agricultural output, no substantial transfer from agricultural to nonagricultural employment seems probable. Moreover, at the same time that annual increments to the nonagricultural labor force are declining, the Soviet regime has promised a reduction in the workweek from 45 to 40 hours by 1962. As a result, no significant increase in the number of man-hours of labor input in the nonagricultural sector appears likely. Thus almost all of the increase in output will have to come from the growth of productivity per man-hour. This will entail not only better job performance but also substantial investment in modernization and automation, intensifying the investment problem described above.

The agricultural sector likewise presents problems for the Soviet economy. A further expansion of the sown area comparable to that obtained during 1954–56 is not possible, because there is virtually no suitable additional land. Increased output will therefore depend on increased yields and on the growth of livestock and dairy production, through increased investment, more efficient management, and greater incentives. It is difficult to estimate how much agricultural output will be increased in the next few years by such measures.

Finally, greater Soviet economic aid to the European satellites, China, and underdeveloped countries outside the bloc may depress the rate of growth of national product, because this aid to a large degree involves the diversion of resources from domestic investment. On the other hand, the present level of Soviet foreign aid is sufficiently small relative to the level of Soviet investment that a substantial increase in the former could be made without a serious effect on the latter and thus on the rate of growth of Soviet national product.

The factors tending, in contrast, to sustain or accelerate the rate of growth can be listed more briefly, although they should not therefore be considered correspondingly less significant than the retarding factors. Of prime importance is the continued concern of the Soviet regime with economic growth, epitomized in the oft-stated Soviet objective of "catching up with and surpassing the United States in per capita output." In view of this objective, a substantial reduction in the rate of investment, or a drastic shift in its composition, in favor of increased consumption levels seems unlikely. Coupled with a continued high rate of investment will be greater emphasis on improvements in technology and on automation, which will tend to increase productivity and the rate of growth. The U.S.S.R. appears to have both the scientific and technical skills and the machine-bulding capacity to develop and produce advanced equipment and processes for modern, automated industry. Finally, allowance must be made for the possibility of greater efficiency in the planning and administration of the Soviet economy. There is ample evidence of Soviet concern with this element in economic growth in the changes in the past few years in planning methods, the reorganization of industry and agriculture, and the extensive discussions among Soviet economists about improvements in the price system. If these and similar measures are successful in increasing the efficiency of Soviet economic planning and management, they will help maintain or perhaps even raise the Soviet growth rate.

It is difficult to assess the likely future impact of the Soviet military program on the growth of national product. Clearly, the defense end use competes with the investment end use for resources, both in a general way and specifically for the output of such industries as machine-building, metal-working, chemicals, and electronics. If there were an across-the-board reduction in the Soviet military effort, say as a result of a disarmament agreement, the probable effect would be to reallocate resources from defense to investment (and possibly to a lesser degree to consumption and to foreign aid) and thereby to increase the rate of growth. However, if this reduction entailed primarily manpower, while emphasis on the development and production of aircraft, missiles, and atomic weapons continued, the favorable effect on the rates of investment and economic growth would be much less. Similarly, if the U.S.S.R. expanded its efforts in the missile and atomic weapon fields, this would tend to depress the rates of investment and economic growth. Hence, the classification of the Soviet military effort as a retarding or accelerating factor in regard to the future rate of growth of Soviet gross national product depends on which of many possible assumptions one makes about the future scale and nature of this effort.

Where does the balance lie between the factors tending to depress the rate of growth of Soviet national product in the next 5 or 10 years and those tending to maintain or accelerate it? To this writer, it appears that there may be some decline in the average annual rate of growth, say from 7 percent in the 1950–58 period to 6 or 6.5 percent in the next 5 or 10 years. Even with such a decline, however, the rate of Soviet economic growth would remain high, substantially exceeding a probable U.S. rate of, say, 4 percent.

One consequence of the higher Soviet rate, of course, would be an increase in the size of Soviet national product relative to that of the United States. For example, if it is assumed that Soviet gross national product grows at an average annual rate of 6 percent and U.S. gross national product at an average annual rate of 4 percent, Soviet gross national product would increase from about 46 percent of the U.S. level in 1958 to about 53 percent in 1965.[21]

Such an increase in the size of the Soviet economy compared with that of the United States need not in itself be considered alarming. More important is the significance of a rapid rate of economic growth for the world position of the U.S.S.R. A larger, and rapidly growing, national product will provide the U.S.S.R. a greater economic base for a strong military posture, for further scientific and technical progress, for greater foreign trade and foreign aid, and for an improvement in the living conditions of the Soviet population. Furthermore, an uninterrupted high rate of growth will be prominently cited in Soviet efforts to convince underdeveloped countries that they should emulate the Soviet "model" in their development programs. In all of these ways, a high rate of growth will strengthen the economic, military, and political position of the U.S.S.R. on the world scene. The consequences of this enhanced Soviet position will be of great importance to the United States and the rest of the free world.

---

[21] Both percentages are the geometric averages of the respective ruble and dollar comparisons.

NATIONAL INCOME AND PRODUCT OF THE U.S.S.R., RECENT TRENDS AND PROSPECTS

(By Francis M. Boddy, University of Minnesota)

INTRODUCTION

While there has been a growth in the publication of economic information by the U.S.S.R. in recent years, the type of national income and product data that economists have come to depend upon for the study of economic structure and growth in the United States and Western European countries is not published by the U.S.S.R.

The result is that we must depend on the research specialists in this area to put together painstakingly the bits and pieces of information that become available in numerous scattered Soviet sources, to give us some estimates of the overall structure and growth of the economy.

In this paper I can at best compare some of the readily available data from Soviet sources with some of the results of such detailed research of others and suggest some crude comparisons with the growth of the national product in the United States.

GROWTH IN SELECTED NATIONAL INCOME DATA, U.S.S.R., 1949–58

A recent working paper, published as a Rand research memorandum, by O. Hoeffding and N. Nimitz,[1] gives estimates of the national income and product of the U.S.S.R. for the years 1949–55 in current rubles and established prices.

In table 1, below, four selected items of these national income estimates are tabulated, and from these data are calculated and tabulated the percentage increase from year to year in these items.

TABLE 1.—*Selected national income data, U.S.S.R., 1949–55* [1]

Year	Total income of households, currently earned (billions of rubles)	Percent increase over preced ng year	Consolidated total charges against current product of government, social, and economic organizations (billions of rubles)	Percent increase over preceding year	Net national product (billions of rubles)	Percent increase over preceding year	Gross national product (billions of rubles)	Percent increase over preceding year
1949	516.2		407.3		894.4		923.5	
1950	549.6	6.5	383.3	−5.9	902.3	.9	932.9	1.0
1951	572.1	4.1	419.8	9.5	958.6	6.2	991.9	6.3
1952	599.7	4.8	436.5	4.0	998.5	4.2	1,036.2	4.5
1953	619.8	3.4	441.9	1.2	1,018.9	2.0	1,061.7	2.5
1954	681.6	10.0	438.1	−.9	1,072.7	5.3	1,119.7	5.5
1955	712.3	4.5	489.9	11.8	1,150.3	7.2	1,202.2	7.4
Percent increase, 1949–55		38.0		20.3		28.6		30.2

[1] From "Soviet National Income and Product, 1949–55," O. Hoeffding and N. Nimitz, Project Rand research memorandum, RM–2101, Apr. 6, 1959, tables 1, 2, and 3.

---

[1] "Soviet National Income and Product, 1949–1955," by O. Hoeffding and N. Nimitz, RM–2101, a Project Rand research memorandum, Rand Corp., Santa Monica, Calif., Apr. 6, 1959.

Since these estimates are in current rubles, the effects of substantial price reductions in the Soviet economy, particularly in the years 1950–54 in retail prices and in 1949 and 1951 in industrial, are not shown in these figures, nor are there yet available appropriate price indices to make the adjustments.

Table 2 presents two statements, from Soviet sources, of the growth of national income over the period 1950–58 (in col. 2) and from 1951–55.

The overall increase in net national product and of gross national product from 1949 to 1955 in table 1 amounts to only 28.6 percent and 30.2 percent, respectively. On the other hand, the Soviet claims presented in table 2, column 2, mount up to a claimed increase in national income of 105 percent over this same period.

While a substantial (but unknown) part of the difference in the growth rates shown in table 1 and table 2 during the first 5 years of this period might be accounted for by the impact of the price reductions, the differences in growth rates in 1954 and 1955 could not be substantially affected by the price changes in the Soviet economy in these years, for by all indications they were of relatively modest proportions.

TABLE 2.—*Percent increases in national income of the U.S.S.R., reported by Soviet sources, over preceding year*

Year	Percent [1] increase in national income (in comparable prices) [2]	Percent [2] increase in national income
1950	21	
1951	12	12.3
1952	11	10.9
1953	8	9.4
1954	11	12.1
1955	10	11.9
1956	12	
1957	6	
1958	9	

[1] Sources: "Annual Reports of Plan Fulfillment," Central Statistical Administration of the U.S.S.R. Council of Ministers, Pravda and Izvestia, translated in the Current Digest of the Soviet Press, New York.
[2] The phrase "in comparable prices" was used in reporting only the increases in 1950, 1951, and 1956 in the Soviet reports.

Source: Calculated from data from "Narodnoe Khozaistvo S.S.S.R. v 1956 Godu," Moskva, 1947, p. 42.

Table 3 gives the Soviet estimates of increases, year by year, in the real income per working person, from 1950 to 1958. If one, by crude interpolation in the years where the overall averages per worker are not given, computes the growth of these claimed increases in real income per worker from 1951 to 1958 (70 percent) and compares this with the growth in total national income from 1951 to 1958 as given in table 2 (90 percent), the results are roughly consistent with the growth of the number of workers over the period.

TABLE 3.—*Percent changes in real incomes in U.S.S.R., 1949–58* [1]

	Reported increases in real income, in percent over preceding year, of—		
	Population, per worker	Workers and employees, per capita	Peasants, per capita
1950	19		
1951	10		
1952		7	8
1953	13		
1954	11		
1955		3	7
1956		3	12
1957		7	5
1958	5		

[1] Sources: "Reports on Fulfillment of State Plan," by the Central Statistical Administration of the U.S.S.R. Council of Ministers, Pravda and Izvestia; translated by the Current Digest of the Soviet Press, New York.

In table 4 are tabulated the total U.S.S.R. state budget revenues and expenses, as reported each year by the Minister of Finance, from 1949 to 1959. The increase by 1958 in total revenues amounted to 47 percent of the 1949 figure and in revenues to 52 percent. The claimed increases in national income from 1949 to 1958 in table 2, however, amount to 166 percent.

TABLE 4.—*U.S.S.R. state budget revenues and expenditures, 1949–59* [1]

	Revenues		Expenditures	
	Total (billions of rubles)	Percent increase over preceding year	Total (billions of rubles)	Percent increase over preceding year
1949	437.0		412.3	
1950	422.1	−3.4	412.7	0.0
1951	468.0	10.9	441.3	6.9
1952	497.7	6.3	460.2	4.3
1953	539.7	8.4	514.8	11.9
1954	557.5	3.3	552.8	7.4
1955	561.6	.7	537.8	−2.7
1956	583.0	3.8	561.0	4.3
1957	614.5	5.4	598.2	6.6
1958	641.8	4.4	626.7	4.8
1959	722.7	12.6	707.2	12.8

[1] Source: "Reports on the Annual State Budget, U.S.S.R. Minister of Finance, Pravda and Izvestia, translated by the Current Digest of the Soviet Press, New York.

One may conclude, on the basis of these crude and imperfectly comparable indexes of growth in Soviet income and product, that the rates of growth claimed by the Soviets over the recent years are substantially exaggerated, but until further research gives us better estimates of the internal price level changes in the U.S.S.R., or direct estimates of the growth in real national income and product, the extent of the exaggeration will remain an open question.

Even a major scaling down of these Soviet claims, however, would still leave substantial growth rates for the Soviet income and product, certainly not to be unfavorably compared (from the Soviet point of view) to the total growth rates of the United States gross national product (in 1954 dollars) from 1949 to 1955 of 34 percent, or from 1951 to 1958 of 17 percent; or to the total growth rates in the United States personal income per capita (in constant dollars) from 1949 to 1955 of 20 percent, or from 1951 to 1958 of 12 percent.

SOVIET PREDICTIONS OF FUTURE GROWTH, 1958–65

The Khrushchev theses on the 5-year plan, 1959–65 [2] predicts:

> The national income will increase by 62–65 percent in 1965 as compared to 1958. with its growth a further increase in public consumption will be effected. It will increase by 60–63 percent in the next 7 years. * * * The real incomes of factory and office workers in the next 7 years, per working person, will increase on the average by 40 percent as a result of the increase in wages, pensions, and grants as well as further price reductions in public catering. The real incomes of collective farmers, too, on the basis of the growth of agricultural production and higher laborer productivity, will increase for the same period by not less than 40 percent, mostly due to the expansion of the common output of the collective farmers.

In comparison with the claimed growth in national income and in real income per worker for the past 7 years (1951–58) these forecasts seem relatively modest, and even a substantial scaling down of the claims on recent performance would not make these forecasts of Soviet growth clearly out of character with the recent growth of the Soviet economy.

In considering the factors that will basically determine the feasibility of such growth in the Soviet economy in the coming 7 years, one must weigh heavily the continued growth in the recent past of capital investments by the Soviets in their national economy, summarized in table 5.

TABLE E.[1]—*Planned capital investments in the national economy*

[Billions of rubles]

	Total	Of which—	
		From the budget	From enterprise resources
1953	156.1	106.7	49.4
1954	184.0	121.1	62.9
1955	167.2	109.3	57.9
1956	160.8	118.4	42.4
1957	178.6	124.9	53.7
1958	203.8	142.7	61.1
1959	231.2	162.1	69.1

[1] Source: "Reports on the Annual State Budget," U.S.S.R. Minister of Finance, Pravda and Izvestia' translated by the Current Digest of the Soviet Press, New York.

Using the Hoeffding–Nimitz estimate of Soviet gross national product of 1,202 billion rubles for 1955 and scaling down somewhat the Soviet claims of growth from 1955 to 1958, the percent of GNP going to investment in the national economy in 1958 is on the order of 15 percent.

[2] "Control Figures for the Economic Development of the U.S.S.R., 1959–65," Foreign Languages Publishing House, Moscow, 1958, p. 98.

The planned investments for the period 1959–65 is summarized by this quotation from the "Control Figures for the Economic Development of the U.S.S.R., 1959–65" (pp. 66–67):

> The forthcoming 7 years will be a period of unprecedented construction in all parts of the country, and particularly the eastern regions. Capital investments by the state will be 80 percent greater through 1959–65 than in the preceding 7 years and will nearly equal the total investments made in the national economy through all the years of Soviet power.

The 7-year plan calls for total capital investments in the national economy in 1959–65 of 1,940 to 1,970 billion rubles, an increase of 81 to 84 percent over the investment total for 1952–58 of 1,072 billion rubles.[3]

The growth of the industrial working force by transfer of workers from the oversupplied agricultural sector, the education and training of professional and skilled personnel on a major scale, and the apparent success of the recent economic reorganization in improving the organization of the industrial sector of the economy are other plus factors, from the Soviet point of view, that suggest that these growth rates are not outside the possibilities of achievement. On the minus side, however, the continued urban housing shortage may put a brake on the transfer of rural workers to industry, the apparent shortages of high quality basic raw materials in some lines, and the ever-present shortage of good agricultural land in good and stable climatic areas may create real handicaps to the planned development. But even a scaling down of these forecasts of Soviet growth will leave possible growth rates that may make it possible for the Soviet income and product to approach the levels of those of the United States in the not too distant future if our growth rates of the recent past are not substantially increased.

[3] Ibid., p. 67.

FOREIGN ECONOMIC ACTIVITIES

AN INTERPRETATION OF EAST-WEST TRADE

(By Robert Loring Allen, University of Oregon)

The term "East-West trade" is customarily the euphemism for the trade of the Soviet Union, Eastern Europe, and mainland China with the non-Communist countries of Western Europe and the Western Hemisphere. This paper deals with this trade and also in part with internal Sino-Soviet bloc trade as well as trade with other non-Communist countries. When the "bloc" is used, all of the Communist countries except Yugoslavia is meant. The statistical appendix includes the relevant trade data and a source bibliography contains references to the literature.

About one-third of the paper is concerned with (1) the value and volume of exports and imports of the bloc, (2) growth and trends in trade, (3) the geographic direction of trade, and (4) its commodity composition. In order for these facts and figures to have meaning, it is also necessary to treat (5) prices and the terms of trade, (6) the bloc's motives for trade, (7) the commercial policies employed by the bloc, and (8) trade experience. Following an evaluation and an examination of the prospects for trade is a brief indication of the problems posed for U.S. policy.

It must be kept in mind that most of the data are based upon the bloc country's national statistics and hence may be subject to error or distortion. The statistics are, however, probably sufficiently accurate that useful general conclusions may be drawn. The systematic use of dollar quotations does not reflect the use of dollars in trade, which is carried on in many currencies and even without foreign exchange through bilateral agreements. The dollar figures, however, are roughly comparable to other dollar magnitudes since the bloc trades at world market prices, regardless of domestic prices or costs.

VALUE AND VOLUME

The Sino-Soviet bloc is not a large world trader. The countries of the free world export less than 3 percent of their total exports to the bloc and acquire less than 3 percent of their imports from the bloc. In 1957, for example, the free world exported $99.8 billion, of which $2.9 billion went to the bloc. The bloc in the same year exported a total of $11.5 billion, of which only $2.8 billion went to the free world, the remaining amount being intrabloc trade. Thus, total exports by bloc countries, including exports to other bloc countries, was about 10 percent of total world exports.

The largest component of bloc foreign trade is Soviet trade. In 1957 total exports were $4.4 billion and total imports were $3.9 billion. This places the Soviet Union in eighth place as an importer, behind the United States, Canada, France, West Germany, the Netherlands, the United Kingdom, and Japan. As an exporter, the Soviet Union is in sixth place, ahead of Japan and the Netherlands but behind the others mentioned. In 1958 the value of Soviet trade remained about the same as in 1957, but the volume increased slightly because of the continued decline in raw materials prices which still constitute the bulk of Soviet imports and exports.

Eastern Europe as a whole—Bulgaria, Czechoslovakia, East Germany, Hungary, Poland, and Rumania—is a larger trader than the Soviet Union. The big three—Czechoslovakia, East Germany, and Poland—imported $4.3 billion in 1957 and exported $4.2 billion. The other East European countries account for both imports and exports slightly in excess of $1 billion. Mainland Chinese trade is about $2 billion each way. Thus, including intrabloc trade, the entire Sino-Soviet area imports slightly less than $12 billion and imports about the same amount. U.S. imports and exports during the same period were substantially higher. The second largest world trader—the United Kingdom—imported and exported slightly less than did the bloc as a whole.

As in the case of the aggregate figures, the physical quantities of various products imported and exported are also small relative to the total amounts of the products produced and exchanged. In 1956 and 1957, for example, the Soviet Union imported 140,700 and 145,500 tons of crude natural rubber. World natural rubber production in 1957 was 1,935,700 tons. Malaya alone produced more than four times the Soviet imports. The free world produced more than 5.5 million tons of cotton in 1957 and more than 2 million tons of wool. In the same year the Soviet Union imported 108,800 tons of cotton and exported 318,400 tons. The Soviet Union imported 57,300 tons and exported 13,800 tons of wool. In 1957 the Soviet Union exported 85,400 tons of aluminum, representing for the United Kingdom about 10 percent of the 1957 rate of imports and less than about 3 percent of free world production in 1957. In 1956–57 the free world produced about 120 million tons of wheat. In 1957 the Soviet Union exported 5.5 million tons, a figure four times higher than 1956 shipments when free world production was slightly higher. The Soviet Union exported 18,300 tons of tin in 1957, mainly of Chinese origin, but free world tin consumption that year was 146,000 tons and production was substantially higher.

It would be possible to go down the commodity list product by product, not only for Soviet trade, but also for East European and mainland Chinese trade, and indicate the small and fractional percentages of imports and exports provided by these countries. For particular countries and particular products, however, the bloc may represent a significant proportion of trade. Finland and Iceland, for example, import nearly all of their petroleum products from the Soviet Union and Rumania. Egypt sells a large proportion of its cotton to the bloc. The large trading partners of the bloc in Western Europe seldom singly buy or sell a significant part of the output of a product category in trade with the bloc.

GROWTH AND TRENDS

Between the two World Wars Soviet foreign trade reflected its policy of autarchy—the drive for internal economic self-sufficiency.

Soviet trade was only enough to insure the fulfillment of its economic plans. The country imported in order to industrialize and exported in order to continue importing. Both imports and exports were below the 1913 czarist levels during the interwar period.

During the first 5-year plan, from 1928 to 1932, the Soviet Union bought significant quantities of machinery and equipment from the industrial countries, such as Germany and the United States. The Soviet Union, selling wheat at sacrifice prices, largely at the expense of literally starving Ukrainians, bought for technical excellence in machinery and in order to acquire technological know-how.

Trade was predominantly carried on in multilateral channels. Before 1929 nearly all Soviet trade was multilateral. During the great depression, the Soviet Union adopted some bilateral agreements, but during the 1930's much of Soviet trade remained multilateral. In 1938 less than 10 percent of Soviet trade was conducted under five bilateral agreements. In 1957 and 1958, the bloc countries were parties to 240 agreements, with the Soviet Union having the most agreements.

The large Soviet deficits which were incurred between 1925 and 1932 were covered by drawing down reserves, with short-term credit, and through the sale of gold. After 1932 Soviet trade declined significantly and the deficit turned to an export surplus. By 1938 Soviet foreign trade, cut by one-half as compared to 1930, was approximately balanced at $268 million imports and $251 million exports.

During the Second World War the most significant element was the large-scale unrequited deliveries of lend-lease aid by the United States. Toward and at the end of hostilities the Soviet Union acquired large quantities of foreign resources by confiscation from enemy countries. After the war reparations were also significant in Soviet imports. By 1946 trade had more than recovered, with exports at $642 million and imports of $761 million.

Beginning in 1948 bloc trade with the free world dropped off sharply, while both intrabloc and free world trade was continuing to expand. In 1948 Soviet-East European trade with the free world had been balanced at about $2 billion each way. The low was $1.4 billion for imports and $1.6 billion for exports in 1953. Since 1953, bloc trade has been rising rapidly.

In 1955 Soviet imports were $3.1 billion and exports were $3.5 billion. Imports went up 18 percent in 1956 and another 11 percent in 1957, while exports increased 4.1 percent in 1956 and 21.3 percent in 1957. The full 1958 trade data have not been released, but indications are that the value remained about the same as in 1957 while volumes increased.

In Eastern Europe the largest trader is East Germany, followed by Czechoslovakia, Poland, Hungary, Rumania, and Bulgaria. East German imports more than doubled between 1952 and 1957. The largest expansion, however, took place in 1957, when imports jumped from $1.3 billion to $1.6 billion. Exports also experienced a large increase in 1957, from $1.4 billion in 1956 to $1.8 billion in 1957. Czechoslovakian trade in 1957 was approximately balanced at $1.4 billion each way, although in 1955 and 1956 that country ran an export surplus. Trade in 1957 was not quite double the 1948 level, which was nearly triple the 1938 level. Polish trade in 1957 ran a serious trade deficit—$1.3 billion in imports and $1 billion in exports. An import surplus has characterized Polish trade for the last 4 years, during which time imports have increased by 38.4 percent and exports by only 13 percent. The trade of Rumania, Hungary, and Bulgaria has also been expanding in recent years. East European exports were $4.6 million in 1955; in 1957 they were $5.5 billion, a 19.6 percent increase. Imports of Eastern Europe increased from $4.3 billion to $5.7 billion between 1955 and 1957, an increase of 32.6 percent.

Mainland Chinese trade has also expanded considerably in recent years. Trade statistics for that country are particularly poor, but Soviet data shows an increase in both imports and exports except Soviet exports in 1957 which fell sharply. The Soviet Union is China's leading trading partner, accounting for about one-fifth of Chinese trade. Other bloc countries, as well as free world countries, show increases in trade with mainland China.

GEOGRAPHIC DIRECTION OF TRADE

Mainland China has been the leading trading partner on the Soviet import side in recent years, except in 1957 when China slipped slightly behind East Germany which has been in the second position. Czechoslovakia is third and Poland is fourth. Mainland China accounted for 18.7 percent of Soviet imports in 1957, while all of Eastern Europe provided 48.6 percent. China has been the leading buyer also, again except in 1957 when both East Germany (normally in second place) and Czechoslovakia (normally in fourth place) bought more Soviet goods. Poland has been in third place in recent years. China bought 12.4 percent of Soviet exports in 1957 (in 1956 it was 20.3 percent). Eastern Europe absorbed 57.6 percent. Thus, other bloc countries (including the Asiatic Communist countries) constituted 70.2 percent of the imports and 73 percent of the exports of the Soviet Union in 1957. There have been relatively small variations in these percentages in recent years, but since the consolidation of Communist power and Soviet influence over the bloc, the overwhelming bulk of Soviet trade has been with other bloc countries.

Among free world countries, only Finland, the United Kingdom, and Egypt, in that order, provided $100 million or more in goods to the Soviet Union. Finland and the United Kingdom only bought $100 million or more from the Soviet Union. Finland in recent years has been the free world country from which the Soviet Union imports most, while the United Kingdom has been the principal purchaser. Because of Soviet punitive action against Finland in 1958 and 1959 Soviet trade with that country probably declined for those years. Other significant trading partners in the free world (more than $50 million in imports and exports in 1957) are Austria (exports only), West Germany, Yugoslavia, France (import side and slightly less on export side), and India (import side, less on export side).

Western Europe (Austria, Belgium, Denmark, Finland, France, West Germany, Italy, Netherlands, Norway, Sweden, Switzerland, United Kingdom, and Yugoslavia) accounted for 13.8 percent ($423 million) of Soviet imports in 1955 and 16.9 percent $667 million) in 1957, a growth of 59.8 percent in the period. These same countries bought 15.3 percent ($532 million) in Soviet exports in 1955 and 16.8 percent ($735 million) in 1957, an increase of 38.2 percent. On the other hand, the underdeveloped countries with whom the Soviet Union trades (Afghanistan, Argentina, Burma, Cuba, Egypt, Ghana, India, Iran, Malaya, Turkey, and Uruguay) provided 5.9 percent ($179 million) of Soviet imports in 1955 and 9.2 percent ($361 million) in 1957, an increase of 101 percent. These countries bought 2.5 percent ($86 million) of Soviet exports in 1955 and 5.4 percent ($238 million) in 1957, an increase of 176 percent.

Thus, while Soviet trade with underdeveloped countries has been increasing rapidly in the last few years, Western Europe has been holding its own. What in effect has been happening in recent years is that underdeveloped countries have been gaining at the expense of smaller rates of growth in trade with bloc countries. In the expansion of trade with Western Europe, Austria, Belgium, West Germany, the United Kingdom, and Yugoslavia have been the leaders. The rapidly growing trade with underdeveloped countries has primarily been with Afghanistan, Egypt, India, Malaya (on the export side only), and Uruguay.

The Soviet Union is East Germany's leading trading partner, accounting for 45.6 percent of the latter's imports and 44.7 percent of its exports in 1957. On the import side, West Germany is next (11.4 percent), followed by Czechoslovakia, Poland, and China (together 19.2 percent). West Germany is the second leading exporter to East Germany (11.3 percent), followed by Poland, Czechoslovakia, and China (together 21.9 percent). Larger than proportionate increases have been registered by such underdeveloped countries as Brazil, Egypt, and India. These three countries together expanded their exports to East Germany five times between 1955 and 1957, and East Germany has tripled its exports to them.

The Soviet Union is also Czechoslovakia's leading trading partner, accounting for 37.2 percent of the latter's imports and 27.1 percent of exports. On the Czechoslovakian import side, East Germany, China, and Poland (Hungary the same as Poland) in that order of importance, provide 19.8 percent of imports. In most recent years exports to Czechoslovakia, Polish exports have been greater than China's exports. East Germany, Poland, and China are the leading purchasers of Czechoslovakia goods, accounting for 22.6 percent of its exports. The Soviet Union claimed 26.5 percent of Polish exports (a declining percentage in recent years) and provided 33.4 percent of Polish imports. On the import side, East Germany is second and Czechoslovakia is third (together 19.4 percent). On the export side, Czechoslovakia is second, with 12.9 percent. Unlike other bloc countries except East Germany, a free world country—the United Kingdom—is an important buyer of Polish goods and is the third largest importer, with 6.5 percent of Polish exports. Imports from the United States jumped from 0.2 percent in 1956 to 4.5 percent (fourth largest exporter to Poland) in 1957. Large imports from the United States continued in 1958 and 1959. In general, East European trade with the Soviet Union has been growing less rapidly than has its trade with mainland China and with the underdeveloped countries. East European trade with Western Europe has made only minor gains.

COMMODITY COMPOSITION

The commodity composition of Sino-Soviet bloc trade strongly emphasizes the export of raw materials and food products and the import of machinery and equipment. This circumstance is even more pronounced in bloc trade with the free world, since much of the machinery exports of the Soviet Union, East Germany, and Czechoslovakia, the leading machinery producing countries, go to other bloc countries.

More than one-half, and in many years substantially more than one-half of Soviet exports and imports are in the raw materials and fuels category. If grain is added on the export side, then about 70 percent of Soviet exports consist of food and various kinds of raw materials. Machinery and equipment exports have increased substantially since the end of the Soviet postwar recovery. Before the Second World War, only 5 percent of total exports were machinery. In the post-recovery period it has characteristically been between 15 and 25 percent. These greater capital goods exports reflect, at least in part, the great expansion of the Soviet industrial base. On the import side, the need for machinery and equipment, as reflected in purchases, has not abated, hovering between one-fourth and one-third of Soviet imports. One of the most striking characteristics about Soviet trade, indeed about bloc trade in general, is the small proportion of consumer goods. In recent years, the Soviet Union has imported less than 10 percent of its total imports in the form of consumer goods, and its exports of these items has been about 20 percent. This phenomenon, like the growing exports of machinery, reflects the basic policy decision emphasizing industrial growth to the neglect of consumer satisfaction.

East Germany and Czechoslovakia are the industrial giants of Eastern Europe. The former's exports of machinery comprise 60 percent of total exports, with most of the remainder fuels and raw materials. Czechoslovakia exports 40 percent of its goods in the form of machinery, proportionately more raw materials, consumer goods, and food than East Germany. Hungary is beginning to export larger quantities of machinery, but nearly one-third of its exports remain foods. Poland, interestingly enough, is a leading consumer goods exporter, proportionately more than four times more than other East European countries. Rumania's exports heavily emphasize oil and Bulgaria, proportionately, is the leading food exporter.

East Germany and Czechoslovakia must import great quantities of food and raw materials, accounting in both countries, for about 80 percent of total imports. Bulgaria, Poland, and Rumania import proportionately more machinery than does the rest of Eastern Europe, and the last has a very high raw materials import bill. Again Poland is in a unique position, importing nearly one-half of its imports as consumer goods, nearly triple the proportion of other East European countries. About 82 percent of Poland's imports are machinery and consumer goods.

The structure of Sino-Soviet bloc trade does not indicate any existing or potentially decisive degree of complementarity which would tend to propel the bloc into a position of leading world traders. Stretching from Berlin to Peiping, the Sino-Soviet bloc contains vast resources which makes it possible for the area to be almost a self-contained unit, if it so desires. Since central planning and the Communist dogma both require a closed system, trade as seldom been viewed simply as a matter of comparative advantage; rather trade was and is an economic necessity. As the area develops the necessity will probably decline and the bloc must decide whether or not to trade to achieve sometimes marginal cost reductions. It is likely, given the Communist system, that this will be primarily a political, not an economic decision.

It is not possible to make a strong case for important complementarity between the bloc and many areas of the world, including Asia, Africa, the Middle East, and Latin America. The strongest trade ties of the bloc are with Western Europe, based upon bloc needs for machinery and equipment. Food products and consumer goods technically could find a large market in the bloc, but only if consumer sovereignty asserted itself in the area. This is a rather unlikely event.

There is, of course, some basis for trade and trade will not only continue but expand. There is no reason, however, to believe that the bloc trade, as a proportion of world trade, will increase significantly or that either the free world generally or the bloc will develop inextricable dependence upon one another. This does not apply, however, for individual countries, which can develop a crucial reliance upon the bloc for a single or a few commodities or depend upon the bloc for a substantial part of its export market.

PRICES AND THE TERMS OF TRADE

The Soviet Union has an independent internal pricing system in which the prices of products do not reflect either their domestic costs (except in a bookkeeping sense) or world market prices. Indeed, it is only by accident if the internal price of Soviet products, translated at the official exchange rate into other currencies, even comes close to the prices of comparable products in other countries. Soviet specialists have argued that domestic prices and costs are not too far out of line and that periodic price reforms perform the function of bringing costs and prices together. Even so, world prices are the guidelines for Soviet-bloc trade, a matter of necessity which has been elevated to principle and embodied in trade agreements. When Eastern Europe came under Soviet influence and when mainland China became controlled by the Communists, these countries followed the Soviet model. But even among the bloc countries, there is no systematic relationship among prices and bloc trade is on the basis of world prices.

Thus, when a bloc country buys a combine and pays $6,000 it pays that amount in foreign exchange or with a credit balance of say 24,000 rubles (the official exchange rate) in favor of the trading partner. The domestic price might be 35,000 rubles or 20,000 rubles. Likewise, when the bloc sells a tractor, the price is determined by comparable machines on the export market produced by the United States, West Germany, and the United Kingdom. The Soviet Union gets say $2,500. The domestic costs may be above or below that amount. Since the ruble is substantially overvalued, as even a cursory examination of Soviet price lists indicates, trade tends to take place at a net bookkeeping deficit to the state trading organizations, presumably paid out of the budget. In a comparative cost sense, however, there is a net economic gain in most cases because Soviet real costs differ from Soviet, as well as world market prices.

While it is the stated policy to trade at world market prices, there are many divergences in practice and in a few cases a conscious departure from the policy. Technically, nine situations could prevail. Soviet exports could be (1) overpriced, (2) market-priced, or (3) underpriced, each in combination with (*a*) overpriced, (*b*) market-priced, or (*c*) underpriced trading partner exports to the Soviet Union. The Soviet Union is best off in the case of (1) (*c*); the trading partner is best off in the case of (3) (*a*); while (2) (*b*) is the stated Soviet policy. In a few cases the Soviet Union deliberately sells at a discount (3) in order to penetrate a market; in other cases the Soviet Union pays a premium (*a*), either in order to acquire some badly needed commodity or to provide the basis for Soviet exports. In many cases these situations are accompanied by bargaining which reduces the trading partner's price (3) (*c*) or by overpricing Soviet exports (1) (*a*). In this event the terms of trade are indeterminate; the relative bargaining strength of the trading partners is all-important. The West European trading partners are strong and pricing tends to be close to (2) (*b*). The Soviet Union is trying to make a favorable impression on its new trading partners in Asia, Africa, and Latin America, so that (3) and (*a*) are frequently offered. In practice, however, the underpriced Soviet exports (3) are either illusory because of the conditions of trade or adverse commercial practices or are accompanied by bargaining which lowers the prices of the products of the trading partner (*c*). When premium prices (*a*) are offered, they are frequently accompanied by overpriced Soviet exports (1).

In practice, every conceivable pricing situation has arisen. The bloc paid premium prices on Egyptian cotton and then overpriced its exports. Indonesia was paid a premium for rubber but the accumulation of nonconvertible balances wiped out the advantage. Argentina, Uruguay, Iceland, and others buy Soviet petroleum at lower than market prices. The Soviet Union sold tin at the world market price (stabilized by the International Tin Council) but in the process used up all of the Council's funds and broke the price after the Soviet tin had been sold. The Soviet Union has sold aluminum at prices 4 to 12 percent lower than that offered by the leading trader, Canada, and has offered timber, pharmaceuticals, and many other products at below market prices.

The bloc has frequently been accused of dumping. This term has no meaning for state trading countries and usually has the meaning simply of unfair competition. A technical charge of dumping can be documented in the tin case, however, since the tin was a reexport from mainland China. The latter was paid a higher ruble price (8,278 rubles per ton) than were charged by the Soviet Union (8,226 rubles per ton).

It is frequently averred that the bloc has a decisive edge in price competition with the free world since the former's state trading organizations can ignore prices and can act quickly and flexibly, if they choose. This is true, but only in a limited sense. There are budgetary and planning constraints, as well as potential conflicts of interest if such a practice is pursued on anything but a relatively small scale. Large-scale price cutting or substantial rapid changes frequently involve an exorbitant cost which even the Soviet Union is unwilling to absorb and may also interfere with plans in a costly way. Overriding political considerations may on occasion dictate substantial price manipulation or a sudden change, but these circumstances are rare.

Insofar as the bloc follows world prices, its terms of trade are fundamentally similar to the average of world terms of trade for the particular product mix of the bloc country. The Soviet Union, for example, is basically a raw material exporter and a capital goods importer. Thus, when primary product prices decline, as they have in recent years, the Soviet capacity to import, in real terms, falls. The trend toward lower raw material prices recently has thus hurt the Soviet Union to some extent, in addition, the secular trend toward the improvement in terms of trade of manufactured products observed by Kindleberger and others has also reduced the Soviet capacity to import. On the other hand, the recent rising machinery exports and greater raw material imports tend to offset, at least in part, the former tendency.

East Germany and Czechoslovakia, as industrial nations, have tended to enjoy the fruits of that position. However, their industrial exports are generally of a lower quality and meet stiff competition in foreign markets, thus lowering the advantage of improving terms of trade of manufacturing countries. The rest of Eastern Europe, mainland China, and the Asiatic Communist states are raw material exporters and industrial product importers. Thus, for the most part, their terms of trade heave deteriorated to some extent in recent years.

Since the bloc countries are state traders, they can and do practice discrimination. The Soviet Union, is of course, in the best position to discriminate. The only systematic discrimination which has been observed has been against Eastern Europe. According to a careful study of recently released Soviet data, Horst Menderhausen (Review of Economics and Statistics, May 1959) indicates that the Soviet Union charges Eastern Europe more for Soviet exports and pays less for its imports from Eastern Europe than for the same products bought from and sold to Western Europe. Limited evidence also suggests that the Soviet Union, by accident or otherwise, has occasionally taken advantage of its superior bargaining power with primary producers. The bargaining strength of the Soviet Union, however, as well as of Eastern Europe and mainland China, is not sufficiently great to discriminate to achieve price advantages to any significant degree against any of its major trading partners in Western Europe.

One element in bloc terms of trade is of some technical but probably at present little practical significance. By remaining aloof from the world market while trading at world prices, and by insulating trade through bilateral agreements and completely nonconvertible currencies, the bloc is able to claim a slight edge in the terms of trade. The absence of an effective demand on the world market from the bloc on a year-to-year basis implies that the world price tends to be lower for those products which the bloc does buy than it would have if the bloc were regularly in the market. By paying the world price, the bloc has a lower import price. On the other side, the absence of regular bloc supplies implies that the world price is higher than it would have been if the bloc had been in the world market. Thus, when selling at the world price, the bloc is paid more than it would have if it had been facing competition with other sellers. This automatic edge is possible only because of the sheltered condition of bloc trade. Three-fourths of this trade is within the bloc—presumably at world prices—and the bloc is not noted as a reliable and systematic buyer and seller in free world markets. To the extent that bloc supplies and requirements are known, they can be accounted for in the world price and the improvement in the terms of trade for the bloc can be eliminated.

It is unlikely that this effect is of any great significant in free world markets, since the bloc supply and demand is not substantial in most cases. It would tend to become more significant when and if the bloc assumes more importance in the free world market generally and for particular products. It is also of greater magnitude in the exchange of bloc capital goods, which tends to have a relatively elastic supply, for primary products, which tends to have a relatively inelastic demand.

COMMERCIAL POLICY

The essential ingredient of Soviet, East European, and mainland Chinese commercial policy is one-to-one bilateralism, conducted through formal trade payments agreements to which governments are the customary signatories. All of the intrabloc trade is carried on through these agreements and much of the bloc's free world trade is so conducted.

It is easy, however, to overestimate the significance of bilateral agreements in the overall trade of the bloc with the free world. As Western currencies have become stronger, the major trading partners of the bloc have increasingly refused to trade under strict payments agreements which avoid the use of foreign exchange. The United Kingdom and West Germany, for example, have agreements but their provisions are such that no agreement is really necessary. Finland, of course, is in a weak trading position and still must trade under agreements. Even there, however, triangular agreements with East European countries in one corner have been tried. The bloc has been most successful with its agreements policy in the underdeveloped countries. Even these countries, however, have begun to revolt. India trades in sterling or convertible rupees. Indonesia abandoned strict bilateral trading. Uurguay's agreement is in effect a convertible currency agreement. Many other countries have been more insistently urging straight cash trade.

The bloc, however, thinks it sees an advantage in bilateral agreements and continues to push them wherever possible, and accepts them completely for intrabloc trade. The intrabloc agreements are coordinated with the plans of the countries involved, all of which are coordinated with Soviet plans. These agreements are quite elaborate. Bloc agreements with nonbloc countries have been increasingly liberalized. Quotas have been abandoned in most of them and as mentioned earlier, there are more provisions for convertible currency payment, rather than through clearing accounts.

Bilateral agreements are generally of two kinds: one, a trade agreement that determines the characteristics, amounts, and conditions of trade, and the other, a payments agreement which specifies the method by which each partner is paid for exports and is to pay for imports. Frequently, the two agreements are in the same document. In a few cases there are only trade agreements.

The trade agreements are usually for a period of 1 to 5 years, providing for annual tacit renewal without specific negotiations, but also permitting unilateral renunciation upon 90 days' notice. The trade agreements now frequently provide only a relatively simple listing of products or product categories to be exchanged. The individual transactions under trade agreements are carried out by ordinary commercial contracts after negotiations on prices and quantities have occurred. Most of the agreements specify an equal value of trade for both countries at a given level. In a few cases, trade is deliberately unbalanced in order to allow for paying off an indebtedness or to permit deliveries on credit. Reexportation is customarily prohibited in agreements with primary producers, but in agreements with some European countries, it is permissible.

The payments agreements specify the financial arrangements by which trade is conducted. They usually have the same duration and renewal provisions as the trade agreements. The principal provisions define whether or not a convertible currency is to be employed, and if not, provide for the establishment of clearing accounts in the appropriate financial institutions of the trading partners. The agreement also specifies the currency unit of account and credit provisions. The agreement also provides for methods of clearing balances in the clearing account, either at specified periods or at the end of the agreement, and for the correction and/or liquidation of seriously unbalanced accounts.

In typical agreement, an account is maintained in the central bank or official clearing office of both trading partners. The accounts are credited in favor of the exporting country by the value of export shipments and debited by the value of imports or other transactions giving rise to payments to the partner country. Official exchange rates are employed. The actual financing of particular commercial transactions involves the use of bank letters of credit, drafts drawn directly on the importer, and other traditional foreign exchange instruments. Banks in free world countries holding drafts on Soviet bloc country importers or their banks sell them to their own central bank, and after verification, these claims are settled by entries in the clearing account. Likewise, commercial banks having to make payments to firms or banks in bloc countries, either on their own account or for the account of customers, make the payments to their own central bank or clearing office in their own currency and the central bank in turn makes the appropriate entry in the clearing account.

Since it is seldom possible to maintain an exact balance at all times, "swing" credit provisions are made. In most of the agreements a specified sum of money is denoted as swing credit. The sum is usually a percentage of total trade, ranging from 5 to 20 percent, with about 10 percent being customary. A wide variety of settlement provisions are contained in the agreements. The four basic methods are: (1) transfer of gold or convertible currency, (2) shipment of goods, (3) triangular arrangements, and (4) reexports. The most common are the first two. Many of the agreements which make regular use of the clearing account specify payment in convertible currencies or gold either at the end of the agreement should there remain a balance, either immediately at the expiration of the agreement or after a specific waiting period, or at regular intervals during the life of the agreement, and/or when the swing credit is exceeded.

For the most part trade and payments agreements are negotiated between representatives of governments, thus committing governments to specified performance. For the bloc this is perfectly natural. It should not be concluded, however, that the agreements are enforceable legal documents, on either trading partner. The Soviet Union has on occasion ignored its agreements. Usually, if any legal action is brought, the Moscow Arbitration Court holds exclusive jurisdiction. In the free world, governments ordinarily make a commitment to make licenses available to private traders but do not guarantee the level of trade. They do, however, perform the vital function of bringing bloc state traders into contact with indigenous private traders and use the Government's good offices to acquaint buyers with bloc goods and export capabilities.

Most of the other elements of commercial policy are either not applicable to state trading nations or these countries conform generally to accepted standards. Most-favored-nation clauses, for example, although used and provided for in bloc agreements, have no meaning when all trade is in the hands of the government. The Soviet Union and other bloc countries have a tariff, but it is nominal and is not used for discrimination, since the state trading organization is a more effective discriminator.

BLOC MOTIVES FOR TRADE

Soviet bloc motives behind international trade are a curious amalgam of economic and political considerations. This is in part due to the persistence of the traditional Communist orientation toward autarky. In principle, the Soviet Union continues to pursue this dream of economic self-sufficiency but has generalized it to embrace Eastern Europe to a certain extent. On the other hand, Soviet leadership is aware of trade serving as a lever for both economic and political influence and exhibits little hesitation in conducting trade for these purposes. Simultaneously, an apparently greater recognition exists for the cost-reducing opportunities that appear in international trade.

Temporary political considerations aside, Soviet bloc trade with most of the free world, which is centered in Western Europe, is conducted primarily for commercial purposes. The Soviet bloc motivation stems basically from the necessity of procuring machinery, equipment, and materials which are either not available from domestic sources or can be had only at prohibitive costs. Its exports, in turn, are of a nature which the bloc's trading agencies feel can be disposed of with a minimum of cost or inconvenience to the national economy and its plans. Trade in itself has been regarded as a temporary necessary evil.

Ultimately, political motivations have a place in all Soviet bloc trade. Since 1953 this has been most dramatically apparent in the developing trade relations of the bloc with its new partners in Asia, Africa, and Latin America. Yet to emphasize this motivation alone would be to obfuscate rather than to illumine the complex nature of bloc motives. The very process of industrialization experienced by the Soviet Union and currently prevailing in Eastern Europe and mainland China has given rise to certain conditions related to economic factors as well.

The Soviet Union continues to need large quantities of machinery and equipment, as well as some kinds of raw materials, in its sustained emphasis on rapid industrialization. The addition of Eastern Europe and mainland China to the Soviet sphere of influence has accentuated this need and has added, at least for the present, other import requirements. It has been necessary for the Soviet Union to be the major source of important supplies for members of the bloc. Meantime, the capital goods needs of the Soviet Union itself have shifted as its economy has grown to the point where primarily the more highly technical and specialized machinery is required more than the basic simple types of capital goods. It is now simultaneously capable of exporting a limited line of standardized capital equipment. Some mineral and metals industries have begun to experience rapidly rising costs. Thus, the bloc needs trade with Western Europe (and the United States) for specialized capital goods and with primary producers for raw materials, possessing raw materials for the former and some capital goods for the latter in trade which is advantageous to the Soviet Union.

While a substantial amount of trade could and does exist on economic grounds alone, the specific conditions of trade, its volume with particular countries, and its conduct and characteristics reflect markedly political conditions. Trade is used in an attempt to create a favorable view of the Soviet Union, to reward friends and punish enemies, and to promote the ultimate aim of Communist world domination.

One of the principal aims has been to establish an impressive reputation for Soviet industry and to prove that the Soviet Union is a great power, worthy of respect and admiration. Related to this objective is the Soviet desire to demonstrate that the Soviet brand of socialism can work and indeed is the best system, because in just a few years the Soviet Union, initially weak and impotent, has risen to challenge the most advanced industrial nation. Furthermore, the Soviet Union seeks to weaken the economic and political position of the United States. The Soviet Union hopes to encourage an always-incipient neutralism, to have in public office those who are favorable to the Soviet Union, and to be able to impress those who control the means of communication. Other important political objectives include the diplomatic recognition of nations not having relations with bloc countries, the promotion of communism and local Communist parties in other countries, as well as political support for its policy positions, particularly where they conflict with those of the United States.

Soviet goals do not all work in the same direction. Frequently they conflict, giving rises to contradictory behavior. These conflicts arise in part from still unresolved internal policy disputes, from the dual position of the Soviet Union as a nation and as the chief pro-

46283—59—pt. 2——4

mulgator of communism in the world, from conflicting priorities in the use of resources—internal versus foreign and Communist versus free world—from inexperience, ineptitude, bureaucratic conflicts, and from competition and conflicts among its trading partners.

While it is clear that the Soviet Union hopes eventually to control the world and that economic relations are one of the means by which this expectation is to be achieved, for the most part the bulk of trade serves at this time the vital economic function of providing the Soviet and bloc economies with needed supplies at a cost advantage. Economic warfare for political purposes in a supplementary motivation, pursued when it can be done without significantly impairing the fundamental goal of building bloc strength.

TRADE EXPERIENCE

Living in an artificial, enforced amicability, it is not possible for the members of the bloc to complain in public about their trade experience with other members of the bloc. On several occasions it has become known that the countries of Eastern Europe and mainland China have been less than fully satisfied with their trade with the Soviet Union. The price disadvantage of Eastern Europe is more apparent to them than it is to the outside and has resulted in forceful presentations to the Soviet Union, culminating several years ago in a Soviet agreement that world prices would be the basis of intrabloc trade. As noted earlier, however, Eastern Europe remains the object to Soviet price discrimination. Mainland China as well as Eastern Europe, has felt that the Soviet Union was not providing enough economic assistance. It is probably that the bloc countries make all of the same complaints about trade with the Soviet Union that free world countries do, and then some, but it is discreetly kept within the family.

In trade with the free world it is necessary to differentiate, with respect to performance, among the bloc countries. In general, Eastern Europe, particularly East Germany, Czechoslovakia, and Poland, are better traders. Partly this results from their greater experience as world traders and partly it reflects that to Eastern Europe trade is more of an economic matter—a vital necessity in the domestic economy. To the extent that these countries sometimes do not measure up in trade, it results from the limitations of their economies, the rigidities of planning, mistakes, occasional lapses into efforts to use trade for political purposes, and the necessity to support Soviet policies, even in matters of trade. Mainland China also is, for the most part, a straightforward trader, but suffers from many of the same problems faced by Eastern Europe.

The Soviet Union is an inexperienced trader compared to Western and Eastern Europe, and even many of the primary producers. The result is a larger number of mistakes. The much-vaunted state trading organizations and planning system used in Soviet trade has revealed little flexibility in performance on most occasions. Clinging to the tattered shreds of bilateralism also does not improve Soviet trade relations. The use of trade for political purposes and the employment of the crude bargaining power which sometimes accompanies state trading also have resulted in some unsavory incidents.

It is also necessary to differentiate among the bloc's trading partners. The Western European countries are nearly all old trading nations, with centuries of experience and a considerable talent even in dealing with such obstreperous trading partners as the Soviet Union. Thus, their experience tends to be relatively satisfactory, because they know what to expect and how to handle the problems which arise. These countries have also rejected bilateralism and not trade principally in convertible currencies. The newer countries frequently not only lack trade experience in general, but also have traded with bloc countries only rarely and in small amounts. Finland and Yugoslavia are special cases. Both have been subjected to Soviet punitive action in trade matters. Finland has generally taken its punishment, at a considerable cost to its economy. Yugoslavia has been more difficult, refusing to bow to Soviet demands, even though, as in the Finnish case, at some cost to its economy.

The most important categories of failures of bloc countries, which of course do not apply either to all bloc countries or to all their trading partners, are: (1) Pricing, (2) failures to meet all trade targets, (3) large year-to-year variations in trade, (4) piling up debit balances, (5) delays and irregularities in exporting, (6) poor quality goods, (7) questionable competitive practices, and (8) unsatisfactory commercial practices. Prices have been commented upon earlier.

It is seldom that trade comes close to the targets specified in the agreements. A shortfall, sometimes of considerable significant, is most common. The Mikesell-Behrman study, "Financing Free World Trade With the Sino-Soviet Bloc," examines the statistical record. Actual imports by the bloc were between zero and 10 percent of target imports in 5 percent of the 240 agreements examined. Imports were between 10 and 25 percent of targets in 8 percent of the agreements and between 26 and 50 percent in 25 percent of the cases. Thus, the bloc imported less than one-half of what it said it would in 38 percent of the cases. Bloc exports have a similar record. The bloc exported one-half or less of agreement targets in 36 percent of the agreements. Eastern Europe performed better than the Soviet Union and West European trading partners fared better than the primary producing countries. The Soviet Union both imported and exported only 38 percent of the targets for the underdeveloped countries of Asia, Africa, and Latin America. Eastern Europe exported 65 percent and imported 72 percent of targets with these countries. On the other hand, Soviet imports from Western Europe were 88 percent of the targets and exports were 93 percent of targets. Eastern Europe's exports were 75 percent and imports 73 percent of targets in trade with West European countries.

The Soviet Union claims that planning and bilateralism lend stability and reliability to trade. The statistical record, however, shows that Soviet trade in general has wider year-to-year variations than the trade of West European countries with the same trading partners. Furthermore, under bilateral agreements in which no foreign exchange is involved, bloc countries have frequently run up substantial balances, thus in effect borrowing from their trading partners. These balances have been most common with underdeveloped countries, since the experience of Western Europe has enabled them to forestall the imbalances or insist upon the use of convertible currencies. In some cases, as in Argentina, Indonesia, and some other countries, the balances have constituted a serious problem.

Except in the case of standardized bulk commodities, bloc countries do not have a good record of quality, durability, and performance characteristics in their exports. Even in the case of East German and Czechoslovakian equipment, much of it is below the quality of machinery and equipment exports of Western Europe. Some bloc products sell at a discount in most markets and in other cases repeat sales are difficult because the first lot did not hold up. The underdeveloped countries have frequently sought redress for inferior goods. Again, however, Western European traders have spared themselves a flood of substandard bloc goods by careful buying, insistence upon guarantees, and scrutinizing each transaction closely. Irregularities in deliveries, most notably delays in shipment and shipping goods with different specifications or of a different quality, also characterizes some of Soviet bloc trade. Rigidities in planning often cause these circumstances and also result in out-of-season shipments or deliveries under other adverse circumstances.

The Soviet Union is often a difficult competitor, unpredictable and unwilling to enter international agreements. Cutting prices has enabled the Soviet Union to break into markets—such as tin, aluminum, petroleum—in which its activities in the past have been minimal. The other supplying countries complain bitterly, but there is little that can be done. The primary producers—Bolivia, Malaya, and Canada, among others—have received the hardest treatment, but even in the machinery field, Western Europe is beginning to feel some bloc competition. Bloc countries also pursue some other unsavory commercial practices, such as reexporting commodities in violation of agreements, changing prices of exports, and so forth.

The above is not intended as a blanket indictment of experiences and performance in bloc foreign trade. The bulk of that trade is in fact more or less normal commercial intercourse, conducted under reasonably satisfactory conditions. The aberrations are tendencies which occur when trading partners are new, inexperienced, or not watchful in trade with the bloc.

EVALUATION AND PROSPECTS

Soviet bloc trade is not of any great significance either in its overall volume or with reference to particular commodities in total world commerce. Most of the trade of each bloc country is with other bloc countries, with the Soviet Union the leading trading partner in each case. Trade of the bloc with the free world is an important marginal element in the trade of many of the West European countries, is of considerable significance to Iceland, Finland, and Yugoslavia, and is of growing importance for a group of primary producing countries, such as Egypt and India. Soviet bloc trade in recent years has been growing more rapidly than world trade, but leveled off in 1958. Except for East German and Czechoslovakian trade, bloc trade is fundamentally an exchange of raw materials and food for machinery and equipment. A reverse trend is beginning for Soviet trade with underdeveloped countries.

The conditions of Soviet bloc trade leave much to be desired, deriving from inexperience, the use of the predatory policies of state trading and bilateralism, and the effort to use trade for political purposes. The more experienced trading partners have managed to avoid the potential deleterious effects of trade with the bloc by carefully monitoring such trade. While state trading is a permanent fixture, bilateralism is weakening as increasing numbers of bloc trading partners insist upon trade in convertible currencies. Nearly all of Western Europe is in this position now and more primary producers are beginning to insist upon this type of payments. Bloc motives for trade have been and remain fundamentally economic in nature, although political factors have intruded increasingly in recent years.

Soviet bloc trade will continue to expand in the years to come. The 7-year plan schedules substantial increases. The plan also, however, calls for large additions to the output level of many items, such as cotton and wool, which are still imported. In the nonmachinery categories, the bloc will tend to become more autarchic in the next decade. More important, however, is that the investment plans call for such an expansion of capital facilities that not only will large-scale capital imports be required to fulfill the plan, but it is also unlikely that substantially enlarged machinery and equipment exports to underdeveloped countries will be possible. Eastern Europe will continue to need raw material and food imports on a large scale and will probably seek these products more outside the bloc than inside.

There exists the possibility that for some particular products, the Soviet bloc, especially the Soviet Union, could begin to assume major proportions in the world market in the near future. If petroleum production increases as scheduled and the internal utilization rate does not increase sharply, it is likely that Soviet and Rumanian oil will become important competitors of the Middle East and the United States within the next decade. Aluminum, possibly tin, and perhaps other products occupy similar positions.

It is frequently speculated that the Soviet Union now and will increasingly possess the capability and desire to use its influence in trade to disrupt world markets. The tin case and a few similar incidents are regarded as forerunners of this eventuality. It is undoubtedly true that the Soviet Union, augmented by its gold store and the production of other bloc countries, have this capability and over time it will increase. But it does not seem likely that the capability will be so used except under unusual circumstances. The bloc looks to trade as an important adjunct to the domestic economy and disruption of markets would not contribute to this goal. Even the bloc's political objectives generally run in terms of making friends, becoming respectable, and winning influence through good deeds. There will unquestionably be instances where the bloc's activities are disruptive, but the general trend at this time seems to be in terms of normalized trade and the economic and political benefits it confers.

IMPLICATIONS FOR U.S. POLICY

Just a few obiter dicta on U.S. policy: At least four important areas of U.S. foreign economic policy are conditioned by Soviet-bloc foreign economic policies. They are (1) foreign economic and military assistance, (2) strategic trade controls, (3) the mechanics of

U.S. foreign trade, and (4) U.S. trade with Soviet Union and the rest of the bloc.

U.S. foreign assistance, at least in part, serves the purpose of preventing those conditions from arising which the Soviet Union can exploit to its advantage. The apparent success of Soviet efforts with foreign assistance have made some wonder whether or not the United States should emulate the Soviet Union in the conduct of its foreign assistance program. It must be remembered, however, that the Soviet program is an imitation of U.S. aid, particularly as embodied in the Marshall plan and Truman doctrine. Furthermore, the objectives of the two nations must be borne in mind. The Soviet Union hopes to break Western alliances and gain political influence by selective use of small amounts of assistance and a great deal of publicity. The United States is interested in economic development, hoping thereby to create conditions helpful to U.S. interests in terms of economically and politically stable democratic regimes. If the United States were to try to imitate the Soviet Union, it would do violence to its basic aims and would probably spend its entire time and substance chasing around putting out fires. The United States requires an assistance program based coordinately upon the public development needs of its friends and allies and those neutrals who share the same general public philosophy, and upon the U.S. ability to supply public loans and grants. Such an effort should be supplemented by large-scale private investment, fostered by whatever public measures are necessary to encourage this development. This program would not be insensitive to what the Soviet Union does, but would not be built around Soviet actions, either in fact or in the minds of the American people or of the potential recipients.

Strategic trade controls now have limited scope and are probably doomed, as they should be. Such measures are best suited for imposition in the likelihood of hostilities within a reasonably short period. Otherwise, the potential enemy insulates himself against the deprivation and in time is better off than would have been the case in the absence of the embargo. An open society such as the West cannot long deprive even a potential enemy of technology and goods unless war is imminent. To attempt to do so gives the opposition a tremendous propaganda weapon and whipping boy for all the world's trade ills, and in fact does little to prevent the development of the opposition. If in the wisdom of the Government, some specialized goods should not be sold to the bloc, this can be handled by an ordinary export licensing system and through informal representations to allies.

It is often thought that the United States is at a decisive disadvantage in trade because its trade is in private hands, whereas in the Soviet Union all trade is controlled by the political leadership. The point is highly debatable on political grounds and on economic grounds there is little or no argument. The use of a state-trading agency by the U.S. Government to meet the Soviet Union in competition would give every advantage to the opposition, most notably the initiative. It would be relatively easy for the Soviet Union, with or without the collusion of its trading partners, to keep a U.S. state trading agency in continual chaos and to bankrupt it almost at will. The strength of the United States lies in the fact that it embodies a better and different system of trading. To adopt the opposition's methods would be to lose before starting.

Within the limits of the security of the United States there is no reason why the Soviet Union should not be able to buy what it pleases in this country. But there is certainly no reason for an intergovernmental agreement—to do so would be to set a bad example and would not be in line with the way the United States does business. Credit extension is also a private matter. There seems to be little advantage in continuing to hold lend-lease and tsarist debts against the Soviet Union. It would seem more desirable simply to let U.S. exporters decide on credit matters on the merits of each case. There can be no justification for U.S. Government credit. It does not make sense for the United States to make loans to the Soviet Union when that country is making loans to other countries for the specific purpose of undermining the United States. Let the Soviet Union buy what it will; let Americans buy what they will; all within the traditional framework of U.S. trade and without favoritism or prejudice by the Government.

U.S. foreign economic policy must have an orientation of its own, built upon U.S. goals and conducted within the framework of U.S. practices. Reliance upon the enterprise system, properly encouraged by the Government, with direct Government action when the activity is clearly not within the scope or capabilities of private individuals, should be the keynote of U.S. policy. The United States should do or not do what is in its interests, regardless of what the Soviet Union does or might do. U.S. policy should not ignore Soviet actions, but these actions should be and in fact are only a part of the considerations involved in the discharge of the global responsibilities of the United States.

BIBLIOGRAPHY

Allen, Robert Loring, "Middle Eastern Economic Relations with the Soviet Union, Eastern Europe, and Mainland China," Department of Foreign Affairs, University of Virginia, 1958, 128 p.

———, "A Note on Soviet Foreign Trade Statistics," Soviet Studies, vol. X, No. 4, April 1959, pp. 360–369.

———, "Soviet Economic Warfare," in press, 1959 publication.

———, "Soviet Influence in Latin America: the Role of Economic Relations," Public Affairs Press, 1959, 108 p.

Berliner, Joseph S., "Soviet Economic Aid," Praeger for the Council on Foreign Relations, 1958, 232 p.

Economic Commission for Europe, "Economic Bulletin(s) of Europe" (quarterly) and "Economic Survey(s) of Europe" (annual), United Nations, Geneva.

Mikesell, Raymond and Behrman, Jack, "Financing Free World Trade with the Sino-Soviet Bloc, International Finance Series No. 8," International Finance Section, Princeton University, 1958, 254 p.

Vneshniaia Torgovila, monthly and statistical supplements, Moscow.

Vneshniaia Torgovlia SSSR co Capitalisticheskimi Stranami, Vneshtorgizdat, Moscow, 1957.

Vneshniaia Torgovlia SSSR co Socialisticheskimi Stranami, Vneshtorgizdat, Moscow, 1957.

Vneshniaia Torgovlia SSSR co Stranami Asii, Afriki, i Latinskoi Ameriki, Vneshtorgizdat, Moscow, 1958.

United Nations, "Yearbook(s) of International Trade Statistics," New York, annual.

U.S. Department of State, "The Sino-Soviet Economic Offensive in the Less Developed Countries," Washington, 1958, 111 p.

STATISTICAL APPENDIX

TABLE 1.—*World exports by origin and destination, 1957*

[Billions of dollars]

Exporting area	Area of destination					
	Total free world	Soviet Union	Eastern Europe	China	Total Sino-Soviet bloc [1]	World [2]
Free world industrialized [3]	65.3	0.64	[4] 1.01	0.30	1.95	70.2
All primary exporting areas	28.1	.35	.34	.23	.92	29.7
Total free world trade	93.4	.99	1.35	.53	2.87	99.8
Soviet Union	.96	----------	2.55	.54	3.23	4.4
Eastern Europe	1.19	1.98	1.41	.30	3.83	5.5
China	.60	.74	.26	----------	1.53	2.1
Total Sino-Soviet bloc [1]	2.75	2.94	4.21	1.34	8.49	11.5
World [2]	96.2	3.9	5.5	1.9	11.4	111.3

[1] Including trade with Mongolia, North Vietnam, and North Korea.
[2] World totals include special categories, unallocated exports, and some statistical discrepancy due to the utilization of various sources of data.
[3] Western Europe, United States, and Japan.
[4] Excluding trade between Eastern and Western Germany.
Source: "Economic Bulletin for Europe," Economic Commission for Europe, Geneva, vol. X, No. 2, August 1958, table 3, p. 38.

TABLE 2.—*Soviet and East European trade, 1938–57*

[Millions of U.S. dollars]

	1938	1948	1952	1953	1954	1955	1956	1957
World: [1]								
Imports	23,200	58,500	79,200	75,800	79,000	88,200	97,200	106,400
Exports	20,700	53,000	72,300	73,300	76,100	82,800	92,000	98,800
Soviet Union:								
Imports	268	--------	--------	--------	--------	3,061	3,613	3,938
Exports	251	--------	--------	--------	--------	3,469	3,669	4,381
Bulgaria:								
Imports	60	--------	--------	200	196	195	248	--------
Exports	68	--------	--------	206	233	230	339	--------
Czechoslovakia:								
Imports	239	757	--------	--------	--------	1,053	1,186	1,385
Exports	295	753	--------	--------	--------	1,176	1,387	1,356
East Germany:								
Imports	--------	--------	773	983	1,096	1,173	1,334	1,615
Exports	--------	--------	739	968	1,280	1,278	1,407	1,811
Hungary:								
Imports	123	167	--------	--------	--------	534	456	665
Exports	155	166	--------	--------	--------	609	493	497
Poland:								
Imports	248	516	863	774	904	932	1,022	1,251
Exports	225	533	780	831	869	920	985	982
Rumania:								
Imports	137	--------	--------	--------	--------	384	352	--------
Exports	157	--------	--------	--------	--------	391	395	--------

[1] Excluding Soviet Union, Eastern Europe, and mainland China. Mainland Chinese data has not been available since 1948.

TABLE 3.—*Soviet trade, 1938–57*

	Imports				Exports			
	1938	1955	1956	1957	1938	1955	1956	1957
Total trade	1,422.9	12,242.2	14,452.5	15,751.3	1,331.9	13,874.3	14,446.3	17,526.0
Afghanistan	13.7	43.7	60.5	82.7	14.8	54.4	73.0	72.5
Albania	--------	21.9	32.6	56.4	--------	60.7	72.9	130.6
Argentina	4.2	112.7	51.8	83.3	.3	95.8	76.5	18.7
Austria	4.6	142.2	258.6	272.4	2.2	55.0	43.7	72.1
Belgium	64.2	60.8	128.2	122.7	116.8	96.5	116.9	112.7
Bulgaria	--------	485.5	578.7	792.4	--------	510.0	433.6	690.1
Burma	1.0	67.3	49.1	36.2	--------	.6	17.1	25.9
Canada	30.6	10.5	98.3	35.6	1.5	7.8	8.6	16.8
China	68.5	2,574.0	3,056.9	2,952.5	44.1	2,993.4	2,932.1	2,176.4
Cuba	--------	143.1	58.5	188.4	--------	--------	--------	--------
Czechoslovakia	19.4	1,546.0	1,585.8	1,542.3	13.2	1,423.8	1,494.8	2,205.2
Denmark	5.1	39.8	25.6	45.5	27.4	30.5	33.1	52.1
Egypt	.3	61.5	201.4	443.7	12.1	44.1	153.7	328.8
Finland	3.4	511.3	584.8	660.8	10.8	424.7	459.1	601.8
France	39.4	144.4	202.3	190.1	59.7	238.8	278.5	268.0
Germany, East	67.2 (East and West)	2,025.7	2,505.3	3,057.4	88.3 (East and West)	1,914.7	2,285.4	3,448.2
Germany, West		95.1	272.5	247.4		117.1	167.2	285.7
Ghana	--------	46.2	33.0	75.7	0	0	0	0
Greece	1.5	9.4	25.2	38.4	17.3	17.1	28.9	48.9
Hungary	--------	586.1	483.3	426.9	.1	461.2	507.4	998.9
Iceland	0	39.9	49.9	55.1	0	41.3	39.7	46.3
India	--------	17.6	73.2	167.8	3.6	29.3	161.6	338.6
Iran	63.8	76.2	60.6	74.1	58.0	89.8	76.7	126.6
Italy	--------	65.2	103.9	181.5	.1	69.9	135.7	116.6
Korea, North	--------	163.0	204.8	250.2	--------	176.6	215.3	239.4
Malaya	--------	87.2	335.9	195.2	--------	0	1.3	2.4
Mongolia	38.5	215.1	217.2	200.5	69.8	486.8	413.6	270.7
Netherlands	102.5	133.7	39.6	81.7	92.8	131.4	167.4	131.0
Norway	9.9	60.2	86.1	72.2	21.6	70.4	78.2	84.3
Poland	1.5	1,146.6	1,133.0	1,023.6	7.8	1,727.4	1,429.0	1,723.4
Rumania	.8	839.3	941.4	760.2	.6	1,070.9	848.1	1,003.0
Sweden	27.4	68.0	104.1	100.8	13.5	114.2	138.6	12.57
Switzerland	11.8	16.4	7.5	14.6	12.2	33.6	46.4	40.0
Turkey	22.7	20.5	26.4	21.9	22.7	29.8	23.9	35.7
Union of South Africa	.6	37.9	51.3	106.8	7.6	0	2.1	1.1
United Kingdom	240.3	284.3	297.6	448.4	375.1	676.6	592.6	755.7
United States	405.9	2.2	19.2	40.6	96.7	95.2	108.7	63.7
Uruguay	--------	39.9	49.2	72.5	--------	1.2	11.4	.5
Yugoslavia	--------	70.0	198.7	227.3	.1	65.6	276.2	292.4

Source: "Yearbook of International Trade Statistics, 1957," vol. I, New York, 1958, p. 576.

TABLE 4.—*Czechoslovakian trade, 1955–57*

[Millions of korunas]

	Imports			Exports		
	1955	1956	1957 January-September	1955	1956	1957 January September
Total trade	7,579	8,537	7,109	8,467	9,988	6,785
Soviet Union	----------	2,808	2,646	----------	3,084	1,837
China	----------	478	369	----------	466	454
Bulgaria	----------	229	246	----------	259	166
East Germany	----------	852	686	----------	1,010	675
Hungary	----------	467	351	----------	424	395
Poland	----------	554	351	----------	714	403
Rumania	----------	205	148	----------	252	181
Argentina	----------	86	43	----------	82	25
Austria	120	155	142	135	144	100
Belgium	57	91	61	61	83	44
Brazil	----------	146	92	----------	145	78
Denmark	43	33	54	40	55	34
Finland	59	80	61	130	157	138
France	53	91	54	51	64	73
West Germany	119	280	317	224	364	282
Greece	13	25	28	18	35	36
Iceland	15	29	19	21	29	23
Italy	61	73	51	84	89	71
Malaya	----------	56	73	----------	11	8
Netherlands	88	135	117	119	133	95
Norway	57	63	48	57	72	35
Portugal	12	10	9	8	7	3
Sweden	37	73	59	48	80	39
Switzerland	144	207	113	139	153	104
Turkey	148	122	97	143	147	129
United Kingdom	202	193	168	163	178	149
Yugoslavia	----------	48	15	----------	97	93

Source: "Yearbook of International Trade Statistics, 1957," vol. I, New York, 1958, p. 165.

TABLE 5.—*East German trade, 1953–57*

	Imports				Exports			
	1953	1955	1956	1957	1953	1955	1956	1957
Total trade	3,930.1	4,690.9	5,334.9	6,461.9	3,870.0	5,112.6	5,629.0	7,243.0
Albania	3.7	5.1	7.7	10.8	12.0	24.6	18.3	17.7
Austria	67.0	51.6	64.9	56.8	51.8	53.4	42.3	54.4
Belgium-Luxembourg	62.7	46.4	45.9	33.2	27.0	25.1	31.6	38.9
Brazil	0	.1	15.5	33.9	.2	2.1	1.8	6.6
Bulgaria	72.1	124.0	137.4	106.4	79.7	85.0	129.7	119.2
China	212.1	346.6	343.6	354.2	241.5	389.6	379.7	423.0
Czechoslovakia	233.4	282.9	421.4	475.6	226.5	375.3	439.0	562.2
Denmark	54.4	60.2	55.4	39.6	49.2	56.1	56.0	50.8
Egypt	14.9	18.2	38.4	69.1	4.9	25.4	31.8	93.0
Finland	33.6	69.1	70.0	64.2	40.4	78.8	81.3	86.0
France	16.4	29.8	37.1	67.0	11.5	16.9	16.3	30.6
Germany, West	250.8	524.4	584.7	735.5	278.8	545.7	616.0	818.6
Hungary	137.3	248.4	156.7	188.3	170.4	184.5	190.7	252.9
India	0	5.3	13.9	31.4	3.1	12.8	23.2	29.2
Italy	21.5	42.0	30.4	20.3	19.6	38.2	31.0	22.1
Korea	0	.4	6.7	10.1	28.4	30.5	33.2	27.2
Netherlands	109.9	117.4	108.5	81.4	71.9	72.9	85.1	84.5
Norway	29.4	32.9	30.6	32.7	30.0	29.0	40.3	27.2
Poland	447.7	458.5	419.4	411.8	434.0	495.0	556.0	604.5
Rumania	59.7	151.6	116.6	84.2	125.0	99.1	114.2	135.6
Sweden	53.2	51.9	49.0	57.6	50.9	54.7	58.3	52.3
Turkey	1.9	46.9	63.1	66.1	8.6	57.1	54.0	72.8
United Kingdom	66.3	69.6	69.5	132.3	37.0	48.3	48.8	59.9
United States	37.9	21.4	23.7	14.5	34.9	29.3	28.4	24.3
U.S.S.R	1,833.5	1,688.5	2,228.3	2,943.9	1,733.6	2,062.7	2,277.2	3,238.8
Yugoslavia	0	6.9	14.1	24.2	0	7.6	13.4	34.7

Source: "Yearbook of International Trade Statistics, 1957," vol. I, New York, 1958, p. 230.

TABLE 6.—*Polish trade, 1947–57*

Regions and principal countries	Imports				Exports			
	1947	1955	1956	1957	1947	1955	1956	1957
Total trade:								
Million rubles	--------	3, 727. 2	4, 087. 4	5, 066. 1	--------	3, 654. 0	3, 899. 1	3, 899. 9
Million U.S. dollars	317. 5	931. 8	1, 022. 0	1, 251. 0	248. 2	913. 5	974. 8	975. 0
	Percentages							
Africa	0. 7	1. 1	0. 6	1. 4	0. 1	0. 6	0. 8	1. 2
United States	16. 0	--------	. 2	4. 5	. 3	--------	2. 4	2. 7
Argentina	1. 0	3. 1	. 5	. 4	. 5	2. 4	. 3	. 3
Brazil	4. 8	--------	. 8	1. 3	. 7	--------	1. 3	1. 3
China	. 0	3. 8	3. 4	3. 0	. 0	3. 8	5. 2	4. 6
Austria	. 7	1. 9	2. 6	2. 8	4. 7	3. 1	2. 5	3. 3
Belgium	1. 8	1. 3	1. 0	1. 1	1. 7	. 4	. 7	. 5
Bulgaria	2. 3	. 7	1. 1	1. 2	1. 2	1. 0	. 7	1. 2
Czechoslovakia	2. 0	8. 5	10. 1	6. 2	6. 0	8. 2	7. 8	6. 2
Finland	2. 3	1. 7	1. 7	2. 0	3. 0	3. 6	3. 4	4. 3
France	4. 0	3. 7	3. 2	1. 8	2. 9	1. 4	3. 2	4. 1
Germany, East	2. 3	13. 1	13. 2	13. 2	3. 9	13. 7	11. 0	12. 9
Germany, West	. 4	2. 5	5. 5	4. 4	. 3	3. 2	5. 4	5. 1
Hungary	1. 2	3. 3	2. 3	1. 7	1. 4	2. 9	2. 5	3. 3
Italy	. 5	. 9	. 7	1. 3	2. 3	. 7	. 8	1. 0
Rumania	. 1	1. 3	1. 4	1. 2	. 3	1. 4	2. 0	1. 7
Sweden	9. 0	1. 6	1. 5	1. 7	16. 6	2. 3	2. 7	1. 7
Turkey	0	1. 3	1. 1	. 9	0	1. 7	. 6	1. 0
United Kingdom	8. 6	4. 5	3. 2	3. 8	5. 4	8. 5	8. 1	6. 5
U.S.S.R	25. 1	33. 7	35. 3	33. 4	28. 4	30. 7	27. 7	26. 5
Australia	0	3. 0	3. 4	3. 4	0	0	0	. 1
Total trade	100. 0	100. 0	100. 0	100. 0	100. 0	100. 0	100. 0	100. 0

Source: "Yearbook of International Trade Statistics, 1957," vol. I, New York, 1958, p. 473

TABLE 7.—*Commodity composition of Soviet trade, 1913–57* [1]

[Percentages]

Item	1913	1928	1938	1950	1954	1957
EXPORTS						
Machinery and equipment	0.3	0.1	5.0	16.3	21.5	14.9
Fuels, raw materials	42.8	63.1	57.7	50.7	58.5	64.1
Coal	.1	.6	1.0	.3	1.1	4.3
Petroleum and products	3.3	13.5	7.8	1.5	4.2	9.1
Ferrous-nonferrous metals	.6	.8	1.6	12.6	18.2	14.7
Lumber	6.3	6.8	14.1	2.0	2.6	3.1
Other timber	4.5	5.1	6.0	.9	1.0	1.2
Cotton	----	----	1.9	11.7	12.1	5.9
Fiber-flax	6.2	3.1	1.7	.5	.1	.3
Furs	.4	15.1	9.4	3.3	1.2	----
Other	21.4	18.1	14.2	17.9	18.0	25.5
Grain	33.3	3.3	21.3	18.5	12.2	12.9
Consumer goods	23.6	33.5	16.0	14.5	7.8	8.1
Meat, dairy products, eggs	12.0	13.1	.3	4.6	.1	----
Sugar	1.8	4.3	2.5	1.0	.9	----
Fabrics	3.0	6.5	4.8	2.7	1.6	----
Other	6.8	9.6	8.4	6.2	5.2	----
Total	100.0	100.0	100.0	100.0	100.0	100.0
IMPORTS						
Machinery	15.9	23.9	34.5	27.1	32.6	23.9
Fuels, raw materials	63.4	67.8	60.7	56.6	46.2	55.5
Coal	5.5	.1	----	2.3	3.7	2.0
Petroleum products	.4	----	1.2	5.5	3.3	3.0
Ores and concentrates	.1	----	2.6	1.7	3.6	11.5
Ferrous and nonferrous metals	6.8	13.7	25.9	9.3	5.8	7.4
Natural rubber	2.9	2.5	3.5	3.8	.4	2.7
Cotton	8.3	16.3	1.8	.2	.2	3.1
Other textile raw materials	10.0	10.3	7.9	5.5	6.8	----
Peanuts, soybeans, and other oilseeds	.1	----	.1	3.1	3.6	2.0
Other	29.3	24.9	17.7	25.2	18.8	25.8
Consumer goods	20.7	8.3	4.8	16.3	21.2	20.6
Meat, dairy products, eggs	.7	----	.3	1.9	6.0	----
Sugar	----	.1	.0	3.8	1.9	----
Fruit, vegetables	2.8	1.8	1.9	1.0	1.6	----
Fabrics	2.7	.1	.4	4.7	4.3	----
Other	14.5	6.3	2.2	4.9	7.4	----
Total	100.0	100.0	100.0	100.0	100.0	100.0

[1] Narodnoe Khozaistvo S.S.S.R.: Statisticheskii Sbornik, Tsentral'noe Statisticheskoe Upravlanie * * * S.S.S.R. (Moscow, 1956), p. 217.

TABLE 8.—*Commodity composition of Soviet and East European trade, 1956*

[Percentages]

	Bulgaria	Czechoslovakia	East Germany [1]	Hungary	Poland	Rumania	Soviet Union
EXPORTS							
Machinery and equipment	3.5	40.3	60.4	30.3	15.6	10.1	19.5
Consumer goods	15.3	15.4	7.8	15.4	63.8	3.5	5.6
Fuels and raw materials	36.9	36.9	29.8	32.2	8.9	62.6	66.1
Food	44.3	7.4	2.0	31.1	11.7	23.8	8.8
IMPORTS							
Machinery and equipment	42.3	17.2	4.7	12.2	33.2	20.5	26.6
Consumer goods	17.3	3.2	17.9	4.1	48.6	4.4	13.1
Fuels and raw materials	38.7	55.0	41.3	70.8	5.8	68.2	55.1
Food	1.7	24.6	36.1	12.9	12.4	6.9	5.2

[1] 1955.

Source: "Economic Survey of Europe, 1957", Economic Commission for Europe, Geneva, 1958, table XXXIII, pp. A53–A59. Categories are not identical for all countries.

SOME FINANCIAL ASPECTS OF SOVIET FOREIGN TRADE

(By Franklyn D. Holzman,[1] University of Washington and Russian Research Center, Harvard University)

Financial factors play a less important role in the Soviet economy than they do in the economies of Western nations. This is also true of Soviet foreign trade in comparison with the foreign trade of other nations. Financial factors nevertheless have osme significance and will continue to have significance for the conduct of Soviet international transactions as long as trade is not conducted on a strictly barter basis, prices and exchange rates are quoted, and gold and foreign exchange are recognized as having value and serving as international legal tender.

The following topics are discussed below: (1) Trends in the official ruble exchange rate, (2) the disequilibrium character of the ruble exchange rate, (3) the reflection of the overvalued ruble on enterprise and budget accounts, (4) Soviet international price policy and the foreign trade accounts, (5) the impact of Soviet foreign trade on internal financial stability, (6) Soviet gold policy, and (7) payments agreements.

1. *Trends in the official ruble exchange rate* [4, pp. 292 ff.; 16, pp 198–199]

An exchange rate is the price of one currency in terms of another or in terms of gold, the common denominator of currencies. In a market in which trade flows freely and prices and exchange rates are allowed to seek their own levels, the relative prices of two currencies will reflect, roughly, the relative purchasing power of each currency in its own country, particularly of internationally tradeable goods. Neglecting the refinements,[2] it could be said that an exchange rate between two currencies which (1) more or less achieves a balance of payments without controls, and (2) roughly reflects the price differentials between countries of "tradeables," is an equilibrium exchange rate.

Since World War I, of course, the exchange rates of many Western nations have failed at one time or another to meet these specifications and have been maintained temporarily at disequilibrium levels by controls. In most cases, disequilibrium has eventually led to devaluation, as a last-resort measure, to achieve equilibrium. It is no exaggeration to say that over the past 30 years the exchange rate of no Western nation has been as far out of line from its equilibrium value as the Soviet ruble exchange rate. And no Western nation has applied such extensive controls to foreign trade, controls which are an integral part of the planning organization and which, among other

[1] I wish to express my appreciation to Edwin Cohn and Herbert Levine for critical comments on a draft of this paper and to the Harvard Russian Research Center for financial support.

[2] Neglecting here capital flows, levels of employment and unemployment, and income-elasticities of demand for imports.

things, make it possible for the Soviets to maintain a balance on current account with a disequilibrium exchange rate. The Soviet exchange rate has typically been so far out of line and controls have operated so successfully, that it seems fair to describe the rate as no more than an accounting device for converting foreign currency prices of Soviet exports and imports into rubles for the purpose of constructing foreign trade accounts in local currency.

While the ruble exchange rate has been a fictitious one in the sense that it has little basis in terms of relative commodity prices, the Soviets have seen fit, from time to time, to make exchange rate adjustments. First, these will be traced briefly and then their relationship to Soviet internal price trends will be indicated.

After the Revolution, the ruble was maintained at its prerevolutionary exchange rate. While the gold content of the ruble was specified at 0.774234 grams, [4, p. 297] it was typically quoted in terms of dollars as having a value of $0.5146. This nominal value of the ruble was maintained until the U.S. flight from the gold standard and devaluation of January 1, 1934. Devaluation reduced the value of the dollar from $20 to $35 an ounce of gold. Concomitantly, the ruble-dollar rate changed from $0.5146 to $0.8712 per ruble. After this date, the ruble was typically quoted in terms of francs (one of the few currencies still tied to gold) at 13.1 francs to a ruble.

The next change occurred when, in a decree of November 11, 1935, the Soviets set a special rate for tourists of 3 francs to the ruble to be effective as of January 1, 1936. On April 1, 1936, this rate was extended to cover all foreign transactions, including primarily commodity trade. The change of April 1, 1936, was, of course, a massive devaluation leaving the ruble worth less than 23 percent (1/4.38) of its previous value. It's dollar value fell from $0.8712 to $0.1992 (and franc value from 13.1 to 3.0 francs).

This situation was soon altered. In October 1936, the franc left gold and was devalued raising the franc-ruble ratio from 3 to 4.5. Ostensibly because of this devaluation, the Soviets redefined the ruble in terms of dollars on July 19, 1937. The new valuation involved a slight devaluation of the ruble from $0.1992 to $0.1887 (or 5.3 rubles to the dollar).

The ruble maintained nominal stability from 1937 until 1950. On March 1, 1950, the ruble was revalued upward by 32.5 percent and specifically defined as having a gold content of 0.222168 grams of gold and therefore worth 4 rubles to the dollar. This change was made, according to the Soviets, because of the loss in value of the dollar as a result of post-World War II inflation. (The validity of this claim will be examined below.) Only one further change has been made since 1950: The tourist rate which had been 4 rubles to the dollar along with all other transactions, was devalued to 10 rubles to the dollar in April 1957. The 4-ruble-to-the-$1 rate remains in force for all other transactions.

2. *A disequilibrium exchange rate: The overvalued ruble* [3]

As we have already noted, the exchange rate which was in force until 1936 was the same, in terms of gold, as that which prevailed

---

[3] The materials presented in this section contain some of the preliminary results of a larger study of Soviet foreign trade pricing which is nearing completion. The empirical part of this study compares Soviet export and import unit values with Soviet domestic prices and world prices, respectively, for a number of prewar and postwar years [8].

before World War I although the rates in terms of individual foreign currencies were often quite different due to the widespread revaluations in Europe after World War I and during the thirties. Under relatively stable domestic conditions, it would appear unlikely that the international value of the ruble could have remained in "equilibrium" without any change of its par value over the 25-year period. As it was, the Russian economy underwent, as is well known, a devastating war and a complete change of government and economic organization. The major consequence of these events from the point of view of the international value of the ruble was the hyperinflation, which gripped the Soviet economy after World War I. Before hyperinflation was finally eliminated by the monetary reform of 1924, the internal price level was many billions of times higher than it had been right after the Revolution [2]. It obviously makes little sense to talk of equilibrium exchange rates under such conditions.

How close to a purchasing power parity equilibrium the ruble was right after the reform in 1924 I cannot say. One observer states that "It was probably sometime in 1926 or 1927 that foreign trade became entirely divorced from the internal cost of export goods or the ruble prices of imported goods" [9, p. 170]. This was certainly the case by 1929 (and probably true for 1926–27). Comparisons of average unit values of a substantial sample of Soviet export goods with internal wholesale prices of the same commodities indicate that, on the average, Soviet exports were being sold at less than 40 percent of cost. Around this average there was a very large dispersion with, for example, manganese and iron ores selling at 50 percent above domestic wholesale price, coal and coke roughly at domestic price, and petroleum products at one-fourth domestic price. One might reasonably ask: Why, on the average, did the Soviets sell so much below domestic wholesale price? The answer is simple: With an overvalued exchange rate, the Soviets, if they were to sell abroad, had to sell at below cost in order to compete on world markets. This did not necessarily involve them in a real loss, however. For they were compensated by being able to import needed goods at a similar or greater percentage below domestic cost or price.

This type of transaction can be handled very expeditiously by a country which has nationalized its industry and foreign trade. With an overvalued exchange rate, the foreign trade monopoly is willing, for example, to export abroad for 500 rubles a commodity which costs 1,000 rubles to produce if it can use the 500 rubles of foreign currency earned to import a commodity which costs, say 1,100 rubles to produce domestically. (The difficulty in defining "dumping" under these circumstances is obvious.) A free enterprise economy, on the other hand, in which exports and imports are handled by entirely different persons and enterprises, would find this an unenviable situation (in the absence of direct controls) as profitable opportunities for imports expanded at the same time that profitable opportunities for exports contracted. Presumably under these circumstances, a capitalist nation would be forced either to devalue or to reduce the volume of trade by restricting imports to an amount which could be financed by exports (abstracting from reserves and capital flows). The foreign trade monopoly, as indicated, would be under no such constraint but could maintain the level of trade undiminished simply subsidizing exports out of profits from imports (the mechanics of this are described below).

The gap between export prices on the one hand and domestic wholesale prices and costs on the other increased during the first half of the thirties. This can be inferred from two sets of observations: (1) Comparison of price trends from 1929 to 1935, and (2) direct comparison of export unit values with domestic wholesale prices for 1935. Over the period 1929–35, a study published by the League of Nations [12] indicates that Soviet export prices declined to one-third of their previous level. This decline was not unique to Soviet exports, of course, but reflected the generally depressed conditions of the period. Unlike the situation in other nations where falling export prices were matched in part by falling internal prices as a result of high levels of unemployment, Soviet internal costs and prices were rising as the result of internal inflation [7]. Consumers' goods prices rose by 400–500 percent over the 6-year period. The prices of basic industrial goods rose very little—by only 6 or 7 percent.[4] These prices did not reflect costs, however. Costs had been rising very rapidly. Wage rates, the basic cost element, rose by almost 300 percent over the period. The small increase in prices of basic industrial goods reflects a deliberate Soviet policy to keep producers' goods prices stable despite rising costs by the use of liberal subsidies. To summarize: The rise in domestic prices, and especially in costs, and the fall in export prices point to an increase in the gap between domestic prices and costs and export prices.

Direct comparison of unit values of a sample of exports with domestic wholesale prices (many of which are undoubtedly below cost) supports the above results. By 1935, every group of items sampled was sold abroad at below domestic wholesale price. On an average, domestic wholesale prices were 8 times as high as export unit values[5] including petroleum products and 5½ times as high excluding petroleum products.

Without doubt, the disequilibrium character of the ruble exchange rate was at a peak in 1935. In 1936, as we have seen, the ruble underwent a 77 percent devaluation and this certainly served to bring the exchange rate closer into line with domestic costs and prices. The devaluation may have been conceived as part of the more general price reform which was accomplished in 1936. As we have seen, prices of basic industrial materials had been kept stable in the face of rising costs for a number of years. In 1936, these prices were increased by more than 50 percent in a general attempt to eliminate subsidies and thereby equalize costs and wholesale prices. This price increase had the effect, of course, of partly offsetting the effectiveness of the devaluation in bringing domestic wholesale prices and export prices into line.[6]

This, in turn, was offset, however, by the upswing in world market prices in general; the prices (measured in the currencies of the major trading nations) which the Soviets were able to obtain for their exports rose by some 50 percent over the next 2 years [12].

---

[4] This excludes petroleum. Inclusive of petroleum products, prices rose by 55 percent.

[5] Domestic cost-prices, adjusting for subsidies, must have exceeded export unit values by a factor of 12.

[6] It did not affect, of course, the relationship between domestic cost-prices and export prices.

The devaluation of 1936, then, may be viewed as an attempt to reduce the disequilibrium character of the ruble exchange rate—to bring export and domestic prices into closer alinement. Whether deliberately or not, the degree of devaluation was not extreme enough to achieve this putative objective. Despite the favorable upswing in export unit values noted above, the ratio of domestic prices to export unit values in 1937 was little less than 3 for all commodities, about 1.5 for basic industrial goods excluding petroleum, and about 2.5 including petroleum. This is considerably closer to equilibrium than the situation which prevailed in 1935 but is still far enough out of line to have necessitated the use of the most stringent controls to keep trade in balance were such controls not required in any case as part of the planning structure.

The Soviets revalued the ruble upward in 1950 by almost one-third from about \$0.19 to \$0.25 (or from 5.3 to 4 rubles to the dollar). As already noted, the reason given for this revaluation was the erosion of the value of the dollar due to inflation after World War II. Furthermore, the Soviets could point to the fact that their prices began a secular decline after the monetary reform of December 1947, while Western prices continued to rise. These trends notwithstanding, the critical fact is that the Soviets experienced very substantial cost and price inflation from 1936 until 1948, and an upward revaluation of the ruble would seem to have been justified only if it tended to bring Soviet costs and prices more into line with costs and prices (especially of traded goods) in other countries (as indicated by the relationship of Soviet domestic prices to export unit values). Precise comparisons for 1950 are impossible because Soviet export unit values are not available. However, rough indicators of the trends from 1937 to 1950 in domestic prices and in export prices provide sufficient clues.

Between 1938 and 1950, the world index of export prices [19, p. 28] rose from 40 to 89 (1953=100). The index of export prices of industrial nations rose from 45 to 85. Since Soviet foreign trade prices more or less follow world prices, it is probably not too far off the mark to assume that the unit values of Soviet exports (in world prices) roughly doubled from 1937 to 1950. Over the same period, the domestic prices of both basic industrial goods and consumers' goods produced in the Soviet Union roughly tripled [7]. Since domestic prices substantially exceeded export unit values in 1937, clearly the gap was increased by the relative price trends from 1937 to 1950 and the exchange rate was even more overvalued in 1950 than in 1937. We must conclude, therefore, that the upward revaluation of the ruble in 1950 increased rather than decreased the disequilibrium character of the ruble exchange rate. It is difficult to find economic justification for the 1950 revaluation. Unlike the 1936 devaluation, the motivation in this case appears to be largely political rather than economic: to boost the ruble for its forthcoming role as the "key" currency in the rapidly growing intra-Soviet bloc trade.

The trend since 1950 has been in the direction of "equilibration." However, the rate of change is slow and the distance to be covered, large. Export prices of industrial nations have risen since 1950 and in 1956 stood at a 20 percent higher level. Undoubtedly, Soviet export prices have risen to a somewhat similar extent. On the other hand, Soviet internal prices have been falling steadily. In 1956, prices of basic industrial goods and of consumers' goods were 15 and 25 percent, respectively, below 1950 levels. Clearly, the gap between domestic prices and export unit values is still far from bridged. A summing up of the trends since 1937 leads one to expect that in 1956 domestic prices should have been roughly 2½ times export prices. In the way of an independent check, direct comparison of a sample of domestic prices and export unit values for 1956 shows ratios of 2 and 2.5, respectively, for nonconsumers goods and for all goods including consumers' goods (adjusted for turnover tax).

The little information available regarding Soviet domestic price trends since 1956 indicates relative stability over the past 2½ years. Nor have world prices, and presumably Soviet export prices, changed very much. This leads to the conclusion that as of mid-1959 the ruble is still a substantially overvalued currency at the official exchange rate as it has been since at least 1929 and probably throughout the whole Soviet period.

3. *Enterprise and budget accounts and the overvalued exchange rate* [18]

The institutional use of an overvalued exchange rate has its reflection in the accounts of export and import organizations and the state budget.

Purchases and sales in international markets are conducted by Soviet export and import organizations. The export and import organizations serve as intermediaries between the domestic producers or sales organizations and the foreign buyers and sellers. There are about 25 of these organizations and they each cover either the export or import of an important group of traded commodities. [11, pp. 256–269.]

The export organizations purchase from the domestic producers, wholesalers or retailers, the commodities they are scheduled in the plan, to sell abroad. The purchase price, in the case of basic industrial goods is the normal wholesale price which any other state enterprise or organization pays for the same commodity. Consumers' goods are also procured at wholesale price. If, however, the export organization purchases consumers' goods from the retailer, this involves excusing it from having to pay the very large sales (turnover) tax levied on almost all consumers' goods sold to the population. This tax amounts, on the average, to a 100-percent markup over wholesale price on all goods sold by state and cooperative stores to the population [6, ch. 10]. The export organizations then attempt to sell their stock of goods abroad presumably at as high a price as they can obtain with certain exceptions of a political nature. (Soviet writers constantly stress that foreign trade organizations should take advantage of capitalist business cycles to buy cheap and sell dear.) In intrabloc Soviet trade, the prices of most imports and exports are determined simultaneously when the bilateral agreements are drawn up. These prices will usually bear some relationship to world prices but, since the ruble has been and is overvalued, very little relationship to domestic wholesale or retail price. The export organization is credited for export sales at the foreign price converted to rubles at the official exchange rate. Again, since the ruble is overvalued, receipts from sales will usually be below cost of purchase and will involve the export organization in a loss. The loss is financed by a subsidy to the export organization from the state budget.

For example, suppose Avtoeksport, the organization which sells motor vehicles abroad, carries out the declared Soviet intention of exporting the little Moskvich to the United States for around $1,200. Assuming transport and other costs amount to $200, the account of Avtoeksport is credited with $1,000, or 4,000 rubles at the official exchange rate. The Moskvich sells in the Soviet Union for 25,000 rubles. Assume, for sake of illustration, that this retail price includes a 100-percent sales tax markup. The wholesale price, or cost to Avtoeksport of the automobile will be 12,500 rubles. Avtoeksport sustains a loss on the transaction of 8,500 rubles (12,500 minus 4,000) which is refunded in due course by a state budget subsidy.

The situation is very much the same in the case of import organizations. Presumably, they attempt to purchase goods from abroad at a low price. The foreign price at which they consummate a transaction is converted to rubles at the official exchange rate and this constitutes the major expenditure item of the organization. In turn, they sell the commodity to domestic wholesalers or retailers at the internal price. Since the ruble is overvalued, this will usually be a much higher price than the purchase price and the organization will earn a large profit which is, after other minor expenses are deducted, paid into the State budget. This difference between the cost of purchasing a commodity abroad and internal price is, as far as I have been able to determine, often labeled by the Soviets a "tariff" and is the major form of tariff levied by them at present.[7]

The case of the import organization is also easily illustrated. Suppose that Mashino import purchases for $50,000 oil-drilling equipment which has an internal wholesale price of 500,000 rubles. Its accounts will receive a credit of 500,000 rubles and a debit of 200,000 rubles, or $50,000 converted at 4 rubles to the dollar. In due course, the 300,000 rubles (deducting minor expenses) is transferred to the budget as customs receipts.

While it is quite clear in the Soviet literature that the losses of export organizations are compensated in the form of budget subsidies and the profits of import organizations are paid into the budget as customs receipts, the actual budget accounts are not usually presented in sufficient detail to make it possible to distinguish these items directly. With respect to exports, the principal difficulty is that budget expenditures on foreign trade and domestic trade are usually not distinguished, and sometimes, apparently, only expenditures on domestic trade are reported. Fortunately, for the year 1956, the Minister of Finance, A. G. Zverev, states that expenditures on internal trade alone, were 1.1 billion rubles [15, p. 25] and another source [4, p. 347] presents a figure of 12.2 billion rubles as the measure of budget expenditures on trade. Apparently the difference, 11.1 billion rubles, was allocated to foreign trade. Now while some of this latter amount must have been devoted to investment in trading organizations, probably the bulk of it repre-

---

[7] Except for tariffs on imports by or gifts to private Soviet citizens from abroad.

NOTE.—I was informed at Amtorg that the prewar tariff schedules are still in effect. But these are ignored in the current Soviet literature on foreign trade and probably because they tend to be absorbed by the much larger differential between the import and domestic prices.

sented loss subsidies to export organizations.[8] The deduced figure of a little less than 11.1 billion rubles as the measure of subsidies to export organizations is unfortunately not substantiated with any precision by direct computation. Total Soviet exports amounted to 14.6 billion rubles in 1956. If domestic prices were from 2 to 2½ times export unit values, as we have estimated, then loss-subsidies should have amounted roughly to from 15 to 20 billion rubles. This is a somewhat larger figure than the estimate from budget data. However, in light of the general crudity of the estimating techniques used, the two figures may be considered to be of the same order of magnitude. Our estimate of the ratio of domestic to export prices was based on a sample of about one-third by value of total exports. If the discrepancy derives from an unrepresentative sample, the implication is that the ratio of domestic price to unit value of the remaining exports is probably somewhat less than 2.

Attempts to detect the amount of the customs receipts item in the budget are less successful. The only direct clue is provided by budgetary data for 1958. Two different breakdowns of planned budgetary receipts have been presented:

	A	B
Turnover tax	301.5	301.5
Profits tax	130.3	130.3
Income tax on co-ops and collectives	15.6	15.6
Receipts from population	72.7	72.7
Social insurance	32.1	}
Income from forests	2.1	}
Income from other enterprises	(1)	} 122.8
Income from foreign trade organizations	(1)	}
Income from machine tractor stations	11.9	(1)
Unspecified residual (not listed)	76.8	0
Total	643.0	643.0

1 Not listed.

Sources: A from [4, pp. 65–66]. B from [17].

From these two sources it can be deduced that income from foreign trade organizations and from "other enterprises" together were expected to return 76.8 billion rubles to the budget. There seems to be no way, unfortunately, of disentangling the two items. Since the ratio of domestic price to unit value is somewhat higher for imports than exports,[9] one would expect income from foreign trade organizations to amount to from 20 to 30 bilion rubles. Satisfactory reconciliation of these figures will not be possible until additional information is discovered or published. It should be noted that the budget report from which the B estimates were taken is the first to my knowledge in the past 10 years to contain any mention of receipts from foreign trade operations.

4. *Soviet international price policy and the foreign trade accounts*

Anyone engaged in a study of Soviet foreign trade sooner or later discovers that different Soviet sources often give quite widely diver-

[8] I have not been able to ascertain whether any part of Soviet loans to other nations is reflected in the budget and, if so, whether it would be reflected in the above-mentioned category or in miscellaneous expenditures. The same problem exists with respect to interest on and repayments of foreign loans.

[9] Imports were roughly 2.5–3.

gent figures for the exports and imports of any given year. For example, Soviet literature provides the following estimates of total Soviet trade in 1929:

[Million rubles]

	Exports (million rubles)	Imports (million rubles)	Date of publication of source
A	924	881	1933
B	4, 046	3, 857	1939
C	3, 219	3, 069	1957

In working with Soviet foreign trade data, it is extremely important to make sure one is using a consistent set of statistics and to be able to reconcile the apparent inconsistencies noted above.

The apparent inconsistencies result from the Soviet practice of revaluing all previous trade statistics every time the value of the ruble is changed in terms of foreign currencies and revaluing by the full amount of change in exchange rate. Thus, the A and B estimates differ by a factor of 4.38, the amount of the devaluation of April 1936. The B estimate is converted into the C figure by first increasing the B figure to account for the small devaluation of 1937 (divide by 0.947) and then decreasing it to allow for the 32½ percent revaluation of March 1950 (divide by 1.325). For some unstated reason, probably its small magnitude, the 1937 devaluation was not used until 1950 to adjust the value of earlier year trade returns.

This Soviet practice is quite unique and, to my knowledge, is not used by any other nation. An example may clarify the issues. Typically, when a nation devalues, the prices in foreign currency of its exports and imports at first fall whereas the prices in domestic currency remain the same.[10] Therefore, the unit value in domestic currency of the devaluing nation's trade may remain roughly the same before and after devaluation. Thus, suppose the United States were selling automobiles to Great Britain for $2,800 or £1,000 and then devalued from $2.80 to $5.60 to £1. After devaluation, the price to Great Britain in dollars would still be $2,800 though the price in sterling would have fallen to £500.

The Soviets rationalize their practice on the grounds that their foreign trade prices are fixed in accordance with world prices and, therefore (by implication) when their exchange rate changes, the world price remains the same but the value in domestic currency changes. This causes a sharp discontinuity in the unit values at which trade in domestic currency is valued (if there has been a currency revaluation). This in turn justifies their practice of revaluing earlier trade returns for comparability. Suppose, for example, the Soviets are exporting Moskvich automobiles to the United States for $1,200 or 4,800 rubles. Suppose they devalue to 8 rubles=$1. By their practice, the foreign currency price of a Moskvich remains $1,200 but increases in domestic currency, to 9,600 rubles. The Soviet trade returns (in rubles) would show, in this case, a doubling

[10] Actually, prices in domestic currency may rise because of the increased demand at the lower price in foreign currency; and for highly competitive products, the price in foreign currency is likely to remain unchanged.

of the value of trade. To avoid this purely statistical illusion of an increase in the volume of trade, all trade conducted during the previous year is revalued upward for comparability with trade returns at the new exchange rate.

No attempt will be made here to evaluate the Soviet statistical practice just described. It seems clear, however, that since Soviet foreign trade prices have no reference in the domestic price-cost structure (if they did, the practice would not be necessary in the first place) changing the value of trade for comparability in world prices is certainly a step toward obtaining a consistent series of the value of Soviet trade for intertemporal comparisons.[11] Users of such series should be careful to employ them only for comparisons of Soviet trade over time and then, for many purposes, they should not be used without further adjustment. They should not be used to compare Soviet trade in some predevaluation period with the trade data of other nations in that period. Neither the revised nor the original trade figures can be used, of course, in Soviet national income accounts without an adjustment for the gap, indicated earlier, between foreign trade unit values and domestic costs and prices. Finally, it is essential to check carefully the price basis underlying any series of trade data published recently by the Soviets. In the past few years, different sources have contained historical figures some in terms of a ruble worth $0.25 and others at the earlier rates which prevailed in the years to which the figures pertain.[12]

Soviet commodity trade

[Millions of 1950 rubles]

	Exports	Imports	Balance		Exports	Imports	Balance
1913	5, 298	4, 792	506	1930	3, 612	3, 690	−78
1917	1, 698	8, 453	−6, 755	1931	2, 827	3, 851	−1, 024
1918	28	367	−339	1932	2, 004	2, 454	−450
1919	0	11	−11	1933	1, 727	1, 214	513
1920	5	100	−95	1934	1, 458	810	648
1921	70	734	−664	1935	1, 281	841	440
1922	284	940	−656	1936	1, 082	1, 077	5
1923	760	499	261	1937	1, 312	1, 016	296
1924	1, 175	906	269	1938	1, 021	1, 090	−69
1925	2, 120	2, 881	−761	1946	2, 600	3, 100	−500
1926	2, 525	2, 440	125	1950	7, 200	5, 800	1, 400
1927	2, 600	2, 642	−42	1955	13, 874	12, 242	1, 632
1928	2, 800	3, 322	−522	1956	14, 446	14, 452	−6
1929	3, 219	3, 069	150	1957	17, 526	15, 751	1, 775

Sources:

1917: "Dostizheniia Sovetskoi vlasti za 40 let v tsifrakh," Moscow 1957, p. 31 (converted).

1913, 1929–38: V. S. Alkhiiov and others, "Vneshniaia torgovlia S.S.S.R. s kapitalisticheskimi stranami," Moscow 1957, pp. 7–11.

1918–1928: N. Liubimov and A. M. Smirnov, "Vneshniaia torgovlia S.S.S.R.," Moscow 1954, pp. 147, 165, 177.

1946, 1950: Vneshniaia torgovlia (monthly), 1958: 4, p. 21.

1955: "Vneshniaia torgovlia S.S.S.R. za 1956 god," 1958.

1956–57: "Vneshniaia torgovlia S.S.S.R. za 1957 god," Moscow, 1958.

5. *Foreign trade and internal financial stability*

As a planned economy, the Soviet economy is much more insulated from the impact of foreign trade than are the economies of other nations. It is convenient to distinguish here between three effects of

[11] For many purposes it would have been more useful to have revalued the trade in terms of domestic prices in those years in which domestic prices were "rational."

[12] It is worth noting that from the 1917 revolution until October 1, 1924, probably because of the hyperinflation which gripped the nation's economy, all trade data published were in 1913 prices and in terms of $0.5146 ruble [3, p. 235].

foreign trade on an economy: (*a*) The comparative advantage effect, (*b*) the employment effect, and (*c*) the financial effect (with which we are here mainly concerned).

(*a*) By the comparative advantage effect is simply meant that nations achieve a higher level of productivity and output by specializing in those activities to which their skills, resources, climate, and factor proportions are best suited and then exchanging some of the domestically produced output for goods which the country cannot produce or can produce only at high cost relative to other nations. Let it suffice to say here that both planned and unplanned economies benefit equally from the comparative advantage effects of trade. These effects constitute, of course, the basic rationale of international trade. Perhaps the one difference here between the Soviet Union and most Western nations has been that the Soviets have preferred in the past, for political and strategic reasons, to be as self-sufficient as possible and to forgo these benefits of trade. Since World War II, this policy has been reversed in trade with other Soviet bloc nations and shows signs of being relaxed slightly in trade with the West and with underdeveloped nations.

(*b*) By the employment effect of foreign trade we refer to the fact that (1) an increase in exports tends to increase the level of employment; and (2) an increase in imports, to the extent that the imports substitute for domestically produced goods, tends to reduce the level[13] of employment. The importance of this effect is dramatically attested to by the so-called beggar thy neighbor policies of the 1930's and the international rejection of such policies today. Most nations are now committed to maintaining a high level of employment through domestic fiscal and monetary policies and not by "beggaring their neighbors."

Though foreign trade has an important impact on the level of employment in Western nations, it has little or no impact on the level of Soviet employment. This is because the Soviets plan for full employment of their labor resources taking into account the foreign trade sector. In theory, should the plan schedule a rise in imports which replace domestically produced products, it should also schedule new jobs for the workers rendered unemployed by the increment to imports; should the plan call for a decline in exports, it should also call for a shift of workers from export industries to those producing for domestic consumption.[14] There is one exception to our proposition regarding the impact of trade on Soviet employment: if Soviet plans for imports of raw materials and other intermediate products are not fulfilled, and if the Soviets do not have adequate reserves on hand, then bottlenecks may develop, factories may have to reduce their activities, and labor will be temporarily underemployed or unemployed.

(*c*) By the financial effect[15] is meant the potentially inflationary or deflationary effect of foreign trade on the economy. The financial effect is virtually indistinguishable from the employment effect in the case of free enterprise economies. Thus, at full employment, an increase in exports relative to imports will create inflationary pressures

---

[13] The comparative advantage effect works through altering the "distribution" as opposed to the "level" of employment.

[14] This may require no actual physical shift, of course, since many domestic industries produce exportables.

[15] The pioneering study of this question is that of Edward Ames [1]. The analysis here differs from Ames' in several respects. A more elaborate analysis of this problem is in preparation.

and a decrease, deflationary pressures. In the Soviet economy, the financial and employment effects are quite distinct. This is because the monetary flows in the economy are not allowed to influence the employment or allocation of resources in any "substantial" way. As we have already indicated, the Soviets plan for full employment. Full employment has a very high priority in their system and they do not allow financial factors to stand long in the way of achieving this objective. While deflation has never been a problem the Soviets have had to face, they have been perennially plagued by inflationary pressures [6, ch. 2; 7]. Inflation, though it has not affected the overt level of employment directly, has had many undesirable side effects on the economy such as encouraging speculative activities; reducing work incentives; requiring, at times, rationing; and providing obstacles to planning [6, ch. 1]. The major purpose of their tax system is, in fact, the elimination of this excess purchasing power in the hands of the population and the prevention, thereby, of these undesirable side effects of inflation.[16]

The financial effect on the Soviet economy of foreign trade, while in fact not very important, in theory depends on the following factors: (i) The relative amounts of exports and imports; (ii) the relative proportions of consumers' and producers' goods in both exports and imports; (iii) the size of the sales taxes on exportables and on import substitutes, respectively; (iv) the extent of the comparative advantage effect, and related to this, the relative labor costs of producing exports and import substitutes.

(i) If exports exceed imports, whether because of long-term credits or due to a short-term imbalance, the effect is inflationary, all other things being equal. The reverse is true if imports exceed exports.

(ii) The impact of inflationary pressures is quite different in the consumers' goods and producers' goods markets, respectively. We need not be concerned here with the latter since the major interenterprise transactions are all carefully regulated by the state and the purchase and sale of important producers' goods are accomplished by direction allocation. Moreover, the state bank has been very successful, in the postwar period, in preventing enterprises from converting excess deposits into cash for the bidding up of wage rates, a practice very prevalent in the 1930's [6, ch. 2; 7]. The impact of inflationary pressures in consumers' goods markets has already been indicated. For financial stability in the consumers' goods markets, then, total exports and imports are not the crucial variables but rather the relationship of exports and imports of consumers' goods. In other words, the volume of exports might be double that of imports but if the exports consist entirely of producers' goods and the imports, of consumers' goods, the net impact on the consumers' goods markets will be deflationary. On the other hand, even if imports exceed exports, the net impact will be inflationary if the volume of consumers' goods exports exceeds the volume of consumers' goods imports.

---

[16] While taxes in the United States also serve these functions, their major purpose, when viewed in light of limitations on increasing the national debt, may be considered the procurement of resources for Government use. In the Soviet economy, resources for Government use are allocated directly and the taxes simply serve to keep the monetary flows in line with planned resource flows and thereby prevent the development of inflationary side effects just mentioned.

(iii) Consumers' goods sold in the Soviet Union almost all bear a sales tax which averages about 50 percent of price (ie., a 100-percent markup) and which varies from 1 percent on some commodities to as much as 80 percent of price on others. The export of a consumer's goods means the loss of sales tax revenue whereas the import of a consumer's goods adds sales tax revenue since imported consumers' goods are sold at the same price as equivalent domestically produced commodities. Therefore, foreign trade will be more (less) inflationary the larger (smaller) the foregone sales tax (markup) on exported goods and the smaller (larger) the markup on imported goods.

(iv) With the exception of small transfer payments, demand for consumers' goods in the Soviet economy derives exclusively from labor income (i.e., wages, salaries, income of peasants). Therefore, the inflationary effect of foreign trade will be affected by the labor cost of producing exports (both producers' and consumers' goods) compared with the labor cost of an equivalent value of import substitutes. In other words, if there have been "real" gains from trade so that the output per person available for consumption (by state and household) after trade is greater than before trade, the volume of goods will have increased relative to the size of household incomes and foreign trade will have had, on this account, a deflationary impact.

A significant fact to be noted, here, is that in discussing the financial impact of foreign trade on the economy, we have ignored both the par value of the exchange rate and the export and import unit values at which Soviet goods exchange in the international market. The reason for this is related to the fact that we are concerned here only with inflation in the consumers' goods markets. The relationship between domestic prices and foreign trade unit values arrived at via the official ruble exchange rate has important implications for enterprise accounts as we indicated in section 3, but very little for the goods-money relationship in the consumers' goods markets. As we have already indicated, since most aspects of the interenterprise markets are thoroughly administered and inflation in the labor market is under control, the inflationary effects of foreign trade in this sector can safely be ignored.

The final question to be considered is: If foreign trade has a net inflationary or deflationary effect in the consumers' goods market, is this effect likely to be very significant? My guess is that it is of no great significance for the following reasons: First, Soviet foreign trade amounts to no more than about 3 percent of gross national product and foreign trade in consumers' goods amounts to an even smaller percentage of the value of consumers' goods sold domestically. Since Soviet trade is usually close to being balanced, the net effect is smaller still.[17] Second, to the extent that exports and imports of consumers' goods are planned in advance, their net inflationary or deflationary impact on the domestic economy can be and probably is offset by adjusting other variables in the financial picture. This is not meant to imply that the Soviets have perfected the science of financial planning. Far from it. They have never succeeded in achieving an

[17] No attempt has been made to estimate the balance of consumers' goods in foreign trade or the relative tax rates on exports and imports of consumers' goods.

equilibrium between the money and commodity flows in their consumers' goods markets with the possible exception of 1949 [7]. It seems doubtful, however, that foreign trade has affected this problem significantly.

6. *Soviet gold policy*

The Soviets are believed to be the second largest gold producer in the world, after the Union of South Africa. The Soviets have not, however, published figures regarding either their gold stock or gold production for at least three decades. Estimates of Soviet gold production which have appeared in the League of Nations Statistical Yearbooks and in the annual reports of the Director of the U.S. Mint agree that (1) gold production fluctuated widely in the 1920's but was substantially less than 1 million fine ounces a year, and (2) increased from about 1.5 million fine ounces in 1930 to over 5 million ounces annually from 1936 to 1939. At $35 an ounce, the Soviets must have been producing close to $200 million worth of gold annually in the late thirties. Since Soviet trade deficits were small and recorded gold exports amounted to less than $700 million they may have accumulated as much as $2 billion worth of gold before World War II. This would have been an impressive stock at prewar prices.

Postwar output and stock of gold estimates are probably less firm than prewar. In its annual Bullion Review for 1955, Samuel Montague & Co. estimated that the Soviets are now producing 10 million ounces, or $350 million worth of gold a year. On the basis of this production estimate, they concluded that the Soviet gold stock is currently (1955) in the neighborhood of 200 million ounces or $7 billion.

While none of the above figures can be considered more than informed estimates, there is no question about the fact that the Soviets mine gold on a large scale and that they are one of the largest producers of gold in the world. They have admitted this much.

Why do they devote so much in the way of resources to the mining of gold? While, legally, the state bank is required to cover its note issue with 25 percent backing in gold, this probably has no significance whatsoever for Soviet practice today. Soviet economists stress that it is not gold which gives their paper currency its real value but rather the goods in circulation which the money can buy. The basic reason for mining gold, they say (postwar), is for use as a foreign exchange reserve. The gold can be used to meet planned deficits in the balance of payments; to make purchases abroad to correct maladjustments in the plan which arise during a planning period; to make payments, under bilateral clearing agreements, when indebtedness exceeds a given amount; and to extend loans to friendly nations. The existence of a reserve of gold thus gives the Soviets considerable flexibility for adjustment in foreign trade and domestic economic matters. There is no question about Soviet use of gold in the postwar period for just the reasons mentioned above. It is well known, for example, that they have made gold loans to a number of nations (e.g., Poland, Czechoslovakia, East Germany); that they have used gold to purchase sterling because of a persistent trade deficit with sterling area countries; and that gold was used to help finance the large unplanned imports of consumers' goods in 1953–54 promised by Malenkov after Stalin's death, and so forth. Gold sales, mainly through Switzerland and London, to finance these transactions have roughly amounted to:

[In millions]

	Ounces	Dollars
1953	4.3	150
1955	2.0	70
1956	4.3	151
1957	7.5	263
1958	6.0	210

Source: 10, 13.

In addition, it has been reported that the Soviets have sold abroad substantial amounts of other precious metals, notably silver and platinum.

There is some question as to whether the mining of gold is an economically profitable operation for the Soviets in terms of the imports which the gold can be used to buy. In the thirties, there is little doubt but that most of the gold was mined by forced labor. Given the institution of forced labor, and given the low world prices of goods, the mining of gold may well have been "profitable." There seems to be considerable doubt concerning its profitability today, however, what with high world commodity prices and, since the reduction in forced labor, probably a shift to use of free labor in many of the mines. Furthermore, it is generally believed that conditions for gold production in Russia are, for the most part, very high cost [5, p. 37]. It might make sense, from an economic comparative advantage point of view, for the Soviets to shift resources out of gold and into other exportables. A labor day in machine tools, for example, might earn more foreign exchange at present than a labor day in the gold mines In any event, recognition of the relatively low purchasing power of gold has led no less a luminary than Deputy Premier Mikoyan to accuse the United States of exacting a tribute from the gold-producing nations and to call for an increase in the price of gold [14].

7. *Payments agreement* [4, pp. 306 ff; 11, pp. 93 ff; 16, ch. 6; 20]

Before 1929, most Soviet trade was conducted on a multilateral basis. The worldwide financial crisis of that period started them on the path of bilateral agreements with the use of clearing accounts; and this form of payment agreement still characterizes most of their financial relationships with other nations today.

The Soviets argue that their use of clearing accounts in trade with capitalist nations is a result of the limitations on convertibility of many western currencies and of the trade controls used by capitalist nations; but that the use of clearing agreements among nations of the socialist camp reflects not inconvertibility or trade controls, but rather the planned nature of intrabloc trade and the long-term agreements on trade among bloc nations. Actually, the ruble is, as we have seen, the most inconvertible of currencies being greatly overvalued at its nominal exchange rate of 4 rubles to $1. For this reason the unit of account in Soviet trade with a western nation is always the currency of that nation or the currency of some other western nation, usually the United States or Great Britain. (Since 1950, trade among bloc nations has been in tems of the ruble.) The western currency, rather than the ruble, is also used to settle persistent trade inbalances and usually these currencies, even where not fully convertible, are guaranteed convertibility in trade with the U.S.S.R. It is hardly fair, therefore, for the Soviets to place the blame for bilateralism on the currencies of nonbloc nations. Furthermore, with respect to the planned nature of Soviet bloc trade, it has been shown that bloc bilateral trade (*a*) has been subject to wider fluctuations than unplanned trade among nonbloc nations and (b) has usually been wide of targets [20].

The clearing account usually encompasses all commodity trade but with many nations provides also for settlement of expenses on invisible account. Since trade between a pair of nations will never balance precisely at all times, even though bilateral balance may be achieved over time, the clearing accounts agreements typically provide either implicitly or explicitly for swing credits. These "technical" credits, as the Soviets call them, allow for a certain percentage of imbalance without an interest charge. The imbalance allowed varies from 5 to 20 percent of the value of trade in each direction, much less than is usual among capitalist nations. The absolute amount of "technical" credit allowed will depend on the value of trade, seasonal character of trade, and other such variables. Should the trade imbalance exceed the limit set, then the usual provision is that either party can ask for payment of the excess in gold or convertible currency. If the trade agreement should be concluded with an imbalance, then the total amount of the imbalance is usually settled in gold or convertible currency. The payments agreements with nonbloc nations usually contain a clause protecting the Soviets against losses from devaluation should they happen to have an active balance with a nation which devalues.

It should be noted that while in most payments agreements with Western nations, the clearing account technique is employed, this is not always the case. In some instances, the agreements provide simply for payment in convertible currencies; in others, the agreement is in strictly barter terms though, usually, with some provision for payment in convertible currency or gold should one or the other side fail to deliver as promised. It should also be noted that in a few instances in payments agreements with Western nations, provision has been made for settlement of bilateral imbalance in terms of mutual trade with a third nation. There are also a few instances of trilateral settlement in intrabloc trade. Multilateral settlement of imbalances based on the ruble seems to be a goal of the Soviets in intrabloc trade. In June 1957 the members of the bloc actually signed an agreement for multilateral settlement as a supplement to the bilateral agreements now in force. There is some question as to whether this agreement has ever been put into operation. In fact, there is considerable doubt that any system of multilateral settlement could be implemented in terms of Soviet bloc currencies so long as they each maintain exchange rates which are not mutually realistic in terms of their respective cost-price structures.

APPENDIX

The most recent complete balances of payment data released by the Soviets are those for 1935 and 1936 and published by the League of Nations. These are presented below (in 1936 rubles):

Balance of payments of the U.S.S.R. for 1935 and 1936

[In million rubles]

CURRENT ITEMS

Receipts	1935	1936	Payments	1935	1936
1. Receipts from sale of export goods (f.o.b. prices)	1,800	1,497	1. Cash payments for imports including overhead charges (c.i.f. prices)	860	1,328
2. Income from marine freightage (balance)	48	72	2. Expenses on technical servicing and assembly	23	23
3. Receipts from harbor dues and for the servicing of ships (balance)	11	2	3. Excess of State expenditures over State receipts abroad	57	55
4. Other receipts from transport (balance)	12	16	4. Interest on loans and credits (balance)	89	44
5. Receipts from insurance operations (balance)	6	2	5. Other expenses	--------	62
6. Receipts from noncommercial transfers (balance)	62	7			
7. Receipts from the tourist trade and money spent by foreigners (balance)	29	35			
8. Other receipts	165	32			
9. Sale of gold	52	--------			
Total (1-9)	2,185	1,663	Total (1-5)	1,029	1,512
			Excess of receipts over payments on current items	1,156	151

MOVEMENT OF CREDITS AND PROPERTY HELD ABROAD

Claims	1935	1936	Counterclaims	1935	1936
1. Repatriation of property held abroad (balance)	--------	71	1. Repayment of State and concessionary loans	--------	46
2. Receipts from State loans sold abroad	8	--------	2. Repayment of import credits granted by foreign firms	694	354
3. Receipts from financial credits	--------	242	3. Reduction of indebtedness made up of short term export and bank credits	319	32
Inflow of credits and property held abroad (1-3), total	8	313	Outflow of credits and property held abroad (1-3), total	1,013	432
Excess of outflow over inflow in the movement of credits and property abroad	1,005	119			
			Net increase of the Soviet banks' foreign currency accounts held abroad	151	32

Source: Alexander M. Baykov, "Soviet Foreign Trade," Princeton 1946, p. 39.

SOURCES

1. Ames, E. "The Exchange Rate in Soviet-type Economies," *Rev. of Econ. and Stat.*, November 1953.
2. A. Z. Arnold, "Banks, Credit, and Money in Soviet Russia," New York, 1937.
3. S. N. Bakulin and D. D. Mishustin, "Statistika Vneshnei torgovli," Moscow, 1940.
4. "Finansy i sotsialisticheskoe stroitel'stvo," Moscow, 1957.
5. Alexander Gerschenkron, "Economic Relations with the U.S.S.R.," sponsored by Committee on International Economic Policy, New York, 1945.
6. Franklyn D. Holzman, "Soviet Taxation," Cambridge, 1955.
7. Franklyn D. Holzman, "Soviet Inflationary Pressures, 1928-57: Causes, Cures, Lessons," ms.
8. Franklyn D. Holzman, "Soviet Foreign Trade Price and Exchange Rate Policy," ms.
9. L. E. Hubbard, "Soviet Money and Finance," London, 1936.
10. International Monetary Fund, "International Financial News," Mar. 29, 1957.
11. G. E. Koftova, D. F. Ramzaitseva and V. B. Spandar'iana (editors), "Spravochnik po vneshnei torgovlei S.S.S.R.," Moscow, 1958.
12. League of Nations, "Review of World Trade," Geneva (annual reports).
13. The New York Times, Mar. 11, 1959, p. 59.
14. The New York Times, Aug. 3, 1958, p. 20.
15. "Planovoe Khoziaistvo," 1957:3, p. 25.
16. V. F. Popov (editor), "Gosudarstvennyi bank S.S.S.R.," Moscow, 1957.
17. Pravda, Dec. 23, 1958.
18. V. K. Shishov, "Osnovy bukhgalterskogo ucheta i analiz khoziaistvennoi deiatel'nosti vneshnetorgovykh ob'edinenii," Moscow, 1957.
19. United Nations, "U.N. Yearbook of International Trade Statistics," vol. 1, New York, 1959, p. 29.
20. R. F. Mikesell and N. N. Behrman, "Financing Free World Trade with the Sino-Soviet bloc," Princeton, 1958.

SINO-SOVIET ECONOMIC ACTIVITIES IN LESS DEVELOPED COUNTRIES

(By Henry G. Aubrey, Project on the Economics of Competitive Coexistence, National Planning Association, Washington, D.C.)

Various U.S. Government publications have previously dealt with my present topic.[1] They have provided the basic statistics and much detail about the Communist moves. No good purpose would therefore be served if I were to summarize what has been said there already. Since the theme of the present study is a comparison of the American and Sino-Soviet economies, it may be more useful if my contribution would center on comparison, interpretation and analysis. Among others, it draws heavily on studies undertaken by the project on the economics of competitive coexistence of the National Planning Association under my direction;[2] but the views expressed in this paper are my own and do not commit anyone but myself.

1. COMPARATIVE EFFECTIVENESS: THE TWO IMPACT EFFECTS

Any comparison must begin with quantities. Hence, in discussing aid and trade in turn, magnitudes will be mentioned. They will make it evident that Soviet foreign economic activities, while growing, lag far behind the Western effort. But an apparent paradox emerges at this point. Although it can be seen that Communist aid and trade are relatively small, they are generally considered an alarming threat to the Western position which by all counts is so much older and therefore ought to be so much more firmly established. This implies that the effectiveness of the bloc's activities is presumed to be high while the West's own aid programs are perennially confronted by doubts about their achievements. It would seem to follow that, dollar for dollar or by any other measure, Soviet activities are deemed to be more effectual. Why should that be so, and is it due to what the Sino-Soviet bloc does, or how it does it, or to the political climate surrounding its effort? Our discussion therefore turns from quantitative to qualitative factors. In particular, differences in techniques and institutions, psychological factors and even imponderables, call for attention. In fact, the problem can be reduced to one fundamental question. If the United States

---

[1] Department of State, "The Sino-Soviet Economic Offensive in the Less Developed Areas," Publication 6632, May 1958; "The Communist Economic Threat," Publication 6777, March 1959; Mutual Defense Assistance Control Act of 1951, "Twelfth Report to Congress," and earlier reports; Department of Commerce, "Exports (Imports) of Free World Countries to (from) Soviet Bloc, Value Series," and "Summary of Country-by-Commodity Series"; and testimony by the Secretary and Under Secretary of State and by the Director of the Central Intelligence Agency before the Congress.

[2] Particularly the three studies with the collective title "Communist Economic Strategy," namely, "The Role of East-Central Europe," by Jan Wszelaki; "The Rise of Mainland China," by A. Doak Barnett; and "Soviet Growth and Capabilities," by Alec Nove; also "Japan, China, and the West," by H. Michael Sapir, and "East and West in India's Development," by Wilfred Malenbaum; all published by the National Planning Association, Washington 1959. A comprehensive volume of analysis on the problems of coexistence is now being prepared by myself. See also Henry G. Aubrey, "Sino-Soviet Aid to South and Southeast Asia," World Politics, October 1959, and "Soviet Trade Price Stability, and Economic Growth," Kyklos, vol. XII (1959) Fasc. 3.

and the Communist bloc appear to do the same thing, could it be that it is not the same, and why?

It has been said that the entry of the Communist bloc into the aid field represents an acknowledgment of the effectiveness of Western programs. Undoubtedly the Communists did not want the West to perpetuate a privileged position it had held so far only by default on the bloc's part. But for every similarity one can detect differences which can be interpreted as deliberate contrasts to the West's handling of aid and trade. This may well be due to different policy aims. But as I am not sufficiently confident of our ability to divine the price intent behind individual Soviet moves, in contrast to a popular line of thought, I prefer to tackle the problem from the other end: the impact upon the recipient countries. For, surely, the effectiveness of a policy instrument can best be evaluated by what it achieves at the point toward which it has been directed.

Consciously or not, the Communists appear to realize that there are not one but two related impact effects which operate on distinct levels of receptiveness. The first is socioeconomic and tangible: the changes which, say, aid achieves in the economic and social fabric of the recipient country. This effect usually takes time to take hold; and while its impact may go deep, the change is gradual and seems unspectacular and therefore unimpressive to the average observer. In fact, for this very reason, there can arise differences between the donor and the recipient country regarding the anticipation of the effects or in its evaluation after the event.

At this point, the first impact effect is linked with the second: the impression aid makes on the minds of the recipients, governments as well as the people. This a psychological-political factor of the utmost importance, since undoubtedly the creation of a receptive and sympathetic climate is one measure of the efficiency of any policy instrument. In this respect, then, it may well be more consequential how aid is given, and for which presumed reasons, than what and how much. Note the emphasis on the term "presumed," because the effective ingredient need not be the true intent but the image evoked in the recipients' minds.

As we now proceed to the discussion of aid and trade, it will become evident that the Communists appear very finely attuned to the second impact effect, while the United States has been resting its case on what, in its view, will eventually be best for the recipient countries. From the short-run political angle it is easy to see that more may be gained psychologically by banking on the immediate benefits of the second effect than by neglecting it in the hope—and there can be no certainty—of being right over the long term. But by the same token, who is right eventually is apt to win the contest, provided he has not lost one battle too many in the meantime—and it is hard to tell in advance which of them would turn out to have been Waterloo.

2. SINO-SOVIET AID

Comparative magnitudes

In the period from mid-1954 to mid-1959, bloc assistance agreements totaled around $2.7 billion (see table 1). About three-quarters of this amount was economic aid and the rest military. Of the total the U.S.S.R. provided about 70 percent and Communist China not more than about 4 percent. In the same period the United States provided to the same group of 20 countries $5.3 billion of economic assistance alone of which about $1.2 billion were defense support. Inclusion of countries to which the bloc has not offered any aid would approximately double the American 5-year assistance total.

TABLE 1.—*Communist-bloc and U.S. Government assistance to selected underdeveloped countries, July 1, 1954, to June 30, 1959*

[Millions of dollars]

	Communist-bloc total assistance			U.S. economic[2] assistance[3]
	Total	Military	Economic[1]	
Middle East and Africa	1,427	580	849	1,197
Egypt	658	315	343	140
Syria	304	128	177	2
Ethiopia[4]	124		124	56
Guinea	1		1	2
Iran	6		6	353
Iraq	257	120	138	15
Turkey	17		17	623
Yemen	60	17	43	7
South and southeast Asia	1,102	195	907	2,495
Afghanistan[5]	245	32	213	85
Burma	17		17	71
Cambodia	34		34	173
Ceylon	58		58	54
India[6]	323		323	1,166
Indonesia	402	163	239	189
Nepal	20		20	19
Pakistan	3		3	738
Europe	114		114	655
Iceland	5		5	25
Yugoslavia[7]	110		110	630
Latin America	106		106	962
Argentina	104		104	345
Brazil	2		2	617
Total	2,748	773	1,975	5,309

[1] Including about $167 million in grant aid to Afghanistan, Cambodia, Ceylon, Egypt, Guinea, India, Nepal, Pakistan, and Yemen.

[2] Data on U.S. military assistance to individual countries are classified and therefore omitted from the table.

[3] Including the following: ICA obligations; Development Loan Fund commitments announced through June 30, 1959; Public Law 480 assistance and agricultural surplus aid under the Mutual Security Act (under agricultural sales agreements, figures represent uses made of local currency proceeds); development loans by Export-Import Bank.

[4] Including a credit agreement for $122 million concluded early in July 1959.

[5] Includes a $3.5 million credit reported during the first half of 1954.

[6] Not including a credit for $378 million promised in July 1959 for the 3d 5-year plan which is not slated to begin until 1961.

[7] Not including $354 million in credits extended in 1956 and subsequently either canceled or allowed to expire.

NOTE.—Details may not add to totals because of rounding.
Sources: U.S. Department of State and ICA.

Actually, this comparison which seems already so favorable to the West is nonetheless biased in favor of the bloc. Under the Soviet system long-term, "bulk" credits are negotiated. They are in effect credit lines, or ceilings under which agreements for individual projects are thereafter negotiated. This takes much time and there may be long delays in acceptance or ratification (about 2 years in the case of Indonesia); and the total is expected to be expended over a period of years (7 years in the case of Syria). This is in striking contrast to the American system of annual authorization and appropriation under which obligations usually follow promptly since funds are chronically short, and disbursements also lag much less.

Moreover, more time passes until the bloc has manufactured and delivered the aid goods. If large projects, such as a steel mill, are involved it may take years to complete. Thus, at the end of 1958 it was believed that not more than one third of the credits had actually been drawn; and an earlier attempt to calculate the rate of disbursement project by project [3] suggests that it was no higher than $160 to $200 million in 1957, less than one tenth of 1 percent of national income though it probably has been rising somewhat since then.

These are, clearly, not large amounts and the actual burden is even smaller since most of bloc aid consists of loans and value will be received in the form of imports in repayment. In some instances, such as Burmese rice and Egyptian cotton, the shipments to the bloc were even received in advance and the bloc in effect enjoyed a credit from these less developed countries.

In a proper East-West comparison non-American Western assistance ought to be also included. In 1957–58 the annual rate of total non-Communist aid, bilateral and multilateral, net of repayment, was estimated by the United Nations as close to $3 billion to which the United States contributed about one third.[4] On grounds of much higher international loan activity a later period would probably show an even higher rate of Western assistance. This makes the discrepancy between Western and Communist aid still wider.

Finally, one may want to include private loans and investments in the total Western contribution of capital. A reasonable, though admittedly rough guess might put the total average annual flow of long-term capital to the less developed areas at about $2 billion [5] over a recent 4 year period. This does not even make full allowance for medium and short-terms credits by suppliers and financial institutions. In all its various forms, Western investments, bilateral and multilateral assistance capital probably exceeded $5 billion a year and will probably increase as multilateral contributions and European exports grow.

This kind of calculation, however, assumes that the impact effect of private investment and of government capital, such as the Communist bloc exclusively supplies, is the same. In the light of the "two-impact-effect" test outlined before, it becomes evident that this is not necessarily so. In the strictly economic sense, any capital inflow increases the supply of inevitable resources and to that extent the first impact effect of private investment ought to be the same as that of public loans, although the servicing of loans or transfers of profits may involve different balance of payment burdens.

But the second impact effect is not the same at all since many recipients take a dissimilar view of a plant the Russians build and leave behind when they go home, and one remaining under the control of

[3] Joseph S. Berliner, "Soviet Economic Aid" (New York, 1958), pp. 41 ff.

[4] Computed from United Nations, "International Economic Assistance to the Less Developed Countries" (Document E/3255, May 8, 1959, mimeographed), table 19.

[5] United Nations, "International Flow of Private Capital, 1956–58" (Document E/3249, mimeographed), pp. 9 and 21. Due to shortcomings of balance of payments statistics the actual amount may be larger, as some of the components are net of repayments. Moreover, reinvested earnings abroad are largely excluded and their inclusion would greatly raise the investment total, even though no new flows of funds are involved. See Emilio G. Collado and Jack F. Bennett, "Private Investment and Economic Development," Foreign Affairs, July 1957.

foreign investors for the indefinite future. Thus, the welcome extended to both varieties is often very different; and it is well to remember that the second impact effect is formed in the recipients' mind and by his own lights, no matter how misguided in our own view.

Technical assistance

Along with the credit program, the Sino-Soviet bloc also ventured forth into technical assistance on a rising scale.

The bloc has an estimated 4,675 technicians engaged in economic development work abroad for 1 month or more during the first half of 1959. This compares with over 6,000 American technical personnel abroad as of June 30, 1959. Of course, American technical cooperation is of much older standing, going back to the time before World War II, but then the number of bloc technicians abroad has lately been increasing at twice the American rate. The bloc also reportedly trained about 3,000 foreign technicians and students over the last several years, while the United States financed the training of nearly 9,000 nationals of less developed areas under the fiscal 1959 program.[6]

If the bilateral programs of other Western countries were included, the numbers would be greatly increased, not to mention the important transfer of skills by business that goes along with foreign investment; but statistics in this respect are unfortunately not available. The expanded technical assistance program of the United Nations alone has sent about 8,000 experts abroad and financed the foreign training of about 14,000 students and officials in the first decade of its existence; and its work continues to grow and is being further expanded by the special fund established in 1958. The contribution of the Sino-Soviet bloc to the United Nations programs is small, both in terms of men and of funds (which are, moreover, tied to bloc goods and services to the extent of better than 75 percent). The bloc contributed only 23 experts in 1958, much less than many less developed countries; for instance, India supplied 146 and even the United Arab Republic 56.[7]

It may be useful to point to some systematic differences between Soviet and American technical assistance. Western services are usually supplied within a framework of individual projects, many of them small and aimed at very specific training results; this aid is typically supplied free in a setting of mutual cooperation in which the recipient takes care of the local cost. Soviet technical assistance is more frequently part of a larger package, consisting of loans, development goods and bilateral trade; the services of experts are not free, but are charged against the loan, if not accounted for separately, and these charges are quite high, sometimes higher than the West's.

Reports on the qualifications of Soviet technicians are mostly favorable though they are not as broadly trained as Western specialists. They seem to behave correctly and the fear that they might be spies or carries of propaganda does not seem to have been borne out. In

---

[6] "The Mutual Security Program, Fiscal 1960. A Summary Presentation" (March 1959); and State Department publications previously cited.

[7] United Nations, "Annual Report of the Technical Assistance Board" (Document E/3226, mimeographed), pp. 117 ff; Robert Loring Allen, "United Nations Technical Assistance: Soviet and East European Participation," International Organization, vol. XI, No. 4 (1957), p. 629.

many instances they have rather more language difficulties than their Western counterparts. But in some Middle Eastern regions experts of Turki or Moslem ancestry were used, perhaps in an attempt to capitalize on an affinity of kinship and language. The Russian experts do not appear to fraternize much with the local people. But in building a steel mill in India, along with other steel mills supplied by Great Britain and Germany, some reports stress the good personal relationship of the Russians with the Indians; others mention that the British are getting along best with the the Indians while the Russians have to operate through interpreters and allegedly are not generous with explanations.[8]

For their part some American experts, as is well known, find it difficult to adjust to foreign conditions and so do their wives.[9] Even if too much can be made of such personality difficulties compared with the impeccable but less newsworthy deportment of the vast majority, it is a fact that Americans abroad tend to gather in tight little groups and that their standard of living is conspicuously higher than that of their counterparts in the recipient countries; moreover, they often seem to live better than Soviet experts, especially with regard to lodging, modern amenities, cars, and imported food.

This is not surprising because the bloc experts are used to less elaborate comforts. But the essential feature is the problem of recruitment the West faces. Under the Soviet system the consent to a foreign assignment is not essential, though we need not assume that it has to be forced on the bloc experts; on the contrary, it is quite likely that the general lack of opportunity for foreign travel and the acquisition of foreign goods makes the chance for foreign work rather attractive. By contrast, the difficulties of recruiting in the West qualified personnel for oversea service are well known, even though the growing participation of university personnel under contracts helps to relieve certain specific shortages.[10]

A further distinction between Communist and Western technical assistance is particularly significant for the impact effect of foreign aid. East and West have come to specialize in different fields, in line with their divergent aid philosophy. Americans accord priority to assistance for basic needs like agriculture, health and education, which generally give rise to contacts with large numbers of people, but also calls for an adaptation of skills to very different socioeconomic conditions. Communist bloc experts serve in mineral development, power and transportation, steel mills and other industries which entail the teachiing of a fairly complex technology to relatively small numbers of people. Thus the Western programs operate on the expectation of a gradual impact over a long term while the Soviet experts' work tends to be completed in relatively short time and is directed toward conspicuous projects that are likely to find recognition and appreciation in short order.

---

[8] Under Secretary Dillon's testimony before the Committee on Foreign Affairs, House of Representatives, Jan. 29, 1959, p. 37; Paul Wohl in Christian Science Monitor, March 1959; Taya Zinkin in Manchester Guardian Weekly, Feb. 22 and Nov. 27, 1958.

[9] See Harlan Cleveland, "The Pretty Americans," Harper's magazine, March 1959; Gerard J. Mangone, "New Americans in Old Societies," the Antioch Review, winter, 1958.

[10] See "Report of the Special Committee To Study the Foreign Aid Program," p. 21, and Louis J. Kroeger and Associates, "Personnel for the Mutual Security Program," study No. 2, Compilation of Studies and Surveys (85th Cong., 1st sess.), pp. 54, 83, 120; Hugh Tinker, "The Name and Nature of Foreign Aid," International Affairs (January 1959), p. 49.

Comparison of assistance terms

Reverting to capital assistance, it is worth noting that bloc contribution is largely in the form of loans, with the exception of Communist China which entered the field with more grants. Western aid has a much higher component of grants, mostly for the purpose of defense support. The impact-effect test once more reveals a discrepancy on which the Communists have tried to capitalize. Economically, a grant should be preferred by the recipient because no interest and no repayment burden are involved. Psychologically, however, a grant is deemed to involve an obligation—mutual, as in military aid, or imponderable but still implying some dependence, as the Russians never tire of saying. And since the fear of dependence, or the supremacy of a stronger power, or "strings" that exist only in suspicious minds, are woven deeply into the political fabric of former colonial countries, the psychological factor will often outweigh economic rationality.

There is apparently not much difference in the length of loans and repayment terms between Sino-Soviet and Western agreements, except for one feature that gives the former an edge on both impact counts. More bloc loans are repayable in local currency or local products. This has the economic advantage of relieving the borrower of the troublesome problem of finding the foreign exchange for repayment, a grave matter indeed because developing countries are, virtually by definition, chronically short of foreign exchange.

As long as sufficient new capital flows in, the repayment problem need not become too acute; and with increasing frequency the United States had to fund maturities or agree to postponement of payments to forestall defaults. The Development Loan Fund provides for repayment in local currency and so would the proposed International Development Association. But the bloc has used this device more systematically and can well afford to do so in the expectation of acquiring local products in due course. In fact, the bloc has a competitive advantage in this respect because its perennially resource-starved economies can well use most products the less developed areas have to offer; the West, in contrast, buys what it needs anyway through impersonal market channels and often, in order to protect its own domestic production, would not be willing to make an effort to increase imports.

But there is a second, a psychological factor of equal importance. By accepting local products the bloc not only frees primary producing countries from the periodic worry where to dispose of their surplus but, in fact, undertakes to create a new market for them. More important, it makes these countries feel that they are given the tools for their development and the chance to pay for them with the fruits of their economic growth and the products of their soil, so that the repayment promises to be painless and the loans virtually self-liquidating.

Finally, the bloc's interest rates are much lower than the West's. This has clearly both an economic and a psychological-political impact. To give an example, the Soviet loan for the Bhilai steel plant in India calls for 2½ percent interest while the World Bank loans for the expansion of the Tata Iron & Steel Co. carry interest at 4¾ and 6 percent:[11] this clearly adds up to sizable sums over time.

[11] International Bank for Reconstruction and Development, 13th Annual Report, p. 62.

In addition, it provides the Communists with a first-rate propaganda issue because the higher Western interests are described as exploitation. Since suspicion is always rife in formerly dependent areas, where colonialism, imperialism, and exploitation are considered virtually synonymous even by many non-Communists, Soviet contentions undoubtedly fall on willing ears.

More sophisticated observers in the less developed countries probably understand that the interest rate has many market functions to fulfill which it lacks in the Soviet system. It would be difficult for the World Bank to quote lower rates without endangering its link with the international capital markets on which it will depend increasingly. And in the United States, too, lower interest rates would require unusual measures, such as, perhaps, subsidization. But this is only one of a number of institutional problems that the West would face once it decides to match the Communist bloc in its simple, but effective, approach.

The impact of Communist aid

While total aid by the Communist bloc, as mentioned before, is much smaller than the West's, it is also centered in a relatively small number of countries. As first it was largely granted to the new countries in Asia who, it was probably hoped, could thus be kept away from Western influence and encouraged in their neutralist course. Then the nationalist turmoil in the Middle East offered new opportunties for military and economic assistance, partly to spite the West, partly to endorse deep-flowing aspiration with an elaborate show of sympathy and respect. More recently, Africa has received increasing attention and generous offers of aid not restricted to countries where anti-Western feelings were rife, as witnessed by the $122 million credit to Ethiopia by the Soviet Union and Czechoslovakia. There is an alert watch for openings in Latin America whenever a country would become sufficiently hard pressed for imports to accept Soviet aid, as in Argentina and quite recently in Bolivia. And, turning full circle, nearly $400 million have lately been offered to India for its third development plan, more than doubling the aid promises to that country.

Nonetheless, as table 1 shows, bloc aid is highly concentrated. About 90 percent of all economic aid (excluding the promise to India for the third plan which is due to start only in 1961) was allocated to only nine countries granted more than $100 million worth of assistance each. As a result, bloc aid promises are greater than American aid in such neutralist countries as Afghanistan, Indonesia, Iraq and the United Arab Republic. But if all Western sources of capital, including private investment were considered, the picture may change. For instance, total Western loan commitments in Egypt during the last 3 years were reported as twice those from the bloc, largely due to German commitments, and there are indications that total Western credits to Indonesia also exceeded the bloc's.[12]

American aid is much more widely distributed. Where it is concentrated, largely in the form of defense support, it is in areas of importance for the cold war, while the bloc's centers in neutralist areas important in competitive coexistence. This implies a significant

[12] The Washington Post and Times Herald, May 30, 1959; and Frankfurter Allgemeine Zeitung, May 25, 1959.

difference in aid philosophy. It reflects the ingrained American stress of the external threat in contrast with the manifest Communist belief in bringing the less developed countries around by economic and political means. This also explains the bloc's alertness in seizing on situations where anti-Western feelings are encountered and, very importantly, its efforts to demonstrate its endorsement of the national aspirations and the Communists' understanding of the needs of uncommitted nations.

This is expressed by a lavish display of respect and friendship, exchanges of high level visits, and by minute attention to details designed to suggest a contrast with the neglect and condescension of which, in remembrance of the colonial era, the West is all too often suspected. Previously discussed departures of the aid agreement terms from Western practice undoubtedly reinforce the impression of greater affinity on the part of the bloc. A "businesslike" relationship, free of interest in profit and poles apart from so-called Western exploitation, is emphasized and unfavorably compared with "degrading" grants that allegedly create an unwholesome relationship of political dependence.

Thus higher Western interest rates on loans are made out as rapacious. The profit motive is disparaged and American "harping" on a greater role for private capital in economic development and in foreign aid [13] is made to provide evidence that Western aid only serves the interests of busines. These contentions capitalize on a measure of intellectual affinity to Fabian or Marxist tenets that is quite frequent even among non-Communist intellectuals in many less developed countries.

The issue of socialism in competitive coexistence

This point is probably important enough to dwell upon briefly. More often than not the much-discussed Socialist tendencies in the new countries have a fundamentally different meaning from what the word seems to imply to observers who view such leanings too much in Marxist-Leninist terms. By the same token, the image of capitalism in some of these areas is that of a 19th century type which has long vanished in most Western countries; and the relatively enlightened business spirit of social responsibility which has come to the fore in the West has barely entered the field of vision of social critics in many less developed areas. Consequently, socialism and other radical-sounding language means no more to many non-Communist leaders and intellectuals than social reform, legislative safeguards, and a mild bias toward public enterprise—not necessarily exceeding the features of a mixed economy that have already become commonplace in quite a few advanced countries, in some respects including the United States.

It would be a grievous, indeed a fateful, error if the Communist bloc were permitted to monopolize for its purposes this latent desire for social betterment and if the West were to permit itself to be identi-

---

[13] Such as the Cooley amendment to the Agricultural Trade Development and Assistance Act; and the call to make more room for private collaboration, including the use of contractors, in American governmental assistance, see e. g., "Report of the Committee on World Economic Politics" (Boeschenstein report), Washington, Jan. 22, 1959: "Expanding Private Investment for Free World Economic Growth" (Straus report), Washington, April 1959; and "Economic Assistance Programs and Administration," third interim report (Draper report), Washington, July 13, 1959.

fied with an image of capitalism that is a caricature of modern conditions. The first precondition for avoiding this evil is a more discriminating understanding of the true aspirations of these countries and a greater willingness to tolerate even those distinctive features which we would not necessarily seek ourselves.

In good part, the apparent conflict is one of 19th century images rather than one of modern economic actualities. The rift between the meaning of words like socialism and capitalism to Americans and to Indians and Burmese is much wider than the difference in actual policy. True, public initiative is more favored in these countries than in the United States today. But, due to a paucity of human and financial resources in early stages of economic development, this has been a common feature in the 18th and 19th centuries, even in the free-enterprise economies of the West, not excluding the United States, where private initiative has nonetheless thereafter taken over.[14]

If these factors were considered, perhaps a premature insistence on private investment, even where the economic and human infrastructure is lacking, might be avoided, lest the ensuing disappointment would strengthen the bloc's strategy. Moreover, repetitive and sometimes nagging representations tend to be interpreted as interference by people who are jealously insisting on their right to adopt their own path to economic development; and this goes no less for the promotion of our system, no matter how superior we believe it to be, than for the advocacy of the Communist ideology which is all too ready to monopolize certain vague preferences for the public system. As a matter of practical policy, as one observer has said, "for most of these countries the critical question is not one of government management versus private management. It is whether totalitarian methods will eventually be resorted to in order to increase the level of saving."[15] At this point, and with the Communist bloc watching on the sidelines, excessive or untimely zeal can easily prejudice the future acceptance of foreign capital in the less developed areas, while a more pragmatic accommodation to the development aspirations of the new nations may, with time, achieve the same end much more effectively.

3. SINO-SOVIET TRADE[16]

Trade as an instrument of foreign policy

Another study is going to deal with East-West trade as a whole. This paper is therefore going to limit itself to those aspects of bloc trade with the less developed areas that are illustrative of its use as a policy instrument and of its impact effect on the bloc's trade partners. Quite frequently Communist trade is discussed in rather vague terms as a weapon that is used for penetration or to induce dependence. It is useful to inquire what these terms mean, to what extent trade can be instrumental in political influence, and what, in particular, Communist trade seems to be achieving in this respect. For the present

---

[14] For historic examples, see, e.g., Henry G. Aubrey, "Deliberate Industrialization," Social Research, June 1949, and "The Role of the State in Economic Development," papers and proceedings, American Economic Review, May 1951.

[15] Thomas C. Schelling in the American Assembly, "International Stability and Progress: United States Interests and Instruments" (New York, 1957), p. 159.

[16] In addition to the sources mentioned in the first and second footnotes, this section has drawn on Raymond F. Mikesell and Jack N. Behrman, "Financing Free World Trade With the Sino-Soviet Bloc" (Princeton, 1958).

task of comparison, two related questions need to be asked. (1) Since the bloc's external trade is so very much smaller than the West's—only about 3 percent of world trade—why should it be suspected of such disproportionate influence? (2) Does the Soviet system of trading lend itself to applications that the free world does not possess or cannot use with comparable effectiveness?

One important institutional difference comes immediately to mind. Decisions on trade, as on most other matters under the Soviet system, are made centrally and can then be put into effect very rapidly. Under Western practice, trade occurs through uncoordinated decisions of numerous private parties. True, in times of war and for security reasons, Western commerce is subjected to controls, but they are essentially negative; in other words, undesirable trade can be prohibited or limited, but private trade cannot be directed into preferred channels without infraction of the West's self-imposed international rules.

The bloc, by contrast, can shift its trade with deliberate intent and has demonstrated that it can turn it on (e.g., Iceland, Burma, Egypt) or off (e.g., Israel, Yugoslavia, Japan) at the spur of the moment. Moreover since the bloc's market potential is naturally large, the quantities involved in individual deals are sizable compared with the West's atomistic and impersonal market operations. This does not mean that all bloc trade is, so to say by definition, planned with malicious intent, an impression too easily fortified by Soviet fondness for adorning policy pronouncements with political rationalizations. Yet, undoubtedly, the bloc is interested in imports to an increasing extent—indeed Communist China vitally so—and imports have to be paid for by exports of merchandise or gold. Thus an assumption that all Communist trade is more politically than economically motivated blocks a more discriminating understanding of the economic advantage that trade can confer even on a totalitarian economy.[17]

It is often said that the Communist bloc does not care about costs and can therefore be expected to dump exports or overbid for imports as its political purpose demands. Sometimes, a feeling of helplessness stems from this line of thought.[18] But it seems to me desirable to question both the premise and its defeatist conclusion.

Undoubtedly, the bloc has the economic potential for disruptive activities if it so desires, but there is no reason to believe that the Communist policymakers would not be acutely aware of the price. Cost calculations are important in the Soviet economy even though their foundation is open to objections by Western standards. As the Russians run into resource limitations they become more and more productivity conscious and make strenuous efforts to reduce costs on all fronts. In foreign trade they have been found to drive hard, sometimes even sharp, bargains. It is therefore necessary to examine the facts and to distinguish between what the bloc has the capability of doing and what it has actually done, between its trade potential and its actual practice. In my judgment, the Soviet bloc in Europe, at least, has so far done little that was not economical from its own point of view, no matter how important the political element in the policy decision might have been.

---

[17] Alec Nove, op. cit., and "Soviet Trade and Soviet Aid" in Lloyds Bank Review, January 1959; Jan Wszelaki, op. cit., and A. Doak Barnett, op. cit.

[18] E.g., Baron Bonvoisin, "Can We Meet the Soviet Trade Competition," Belgian Trade Review, March 1959. "We are therefore led to believe that the Western World is largely powerless in the face of Soviet commercial policy" (p. 21).

Trade or aid?—Trade as aid

On of the most significant (and least discussed) features of the Soviet trade system is its ability to combine trade and aid in such a manner that the bloc manages to make the best of both. Since aid is eventually repayable in local products, it is made to appear as deferred trade. And at the same time the bloc manages to make trade look like aid by appearing on the scene when its custom is most welcome. The West, by contrast, sometimes seems to get the worst of both worlds psychologically, in the sense of the second impact effect.

Paradoxically, the slogan "trade, not aid" was coined in the West to denote a preference for letting the developing countries earn more foreign exchange through exports rather than unilaterally through assistance. Even though the imports of industrial countries have increased sharply, the intended shift was impeded by the vocal protests of domestic producers and the resulting imposition of restrictions, especially in the United States. To be sure, some of the most objectionable measures were avoided, but the adverse political impact abroad of those adopted was much greater than statistics alone may seem to justify.

In the context of competitive coexistence three elements were bound to leave an unfavorable impression by comparison with Soviet practice: Public display of dissension and the ascendancy of policies that, in a pinch, would harm rather than help the trade of primary producers; a cleavage between the philosophy of free trade and nondiscrimination that is being expounded to the less developed areas, and the actual practice applied to some of their own vital exports; and certain painful limits to trade complementarity between primary producers and the industrial West, in contrast to the standing claims that the Western system offers the best prospect for a stable and growing world trade.

While the bloc has used its capacity to increase imports to the hilt—and thus made the instances of Western reluctance stand out even more sharply—the United States possesses the inverse capability of supplying its surpluses to a needy world with a generosity the Communist bloc cannot begin to match. But the American surplus disposal has been set up in a manner that deprives this country of most psychological-political benefits. Although the largest part of the local currency proceeds from the sale of surpluses is promptly loaned to the recipient countries for economic development, the transaction is called a sale. As a result, some recipient countries feel they are doing the United States a good turn by ridding it of its surpluses. By the same token, the appreciation due to a loan or grant is forfeited by insisting that the deal is a sale. The institutional origin of this procedure is clear and need not be discussed here; but this is an instance of the difficulty in this country—and the contrasting ease in the Communist bloc—in adapting programs with immense impact abroad to the exigencies of foreign policy rather than to domestic convenience.

The Sino-Soviet bloc as a "buyer of last resort"

The most impressive instances of shrewd and timely trading decisions on the part of the bloc occurred when a country ran into trouble through inability to sell enough of its main exports in the non-Communist world. Since the events are well known, the implications rather than the chronology will be discussed here.

When Iceland's fish was barred in Great Britain in 1952 as a move in a dispute over the extension of territorial waters, the Soviet bloc increased its purchases so that its share in Iceland exports rose from 7 percent in 1952 to 25 percent in 1954. This dispute between two partners of the Western alliance is continuing and in 1958 the bloc held no less than 35 percent of Iceland's exports and 32 percent of its imports. This thorn in the side of Western unity thus remains.

The West is not a large factor in the world's rice markets, though the sale of American excess stocks at the time when Burma's concern with its surplus reached its peak may have been a disturbing element, at least psychologically. In fact, Burma's failure to recognize the trend toward market saturation and reduce its price in good time was the major cause why Burma had accumulated much larger unsold stocks than its competitors. But in any event, the timely offer by the block in 1955 to buy up 750,000 tons of rice appeared like a godsend, even though the quantities actually shipped were much smaller. This was not the bloc's fault, but the rice market had turned and rice could again be sold for cash. This fortunate development, for which the West can really not claim any credit, provided a rare demonstration of the drawbacks of bilateral trade in comparison with free markets which were again functioning; this lesson was publicly acknowledged by the Burmese leaders, who were, moreover, in some respects disappointed by the price or the quality of the goods received in turn from the bloc.

An oversupply of cotton gave an opening to the bloc in Egypt and Syria which have now joined in the United Arab Republic; but there is no such happy ending to the story as in the case of rice—at least not yet, even though it seems that Syria's trade with the bloc has fallen off sharply in the first part of 1959.[19] The bloc has become by far the largest customer of Egypt and Syria, absorbing 44 and 31 percent, respectively, of their exports in 1958. Reportedly, there was some friction over resales of cotton by the bloc at lower prices, not surprisingly, since the price of cotton in Alexandria had been driven above the world price as a result of Soviet purchases. In the Sudan, too, where surpluses of long staple cotton have been increasing, the bloc has made offers to buy on a large scale and pay with development goods and technical assistance but, so far at least, the Sudanese Government has not gone along with these attempts.

The common element of these three instances is clear. It was the inability of primary producing countries to sell their products at what they considered remunerative terms. True, if they had slashed their prices to the bone they might have sold more, but in that event their export receipts would have been greatly reduced as, unhappily, the demand for most primary commodities is so rigid that drastic reductions are necessary to achieve significantly higher sales. Since most of these countries are bent on economic development that calls for rising exchange receipts to pay for larger imports year after year, any sharp drop of export volume or prices is sorely felt; and any

[19] Harry B. Ellis in the Christian Science Monitor, Aug. 6, 1959.

recession in Western industrial countries is particularly feared because it usually means both less volume and lower prices.

The Soviet bloc is taking advantage of such situations in two ways: by becoming known as a friend in need, and by driving home the point that the capitalist system is inefficient, cannot avoid crises, and makes the less developed countries shoulder the burden by pushing down the prices of primary products they sell while maintaining or raising the prices of manufactures they have to buy. Anyone who has followed the relative price movements during the recent recession will have to admit that this was the outcome even though there was certainly no malicious intent on the part of the industrial countries; thus, between 1956 and 1958 the terms of trade of industrial countries improved by 5 percent, while those of other countries deteriorated by 7 percent.[20]

The bloc has made the most of these opportunities through shrewd timing and considerable flexibility. When the Burmese needed outlets, the bloc was ready. When they wanted to sell less because the market for cash sales had expanded, the bloc was willing. Either way they acted like a disinterested friend, and this is just the way the Communists always picture themselves. The implication is that another time they will help again, true buyers of last resort, in contrast with the West where instability seems to originate and where moreover—as with American cotton and rice—competition rather than relief is often found. It is not hard to see that the psychological-political impact effect of such trade can be much greater than the amounts involved would seem to justify.

Purely economically speaking, one might be inclined to wonder whether the emergence of a buyer who is able and willing to absorb worldwide surpluses is not a good thing. In some commodities, e.g., rubber and wool, bloc purchases have tended to raise or stabilize commodity prices. This effect is most marked, and perhaps most welcome, where the bloc buys on established exchanges or auctions and thereby improves the "tone" of the Western market system. But if the bloc's trade partner is enmeshed in bilateral agreements, the more frequent form of Communist commerce, the free world's trade will rarely benefit.

The obvious response for the West is to reduce the opportunities from which the bloc could benefit. The case of rice shows that the reemergence of sufficient demand provided a timely escape from bilateral shackles for Burma. Perhaps this course of events is not typical because the surplus had been largely due to a few exceptionally good crops; and if Communist China ever emerges as a major exporter of rice—and this could happen if a mere fraction of its vaunted production increases became true with time—the situation may again become quite serious. In that event, the bloc's opportunities will rise in inverse proportion with the West's ability and willingness to help Burma or other producers with their problems in an alternative manner.

It is equally relevant for a sober evaluation of the surpus problem that Egypt and Syria have still not found enough alternative mar-

[20] United Nations, Monthly Bulletin of Statistics, July 1959, p. X.

kets to reduce the importance of the bloc for their trade. It does not help the West's cause that the United States is a competitor who keeps piling surplus on surplus that must be unloaded on the world markets; and this country is far too large a factor in world cotton to avoid having its subsidized export sales make themselves felt adversely, no matter how circumspectly they may be conducted. Thus, domestic political-institutional factors aggravate the world impact, to the detriment of the West's position, while in the case of fish from Iceland inability to subordinate a relatively minor dispute to the overriding goal of Western unity continues to have similar debilitating effects.

In all instances the bloc had an important structural advantage: it could absorb these surpluses at little cost and usually with economic benefit. More fish, cotton, rice, and, in other cases, more cocoa from Ghana and Brazil, wool and meat from Argentina and Uruguay, copper wire from Chile, or perhaps some more coffee from Latin America—all these goods could be well used in economies under perennial pressure of excess demand, even if they are not prime necessities. The occasional reexport by the bloc does not necessarily prove the contrary, but may well be due to a need for additional foreign exchange. In any event, the bloc's ability to accept goods the West cannot use suggests a welcome degree of complementarity that is bound to make a favorable impression on primary producers in general.

The peril of overdependence

Whatever the individual circumstances—and each case is different—the broad issue from the angle of competitive coexistence is the danger that a producer of primary commodities may first seek relief in relation with the bloc and then become so dependent on it that a threat, or perhaps the mere possibility, of losing this market would make him vulnerable to political pressure. To be sure, expanded trade provides other more subtle benefits to the bloc as well: the novelty of interchange, broader contacts, friendly relations, prestige; but all these are most effective initially and are bound to wane with time as they become familiar and tend to be taken for granted.[21] But, on the whole, dependence is surely the most critical issue in the long run.

It would be useful if a condition of approaching overdependence could be diagnosed by a simple statistical measure, such as the ratio of total trade that is directed to the Soviet bloc. Table 2 provides this information for selected countries whose exports to or imports from the Sino-Soviet bloc exceeded 10 percent of the total in any one of the last 5 years. Afghanistan could not be included for lack of reliable data, although the proportion of bloc trade is rather high; indications are that it has been in the neighborhood of 30 percent in recent years.

---

[21] Large embassy staffs ostensibly related to economic matters may also open channels for subversion, perhaps even espionage; the large Soviet staff in Uruguay, for instance, is suspected of being the nerve center of all operations in South America.

TABLE 2.—*Percentage of total exports and imports of selected countries held by the Sino-Soviet bloc, 1954–58*

	1954		1955		1956		1957		1958	
	Exports	Imports	Exports	Imports	Exports	Imports	Exports	Imports	Exports	Imports
Iceland	25	18	28	22	30	26	34	33	35	32
Finland	28	28	26	27	27	25	28	31	25	26
Greece	7	3	5	4	10	5	11	6	16	7
Turkey	17	9	22	18	20	15	18	17	24	18
Yugoslavia	3	1	14	8	24	23	28	23	29	28
Egypt	14	6	27	7	34	14	47	26	44	29
Syria	(1)	3	1	3	8	4	17	8	31	12
Iran	18	10	10	9	17	10	23	11	26	9
Burma	(1)	2	19	2	14	19	12	11	3	12
Ceylon	12	11	6	6	11	9	10	5	6	9
Uruguay	10	1	6	1	4	5	8	2	21	5

[1] Less than 1 percent.

Source: State Department, Mutual Defense Assistance Control Act of 1951, "Reports to Congress."

It is immediately apparent that no country has directed as much as 50 percent of either exports or imports to the bloc, only one (Egypt) more than 40 percent, and none as much as 40 percent, if the total volume of trade (exports plus imports) is used as a yardstick. But there is no reason why 50 percent, 40 percent, or for that matter any other figure, should be singled out as a generally valid danger line. On the contrary, quite different figures may be related to potential danger, depending on such factors as the composition of trade, the strategic position of a country, its economic structure and internal political vulnerability, and many others. Most observers would feel intuitively that Turkey's 24 percent of Iran's 26 percent mean less in the case of allies with such a stanch record of independence and anticommunism than the sudden jump from 8 to 21 percent in Uruguay whose inability to sell its meat and wool (partly due to a countervailing duty on wool tops invoked by the United States) has been responsible for some spectacular deals with the bloc.

It is also revealing that the table does not include the bloc's two largest beneficiaries from Soviet loans, India and Indonesia. Though rising, their trade remained below 10 percent, and yet these countries are surely of prime political interest to the Communists—indeed, to the West and East alike. But the list does include Middle Eastern areas where trade, though important, is only one factor, while the bloc's arms deliveries and the unequivocal endorsement of anti-Western sentiments and nationalistic aspirations were probably much more decisive for the successful Soviet penetration into this strategic area.

This line of thought indicates that the problem of dependence cannot be comprehended in statistical terms alone. Commonsense suggests that a large customer will not be lightly spurned if promising alternative markets are lacking. Hence, the degree of dependence, whatever this might represent in specific instances, is primarily a function of the opportunities on which a country can fall back in case of friction with the bloc. If these alternatives are kept open, chances are the bloc would not even attempt excessive pressure for fear of standing accused of the same kind of "imperialistic methods" with which it has labeled the historic "dependence" on Western markets.

Finland and Yugoslavia may serve as examples. The first has developed industries to which the Russian market is truly indispensable; yet, although political pressures have not been absent, the Soviet Union has refrained from using its unquestioned economic power to the hilt in order to achieve political control. And in Yugoslavia, the recent political break was hardly felt at all in the share of Soviet trade.

The limit to the bloc's influence through trade thus depends on the West's success in keeping its own trade healthy and rising, thus denying the bloc the opportunities to obtain strangleholds. The West cannot shirk this effort, since the functioning of the free markets is after all the West's very own concern. This is not the place for the detailed discussion of complex matters and concrete techniques. But it is evident that the task includes most prominently the prevention of recessions or the alleviation of their effects on the weaker countries if they occur nonetheless. And it involves also a coordinated effort to mitigate the instability of commodity prices. This is a difficult problem for which no easy solutions are in sight. But until recently American policy has evaded the issue and this aloofness has been widely interpreted abroad as lack of interest, sometimes as callousness. Without the active participation of the United States, the world's largest importer, these problems cannot be attacked with any hope for success. But a serious and persistent effort, even merely partial solutions, promise to diminish the danger of Communist influence through trade dependence below the threshold of danger on a worldwide scale.

The bloc as a supplier

In its trade regulations with the less developed areas three types of bloc exports can be distinguished: tied sales of manufactures under credit agreements; competitive sales, whether covered by trade agreements or not; and sales of primary commodities in the industrial countries which have repercussions on the less developed primary producers. The Communists usually claim that they are selling at "world prices." This does not seem too far from the truth as a guide to Soviet pricing because the artificial exchange rates maintained by the bloc would make a rational link with domestic costs and prices extremely precarious. The bloc members, therefore, usually keep close to the prices of their competitors, shading them sufficiently to secure the business they want. To be sure, there have been reports of sizable price cuts, some of which cannot always be fully substantiated; from the vantage point of the United States they may appear larger than in comparison with other suppliers, when American prices happen to be higher in the first place. But, on the whole—at least up to now—systematic and large-scale price cutting appears to be the exception rather than the norm for the Soviet bloc in Europe.

Soviet credits are, of course, firmly tied to bloc merchandise.[22] The recipient of aid may find it difficult to argue about the price of goods received and instances of overcharging have leaked out. The bloc, however, seems intent on minimizing such instances and, as in the case

[22] In fact, the strict bilateral system employed makes it usually difficult to switch even from one supplier to another within the bloc, and where such arrangements had been stipulated, as in the case of Finland, the system did not work well.

of Egypt, has been known to respond to complaints. Moreover, where bilateral trade is involved, the price of exports alone means little unless import prices are also considered; in such transactions it is not unusual for the bloc to offer higher-than-market prices and recoup the difference in reverse deals. As the bloc exports are often delayed, it takes time for the facts to become known. But in Burma and Indonesia official statements indicate that the terms of trade with the bloc were unfavorable. There have been hints of dissatisfaction in Egypt, and no one can tell whether diplomatic niceties do not obscure similar sentiments elsewhere. In any event, even where Soviet prices in bilateral transactions were not higher than in free markets, chances are that the bloc's purchases would have raised the price had they been placed on the world market instead of through sheltered channels.

Regarding Communist Chinese exports, reports of price cutting are more plentiful and consistent than in the instance of the Soviet bloc. The reasons are probably both economic and political. China is much more dependent on imports than the Soviet bloc, and while most of its trade is directed toward the latter, all imports from the free world have to be paid by exports. Southeast Asia is a natural outlet geographically, but it is not unlikely that mainland Chinese exports to these areas were stepped up deliberately in order to hurt Japan against whom the Chinese Communists had instituted an embargo following the latter's refusal to give de facto recognition of their flag. It is also possible that they wanted to establish a "presence" and stake a claim in this area, sometimes with the help of pressure on the important overseas Chinese community in southeast Asia; and this effect may well survive the recent sharp drop of Communist exports that seems to have resulted from domestic difficulties.[23]

On the whole, the performance record of bloc trade appears to be neither very good nor all bad from the angle of its trade partners, and this is where the relevant impact effect arises. Deliveries are often delayed, regardless of embarrassment to the buyer. There have been numerous reports of dissatisfaction with the quality of the goods supplied. Partly they may be attributed to inexperience with foreign requirements, partly to bureaucratic inflexibility. But such shortcomings may not be beyond remedy and the more advanced East-Central European countries are recovering their prewar status as exporters and expanding their activities. How well bloc exports would fare in free multilateral trade may well be in doubt. But as long as the greatest part follows the purchase of commodities the West cannot use, the bloc's partners have little choice but to take what they can get in return for their sales. Hence, as in the past, an important part of Communist trade will depend significantly on Western import policy; and to that extent the direction of the less developed area's trade with the bloc will be a function of the growth and flexibility of the Western market system.

These qualities may well be tested by the bloc in still another direction. The Soviet Union has recently emerged as a major exporter of metals and minerals, in some respects in competition with certain

[23] Reexports of Communist goods through Hong Kong and Singapore, major transit channels from the mainland to southeast Asia, have reportedly dropped by 25 percent in the former, and 73 percent in the latter case in the first 5 months of 1959 (Time, Aug. 3, 1959, p. 72).

less developed countries. When the Council of the International Tin Agreement had to absorb large quantities of Russian and Chinese metal in 1957, it was compelled to invoke the statutory export quotas by which the price could be maintained fairly successfully, except for a short period when the agreement's buffer stock manager temporarily ran out of funds. Even though the Soviet Union informally agreed to reduce its tin exports in 1959, the exports of Thailand, Indonesia, Malaya, Bolivia, and Nigeria were reduced to less than half of the preceding year. The impact effect of this incursion by the Soviet bloc has been adverse and quite vocal; and this is a good example of the see-saw character of trade competition.

On the reverse side of the ledger are growing sales of Soviet bloc petroleum in the less developed areas, especially of Latin America. They fill an important gap in the trade of such countries as Argentina, Brazil, and Uruguay. Their erstwhile complete dependence on Western oil has long been a sensitive point in the internal politics of these countries. The negative American attitude toward the ambitions of the government monopoly in Brazil to develop its oil resources without private foreign capital was also involved. Whenever the Soviet bloc injects itself into such a situation, as it recently did also in Bolivia,[24] fuel is poured on this long smoldering disagreement; and in countries where private enterprise fares well in other respects, nationalistic sentiments are fanned by this one issue on which American policy has been more inflexible than on virtually any other. This example illustrates the close interrelation of all kinds of policies to which the Communist bloc is so much more finely attuned, with trade just one convenient instrument.

4. SUMMARY AND CONCLUSION

In the period from mid-1954 to mid-1959 assistance granted by the Sino-Soviet bloc to 20 countries totaled about $2.7 billion. About three-quarters of it was economic aid. Five of the recipient countries received only small amounts (less than $10 million each) while about 90 percent of the total was concentrated in only nine countries receiving more than $100 million each. In the same 5 years the United States gave the same 20 countries about $5.3 billion of economic assistance, more than 2½ times the Communist economic contribution. If aid to the other countries absent from the Soviet list were included, the American assistance amount would be doubled. Total non-Communist bilateral and multilateral assistance is being given at an annual rate of close to $3 billion. If private foreign investment were included, the total yearly flow of capital from non-Communist sources to the less developed areas probably exceeded $5 billion, at least 15 times the actual annual bloc expenditures for foreign assistance.

While this ratio appears comforting, it is questionable whether quantities count for so much. For if they did, why should one be worried about Communist aid that is relatively so small? Actual-

[24] Reportedly the Soviet Union has offered a large loan ot the state oil company in Bolivia, thus capitalizing on criticism of U.S. refusal to finance the reequipment of the state-owned petroleum or mining industries (Juan de Onis in the New York Times, Aug. 19, 1959).

ly the impact of aid is not necessarily proportionate to the amount and it is desirable to distinguish between two very different impact effects.

The first is the direct economic and social impact, a slow change induced over time, often unspectacular, sometimes intangible. The second is the impression aid makes upon the recipient's mind. It is subjective and conditioned by sentiment and prejudice; its impact is direct, immediate, and politically potent. The U.S. development aid programs have been fashioned with the first impact effect in mind. The Communists have shown themselves much more finely attuned to the second.

Due to the second impact effect, it matters at least as much how capital is provided, as how much. For one instance, in many underdeveloped countries private foreign investment included in the above totals is frequently not accorded the same reception as loans. A plant built by the Russians and left behind when they go home may be more welcome than one remaining under foreign control indefinitely. No matter whether right or wrong, the recipient's attitudes shape the political impact, and the Communists have cleverly used the latent suspicion of Western business that rests on anticolonial and nationalistic sentiments. Therefore a nagging insistence on linking assistance to private business tends to support the Communists' taunts that Western aid is a pretext for profits whilst theirs, as they maintain, is disinterested and free of strings.

"Strings" are a psychological and political element, not determined so much by the donor's real intent than by the image in the recipient's mind. There must be conditions to foreign aid, but those that are congenial to the recipient's aspirations are not viewed as strings, while others are considered as interference. Therefore the Communist bloc has catered to the sensitive ego of new nations in both the substance of aid agreements and the pomp and circumstance surrounding the negotiations.

Communist assistance terms strike the observer as being made to appear as different as possible from Western practice. Most bloc assistance takes the form of credits rather than grants which are pictured as entailing debasing obligations. Loans are usually repayable in local products, or in local currency for which local products are to be acquired later. This relieves the recipients of the problem how to muster enough foreign exchange to transfer investment profits, interest, and repayments that burden them in connection with Western capital. It also makes them feel secure in the belief that Communist loans are self-liquidating and that development assistance from the bloc can be paid for with the fruits of development itself.

Interest on bloc loans is much lower than the West's. This bolsters suspicions of exploitation that are rife in formerly colonial areas where imperialism and exploitation are considered inseparable even by many non-Communists. This reinforces the picture of greater affinity between the less developed countries and themselves which the Communists have been trying to create, in order to make the Soviet system appear more suitable for rapid economic growth than the democratic method.

Identification of public enterprise with "socialistic" tendencies also tends to play into the hands of the Communists. In the free-enterprise economies of the West governmental initiative has also been far broader in early stages of economic development than now. And even today the economic structure of countries like India or Burma differs much less from many European countries than the term "socialist" they like to apply to themselves seems to indicate. It would be tragic if a mere antagonism toward words, or a variance of social imagery, would block the Western understanding of the prevalent aspirations for economic and social betterment which the Communists would dearly like to monopolize.

The number of Soviet technicians, an estimated 4,700 working abroad for more than a month in the first half of 1959, is not too far below the number of American Government technicians abroad. If all Western countries and international agencies, and privately employed technicians were included, the West would, of course, be far ahead of the bloc. But, again, numbers may not be a true measure of impact. The choice of projects for Soviet capital and technical assistance gives also evidence of a desire to be identified with the recipient's aspirations. Sino-Soviet technical assistance is usually linked to large projects, such as mineral development or industry that are close to the heart of developing countries. Moreover the bloc technicians' own background in recently still underdeveloped countries gives eloquent testimony for the feasibility of rapid growth which the new nations also crave.

Communist aid is always closely linked to trade, but trade alone is also made to impress less developed primary producers with the extent of complementarity between them and the bloc. Government monopolies can conclude large transactions quickly, in contrast to the atomistic and uncoordinated trading decisions characteristic of the Western system. Most importantly, the bloc has displayed a superb sense of timing, by appearing as a buyer of last resort when primary producers could not sell their output in Western markets at remunerative prices. Fish from Iceland, rice from Burma, cotton from Egypt and Syria, wool and meat from Uruguay and Argentina—all these deals point to the bloc as a powerful new factor in world trade, even though the bloc's share is no more than 3 percent of the total.

In return, the bloc is able to supply the kind of things the primary producers need, including capital goods for development. The value received was sometimes disappointing to the uncommitted countries, and the lesson has been learned by some that cash is better than bilateral trade whenever it can be obtained. But a continuation or recurrence of surpluses will give the bloc similar opportunities whenever non-Communist markets cannot, or are unwilling, to absorb all output. Hence the bloc's opportunities to capitalize on other countries' embarrassments will be a function of the West's neglect in looking after the health and smooth functioning of the world's free markets.

This is also the answer to the question whether the bloc could attain political control through its power over the trade of smaller nations. The bloc holds a quarter or more of some countries' trade. Where the danger point is depends on many factors, but no government need yield to excessive pressure if it knows that alternative opportunities will again become available, through a turn of the market or through deliberate Western policy. As a result, no instance of subservience through trade with the bloc has yet arisen and the West has the capability, if it has also the will, to develop policies that will deny the bloc the use of its bargaining position for obtaining strangleholds.

Such policies include maximizing the imports of the industrial countries and collaborating in attempts to stabilize the markets for commodities which the less advanced primary producers have to sell, in order to pay for imports of necessities and of development goods. These are really policies the West should want to pursue even in the absence of the Communist threat, for the viability of the world's free markets are the West's very own concern. But, of course, with the Communist bloc waiting to capitalize on the West's mistakes, the penalty for neglect is so high that aloofness is no longer feasible and concerted action indispensable. The United States, the world's largest trading nation, would do well to recognize the trend and to lead rather than lag on the road to better Western economic collaboration with the less developed areas.

EVALUATION OF THE RUSSIAN ECONOMIC THREAT BY PRIVATE POLICYMAKERS

EVALUATION OF THE RUSSIAN THREAT IN THE FIELD OF ELECTRIC POWER

(By Edwin Vennard, Edison Electric Institute, New York, N.Y.)

I. Introduction

Two visits to inspect electric power installations and facilities for the manufacture of electrical equipment in the Soviet Union have provided Americans in the power industry with new statistics, facts, observations and impressions upon which an appraisal can be based. These trips were arranged by the U.S. Department of State and its counterpart in the U.S.S.R. They were part of the technical and cultural exchange program between the two countries. Our group represented the electric utility industry and the manufacturers of electrical equipment.

The tours were conducted under the auspices of the Edison Electric Institute and the Association of Edison Illuminating Companies, trade associations of investor-owned electric utilities.

The first visit was from August 14 through August 30, 1958. There were seven electric utility executives and three executives of manufacturing companies on this tour. Aside from myself, the members of the delegation were—

Mr. Harvey E. Bumgardner, assistant to the president, the Detroit Edison Co., and chairman, committee on technical exchange for overseas visitors of the Edison Electric Institute.

Mr. Walker L. Cisler, president of the Detroit Edison Co. and the leader of the group as appointed by the Edison Electric Institute.

Mr. J. F. Davenport, executive vice president, Southern California Edison Co.

Mr. D. S. Kennedy, president of the Oklahoma Gas & Electric Co. and past president of the Edison Electric Institute.

Mr. Gwilym A. Price, chairman of the board, Westinghouse Electric Corp.

Mr. Philip D. Reed, chairman, finance committee, General Electric Co.

Mr. R. G. Rincliffe, president, Philadelphia Electric Co., and vice president of the Association of Electric Illuminating Companies.

Mr. J. L. Singleton, executive vice president, Allis-Chalmers Manufacturing Co., and president, National Electric Manufacturers Association.

This tour covered European Russia.

The second trip was from July 23 through August 4, 1959, at which time we visited facilities in Siberia, the Urals, and in Armenia. On this trip were seven representing the utilities, two the manufacturers, and one representing an engineering construction firm. Besides myself, they were—

Walker Cisler, president of the Detroit Edison Co. and the group leader.

Harvey E. Baumgardner, assistant to the president, the Detroit Edison Co.

Charles E. Eble, president, Consolidated Edison Co. of New York.

Lewis R. Gaty, vice president, research and development, Philadelphia Electric Co.

Donald S. Kennedy, chairman of the board and president, Oklahoma Gas & Electric Co.

Francis K. McCune, vice president, atomic business development and marketing services, General Electric Co.

Alexander C. Monteith, vice president and general manager, apparatus products, Westinghouse Electric Corp.

J. Perry Yates, executive vice president, Bechtel Corp.

In 1958 the host organization was the Ministry of Power of the U.S.S.R.[1] Between the 1958 and 1959 visits there was a slight change in the system of administering the electric power industry. Accordingly, the host organization for the 1959 trip was the Ministry of Construction of Power Stations.

Twelve executives and specialists representing the Ministry of Construction of Power Stations in the U.S.S.R. will visit facilities of electric utility companies and electrical manufacturing companies in America, beginning October 5, 1959.

This paper is a summary of the facts respecting the power facilities in the U.S.S.R. It includes what we saw and what we were told. To assist in an evaluation, suitable comparisons have been made with the electric power facilities in America. In addition, the report includes an opinion as to the economic significance of the facts, especially as they relate to the electric power business.

The Americans found the Russians they met to be friendly, courteous, and hospitable. They were eager and sincere in their efforts to give us information about the status of the electric industry in Russia. They were equally anxious to learn about similar facilities in America. On the first trip after a briefing by the heads of the Ministry of Power, we visited—

Moscow Research Institute.

All-Union Institute for Thermal Research.

Nuclear research center at Dubna.

Industrial and agricultural exhibit in Moscow.

Three typical thermal power stations.

Two of the larger hydroelectric stations.

Atomic prototype powerplant at Obnisk.

State planning commission.

A principal substation near Moscow.

A large plant for the manufacture of turbines, generators, and transformers.

A principal dispatching center.

---

[1] App. A contains the names of the principal hosts on each of the tours.

At the close of the trip there was a final meeting with the officials of the Ministry of Power.[2]

On the second tour, we again had a briefing by the officials of the Ministry of Construction of Power Stations, following which we visited [3]—

Hydroelectric station at Irkutsk.
Construction site of 4,500,000 kilowatt hydro plant of Bratsk.
Hydro plant and generator works at Novosibirsk.
Thermal stations at Youzhno-Kuzbass and Youzhno-Uralsk.
Atomic powerplants at Beloyarsk and Voronezh.
Hydro plants at Sevang-Razdan Cascade.

II. Russia's Electric Power

THE MAIN SYSTEMS

There are 52 power systems in all of the U.S.S.R. Many of these are individual plants, not interconnected with any power grid. Within European Russia the three principal, interconnected systems are the central (including the Moscow, Yaroslav, Ivanova, and Gorky systems), the Urals (including the Molotov, Sverdlovsk, and Chelyabinsk systems) and the southern (including the Dnieper, Donets, and Rostov systems). Each of these main systems has a capacity of 6 or 7 million kilowatts. At some indeterminate time in the future, these three systems are to be linked with other systems in European Russia and the six systems in central Siberia to form a single power grid.

Transmission, capacity, and generation—United States compared

Figure 1 shows a transmission map of the Russian systems as of 1958. For comparative purposes, figure 2 shows the principal interconnected electric transmission lines of the power facilities in the United States. The following table shows the kilowatts of capacity and the kilowatt-hours of electric energy generated in the United States and the U.S.S.R. for the year 1957 [4] both for hydro and steam:

---

[2] See app. B for the dates of these visits.
[3] See app. C for a more detailed outline of this second tour.
[4] We do not yet have the 1958 figures for U.S.S.R. power capacity.

FIGURE 1

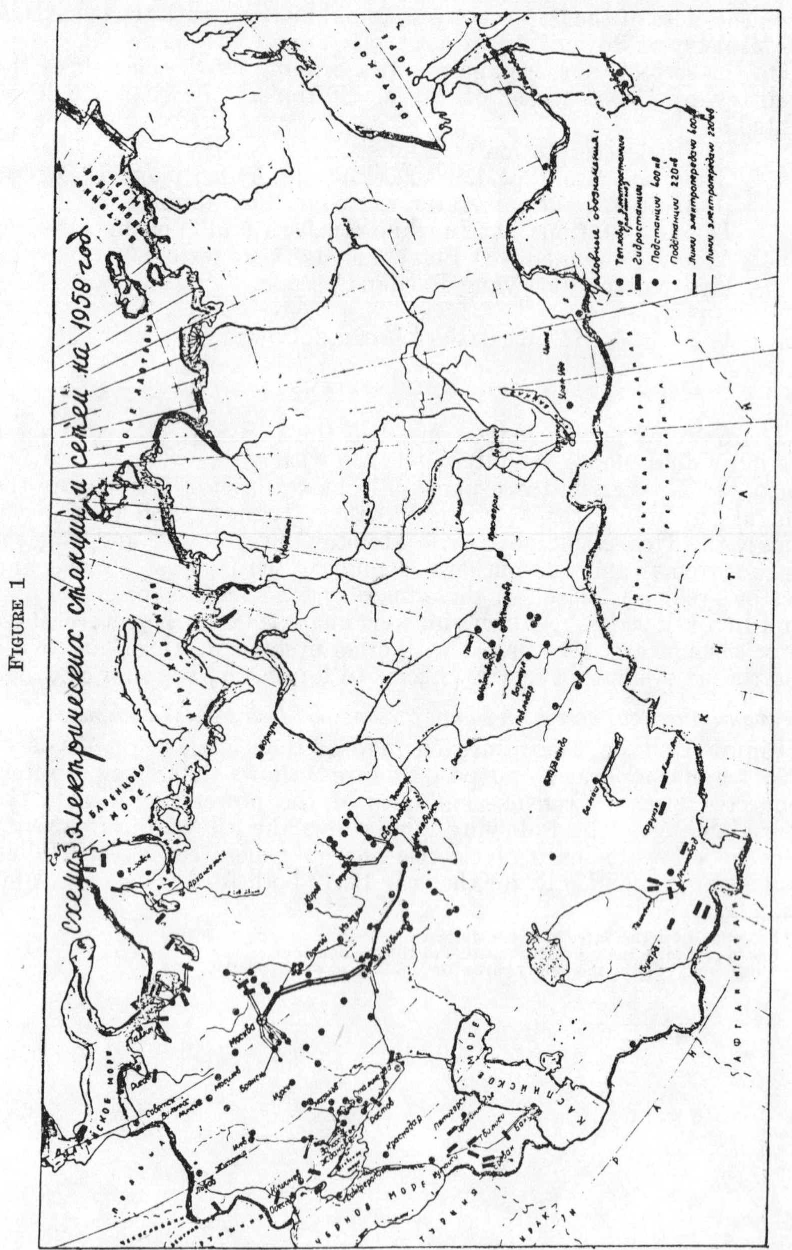
Схема электрических станций и сетей на 1958 год
Условные обозначения
Тепловые электростанции
Гидростанции
Подстанции 400 кв
Подстанции 220 кв
Линии электропередачи 400 кв
Линии электропередачи 220 кв

FIGURE 2

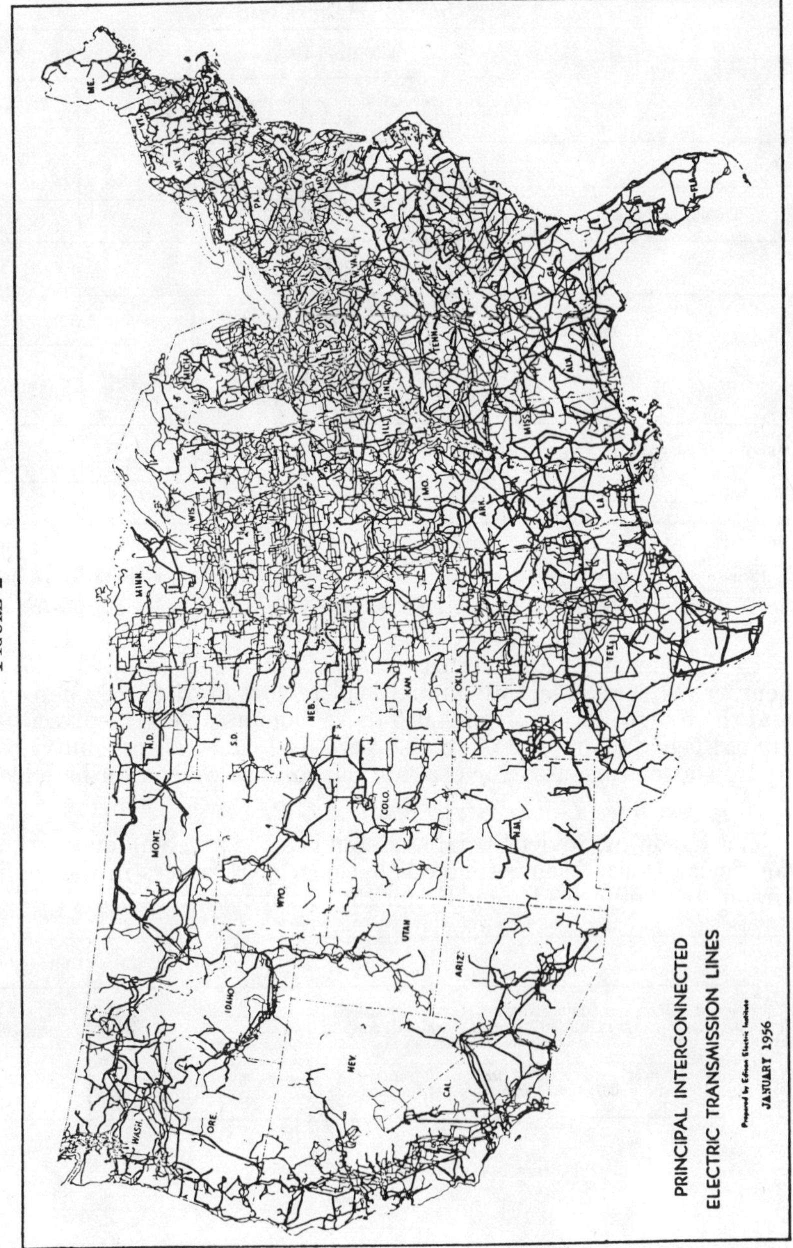
PRINCIPAL INTERCONNECTED
ELECTRIC TRANSMISSION LINES
Prepared by Edison Electric Institute
JANUARY 1956
ME.
VT.
N.Y.
PA.
VA.
W.VA.
N.C.
GA.
FLA.
KY.
TENN.
ALA.
MISS.
MICH.
IND.
ILL.
WIS.
MO.
ARK.
LA.
MINN.
TEX.
OKLA.
KAN.
NEB.
S.D.
N.D.
COLO.
N.M.
MONT.
WYO.
UTAH
ARIZ.
IDAHO
NEV.
CAL.
ORE.
WASH.

Kilowatts, installed capacity, 1957

	United States [1]		U.S.S.R.	
	Millions of kilowatts	Percent	Millions of kilowatts	Percent
Hydro	27.8	19	9.9	19
Steam	118.4	81	38.5	81
Total	146.2	100	48.4	100

Kilowatt-hours generated, 1957

	United States		U.S.S.R.	
	Billions of kilowatt-hours	Percent	Billions of kilowatt-hours	Percent
Hydro	130.0	18	39.3	20
Steam	590.0	82	170.2	80
Total	[2] 720.0	100	[3] 209.5	100

[1] Total United States, including 17, 1,000,000 kilowatts in industrial, mine, and railway electric powerplants. The 1958 total was 160, 2, 000,000 kilowatts.
[2] Including net imports of 3,600,000,000 kilowatt-hours. In 1958, the kilowatt-hours generated amounted to 727,400,000,000 kilowatt-hours.
[3] The 1958 U.S.S.R. electricity production figure has been reported to have been 235,000,000,000 kilowatt-hours.

In the Soviet Union thermal stations operate from 4,500 to 7,000 hours a year (representing annual load factors of 51.4 to 80 percent) and the hydro stations from 4,000 to 5,500 hours a year (representing annual load factors of 45.6 to 62.8 percent). As in this country, the hydro stations are used for peaking purposes as well as for base load.

Energy resources, United States and U.S.S.R.

The Union of Soviet Socialist Republics has an abundance of coal for fuel. It has been estimated that energy resources in the Soviet Union are as follows (United States shown for comparison):

	U.S.S.R.	United States
Coal reserves, billion short tons (National Coal Association)	1,763	1,895
Crude petroleum reserves, billion barrels (World Oil, Aug. 15, 1959)	24	30.5
Proven gas reserves, trillion cubic feet (American Gas Association, World Oil, supra)	706	254
Potential waterpower, mean flow, million horsepower (U.S. Geological Survey Circular No. 367, U.S. Department of Interior)	375	116

Figure 3 shows the production of electricity in kilowatt-hours per capita for each of the two countries from 1940 through 1957.

FIGURE 3

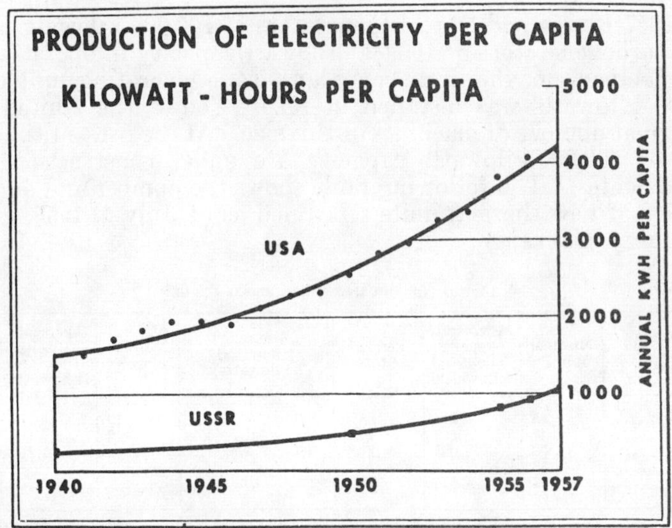

Russia places great emphasis upon the building of the industrial plant or the machinery of production. As a consequence, about 80 percent of the total production of electricity is for industrial purposes. The remaining 20 percent is used by commercial establishments, the homes, and the farms.

For comparison, the following table shows the use of electricity in the United States by the major classifications for 1958.

	Billions of kilowatt-hours	Percent
Residential	159.0	27.9
Commercial	101.2	17.8
Farm (rural)	11.0	1.9
Industrial	275.0	48.4
All other (street and highway, other public authorized railroads, etc.)	22.8	4.0
Total	[1] 569.0	100.0

[1] The difference between this figure and the 727.4 billion kilowatt-hours shown on p. 8 represents generations of industrial, mine, and electric railway powerplants plus company use and losses.

STEAMPLANTS

Cherepetz and Youzhno-Uralsk

Probably the most modern steamplant operating in Russia today is the 450,000-kilowatt station at Cherepetz, about 2 hours' drive from Moscow. It has turbines of 150,000-kilowatt capacity, and operates at a pressure of 2,490 pounds per square inch and 1,040° F.

At the Youzhno-Uralsk Thermal Station, near Chelyabinsk, we saw a present capacity of 600,000 kilowatts with four 50,000-kilowatt units and four 100,000-kilowatt units. An addition to the plant is being built to contain two 200,000-kilowatt units, bringing the total capacity to 1 million kilowatts in this station.

We were told that units of 300,000 and 600,000 kilowatts are now being designed.

In 1957 Russia had 56 turbogenerators of 100,000-kilowatt capacity and 3 turbogenerators of 150,000-kilowatt capacity in operation.

By comparison, the first American steam-generating unit of over 200,000 kilowatts was installed in 1920. Today, the United States has a great number of machines of this size. At the present time, three units of 500,000-kilowatts capacity are under construction in the United States. The following table shows the number and aggregate capacity of new thermal units scheduled as of July 1, 1959, grouped according to size range.

[In terms of manufacturer's ratings of the units]

Size range (thousand kilowatts)	Number of units	Aggregate capacity (thousand kilowatts)	Percent of total	Size range (thousand kilowatts)	Number of units	Aggregate capacity (thousand (kilowatts)	Percent of total
Under 100	85	3, 218	8. 4	300 to 399	19	6, 068	16. 2
100 to 149	49	5, 562	14. 9	400 to 499	2	900	2. 4
150 to 199	50	8, 065	21. 6	500 and over	3	1, 500	4. 0
200 to 249	36	7, 600	20. 4				
250 to 299	17	4, 525	12. 1	Total			100. 0

An order has recently been placed for a single unit of 600,000 kilowatts.

Pressures and temperatures

Russia makes use of high pressures and temperatures. At the thermal stations in service today, 58.7 percent of the installed equipment operates on steam of high pressures and temperatures, in the range of 1,420 pounds per square inch and of 930° F.

In the United States, the newer stations are being built with steam pressures of 2,400 pounds per square inch and temperatures of 1,500° F. The highest temperature and pressure planned for a plant in the United States will be in the Eddystone Station of the Philadelphia Electric Co., which will operate at the supercritical pressure of 5,000 pounds per square inch and the temperature of 1,200° F. A plant is in operation today at a pressure of 4,500 pounds per square inch and temperature in the 1,150° F. range.

HYDROELECTRIC STATIONS

The Soviet Union has developed a number of large efficient hydroelectric stations. We visited Kuibyshev on the Volga River, located about 560 miles southeast of Moscow. It has 20 units, each having an operating capacity of 115,000 kilowatts, for a total capacity of 2,300,-000 kilowatts.

About 1,250,000 kilowatts of the station's capacity is transmitted to Moscow over a 400,000-volt transmission line. The rest of the capacity goes to the Urals, over transmission lines of similar voltage.

The Stalingrad hydroplant, also on the Volga, was under construction when visited in 1958.

A 4,500,000-kilowatt hydroelectric station is under construction at Bratsk, located in a very thinly populated area in Siberia. It is expected that the first units of this plant will be in operation in 1961. The plant will be completed by 1963. We were told that Russia plans to move industry into this area to utilize the power. Also, part will be used in the further electrification of the Transsiberian Railroad.

ATOMIC POWER STATIONS

The following is a brief description of the known atomic power stations in the U.S.S.R. The capacities shown are in electrical kilowatts.

Operating

1. Five thousand-kilowatt enriched uranium-fueled graphite moderated light water cooled reactor. It is located at Obnisk, near Moscow, and has been operating since 1954. We visited this station in 1958.

2. One hundred thousand-kilowatt dual purpose natural uranium-fueled graphite moderated light water cooled reactor. This station was announced at Geneva in 1958 by U.S.S.R. It is located in Siberia. We did not visit it.

Under construction

3. Four hundred and twenty thousand-kilowatt two-reactor pressurized water slightly enriched uranium oxide fuel with zirconium cladding. It is located at Voronezh in the central industrial region. The first phase of this plant is now under construction, for a total of 210,000 electrical kilowatts in three 70,000-kilowatt units. We were told that the second stage of 210,000 kilowatts will not be constructed until it is determined how the first stage will operate. We were told this first unit will be in operation in 1961.

4. One hundred thousand-kilowatt boiling water reactor located at Beloyarsk in the Urals. We saw this station under construction. We were told that it will be in operation in 1961.

5. Fifty thousand-kilowatt boiling water slightly enriched uranium fuel reactor. It is located in the Ulyanovsk region. We did not visit this station.

Summary of atomic power

	Electric capacity-kilowatts
1. Obnisk	5, 000
2. Natural uranium	100, 000
3. Voronezh (1st stage)	210, 000
4. Beloyarsk	100, 000
5. Ulyanovsk	50, 000
Total	465, 000

U.S. program compared

For comparative purposes we list below a summary of the present atomic power development program in the United States.

By the end of 1958, a little over 4 years since the passage of the 1954 Atomic Energy Act (which permitted industry for the first time to engage in development and construction of its own atomic plants), a total of 131 electric-power companies and associated service organizations were participating in projects for the development and construction of 16 atomic powerplants and 11 major research, development, and study projects.

The 16 plants in which electric-power companies are participating will have a combined capacity of about 1,400,000 kilowatts and will require an estimated expenditure by the companies of more than $570 million.[5]

PLANTS IN OPERATION

Company	Type of reactor	Electrical capacity of plant, kilowatts	Operation
Duquesne Light Co	Pressurized water	60,000	December 1957.
Pacific Gas & Electric Co	Boiling water	5,000	October 1957.
Southern California Edison Co	Sodium graphite	7,500	July 1957.
PROJECTS UNDER CONSTRUCTION, DESIGN, OR CONTRACT NEGOTIATIONS			
Commonwealth Edison Co. Nuclear Power Group.	Dual cycle boiling water	180,000	1960.
Consolidated Edison Co. of New York, Inc.	Pressurized water thorium converter.	275,000	1961.
Northern States Power Co., Central Utilities Atomic Power Associates.	Boiling water with nuclear superheater.	66,000	1962.
Pacific Gas & Electric Co	Advanced boiling water	50,000	1962.
Detroit Edison Co.-PRDC	Fast breeder	100,000	1960.
Yankee Atomic Electric Co	Pressurized water	134,000	1960.
Carolinas-Virginia Nuclear Power Associated.	Heavy water moderated and cooled.	17,000	1962.
East Central Nuclear Group, Florida West Coast Nuclear Group.	Gas cooled, heavy	50,000	1963.
Philadelphia Electric Co.-HTRDA	High temperature, helium cooled, graphite moderated.	30,000	1963.
General Public Utilities Corp. System	Water	5,000	1961.
Consumers Power Co	Boiling water, high power density	50,000	1962.
PLANTS IN VARIOUS PLANNING STAGES			
New England Electric System	Not yet selected	200,000	Mid-1960's.
Pacific Gas & Electric Co	do	200,000	

NOTE.—These projects involve investor-owned companies only. In addition, public power organizations, in cooperation with the AEC, will participate in the building and operation of 3 nuclear powerplants having a combined capacity of about 110,000 kilowatts. These plants will require an estimated expenditure by these public power organizations of about $32 million.

U.S.S.R. policy on atomic power

We were told by the U.S.S.R. scientists that the atomic power program in Russia is still in the research and development stage, just as it is in the United States. Russia expects its cost of producing power from atomic fuels to be above its costs from conventional fuels. Likewise, this has been the case in the United States. As a consequence, Russia does not plan any large-scale development of atomic powerplants until it is possible to make energy from atomic fuels as economically as from conventional fuels.

Russia feels as we do that ultimately a way will be found to make economical power from atomic fuels. Consequently, they are going forward with their research.

[5] The knowledge, experience, and financial assistance of the Atomic Energy Commission have been valuable in the development of all these projects. In two of the operating projects the AEC has paid for the reactor portion of the plants. The cost of construction, research, and development of several other plants is being borne by the electric companies involved. But in the majority of the projects valuable assistance in the form of research and development grants and waiver of charges on special nuclear material is being given to the electric-power companies by the AEC.

TRANSMISSION

From a technical standpoint some of the most interesting work going on in Russia today is in the field of high voltage transmission. Eleven hundred miles of lines are now operating at 400,000 volts and it is expected that these lines will shortly be converted to 500,000 volts.

The construction of an 800,000 volt direct current transmission line from Stalingrad hydroelectric station to the Don Basin is expected to be completed in 1962. This is a distance of about 300 miles. The transmission capacity is to be 750,000 kilowatts.

In the United States the highest voltage transmission lines are 345 kilovolts. The next higher step will be 460 or 500 kilovolts. Tests are being made at the present time on a high altitude 500-kilovolt transmission line at Leadville, Colo.; at Pittsfield, Mass., the General Electrict Co. is building a 4½-mile line which will be operated at 750 kilovolts. No high-voltage direct current lines are as yet planned.

At the end of 1957 the total length of transmission lines in the U.S.S.R. of 35,000 volts and above was about 62,140 miles. In the United States the total length of lines 35,000 volts and above was 240,000 miles in the same year.

APPRAISAL OF RUSSIAN TECHNICAL SKILL

Russia's power specialists

In the field of engineering and construction of power facilities, we believe the Russians are good. They are making good turbines and generators. We were unable to get any figures on the efficiency of manufacture, but the resultant product is good. We believe the Russians capable of building the larger units. Also, in the fields of transformation, transmission, and dispatching we believe the Russians to be competent. Their research facilities are good.

III. Forecasts

CONSTRUCTION PLANS, ELECTRIC INDUSTRY

We were told that Russia plans to install 60 million additional kilowatts by the end of 1965, which would bring U.S.S.R. total capacity to something over 108 million kilowatts.

By comparison, we have under construction in America 51 million kilowatts of new capacity for the 4 years ending 1961. The new capacity we will have installed from 1958 to 1961 is slightly greater than Russia's present total. The following table shows the announced and estimated Russian plans to 1965 as compared with the United States for the same period.

Millions of kilowatts of capacity

	United States	U.S.S.R.
1957	146.2	48.4
1965	245.0	108.0

Figure 4 shows the kilowatt-hours per capita extended to 1965. The Russian figures are based upon the capacity quota of 108 million kilowatts. The U.S. figures are our forecast based upon past performance.

FIGURE 4

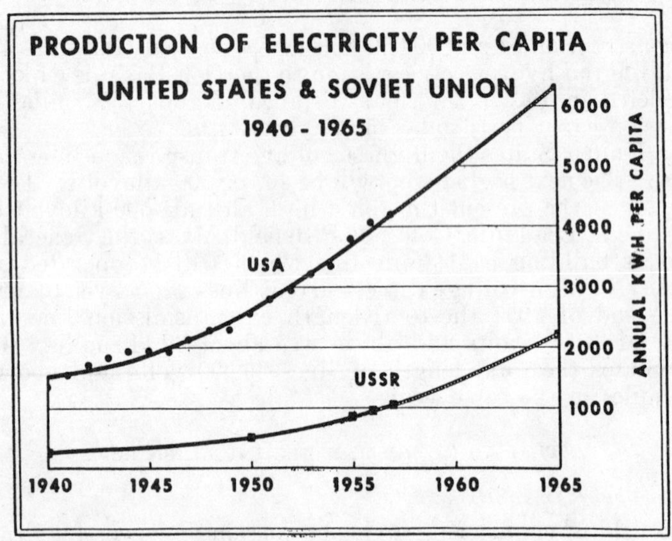

Will Russia meet its goal of 108 million kilowatts by 1965? Russia places great emphasis on goals or quotas. Managers and workers are encouraged to strive for these goals. It is not known whether the 108 million kilowatt figure is an estimate of what will occur or whether it is a budget or quota.

Russia's "goal" for 1957 was 230.2 billion kilowatt-hours. The actual was 209.5 billion kilowatt-hours, or about 9 percent under the goal.

THE U.S.S.R AND THE FUTURE

Planning to meet industrial needs

It is understandable that the various ministers who plan for the Soviet economy can determine the size of the total industrial plant for any given time in the future and design a plan to reach that goal. Supplying the electric power to fit in with such a plan is not an insurmountable problem; it is fairly simple to state that the light metals industry, for example, will require a certain number of kilowatts, and then to plan for the construction of those kilowatts according to a time schedule.

Problem of nonindustrial use

Bringing about an increase in the nonindustrial use of electricity is more difficult. For example, the average home use of electricity in Russia is about 400 kilowatt-hours per year, as compared with an average of about 3,400 kilowatt-hours per home in the United States in 1958. The use of electricity in the home depends to some extent upon the purchasing power of the people—the purchasing power to buy appliances as well as electricity. In some respects the use of electricity in the home reflects the well-being of the people in the home. It is a good indication of the standard of living. There is a definitive correlation between the purchasing power of people and the use of residential electricity.

We were told that Russia plans to continue to emphasize the building of the machinery of production. We heard of no plans for the promotion of the increased use of electricity for commercial establishments, for the home, or for the farm.

Goals for 1965

Knowing of Russia's technical and scientific ability, it would be safe to assume that she is capable of reaching a total of 108 million kilowatts in power capacity by 1965.

OPERATION OF THE RUSSIAN SYSTEM

To make a proper appraisal of Russia's productive capacity and potential growth, it is necessary to inquire into the Russian system and how it operates.

System of Government ownership

In Russia all industry is owned and operated by the Government. The Government owns and operates all steel plants, aluminum plants, textile mills, railroads, transportation facilities, power systems and clothing manufacturing plants. The Government is the sole supplier of goods. It owns and operates all stores. Practically everyone works for the Government—all managers, all scientists, all engineers, all doctors, all lawyers, all white-collar workers, all factory workers.

All prices are fixed by the Government. The Government manufactures and sells all goods and services. The margin between selling price and cost of production constitutes the major income to the Government. Other income is obtained through direct taxes.

The Government fixes all wages; there is a set wage for each job. The wages are graduated so that those of lesser ability receive less. Those of greater ability, knowledge, training, and schooling receive more. The bonus or incentive system is used to encourage workers individually and collectively to reach and exceed set quotas.

To the extent that Russia utilizes the incentive wage and pays according to ability, it does not follow the Marxian tenet "From each according to his ability, to each according to his needs."

U.S.S.R. administrative organization

In Russia there are 24 ministries. Included among them are the Ministries of Foreign Affairs, Home Affairs, Finance, Higher Education, Culture, Power, Grain Products, Geology and Conservation of Resources, Agriculture, and Defense.

In 1958 we were the guests of the Ministry of Power. At that time all aspects of the power industry were directed by this Ministry.

When we returned in 1959, we found that the administration of the industry had been changed. Now, the Ministry of Construction of Power Stations is responsible for construction. The operation of the plants is in the hands of local commissions.

The whole Rusian system is subject to the control of the Council of Ministers. The Council of Ministers has a staff organization known as

46283—59—pt. 2——8

the State Planning Commission which works with the Council in planning all economic and production activities. We visited with the State Planning Commission and its operation was explained to us.

There are 15 separate republics making up the U.S.S.R. These in turn have been divided into 105 economic regions. In some instances these regions overlap the boundaries of the 15 republics. Each of the 105 regions has a regional economic council, and under it is a regional board of power. It is the regional power board which oversees the activities of the various powerplants in the regions.

The regional economic councils draw up individual plans for their districts each year. These plans are intended to cover all phases of economic activity and call for the amounts of material and manpower that will be required to meet industrial objectives. These plans are sent to the Council of Ministers, where they are coordinated and the overall plans established.

In each of the regions the regional economic council is made up of directors representing the basic industries operating in the region. Together they plan the activities of their region. One of these directors is the chief of the regional power board. Under him will be found the individual directors of the various powerplants in the region.

IV. Economics

EXCHANGE RATES

The official exchange rate is 4 rubles per dollar, but Americans are given 10 rubles per dollar. We tried to estimate the proper exchange rate by pricing staple articles in Moscow—clothing, food, a few services, a few appliances. By and large our dollars at 10 rubles per dollar would buy substantially the same as they would buy in New York in terms of staple articles. Of course, there was not the variety nor the quantity available in Moscow that one finds in New York. There were notable exceptions where scarce articles carried unusually high price tags, but generally speaking, the 10-to-1 ratio appeared to be about right as a measure of the cost of living. We had no way of knowing whether, in the cost of building powerplants or other industrial establishments, it was proper to use a ratio of 4 to 1 or 10 to 1, or some other ratio.

Black market

We heard that there is a black market which would give possibly 20 rubles or 30 rubles per dollar. We did not encounter this. But even if there were, this would not alter the fact that the 10-to-1 ratio appears about right in the measure of the standard of living. Russian tourists planning to visit America are limited in the number of dollars they can take out of Russia. Such tourists may be willing to give more than 10 rubles per dollar just for the purpose of buying American articles.

POWER INDUSTRY COSTS

Investment per kilowatt

We asked and were told about certain capital costs in the building of power stations and certain operating costs. Although they are shown here, care should be used in assessing them owing to the different exchange rates in use.

Following are a few examples of investment costs of power stations:

Station and location	Type	Investment per kilowatt [1]
Station 20, Moscow	Steam	$180
Kuibyshev	Hydro	87
Irkutsk	do	200
Bratsk	do	133
Novosibirsk	do	225
Youzhno-Kuzbass	Steam	110

[1] Converted from rubles at 10 to 1.

These costs per kilowatt are not greatly dissimilar from unit costs in the United States.

Production cost, steam plant

The following table shows the cost of producing power at the Cherepetz steamplant.

	Kopeks per kilowatt-hour
Fuel	5.93
Wages	.56
Amortization	1.77
Materials	.49
Maintenance labor	.16
All other	.09
Total	9.00

A kopek is one-hundredth of a ruble. If there are 10 rubles to the dollar, a kopek is then one-tenth of a cent or 1 mill.

Note that amortization takes 1.77 kopeks per kilowatt-hour.

Amortization

We were told that all power stations must be amortized over a period of years; that is to say, the investment is paid back to the Government. The investment in machinery is repaid in 25 years. The costs of other facilities, such as the dam in a hydroelectric station, are paid back in 50 years. Consideration is now being given to a reduction from 25 to 20 years for the repayment of machinery and for extending the repayment period to 100 years for other facilities.

At the Luganskaya thermal plant, the total operating cost including amortization is said to be 4.9 kopeks per kilowatt-hour. Fuel accounts for about one-half of this cost.

Interest and taxes

It is noted that Russia does not consider interest as a cost of doing business. Notice also that there is no provision for taxes in the operation of these plants.

Because of the absence of interest and taxes, we found the reported cost of producing hydroelectric power in some stations to be quite low—as low as 1 mill per kilowatt-hour in some cases.

FUTURE PLANS FOR HYDRO

Emphasis on thermal plants

We were told that in the future Russia will place less emphasis on the development of hydro and more emphasis on thermal plants. Of the 60 million kilowatts of new capacity planned by 1965, we were told that 85 percent is expected to be thermal and 15 percent hydro, compared to the present ratio of 81 percent thermal and 19 percent hydro. This information is supported by a statement made by Premier Khrushchev in his address at the dedication of the Kuibyshev hydroelectric plant. We were told that the reason for the change in policy is that the hydroelectric plants are more expensive and they take longer to build.

This experience in the relative value of hydro and thermal stations is similar to the experience of the power companies in America. Great improvements have been made in the efficiency of thermal stations, whereas by comparison the increase in efficiency of hydroelectric stations has been slight in the last 25 years. Some years ago hydroelectric power was in most cases cheaper than thermal power. Now with notable exceptions the reverse is true. Also, in America, a primary factor favoring thermal power is that steamplants can be built closer to the load centers, while hydro stations must be built where there is a sufficient head and volume of water. Since most of the good hydro sites have already been developed, remaining sites are likely to be comparatively remote. This generally necessitates a higher investment in transmission to bring the power from the water site to the load centers.

ATOMIC POWER COSTS

In reply to our questions we were told by the Russian atomic scientists and engineers that they did not know what their costs would be in producing power from atomic fuels. One reason is that atomic fuels come from other departments and these engineers did not know what they would be charged. They did say that they, as we, have found the costs higher than originally anticipated. Also, they stated that they expect their costs to be considerably higher than the cost of equivalent power made from conventional fuels. Any large-scale development of atomic powerplants in Russia will wait until such time as research and development enable the production of power from the atom at a cost competitive with conventional fuels.

WAGES

As we traveled from plant to plant we were able to ask many questions. Naturally we were interested in how the employee was fairing under this planned economy, how much he earned, how much he could buy with his salary, how his life compared with that of an American worker in a similar job.

We found, for example, that a turbine operator in Russia earns about 1,200 rubles a month as a salary. At the average rate of 10 rubles to a dollar, this means that he is earning about $120 a month. In addition he could earn a bonus that would increase this to $140 to $160 a month. An American worker with the same sort of a job earns about three times as much. On the average the Russian worker receives about 800 rubles a month.

A graduate engineer receives about 2,500 rubles a month. The director of a plant receives 4,000 rubles or $400 a month. With bonus, his salary may be about $500 a month.

In appraising these wages it should be remembered that the rent paid to the Government, the owner of practically all housing, appears to be low and possibly below the cost of furnishing the housing service. In this respect the low rent might be considered part of income. In America the average worker may pay something like 20 percent or 25 percent of his total income for housing. Also, taxes paid by the Russian worker appear to be somewhat less than taxes paid by the American worker. After taking all of these factors into account, it would appear that the average income of the Russian worker is something like one-third of the income of the American worker.

HOUSING

By our standards Russian housing is rather poor. However, it must be remembered that much housing was destroyed in World War II.

Today Russia has 79 square feet of housing per capita in urban areas. For a family of four this is 316 square feet. This is an area a little less than 18 feet by 18 feet. In America we have 370 feet per capita or, for a family of four, 1,480 square feet. This is an area about 38 by 38 feet.

Russia now has a program for expansion and betterment of housing facilities. Under the new housing plan a family of four will have 400 square feet of housing, or a square area of 20 feet by 20 feet. The family will share a kitchen and bath with one or two other families.

Lately individuals have been allowed the privilege of building a home in the country on their own.

ELECTRIC RATES

We did not obtain the prices of electricity to industry. We were told that the price covers the cost of making the power plus some margin. Since the Government owns the power facilities and the industry, the price is not of much significance.

The price of residential electricity is a flat 40 kopeks per kilowatt-hour. At 10 rubles per dollar, this is equivalent to 4 cents a kilowatt-hour for all use. In America we follow the practice of providing a sliding scale rate for all use of electricity. For residential service this may start in the neighborhod of 4 to 6 cents a kilowatt-hour and scale on down to 1½ to 2 cents a kilowatt-hour. The average price of all residential electricity in the United States is about 2.53 cents a kilowatt-hour.

EDUCATION

In the field of education it appears that the Russians have made considerable progress. We were told that some of the educators receive among the highest salaries paid in the U.S.S.R. Because of this there is a tendency for the more intelligent and more able people to move into the field of education and science.

High school students are given tests to measure their aptitudes and abilities. Those with abilities, intelligence, and good grades are then chosen by the state to go to college. Those chosen are paid while obtaining their higher education. When graduated they command a higher salary than those of less education. These incentives lead the students to strive for good grades so that they will be eligible for college. Education is taken seriously in Russia.

V. Evaluation of the Russian System

ELECTRIC POWER

In the field of electric power it appears that Russian production will be considerably behind that of America for at least as far as we can foresee in the future. This in some respects is a measure of the total industrial capacity of the two countries. Obviously a country with a lower productive capacity can concentrate on certain items and excel in these fields. This Russia has done.

WELFARE STATE ECONOMY

Russia has demonstrated, as other countries in history have demonstrated, that this system of government ownership and operation of the machinery of production can be made to work for a while. The people are employed and they appear contented with their system. It is the complete totalitarian state, the planned economy, the welfare state. Under the new regime in Russia the people have a great deal more freedom than they had previously, but their individual freedom is not at all comparable to the individual freedom enjoyed by the American. In Russia all wages are fixed by the Ministry of Finance. The workers do not bargain for their wages. They cannot strike when they are dissatisfied. The individual does not go into business for himself to make some new article which he thinks might be better than something now being made. There is no competition as there is in America. The individual has not the same incentive to save and to invest in the machinery of production in hope of a profit or reward for the use of his savings.

In America the individual has these freedoms and more.

THE ECONOMIC SYSTEM AND STANDARD OF LIVING

The whole problem relates back to the basic question, "How best can man raise his standard of living?" We here in America long ago adopted a system of freedom and market incentives. Let man do what he wants, as long as he respects the rights of others, and reward him as his efforts contribute to society's needs. Thus a man will seek to make his highest possible contribution to society, for that is where he will earn his highest possible reward.

Russia has seen how this system has worked for us, and is adopting our incentive system. Where the Soviet Union has applied these incentives, she has made her greatest progress.

Russian successes and failures

The Russians have been successful and competent in selected areas; in others, they have not done as well. Steel production is an area, for example, in which Russia has done well. Missiles and rockets represent another area of Soviet success. By contrast their record in agriculture has been a sorry one indeed. With five times as many people working on farms, Russia has a hard time feeding itself. Russia still has a severe housing problem, brought about in part by the devastation of World War II. These are but two areas in which Soviet performance is deficient. The Russians are working hard to correct this.

United States compared

By contrast, the United States is competent in many areas. We have a farm problem, but it is that 7 percent of our population can produce much more food than the rest of us can eat. Our industrial machinery is remarkably responsive to the needs and desires of the American people and Nation. In general we have fewer weak spots, economically speaking. Not only will the Soviet economy have to grow some to reach the standard of ours, but it will have to get more in balance if it is to show stability.

RUSSIAN GROWTH BY DECREE

Where the planners have decreed growth, there has been growth. The growth has not always been in the quantity ordered or of the best quality, but there has been growth. In a number of instances, Russian growth has been greater than ours when expressed in terms of percent increase. Much of this is due to the extreme low level of the starting point; some is due to the different state of development of the two economies; some is due to the manner in which growth can be engineered by the planners.

Many people feel that Russia is not likely to overtake us at all unless there is a substantial change in the ground rules. I am inclined to support this theory. I do not believe Russia will catch up with us unless Russia adopts the incentives and rewards of the free enterprise system, or we abandon that system.

Russia adopting our system

As pointed out we have noted a certain tendency in the Russian system to gravitate toward some of the principles that we employ, such as incentive wages, although we have noted no tendency toward the two-party system and free elections. On the other hand, many economists and students of political economy have noted a trend in America under which more and more Americans are calling upon their Government to do for them those things which traditionally Americans have done for themselves. As a consequence, we have witnessed an increased emphasis on Government spending, and Government taking care of people and Government entry into fields which traditionally have been carried on by individuals as such or in groups. If this trend continues, it is entirely possible that Americans, unwittingly perhaps, may gradually bring about a conversion of their system to one of Government operation of the economy. If this comes to pass, our productive capacity will level off and we will find that the system we have adopted, by its nature, results in a lower standard of living.

But in recent months we have seen evidence here in America of a swing in popular sentiment favoring less Government and more freedom. This is encouraging.

APPENDIX A

Hosts on 1958 visit to U.S.S.R. (all of Ministry of Power Stations):
- A. S. Pavlenko, Minister of Power Stations.
- D. G. Chizhov, Deputy Minister of Power Stations.
- Nikolai P. Galochkin, Chief of Department of Foreign Relations.
- A. M. Nekrasov, Chief of Technical Department, Ministry of Power Stations.

Hosts on 1959 visit to U.S.S.R. (all of Ministry of Power Station Construction):

I. T. Novikov, Minister.
A. A. Belyakov, Department of Hydroelectric Power Construction.
A. U. Buchover, Secretary, Ministry of Construction of Power Stations.
A. E. Finogenov, Second Deputy Minister.
N. P. Galochkin, Chief Engineer, Department of Foreign Relations.
K. D. Lavreneinko, Deputy Minister.
F. B. Sapozhinikov, Chairman, Design Department.
N. A. Tarasov, Chairman of South and West Power Stations.
N. D. Veselov, Chief, Foreign Relations, MCPS.

Appendix B

Itinerary in the U.S.S.R., August 14–30, 1958

August 14.—U.S. party was met at Vnukovo Airport in Moscow by Mr. Andrey M. Nekrasov, Chief of the Technical Department, and Mr. Kilolai P. Galochkin, Chief of the Department of Foreign Relations, both of the Ministry of Power Stations, and other officials.

August 15.—Met with Mr. A. S. Pavlenko, Minister of Power Stations; Mr. D. G. Chizhov, Deputy Minister of Power Stations; Mr. A. M. Nekrasov.

August 16.—Visited Station No. 20 near Moscow—a thermal plant. Also visited Moscow Supply Center.

August 17.—Visited Suvorov thermal plant (station No. 19) in Cherepet, near Moscow.

August 18.—Visited the Moscow Research Institute.

August 19.—Visited Noginsk 400-kilovolt substation and the State Planning Commission (Gosplan).

August 20.—Visited the atomic powerplant (5,000 kilowatt) at Obinsk, outside Moscow.

August 21.—Visited the All Union Institute for Thermal Research (Moscow).

August 22.—Visited the Nuclear Research Center at Dubna, 120 kilometers outside Moscow. Also visited the Industrial and Agricultural Exhibit in Moscow.

August 23–24.—Visited Kuibyshev, a 2,300,000-kilowatt hydro plant which was 1,000 miles east and slightly south of Moscow.

August 25.—Stalingrad—group divided into two sections. First section visited the Dnepropetrovsk hydro plant on the Dnieper River. Second section visited the Stalingrad hydro plant.

August 26.—First section visited the Zaporozhskiy transformer works. Second section visited the Lugansk thermal plant in Stalino.

August 27.—Second section visited dispatching center at Garlovka, 60 kilometers out of Stalino.

August 28.—Party visited Leningrad metal works which produce thermal and hydro turbines. Also visited Electrosila, generator works in Leningrad.

August 29.—Final meeting with Ministry of Power in Moscow followed by dinner with Mr. A. S. Pavlenko, Minister of Power Stations.

August 30.—Party departed for either Copenhagen or Amsterdam in TU–104 Russian jet.

Appendix C

Itinerary: 1959 Trip to Russia

July 23.—Arrive Moscow.

July 24.—Dedication and opening of the American exhibit.

July 25.—Exhibition of U.S.S.R. national economy achievements.

July 26.—Arrive Irkutsk. Hydroelectric plant on the edge of Baikal Lake. Arrive Bratsk.

July 27.—Construction site of Bratsk hydroelectric plant. Arrive Novosibirsk.

July 28.—Hydroelectric plant and generator works at Novosibirsk. Arrive Stalinsk. Youzhno-Kuzbass thermal power station.

July 30.—Arrive Sverdlovsk. Beloyarsk atomic powerplant. Arrive Chelyabinsk.

July 31.—Youzhno-Uralsk thermal power station.

August 1.—Arrive Voronezh. Voronezh atomic powerplant.

August 2.—Arrive Yerevan.

August 3.—Hydroelectric plants of the Sevang-Razdan cascade.

August 4.—Arrive Moscow.

AN AGRICULTURAL VIEW OF THE SOVIET THREAT

(By Charles B. Shuman, president, American Farm Bureau Federation, Washington, D.C.)

In this paper we have chosen to use the terms "U.S.S.R." and "Soviet" in preference to "Russia" and "Russians" in most instances. This choice of words is based on a belief that the threat to the United States, which we are to discuss, is a threat that arises out of the Soviet system, whereas Russia is a geographic threat.

In evaluating the Soviet threat from the point of view of agriculture, comments will be made on—

I. Why the U.S.S.R. is a threat;

II. Agriculture in the United States and the U.S.S.R.;

III. Developing trends in Soviet international trade in farm products and

IV. Implications of Soviet economic offensive to U.S. policies.

This paper has been prepared in the light of Farm Bureau philosophy of government. This philosophy emphasizes the God-given liberties of every individual and the necessity of being alert to the destruction of individual freedom by the domination of government It recognizes that the centralization of power in the United States or any other area of the world is one of the greatest dangers faced by individuals. A statement of beliefs set forth in Farm Bureau's policy resolutions reads in part as follows:

> That the trend toward increased centralization of power in the Federal Government, if left unchecked, will lead to socialism and thus to communism.
>
> That such "planned economy" concepts as socialism, fascism, communism, and other forms of totalitarianism should be opposed wherever and in whatever form they may be found.

The Farm Bureau regards the U.S.S.R. as a threat because of (*a*) the nature of communism and (*b*) Communist desires for world domination. In evaluating this threat it must be recognized that communism involves a struggle to the death for men's minds, and a consequent danger that we might lose our freedom by unwittingly adopting Communist program bit by bit.

WHY THE U.S.S.R. IS A THREAT

The nature of communism

Marxism-Leninism, as practiced in the Soviet Union, is a collectivist, totalitarian, socialist police state, officially based on the following concepts:

(1) Atheism promoted by government, with religion and ethics being treated as something to be destroyed as "the opiate of the people."

(2) Government ownership and control of virtually all of the primary means of distribution and all means of production including

all property, homes, and land. (Since in the last analysis the most essential means of production is human beings, this means complete control of all humans.)

(3) Centralization in government of all power and authority over every aspect of life, which vests in a small group or individual the determination of all policy and transmits policy to the people through the single "political party" permitted to function.

(4) Morality consists of promoting communism, and any course of action which furthers this is moral.

(5) Communist concepts are to be extended by every feasible means to other peoples in all countries.

In addition to the above official concepts, the leaders of communism have specifically stated that it is a conspiracy to impose its will on the rest of the world by subversion, violence, deceit, legal and illegal means.

The writings of present-day Communists make it clear that the official religion of the U.S.S.R. is "worship of government." The conspiracy depends upon illusions of scientism and intellectualism, with its central thesis for the rest of the world being revolution, dissension, hatred, and the exploitation of misery and trouble.

Communism is a substitute for religion and a belief in the ultimate complete perfection of humans here on earth, compounded with the contradiction that individual freedom as a way of life will not work; it is a belief that government is far more capable of running your life than you are; it is a contention that if people are free to manage their own affairs, most of them will go hungry and be cold; it is a repudiation of the free market where willing buyers and willing sellers voluntarily arrive at prices agreeable to both; it is a false thesis that employers and employes belong to different classes and are natural enemies; it is a process whereby some people use the power of government to make other people conform to their views and desires; it is a coerced debasement of the intelligence and integrity and dignity of the individual human being who must bow his head in deference to the views of political masters; it substitutes for the present owners of property a "new class," i.e., the government functionaries, who have the beneficial use of the expropriated property; it is a throwback to a system of tyrannical power over individuals—a system wholly repudiated by our Founding Fathers in the early days of this free Republic. It is the ultimate in concentration of political power and represents naked government force at its worst.

Communist desires for world domination

(1) The evidence of the desire of the Communists to dominate the world is cumulative from the Communist Manifesto of 1848 down to the current day. In the Communist manifesto the following appears:

> In short, the Communists everywhere support every revolutionary movement against the existing social and political order of things * * * they openly declare that their ends can be attained only by the forcible overthrow of all existing social conditions. Let the ruling classes tremble at a Communist revolution. The proletarians have nothing to lose but their chains. They have a world to win. Working men of all countries unite.[1]

[1] Karl Marx and Frederick Engels, vol. I, Foreign Languages Publishing House, Moscow, 1951, p. 61.

(2) Lenin persistently carried forward the idea of world revolution and world domination. The following is a typical example of his thinking:

The victorious proletariat of that country, having expropriated the capitalists and organized its own socialist production, would rise against the rest of the capitalist world, atract to itself the oppressed classes of other countries, raise revolts among them against the capitalists, and in the event of necessity come out even with armed forces against the exploiting classes and their states.[2]

(3) Stalin sounded the same note in numerous works from which the following is one example:

Lenin never regarded the Republic of the Soviets as an end in itself. To him it was always a link needed to strengthen the chain of the revolutionary movement in the countries of the West and East, a link needed to facilitate the victory of the working people of the whole world over capitalism. Lenin knew that this was the only right conception both from the international standpoint and the standpoint of preserving the Soviet Republic itself.[3]

(4) Even though Khrushchev has castigated Stalin, he makes it clear that he and the Communists are following Marx and Lenin in an effort to obtain world domination. An example of his statements follows:

If anyone thinks we shall forget about Marx, Engels, and Lenin, he is mistaken. This will happen when shrimps learn to whistle.[4]

(5) Those who think we can trust the Russian leadership to peacefully coexist with us should seriously consider the following statements of Lenin, Stalin, and Khrushchev.

We are living not merely in a state, but in a system of states and the existence of the Soviet Republic side by side with imperialist states for a long time is unthinkable. One or the other must triumph in the end. And before that end supervenes, a series of frightful collisions between the Soviet Republic and the bourgeois states will be inevitable.[5]

But as soon as we are strong enough to defeat capitalism as a whole we shall immediately take it by the scruff of the neck.[6]

Who will conquer whom? That is the whole question * * * the world is divided into two camps—the capitalist camp, headed by Anglo-American capital, and the Socialist camp, headed by the Soviet Union. The international situation, therefore, will be more and more determined by the correspondence of forces between these two camps. * * *[7]

Whether you like it or not, history is on our side. We will bury you.[8]

As long as capitalism and socialism exist, we cannot live in peace; in the end, one or the other will triumph—a funeral dirge will be sung over the Soviet Republic or over world capitalism.[9]

The struggle for men's minds

The conflict with communism is a conflict of opposing ideologies; consequently, it is a struggle for men's minds. In such a struggle the continued existence of either ideology is an actual or potential threat to the continued existence of the other.

---

[2] V. I. Lenin, "The United States of Europe Slogan" (1915), "Selected Works," International Publishers, New York, 1943, vol. V, p. 141.
[3] Joseph Stalin, "On the Death of Lenin" (Jan. 26, 1924; Pravda, Jan. 30, 1924).
[4] "International Affairs," Moscow, January 1956, p. 2.
[5] Joseph Stalin, "Problems of Leninism" (Foreign Languages Publishing House, Moscow, 1953), pp. 192–193.
[6] V. I. Lenin, "Speech to Moscow Party Nuclei Secretaries" (Nov. 26, 1920), "Selected Works" (International Publishers, New York, 1943), vol. VIII, p. 282.
[7] J. Stalin, "Results of the Work of the XIV Conference of the RKP (B)," May 9, 1925, Sochineniya (Gospolitizdat, Moscow, 1947), vol. 7, pp. 95–98.
[8] Nikita S. Khrushchev at Kremlin reception, Nov. 17, 1956 (Time, Nov. 26, 1956).
[9] Lenin, "Speech to Moscow Party Nuclei Secretaries" (Nov. 28, 1920), "Selected Works" (International Publishers, New York, 1943), vol. VIII, p. 297.

Western civilization is based on Judeo-Christian ethics such as those expressed in the Ten Commandments and the Sermon on the Mount. In the ethics of Western civilization, truth is of transcendent importance. The Communist brand of tyranny (like fascism under Mussolini and state socialism under Hitler) cannot permit truth as we know it to exist.

Christian ethics are grounded in the belief that certain fundamental truths are permanent and fixed. On the other hand, the Communists, and Socialists who vigorously insist they are anti-Communists, both generally take the point of view that there are no absolute, unchanging truths. Lenin, for example, commenting on the ideas of Marx and Engels, wrote:

> For dialectical philosophy nothing is final, absolute, sacred. It reveals the transitory character of everything and in everything; nothing can endure before it except the uninterrupted process of becoming and of passing away, of endless ascendency from the lower to the higher. And dialectical philosophy itself is nothing more than the mere reflection of this process in the thinking brain.

The Communists and the Socialists contend that "the end justifies the means." The Communists treat the truth not as something sacred or to be revered in itself, but merely as a tool of the party to get on with the work of the revolution.

Once the unsuspecting person accepts the philosophy that there are no absolute truths he is lost, and from that point onward is an easy prey to the propaganda of the skillful Socialist.

The Communists cannot permit the existence of the idea that the individual is made in the image of God and obtains unalienable rights from the Deity. Such an idea presupposes a power greater than that of the state.

The danger that we might lose the struggle by unwittingly copying the Communist program bit by bit

Everyone who cares earnestly about freedom is aroused against communism. But it is not only the Communists, it is in a more subtle way the Socialists, who are pushing the free world (including the United States) toward the excessive centralization of power in government. This is the road to totalitarianism. It is difficult in a brief paper to fully explore the means by which the Communists and Socialists are weakening the United States by boring from within. One of the real problems is that many people who have no intention of helping to destroy our system and bring about the "new economic order" advocated by the Communists and Socialists, are nevertheless unwittingly doing so.

The average American citizen, and for that matter many of our best-informed citizens, appears to be unable to relate day-to-day instances occurring here in the United States to the combined Socialist-Communist conspiracy. This inability to understand the Socialist-Communist conspiracy in operation here may be due to a lack of knowledge concerning—

(1) The objectives and goals of communism and the objectives and goals of Fabian socialism, which in many instances are one and the same;

(2) Similarities of the pattern of attack that the Socialists and Communists are making on our institutions by such actions as interfering with the free choices of buyers and sellers;

(3) "Lack of a thorough understanding of the moral and political basis of the system that has made the United States the envy and standard of comparison throughout the world";[10] or,

(4) The direct personal interest of some individuals, and the less personal interest of well-meaning planners and reformers, in the diversion of money from those who earn it to those who do not.

For most of the last 4 decades a gradual change has been occurring in our economic system. This change has been brought about by many small steps, but the cumulative effect has been a long step away from the morally and economically sound concept of individual responsibility to the immoral and economically unsound concept of government responsibility.

In order to understand the situation, not only must we understand the moral and political rightness of our basic system of free choice, but it is necessary to study the literature of the Communists and the Socialists to see how they bring their schemes into effect. In other words, it is necessary to know our enemy. If a person will examine the situation thoroughly, he will finally see the pattern of conspiracy shining through day-to-day programs that are being advanced in the United States. This examination will also reveal how the activities of Socialists, who are looked upon by many as respectable, intertwine and reenforce the program of the Communists, who are generally considered disreputable.

The House Committee on Un-American Activities published a series of five reports under the heading "Communist Conspiracy—Strategy and Techniques of World Communism." If a person will familiarize himself with this information, he will be well armed to understand how the Communist conspiracy is being advanced throughout the world.

Marx was not sincerely interested in reforms as such, but proposed to use campaigns for reform measures in order to push non-Communists step by step "to the extreme" and ultimately to actual ruin.

> At the beginning of the movement, of course, the workers cannot yet propose any directly Communist measures. But they can: (1) Compel the democrats to interfere in as many spheres as possible of the existing social order, to disturb its regular course, and to compromise themselves, as well as to concentrate the utmost possible productive forces, means of transport, factories, railways in the hands of the state; (2) they must drive the proposals of the democrats, who in any case will not act in a revolutionary but in a merely reformist manner, to the extreme and transform them into direct attacks against private property * * * If the democrats propose proportional taxes, the workers must demand progressive taxes; if the democrats themselves put forward a moderate progressive tax, the workers must insist on a tax with rates which rise so steeply that large-scale capital is ruined by it; if the democrats demand the regulation of state debts, the workers demand state bankruptcy * * *[11]

What makes the problem exceedingly difficult is that the goal of the Socialist is generally the same as the Communist, namely, the elimination of both the private ownership of property and the impersonal distribution of goods and services by free choice in the market. Of course,

---

[10] London Economist, Aug. 15, 1959, p. 409.

[11] Karl Marx, "Address of the Central Council to the Communist League," London, March 1850, Karl Marx, "Selected Works," vol. II (Cooperative Publishing Society of Foreign Workers in the U.S.S.R., Moscow, Leningrad, 1936), pp. 167–168. Reported in "Contradictions in Communism."

the Socialist advocates the transfer of control of private property to or by the government by gradual legal means, while the Communist advocates the same thing through violent revolution.

Prof. G. D. N. Cole, a leading British Socialist, writes in the Encyclopaedia Britannica as follows:

> The distinction between socialism, as represented by the various Socialist and Labor Parties of Europe and the New World and communism, as represented by the Russians and the minority groups in other countries, is one of tactics and strategy rather than of objective. Communism is indeed only socialism pursued by revolutionary means and making its revolutionary method a canon of faith.

In other words, the Socialists admit that the goals of the Communists and the Socialists are the same.

One of the schemes that the Communists use to convince people that they should give up their individual rights and turn them over to the Government is the argument that as civilization becomes more complicated, the more restricted must be the freedom of the individual. The argument for totalitarianism is basically the same. For example, Mussolini said:

> We were the first to assert the more complicated the forms assumed by civilization the more restricted the freedom of the individual must become.

The unforeseen but inevitable consequences of socialism create a state of affairs which if pursued will enable totalitarian forces to get the upper hand.

The essential point is that bit by bit and little by little we can gradually destroy here in the United States the freedom of the individual in return for illusory promises that individuals will gain greater personal security by abdicating their responsibilities to an all-powerful Federal Government.

The men who established our constitutional system here in this country thoroughly understood that tyranny was the result of centralization of power in the hands of the state.

Franklin is quoted as having said:

> Those who would give up essential liberty to purchase a little temporary safety deserve neither liberty nor safety.

The whole theory of limited government is threatened by those who think that the essential problem to be resolved today is redistribution of the wealth by the Federal Government, taxing those who have earned it—distributing to those who have not earned it.

The appropriate attitude for U.S. policymakers to take toward the U.S.S.R.

In view of the nature of communism; the announced desire of the Communists for world domination; the clear record of Communist duplicity; and the irreconcilable nature of the conflict between communism and a philosophy that stresses freedom and the worth of the individual; U.S. policymakers should regard the U.S.S.R. as an enemy which is waging a form of total war against us and all free people of the world. The record is clear that Communist promises cannot be relied upon. Under the Soviet system every transaction is subject to Government policy. The Soviets are not interested in developing trade or other relations with other countries on a normal basis, but only on a basis that will advance Communist objectives.

Communism and socialism are forms of deadly infection that must be fought externally and internally. This does not mean that we should seek to avoid all contacts with the Soviets, but it does mean that we should constantly be on the alert to safeguard our own interests. We must know the mainsprings of our own strength—improve and guard them—through our schools, churches, public institutions. To drop our guard would be fatal. Trying to do business with Hitler enslaved Germans, betrayed others who tried to appease him, and ended in the most devastating war in history. Trying to appease the Communists would also lead to disaster.

SOME OBSERVATIONS ON AGRICULTURE IN THE UNITED STATES AND THE U.S.S.R.

Any effort to compare American and Soviet agriculture is fraught with difficulty and also with the dangers of oversimplifying or creating misleading impressions. Soviet statistics are incomplete and often of questionable reliability. Official Soviet reports are colored by propaganda and boasts of things that are yet to be accomplished. The reports of U.S. visitors to the Soviet Union generally are based on limited observations in a vast country, where economic, social, and climatic conditions compound the difficulty of making valid comparisons with the situation that exists in the United States. Furthermore, the conditions that now exist and the statistical record of the past do not necessarily provide a valid basis for appraising future potentials.

In spite of these limitations, a few general observations appear to be in order.

The outstanding difference between American and Soviet agriculture is the fact that our agriculture is characterized by independent, family-type units operating under a private, competitive enterprise system, while Soviet agriculture is characterized by collectives and state farms operating under a centralized system of bureaucratic planning.

The major problem of Soviet agriculture is to increase production to provide a better diet for an expanding population and a surplus that can be exported to acquire needed foreign products and exchange. In the United States we are plagued with surpluses because agricultural production has been expanding more rapidly than effective domestic and foreign demand. While our present agricultural surpluses are largely a result of governmental policies that have stimulated the flow of capital into agriculture and have retarded needed adjustments, they are nonetheless an indication, not only of the present productive ability of American agriculture, but also of our capacity to expand agricultural production. Present trends suggest that the day when the United States will have to worry about its capacity to produce farm products is far in the future. The Soviets apparently have been increasing agricultural production at a rapid rate in recent years, and it seems clear that their potential for further expansion is substantial—particularly for some products.

Agricultural resources [12]

Both the United States and the U.S.S.R. have very great natural resources for agricultural production; however, we have some definite advantages in this area.

> * * * more than 70 percent of the total area of the Soviet Union is nonagricultural as compared with an estimated 42 percent for continental United States.

Despite this high percentage of nonagricultural land, the Soviet Union, with a land mass three times that of the continental United States, has a very large acreage that is suitable for agricultural purposes.

The area sown to crops in the U.S.S.R. is reported to have increased from 371.6 million acres in 1940, to 410.5 million in 1954, and 483.1 million in 1958. A part of this increase, of course, reflects territorial changes. By way of comparison, the U.S. Department of Agriculture estimates that the total cropland available for crops in this country in 1954 was 465 million acres. Acres of cropland are not necessarily a good measure of agricultural potential as soil, topography, climate, technology, and the availability of new land that can be brought into production through drainage and irrigation are also important.

Soil scientists have reported that the U.S.S.R. has great soil resources and that much of the land now under cultivation has a high natural fertility.

Adverse climatic conditions are the most serious natural handicap faced by Soviet agriculture. This reflects the northern location of the U.S.S.R. and other geographical factors, such as the size of the Soviet land mass and the location of mountains which affect rainfall.

The southernmost point in the Soviet Union is in the same latitude as Memphis, Tenn., and Albuquerque, N. Mex.

> * * * Yalta, at the southern tip of the Crimea, is approximately in the same latitude as Rochester, Minn.; and Odessa, on the Black Sea, is in the same latitude as Duluth, Minn.

Important Soviet cotton areas are located in approximately the same latitude as Chicago.[13]

> * * * the crucial disadvantage of the continental Russian climate is the inverse relationship in the distribution of heat and moisture, both of which are essential for plant life. As the amount of heat increases, from north to south and west to east, moisture tends to diminish and the maximum of heat is accompanied by a minimum of moisture.

There are, of course, local exceptions to the above generalization. Where water is available and other conditions are favorable, the absence of adequate rainfall can be overcome by irrigation. The Soviets have a large irrigated acreage which they probably can expand to a considerable extent if they are willing to make the necessary capital investment. The entire Soviet cotton crop is produced on irrigated land, and irrigation is being expanded in the cotton areas.

---

[12] The comments on the agricultural resources of the United States and the U.S.S.R. which are set forth in this section are based on information from many sources; however, heaviest use has been made of a bulletin entitled, "Economic Aspects of Soviet Agriculture, Report of a Technical Study Group," published by the Agricultural Research Service of the U.S. Department of Agriculture in May 1959. Except as otherwise indicated, all direct quotations relative to the U.S.S.R.'s agricultural resources are from this pamphlet.

[13] "Cotton in Russia," Leonard A. Mobley, Foreign Trade Division, National Cotton Council, p. 7.

This suggests that the Soviets have a substantial potential for the expansion of cotton production, although irrigated land is also used to produce sugar beets and other crops.

In the western and north-central European areas of U.S.S.R., a considerable acreage of marshland and swamps can be reclaimed and turned to productive use, as meadows, pasture, and cropland. Indications are, however, that reclamation operations are proceeding slowly, and sometimes with a subsequent considerable gap in the utilization of the reclaimed land.

Much of the expansion that has taken place in recent years in the area seeded to crops in the Soviet Union has been in the so-called new lands in central Asia and western Siberia. These lands are subject to wide variations in rainfall, and it remains to be seen whether they can be kept in production over an extended period of time.

It has been suggested both that cropping of the new lands may lead to a "dust bowl" problem, and that the possibility of retaining these lands in production could be increased by adoption of the summer fallow system, which is used in some of the dry land areas of the United States.

In the past, the Soviet diet has leaned heavily on cereals, potatoes, and other vegetables that are grown in household gardens.

Soviet leaders have announced ambitious plans for the expansion of meat production; however, the agricultural resources of the Soviet Union are better adapted to the production of food grains than to the production of the feed grains that are essential for meat production. In recent years the Soviets have made a considerable effort to expand corn production; however, a large part of their corn crop is harvested for silage and green feed, rather than grain. This reflects the fact that climatic conditions are unsuitable for the production of ripe corn in large areas of the U.S.S.R.

While steps can be taken to expand feed production, the adjustments necessary to accomplish this may require considerable time. In the meantime population growth will increase the production needed to maintain present diets.

The following table indicates the gaps that now exist between the per capita production of some important livestock products in the United States and the U.S.S.R. It will be noted that the United States is far ahead on meat, poultry, and eggs, and slightly ahead on factory butter. The significance of the factory butter comparison is reduced by the much heavier consumption of competing fats in the United States.

Comparison of per capita production of meat, eggs, wool, and butter in the Soviet Union and United States, 1956 [1]

	Soviet Union	United States
Livestock and poultry slaughtered, live weight......pounds..	117.9	345.7
Meat production, including poultry, dressed weight......do....	72.9	214.9
Beef and veal, dressed weight......do....	26.0	96.1
Pork, including lard, dressed weight......do....	29.5	83.6
Lamb, mutton, and goat meat, dressed weight......do....	9.0	4.4
Poultry meat, dressed weight......do....	8.5	31.0
Egg production, number of eggs......	97.4	392.2
Wool production......pounds..	2.87	1.67
Factory butter production......do....	6.1	8.4

[1] Derived from data published in "Economic Aspects of Soviet Agriculture, Report of a Technical Study Group," Agricultural Research Service, U.S. Department of Agriculture, May 1959, p. 26.

Since it takes more resources to produce meat than cereals, it would appear that Soviet income levels will have to rise if the average Soviet citizen is to be able to afford a higher level of meat consumption.

Dairying is the most advanced livestock enterprise in the Soviet Union. In 1957, production per cow was reported as averaging about 4,000 pounds, in comparison with a U.S. average of 6,162 pounds. Total Soviet milk production, including 4½ billion pounds from sheep and goats, was reported as 121 billion pounds in 1957, in comparison with a U.S. production of 126 billion pounds.

Inadequate transportation apparently limits the marketing of whole milk.

> * * * outside the radius of large cities, all milk is separated into cream on the farm. The cream is then hauled to a creamery and the skim milk is fed to hogs on the farm. This system is identical with that which prevailed in the United States 30 years ago. It is wasteful of milk solids other than fat—a serious waste in a nation that needs to put more animal proteins into its high cereal diet.

In this connection it probably should be noted that, while we have gone a long way toward developing a marketing system for whole milk, this—plus our dairy price-support program—has resulted in a burdensome surplus of nonfat milk solids.

Other factors affecting agricultural production

Although important, natural resources are only one of the factors that affect a nation's capacity to produce farm products. It has been said that resources are a function of human knowledge. Stated another way: "Technology is our primary resource. Without it, all other resources would be economically nonexistent." [14]

This is true in agriculture as well as in industry. At the present time the United States appears to be far ahead of the U.S.S.R. in agricultural technology. The present advanced stage of our agricultural technology reflects the results of years of public and private research, widespread educational programs including specialized programs to spread the knowledge of scientific agriculture, and a private enterprise system which stimulates individual initiative. American agriculture also has benefited a great deal from progress in other sectors of the economy. For example, it takes a great deal more than a capacity to produce farm products to make a high quality diet available to millions of urban consumers in a large country such as the United States or the U.S.S.R. A highly complex industrial system is also necessary to process, package, transport, store, and distribute farm products. As has already been pointed out with respect to milk, Soviet agriculture apparently is handicapped by inadequate facilities for refrigeration, transportation, and distribution of perishable products.

An important contributing factor to the economic growth of the United States has been the fact that the increasing productivity of American farmers has made it possible for a smaller and smaller percentage of our total population to produce needed farm products. In other words, the advance of agricultural technology in the United States has released labor for industrial and service activities. In this

[14] J. F. Dewhurst, "America's Needs and Resources," quoted by Yale Brozen of the University of Chicago in a paper presented to the Sixth Conference on Scientific Manpower, Indianapolis, Ind., December 1957.

respect we are now far ahead of the Soviets. It has been estimated that 43 percent of Soviet population is engaged in agriculture. In the United States the farm population is estimated to be 12 percent of total population; however, U.S. statistics on farm population include a very sizable number of people who live on residential, or subsistence units, that produce little or nothing for sale.

The large percentage of the Soviet work force which is now engaged in agriculture means that the Soviets have a very great potential for strengthening their economy by improving efficiency in agriculture and, thereby, releasing labor for other activities.

One observer has gone so far as to say that—

> * * * the possession of knowledge by the Russians which enables them to build an ICBM may be less fearful than the development of higher productivity in the agricultural sector of their economy. When we furnish hybrid seed and models of agricultural machinery to the Russians, a graver threat to security is involved than open publication of atomic secrets. If manpower requirements in Russian agriculture were reduced as radically as they have been in American agriculture, the release of resources to the military and to armaments production would make Russia a far graver threat than she now is.[15]

There is no question but what progress in agriculture which enabled the Soviets to reduce the percentage of their labor force that is required to maintain a desired level of farm production would strengthen the U.S.S.R. There is, however, little that we can do to prevent the Soviets from obtaining technical agricultural information either from the United States or from other advanced countries. There are very few trade secrets in agriculture. The important thing in regard to hybrid corn is not the seed itself, but the technology that is used to produce it. Seed that has been developed for use in the United States may do very poorly under Soviet conditions; however, the technology that is used to produce hybrid seed can be used by the Soviets to develop varieties that would be better adapted to their conditions. The principles back of hybrid seed and many other technological advances in agriculture are widely known and freely available in published literature.

The advantages of an incentive system

From a long-run standpoint, our greatest advantage over the Soviets in agriculture, as well as in other fields, is not to be found in natural resources or technology, but in the fact that we have an incentive system, while the Soviets have a planned economy. Under our system every individual farmer has an economic incentive to improve his utilization of available resources. The individual farmer must constantly improve his efficiency in order to survive competition in a period of rapidly changing technology. The great profusion of consumer goods available in the United States makes it clear that the individual can improve his living standards by increasing his efficiency. This is not always clear in the U.S.S.R., not only because the planners may decide otherwise, but also because of the limited availability of consumer goods.

The Soviets have recognized the need for individual incentives to a degree, but collective farmers and employees of state farms cannot possibly have either the opportunity to exercise individual initiative

---

[15] Yale Brozen of the University of Chicago, op. cit.

or the incentive to improve efficiency that the individual farm operator has under our system.

Competition and the incentive system also stimulate industrial developments which enable farmers to reduce costs and expand output.

Centralized planning can produce spectacular results in individual undertakings, but it cannot mobilize the total energies and abilities of individual citizens as effectively as an incentive system. In a market system the mistakes of individuals tend to cancel out with little effect on overall progress of the economy, but when the planners make a mistake in a planned economy, the result may be nationwide and disastrous.

The Soviets have challenged us to war on the economic front. As we ponder the meaning of this challenge, it is well to remember that economics is the science which deals with the utilization of scarce resources. The economic strength of a nation depends not only on its resources, but also on the ways in which these resources are utilized. The Soviets probably are capable of making some spectacular advances in agriculture as they have in other fields, such as space satellites, but such advances will not necessarily represent an efficient utilization of scarce resources. Consequently, they will not necessarily add to the long-run strength of the Soviet system. For example, marginal land can be brought into cultivation through costly irrigation and drainage projects, and crops can be seeded in areas which are ill adapted to their production, but these practices do not necessarily represent an economic use of scarce resources. Projects that are not economic reduce rather than increase the strength of an economic system.

Despite the limitations inherent in a planned economy, the Soviets have a great potential for increasing the productivity of their agricultural workers. If we are to maintain the margin of advantage which the United States now has over the U.S.S.R. by reason of the greater productivity of our agricultural workers, we must avoid hamstringing the further growth and development of American agriculture. This means that we must avoid policies that substitute Government planning for the operation of an incentive system and policies that attempt to freeze farming in a rigid historical mold, or otherwise prevent needed adjustments in the resources (including human resources) devoted to agriculture. This can be accomplished by moving away from Government programs that attempt to fix prices and allocate the right to produce farm products, and by allowing increased opportunity for market prices to help to guide production and consumption.

Although a market system does not always work as smoothly and as painlessly as we might wish, it is still the most efficient system that has ever been developed for determining what things are really worth and how scarce resources can best be used. There have been many cases in this country in which the Federal Government has interfered with the operation of the market system, with a resulting waste of resources, but we are still able to evaluate the results of Government intervention on the basis of values established by a market system which covers most of our economic activities. The problem of allocating scarce resources on an efficient basis is far greater in a country where there is no market system and where all basic economic decisions must be made by a planning bureaucracy.

Significance of possible Soviet progress in agriculture

The present and potential productivity of Soviet agriculture suggests that Soviets can meet their basic needs for agricultural products even with an expanding population, but that they will have great difficulty in providing their people with a diet of the quality that is now available to American consumers in the foreseeable future. Self-sufficiency in agriculture has been an advantage to warring countries in the past when prolonged hostilities have sometimes shut off outside supplies. The importance of self-sufficiency in agriculture in case of an atomic war, which might result in great devastation in a short time, is open to question.

Assuming that it is the intention of the Soviet Union to continue the cold war without provoking a full-scale shooting war, the future progress of Soviet agriculture is of concern to us primarily from the standpoint of its potential impact (1) on the Soviet economy, which has already been discussed, and (2) on international trade in farm products.

The fact that the Soviets have some very definite limitations in agriculture creates a basis for trade with the so-called underdeveloped countries—many of which have exportable supplies of agricultural products. This can create some problems for the United States, particularly in cases where other countries feel that our surplus disposal policies are reducing their access to free world markets.

From the standpoint of U.S. farmers, a matter of important concern is the prospect of increasing Communist competition in the international market for some of our major agricultural commodities.

This will be discussed in the following section of this statement on the basis of information received from the Farm Bureau foreign trade office at Rotterdam, Netherlands.

DEVELOPING TRENDS IN SOVIET INTERNATIONAL TRADE IN FARM PRODUCTS

During the last few years the Soviet Union has moved into a leading position as an exporter of grains, principally wheat. It must be remembered, when attempting to assess the trend of Soviet trade in farm products, that Russia was one of the principal exporters of wheat during the period prior to World War I. Russian wheat exports, including flour, reached an average of 165 million bushels per year during the 1910–14 period. For many years following the Soviet takeover Russian exports were a negligible factor in the world wheat trade; however, in 1957 and 1958, Soviet shipments of wheat moved up to aroundt 150 million bushels. Thus, after about 40 years of Soviet rule, Russian wheat exports are again reaching the high volume attained during the early nineteen hundreds.

The Soviets need foreign exchange. Wheat exports bring exchange when sold for cash and needed goods under barter arrangements. During the last few years the Soviets have also been active in exporting oats, barley and, to a lesser extent, corn. Much of the corn, however, has been of Bessarabian or Rumanian origin.

Responsible observers in the European grain market uniformly are at a loss to forecast future Soviet exports with any real hope of accuracy. The Soviets have an expanding population which must be fed. They have made a definite and, to a certain extent, successful effort to stimulate production. Accordingly, output at current levels has greatly increased available supplies. The quantity of Soviet wheat and feed grains which may at any given time flow into European or other markets is largely a matter of U.S.S.R. Government policy; therefore, any attempt to forecast such exports as firm annual figures is wishful thinking.

The cold, clear fact remains that production has increased rapidly, largely as a result of some good harvests and the development of new lands east of the Volga River and Ural Mountains. With these increased supplies the Soviet Union possesses the means to seriously disrupt the European market, or for that matter, the world market whenever she so wishes—assuming a normal harvest in that year.

Soviet wheat exports to Western Europe

In the past 2 years the Soviets have sold wheat to France, the Netherlands, Norway, Sweden, Austria, the United Kingdom, Denmark, and Belgium. They have disrupted U.S. sales in one important European country this year. As an example of what can be done by the Soviets, let us examine what has happened in the Netherlands. To a lesser extent it has also happened in other Western European countries.

The Netherlands has been a traditional market for American and Canadian wheat. Soviet exports to the Netherlands have been unimportant. In 1957, the U.S.S.R. moved about 2,000 metric tons to the Netherlands. In 1958, the total increased to 5,000 tons. On the basis of the record for the first 6 months of 1959, the Farm Bureau Foreign Trade Office estimates that the U.S.S.R. may move as much as 300,000 metric tons of wheat to the Netherlands this year along with a substantial amount of feed grains. These sales represent lost markets for American farmers and also for our competitors in such countries as Canada and Argentina.

In the fall of 1958, a group of Dutch wheat importers began negotiating seriously with the Soviet trade mission in Amsterdam.[16] After negotiations, sales were finalized. Soviet wheat began to arrive in substantial amounts by around the first of the year. Dutch bakers began to plan mixing and baking schedules for Soviet grain. Quality was reported to be irregular, but satisfactory. Farinograph reports indicated that the Soviet wheat was somewhat easier to work than U.S. wheat. It was comparable to a mixture of American Red and Hard wheats.

No accurate information is available as to the prices that were paid for the Soviet wheat—the data are still a closely guarded trade secret. Published Soviet wheat prices usually ride only slightly below CCC quotations; however, the consensus is that the sales to the Netherlands were barter transactions involving coffee from Brazil, German steel (through Dutch intermediaries), nylon, chemicals, and hides. It is reported that, in addition to the prices established for Soviet wheat in the barter transactions, premiums or bonuses (as much as 6 percent) were paid for the coffee, steel, nylon, and so forth. These premiums allegedly were "kicked back" to exporters, who in turn allowed

[16] Soviet missions are spread all over Western Europe and are located in Belgium, Luxembourg, France, Italy, the United Kingdom, Denmark, Norway, and West Germany. It is understoon that these missions have a loose, but official tieup with Soviet Embassies, and that the chief of the mission reports directly to the Ambassador.

the importers of the Soviet wheat part or all of the premium. The effect of such transactions is to move wheat at prices below existing world market levels.

The Canadians have sold wheat to the Soviets[17] (reportedly for credit), only to have their customers turn around and export substantial quantities of wheat to Western Europe. It can be argued that the Russians import hard Manitoba varieties and export softer varieties to Western Europe, and that one does not displace the other. Indications are, however, that "wheat is wheat" as far as the Soviets are concerned.[18] They are perfectly willing to sacrifice optimum bread-mixing formulas to accomplish other objectives. The Canadian wheat has, in part, enabled the Soviets to accomplish three important objectives:

(1) Conserve rail transportation which would have been required to move Ukrainian wheat to the eastern parts of the Soviet Union (Canadian wheat arrives at Pacific ports);

(2) Displace corresponding quantities of American and Canadian wheat in Western European markets; and

(3) Establish direct contacts with Western European business interests, which obviously is valuable to them, for political and economic reasons.

The problems created by increasing Soviet sales in international markets cannot be solved by criticizing Western European participation in such transactions.

Obviously not all Western European business interests relish trading with the Communists, but they have little choice as long as their competitors are free to do business with the Communists, and to obtain attractive terms. It is imperative that our farmers, the grain trade, and the U.S. Government clearly understand what is going on, and the need to compete vigorously in the European market.

European criticism of Public Law 480

There has been no little criticism by European importers of the Public Law 480 program and U.S. barter programs. The Dutch importers who purchased Soviet wheat (but who might have purchased American wheat) are willing and able to buy wheat with dollars; but they question the wisdom of paying with dollars when the United States is offering such vast amounts of wheat for local currencies of very limited value. What disturbs them even more is the negotiation of U.S. barter transactions at, to quote directly, "absurdly low prices." For example, it was reported by the Dutch trade that last year Sweden, a dollar-rich country, paid $64.60 per ton for U.S. spring wheat under a barter arrangement, while the Dutch would have had to pay $67.50 for a similar quality. This simply does not make sense to many European traders. They do not understand why they cannot get the best deal pricewise for cash payments rather than through complicated barter transactions. If they cannot get the best deal pricewise for cash payments in dollars, cash purchases with dollars cease to be a preferred way of doing business.

There also have been persistent, although unconfirmed rumors, that shipments of surplus U.S. commodities have crossed back and forth

[17] Under a 3-year pact which ended earlier this year, the Russians agreed to buy a minimum of 14.8 million bushels a year for 3 years from Canada.

[18] Canadian wheat reportedly was offered to Dutch traders by Poland last winter.

through the Iron Curtain. In some cases such movements would violate Public Law 480 agreements; however, these cases are extremely difficult, if not impossible, to confirm. It is clear, however, that commodities exported under Public Law 480 can reduce dollar sales. For example, German trade reports indicate that immediately following the announcement of a Public Law 480 sale of U.S. soybean oil to Poland, the Poles offered to sell lard in West Germany. Any such sales would displace U.S. lard which was being sold for dollars.

The United States must be prepared to compete

The situation can be summed up as follows: The U.S.S.R. is making a considerable effort and probably will make a greater effort to establish permanent cash markets in European importing countries. It must also be recognized by the United States that the first trial shipment of Soviet wheat to Japan was announced recently, and that some gift wheat has gone to the Middle East. Therefore, the United States must be alert to competition in other markets besides Europe.

The U.S.S.R. is increasing production of wheat. A substantial part of the increase that has already taken place in Soviet wheat exports has gone to satellite countries. It is unlikely that the requirements of the satellite countries will increase—they probably will decrease somewhat. Therefore, we should be prepared for a substantial rise in Soviet wheat exports to the free world. Such exports apparently reached the 35- to 40-million-bushel level in 1958–59. Whether or not they go higher depends in large degree on a basic Soviet policy decision; namely, how much emphasis to put on the expansion of feed production in order to make possible an enlarged livestock industry. This could be an important limitation on future wheat production and exports.

Future Soviet trade policies regarding cotton are uncertain. Cotton export and import levels can be altered at ease without regard to basic economic factors. If deemed essential by Soviet leaders, cotton production probably could be increased faster than consumption so as to provide an exportable surplus. It is also important to note that the Soviets undoubtedly will realize some increases in yields because of technological improvements (as we have done).

Soviet trade policy in farm commodities is tied to an extent with the export policies of Communist China. Needless to say, government policies are all important and are the overriding factors with China, as well as with the Soviet Union.

European oil crusher contacts reveal that soybeans from the Manchuria area are becoming increasingly popular in Western Europe. The best beans consistently yield as high as 18½ percent oil, and have a very low "foreign matter" content, often down to one-fourth of 1 percent.

It must be noted that Red China's exports of soybeans increased from about 700,000 metric tons in 1957 to an estimated 990,000 tons in 1958. During the same period U.S. exports fell from 2,395,000 to 2,295,000 tons. Most Chinese beans have been sold to Western Europe through Hungary and now Yugoslavia. Further inroads in the European market are likely, as Communist production is expected to rise by more than 1 million metric tons in 1959. Informed German sources indicate that the recent flood damage in China, especially in the soybean area, was not substantial and should be minimized. With no little concern the Farm Bureau foreign trade office reports that reliable European traders are forecasting that Red China's soybean exports will amount to around 1,350,000 tons in 1959, an alarming 30 percent increase over the 1958 movement. Production of soybeans undoubtedly will continue to increase and American producers must expect severe competition in this area.

It is believed also that the Chinese Communists have serious future export intentions for other oilseeds and tobacco. They also have made small trial shipments of frozen poultry to Western Europe. Livestock product exports from Eastern European countries are also of increasing significance.

IMPLICATIONS OF THE SOVIET ECONOMIC OFFENSIVE TO U.S. POLICIES

On the basis of the foregoing, it obviously is extremely important that the United States be alert to developments in the commercial markets for farm products, especially in the so-called free (and very important) dollar markets of Europe.

During the coming years competition from the Soviet Union, satellite countries, and Communist China will be extremely keen. Moreover, the Common Market is now a fact and may present real problems if it turns out to be restrictive regarding imports. The outer seven is rapidly becoming a reality. It is well also to remember that an annex to the Common Market agreement (protocol 2) enables countries such as West Germany and others to continue to trade freely with Soviet-dominated areas. We must be alert and vigorously merchandise our products if we wish to maintain an appreciable export market for farm commodities.

The United States cannot and should not rely upon political friendships to guarantee markets for our farm products. We must compete on tough commercial terms with quality products.

It must be recognized that trading in farm commodities, especially in grain, is a highly technical and complex business. To be successful grain exporters must be able to follow and observe markets closely on a daily—even an hourly—basis. This can be done far better by the private trade than by the Government.

The Soviet trade offensive—A challenge

We view Russia's entry in the world agricultural market with wheat, or other farm commodities, as a challenge. In response to such a challenge we must determine whether or not U.S. agriculture can compete. We have three possible choices. First, if we cannot compete we could let the Soviets push us out of international commercial markets and store the production which formerly was exported, or attempt to give away the major portion of such production to various countries who are willing, or who could be induced, to accept it. There are some who would advocate such a course for American agriculture. Farm Bureau does not.

The second possible choice would be for agriculture to turn over its export problems to the U.S. Government, which would in turn fight and all-out trade war with Russia on a government-to-government basis. In simple terms this would be an attempt to "out state trade" Russia by offering to undercut prices or enter into bilateral trade arrangements. It is Farm Bureau's contention that the totalitarian

Soviet Union is better equipped politically than the United States to engage in state trading. If the United States made such a choice it would in effect be allowing the Soviets to choose the field of conflict and the implements of battle.

The United States and the American farmer sacrifice a great deal when we turn over to Government the right to engage in trade in the world market.

The third possible choice—and in our opinion the most desirable—is to meet this challenge of Soviet Russia with the economic advantages that are at our disposal under our economic system. The American farmer is the most efficient producer in the world. We can become even more efficient and we must. This means the end to unrealistic domestic farm price support programs and a return to the farmer of those opportunities and incentives which permit and induce him to produce for the market as economically as possible. We should meet the challenge of Soviet Russia with all the force of a vigorous private, competitive enterprise system. We are confident that outcome will prove our economic system superior.

The U.S. advantage in foreign trade

From an overall standpoint, it should be emphasized that at the present time the Soviet economic offensive is still in the nature of a "threat" rather than an actuality. This is not to say that the threat is not real and that the United States should not take positive steps to meet the offensive.

It should be borne in mind that in the field of international trade the United States can have a great advantage. In 1958, total trade to and from the United States was in excess of $30 billion. Total free world trade amount to $95 billion. In the same year Soviet Russia, the satellite countries, and mainland China, considered as a whole, had total exports of $2.96 billion and total imports of $3.18 billion, excluding trade within the area. Thus, the total trade of the Communist bloc with outside countries was equal to only about 20 percent of total U.S. trade and only 6 percent of total world trade.

The United States is a tremendously important international market. It is elementary that trade is a two-way street; that if we wish to hold our export markets, we must allow our customer nations access to the U.S. market. The United States should make firm its offer to all countries of the free world to become a trading partner and to expand trade on the basis of mutual advantage. It is through the inducement of offering other countries the opportunity to expand trade with us that the United States can best thwart the U.S.S.R.'s so-called trade offensive.

Renewed emphasis on the reciprocal trade agreements program could make this program one of the most effective of the devices available for meeting the Soviet challenge. This is in direct refutation of the position held by some that our national security demands greater trade restrictions. In our opinion mandatory import quotas on oil, lead, and zinc decreased rather than increased our national security, in that we have tended to alienate allies and, indeed, customers. Such restrictions on imports inevitably reduce markets for efficient U.S. export industries, including agriculture, and at the same time waste scarce domestic resources by channeling them into marginal operations that otherwise would be unprofitable.

Through our national trade policy, we have chosen to take a multilateral rather than a bilateral approach to foreign trade. In this manner we should work at opening up the total market of the free world, a market 30 times greater than that of the Soviet bloc. In such an environment Russia's puny bilateral offers could have little attraction to free countries.

To achieve such results the United States must do more than adhere to its trade agreement commitments. It must insist that other countries do the same in order to receive the benefits of U.S. concessions. For example, there are still numerous discriminatory restrictions against dollar imports in certain countries, although some progress has been made in removing them. In many cases these discriminatory restrictions are without justification. Countries with substantial dollar and gold reserves should not be given 3 years, 2 years, or 1 year to remove discriminatory dollar import restrictions. They should be required to remove such restrictions immediately if they are to continue to enjoy the full benefits of U.S. policies with respect to the reduction of trade restrictions.

It cannot be argued that we cannot compete with the Soviets as long as they are able to price their goods on a political basis without regard to costs. While there is something to be said for this view, it would be a mistake to overemphasize it. One thing is certain: We are in a weak position either to criticize Soviet pricing policies, or to urge that other countries take countervailing action against disruptive Soviet pricing tactics as long as we subsidize the bulk of our agricultural exports.

If we were to get our own house in order so that we were prepared to enter the world market on the basis of comparative advantage—rather than through subsidies—we would be in a far better position to rally other nations to a program of coordinated action if the Soviets should threaten the demoralize world markets by dumping their products. Every non-Communist country that is trying to develop export markets on an unsubsidized basis has an interest in helping to see that international markets are protected against disruptive tactics such as dumping.

Finally, if we are to retain the opportunity to compete in international markets on the basis of comparative advantage, we must protect the integrity of the dollar by effectively counteracting inflationary pressures here at home. If we fail to do so, we inevitably will be priced out of international markets by a wage-price spiral.

Representing 1,600,000 farm families engaged in an American industry which produced 22 percent of U.S. exports in 1958, Farm Bureau believes that the United States can meet and defeat any Soviet trade offensive as long as it adheres to, and vigorously implements, the principles of private, competitive enterprise that have contributed so much to the development of our Nation.

STATEMENT OF INDIANA FARMERS UNION

(By John Raber, Indiana Farmers Union, Indianapolis, Ind.)

As an Indiana farmer traveling in Russia in July of 1958, I had the opportunity to talk with Russian farmers, to see and evaluate their system of agriculture as it compared to our own.

Since our itinerary was made for us and our time limited, we were not able to see enough of Russia to make our experiences as comprehensive as I feel would be necessary to determine solid concepts about their system. But, even under these circumstances, we could see that all collective farms were not equally managed and that production varied widely.

I felt that Russian state farms had not settled on a procedure or even a standard approach to agriculture. Instead, there was evidence that collective farms were duplicating what we, in this country, would call an experimental farm pattern.

The farms we visited were exceptionally clean. Even hog and cattle barns were decorated with flower pots and white paint. The people who worked these "experimental stations" were proud of their progress and spoke warmly of their Government. They had a deep sense of dedication and accomplishment.

In comparing the American system and economies in agriculture with those of the Russians, I found the Russians had nothing new in equipment and farmer know-how. Russian equipment was lacking in mechanical perfection and Russia was still behind us in our professional approach to production. However, the state of mind of the Russian should give us concern. The Russian farmer feels he is needed and wanted. Each of his successes is met with Government praise and reward. He feels Russia has the better system, and he is pledged to outstrip us in production and in quality. For example, I asked a wheat farmer what Russia would do when they learned how to produce a surplus; his reply: "Then we will use it to make friends for Russia."

The American farmer, on the other hand, feels rejected. He is dedicated to individual ownership of America's farms, and he fears there are forces in the land that want to drive him off the farm. He feels our present farm program is a failure, that local taxes are unfair, that the Government doesn't care about his future.

In comparing the Russian farm economy with our system, I have concluded that the American farmer and his equipment is superior to the Russians. But the attitude of the American farmer today is lacking in enthusiasm and purpose, and his will to succeed is dying. The Russian, on the other hand, accepts this comparison and is dedicated to his task. He has confidence and he is living for his future.

It was William James who said, "You can measure everything about a man except his will to win." We in America must recognize the limited attitude of American agriculture as compared to the "will to win" of the Russian, and we must plan our future accordingly.

SOME COMPARISONS BETWEEN THE SOVIET AND THE UNITED STATES ECONOMICAL COMMITMENT TO EDUCATION

(By W. W. Eshelman, National Education Association, Washington, D.C.)

It is a privilege to appear before this committee in behalf of the National Education Association. My remarks will be confined to one aspect of the important overall theme that this committee is investigating. I would like to spend a few minutes with you on some comparisons between the Soviet and the United States commitment to education in terms of economic capacities.

I am sure that many of the distinguished speakers who have appeared before this committee have cautioned against quick or black and white comparisons. Comparisons are difficult and at best tenuous; nevertheless, they are necessary. Perhaps the word of caution mentioned by Sir Michael Sadler in 1900 might be appropriate. Sir Michael said:

> We cannot wander the pleasure among the educational systems of the world, like the child strolling through a garden, and pick off a flower from one bush and leaves from another, and then expect that if we stick what we have gathered into the soil at home, we shall have a living plant. A national system of education is a living thing, the outcome of forgotten struggles and difficulties and of battles long ago. It has in it some of the secret workings of national life. It reflects, while seeking to remedy, the failings of national character. By instinct it often lays special emphasis on those parts of training which the national character particularly needs.[1]

Turning to the United States, what is our commitment to education? Almost without exception every national leader believes in good health, happy marriages, and good education; yet in that we need to do much more. With a shortage of 140,000 classrooms and 135,000 teachers, this great Nation of ours is entering one of the most decisive periods in its history with an unswerving belief in the importance of good education to our Nation's survival yet unwilling to pay for it. Our total expenditures for all regular school education is roughly about the same as that of the Soviet Union—about $16 billion per year, but, according to Nicholas De Witt's calculations, the percent of our educational expenditures in the gross national product is about 3.7 percent, as compared with 6.5 percent for the Soviet.[2] Realizing the possibilities of error in this comparison, nonetheless it is generally agreed by scholars that the Soviet Union, within the context of its resources and goals, is making a proportionally greater commitment to education than is the United States in terms of our resources and goals.

---

[1] Sadler, Sir Michael, "How Far Can We Learn Anything of Practical Value From the Study of Foreign Systems of Education?" Guildford, 1900, p. 11 f.

[2] De Witt, Nicholas, "Basic Comparative Data on Soviet and American Education," Comparative Education Review, 2:9–11, June 1958.

46283—59—pt. 2——10

The overriding characteristic of the Soviet system is its fervent dedication to world communism and its strong belief that communism will inevitably dominate the world. They believe their way of organizing society represents a higher social system than capitalism and they believe their dialectic will in time replace capitalism. In the Soviet system, with its overriding commitment to a political "end," economics serve as a "means" to the "end"—an "end" that believes in man as master of men as opposed to our belief in man as master of man.

The Soviet emphasis on education is based partly on the Marxist principle that all cultures reflect their economic environment, and on Lenin's practical opinion that "you cannot build a Communist state with an illiterate people." To expand these points somewhat: Soviet leaders long have considered education as an essential part of the Communist scheme. They believe in the validity of scientific materialism, which, simply stated, refers to a view of the world which believes entirely in the ability of knowledge to conquer all obstacles, given time. Education, therefore, is the key to all doors. Education can eliminate superstitions and backward beliefs; education can promote the culture and language arts; education can be used to mold minds into desired ideological grooves; and education can provide the skill to build machines. A recent visitor to East Germany noted an interesting parody upon the Lenin theme. The sign read: "Study, study, and, once again, study."

What about Soviet education?

Let me begin by stating what seems to me a case of bordering on the ridiculous if it were not so serious. Today we simply do not know enough about Soviet educational finance to make anything more than intelligent guesses about this important problem. One of our leading authorities on Soviet manpower and education, Dr. Nicholas DeWitt of Harvard's Russian Institute, recently told an NEA staff member that he had six Soviet books and many journals waiting to be translated. We should view with alarm this situation. While we talk much about the challenge and threat of communism, our scholars do not have sufficient help to translate those works which are necessary to assess the extent and direction of the Soviet effort. Dating back to Biblical times, the adage "Know thy enemy" has been important to survival. I submit to this distinguished group that we do not know our enemy in the important field of educational finance. Therefore, it would seem highly fitting for this committee to explore measures that might be taken to provide our researchers with sufficient assistance to have important Russian sources translated into English.

Considering the insufficient evidence that is available at the present time, what can we say about the financing of Soviet education?

As mentioned before, DeWitt has found that the Soviet Union spends about 6.5 percent of the gross national product on education. This figure is somewhat below the 10 to 15 percent estimates given in the latest Office of Education report.[3] The problem lies primarily in the definition of education. Without going into technical aspects of this question, it can be mentioned that funds for education in the

[3] Report of the first official U.S. Education Mission to the U.S.S.R., "Soviet Commitment to Education." Washington, D.C.: U.S. Government Printing Office, 1959, p. 13.

U.S.S.R. come under the division of the planned budget which is for "health and educational-cultural activities and social services," regardless of the national, republic, or other government channel through which moneys are distributed. Soviet news releases announced 26.1 percent of the 1955 planned budget for such services and activities as a whole.[4]

Under the centrally controlled, planned economy of the U.S.S.R., the educational budget relates to public funds from the general revenue of the state. Taxes are not levied specifically for educational purposes and there is no privately financed educational system. The state budget for education provides for building construction and maintenance, supplies and equipment, salaries of teachers at all levels, stipends for students in institutions of higher education, special programs in education, and miscellaneous expenses. Industrial enterprises and collective forms also provide considerable supplementary support for education, primarily in equipment and facilities.

The supplementary support of Soviet education is very difficult to estimate. For example, if a Soviet community decides to paint its schoolhouse, not an infrequent occurrence, this should be counted as part of the total cost of education; yet it is almost impossible to make even an educated guess at present regarding this extracurricular community participation. Recent educational reforms will tie the schools even closer to industry, thereby promoting even greater impromptu or nonauthorized support than ever before, making the task of comparison even more difficult.

And even if a quantitative comparison could be assessed with some accuracy, its qualitative significance is another matter. For example, the Soviets are, roughly speaking, producing two or three times as many engineers as the United States. Yet this does not tell the whole story. In the first place, the Soviet level of development—across the board—is about where we were at the turn of the century. They need many more engineers in order to industrialize than we—already a highly industrialized nation—need to sustain and develop further our economy. Also, the Soviet population is approximately 12 percent greater than ours. And finally, the key figure may not be the numbers of engineers produced, but the numbers of skilled and semiskilled workers that are being turned out. In this category the Soviets are deficient, but they recognize the need and are expanding their program.

Turning for a moment to teachers and teachers' salaries: I am not happy to report that the Soviet society seems to treat its teachers better, financially and prestigewise, than we do. In his statement before the National Press Club, the U.S. Commissioner of Education noted about his mission's trip to the Soviet Union:

> * * * We saw no evidence of any teacher shortage. Teacher workloads and other working conditions are advantageous. Teacher prestige is high; only the best are chosen to teach—one out of six who apply for training. Salaries are at the levels of those of doctors and engineers; in fact, a fully trained doctor and nurse are regular members of each school staff.[5]

---

[4] U.S. Department of Health, Education, and Welfare, "Education in the U.S.S.R." (Bulletin 1957, No. 4) Washington, D.C.: U.S. Government Printing Office, 1958, pp. 23–24.
[5] Derthick, Lawrence G., "The Russian Race for Knowledge," School Life, vol. 40, pp. 3, 4.

Commenting upon salaries of American teachers, the Rockefeller Report on "The Pursuit of Excellence" states forcefully the American problem in this manner:

* * * The root problem of the teaching profession remains financial. More perhaps than any other profession, teaching needs dedicated men and women to whom pay is not an overriding consideration; but until we pay teachers at least as well as middle echelon of executives, we cannot expect the profession to attract its full share of the available range of talents. Salaries must be raised immediately and substantially.[6]

Before turning to some general conclusions, I would like to spend a few minutes on the financing of American education. Generally, expenditures for American education are computed by adding up to total cost for public and private elementary, secondary, and higher education plus a small miscellaneous category and dividing this total by the gross national product. This is one way of doing it and it is statistically proper to do so. It overlooks, however, the larger societal commitment that we have made to education. Today, we really have four systems of education. A recently completed, and, as yet, unpublished study by an educational economist—Prof. Harold Clark—discusses American education in terms of these four systems, which are: the regular school system, business and industrial courses, organized group study, and systematic self-study.[7]

I think American education, viewed in this broader context, makes more sense for the purpose of this paper because it tells something about our society as a whole, and the Soviet challenge must be met by the whole society. The amount of education that can be provided by a society depends upon its overall efficiency as well as the efficiency of the educational system itself.

In William Benton's provocative book on the Soviet challenge, he mentions that public school education has traditionally depended on the general property tax. This tax is inflexible. It does not respond to rising income or inflation. It now contributes about one-eighth of all revenues. Its importance has steadily declined. Relative to other taxes, it provides but 25 percent as much revenue as it did 25 years ago.

State and local debts have trebled. Further, putting increased burdens on State and local governments tends to strike most heavily against low-income groups; whereas 80 percent of Federal taxes are on income, less than 10 percent of the State and local taxes are on income, and more than 90 percent are on property and consumption taxes that weigh heavily on low-income groups.

The inadequate fiscal capacity of State and local government, the unequal capacities of States, and the urgent requirements of national defense are among the reasons for Federal support of schools. Poor States try harder but they are necessarily bound to lower standards, as the system works today. Thus in relation to income, Mississippi spends twice as much for school aid as New York. Yet in 1953–54, expenditures per pupil averaged $110 for Alabama and Mississippi and $341 for New York State. In a recent year, 12 richer States had

---

[6] "The Rockefeller Report on Education," "The Pursuit of Excellence: Education and the Future of America." (America at Mid-Century Series) Garden City, N.Y.: Doubleday & Co., Inc., 1958, pp. 25, 26.

[7] Clark, Harold F., and Ruth E. Sobkov, "How Much Can the People of the United States Afford To Spend on Education? (Unpublished report) 1959. (141 pp.)

fewer than 5 percent of their registrants failing the selective service education test; but from 13 poorer States 20 to 49 percent failed.[8]

Carrying Benton's point on Federal support one step farther, the recent Rockefeller report on "The Pursuit o f Excellence," a pursuit fully realized in the report, it goes directly to the heart of the matter when it points out that—

> Excessive dependence upon State and local revenues—particularly the latter—upon the real property tax * * * more than anything else * * * gives rise to current proposals for increased Federal support of education. For those who wish to resist or postpone the resort to Federal funds and at the same time not constrict educational service there seems to be only one alternative: a thorough, painful, politically courageous overhaul of State and local tax systems.[9]

Even allowing for considerably greater efficiency in the use of educational funds, it is likely that 10 years hence our schools and colleges will require at least double their present level of financial support to handle our growing student population. In other words, by 1967 the entire educational effort is likely to call for expenditures on the order of $30 billion, measured in today's prices. Since the gross national product by 1967 has been estimated to be around $600 billion, educational expenditures would absorb about 5 percent of gross national product in contrast with the current 3.6 percent level.[10]

In conclusion, one can say that the Soviet Union is quite totally committed to communism as a way or organizing people, and to education as a tool or instrument to that end; the United States is quite committed to democracy as a way of organizing society, which allows the individual that degree of freedom compatible with the society as a whole.

We must always be openminded about learning and borrowing something of value from the Soviet system. From the early days of our Union, Americans have been adopting other ideas as well as inventing their own. If the Soviets have an educational technique or idea that can improve our system, by all means we should adopt it. Not to do so weakens our system—a very unwise and perhaps fatal price to pay to pride and self-satisfaction.

Within the context of their system and their objectives, the Soviets may well be achieving more progress toward their ends than we are toward ours. Our decentralized and diversified society has done remarkably well in educating the people. Our free, public school education is unique in history. Our commitment to education has paid us back manyfold in our amazing agricultural and industrial growth. Yet, as we enter the second half of the 20th century, our Nation is faced with internal and external problems that will force us to do a better job of education than we have done at any time in our history. In this context, I close with a short paragraph from the "Rockefeller Report:

> The Nation's need for good education is immediate; and good education is expensive. That is a fact which the American people have never been quite prepared to face. At stake is nothing less than our national greatness and our aspirations for the dignity of the individual. If the public is not prepared for

---

[8] Benton, William, "This Is the Challenge." New York: Associated College Presses, 1958. Pp. 136–137.

[9] "The Rockefeller Report," op. cit., p. 35.

[10] Ibid., p. 34.

this, then responsible educators, business leaders, unions, and civic organizations must join in a national campaign to prepare them.[11]

Percent of national income going to education

	Total in millions of dollars	Percent of national income
I. Direct expenditures for education:		
A. Regular system:		
1. Public elementary and secondary schools	$11,737	3.33
2. Private elementary and secondary schools	1,748	.495
3. Miscellaneous	90	.003
4. Higher education, public and private	4,404	1.25
Total	17,979	5.097
B. Business and industry	10,000	2.83
C. Group	5,000	1.42
D. Self	1,500	.42
Total direct cost	34,479	9.77
II. Support of students in regular system	24,200	6.86
40,286,000 at $600 [1]	58,679	16.83

[1] Excludes approximately 1,080,000 college students whose room and board is included under auxiliary expenditures of institutions of higher education.

[11] Ibid., p. 33.

SOVIET ECONOMIC GROWTH AND UNITED STATES POLICY

(By Howard C. Petersen, Committee for Economic Development)

The rapid growth of the Soviet economy is one of the leading facts of our lifetime. It is an important fact for everyone, including the United States, who shares this little globe with the Russians. But just how it will affect us and how we should respond are, in my opinion, far from clear or certain. Therefore I welcome the effort of the Joint Economic Committee to explore these questions.

I submit this paper in the spirit of participation in an exploratory discussion. I am not an expert on the Soviet economy or on the intentions of the Soviet leaders. Neither is the Committee for Economic Development,[1] on whose behalf I respond to the invitation of the Joint Economic Committee to present a paper. Although I am testifying as CED's representative, the views I am expressing here are my own responsibility, and do not necessarily represent the views of the Research and Policy Committee or other CED committees or individuals. However, the Research and Policy Committee of CED, in a number of statements on national policy, has encountered the fact of the growing Soviet economy. This was notably true in our work on national security, foreign economic assistance and U.S. economic growth.[2] We have had to form some judgments, based on information we could readily obtain, about the significance of the Soviet economy for our policy. This paper reflects these judgments as well as presenting additional views of my own.

I. GENERAL ECONOMIC ASSUMPTIONS

Let me begin with three assumptions about the size and growth of the Soviet economy in relation to our own. I base these mainly on previously published information since estimates contained in the papers in this compendium are largely unavailable to me at the time of writing.

First, I assume that at the present time the total gross national product of Russia is at least two-fifths that of the United States and its per capita output at least one-third ours, but not much more.

Second, I assume that the yearly percentage increase in Russian gross national product during the past decade has significantly exceeded that of the United States. In this period the Russian growth

[1] The Committee for Economic Development is composed of 185 leading businessmen and educators. Its purpose is to conduct objective economic research, to support and promote economic education and to formulate and publish recommendations on major economic problems that will contribute to growth and stability in the American economy, higher living standards and increasing opportunities for all Americans, and to strengthening the institutions and the concepts essential to progress in a free society.

[2] Committee for Economic Development, "The Problem of National Security—Some Economic and Administrative Aspects" (1958); "Economic Development Assistance" (1957); and "Economic Growth in the United States—Its Past and Future" (1958).

rate may have been 6 or 7 percent a year. Recent changes in this country have been quite irregular. Our average long-term rate, in which there is no clear evidence of change, has been about 3 percent, and I use that figure as measuring our current trend. On that basis, the average absolute yearly increase in total Russian gross national product is less than that in ours but is approaching it and if recent growth rates continue may soon exceed it. On the basis of the same estimates, the absolute yearly increase in Russian per capita gross national product already is larger than ours. I am not making a judgment that investigators who suggest a much lower rate of Soviet growth than these comparisons imply are necessarily wrong, but to base policy upon their findings does not seem to me prudent unless the evidence becomes more conclusive than it is now.

Third, I assume that the difference between the growth rates of the two countries cannot be extrapolated into the distant future. It is easy enough to show arithmetically that if one country maintains a higher growth rate than another, eventually it will reach and surpass it. If the Soviet gross national product is now two-fifths as large as ours, and if the Russians maintain a growth rate 1 percentage point above ours—say, 4 percent against 3—their gross national product will match ours in 93 years. If the difference is 2 percentage points, it will take 47 years; if 3 percentage points, 31 years; and if 4 percentage points, 24 years. Such calculations are startling but provide inadequate basis for present policy. While economic growth results from a complex of influences, the exceptional height of the Soviet growth rate, if it really exists, is evidently made possible in the main by five forces. These are—

1. Russia has devoted a large proportion of her output to investment. On a comparable basis, gross investment in real assets, public and private, represents perhaps 25 percent of gross national product in Russia and 20 percent in the United States. The difference in net investment rates is larger.
2. The Soviet authorities have been able to control demand patterns in a way that has diverted production and supporting investment from activities where the value of output per employee is low, calculated on the basis of controlled internal relative prices, to activities where it is high.
3. The Russians have experienced a large expansion of the nonagricultural labor force, based on the shift of workers from agriculture.
4. Russia has experienced the large gains made possible by the spread of a basic education among a previously largely illiterate population, and the initial training of a quickly expanding industrial labor force.
5. Russia has had opportunities to increase productivity greatly by the introduction of techniques already prevalent in Western countries and, increasingly, in the technologically advanced sectors of the Soviet economy. This is probably the most important element of all in making possible her large output advances.

These advantages are not, of course, unique with Russia; they are at least potentially available in varying degrees to all but the most advanced countries. Unlike most other countries, however, Russia has had an all-powerful centralized authority with the drive to take full advantage of them to push growth regardless of the present sacrifice imposed upon her population.

Can Russia's high growth rate be maintained? Despite internal pressure for better living conditions, Russia may continue indefinitely to devote the present high proportion of gross national product to investment. This would permit consumption to expand in proportion to gross national product, which may be sufficient to satisfy her population. But the other four elements permitting exceptionally rapid growth are essentially transitional advantages which will become of decreasing importance as the stage of development of the Russian economy becomes more similar to ours. As the differential in the level of output is reduced, it is likely that the differential in growth rates will also narrow. The realistic expectation as of the present time is that our relative advantage over the Russians will continue to diminish but at a slackening rate. Since information concerning production technique available to all countries is about the same, and since Russia is well endowed with natural resources and may eventually match the size of our capital stock and the diffusion of education over the whole population, there is no sufficient reason to feel sure she cannot some day match us in per capita output, although most of us may properly have sufficient confidence in the superiority of our own system to doubt that she can do so.

If we compare the output of the NATO alliance as a whole with that of the European bloc countries as a whole, the comparison with respect both to present level and to growth appears more favorable to us. Some of the Western European countries have been growing about as fast as Russia, and the total economic potential of our NATO allies greatly exceeds that of the European satellites.

II. WAYS IN WHICH SOVIET ECONOMIC EXPANSION MAY AFFECT US

The relative size and growth of the Soviet and American economies may affect the Soviet threat to us in a number of ways. The principal points of possible impact include—

(*a*) The ability to bear the burden of military programs and to progress in military strength;

(b) Aid and trade with the underdeveloped world;

(*c*) The Soviet ability to conduct an offensive economic policy against the United States and other industrial countries and our ability to withstand or retaliate;

(*d*) The attitudes of the "neutrals," mainly underdeveloped countries;

(*e*) The attitude of the U.S. population and Government;

(*f*) The attitudes of our Allies;

(*g*) The attitudes of the Soviet satellites; and

(*h*) The internal Russian political situation and the international objectives of Soviet policy.

The prospect of faster economic growth in the Soviet Union than in the United States probably is adverse to our position in almost all of these areas. Nonetheless, it does not seem to me likely to be the decisive factor in the outcome of the East-West struggle, provided that our own performance is at least as satisfactory as in the past.

Military strength

The larger a nation's national income, the smaller is the burden of financing military expenditures at any stated level. Economic growth clearly increases the size of the military program it is possible for a nation to support. Among countries with at all comparable resources, however, differences in actual military strength are much more closely related to their appraisals of need and willingness to sacrifice than to rates of economic growth or absolute limits imposed by the size of their economies. If we were devoting the same proportion of gross national product to national security in fiscal year 1953 as we would be if defense expenditures had kept pace with economic growth over the intervening period, we would now be spending $66 billion a year for national defense instead of $46 billion. Were our Government convinced that it was necessary, we could and would spend a good deal more than that.

Despite a much smaller economy and a larger population to support, the Soviet Union maintains a powerful and diversified military machine sufficient to provide approximate military parity with the United States. She does so by devoting a larger portion of her gross national product to this purpose than we do, by eliminating features that add more to the comfort and safety of her armed forces than to their striking power, and by paying her armed forces a great deal less, as well as by less obvious means.

Clearly the size and rate of growth of the United States and Soviet economies, though important variables, are not the decisive ones determining their relative military strength.

Aid and trade with underdeveloped countries

Soviet aid has very largely taken the form of loans at rather low interest rates. Whether, and under what conditions, Soviet loans to underdeveloped countries outside the bloc are adverse to our interests is itself a complicated question. If they actually contribute to economic progress in these nations, which certainly is an objective of our own policy, they may even be in our long-term interest. In any case, even more than that of military programs the scope and character of economic aid to underdeveloped free nations will be determined by considerations other than the capacity to provide aid. In neither Russia nor the United States does such assistance amount to more than a fraction of 1 percent of gross national product or to any considerable proportion of defense spending. Heavy concentration on aid requiring use of a particular type of facility, such as the provision of steel mills, might well tax Russian capacity at present. But this is a matter of foresight in arranging for expansion of specialized capacity in such areas or in scheduling aid programs rather than of general economic growth.

Trade of most underdeveloped free countries with the Soviet Union is presently trivial in comparison with their trade with the West. Russia accounts (based on 1956 data) for more than 10 percent of imports only in Afghanistan and Yugoslavia, and of exports in these two countries and Iran. Measurement by trade with the bloc as a whole would add only four other countries to such a list. Soviet trade is small primarily because Russia has followed a policy of extreme autarchy. The Russian policy of self-sufficiency has been relaxed in recent years but only slightly insofar as countries outside the bloc are concerned. If Russian trade with most countries were doubled or tripled as a result of Soviet economic growth, it would still be tiny in comparison with their trade with the West. The volume of her future trade, conducted for ordinary commercial purposes, will depend far more on future Russian trade policy than on her rate of economic growth.

Most underdeveloped nations are greatly dependent on the export of one to three raw materials. A sharp drop in the volume or price of exports of these commodities has catastrophic consequences for their balance of payments and hence for their development programs. In the past few years Russia has stepped in with offers to buy whenever such situations have developed. In some well-publicized cases these commodities have reappeared in markets outside Russia to compete in the original exporter's usual markets, and the transaction has neither helped the underdeveloped nation nor earned good will for the Soviet. It is evident, however, that real opportunity exists for Russia to advance her influence by buying raw materials in depressed markets in good faith. Consumer commodities like coffee and fish can be offered to Russian consumers. Industrial raw materials can either be permitted to replace Russian production or, if she is unwilling to relax her policy of self-sufficiency, stockpiled or destroyed. Only in the last case is any real cost imposed upon the Russian economy by this type of purchasing; it then becomes, in effect, a form of aid.

Russian growth will contribute to Russia's ability to expand trade on a commercial basis. It may result in a wider variety and better quality of goods offered for export. It will increase her ability to absorb imports. It will increase her economic capacity to provide aid through purchase of unwanted commodities, just as in other forms. But the future course of all forms of Russian trade with underdeveloped countries will be determined much more by her policy decisions than by the rate of her economic growth.

Ability to conduct an offensive economic policy against industrial nations

The larger the Russian economy, the greater will be her ability to incur the costs of a policy of economic warfare against the United States and other industrial nations. This might involve dumping commodities to disrupt western markets, preclusive buying of commodities in short supply, and possibly attempts at manipulation of foreign currencies. But there is little evidence of any deliberate Russian policy to engage in such activities. Such practices would necessarily involve costs to her. In fact, the aggressor in this type of warfare is not likely to inflict as much loss on an opponent as he himself incurs, except, perhaps sporadically in unusually favorable circumstances. Moreover, defensive steps are possible. I do not see strengthening of Russia's capacity to engage in this kind of activity as an important consequence of her higher growth rate.

Attitudes of peoples throughout the world

A situation in which the Soviet economy is generally recognized to be growing faster than ours, not only in percentages but also absolutely, not in spurts but steadily, and is approaching ours in total size, could, it may be supposed, greatly affect the attitudes of peoples throughout the world. It might greatly strengthen the confidence of the Russians in their own system, strengthen the dependence of their satellites upon them, increase the attraction of the Communist system for the independent, underdeveloped countries, worry our allies about their reliance upon us, and weaken our own morale. Yet I think all of these things are either unlikely to occur as a result of comparative U.S.-Russian growth rates or unlikely to be important to our position.

Consider the underdeveloped nations of the free world that are either emerging into a phase of sustained economic growth or hoping to do so. Their success is of the utmost importance to us. If they achieve vigorous growth and visibly rising living standards, they are not likely voluntarily to abandon freedom for communism; if they do so it will be for other reasons, such as the inability of the masses to eliminate by other means an unacceptable distribution of income or system of land tenure. If their plans for economic development are badly disappointed, they will, indeed, consider the Communist alternative. But they are more likely to compare their experience with that of China, Mongolia, North Korea, or Vietminh than with that of Russia or the European satellites. Insofar as third-party comparisons are made at all, comparison of the growth rates of India and China, the largest underdeveloped countries of the free and Communist worlds, is likely to seem more relevant than that of Russia and the United States.

That in the United States, Canada, or the Western European countries—some of which themselves have had postwar expansion comparable to that of Russia—any considerable number of people other than those already enrolled in Communist Parties could be attracted to communism by a fast Soviet growth rate seems scarcely credible. Educated peoples with full access to information are not likely to barter freedom for slavery to gain even real economic advantages unless their own conditions are intolerable. If any economic development does produce such a result, it will be a major domestic depression, involving widespread unemployment, or else stagnation in per capita incomes of the mass of the people. It would be, in other words, because of the failure of the Western societies as judged by their own standards.

We could lose our allies not because they are attracted to communism but because of loss of confidence in us. Failures in our foreign policy, an inadequate military posture, or the sheer terrorism of the mutual power of destruction provided by modern weapons might lead to this result. But it is hard to see how changes in relative economic potential could do so, particularly since there is so little chance that, with present borders, the size of the economies of the Western Communist countries can come to match that of the combined NATO Powers, nor that of the whole Communist world that of the free world.

The attitudes of the peoples of the satellite countries also will be influenced mainly by conditions within their own borders, not by comparisons of the Soviet and U.S. growth rates. In addition, before Russia can command popular support there, she must somehow escape the onus of representing the imposition of an alien power and her past record of terrorism.

It is the effect upon Russian attitudes that is most open to question. Surely, the Russians may be expected to take pride in their progress and to exult if they ever succeed in their goal of overhauling us in what they view as an economic race. But it is hard to see how the Soviet leaders could become more implacable enemies of the Western democracies than they have been in the past. And it is hard to see why their own success should increase hostility toward us among the Russian people.

On the other hand, there is at least reason to hope that rising living standards will lead to humanizing political and economic changes within the Soviet society, the emergence of a different type of leadership, and a less truculent attitude toward the outside world. This must, indeed, be our principal hope for a more assured peace in some future period. But this hopeful prospect is far too hypothetical to permit us to rest policy upon it now.

III. IMPLICATION FOR U.S. POLICY

The rise of Russian economic power is one of the great developments of world history. It was probably inevitable regardless of the form of Russian government. It is important that we understand it and that the peoples of the world understand it and place it in its proper perspective.

Our reaction should not be one of amazement or despair. What Russia is doing other nations have done, though other nations have done it with less feverish haste and far less human cost. Our reaction should not be to attempt to match the present Russian growth rate simply because the Russian rate is higher than ours. Those suggesting such a course have not, in my opinion, even begun to explore its implications or its costs.

In general, there are four broad types of action we might consider to accelerate our own rate of growth.

First, we can try to reduce involuntary unemployment of resources, especially to minimize the depth and duration of recessions.

Second, we can try to make our economic system work more smoothly so as to get more real product from the resources now going into production. We can try to make our system more competitive, and remove public and private impediments to the mobility of resources and to the introduction of improved techniques. We can reduce barriers to trade. We can reexamine our tax structure with a view to improving incentives and reconsider various governmental subsidies and price supports.

These are desirable things to do. In our own interest we should try to reduce unemployment and increase the efficiency with which we use resources regardless of the Russian threat. But the reduction of unemployment and elimination of most of the barriers to efficiency we can readily think of would mainly provide one-time gains. They would yield a limited nonrecurrent increase in output but not an increase in the rate of growth. These are quite different things.

Suppose, for example, that unemployment had not exceeded 4 percent of the labor force in any year from 1947 to 1957, and had been what it actually was in the years when it was lower. This seems a reasonable interpretation of what is meant by sustaining a higher level of employment. In that case, employment over the period would have averaged about one-half percent higher than it was. Output would probably have been bigger by a somewhat larger percentage—say 2 percent as a high estimate.

If we could do that much better in the future, output might be 2 percent higher than otherwise. But this would not be equivalent to the difference between a 3 percent and a 5 percent growth rate. It would be a once-for-all increase, equivalent to growing 5 percent rather than 3 percent in 1 year, not over any longer period. The 2-percent higher output would presumably permit some increase in the amount of saving. As a first approximation this might be a 2-percent increase in the amount of saving. Under certain assumptions this would contribute to faster growth. But the contribution would be insignificant.

Nonrecurrent gains, though well worthwhile, will not go far toward matching the Russian growth rate.

The third possibility, then, is to increase the amount of work done in our society. In the past, average annual hours of work have declined about one-half percent a year. If we stopped this reduction now, we might thereby hope to add to our past growth rate about one-half percent a year, on the very favorable assumption that none of the past increase in output per man-hour was the result of shortening hours. The other possibility of increasing total man-hours is through faster expansion of the labor force, but the possibilities for cumulative effects here except by affecting the size of the total population, appear much smaller.

Fourth, we can increase the rate of economic growth by devoting more of our output to uses that promote growth.

More investment, more research, more education are needed for growth, but they are needed just to sustain the rate of growth we have been getting. We have achieved an average growth rate of 3 percent per annum over the past 50 or 75 years by increasing our annual devotion of resources to investment, research, and education. In order to increase the rate of growth it is not sufficient just to increase these things; it is necessary to increase the rate of increase.

The amounts of increase in the rates of savings, investment, education, and research needed to get any given increase in the rate of growth are literally unknown. There is great need for much more information before we can talk sense about this subject. Some crude calculations of what might be necessary give staggering results. They suggest that we have to find out not whether it would take $3 billion or $5 billion or even $10 billion more a year of investment, research, and education to get our growth rate up from 3 percent to 5 percent, but whether it would not take something like $75 billion a year.

Suppose the 3 percent growth rate results from an annual increase in the labor force of 1 percent a year and an annual increase in output per worker of 2 percent a year. Unless we speed up the increase in the labor force, to raise the 3 percent growth rate to 5 percent would require the annual increase in output per worker to be raised from 2 to 4 percent—that is, to be doubled.

To obtain the present increase in productivity we are spending something like $75 billion a year, or 15 percent of our total output at high employment, on net investment in productive assets, public and private, on education, and on relevant research. The simplest estimate is that to double the increase in output per worker we would have to double these expenditures to $150 billion a year, or 30 percent of our output. An increase of $75 billion in these private and public outlays implies, of course, a corresponding increase of $75 billion a year in the sum of the Nation's saving and tax payments. To get a simultaneous increase in taxes and savings on such a scale without seriously impairing incentives important to growth would clearly be extremely difficult.

I do not wish to place any great burden on the figures I have used for illustration. But the main point is that the requirements for an increase in the rate of economic growth, say from 3 percent to 5 percent—which still would not equal the present Russian rate—may be very large, much larger than seems to be contemplated in current discussion. There are many different facts, estimates, and assumptions that could be introduced to change these figures. But we are not now in a position to decide that we want a significantly higher growth rate on the assumption that it will be easy to achieve. It will obviously take some doing.

There is no reason to think that the United States is exempt from the law that we are preaching to underdeveloped countries all over the world—that more growth in per capita income requires more savings and more investment in productive facilities, education, and research. And there is no reason to presume that the proportionate increase required is smaller than the proportionate increase in the growth rate desired. In fact, this assumption is in all probability overoptimistic, since it is not likely that an increase in growth-supporting expenditures will yield a fully proportionate return.

To increase the long-term growth rate by one or two percentage points is a formidable undertaking, requiring some really basic changes. It probably can be done, if this is accepted as a sufficiently urgent objective of national policy to give it an overriding priority. My interest here is in showing that if the crude estimates presented above are anywhere near correct there has not yet been in this country any serious consideration of the steps that would be necessary. I shall not attempt here to spell out any steps by which the result might be achieved, though it seems obvious they would be drastic. What seems to be involved is a degree of governmental intervention in economic life that would change the very character of our free economy.

The implication I draw from all this is that the United States should promote its own growth by reasonable means, not by all means. Our past performance has given us an economy that has long been the envy of the world and that has given us the highest living standard ever known. Surely we wish to progress as rapidly as in the past, and to do better if we can—but not at any cost. There is no necessity for us to match the present Russian growth rate.

We are engaged in a competition of systems, not a competition of growth rates. Our strategy in this competition should be to make our own system work as well as we can, in terms of its own values. The values that our system serves are the values that men everywhere would choose if given the chance. Men want freedom, security, rising living standards for themselves and their families, relief from the burdens of toil, fair treatment, and personal dignity. If they did not we would be faced with an awful dilemma. But I believe that we are justified in believing that people everywhere want the basic things that we want, and that the attractiveness of our system is enhanced by its demonstrated success in achieving these goals.

More rapid growth contributes to the success of the system, but is not identical with success or the sufficient means to its achievement. For us to seek to force our rate of economic growth by a great expansion of the role of government, and by curtailing the freedom of families to choose between consumption and saving and between work and leisure, would be inconsistent with our own values. And it would not make our system more appealing to others.

The Russian threat is grave. It demands from us a strong and varied response. The response should not be imitative. Our danger is not that our total economic resources are, or will be in the foreseeable future, too small for the promotion of U.S. policy. Our great need is not for larger resources but for the best use of the resources we have.

We should use the resources we have—which are superior to those of the Russians now and will be at least equal to them for the foreseeable future—to promote U.S. policy better.

I do not know whether our military strength is adequate to meet the tests it may face, but if larger defense expenditures will add to our security, they should be made. Our greater economic strength gives us the ability, if we wish to use it, to seize the initiative in the development of large and varied military forces and in the deliberate obsolescing of equipment and to place pressure on the Russians to maintain equality with us. Whether we should do so is a political question, not a matter of economic potential.

We should be providing much more economic development assistance to the underdeveloped countries of the world than we are doing now. Their success is vital to us, and our assistance to them may be critical to their success.

In neither of these fields should we hold back because of vaguely felt fears that we cannot afford to do what is necessary, that financing adequate defense and assistance programs will somehow damage our economy or impair our growth. Any additional public expenditures for these purposes must be matched by higher taxes to avoid feeding inflationary pressures. Stability of the value of the dollar is properly an important objective of our economic policy. Attention must be given to the way in which taxes are raised so as to minimize any curtailment of private saving or incentives to work. Given the exercise of a reasonable degree of common sense and responsibility in these matters, however, such fears have little foundation.

We should be acting vigorously to counter the Soviet drive for foreign expansion in all its aspects—not only the Soviet use or threat to use force, but their propaganda, their use of foreign trade as a political weapon, their support of subversion of government, and their meddling in domestic politics everywhere, often combined with the supplying of money and arms. Wherever possible we should be seizing the initiative.

We should be moving vigorously to reduce international trade barriers. We should utilize fully the powers granted by the Trade Agreements Act to achieve gradual and selective reductions in our own tariffs and, by negotiation with other countries, to secure reductions in their barriers to international trade. Aside from the direct advantage of such a policy to us and to other advanced countries, we must insure a structure of international markets that will provide newly developing nations opportunity to participate fully and fairly in international exchange. Our new addiction to the imposition of quotas when foreign countries successfully penetrate our markets is the worst possible course for us to follow, one that is especially well designed to harm our friends and to create opportunities for the politically inspired Russian trade offensive.

At home we and other advanced Western nations should adhere to our own values of what is good and desirable, and manage our domestic affairs in the light of our own criteria of success, not by the criteria of Soviet communism, if we wish to maintain vigorous and self-confident societies. Of course, economic growth decidedly continues to be one of the central objectives of domestic policy in our own interest. Public policies must be reviewed from the standpoint of their effect upon growth. It is the source of our ability to provide better living standards, more freedom of choice, more leisure, and better educational opportunities, and to protect the less fortunate against the hazards of life. We are far from having reached the state where additional income is of little interest to us. But economic growth is not an overriding objective that calls for drastic changes in the way we organize our society and allocate our resources. The resources we allocate to growth should be based upon our own interest, as determined in part by the amount private citizens wish to save or invest and to spend for education and research, and the valuation they place upon income as against leisure, and in part by our political decisions, reached through the democratic process, as to how much we wish to pay in taxes for public expenditures that promote growth.

Our success in the continuing struggle against Communist imperialism will be determined by our faith, determination, willingness to sacrifice, intelligence, and ingenuity. If we fail it will not be the result of an inadequate economic base, unless future changes in relative economic growth are much different from what we can now foresee.

46283—59—pt. 2——11

EVALUATION OF THE SOVIET ECONOMIC THREAT

(By Gerhard Colm,[1] assisted by Joel Darmstadter, National Planning Association, Washington, D.C.)

SUMMARY AND CONCLUSION

A statistical "thaw," following Stalin's death, has provided increased knowledge about the Soviet economy. While some statistical exaggerations and distortions persist, Soviet claims must not be shrugged off, but carefully evaluated. Tangible Soviet achievements in science, education, and weapons technology bear this out.

Soviet economic growth is a threat to the extent that it serves as an instrument of military buildup and militant foreign policy. The comparison between Soviet and United States economic strength indicates that the United States can, for decades, still have the greater economic capacity. What is decisive, however, is not only potential economic capacity but also the extent to which the potential is realized and the allocation which is made to purposes of defense and foreign economic policy.

In recent years, Soviet output—both total and per capita—has grown at rates considerably in excess of those in the United States. With proper measures by government, business, and labor it should be possible to increase the annual rate of growth in the United States to 4–5 percent. At the same time there are grounds for believing that Soviet growth rates will diminish somewhat, say to 6 percent. This differenct in growth rates is not enough to justify Soviet boasts of equaling U.S. output in the foreseeable future. However, the difference in annual increments will decline substantially. Both in Russia and the United States, the increase in production makes it economically possible to increase substantially national security and foreign economic activities and at the same time add to productive capacity and improve the standard of living. Political determination appears to be more important than the economic potential.

The highly publicized Communist economic aid activities of the past several years have been far below comparable U.S. or Western efforts. Yet, the Communists seem to have achieved a relatively large measure of success, both because of their capacity to combine aid with trade and because they can exploit latent fears and suspicions rooted in the colonial heritage of many underdeveloped nations. In addition to foreign assistance, the Communists have engaged in some practices—for example, massive sales of tin and aluminum on Western markets—which may not have been politically motivated but which

[1] This paper is based largely on the monographs which have been published by, or prepared for, the National Planning Association's research project on the "Economics of Competitive Coexistence." Use has been made also of several chapters of the final volume which the research director of that project, Dr. Henry G. Aubrey, has in preparation. Nevertheless, the views expressed in this paper are our own and do not necessarily reflect those of the National Planning Association or of Dr. Aubrey.

constitute tools for disrupting the free world economy, available for recurrent use.

In evaluating the potential economic threat in years to come, one must reckon with the continuing importance of Marxist dogma in Communist policies. Capitalism is still pictured as driven to imperialism and wars as "solutions" for the problem of overproduction. And militant Marxism still believes that the Soviet-Chinese "avant garde" has the mission of supporting the Communist struggle everywhere in the world, by whatever means are available and whenever it is promising.

In the underdeveloped countries the Soviets have been at least partly successful posing in the role of the advocates and supporters of rapid economic growth and independence in contrast to the West, which is pictured as advocating "go slow" policies and using these countries as a "dumping ground" for surplus products.

The analysis of the Soviet economic threat raises a number of policy questions:

1. Without engaging in a gross national product race, what can the U.S. Government, business, and labor do to support a rate of growth adequate to meet the urgent requirements in defense and nondefense, domestic and international?

2. What defense posture is needed to convince the Soviets that every aggressive move at the center, or the periphery, will be met by force?

3. What foreign programs are best suited to support effectively economic development in underdeveloped countries in a manner which convinces these countries that they will remain masters of their own destinies?

4. How can we make the world understand that we are developing an economic system suitable to meet the material and nonmaterial requirements of our age and still recognize that other countries may need institutions and policies different from our own?

1. INTRODUCTION: THE MEANING OF "ECONOMIC THREAT"

Classical economics suggested, and the 19th century experience by and large confirmed, the view that economic gains in one country bring economic advantages also to other countries. This theory and experience were in contrast with the views and historical facts of the earlier period of mercantilism when the ascendancy of one empire usually was associated with the decline of another

However, even in the 19th and 20th centuries economic power has often continued to be used as an instrument of political power, as when economic penetration served as a first phase of colonial domination. To that extent, economic growth may have involved conflicts among various national interests. Also, industrial development in one country often forced other countries to make painful readjustments in their own production and trade. Nevertheless, on balance it is still true today that a nation can gain more by economic prosperity in other nations than by their economic stagnation or deterioration.

This applies clearly to the economic relationships among the nations of the free world. But does it apply also to the relationships between the nations of the free world and the Soviet bloc?

The subject of these hearings could be interpreted as suggesting that economic development of the countries under Soviet rule in itself presents a threat to the non-Soviet world. This is not a necessary interpretation of the Soviet economic threat. On humanitarian grounds, an increase in the welfare of people anywhere would be welcome. Furthermore, domestic misery rarely has made a country easier to deal with. On the contrary, it must be our hope that a rising standard of living and growing economic maturity in the Soviet world will force its political leaders to change their attitudes and convert peaceful coexistence from a slogan to a reality. This, in turn, would also make it possible for the West to relax its defense effort and to devote a larger share of growing production to peaceful purposes.

Economic development in the Soviet bloc is a direct threat to the West to the extent that growing economic strength is used not for raising the standard of living and the welfare of the people but as support of an aggressive military and economic policy. It is an indirect threat to the extent that steady growth might appear to the underdeveloped countries as a predominant feature of the Communist system.

For appraising the free world's and particularly the U.S. political and economic defenses vis-a-vis the Communist threat, it is essential to have an evaluation of the Soviet bloc's probable economic development and of the likelihood that growing economic strength may be used in support of an aggressive military and economic policy. This paper will not deal with the full breadth of that problem. It will give a picture of Soviet economic development in the recent past and the outlook for the coming decade and discuss the relative economic capabilities of the Soviet Union and the United States. It will survey some of the uses which the Soviet Union has made of its growing economic strength for what has been called the "economic offensive." Finally, a few comments will be made evaluating the Soviet economic threat on the basis of these experiences of the past and raising some questions with respect to our own policy. In line with the subject of the hearings, the report will concentrate on the Soviet-United States relationship, with only occasional references to other Communist countries and the Soviet bloc and the free world as a whole.

2. SOVIET-UNITED STATES ECONOMIC STRENGTH

Comparative growth and coexistence

The very brashness with which Khrushchev and other Soviet leaders herald Soviet economic plans and attainments is perhaps sufficient to invite a healthy dose of skepticism. Economic pronouncements, no less than military claims, are clothed in threat and intimidation. In the past few years, however, it has become increasingly clear that loud claims, no matter how embellished by propaganda, have not been without demonstrable accomplishments. A broad range of achievements—from sputniks to economic activities in underdeveloped countries—attests to the resourcefulness and imagination of the Soviet Union. These events have understandably stirred the West into reassessing the adequacy of its own long-range policies.

In the economic field such reassessment has particular significance since it is in competitive coexistence of economic systems that the

Soviet Union has thrown down a major challenge to the West. An understanding of this challenge—if, indeed, it is only a challenge and not a threat—is basic to policy formulation designed to meet it. Accordingly, Western economists have, in the past few years, intensified their researches on Soviet bloc economic performance.

The reliability of Soviet statistics

By and large, such studies have benefited, in the period since Stalin's death, from a lessened degree of statistical exaggeration, though the very shift from a higher to a lower amount of statistical manipulation impairs historical economic comparisons. Alec Nove, in his study for the National Planning Association,[2] discusses reliability for three groups of Soviet economic statistics: (*a*) Industrial output statistics in physical terms, which, to the extent reported, he finds fairly reliable and for whose interpretation he advises "care rather than incredulity"; (*b*) agricultural statistics which are somewhat less reliable for a number of reasons—poor sampling, unreported home consumption, and the political importance of agriculture for Khrushchev's power status; and (*c*) indexes of industrial output and national income, which are regarded as least reliable for a variety of computational reasons, through here, too, current reporting is by no means pure invention, and while "firmly rejecting propagandist exploitation of unacceptable claims," we are asked not to "fall into the opposite error of ignoring current 'aggregate' claims entirely."

Unfortunately, it is precisely a long-term aggregative measure—item (*c*) above—which is necessarily for the construction of historical growth rates. Since Western scholars have necessarily had to construct such series from very scattered evidence and often by inference and personal judgment, it would be highly improbable to find complete unanimity in Western attempt to delineating Soviet rates of growth. Yet the vocal and frequently conflicting claims of different "schools of thought" should not obscure for us broad areas of agreement and reasonable deductions.

Soviet economic performance: Present, past and the outlook for 1959–65

The Soviet 7-year (1959–65) plan, adopted by the 21st Communist Party Congress early in 1959, calls for the following average annual rates of growth:

	Percent
Industrial production	8. 8
National income	7. 2

To judge the degree of realism in these objectives, it is necessary to relate them to some sort of historical trend line, one that takes in a period of at least some stability. Recounting the vast internal upheavals of the first several decades of Soviet power and wartime chaos, Alev Nove, in his NPA study cited earlier, writes:

> At the cost of stirring up some criticism, it seems not unreasonable to take the period 1951–55, extend it as far as possible to 1958, and base our future appraisal upon it, not by projecting the 1951–58 rate into the future but, rather, using it as a basis for comparison, as a period of relative normality, insofar as this word has any meaning at all.

[2] "Communist Economic Strategy: Soviet Growth and Capabilities," Washington, 1959.

A close examination of various Western analyses and of Soviet claims, which are rejected as being exaggerated by several percentage points, suggests that average annual rates of increase for the period 1951–58 may be cautiously put forth as follows:

	Percent
Industrial production	9½
National income	8 to 9

Does this achievement—if accurately gaged—cast doubt on Soviet plans? The Soviets themselves admit some slowdown. Is their allowance sufficient? Numerous "growth-inducing" factors of the recent past will contribute less in the future: the ruthless concentration on heavy industry—itself the instrument of fast growth—has to be somewhat mitigated; a growing share of output will be required for depreciation of capital; natural resources, while considered abundant, are more remote and will require greater capital investments for utilization; low wartime births will create a labor stringency for some years to come, with resultant need for very large productivity improvement; there is less scope for "borrowing" Western technology. On the other hand, agriculture, while still a weak link in the Soviet economy, will perhaps benefit from the switch "from coercion to incentives," and the Soviet educational effort of the past decade must be expected to bear some fruit. Balancing the pros and cons scarcely allows one to make an intelligent guess as to what real rates of growth will be. Without any attempt at precision, the balance of the evidence suggests the following orders of magnitude in average annual rates of growth:

	Percent
Industrial production	7 to 8
National income	6

It may be convenient to combine the Soviet claims and Western "guesstimates." This is done in table 1.

TABLE 1.—*Soviet growth 1951–58 and planned 1958–65: Claimed and "probable"*

[Average annual percentage rates of increase]

	1951–58		1958–65	
	Claim	"Probable"	Claim	"Probable"
Industrial production	11.9	9½	8.8	7–8
National income	10.1	8–9	7.2	6

Source: Alec Nove, "Communist Economic Strategy: Soviet Growth and Capabilities," Washington: National Planning Association, 1959.

Two observations are, perhaps, relevant: (1) Soviet claims—past and projected—are by no means outlandish compared to the Western "probable" estimates. (2) Even a declining rate of growth will, at the relatively high levels deemed reasonable, often yield impressive increases. This means, for example, that even with Soviet steel capacity equal to one-third that of the United States, a Soviet rate of increase three times as high as ours, will produce annual increments to output as high as those of the United States. The comparison cannot be made for recent years, since annual U.S. steel output has been falling ever since 1954 while that of the U.S.S.R. has risen over

30 percent over the same period. This illustrates, incidentally, the misleading conclusions which can be drawn from a "lag" analysis. Although current Soviet output of a given commodity may represent the U.S. level of 20 years ago, at growth rates considerable higher than ours (for that commodity), or with a rate of utilization greatly exceeding ours, the "catching up" period may be subsantially less than 20 years.

Soviet-U.S. economic comparisons: Aggregate and per capita; past and projected

This leads us into a brief comparison of Soviet economic performance with that of the United States. The preceding paragraphs attempted to throw some light on the Soviet economic record in terms of Soviet statistical concepts. "Industrial production" and "national income" are not comparable to similar terms employed in the West. The Soviet "industrial production" index, for example, is a gross—rather than net—concept which can, though need not necessarily, artificially exaggerate real output by organizational shifts in the economy. The Soviet "national income" concept, in addition to some conceptual difference with U.S. usage, suffers from being reported solely in terms of percentage changes.

In order to portray Soviet economic growth in the more familiar social accounting framework of the Western nations, we shall indicate what the previously cited data signify in terms of U.S. economic growth, expressed in GNP and its components. It should be carefully noted, however, that such a comparison involves even greater statistical hazards than does the unraveling of Soviet data in terms of Soviet concepts. To name only two difficulties, Soviet economists—in accord with Marxist theory—do not include certain services in aggregate production as we do in the West; and it is very difficult to translate Soviet output into dollars using exchange rates which adequately reflect purchasing power equivalents. Nevertheless, the comparison, presented in table 2, signifies the general order of magnitude.

TABLE 2.—*Comparison of United States and Soviet GNP, 1950–70*

	Actual				Projected		Average annual growth rate (percent)	
	1950	1955	1957	1958	1965	1970	1950–57	1957–70
Soviet GNP (billions 1958 dollars)	117	158	179	190	286	378	6.3	6.0
U.S. GNP (billions 1958 dollars)	352	435	452	442	633	790	3.6	4.4
Ratio U.S.S.R.: United States (percent)	33	36	40	43	45	48		
Soviet population (million)	182	198	204	207	233	250	1.6	1.5
U.S. population (million)	152	165	171	174	196	214	1.7	1.6
Soviet GNP per capita (1958 dollars)	643	798	877	918	1,227	1,512	4.5	4.3
U.S. GNP per capital (1958 dollars)	2,316	2,636	2,643	2,540	3,230	3,692	1.9	2.6
Ratio U.S.S.R.: United States (percent)	28	30	33	36	38	41		

Source: U.S. Department of State, "Soviet Economic Growth in the Struggle for the Underdeveloped World," unclassified document, Mar. 11, 1959. Data in this document have been converted from 1957 to 1958 values, and the U.S. GNP data slightly altered onthe basis of recent revisions. Projected Soviet figures are State Department estimates; projected U.S. data represent estimates of the National Planning Association.

The table serves to restore some perspective to United States-Soviet GNP comparisons. Particularly, the figures lend scant support to Khrushchev's boast of Soviet equality in per capita production by 1970. Even equality in total production by 1970 would require, on the one hand, still higher rates of growth for the Soviet economy than those projected in the table, and, on the other, stagnation in the U.S. economy. Yet, little complacency is called for. For example, had our tabulation of recent growth rates taken 1955 and 1958 (instead of 1950 and 1957) as terminal years, the United States would show virtual stagnation in GNP. On the other hand, the rate for Soviet GNP would be high no matter what combination of years had been chosen. And the "erratic nature of capitalist growth," of course, comes in for its share of Communist propaganda.

A similar point can be made for the years ahead. Projected data for U.S. GNP are based on reasonably full utilization of technology and manpower, and a pursuit of policies in support of economic growth. But suppose the actual rates of increase to 1970 averaged out to only about 3 percent. It would mean, should the Soviet Union be able to sustain its rate at about 6 percent, that annual increments to GNP would be as high in the U.S.S.R. by 1970 as in the United States. The impact of compound interest bears reckoning.

Uses of production: U.S.S.R. and United States

Table 2 showed that Soviet GNP, very approximately estimated at 40 percent of U.S. GNP in recent years, can be projected as approaching 50 percent by 1970; and per capita output, recently in the order of 33 percent, is shown as exceeding two-fifths by 1970. These data must be interpreted, however, in the light of the uses to which national productive capacity is put. A very approximate idea of United States versus Soviet expenditures for major components of GNP appears in table 3.

TABLE 3.—*Expenditures on major GNP categories, U.S.S.R. and United States, 1957*

	As percent of GNP		U.S.S.R. as percent of United States
	U.S.S.R.	United States	
Total GNP	100	100	40
Consumption [1]	60	67	25
Investment [1]	25	21	66
Industrial	(21)	(9)	(90)
National security [2]	14	10	56
Government administration	2	2	40

[1] Including private and public.

[2] In addition to being an extremely rough comparison, the national security data should be qualified in a further sense. Shares of national security in GNP tell nothing of the relative destructive power of the resulting output. It is worth noting that (1) if Soviet military output, maintenance, and pay were valued at U.S. prices, the absolute money total of $40,000,000,000 would be about equal to the value of U.S. defense expenditures, and (2) that the Soviet armaments industry is considered to be among the most efficient of all its industries while its military personnel live much more modestly than U.S. soldiers. Consequently, the Soviet military establishment is described by the U.S. State Department as requiring "fewer resources to produce the same destructive power as its American counterpart." Similar conclusions were reached by the President's Committee To Study the U.S. Military Assistance Program (Draper Committee), Final Report, Aug. 17, 1959, p. 15. The Draper report does not give the basis for its estimate.

Source: U.S. Department of State, "United States Versus Soviet Spending for Major GNP Categories," Intelligence Information Brief No. 87 (unclassified), Feb. 24, 1959.

The relatively low ratio of Soviet to U.S. consumption ($525 as opposed to $1,770 on a per capita basis for 1957) brings up the question whether increases in national product necessarily lead to higher living standards. In the early period of Soviet industrialization, substantial increases in total output were accompanied by a drastic fall in personal living standards. The plans of the Soviet leaders do, however, reflect the necessity to devote additional resources for improvements in standards of life. As Alec Nove remarks in his study for the National Planning Association:

> To admit that Communist chiefs are interested in welfare does not, of course, imply any kind of moral approbation. More than one dictator has taken much trouble to clothe, feed, and pay his men, and indeed this is usually best from his points of view. Farmers have been known to feed their animals well, too, without wishing to give them votes.

While centralized control seems effective in putting a brake on meeting the wishes of the people, as they can be expressed in a free-market Western economy, a higher priority than heretofore has now been assigned to an increase in agriculture, housing, and consumer goods production. If these efforts are carried through, some genuine improvement in consumption and housing appears likely.

Soviet consumption, in 1957, is seen to have been markedly lower than U.S. consumption, but investment—particularly in producer economy. The Soviet "national income" concept, in addition to some durables—came much closer to the U.S. total. Still, there is no 1950, and once again, we should note that a continued high share in military expenditures and investment need not rule out a gain in living standards. Even with its neglected relative position in Soviet GNP, substantial increases in total output can carry consumption forward to more respectable levels in the future.

3. ECONOMIC CAPACITY FOR WHAT?

Economic growth of the Soviet Union must be regarded as a threat to the extent that it adds to the economic capacity for increased armaments and for an expanded "economic offensive." If each nation could afford to spend only a certain percentage of total production—and not more—for armaments and other noneconomic purposes, the comparison between present and prospective levels of total production in the Soviet Union and United States would insure a superior U.S. potential. However, before too much comfort is derived from the comparison some important qualifications are needed.

First, the projections of total output for the United States (in table 2), which are based on the NPA's long-range projections, imply a GNP growth rate exceeding 4 percent. This growth rate appears feasible but is likely to be achieved only if government, business, and labor adopt measures in support of a higher rate of growth than that of the last few years.

Second, what may be more significant than the level of total production is the annual increase in total production. The difference in annual increments between the Soviet and the U.S. economy is declining faster than that in production levels of the two countries. Still, with an increase in the United States and U.S.S.R. as projected in our tables, the United States would maintain a considerable margin for years to come.

Third, military capabilities are not adequately measured by only aggregate production, actual or prospective. For instance, the scarcity of manpower in the 18 to 20 age group will pose a serious recruitment problem for the Soviets during the next few years and probably contributed to their efforts to develop manpower-saving technological methods both as weapons and in industrial production.

Fourth, and most important, what counts is not the increase in economic capabilities, irrespective of the method of measurement, as much as the allocation of resources to the satisfaction of consumers' welfare, to economically determined investments, and to political purposes. It was noted in the preceding section that, in spite of the much-lower level of total production, the Soviets devote a much-higher percentage of resources to defense than the United States. The United States certainly could economically support a higher level of expenditures for defense, but U.S. policymakers either believe that the world situation does not require a higher level of defense programs or that the people would not support such higher programs. In any case, the size of the defense effort is not directly related to economic capabilities but to decisions regarding national priorities which guide the allocation of resources. It was noted, in the preceding section, also, that the Soviets, for reason of domestic policy, will probably be impelled to increase the level of consumption. That share is still so low that a very substantial rise in the absolute and relative level of consumption is possible without preventing a simultaneous and substantial further rise in the level of defense expenditures. Thus, the Soviet defense effort certainly can be stepped up also if the leadership should determine that it would be in the Soviet interest. However, on grounds of economic capabilities, the United States could increase its effort even more, given the political determination that it is needed.

4. THE SO-CALLED SOVIET ECONOMIC OFFENSIVE

In recent years, the impression has been created that the Soviet military threat is supplemented by an economic offensive. In this respect three types of activities are prominently observed: The dumping of products on world markets, bulk purchases of commodities, and the extension of financial and tchnical assistance in general. Each of these activities will be briefly touched upon. It is worth noting, however, that frequently—and characteristically—the Communists have managed to coordinate these policies in a functional whole. This is particularly true of the second and third elements, that is, trade and aid.

Dumping of products on world markets

The principal examples are the exports of tin and aluminum sold for sterling in Europe. Nove believes that these sales were most immediately motivated by the Soviet effort to meet a substantial sterling deficit. Nevertheless, the disruptive effects of such forced sales remain no matter what the primary motive. A totalitarian regime always has the power—and a Communist regime also the trade organizations—to engage in such sales whether primarily motivated by economic or political considerations. Therefore, they must be expected to recur, possibly on a growing scale, in the future and measures, designed both to protect the economic defense of Western countries and viability of primary-producing countries, are called for to mitigate the disruptive effects of such sales.

Bulk purchases of products as a political instrument

The best known examples are the purchase of large quantities of cotton in Egypt, fish in Iceland, rice in Burma. Besides these striking instances, in which the political motivation was fairly evident, there are many other cases in which the political and economic elements are more interwoven. Soviet imports from many underdeveloped countries, particularly Latin America, the United Arab Republic, and India have increased rather sharply in recent years. To some extent, this increase in imports is related to domestic Soviet growth; to some extent, it is one aspect of the "aid with trade" program.

Between 1955 and 1958, Soviet gross national product is estimated to have risen about 20 percent, Soviet foreign trade turnover by about 30 percent. Soviet foreign trade is extraordinarily small in relation to gross national product (in the order of 3 percent), much lower than the relatively small proportion in the United States (4 to 5 percent). If trade restrictions in the West are relaxed, some increase in the proportion is likely to occur. However, in the longer run, Soviet trade policy, while somewhat freed from the rigidity of Stalinist isolation, is still very much guidde by autarchic thinking. The new 7-year plan sems to continue this marginal reliance on foreign trade. Even if trade remains the same low proportion of domestic production as heretofore, its relative position in world trade may rise, particularly in those areas where it is pushed.

Actually, the European satellite countries have generally played a greater role than the Soviet Union in foreign trade—always speaking in terms of trade relative to the rise of domestic production. Wszelaki [3] notes that "spectacular Asian journeys of Soviet leaders notwithstanding, it is the east-central European countries which have opened the Afro-Asian non-Communist markets to the Soviet bloc's economic offensive. * * * In 1955 the satellite area outranked the Soviet Union in Afro-Asian trade by about 4 to 1; the ratio in 1957 was still about 6 to 4." Lately, however, imports of the U.S.S.R. from nonindustrial areas have been approaching the level of the European Communist countries.

The complementarity between the U.S.S.R. and other industrialized bloc members and the underdeveloped areas of the world encourages this trade. Jute, raw cotton, wool, hides, fish, and some tropical foodstuffs all find an eager market in the bloc, and Soviet bloc experts of development goods find a ready market in underdeveloped countries. This does not mean that the U.S.S.R. would not wish to import many manufactured goods from the West. But it is severely limited by what it can export in exchange.

However, economic rationality does not govern all Communist trade policies. It has been evident that Communist China, both in her trade relations with Japan, and in her exports to southeast Asia, has used trade as an important political weapon, on balance perhaps to her

[3] "Communist Economic Strategy: The Role of East-Central Europe," Washington, National Planning Association, 1959.

economic detriment.[4] In final perspective, one must therefore assess economic and political factors in conjunction. Nove says: "The expansion of bloc trade with the underdeveloped world carries with it some very obvious political advantages. Certainly the development of economic ties gives political opportunities. It lessens dependence of these countries on the West, it has psychological-political consequences desirable from the Soviet point of view. This is particularly to the Soviet advantage if a given country has run into trouble with the West—as for instance was the case with Egypt and Iceland."

Soviet aid-with-trade programs

Total Soviet bloc economic credits and grants to underdeveloped countries, between June 30, 1954 and June 30, 1959, are estimated at $1,853 million which compares with credits and grants of at least $10 billion extended by the United States. The total number of Soviet technicians deployed on economic projects in underdeveloped countries was about 4,675 in early 1959 compared with about 6,000 from the United States. If the U.S. totals were combined with activities of other Western industrial nations and those of international agencies, the aggregate of free world economic assistance would be far greater than Soviet commitments, which, in any case, lag conspicuously behind actual expenditures. Thus, even though Soviet activities have been stpped up in the last year, the present level is far below that of the Western countries.

There is, however, the impression that the Soviets achieve more for each dollar spent than does the West. Henry Aubrey has dealt with the possible reasons for the apparent success of the Communist aid program in his paper for this committee. His main conclusions point to—

(*a*) Soviet and Chinese concentration of efforts on relatively few countries.

(*b*) Latent suspicions against Western assistance—particularly when linked to the private sector of the economy—that hark back to anticolonial and nationalistic sentiments.

(*c*) The image of aid "with strings" when it comes from the West, even though this identification is often more imagined than real, the product of the very bias mentioned under (*b*) above.

(*d*) The Communist emphasis on big industry, to which, underdeveloped countries, by virtue of their growth ambitions, are very receptive.

(*e*) The Soviet link of aid to trade, of special appeal to countries subject to recurrent difficulties in marketing commodity exports.

(*f*) The Soviet claim to "businesslike" low-interest loans, as opposed to "debasing" charitable grants, "hardship sales" of surplus food, or prohibitive rates of interest from the United States.

The "no strings attached" principle, so fatuously preached by the Soviets, has been violated in some conspicuous cases, such as the unilateral "postponement" of the $285 million credit to Yugoslavia, which the Yugoslav press described as "a purely political attempt to link economic aid with political considerations" and evidence that

---

[4] See H. Michael Sapir, "Japan, China, and the West"; and A. Doak Barnett, "Communist Economic Strategy: The Rise of Mainland China," both Washington: National Planning Association, 1959.

an agreement with the U.S.S.R. "will hold good only to the extent that Belgrade is ideologically acceptable." [5]

5. EVALUATION OF THE FUTURE ECONOMIC THREAT

Reviewing what the Soviets have undertaken in their "economic offensive" one could say that they have, in the pursuit of their foreign trade policies, occasionally arranged their exports and terms of financing in a manner that fits into their foreign policy objectives, namely: an attempt to drive a wedge between the Western countries and countries friendly toward the West; and to forge closer links between other countries and the Soviet orbit. In foreign aid, and particularly technical assistance, the Soviets have, on a smaller scale, initiated policies launched by the West a decade ago. Why should these activities be interpreted as a threat? Certainly the Soviets could step up these activities should they decide that they fit into Communist world strategy. In relation to total production, the outlays for these purposes are insignificant. Moreover, the same policies pursued by any other country might simply be interpreted as indicating that another nation is becoming one of the great world powers; it need hardly be interpreted as a threat for the rest of the world. Soviet bloc activities do appear as a threat only because they must be interpreted as elements in Soviet strategy. It must be assumed that this strategy is still influenced by important aspects of the Marx-Leninist creed.

1. *Capitalist contradictions.*—The capitalistic countries, according to the Marxist creed, cannot solve the problem of internal overproduction which drives them into the armaments race and the exploitation of foreign markets. According to Marx and Lenin, militarism and imperalism are the unavoidable consequence of internal capitalistic contradictions. Thus, Communists will always be suspicious of the foreign policies of countries which they label as capitalistic. They may not necessarily question the personal motivations of Western leaders, but condescendingly regard these leaders as people who are unaware of the forces which will drive them sooner or later into an aggressive policy.

2. *Militant communism.*—The Communist creed is revolutionary. A Communist must believe the Communist system of production is superior to any other social and economic system and that it will in the end prevail on the entire globe. The victory of communism does not, however, simply come about by the collapse of the other systems. Just as a small Bolshevik "elite" first established a dictatorship over the majority of the Russian people, so the Communist minority of nations, representing the "avent-garde" of communism, feels itself bound to assist the historical process by all means available. Thus, the slogan of "competitive coexistence" is incompatible with the Marx-Leninist doctrine even though the strategies of militant communism may be adapted to changing circumstances. With the development of a nuclear statemate, it is likely that the emphasis will shift from all-out war to local "incidents" and to economic warfare

The theory of imminent imperialistic tendencies in capitalism leads the Communists to maintain a strong defense at all times. The exact

[5] Quotation cited by U.S. Department of State, "The Communist Economic Threat," publication 6,777, March 1959, p. 22.

time when history will call on them to perform their midwife services in the birth of communism in one particular country or all over the globe depends on the interpretation of whether circumstances are ripe for the final push. Thus, if an underdeveloped country, with a government now friendly to the West, fails in solving pressing economic and social problems, it may, in the wake of rising discontent and political instability, easily become a fertile ground for Communist agitation and possible "internal" revolution with whatever "outside" assistance may be needed.

In the light of these elements of the Marx-Leninist creed it may appear hopeless that the threat can ever be removed short of total—and suicidal—war. The only ray of hope can be derived from the fact that there have been other powerful movements in history which felt that they had the mission of conquering the world. When these movements realized that their goals were unattainable they gradually adapted themselves to less aggressive objectives.

However, there are not yet clear indications that we are near that situation with respect to the Communist bloc. There are no signs of any compromising, particularly on the side of Communist China, which is still in the unmitigated phase of militant communism.

It must be the aim of Western policy to impress the Communist leaders with the futility of any aggressive move and at the same time express the willingness to deal with them as great powers if they drop their aggressive aims. It is a fact that nations like the U.S.S.R. or China are not merely embodiments to the Marx-Leninist ideology but are also countries beset with the ordinary problems any growing nation has to meet. These problems are determined by history, geography, size, character of population, and economic resources. The essential question is whether the Communist ideology remains the guiding spirit of the Soviet system determining its world strategy or whether this ideology will be gradually relegated to oratorical use, with strategy becoming more comparable to that of any other great power. If the latter becomes the case, international problems do not disappear but they become manageable.

The aggressive Marx-Leninist strategy can be contained only if the Soviet people and their leaders realize that different systems of political, economic, and social structure can be equally or more effective than communism and that these other systems need not resort to aggression in order to postpone their own disintegration. The Soviet leaders would have to be convinced that the rival systems, far from disintegrating, are not "pushovers" but are ready to meet force with force.

At the same time, the spreading of communism to the uncommitted countries can be prevented if the leaders and the people of these countries firmly recognize (1) that the Communist system does not have a monopoly on fast growth and maximization of welfare; (2) that planning is not a monopoly of communism but that there can be developed what we might call "democratic planning"; and (3) that they nevertheless have a free choice in developing their resources in accord with their own needs and in the manner which they believe is most suitable for them.

6. U.S. POLICY QUESTIONS RAISED BY THE SOVIET ECONOMIC THREAT

From the preceding evaluation, it follows that Western strategy must be designed to meet two interrelated challenges, namely (1) the worldwide strategy of communism based on the conviction that sooner or later all countries "must" become communistic, with or without "help" from the Soviet regime; and (2) the fact that the U.S.S.R. has entered the group of great industrial nations. These are formidable issues, and in the present paper we can hardly do them full justice. We have chosen to limit ourselves to some of the questions that these issues raise for U.S. economic policy.

1. From what we have said about the nature of the Soviet economic threat it should be clear that an economic growth race per se would not contribute to meeting the Soviet threat. There is, however, a big difference between engaging in a "gross national product race" and promoting a rate of steady economic growth which would permit meeting the needs of national security and, at the same time, enable desirable increases in the standard of living and pursuit of other economic and social objectives. Such a rate of growth, appropriate in the light of U.S. conditions and objectives, would be less than the current or prospective Soviet rate of growth, but higher than the rate of growth of the U.S. economy in recent years.

Nothing has helped the Soviets in the underdeveloped countries as much as the fact that they can point to their success in industrial development (without, of course, mentioning the sacrifices in human lives and freedom). For the Western countries it is of utmost importance to demonstrate that they are developing an economic system to which the Marxist theory of inevitable decay is not applicable and which promises to eliminate poverty without sacrifice of human dignity and freedom.

Through the incessant emphasis on growth, theirs and others, the Communists, so to say, appropriate for themselves the advocacy of fast growth, while the West may find itself maneuvered into the role of pursuing "go slow" policies, for themselves and the new countries, too. Thus, the Communists identify themselves with a dynamic aspiration bordering on obsession in many new countries, and the West is cast in the role of the aging generation that can no longer grasp, and seems not to care, what to the younger peoples appears to be the most vital need.[6]

It is not necessary to discuss here the policies which could promote a steady rate of economic growth because the Joint Economic Committee is devoting a special study to this crucial task. However, it cannot be emphasized enough that a satisfactory solution of our domestic economic problems would make a most important contribution to our international problem. The relative neglect of policies encouraging higher growth among the Western nations in the past few years was recently commented upon by the U.N. Secretary General when he asked: "Are we not, perhaps, rather inclined to resolve the conflict between stability and growth too exclusively in favor of stability—to

---

[6] This subject receives more elaborate treatment in Henry G. Aubrey's forthcoming summary volume growing out of the National Planning Association's project on the "Economics of Competitive Coexistence."

the detriment of the vigor and dynamism so characteristic of the world economy during the first postwar decade?"[7]

2. It is hard to say what portion of our natural resources has to be devoted to national security and military and economic foreign assistance. But it is important for Americans to recognize that our productive resources are adequate for any requirement needed to meet the Soviet threat. The Soviets, too, must recognize that we can stand an armaments race better than they can, so that it becomes more prudent not to engage in it.

3. It is important that the conviction in underdeveloped and politically noncommitted countries is maintained that they are masters over their own destinies. Technical assistance should give them advice about methods for planning their best use of resources. We should recognize that economic and social policies under conditions of extreme scarcity of capital will be different than those in the United States where we are enjoying relative capital abundance. How far governments must go in supporting economic development should be decided by these countries and their governments. The only "strings" that we should attach to our assistance should be that our support is directed to economically and socially justified and soundly conceived projects.

But assistance to underdeveloped countries implies more than the extension of credits and the recruiting of staff for technical missions. It requires a much greater effort in training a large number of technicians for effective service abroad and orienting some part of our own research effort toward the problems to be met in the underdeveloped countries.

The Soviets have been skillful in exploiting the impression that the United States tries to promote the export of our specific political and economic institutions along with foreign aid. In contrast, the Soviets have attempted to create the impression that their aid is given without political motivation and without any strings attached (except when they canceled credits for political reasons). It requires great tact to let the world know about, and profit from, American experience and yet recognize the different political, social, and economic conditions in other countries which often require different approaches.

In conclusion, the Soviet threat requires two kinds of long-range measures: first, to discourage any offensive move by Soviet knowledge that we are devoting to defense whatever portion of our resources is needed to meet force with force; and second, to conduct a vigorous domestic and foreign economic policy as required by the objectives which we should pursue even in the absence of the Soviet threat—only in a more perfect manner, realizing that every failure on our side will be exploited by the Soviets and turned to their advantage in their long-range strategy.

---

[7] Statement by United Nations Secretary General Dag Hammarskjold before the Economic and Social Council at Geneva, in July 1959.

COMPARISONS OF THE UNITED STATES AND SOVIET ECONOMIES

Papers Submitted by Panelists Appearing
Before the
Subcommittee on Economic Statistics

JOINT ECONOMIC COMMITTEE
CONGRESS OF THE UNITED STATES

PART III

Printed for the use of the Joint Economic Committee

JOINT ECONOMIC COMMITTEE

(Created pursuant to sec. 5(a) of Public Law 304, 79th Cong.)

PAUL H. DOUGLAS, Illinois, *Chairman*
WRIGHT PATMAN, Texas, *Vice Chairman*

SENATE

JOHN SPARKMAN, Alabama
J. W. FULBRIGHT, Arkansas
JOSEPH C. O'MAHONEY, Wyoming
JOHN F. KENNEDY, Massachusetts
PRESCOTT BUSH, Connecticut
JOHN MARSHALL BUTLER, Maryland
JACOB K. JAVITS, New York

HOUSE OF REPRESENTATIVES

RICHARD BOLLING, Missouri
HALE BOGGS, Louisiana
HENRY S. REUSS, Wisconsin
FRANK M. COFFIN, Maine
THOMAS B. CURTIS, Missouri
CLARENCE E. KILBURN, New York
WILLIAM B. WIDNALL, New Jersey

RODERICK H. RILEY, *Executive Director*
JOHN W. LEHMAN, *Clerk*

SUBCOMMITTEE ON ECONOMIC STATISTICS

RICHARD BOLLING, Missouri, *Chairman*

JOHN SPARKMAN, Alabama
J. W. FULBRIGHT, Arkansas
PRESCOTT BUSH, Connecticut
JACOB K. JAVITS, New York

HALE BOGGS, Louisiana
FRANK M. COFFIN, Maine
THOMAS B. CURTIS, Missouri

JOHN W. LEHMAN, *Economist*
JAMES W. KNOWLES, *Economist*

LETTERS OF TRANSMITTAL

NOVEMBER 10, 1959.

Hon. PAUL H. DOUGLAS,
Chairman, Joint Economic Committee,
U.S. Senate, Washington, D.C.

DEAR SENATOR DOUGLAS: Transmitted herewith is part III of a series of papers submitted by the panelists invited to appear before the Subcommittee on Economic Statistics in connection with the subcommittee's current study of "Comparisons of the United States and Soviet Economies." These papers are based on materials released October 2 and October 26 in parts I and II.

This study is being conducted in accordance with instructions from the full committee as announced in the Joint Economic Committee's Report on the 1959 Economic Report of the President. The study grows out of previous work of the Joint Economic Committee during the 83d and 58th Congresses.

It should be recognized, as was stated in the earlier studies, that the problems of making comparisons between any two national economies are exceedingly complex and even more so when those economies are at different stages of development and have different policy objectives. Such limitations are carefully set forth in the papers of the opening panel in part I.

The papers are presented in advance of the subcommittee's hearings in accordance with the Joint Economic Committee's usual practice in order to provide members of the subcommittee and the participating panelists an opportunity to examine thoroughly the analyses and findings in preparation for the discussions at the hearings.

RICHARD BOLLING,
Chairman, Subcommittee on Economic Statistics.

OCTOBER 15, 1959.

NOVEMBER 4, 1959.

Hon. RICHARD BOLLING,
Chairman, Subcommittee on Economic Statistics,
House of Representatives, Washington, D.C.

DEAR REPRESENTATIVE BOLLING: Transmitted herewith is part III of the series of papers submitted by the panelists invited to appear before the Subcommittee on Economic Statistics at the hearings to be held November 16–20.

The first paper in this volume is a continuation of part II since printing complications did not permit it to be included in part II with the rest of the papers from private policymakers.

The following three papers present a summary and analysis of the policy implications of the subject papers published in parts I and II.

Part I contains papers dealing with the subjects of "Problems of Soviet, United States Comparisons," "Population and Labor Force," "Industry," "Transportation," "Agriculture," and "Levels of Living and Incentives in the Soviet and United States Economies." Part II deals with "National Income and Product: A Comparison of Economic Structures, Trends, and Prospects"; "Foreign Economic Activities"; and an "Evaluation of the Russian Economic Threat by Private Policymakers."

The papers are presented as submitted by the panelists without deletions.

John W. Lehman,
Economist, Subcommittee on Economic Statistics.

CONTENTS

EVALUATION OF THE RUSSIAN ECONOMIC THREAT BY PRIVATE POLICYMAKERS (PART II—Continued)

SUMMARY AND POLICY IMPLICATIONS

LIST OF CONTRIBUTORS

PART I

Part II

Part III

EVALUATION OF THE RUSSIAN ECONOMIC THREAT BY PRIVATE POLICYMAKERS (PART II—CONTINUED)

COMPARISONS OF THE UNITED STATES AND SOVIET ECONOMIES

EVALUATION OF THE RUSSIAN ECONOMIC THREAT BY PRIVATE POLICYMAKERS (PART II—CONTINUED)[1]

BASIC DISTINCTIONS BETWEEN THE SOVIET ECONOMY AND AMERICAN ECONOMY

(By Jay Lovestone, Director of International Publications, CIO–AFL, Washington, D.C.)

The economy of a country is much more than a compilation and comparison of production figures. The men and women who work in industry, agriculture, and the services are more important. They are the people behind the figures. The human element is the decisive factor in the economy of every nation.

In the last resort, production is dependent on the material and spiritual well-being of those who work. With the development of industrialization and modern technology, rising living standards, reduction in the hours of work, decent conditions of labor, a voice in the economic process and respect for human dignity, take on decisive importance as the criteria for evaluating an economy.

Toward furthering these ends there exists in the American economy a system of checks and balances—a system of countervailing powers. Within this system, big economic power is checked, regulated and limited by trade unions, farmers' cooperatives, and the State. The enactment of antitrust legislation, establishment of the Securities and Exchange Commission, Federal farm price support, the Wagner Act, minimum wage and other labor legislation dealing with the rights and prerogatives of labor, social security provisions, and the graduated income tax symbolize the role of the State in the American economy.

In view of these facts, the conception of American capitalism expounded by Khrushchev during his recent sojourn in our country, does not correspond with reality. In fact, the very characteristics he attributes to the American economy are inherent features of the Soviet economy. In the economic system of the U.S.S.R., there is a terrific concentration of monopoly power in the hands of a few persons. The Soviet state is solely their instrument. In the Soviet economy, the workers are defenseless and exploited. What they call trade unions in the U.S.S.R. are nothing but lackeys of the Communist Party monopoly State as the sole employer. And the gulf between the social classes is deep.

In the United States, economic progress is becoming more and more synonymous with social progress. The American worker has the

[1] Because of printing complications the following paper could not be included in order in pt. II.

means of striving for, and has been securing an, increasing share of the Nation's wealth.

On the other hand, the Soviet economy serves first and foremost the interests of the Communist dictatorship. At home, the Soviet economy is geared above all else to maintaining and strengthening the power of the Communist Party ruling clique. Abroad, the Soviet economic system is harnessed to aggression, imperialist expansion, and world conquest. The Soviet economy rests on top priority for the development of heavy industry—at the expense of consumer goods industries and agriculture. The Soviet economy is essentially a war economy financed and maintained through intense exploitation of the workers (low wages and speedup), the peasants (compulsory deliveries at low prices) and the consumers (high prices and scarcity of goods).

While there have been changes in the Soviet economy since Stalin's death, these have not been basic. American labor has watched Soviet economic developments with keen and continuous interest. In August 1958, AFL-CIO President George Meany analyzed and evaluated the Soviet and American economies in his study entitled "American and Soviet Economy—Contrast and Comparison." On October 26, 1958, Trud, central organ of the so-called Soviet trade unions, issued a special supplement in which it sought at length to refute this American labor evaluation. In the January 1959 issue of the AFL-CIO Free Trade Union News, Mr. Meany replied to the Trud rebuttal. There soon followed an enraged Trud rejoinder which dripped sulfuric invective and slander.

From the viewpoint of American labor, an understanding of the basic differences between the two countries is most urgent at the present juncture of our country's history. In regard to American labor's attitude toward the economy of our Nation, AFL-CIO President George Meany, in his address of October 17, 1957, before the International Industrial Development Conference, made it clear that:

> American labor believes private enterprise has been and can be a great force for economic and social progress. Nor do we rule out Government intervention, regulation, or enterprise when the people think conditions require it. Private and public enterprise can get along together well in a free society.
>
> While we take the position that labor has a vital interest in the preservation of our free enterprise system, we do not seek to impose American economic forms on any other country * * *. We point to the fact that without benefit of dogmas or cliches, without a political party of our own, we of American labor have steadily reduced the gap between the great productive capacity of our country and the economic capacity (purchasing power) of our working people. We take pride also in the fact that our trade union movement has played a major role in assuring that improvement of the economic conditions of the people should keep pace with * * * industrial development, technical progress, and higher productivity.

The American economy differs from the Soviet in two basic ways: (1) The Soviet economy is virtually a total state economy. Whatever farm cooperatives still remain, own their land only in name. In the U.S.S.R., the state has final and complete authority over every phase and expression of economic life and activity. (2) The Soviet state is controlled and run by a single monolithic political party.

In the U.S.S.R., there exists a political machine with absolute power to determine completely and to direct forcefully the economic and social structure of the country, the way in which its people get their livelihood and may live. This political machine—the Communist

Party—is the residuary of all power—economic, military, social, political, cultural, religious. Regardless of the liberal-sounding phrases which might be used by those who happen to control the Communist Party, at any particular moment, such a society and its economy are totalitarian to their core, antidemocratic.

Unless we keep uppermost in our minds this overriding feature which distinguishes the Communist economy from ours, all comparison and contrast of the two industrial systems would be conducted in a vacuum and would be worthless or even dangerously misleading. Consequently, in judging the trends or the progress of the Soviet economy, we should guard against applying mechanically and arbitrarily the yardsticks or criteria of evaluation we employ in appraising our own economy.

1. SOVIET ECONOMIC AIMS

The Soviet economy is dual in character. It is national. It is, at the same time, Communist and, therefore, worldwide in its overall and ultimate objective. Given this dual character, the aims of Soviet economy are:

1. To speed the building of heavy industry as the base of the country's economic development and strength.
2. To secure the development of heavy industry so as to make the U.S.S.R. ever more independent of countries outside of its area of control.
3. To gear the development of heavy industry to the creation of a gigantic military machine which can aggressively extend and not only defend the Soviet domain.
4. To utilize its technological progress and industrial prowess for the purpose of infiltrating, penetrating, and subverting, especially the industrially underdeveloped lands through trade, outright grants, and technical assistance.
5. To attain such economic progress and strength as will make the Communist system serve as a magnet and model especially for the industrially underdeveloped countries and, thereby, further hasten Moscow's conquest of the world and its remolding on the Soviet pattern.

According to Khrushchev, the "growth of industrial and agricultural production is the battering ram with which we shall smash the capitalist system, enhance the influence of the ideas of Marxism-Leninism, strengthen the Socialist camp and contribute to the victory of the cause of peace throughout the world." In his talk, in January 1957, at a reception in Mao Tse-tung's Embassy in Moscow, the Soviet dictator struck this keynote: "We will, of course, contribute to a certain extent to the more rapid victory of the new by our activities in building socialism and communism in our countries. The force of example is a great force." Even more explosive emphasis on this objective of Soviet economic development was placed by Khrushchev in May 1957 when he boasted that the Soviets would "soon catch up to the U.S. level of per caipta output of meat, milk, and butter; then, we shall have shot a highly powerful torpedo at the underpinnings of capitalism."

The last boast is rather revealing. The United States is, according to Khrushchev, a capitalist country with which he wants his dictatorship to coexist. For years, the United States has far exceeded the Soviet Union in the production and consumption of these and other necessary consumer goods. But the U.S. Government never utilized this overwhelming American economic superiority to "torpedo the underpinnings" of the Soviet system. This Khrushchev threat takes on special import in the light of his repeated expressions of devotion to "peaceful coexistence" with other countries regardless of their social system.

6. To provide its people with at least the minimum consumer goods so that they can sustain life and produce.

7. To further these ends without regard for human cost to the people at home and the rest of the world.

Denial of trade union and other rights of democratic organization to workers and farmers, law wages, speedup, poor housing, famine conditions for millions in rural areas, marked differences in remuneration for various sectors of the productive forces, very heavy taxation (turnover or sales tax), persistent shortages of consumer goods, forced labor, severe punishment for those resisting any economic measure, and militarization of economy as a whole—these are only part of the price paid by the Soviet peoples for the growth of their economy.

For more than 100 years, Socialists of every hue and cry have told the world that what mankind needs most is an economy in which production would be for use. They have emphasized that they seek to establish an economy in which production would be developed planfully and scientifically, for use, and not for private profit or war. According to official Kremlin decree and dogma, the Socialist society has already been established in the U.S.S.R. Inside the Soviet Union, no one would dare to challenge this Kremlin claim, unless he craved disaster. So once powerful a political figure as Molotov, Lenin's associate and Stalin's closest collaborator, was publicly humiliated and severely punished for having used a formulation which did not specify clearly that socialism had already been built and that communism was begining in the U.S.S.R.

Yet, it is precisely in the U.S.S.R., where socialism is allegedly established and the building of communism is proceeding apace that production for use continues to take a back seat. The quantity of consumers' goods and the housing now available are so inadequate and shoddy that Khrushchev has just had to issue a special decree promising improvement. The overwhelming concentration on heavy industry, geared to developing capacity for waging aggressive warfare, has created an imbalance in Soviet economic development and growth. The resulting acute shortage of consumer goods and the low wage scales even in the urban areas are in part confirmed by the fact that about 3 million city folks have, for years, been engaged in the "private subsidiary economy" of owning cattle. Sensing danger in this situation, the Kremlin issued a decree prohibiting—as of October 1, 1959—all residents of large cities, except in some eastern areas, from owning privately such cattle.

The primary purpose of Communist production is not to provide consumer goods, housing and the material base for cultural enrichment. The motivating force of Soviet economy is the strengthening of the Communist dictatorship and its oppressive powers at home and aggressive powers abroad.

2. JUSTIFYING HUMAN COST

Some who defend the forced collectivization of agriculture and rapid heavy industrialization—even at the catastrophic cost entailed in human as well as material resources—seek a historic justification of the economic policy laid down by and carried out under Stalin and now zealously pursued under Khrushchev. They contend that all progress has its cost and that such cost is historically unavoidable. They argue, for example, that in order to have its industrial revolution, Britain had to pay a heavy price in human misery—child labor, long hours, low wages, miserable standards of consumption, and generally degrading standards and conditions of life and labor for the great mass of the people.

Whether Britain had to pay so heavy a human price for the economic achievements of its industrial revolution is debatable. Few would today deny that many avoidable mistakes were made in the advancement of this industrial revolution. However, it must be remembered that Britain was a pioneer in the industrial revolution. It had practically no experience of others on which to draw and from which to benefit.

But, for the U.S.S.R., the situation has been quite different. The Bolsheviks, though seeking to build a new and different type of economy, had considerable experience on which to draw—Russian, British, German, American, French, Japanese among others. It could and did call upon the technical and engineering skills and assistance of the more industrially developed countries. It secured substantial credits from other lands to help its capital development and accumulation.

Last, but not least, the Communist rulers have designated themselves the champions of humanity and enemies of "capitalist inhumanity." Champions of humanity should certainly not resort to dooming to death millions and to sentencing even more to concentration camps and prisons in order to assure speedy collectivization of agriculture and heavy industrialization. The sundry crimes of the "cult of the individual" attributed to Stalin by Khrushchev were largely rooted in the fanatical and ruthless pursuit of this economic program.

What is more, the forced pace of Soviet economic growth—overwhelmingly in heavy industrialization—has, from its very outset, been motivated by and calculated to serve the imperialist expansionist foreign policy of the U.S.S.R. The Soviet economy continues to give secondary and inadequate consideration for the welfare of its own people at home in order to utilize its maximum resources for the pursuit of a policy of cold and hot warfare against other peoples abroad. In this situation, the rate of Soviet economic growth has a sinister import for the American standards of life and labor, for human rights and for world peace. We face a challenge and threat involving not only the two economies, but two ways of life.

Wherein the Threat

The world has now had more than 40 years of the Soviet system and its economy. No matter what fallacies one may see in Communist economics, no matter how utterly inhuman the foundation and practices of the Communist economy may be, no matter what serious weaknesses may have characterized its development, it is a fact that this totalitarian system has been able to develop large scale production.

It is not the rate of Soviet economic growth, or the size of its gross national product, which disturbs American labor or need disturb our country. If India, Britain, Germany, or Japan were now chalking up the achievements claimed or achieved by the Soviet economy, none of us would be really disturbed. Only the nature and aims of the Soviet economy, only the driving purpose behind its rate and volume of growth, provide cause for concern. Here lies the real threat of the Soviet economy. Were its capacities and talents geared primarily to the production of consumer goods and higher living standards for the Soviet peoples, were its nature and overriding international purpose different, there would be no such fears.

American labor seeks to win for itself the highest living standards. We strive and, if need be, strike to secure continuous improvements of our conditions of life and labor under our economy.

On the basis of our experience and the experience of our colleagues in other lands, we have learned that in no country can the workers receive their just share of the national product, fair play, and decent conditions unless they enjoy the fundamental democratic rights of freedom of association and organization—such as the right to organize into free trade unions, to bargain collectively and effectively, and to strike. This means the right to organize and build unions free from control by employers—private, corporate or government—political parties, or any other outside interests or agencies. Under the Soviet system and in its economy, the workingmen and workingwomen are denied this right.

American labor would like to see the workers of all countries—and that includes the workers of the Soviet empire—enjoy human freedom, get higher wages, shorter hours, and increased benefits of modern technology. Our attitude is motivated not only by humanitarian considerations, but also by a measure of enlightened self-interest. Furthermore, the workers of such countries, suffering from low pay and degrading standards of work, turn out goods for the world market at murderously competitive prices. Such low-wage competition tends to undermine our own wage scales and conditions. Furthermore, impoverished hungry nations are not good customers in international trade.

In short, American labor is deeply concerned because of two grave dangers which emanate from the degraded and degrading position which the workers occupy in the Soviet economy. These dangers are the potential competitive menace of the growth of Soviet production based on low pay and poor standards, even on forced labor conditions; and the enhanced power for aggression and war which such exploitation and oppression give to the Communist Party dictatorship.

A Totalitarian State Economy

The dictatorships which have come in the wake of the two World Wars have systematically perverted and distorted the meaning of words which, for years, had a comparatively clear connotation. "Socialism," "communism," "capitalism," "right," and "left," have lost the meaning they once had. It is necessary to keep this in mind, if we are to characterize properly the type of economy under which the Soviet people are now working, and hoping to get more out of life.

The late Rudolf Hilferding was eminently qualified to aid our understanding the nature of the Soviet economy. Hilferding's Das Finanzkapital was utilized extensively by V.I. Lenin in developing his theory of imperialism. This outstanding scholar of the international social-democratic movement also had practical economic experience as Finance Minister under Streseman in 1923. His clash with the former Reichsbank President Hjalmar Schacht had more significants for coming events than realized at the time. Hilferding had to flee Nazi rule and was murdered in a Paris prison by Gestapo agents. These are no mean credentials for anyone called upon to evaluate the nature of the Soviet economy. In his essay on "State Capitalism or Totalitarian State Economy", Hilferding wrote:

> The Marxist sectarian cannot grasp the idea that present-day state power, having achieved independence, is unfolding its enormous strength according to its own laws, subjecting social forces and compelling them to serve its ends for a short or long period of time.
>
> Therefore, neither the Russian nor the totalitarian system in general is determined by the character of the economy. On the contrary, *it is the economy that is determined by the policy of the ruling power and subjected to the aims and purposes of this power. The totalitarian power lives by the economy, but not for the economy.* * * * [Our emphasis.]
>
> *Once subjected to the state, the economy secures the continued existence of this form of government.* * * * [Our emphasis.]
>
> For this reason, the controversy as to whether the economic system of the Soviet Union is "capitalist" or "socialist" seems to me rather pointless. It is neither. It represents a totalitarian state economy, i.e., a system to which the economies of [Nazi] Germany and [Fascist] Italy are drawing closer and closer (Socialist Courier, New York, May 1940).

The nearly two decades which have elapsed since this evaluation was made have confirmed its basic soundness. The latest changes in the administration of the Soviet economy bring into bold relief its totalitarian state character.

Talk about the state withering away with the "building of socialism" is being heard less and less in Soviet ruling circles these days. Instead, there is increasing talk about the state becoming the dominant force in determining the "factors of ideological and moral influence in all spheres of life." We quote:

> *As we approach communism, the role of the Communist Party, which is the directing and guiding force of the Soviet state, the directing nucleus of all the oragnizations of the workers, both communal and state, increases and will continue to increase in the future.* This is due to the fact that in the period of transition from socialism to communism, the factors of ideological and moral influence in all spheres of life become more important and at the same time the factors of the administrative influence become weaker."
>
> (P.S. Romashkin, Moscow University Bulletin (July 1959).) [Our emphasis.]

But according to Lenin, not only the state but also the Communist Party will "wither away" in the Communist society. At the 21st Congress of the C.P.S.U., Khrushchev acknowledged that: "Marxism-Leninism teaches that under communism the state will wither away and the functions of public administration will lose their political character and turn into management of society's affairs directly by the people."

Not only Romashkin but Khrushchev has abandoned this Lenin theory. The Soviet dictator has been stressing that the Communist Party will exist much longer than the state. Khrushchev holds that the Communist Party is needed to build communism. Therefore, he insists that the Communist Party should be strengthened and its role enhanced. According to Khrushchev, the Communist Party will function as the integrating organ of society for a long time after the state has "withered away."

In this spirit, Khrushchev admonished his 21st Congress that: "We cannot oversimplify and conceive of the process of the withering away of the agencies of state as something like the turning of leaves in autumn when the branches are left bare as the leaves fall." He acknowledged that the "withering of the state" would not bring the Soviet people greater democracy which he held up to contempt for "glittering parliamentary oratory," "political deals among the parties," "setting up a flowery screen of 'free elections' behind which capital is omnipotent and the people are actually disenfranchised." He stressed that the Soviet state—particularly its security agencies and armed forces—will be strengthened and not "wither away." And why? Because the U.S.S.R. was threatened by "imperialist attack." This is what Stalin always said.

What is involved in this discussion is no mere quarrel over sterile dogma but the future of mankind.

1. ROLE OF BUREAUCRACY

The growth of Soviet industry has led to a change in the social composition of the U.S.S.R. There has been an increase in the number of workers. The section of the population consisting of managers, technicians, engineers, scientists, and government administrative and industrial experts has likewise grown considerably. The latter constitute a vast bureaucracy enjoying marked social and economic privileges. Since this sector of Soviet society is more educated, better paid and more privileged than the others, some have developed the notion that they are becoming the "new class" of rulers. Some experts have even embraced the notion that this group of bureaucrats will lead Russia toward democratization of the state, liberalization of the economy, and a peaceful international course. Hilferding has shown why such notions have no foundation in reality:

> In reality, the "bureaucracy" is not an independent bearer of power. In accordance with its structure as well as function, it is only an instrument in the hands of the real rulers. It is organized as a hierarchy and subordinated to the commanding power. *It receives but does not give orders.* Any functionary, as Trotsky justly put it, "can be sacrificed by his superior in the hierarchial system in order to decrease any kind of dissatisfaction." And these are the new masters of production, the substitute for the capitalists. Stalin thoroughly exploded this myth when, during the last purges, he ordered shot, among others, thousands of industrial managers.
>
> *It is not the bureaucracy that rules, but he who gives order to the bureaucracy.*
>
> This is the reality which should not be obscured by constructing alleged domination by a "bureaucracy" which is in fact subordinate to the government to the same extent as are the rest of the people. This is true, even though some modest crumbs from the master's table may be doled out to it—without, of course, a guarantee that other crumbs are to follow and at the price of constant danger to their very lives. Their material share does not constitute any important portion of the social product. Nevertheless, the

psychological effect of such a differentiation may be quite considerable. (Socialist Courier, May 1940.) [Our emphasis.]

2. BUREAUCRATIC PLANNING FROM ABOVE

The totalitarian state economy of the U.S.S.R. cannot be understood or judged on the basis of the criteria applied to other economies. Why? Hilferding has very correctly pointed out that:

It is the essence of a totalitarian state that it subjects the economy to its aims. The economy is deprived of its own laws; it becomes a controlled economy. One this control is effected, * * * the character and extent of needs are then determined by the state. * * * [Our emphasis.]

Prices lose their regulating function and become merely means of distribution. The economy, and with it the exponents of economic activity, are more or less subjected to the state, becoming its subordinates. The economy loses the primacy which it held under bourgeois society. * * *

Policy is actually determined by a small circle of those who are in power. It is their interest, their ideas as to what is required to maintain, exploit, and strengthen their own power that determines the policy which they impose as law upon the subordinated economy. (Socialist Courier, May 1940.) [Our emphasis.]

A totalitarian state economy may enjoy certain advantages of centralized direction and capacity for concentrating all-out effort and resources on the attainment of a particular target. But the totalitarian state economy is inevitably ridden with a topheavy bureaucracy and all the evils and shortcomings that this implies. Bureaucratic planning is not as wonderful or efficient as some would like us to believe it is. In fact, bureaucratic planning has hurt the quality of production and impeded economic progress in the Soviet Union.

On June 29, 1959, at the plenary session of the Central Committee of the C.P.S.U., Khrushchev himself gave some examples of bureaucracy at work in the Soviet economy. He showed that, since the fulfillment of the production plans by a factory is measured by tons, then the bigger the tonnage of a factory's output the more it has fulfilled its assignment. To what absurdities this can lead was thus disclosed by Khrushchev when he discussed the production of chandeliers:

It became the tradition to produce not only beautiful chandeliers to adorn the house, but the heaviest possible. This was because the heavier the chandeliers a factory produces, the more it gets, as its output is calculated by the ton. So factories made chandeliers weighing hundreds of pounds and fulfill the plan. But who needs such a plan?

The same problem plagues the furniture industry. According to Khrushchev, the Soviet furniture factories prefer to make "massive armchairs" because these weigh more and their plans are thus fulfilled. However, the Soviet people prefer ordinary chairs and, therefore, seek foreign furniture.

At the same June 1959 session of the Central Committee of the C.P.S.U., Khrushchev made the following criticism:

We have bought several hundreds of millions of rubles worth of chemical and other equipment * * *. During the past 3 years several thousand different machines and instruments have been bought abroad. The plan provides for erecting an installation made of imported equipment at the Novo-Kuibyshev Oil Refinery to supply the Stalinogorsky Plant with raw materials. All the equipment has arrived, but actual construction has not been started * * *. Imported equipment for the Dnepropetrovsk Tire Plant has been lying around since last November. It is already beginning to rust, yet the Committee for Chemistry has not yet finished drawing up the technical blueprints. It is not clear what technical blueprints have to do with it. We bought the plant together with all the equipment.

In 1955–56, cardboard machines bought in Sweden and Finland arrived for the Kotlas Pulp and Paper Mill of the Archangel Economic Council. Yet it is planned to put these machines into operation only in the fourth quarter of 1961.

The prevailing wage system for engineers and technicians does not tend to enhance their interest in developing new production techniques and modernizing the plants. V. T. Zabaluyev, chairman of the Novosibirsk Economic Council put his finger on this situation when he pointed out that the State Labor and Wages Committee of the U.S.S.R. Council of Ministers divides enterprises in different categories on the basis of the number of workers employed. The greater the number of workers it has, the higher is the wage fund received by the enterprise.

However, to be modern and efficient, a factory must turn to automation with its consequent reduction of the number of workers employed. Precisely for this reason, the technical cadres of a given enterprise are afraid to modernize their factory. When they employ fewer workers, they are put into a lower category, their wage fund is cut, and their wages, therefore, lowered.

The aforementioned are typical difficulties inherent in and the consequence of the system of bureaucratic planning from above. Such practices are not merely the isolated mistaken acts of old and rigid individual officials, as Khrushchev would have us believe. The June 1959 plenary session show that the 1957 reorganization plan did not solve this problem. It, therefore, decided to institute stricter control of management by Communist Party Control Commissions. But this is no solution either. Increased party control will only stifle still more personal initiative and criticism and prevent the growth and exercise of personal responsibility and initiative.

This situation cannot be remedied by even the strong Communist Party demands that management and workers assume greater personal responsibility. Personal responsibility is identical with personal initiative. In a totalitarian state where one party controls and directs all life, the development of personal responsibility and individual initiative—especially in the economy—would endanger the entire totalitarian structure. Consequently, even the most earnest steps in the direction of greater economic freedom are very seriously limited in a totalitarian society. The Yugoslav trend toward increased restrictions on the works councils and the latest antiliberal policies for tightening economic controls in Poland confirm this fact.

Recent Changes in Administration of Soviet Economy

Because of the nature of the Soviet dictatorship and its totalitarian state economy, it is often hard to distinguish between fact and fiction in government or party statements. Not infrequently, that which is hailed as an absolute truth at one Communist conclave is branded by the following conference as a total fraud and calculated deception.

A significant example of this application of the strategy of political factionalism to economic policy was cited by AFL-CIO President George Meany when he wrote:

For example, in his address to the plenary meeting of the Central Committee of the Soviet Communist Party on December 15, 1958, Khrushchev admitted that his former intimate friend and leader, his predecessor as Party General Secretary, Malenkov, "deceived the Communist Party and the Soviet people when he told the 19th Party Congress (1952) that the grain harvest in the country had reached 8 billion poods—whereas it actually had been less than * * *."

At the closing session of the Supreme Soviet in August 1953, Malenkov, in his report (for which Khrushchev and all the others in the Kremlin ruling clique voted) boasted before the entire world that "our country is assured of grain." But 6 months later, Russia was in the throes of a grain crisis" (American and Soviet Economy—Contrast and Comparison.)

I. WHAT, WHEN AND WHY

In view of the basic Soviet aims persistently proclaimed and ruthlessly pursued by Lenin, Stalin, and Khrushchev, wishful thinking in regard to the changes that have recently taken place in the Soviet economy would be very dangerous. Exaggeration or underestimation of Soviet economic strength on our part could only lead us to misjudge the direction and misunderstand the social consequences of these changes.

Moscow's shot at the moon, timed at the start of his westward trip, was described by Khrushchev as merely "a pleasant coincidence." Most of us took the Kremlin's moon shot as a rude and not so pleasant, though effectively timed, reminder of Soviet industrial achievements and even superiority in certain technological spheres—especially in the technology of outer space operations. During his recent tour of our country, Khrushchev repeatedly boasted about Soviet technological achievements. Yet, on June 29, 1959, only about 10 weeks before his departure for the United States and Camp David, Khrushchev told a full meeting of the Central Committee of the C.P.S.U. that: "We must wage a determined struggle against waste, slovenliness, and lack of discipline in our enterprises, as well as against absenteeism and loafing." And Aristov—Khrushchev's expert on automation—went even further and said:

> There are roughly 80 steel rolling mills in the plants of the R.F.S.R., of which only 3 are modern ones, while the rest of them—77—are antiquated machines built in the 19th and even in the 18th centuries. Labor productivity in some of them are 20 to 30 times lower than in the modern ones. In some of them, unfortunately, rolling cages are still being used to roll roofing iron according to the old Ural manner * * * which entails heavy physical strain.

This is certainly not the picture of an economy whose overall capacity could be measured or symbolized by sputniks and luniks. Nor is it the model, up-to-date, Soviet economy which Khrushchev, Mikoyan, and Kozlov have shown to prominent tourists in the U.S.S.R. Where is the contradiction? And why? Under the Soviet system, the ruling group, especially the topmost dictator decides which phase of the Soviet economy (or anything else) in the U.S.S.R. should be brought into the foreground of public attention at any particular moment. With Khrushchev, as with other totalitarian dictators (like Mussolini, Hitler, and Stalin), the why and wherefore of what he says at a specific moment, the timing, can be even more significant than its contents. When he thinks it is necessary to impress some prominent foreign visitor or visiting expert—or some country which is industrially underdeveloped—Khrushchev emphasizes the prowess and bright side of the Soviet economy. However, when he finds it necessary to have the Central Committee of the C.P.S.U. approve certain changes in economic policy, Khrushchev turns his attention to the darker side.

2. ALL ROUND EXPANSION OF PARTY CONTROL

On July 2, 1959, Pravda gave the real reason for Khrushchev and Aristov having painted the above gloomy picture. Pravda had the following headline in reporting the most important excerpts of Khrushchev's address of June 29: "All-round expansion of social control concerning the execution of decisions taken." In order to change this gloomy picture, Communist Party control of the industrial, technological, and economic fields was to be greatly extended and intensified. Toward this end, the Central Committee of the C.P.S.U. decided upon a most important change in the administration of the Soviet economy. We quote:

> So as to increase the control over the activities of the administration, the Central Committee of the Communist Party of the Soviet Union has found it advisable to set up at the lowest levels of the party organization (party cells) in the industrial plants, transportation, the building industry, trade, as well as in the planning organizations, design offices, and scientific research institutes, carrying out orders for plants and building projects, committees drawn from members and candidates of the party *for the purpose of establishing controls by the party* organizations over the activties of the administration (Pravda, July 13, 1959).

Why was this sweeping decree issued? What does this decree mean for the Soviet economy? For one thing, the huge growth and the modernization of Soviet industry require some degree of decentralization of the economy. Furthermore, the hopes Khrushchev had placed in 1957 in his production conferences curbing the power of the local and regional economic bureaucracy did not materialize. That is why, at the June 1959 plenary session of the Central Committee of the C.P.S.U., Khrushchev lashed out at the regional economic officials and managers. He charged them with negligence, irresponsibility, bureaucratism, technical conservatism, and selfish local interests.

To overcome such weaknesses, the party was to strengthen its control over the entire Soviet economy by setting up control commissions within the party organizations of enterprises in industry, transportation, construction, and trade as well as design organizations, drafting bureaus, and research institutes. Through its "control committees" at the lowest levels, the Communist Party will have greater control of the managers, manufacturers, engineers, technicians, scientists, and their research institutes and exercise systematic control of the fulfillment of production targets, export orders, quality of products, housing, production costs, transportation, and the introduction of new technological and automation devices.

In addition, "they must look after the observance of state discipline by all enterprise officials and must fight against the appearance of local interest or a narrow departmental approach." Thus, these new commissions have economic and political tasks. They are to be subordinated to the party secretaries in the enterprises and account for all their activities to them. Khrushchev aims to strengthen the authority of the party secretaries in dealing with any manager who may be rebellious. Significantly, the production conferences play no role in this latest reorganization. After only one year of existence, they outlived their usefulness to Khrushchev. Communist Party organs have replaced them. Thus ended one of the best ballyhooed liberalization measures introduced by Khrushchev.

This extension of Communist Party domination over the Soviet economy is a move calculated to enhance the authority and enlarge decisively the power of the Communist Party and the omnipotence of its top leader. The total subordination of the economic and technical experts to the professional party bureaucrats (who owe their privileged position and very existence to Khrushchev and his machine) is not an act of genuine decentralization or liberalization of the Soviet economy.

It is rather significant that this Communist Party move on the economic field comes right after the C.P.S.U. has firmed up its stranglehold on the State Security Services, on the Government bureaucracy (abolition of several ministries), on the Red Army (Zhukov), and on the intellectual and academic arena (educational reform).

3. SOME IMMEDIATE CONSEQUENCES

One of the reasons given by Khrushchev for his decentralization program was that it would increase the responsibility of the local officials. As if to prove the validity of this argument, there soon manifested itself, especially in the border republics, a tendency to have local nationals replace the Russian officials. In some areas, efforts were made to give priority to local needs in the process of fulfilling the State economic plans. But the Kremlin lost no time in denouncing these manifestations as "nationalistic." On July 13, 1959, the very day of the launching of the latest revision of industrial administration, there was reported a serious purge of the Azerbaidjan Communist Party. I. D. Mustafayev was fired as First Party secretary, the party bureau was purged, and a major shake-up hit the top Communist Party and Government officialdom.

The purged comrades were punished for not carrying out the decisions of the 20th and 21st Party Congresses, for having neglected the raising of livestock and cotton—the two principal pillars of agriculture in this Republic, and for the lag in oil production. They were castigated with special severity for their "improper attitude toward the selection, training, and promotion of cadres," "localism," and failure to struggle against sundry manifestations of capitalist ideology—especially in regard to tendencies toward private ownership. The very comrades who took seriously Khrushchev's promise that the decentralization program would permit them more initiative were now accused of local nationalist tendencies leading to lack of regard for "proletarian internationalism" and a wrong attitude toward "the idea of friendship of the peoples of the U.S.S.R."

According to Pravda, August 13, 1959, the Republic Conference on Ideological Questions, called by the Uzbek Communist Party, revealed tendencies toward private ownership, theft of Socialist property, hooliganism, drunkenness, and all else that goes under "survivals of the past." The Tashkent Party Committee secretary, F. Hodzhaev warned the conference that nationalist survivals were especially dangerous in the economic field where "for the sake of local interests, state interests were relegated to oblivion." Taking the cue, the conference emphasized the urgency of the Soviet and Uzbek people choosing cadres on the basis of their technical qualifications and without nationalistic prejudices.

Khrushchev has dispatched many thousands of Russians, skilled Bulgarians, and deported Hungarian craftsmen to Kazakhstan. In recent months, there has been more widespread discontent here than even in Azerbaidjan and Turkmenistan where Moscow had to appoint new security chiefs in September 1959. In the latest issue of the Soviet journal, Kommunist, N. Djandildin, Kazakhstan Party secretary, complains against secret opposition to the Soviet Union's exploitation of this Republic's great natural wealth and against the hostility to the "participation in this matter of representatives of other brotherly republics." Konstantin F. Lunev, deputy chairman of the Soviet State Security Committee, has been rushed to Kazakhstan where he is to take full charge of all security operations. For Khrushchev's political career, Kazakhstan, with the third largest population of the constituent republics of the U.S.S.R. is very vital. It contains many of the virgin lands whose development has been a dramatic and decisive part of the dictator's agricultural program.

Enthusiasm for the Kremlin's "proletarian internationalism" seems to be lagging also in the Baltic republics. In mid-July 1959, the Lithuanian First Party secretary, Antonas Snechkus, found it necessary to pay tribute to the "great historic achievements of the Russian revolutionary proletariat" and to rant against "hostile propaganda from abroad." Recently the Deputy Prime Minister of Latvia, E. K. Berklov, who is also a member of the Latvian Party Presidium, was removed from his high post on the ground that he was opposed to the development of heavy industry.

The objective effect of Moscow's latest industrial program has been to stimulate growing resentment against Russification and all that it implies for the minority nationalities. The above-cited removals reveal more than teething troubles in the childhood stages of "decentralization." Here might well be the seedbed of new difficulties for the Soviet economy as a result of the party taking over direction of economic operations.

Trade Union and Management Control in the U. S. S. R.

At every stage and in every phase of their struggle for power, the Bolsheviks realized the great importance of the trade unions as basic organizations of the working people. It has always been cardinal to the Bolsheviks' doctrine that with their seizure of power, their party was to have complete control of these labor organizations. In pursuit of this unalterable course, the Bolshevik Party line, on the field of labor, has evolved from the militant policy of "workers' control of production" (Lenin, in June 1917) to the present complete control of workers for production.

After much debate, the Tenth Congress of the Soviet Communist Party (March 1921) adopted a resolution offered in the name of Lenin and nine others—"The Platform of the Ten." This resolution laid down the Communist doctrine that the trade unions are to be "auxiliary organs of the proletarian state" and, as such, were "schools for communism." It spelled the doom of free trade unionism under the Soviets and stressed that, ideologically, these labor organizations were to follow the leadership of the Communist Party through the medium of Communist fractions. Moreover, the Communist Party was to supervise all appointments to trade union posts and all union nominations to leading positions in the economic apparatus.

1. ROOTS OF BASIC COMMUNIST POLICY

At the eleventh party conference, December 1921, the final nail was hammered into the coffin of free trade unionism in the Soviet domain. The resolution it adopted set the rules for welding firmly and permanently the domination of these organizations by the Communist Party. We quote:

Taking into consideration the enormous significance of the trade union movement and the danger of opportunist deviations therein without the constant and firm leadership of the party, the conference resolves *to direct to trade union positions of responsibility only experienced party members of long standing, who in the past have not belonged to any other political party.* The *replacement* of leading trade unionists must be carried out with the necessary gradualness and caution. The minimum length of party membership required for an appointment is:—pre-October 1917 membership for chairmen and secretaries of union central committees; 3 years membership for secretaries of provincial trade union councils.

This Leninist resolution has served as the foundation of all Soviet "trade union" policy down through the subsequent years. The "trade union" reforms promulgated under Khrushchev are rooted in the above Leninist policy.

At the time of the February 1917 democratic revolution in Russia, factory and works committees emerged spontaneously and raised the slogan—"workers' control" of management. This slogan was very popular and won them much support. The Bolsheviks hastened to champion and take over this slogan. They soon won control of the factory committees and exploited them for conquering the trade unions which were then under Menshevik leadership. Then, the moment they grabbed all power in Russia and took over the trade unions, the Bolsheviks lost no time in changing the character of the factory and works committees by stripping them of all influence on the administrations of enterprises.

In the twenties, the Communist Party increasingly limited the activities of these committees to the strengthening of labor discipline, and the raising of the workers' productivity. By the end of the twenties, the Soviet "trade unions" branded as heresy any attempt by these committees to defend the interests of the workers in regard to the determination of wage scales and the hiring and firing of workers.

At the plenary session of the Central Council of Trade Unions (July 1933), its secretary, G. D. Weinberg, declared that only the leaders of the economy, administration, and management could determine wages. Otherwise, he insisted, the principle of one-man rule in the enterprises would be endangered and emphasized that:

Too many comrades in the enterprises take the position that trade unions should have as much to say regarding wage questions as management. This is basically wrong * * * This position * * * is a left opportunist's deviation which must be liquidated.

In the thirties, the decline of the "trade unions" proceeded apace. Their overriding objective became the promotion of production. The factory and works committees were likewise geared to the same objective and became rather unpopular with the workers.

During World War II, the factory and works committees occupied themselves mainly with the needs of the workers and their families outside the factories by making available to them homes, canteens, clubs, libraries, health ambulatories, etc. They paid no attention to the job interests of the workers. At best, they took a passive attitude toward wage issues. In the factories, they played more and more the role of agents of management—slave drivers.

There was no immediate change in the situation after Stalin's death. But by 1954, the 11th Congress of the Soviet "Trade Unions" decided that—in order to secure the maximum increase in prouction—the factory and works committees were to concentrate on introducing "progressive, technically justified, production norms." It only emphasized the role of the factory and works committees as auxiliaries of management.

2. TWO MORE DECREES

Two important decrees affecting "trade unions" in the U.S.S.R. were made public in July 1958. These were: (1) the "Rights of factory, works, and local trade union committees" and (2) "Permanent production conferences in industrial enterprises, on construction sites, in Sovchozes, MTS, and RTS." They were hailed as expanding the rights of workers' representatives in the factories, and heralded as vital elements of "industrial democracy." It is important to examine the background of these decrees.

In December 1957, the plenary session of the Central Committee of the C.P.S.U. decided to modify the functions of the factory and works committees. Its resolution on the "Activities of the Trade Unions in the U.S.S.R." again emphasized that the central task of the "trade unions" was the "mobilization of the masses for the struggle for a mighty upswing of all branches of the economy." It also decreed that the fulfillment of this task required the "participation of the workers in the management of production." Toward this end, the functions of the factory and works committees of the "trade unions" were to be expanded.

Henceforth, management was to be permitted to decide on wage questions only "after coordination" with the factory and works committees. The subject of "wage questions" included the revision of the old and the setting of new production norms, wage classifications of workers and salaried employees, job classification in regard to hourly payments, piece rates and bonuses for engineers and technicians. The noted student of Soviet labor, Dr. Solomon M. Schwarz, maintains that "after coordination" does not mean joint decision by management and the factory and works committees. Management continues to make the decisions. The fact that management is to obtain their agreement "after coordination" does not mean that the final decision depends on its securing agreement with the factory and works committees.

The decree further stipulated that works and salaried employees could not be dismissed without the consent of the committees. This represents an enlargement of their rights. The committees were also to deal with the needs of the workers outside the plants. Apartments owned by the enterprises were, henceforth, to be assigned only after a joint decision by management and the committees. Hitherto, management alone exercised this prerogative. These are the two relatively minor concessions made to the "trade unions."

More importance should be attached the provision in the decree that participation by the factory and works committees must be sought in the establishment of production and capital investment plans. The committees had this right previously, but it was mainly on paper. Now management has the duty to report to the committees about the fulfillment of the production plan; the obligations resulting from collective agreements; measures for improving working conditions, and the material and cultural care of workers and salaried employees. The factory and works committees could now call for the elimination of whatever weaknesses these reports disclosed. They could propose to higher organs measures for improving the factory operations and the living and working conditions. Then, these higher organs would examine such proposals and inform the committees about any corrective action to be taken.

Management was under obligation to consult the committees regarding the appointment of personnel to leading positions, but it was not obliged to heed their advice.

Finally, the factory and works committees were to have the right to propose to the appropriate organizations the dismissal or punishment of leading personnel for violating the provisions of the collective agreement or labor legislation. Here too, these appropriate organizations would report their findings to the committees.

The Permanent Production Conference was the new organ created for enabling the committees to carry out their responsibilities. These conferences were to meet only once in several months, but they would have a permanent presidium to work under the guidance of the committees. The production conference was charged with the task of securing the fulfillment and overfullment of the production plan. Management had the duty to eliminate the weaknesses in the work at the plants as disclosed by the production conference and to inform the conference about the situation in the enterprise. The regional economic councils, ministries, and other economic organs were to help the production conferences in their activities.

3. IS KHRUSHCHEV INTRODUCING INDUSTRIAL DEMOCRACY?

Did these decrees signify moves toward industrial democracy? The answer is: No. The much ballyhooed-expansion of the committees' rights is neither extensive nor decisive. The most important issue confronting any organization which calls itself a trade union is wages. Relative to this issue, the decree provides only for "coordination" between committee and management. In case of any dispute or conflict over wages, management has the last word.

And in regard to most of the other labor problems and needs involving improvement of working conditions, the committees have the right only to propose. In respect to the appointment of the leading personnel, management makes the final decision. The old Communist principle of one-man rule in the enterprise is maintained.

In evaluating the importance of these conferences, we must keep in mind that they were set up in connection with the comprehensive industrial reorganization which took place in the summer of 1957. It will be recalled that Moscow had then ordered the dissolution of a number of economic ministries and the transfer of their functions to 105 regional economic councils.

This entire course was dictated by political party interests, no less than economic considerations. In an economic sense, this was a major move to streamline the Soviet economy by decentralizing it and cutting down the power of the bureaucracy. Politically, this was an integral part of the campaign waged by Khrushchev against his rivals in the struggle over who shall succeed Stalin. Malenkov had the support of the economic bureaucracy and this base of his support had to be weakened.

But soon after the new setup was completed, the regional economic councils and the managers of the large enterprises were subjected to charges of "local selfishness", autonomous aspirations, lack of co-operation with other regional councils, and lack of "state discipline." Khrushchev had counted on the production conferences as a means of preventing such deviations and trends toward independence on the part of local and regional economic officials. Through these new organs, Khrushchev had hoped to exercise adequate control of the managers who were, (in consequence of the "decentralization" program), supposed to be removed from direct and strict supervision by Moscow.

In this light, it is clear that the new "rights" conferred on the factory and works committees and the establishment of the production conferences cannot be considered as concessions by the Kremlin to the desires of the Soviet workers for more freedom. These bodies are even more impotent than the Yugoslav works councils. And the latter, contrary to Tito's claims, do not at all assure workers' participation in the management of enterprises.

The Soviet factory and works committees and the production conferences are not at all like the works councils in the free world or the shop committees and shop stewards as we know them in our country. Moreover, when Moscow issued even the anemic decrees of July 1958, it acted to prevent any development toward industrial democracy as we know it or codetermination as practiced in Germany. The Kremlin simultaneously expanded and intensified Communist Party control over all economic organs—including the so-called trade unions.

Much Ado About Very Little

The last 2 years have been a hardening of Communist policies towards the workers in the U.S.S.R. Since 1957, there has been an increasingly strong emphasis on the fulfillment of production plans. There has also been a marked stepping up of "Socialist competition" which has taken the new form of "Brigades of Communist Labor." There are already 60,000 such "Brigades."

To cap it all, Communist Party control is being expanded and intensified on the field of labor and economy in particular.

1. KHRUSHCHEV CONTROL COMPLETE

The 12th Congress of the Soviet "Trade Unions" was held in March 1959. It elected a new central council of 197 members instead of the 174 its predecessor had. But a very high proportion of the former members was not re-elected. Only 36 of the preceding 174 members were re-elected. All the others are new. This sweeping change in the Soviet "Trade Union" leadership reflects and is part of Krushchev's systematic drive to man and control the leading body of all Soviet organizations and authorities. The Kremlin dictator is staffing all such organs with new personnel that is absolutely loyal to him and dependent on him for their future.

In some circles there has been much talk about some insignificant changes made during the last 4 years in respect to the status of the Soviet worker. An examination of the Khrushchev labor reforms relative to the freedom of labor will show how little they mean. A case in point is the decree of April 25, 1956, which was supposed to lift the ban against changing employment and the compulsory shifting of workers from one plan to another. In this connection, Paul Barton, the well-known student of Soviet labor conditions, has pointed out that:

> * * * The freedom to choose and change employment have not, in fact, been restored at all. A worker who leaves his job against the wish of the director runs the risk of being entangled in a whole network of constraint and administrative chicanery, which may finally prevent him from being hired where he wished. The police, from whom, on the presentation of his internal passport, he must obtain permission before every change of residence can forbid him to leave his home. Even if he manages to find work where he lives, he may be threatened by "organized recruitment," a process by which the authorities obtain labor for the sweating industries.
>
> Besides this, he will lose, for 6 months, the right to sick pay and, permanently, his seniority on which depends the extent of various social benefits. A revealing fact is that on March 23, 1956—that is, 1 month before abolition of the ban on change of employment, the Soviet of the city of Moscow passed a special decree to enforce the strict observance of the rules relating to interior passports; a new decree was passed to this effect on April 18, 1958 (Bulletin of the Executive Committee of the Moscow City Soviet of Workers' Deputies, 1958, No. 11).
>
> To be sure, these modifications of the legislation make the workers' lives a litle easier. But at the same time, that is clearly not its aim. This lies in enabling the managers and the authorities to apply restrictions on the wage earners in a more varied, subtle and hence more efficient manner; drastic measures are not always the most effective.
>
> The same applies to all the other changes which have occurred in recent years. There is no question at all of ending the exploitation and servitude imposed on the workers by Stalin; Khrushchev simply wants to eliminate the disorganizing effects which a rigid policy has on industrial relations and even on production.
>
> After all, Stalin himself did as much during the period of spring 1934 to summer 1938; it did not prevent him from crushing the workers again, and more than ever, from December 1938 onward, when he judged that industrial relations were in sufficiently good order (AFL-CIO Free Trade Union News, July 1959).

2. CHANGING THE WAGE SCALES

During the last 4 years, the Soviet Government has been changing the wage scales. Many of these had been in force since before the war; some, even date back to 1932. The new wage scales, though better adapted to the current price level, actually differ little from the old in their structure. Again, Paul Barton has shed welcome light here:

> A very great wage differential is still the basic feature. Thus the new scales applied to the building trade include seven grades of skill; the rates for the seventh grade being 2.8 times higher than those for the first (Soviet Trade Unions 1955, No. 11). For the chemical industry, eight grades have been set up—the highest of which is paid according to a rate 2.6 times, and for certain categories of work (the extraction of and enriching of ores) even 3 times

higher than that of the lowest (Socialist Labour, 1958, No. 2). In the production of slate, four scales with eight grades each have been introduced—with the following coefficients of the eighth: 2.97, 2.56, 2.39 and 2.38 (Socialist Labour, 1958, No. 2). For the oil and gas industry, there are six to seven grades and the coefficient of the highest varies between 2 and 2.6 (Socialist Labour, 1958, No. 7).

Although the reform tends to simply the wage system, the number of rates clearly remains too high * * *.

Furthermore, the working out of the new wage scales is extraordinarily lengthy and the authorities concerned do not seem to have a very clear idea in accordance with what principles they should proceed. Thus, in his speech at the recent National Congress of Trade Unions, the president of the State Commission for Questions of Labor and Wages declared that an effort would, henceforth, be made to reduce somewhat the difference between the lowest and the highest wages. But, at the same time, he asserted that any tendency toward egalitarianism must be rigorously suppressed. On the other hand, he announced that wage scales would, in the future, be set up for individual districts (economic areas) rather than for individual industries (Trud, March 27, 1959). Obviously, such a method is likely only to increase the chaos which already reigns in this field (AFL–CIO Nouvelles du Mouvement Syndicale Libre, August 1959).

3. ANOTHER UNFULFILLED PROMISE

One of the first demands of labor everywhere has been for the shorter workweek. From the human and cultural viewpoint, this has always been desirable. Thanks to modern industry, the shorter workweek is not not only practical but even necessary, economically speaking.

Among the very first decrees of the Soviet dictatorship was the one limiting the workday to 8 hours (October 29, 1917). However, the 12th Soviet Communist Party Congress, held 6 years later, stated that the labor laws regarding the "length of a working day for the various categories of workers" were not really enforced. By October 15, 1927, the Soviet Communist Party Central Committee, headed by Stalin promised a 7-hour day in order to win support in the fight against Trotsky.

But by January 26, 1940, the 8-hour day was officially reestablished because "the strained international situation and the threat of war compelled the Soviet state to abandon temporarily the level of legal guarantees already reached."

The Khrushchev promise for a 7-hour, 5-day week—the shortest in the world—should be judged in the light of similar promises for a shorter workweek made in the past. What is more, this promise, like all the others he has made in regard to labor sharing in the benefits of Soviet industrial progress, is contingent upon an intensified speedup of production; that is, upon intensified exploitation of the worker. In order to have a shorter workday, the workers would have to work much harder to receive the pay they received before. This is confirmed by the U.S.S.R. State Planning Committee's Economics Research Institute which recently declared that—

three-fourths of the total increment of industrial output in the next 7 years will be obtained from increased labor productivity (World Economics and International Relations, June 1959, No. 6, pp. 3–20).

4. CONSUMERS' GOODS—STILL ANOTHER PROMISE

Recently orders have been handed down by the Kremlin to raise the quantity and quality of consumers' goods. The dearth of consumers' goods has reached a point where even Pravda recently had to say:

> We have mastered the sputniks. We have mastered the atomic icebreaker. We have mastered the greatest atomic power stations in the world. Let us now take the trouble to produce a down pillow or a pair of pliers that will draw a nail.

Toward overcoming this terrible situation, there has been proposed a 3-year plan for increasing the production of consumer goods. It is proposed to increase, by 1961, the production of such goods by about 40 percent as compared with the 1958 total of 45,500 million rubles. If fulfilled, this plan would, by the end of 1961, provide every Soviet subject with an additional 97 rubles' worth of consumer goods. Whether the ruble be 10 or 4 to the dollar, this 3-year plan will provide a pitiful addition to the average Soviet subject.

The Soviet budget for 1960 reveals that Khrushchev is intensifying the Kremlin policy of emphasizing heavy industrial development rather than providing consumer goods. Less than 25 percent of the Soviet gross national production goes into consumer goods. In contrast, about 70 percent of our country's gross national product goes into consumer goods and services.

Moscow is able to finance its heavy industrial investment largely through miserably low wages and a very high turnover tax (sales tax) on consumer goods. On the average, present Soviet sales taxes constitute 40 to 50 rubles out of every hundred spent on consumer goods in state stores. More than that. Though Soviet industry has, in the last 5 years, been increasing its production and decreasing its costs, practically none of these benefits has been passed on to the consumer public in the form of lower prices.

From all of this, it is clear that, with all its "reforms" and promises, the Communist economy is based on increasing exploitation of the workers.

Summary

The well-being of the American people urgently requires that our Nation step up the rate of its economic growth. The Soviet threat only makes American economic expansion still more urgent.

Labor, management, the farmers, the scientists and technicians, and our educators should cooperate to foster a higher rate of growth. Wherever necessary, Government aid should be enlisted toward this end. Such a Government role and assistance, in cooperation with the voluntary forces of our national community, can only strengthen our economic system and our free society as a whole.

In the Soviet economy, the rate of growth has been attained more rapidly in gross national output than in increased per capita productivity. Furthermore, in comparison with its rate of increase in gross national product and per capita productivity, the rate of increase in per capita purchasing power has been lagging in the U.S.S.R.

The high rate of Soviet economic growth has also been attained in very great measure at the expense of labor's democratic rights and by denying the Soviet peoples freedom.

American labor is for an expanding economy in freedom. Our Nation has the natural resources, the skilled labor force, the vitality, the seriousness of purpose, and sense of direction to achieve a greater rate of economic growth without being forced into it. AFL–CIO President George Meany has thus summed up the viewpoint of American labor:

> We believe that a higher rate of growth will produce a greater degree of price stability, particularly if the Nation's preoccupation is shifted from the fear of inflation to the need for economic growth. * * *
>
> The AFL–CIO has always indicated a concern over price rises, but has emphasized that growth, not inflation, was the greatest challenge before this Nation. Without growth, we will jeopardize our strength as a Nation both at home and abroad.

In our free society, the trade unions play a vital independent part in the economy of the land. The free trade unions will continue to be the decisive factor in reducing any gap which may develop between increased national productive capacity and the Nation's capacity to repurchase the products for consumption. Without free trade unions, there is always the danger of such a gap developing, especially as a result of an accelerated rate of economic growth. As the primary and decisive force for assuring rising standards of living commensurate with a rising technology, America's free trade unions serve to stabilize and strengthen our economy, and also to spare our economy the inhuman features attendant to the high rate of Soviet economic growth.

Through promoting full employment, production, and purchasing power for millions of Americans who still have inadequate income, housing, education, and health facilities, our country can accelerate its rate of growth.

Through systematically eliminating and abolishing race prejudice, we can end one of the most costly and wasteful ailments afflicting our economy.

Through helping the industrially underdeveloped nations develop their economies and improve their living standards, we can assist in creating a greater area of free world prosperity.

The AFL–CIO has repeatedly urged the holding of a free world economic conference to work out a common program for promoting world prosperity in freedom. Such a common program can strengthen our economy, help its growth and assure its playing an increasingly constructive world role.

American labor believes that a free society can be far more creative and stronger in the economic and in every other field of human endeavor than the most total of all totalitarian societies (communism). Individual freedom and initiative may not be measureable statistically, but they are priceless assets and provide human intellectual resources and capacities far superior to the regimented society.

American labor has never and will never be sparing in its efforts to make our economic system, our free society, far more attractive to the rising new nations of Africa and Asia than any totalitarian state economy and dictatorship.

The reserves of vital forces in our Nation and its economy are enormous. We have nowhere near tapped them. We can and must do so, not only for the sake of our own people, not only for the sake of the entire free world, but also for the sake of the Soviet peoples whose great creative genius can truly serve world peace and social progress once they enjoy democratic rights and live and work in freedom and at peace with all their neighbors and the rest of the nations.

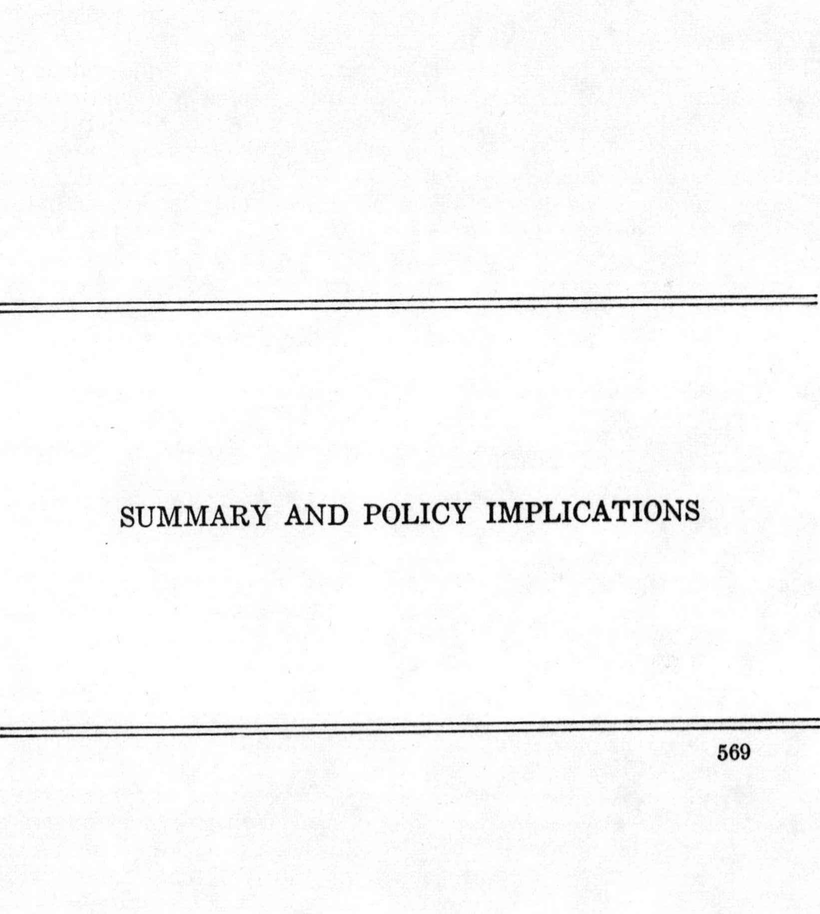

SUMMARY AND POLICY IMPLICATIONS

46283—59—pt. 3——5

SUMMARY AND POLICY IMPLICATIONS

SOVIET ECONOMIC GROWTH AND U.S. POLICY

(By Willard L. Thorp, Merrill Center for Economics, Amherst College, Amherst, Mass.)

THE CHALLENGE

The slogans

"To catch up with and surpass the United States" is an incessant Soviet slogan. Sometimes it is put in rather specific terms, as when Nikita Khrushchev a little more than 2 years ago announced a campaign to overtake the United States in the per capita output of butter, milk, and meat by 1961 at the latest (Johnson and Kahan, p. 220). Or the prediction may be in more general terms, such as "In the next 10 to 12 years we will surpass the United States both in physical production and in production per head of the population while in agriculture this will be accomplished much earlier."[1] Still another declaration made very recently in Vladivostok runs as follows: "The United States produces for the time being more output than we do and has a high standard of living, but the time is not far distant when we shall catch up with and surpass the United States. Soviet people are firmly convinced of this."[2]

These calls for systematic economic competition as the expression of "peaceful coexistence" are not suddenly manufactured for the moment. Communists have always believed that their system would prove to be superior to "capitalism" and that time was all that was required for this superiority to be demonstrated. Khrushchev has transformed "the long-held and prestige-laden Soviet objective of 'catching up with America' * * * into something approaching a national obsession" (Heymann, p. 1). The Soviet emphasis on economic growth is probably of greatest importance for domestic consumption as a continual indication of achievement and of ultimate benefit. To become the richest and most powerful nation in the world is the goal which justifies all present sacrifices.

The slogans may also be important in their effect on the less developed countries. The Soviet Union says, "We were like you, and see where we are now." Its representatives continually point to its success in industrial progress, without of course mentioning the sacrifices in human lives, the compulsions applied to the population, or the relatively slow rate of improvement in the level of living. In areas where economic development has come to be the dominant national objective, the Communist presents himself as representing a demonstrable and successful means to this end (Colm, p. 542).

---

[1] Address by Nikita Khrushchev, National Press Club, Washington, D.C., Sept. 16, 1959.
[2] Thomas P. Whitney, "Crossed Fingers Didn't Nullify Mr. K.'s Threat," the Washington Post, p. E 1, Oct. 18, 1959.

It is hard to see any purpose in presenting this same challenge in the United States, as Khrushchev did so repeatedly. It might be expected that, if any reaction were felt at all, it presumably would be either to disregard the claim as a normal Slavic overstatement, or to take it seriously and set under way an enormous effort to protect our way of life. The fact is that in the United States there is no comparable drive to keep ahead of Russia. To be sure, in special areas the Soviet bogey is produced by one group or another in the effort to stir us to action—in connection with military and space matters, in education, and in foreign aid. But no one is concerned to make sure that our per capita production of butter continues to exceed that of the U.S.S.R. Perhaps Khrushchev regards this as a symbol of catching up with the United States in general, but Americans and Russians may have rather different ambitions concerning the use of butter. Furthermore, the butter comparison will always be inadequate since the United States meets the demand in part by an output of margarine far greater than that of the Soviet Union (Campbell, p. 25). And anyway, if the Soviet Union produced twice the amount of butter per capita as the United States, it would seem to be irrelevant to us and our requirements. In fact, in the United States, butter has been regarded from time to time as a "surplus commodity."

The problem of definition

If the contest is not one of butter production, what is it to cover and what is to be the scoring system? We have gradually developed certain national accounting measures for comparing our own progress over periods of time, gross national product (or national income) and national wealth. They require masses of specific data relating to all kinds of economic activity and a means of aggregating such varying items as the production of sugar, steel, professional baseball games, police protection, and the services of retail stores. Although it will be suggested in a later section that intercountry comparisons of gross national product are virtually meaningless, and there are reasons for being skeptical of such comparisons over time even for the same country, a number of contributors have struggled with the problems of trying to put together comparable measurements of economic growth of such kind.

Over and over they point out that the specific data concerning production and consumption in the Soviet economy, while considerably improved in both quantity and quality in the last few years, still involve important gaps and uncertainties. Secondly, the task of aggregating these separate indicators into total measures is extremely difficult because of the absence of any meaningful price system to use for weighting purposes. Third, the projection of past trends into the future is extremely hazardous. And, fourth, comparisons between the Soviet and American economy really involve an attempt at comparing two quite different economic structures and situations. Much depends upon the system of valuation. If the test was personal prowess, we should have to recognize that the Soviet Union puts out a better team of women's track athletes and usually wins at chess, but there are no Russian stars in golf or tennis. How make an overall comparison with us? Similarly, the Soviet Union is rapidly increasing its production of steel, but obviously has no interest in trying to exceed our output of automobiles in the foreseeable future. What is important in the summation?

Still another problem in any competition is how to score. Are points to be awarded solely for rate of growth without regard to the level of the base or the width of the gap? For example, how score the record for electric power (Vennard, p. 477)?

Millions of kilowatts of capacity

	United States	U.S.S.R.
1957	146.2	48.4
1965	245.0	108.0
Actual increase	98.8	59.6
Percent increase	67.6	123.1

In spite of the substantial percentage increase in the U.S.S.R., it is still further behind at the end of the period than at the beginning. If one is talking of surpassing, then the problem becomes one of estimating rates of growth in the distant future under conditions which are bound to change as a result of developments of the present and immediate future.

Gross national product comparisons

Having all of these difficulties in mind, let us look at a typical calculation of Soviet and American gross national product, even though we may feel that it is the wrong way to score a game which cannot be played (Colm, p. 534):

[1958 dollars]

	Actual		Projected	
	1950	1958	1965	1970
Soviet GNP per capita	643	918	1,227	1,512
U.S. GNP per capita	2,316	2,540	3,230	3,692
Percent Soviet to United States	28	36	38	41

As a first approximation of an answer to the predictions, these figures certainly do not suggest much likelihood for Soviet primacy being achieved in the immediate future. It should be noted that these figures may be somewhat optimistic for the United States, since there is no allowance for any significant periods of interruption of American growth. At a slower rate, it might be that the gap would stop widening in about 1970. There still would be an enormous difference in level to be overcome.

It should be noted that any specific comparisons of rates of past growth of gross national product depend upon the periods under examination, and there are no prolonged "normal" periods. If one compares gross national products in the last few years, say 1955–58, the results are exceedingly favorable to the U.S.S.R., due to its own extraordinary harvest in 1958 and the recession in business activity in the United States at the same time (Bronstein, p. 391). If one takes very long periods, 1870–1913 and 1913–55, the average annual growth rate in Russia in both of them seems to have been only slightly higher than in the United States (Nutter, p. 105). There are various reasons why it is hazardous indeed to project figures like these very far into the future. But there still remain some reasons to suggest why they have very little meaning even for the present.

Reasons for noncomparability

In actual fact, there are several basic reasons why simple statistical comparisons of growth rates in the United States and U.S.S.R. economies are likely to be meaningless, even if one disregards the statistical pitfalls which have been so clearly pointed out by various contributors. (See, for example, Campbell, pp. 13–30; Nutter, p. 95; Gale and Johnson, p. 201; Colm, p. 532.) The first is the different pattern and purpose of the economies. The two economies are producing different things. The planners of the Soviet economy have put their emphasis on the development of basic industries as a basis for military strength and a potential source of an expanded supply of consumer goods. Heavy industry is a necessary power base for the attainment of political-military objectives (Hardt, p. 122). The basic industries in the American economy are growing as a part of a more balanced operation with consumer goods as the center of the development. The Soviet economy therefore has much more uneven growth rates, with less emphasis (until very recently) on housing, clothing, and the more highly nutritive foodstuffs, and yet we might argue that these, should be the chief measures of progress. One ingenious calculation which pictures the basic difference in emphasis gives the following approximations (Bronstein, p. 385):

U.S.S.R. gross national product as percent of United States, 1955

Consumption	28.5
Investment	57.7
Defense	84.3
Government administration	152.3
Total	37.8

In the comparisons, it should be remembered that there is about a 20-percent difference in population, which presumably would influence the consumption figure more than any of the others. Also, consumption covers many items, and Soviet per capita consumption levels are nearer the United States in food and clothing than in durable consumers' goods, housing, and personal services. In the United States, added income is likely to be spent on travel, including the automobile, rather than on added food and clothing (Turgeon, p. 338). Another indication of different treatment of the consumer is shown in the statistics of the use of electricity, where 80 percent in U.S.S.R. goes for industrial purposes as compared with 48 percent in the United States (Vennard, p. 473). In comparing the two economies, one must keep in mind that increases in heavy industry can be done on a massive basis with no problems of variety of items or manifold technologies as in the case of consumer goods. On the other hand, the higher the level of consumer goods, the more luxuries and frivolities are included.

A second difference is the continued existence of a much larger part of the Soviet population on the farm, in spite of the rapid growth of industrial centers. The fluidity of the American population tends to prevent wide gaps in living standards between urban and rural. In Russia the evidence would indicate that there has been little gain in the level of living in the rural area, where slightly more than half the population still lived in 1959 (Kantner, p. 64). The process of shift to the city is likely to be related to a rapid rate of growth, but growth measures fail to indicate how widely the benefits are distributed.

A third difference is in the degree of economic maturity. While economic development clearly is not a uniform process for all countries, the populations in the lesser developed countries are largely engaged in agriculture. As the percentage devoted to agriculture declines, industry moves up; the third stage is the appearance of services as a major economic activity. And at this point, increases in productivity by means of capital additions are not only much more difficult but also not necessarily recorded in national product, for example, improved medical care. This difference in maturity is clearly shown in the following table (Bronstein, p. 383):

Percent of national income by sector of origin, 1955

	U.S.S.R.	United States
Agriculture	27.1	4.6
Industry and construction	36.6	40.7
Transportation and communications	5.0	6.5
Services and trade	31.3	48.2

These figures may underestimate the importance of agriculture in the Soviet GNP because of an inadequate allowance for land rent. A similar contrast between the economies would appear if the labor forces were compared. Figures for the Soviet Union in terms of the percentage of the total population dependent on agricultural occupations are: 1928, 74.8 percent; 1940, 53.7 percent; 1955, 44.1 percent (Eason, p. 89). Growth rates are likely to be higher during the shift from agriculture to industry than in the later stages when services and trade become important.

The fourth difference has to do with services rendered by past accumulations of social capital. Thus, measures of gross national product do not fully reflect the benefits of past savings, be they in the form of thousands of miles of surfaced roads or used automobiles and washing machines still giving service. Even if two individuals or economies have equal current incomes, their actual level of living reflects their accumulations of wealth, much of which is productive or at least provides satisfactions, but is not reflected in the current income record.

A fifth difference has to do with the percentage of the two populations in the labor force. The statistical evidence is exceedingly limited, but estimates made for 1955 put 95 percent of the males and 62.8 percent of the females aged 16 and over in the Soviet labor force (Eason, p. 79). Compared with other countries including the United States, this is very high. In part it reflects the high percentage of the population engaged in agriculture, but it also reflects the industrialization drive, and the fact that women have always comprised an important part of the Russian labor force, even in Czarist days. In comparing countries, it seems clear that the age at which the youth enters the labor force (a function largely of the education system), the treatment of the aged, and the distribution of leisure time all should be part of the consideration.

One other difficulty for any statistical comparison arises directly from the fact that the Soviet Union is a planned economy, and that is the difficulty of relying for weights upon an arbitrary price structure. In a market economy, one has some basis for feeling that values have some relationship to use, that production and consumption have a rather close connection. In a planned economy, the measure is "production" and this corresponds to activity. The digging and refilling of useless holes in the ground might be included in the national product if it were part of the national plan. In such case, the effort to provide an aggregate measure of production is particularly confusing, since the pattern is whatever the planners wish to make it (Nutter, p. 118).

For these and other reasons, the notion of surpassing the United States and the efforts to calculate comparable rates of growth are not very meaningful. Presumably, Khrushchev will feel that this has been achieved when the statistical records of the U.S.S.R. on a per capita basis show higher figures than the United States in the production of some such list of products as oil, coal, electric power, steel, butter, milk, meat, and sugar. But what about neckties, pianos, washing machines, bicycles, electric shavers, cosmetics, picnic plates, cameras, evening dresses, and a thousand other more or less important items which are part of the American national product? And what about the backlogs of several suits of clothes or several pairs of shoes per person and more than one radio per home? Perhaps the widest gap of all is that in housing, where the American standard far exceeds that of the Soviet both in quantity and quality, and where any year's production is only a tiny fraction of the total group of structures inherited from the past. It would appear that the Soviet definition of surpassing the United States is primarily in their terms of certain selected items which are important as basic to the economy, but which certainly do not measure the total achievement of an economy in our terms.

RUSSIA'S ECONOMIC GROWTH

The record of the past

Even though we must regard with great skepticism the efforts to make national comparisons, it is useful to consider what the contributors had to say concerning Russia's own record of development. In general, there seems to be agreement that a rapid rate of growth has been maintained in the industrial sector, that agricultural output has shown little expansion until the last few years, that there are many more urban services, and that great emphasis has been placed upon economic growth at points which would contribute to military strength.

Growth has been most rapid in industries which have contributed to the industrial base, with electric power having very high priority along with metallurgy (ferrous and nonferrous), machine building, and chemicals. Investment in transport facilities seems to have ranked low, though above raising the level of living, including residential and commercial construction. Agriculture has only recently come in as a claimant for much added investment. The emphasis upon structural changes which are related to electrification as the "leading sector" seems to have minimized certain other structural changes common to other countries—the shift from solid to liquid fuel, the shift from ferrous to nonferrous metals for a number of uses, and the rise of service industries (Hardt, p. 126).

A number of elements have contributed to the high rate of expansion in the past. By deliberate plan, consumption has been restricted and economic growth has been given priority. The state has been able to devote a high percentage of the national income to investment in plant and equipment. The basic elements of the rapid growth have been this high rate of investment plus a large expansion in the labor force, made possible by the shift in population from the farm to the industrial centers. These factors have been utilized in accordance with the available Western technology already tested and demonstrated elsewhere. For agriculture, there has been recently a large increase in the sown area, a small increase in the total labor input, and a marked increase in the use of fertilizer (Johnson and Kahan, p. 210; Bornstein, p. 392; Petersen, p. 518).

Prospects for the future

The key problem is of course not so much one of the past as of the future. Can these high rates of growth be expected to continue? Even if one were merely projecting past trends, this would be difficult because of the absence of any moderately long period of undisturbed development. In addition, all the earlier comments about difficulties of comparison come into play. How much will the U.S.S.R. follow the pattern of the United States, or will it develop a different pattern of production and consumption? If, for example, the automobile continues to be deemphasized in the Soviet Union, this may mean that they will depend upon mass transportation facilities, without the same sort of highway development or the garages, filling stations, and traffic policemen required by a country on wheels, not to mention the production of millions of new cars every year. To what other ends will all these resources be put?

A number of contributors have pointed out considerations which may tend to retard the Soviet rate of growth in the future, although there is no suggestion of any sudden or sharp change. First, the large expansion in the industrial labor force which has played such a part in the past will be difficult to maintain, particularly during the next decade. The annual increase in population 16 to 59 years is falling rapidly under the delayed impact on the labor force of the enormous birth deficit of the war, to a point of virtually no change in 1961, after which it increases again but slowly (Kantner, p. 38). This shortage may be met in part by further reducing household and private activities, putting the school population to work, and further urban migration (housing shortages may impede this (Boddy, p. 401)). However, there is not much room for expansion. Compared to other countries, the percentage of the population engaged in economic activity is already very high, being estimated for 1955 at 95 percent of the men and 62.8 percent of the women over 16 years of age (Eason, p. 79). Furthermore, a reduction in the workweek has been promised from 45 to 40 hours by 1962 (Bornstein, p. 393).

For agricultural expansion, the retarding influence may be in terms of land. Much of the increase in agricultural yield in the last several years has come from increasing the crop area, and there now is virtually no additional suitable land. Increased output will therefore depend on increased yields and on the growth of higher cost but more valuable livestock and dairy production (Bornstein, p. 393). In the latter case, the required expansion in feed availability is an enormous task, quite improbable of achievement (Johnson and Kahan, p. 227). The agricultural resources of the Soviet Union are better adapted to the production of food grains than of the feed grains which are essential for meat production (Shuman, p. 497).

Soviet per capita production of meat, poultry, and eggs is far below that of the United States. Not only are the problems of growth in these areas a matter of widespread application of technology, but a supplemental industrial system is necessary to process, package, transport, store, and distribute farm products. The limited amount of milk reaching consumers is an illustration of the fact that facilities are inadequate for refrigeration, transportation, and distribution of perishable products. Forecasts in the agricultural field are difficult to make, but, while some increase in farm output is to be expected, the increases probably will be at a slower rate (Volin, p. 288).

The development in industry has required tremendous investments of capital. It may not be possible to continue such a heavy emphasis upon investment since concessions may have to be made to the demands for greater increases in the level of living. The increase in cultural exchanges may be one source of this demand. Furthermore, investment cannot continue indefinitely to be devoted to basic industries but must go ultimately into the making of final products—if steel capacity keeps on expanding it cannot go entirely into machinery to make machinery. If there is a trend to shift toward consumers goods, and Khrushchev has declared this to be so, it will require capital to go into a much wider variety of uses than in the past, and greatly increase the problem of efficient operation when compared with a simpler input-output pattern.

Even if the rate of investment remains high, some retardation of industrial growth may be expected. The increasing emphasis upon labor-saving, the extension of investment to lower priority uses and locations, and the rapid rise in maintenance and replacement requirements will all tend to employ capital without increases in output at earlier rates. On the other hand, administrative and planning improvements may offset these added costs (Hardt, pp. 138, 140).

This raises the question of technology and what can be expected to happen to productivity, an extremely difficult question. Presumably, labor productivity will rise as capital increases more rapidly than labor force. But even here there may be a sort of diminishing return, particularly as expansion is directed to the consumer goods industries. The programs to increase per capita supplies of food and clothing and added housing space imply a shift in the assignment of investment, with more going to agriculture, light industry, and housing and less to producers' goods and basic industries. While investment may provide as high a return when used in the former as in the latter, it no longer is dedicated to producing more investment goods and thus operating on a compounding basis (Bornstein, p. 393). It is suggested also that shortages may be developing in some lines of high quality basic raw materials, which may, of course, increase real costs (Boddy, p. 401).

As to new technology, there is very little evidence of Soviet innovation except the demonstrations of the sputniks. In the past, the U.S.S.R. has been able to take over much of scientific and engineering discovery at virtually no cost. It seems to be true that important technological developments cannot long be suppressed by any nation. Presumably, with the emphasis upon engineering education, Soviet industry should be able to take advantage of any new industrial developments. However, they started with a huge backlog of unexploited but known technology, and it may be that some of their progress has been in the form of catching up—a process which cannot go on forever. Of course, their own scientists will undoubtedly make contributions which may provide temporary advantages from time to time.

A still added deterrent to growth, in the sense of additions to productive capacity, may come from Soviet policy choices of how much national product to devote to military and space development, how much aid to other countries in the bloc and China, and how much credit to extend to certain of the less developed countries. Any of these purposes, like a shift in concern about Soviet consumers, will direct resources away from use for increasing industrial capacity. On the other hand, it is conceivable that international tensions will lessen and that military requirements might be reduced. Given the threatened labor shortage in the Soviet Union, any reduction in military manpower requirements will not only ease the burden of carrying military establishments in the national budget but would contribute added bodies directly to the labor force.

One may note these various retarding factors, yet certainly one cannot conclude that the rate of Russian economic growth is likely to fall at all sharply. The Soviet system has had certain advantages in the past of available labor, land, and the capacity to maintain a high rate of investment. As it advances, it will face more and more difficult problems of organization and balance. Nevertheless, it seems clear that the Soviet system has not become rigid in structure and procedures, and there is still room for considerably greater productivity and efficiency in its operation. The great emphasis upon education and technical training has not yet had a full opportunity to demonstrate what its significance will be. The apparent success of the recent economic reorganization of the industrial sector of the economy suggests the possibility of further steps from time to time in improving its operation (Boddy, p. 401). It is worthy of note that Soviet economists are beginning to take note of input-output analysis and advanced computer methods for application to problems of planning (Levine, p. 173).

The new 7-year plan does not suggest any major changes from the past. Investment still is to go largely into industry, and mostly into the basic industries. Of the 65 percent of total investment which is to go into industry, the four leading subdivisions are petroleum and natural gas, electric power, chemicals, and ferrous metallurgy. While housing is supposed to get 15 percent of the total, agriculture will get only 8 percent and transportation 6 percent (Hardt, p. 141). For any discussion of U.S. policy, it seems only prudent to assume that the U.S.S.R. will continue her rapid growth, even though there may be a gradual decline in the rate of increase over the years.

THE ECONOMIC SIGNIFICANCE OF SOVIET GROWTH

The requirement of security

For purposes of U.S. policy considerations, then, let us assume that Soviet growth will continue at something like its present rate. This does not mean the "surpassing" of the United States in the foreseeable future according to our criteria, but it does mean a continued rapid increase in industrial capacity and a considerably slower increase in agricultural production. What is the significance of this for the United States?

We believe in economic growth for ourselves and for other countries. The Marshall plan was directed at the reestablishment of Western Europe's productive capacity, and our aid to less developed countries is directed at reducing disease, ignorance, and poverty—objectives which require economic support for their achievement. We are happy to see the advance in productivity and the level of living in France, Germany, Italy, and Japan. We would undoubtedly be unconcerned about Russian progress were it not for the presence of a threat of aggression. But the cold war is a fact, and even hot war comes to the surface in a limited way from time to time. We cannot sit back comfortably in a world which also contains Communist countries whose goal is world domination and whose means are everything which is available.

Economic growth means a greater control over the production of goods and services, a higher potential to use economic resources in any direction. A larger and rapidly growing national product will provide the U.S.S.R. with a greater economic base for military purposes, a possible improvement in the level of living of the Soviet population, resources for further scientific and technical progress, and a higher potential in foreign aid and trade. It would provide a demonstration of the practicality of communism as a way to economic development (Bornstein, p. 395). In what ways can this affect us?

Without any doubt, the area of our greatest concern must be that of security, and to that end we are already maintaining an enormous peacetime military budget. We know that military strength has priority in the Soviet scheme of things. While economic growth increases the size of the military program which is possible, no country in peacetime ever approaches the limit. In fact, expenditures on national defense among countries with comparable resources are much more a function of a sense of urgency and willingness to sacrifice than of rates of economic growth. Our own estimates of defense requirements have varied from time to time with little relationship to our ability to spend (Peterson, p. 520).

Similarly, it is not clear that the Soviet military effort is limited by the capacity of its economy. Everything points to its being given absolute priority, and other demands having to take a poor second place. But the other demands are there and undoubtedly growth does tend to ease the conflicts among claims on the budget. Nevertheless, we probably should assume that the Soviet military threat, in terms of those things which an economy can provide, is already well serviced, and our policies must not assume that there are economic limitations on Soviet military planning. The direct military threat to us will not be greatly increased by further economic progress in the Soviet Union.

U.S.-U.S.S.R. trade

The direct economic contact between the U.S.S.R. and the United States is small and economically unimportant. To be sure, if the United States removed its bans on furs and crabmeat, there might be some increase in trade, but postwar U.S. exports to the Soviet bloc have been extremely small. While some exports to the Soviet bloc are on our list of strategic goods subject to export licensing control, this list is limited and wide areas of trade are unrestricted. Since 1951, U.S. tariff rates have been higher on imports from the bloc than from other countries, but only a small portion of Soviet exports are affected. While the United States used to import manganese and chrome from the U.S.S.R. new sources have been developed during the last decade and there is no reason to expect that this trade would be resumed on any considerable scale.

The strategic trade controls were never as important in their effect on U.S. trade as on the countries of Western Europe, which historically carried on much greater trade with the countries in the Soviet bloc. Probably the controls did delay the Soviet armament effort at the time they were imposed. Their later impact was to cause the bloc to develop its own production of the products which were subject to restriction. Today there is no evidence that trade restrictions are even a pinprick, and it may well be that the countries of Western Europe would gain more through exchanges with the bloc than would the bloc countries—it being assumed that trade would not take place unless both parties benefited. Of course, there are items in which trade should not take place, but any such list is small indeed in these days when technical and engineering information is so readily available. There is much to be said for reducing to the absolute minimum the effort to maintain strategic trade controls. This does not mean, of course, that there is any argument for promoting trade with the U.S.S.R. by such methods as credit extension. Trade with the satellites is a different matter, for there may be good reasons for increasing our economic relations with them, in the hope of encouraging some degree of independence on their part (Allen, p. 420).

Third country trade

The direct impact of Soviet growth on international economic relations will be potentially greatest on third countries through the possible expansion in trade and credits. Since 1953, Communist bloc trade has been rising rapidly, although it still is small compared with the volume of exchanges among free world countries. There are no important products whose trade is dominated by the bloc, although in a few cases, if one considers particular products and particular countries, the bloc may represent a significant proportion of trade (Allen, p. 404). Raw materials, fuels, and grain constitute perhaps 70 percent of the exports, though foreign sales of machinery and equipment are increasing. On the import side, bloc purchases of machinery and equipment are between one-fourth and one-third of imports, the balance being chiefly raw materials. In fact, one of the striking characteristics of Soviet and bloc trade in general is the small proportion of consumer goods which is involved.

To some extent, the Communist drive for self-sufficiency has reduced the need to import raw materials—expanded cotton acreage and the erection of synthetic rubber plants demonstrate this tendency. The 7-year plan schedules substantial increases in imports. Eastern Europe will continue to need raw material and food imports on a large scale. On the other hand, there can be no question but that facility to export has increased. That the Soviet Union can be an exporter of machinery is a definite result of the building up of its own capital goods industries. Furthermore, during the last few years, the U.S.S.R. has moved into an important position as an exporter of grains. Wheat exports have risen to the levels reached during the early years of the century, replacing wheat from the United States and other western suppliers in several free world markets (Shuman, p. 502). Pressure for further industrialization has created a Soviet demand for more highly technical and specialized machinery, even though it may at the same time be exporting simpler types of capital goods. Exports also may expand of wheat, petroleum, aluminum, and possibly tin (Allen, p. 419).

In presenting the 1960 budget to the Supreme Soviet, the Soviet planning chief, Mr. Kosygin, is reported to have told of a planned 25 percent gain in foreign trade, this on top of an earlier report that Soviet foreign trade during the first half of this year was 20 percent above that in the same period of 1958. He particularly mentioned increased oil production as permitting an expansion of exports in that commodity.[3]

While there may be economic motivation underlying the expansion of Soviet trade, it is undoubtedly entwined with political considerations. Centralized control makes trade more readily subject to manipulation. Friends can be rewarded and enemies punished by shifts in the trade pattern. The Soviet Union has demonstrated that it can turn trade on (Iceland, Burma, Egypt) or off (Israel, Yugoslavia, Japan) at the spur of the moment (Aubrey, p. 455).

One can fear this increase in Soviet capabilities as creating a greater capacity to disrupt world markets, as happened recently in the case of tin and a few similar incidents. However, there are not many commodity situations which are very vulnerable. Furthermore, the bloc now looks to trade as an important adjunct to the domestic economy and disruption of markets would not contribute to this goal. Trade is more important for purposes of making friends, becoming respectable, winning favor through good deeds, demonstrating technical capacity and operational skill, and, incidentally, undercutting the leading position of the United States. Economic warfare for political purposes seems to be the exception rather than the rule. (Allen, p. 416; Aubrey, p. 455.) Efforts to use trade to win friends among raw material producers have appeared in the case of fish from Iceland, rice from Burma, cotton from Egypt and Syria, wool and meat from Uruguay and Argentina (Aubrey, p. 465).

The Soviet aid program

The expansion of Soviet trade cannot be discussed properly without including the recent development of long-term credit extension,

[3] Harry Schwartz, "Soviet Spurs Its Exports," New York Times, Oct. 28, 1959, p. 12.

sometimes called aid. Here the problem is primarily that of relations with the lesser developed countries, many of which are politically neutralist, undecided, and unshaped as to their economies. It is clear that the amount of western trade and aid far exceeds that of the Soviet bloc, except in a few areas where the bloc has concentrated its efforts, such as Afghanistan, Indonesia, Iraq, and the United Arab Republic. Whether such aid will greatly expand in the future is difficult to guess. The economic growth of the U.S.S.R. gives it the capability, but there are other demands on the output which may be stronger. Certainly there is no prospect that Soviet bloc aid will come anywhere near equaling in scale that of the free world.

The subject might be dismissed at this point, were is not that there is some evidence that the much smaller Communist trade and aid activities are particularly effective in their psychological-political impact, a short-run reaction quite different from long-run economic benefit (Aubrey, p. 445). Changes which are important to the economic and social fabric of the recipient country are likely not to be spectacular and the results appear so gradually as not to impress the ordinary observer. The Soviets seem to place much more weight that does the West on the process of giving and the effect of conspicuous projects. It hopes to break western alliances and gain political influence by the selective use of small amounts of assistance and a great deal of publicity (Allen, p. 420). There are lavish displays of respect and friendship, exchanges of high level visits, presentations of conspicuous gifts, and efforts to demonstrate how timely and unconditional Soviet aid is.

Another difference appears in the case of technical assistance, where the West is apt to give priority to basic needs like agriculture, health, and education, while Communist bloc experts serve in mineral development, power, transportation, heavy industry, and the like. Bloc assistance in this form has been increasing rapidly. Frequently it is part of a larger package consisting of loans, development goods, and a bilateral trade agreement. The services of experts are not free, but are charged against the loan or separately, at relatively high charges. While the United States contributes in both dollars and manpower to the United Nations expanded program of technical assistance, the participation of the Sino-Soviet bloc in this program is very small (Aubrey, p. 449).

The difference in the aid field are well known. The much larger American program is widely distributed. A considerable part of the program consists of military assistance and defense support—a direct recognition of the cold war and the importance of joint security. The Soviet focus in its aid program is first aimed at knitting together the members of the Soviet bloc and then at winning friends and influencing uncommitted nations. In general, it appears that the Soviet Union has been skillful in creating the impression that the objective of the United States is to export our specific political and economic institutions along with our aid, while they allege that Soviet aid is free from political motivation (Colm, p. 543).

There is considerable room for increasing the actual effectiveness of the American aid program. One illustration of the ineptitude of American policy in action is evidenced in our surplus-disposal legislation. While the bloc has purchased surpluses from time to time from raw material producing countries, the United States is in the fortunate position of possessing surpluses in commodities for which many countries have a shortage. We talk about this program as surplus-disposal rather than aid, and regard the transfer as a sale even though we promptly lend most of the local currency proceeds back to the recipient country for its economic development. Not only is the impression given that aid is being given by the recipient to the United States by ridding it of a burdensome surplus, but the notion of aid is negated by the insistence that the transaction is a sale.

U.S. policy

Neither trade nor aid activities for either the U.S.S.R. or the United States are related in any close degree to our rates of economic growth. They are matters of international policy which are determined on other grounds. If the United States growth rate were higher and the U.S.S.R. growth rate were lower, it is doubtful if this would affect in any way the volume of trade and aid in either country. What is important for U.S. policy is the shift in Soviet policy away from its autarchic orientation to more active participation in international transactions. This may be largely a strictly economic development, but it does open up the possibilities of economic warfare (Peterson, p. 520).

One cannot argue that trade with the Soviet bloc is necessarily a bad thing. In the normal course of trade both parties obtain a benefit. If there are surpluses of certain commodities in the free world which can be exchanged with the bloc for other products for which there is a greater demand, it would seem to be economically desirable. In the best known cases of the Soviet purchases of surpluses—rice from Burma, cotton from Egypt, fish from Iceland—the markets of the free world were clearly less attractive than the Soviet's, whose system and situation permitted it to absorb such products without much thought of profit or loss. Conversely, in the case of Yugoslavia, the problem was to find ways and means to help it break away from its dependence on trade with the Soviet bloc (Aubrey, p. 458).

The real problem arising from trade and credits does not lie in the particular transaction but in the effect upon the independence of the country involved. If the bloc as a purchaser obtains such a preferred position as to be able to use it for political pressures, then the consequences may be serious. The power of the Soviet bloc over those who sell to it will vary inversely with the alternative markets available to the suppliers. The degree of dependence is related to the opportunities on which a country can fall back in case of pressure from the bloc. No country needs to yield to economic pressures from the Soviet if it knows that alternative opportunities will be available either through the operation of the market or through deliberate western policy. This then relates to the degree to which the West provides trade opportunities and healthy markets. From this point of view, the western position is weakened by fluctuations in demand due to recessions, by wide variations in commodity prices, by shifting inventory holdings, and finally, by the lack of any machinery to deal quickly with an emergency in some commodity market. American policy has shown only sporadic interest in the problem of stabilizing markets, but price and volume fluctuations are emerging as a most important matter for many lesser developed countries.

Much the same can be said about the possibility of the bloc using its position as a supplier to disturb the world's markets. Russian exports can create problems; for example, in the case of both petroleum and wheat, the free world's markets are adequately supplied and any substantial additions by the bloc would be disturbing. The basic problem here is not new, and no easy answer for dealing with surpluses has yet been discovered. However, since less developed countries would often be the competitive supplier subjected to any new price squeeze resulting from Soviet exports, the political advantage to the bloc of such actions is not clear. Again, the answer has to lie in bringing more stability into the Western World and in reducing trade barriers. It does not lie in any attempt to isolate the bloc from the world's markets.

Finally, as to Soviet aid (trade based upon credits) again one cannot conclude that this is necessarily undesirable. The lesser developed countries have a great capacity to absorb aid. It does not follow that aid from the United States has no beneficial effect in our behalf while Soviet bloc aid is greatly to its advantage. In fact, given the much greater pressure upon Russian resources for military security and for investment purposes, the extension of credit to foreign countries is a much greater burden than for the West. The problem again is not so much one of the transactions being undesirable as of their ultimate effect in creating dependence of the recipient upon the Soviet bloc.

It seems clear that both the United States and the U.S.S.R. are strong enough so that they can fully support such military requirements and foreign economic policies as they require. The relative rates of economic growth are not the key elements in either of these areas.

In the face of a potentially greater volume of bloc trade and credits, there seems to be no basic reason for any new directions in American foreign economic policy except to give more consideration to the importance of market stabilization. The policies of lowering trade barriers and of cooperating in economic development programs through loans and technical assistance are both basic to the strengthening of the free world and the limiting of dangerous dependence on the bloc. These are programs which were developed in their own right and not as defensive countermeasures. We should certainly wish them to be as efficient and effective as possible, and the Soviet challenge may serve to point up inadequacies which otherwise might not be uncovered. The fact that the Soviet bloc may devote more and more of its resources to trade and aid is no reason for us to become doubtful about our own programs. If we can find ways to strengthen them, we should do so in any event.

THE AMERICAN IMAGE

The images of the United States and U.S.S.R.

What is very important is the image of each country which is created in people's minds throughout the world. The great danger is that the Soviet Union will become associated with growth while the

Western countries will be maneuvered into positions where they seem to be more interested in security and stability. To be sure, the United States has taken the lead in giving actual assistance to the less developed countries, but the representatives of the Soviet Union have talked incessantly of growth. Through their emphasis upon growth and their use of selected figures and soaring charts in speeches, trade fairs, and propaganda generally, the Communists have tended to appropriate to themselves the association with such a purpose. This is further supported by demonstrations of machinery with moving parts which are certain to impress the nonsophisticated audience. Nothing has helped them more in the underdeveloped countries than to point over an over to their own success in industrial development (without describing the human costs, of course) (Colm, p. 542).

It is of course true that the actual comparisons between the rate of growth of the U.S.S.R. and the United States probably will have very little direct impact on the loyalties of individuals in the committed areas. It will not add members to the Communist parties in the free world nor create opposition in the Soviet-Sino world. If any rates of growth are significant, they might be those providing a reasonably direct comparison between countries at more or less the same stage of development—India and China, South and North Korea, West and East Germany. Assuming that the basic statistical data were comparable, probably an impossible assumption, these might have some meaning. The economic growth record in numbers with decimal points of distant countries such as the U.S.S.R. and the United States will seem quite irrelevant to most people, except as meanings are read into them through propaganda channels. They can be impressive as symbols of some broader characteristics (Petersen, p. 522). There might be more sense, for some limited purposes, in comparing the total strength of the Soviet bloc with the combined NATO powers. But even here any measure of economic strength needs very careful definition and it is doubtful if statistical measures will command or repel support. Their greatest use probably would be to arouse people to greater efforts within each country.

Actually, a great many elements contribute to the creation of an image of a country in the minds of people in other countries. So far as the United States and the Soviet Union are concerned, it has been suggested that "the apparent conflict is one of 19th century images rather than of one of modern economic actualities" (Aubrey, p. 454). At any rate, the Communists are ready to appeal to anticolonial and nationalistic sentiments, raising old suspicions of imperialism against the West. Or they stress the false idea that Western aid is loaded with political conditions, that it either is a debasnig charitable gift or a usurious loan, while dealings with the Soviet Union will be "businesslike." Somehow, the West is trying to promote its own specific political and economic institutions while the Communists claim to have no such thought in mind. Woven through all this is the notion of economic growth because that is what the critical countries are interested in. And it is because of the contribution that this makes to the images that our rate of growth and that of the Soviets need to be understood and appraised in their proper settings. We need to consider most carefully all the elements that tend to create unfavorable impressions of us. Some of them need only to be explained; others may represent weaknesses which can and should be corrected.

A sense of purpose

It is possible to carry this problem of images a bit further. Two of our major prophets, Walter Lippmann and George Kennan, have recently given us their reactions to their own images of the two countries. Lippmann said:

The critical weakness of our society is that for the time being our people do not have great purposes which they are united in wanting to achieve. The public mood of the country is defensive, to hold on and to conserve, not to push forward and to create. We talk about ourselves these days as if we were a completed society, one which has achieved its purposes, and has no further great business to transact.

The strength of the Soviet regime, which accounts for its hardness and its toughness and also for its cruelty, is that it is above all else a purposeful society in which all the main energies of the people are directed and dedicated to its purposes. This sense of purpose accounts for the astounding success of the regime in science and in technology both civilian and military. The Soviet nation has its energies and its resources focused on purposes which its rulers define, and all else must make way for the achievement of these purposes.

Thus in our encounter with the Soviet rulers, in the confrontation of the two social orders, the question is whether this country can recover what for the time being it does not have—a sense of great purpose and of high destiny. This is the crucial point. For without a revival of American purpose, Mr. K. is likely to win the competitive race in which he is the challenger.[4]

Kennan said:

If you ask me—as a historian, let us say—whether a country in the state this country is in today: with no highly developed sense of natural purpose, with the overwhelming accent of life on personal comfort and amusement, with a dearth of public services and a surfeit of privately sold gadgetry, with a chaotic transportation system, with its great urban areas being gradually disintegrated by the leading switch to motor transportation, with an educational system where quality has been extensively sacrificed to quantity, and with insufficient social discipline even to keep its major industries functioning without grevious interruptions—if you ask me whether such a country has, over the long run, good chances of competing with a purposeful, serious and disciplined society such as that of the Soviet Union, I must say that the answer is "no".[5]

Both statements are probably too complimentary to the Soviet Union and too harsh on our own society. If the order and discipline in the U.S.S.R. is the result of fear and coercion, the dedication to the leaders' purposes is perhaps not quite so admirable, though it may be frightening. Our national objective has been one of maximizing individual development and this almost by definition does not lead to a specific social objective except that of individual freedom. We have recognized social objectives largely in negative terms—to prevent serious depressions or to provide for our national defense. But in today's world, there are purposes to be achieved and one can question whether we have been sufficiently committed to them. Three of them have been discussed earlier in this paper—the assurance of adequate defense, the strengthening of the international trading system, and the providing of assistance to countries for their economic development programs. In all three cases, there are some fine pages in the record, but too many are blank and some are spotted. Clearly we can do a great deal better in our international relations and many specific suggestions have been presented by the contributors to this series of papers.

Our relations with the less developed countries are particularly important, for these are the "swing" areas. It is all complicated by

---

[4] Walter Lippmann, "Today and Tomorrow," Sept. 17, 1959.
[5] George F. Kennan, address before Woman's National Democratic Club, Oct. 22, 1959.

many crosscurrents of history, prejudice, and the difficulty of adapting our own procedures to new problems. But if we decide that this is a really important matter for the future of the free world and ourselves, we should be able to make the objective of economic development a unifying force in the free world. In such case, the statistics would matter little if the purpose was clearly evident.

One further aspect of Soviet growth needs to be noted—the possible impact of Soviet growth upon the Soviet Union itself. What will be the effects of higher levels of living and expanded education on Soviet motivations and goals? Under such circumstances, will the ambition to bring the rest of the world to communism be strengthened or lessened? It has already been suggested that further economic growth will not greatly enhance the ability of the Soviet to express its hostility toward the West. Perhaps rising living standards may lead to humanizing political and economic changes within the Soviet society, the emergence of a different type of leadership, and a less truculent attitude toward the outside world (Petersen, 523). Speculation along these lines may be of great importance to one seeking optimistically for some ultimate basis for peaceful coexistence, but clearly any such development is a long run away. If the contributors to the series of papers are correct, the goal to surpass the United States will take a long time to achieve, although even the goal may fade in its intensity if there is substantial improvement in the provision of comforts and necessities. The distant hope cannot be given much weight in the consideraton of present policies.

SUMMARY AND POLICY IMPLICATIONS

(By W. W. Rostow, Massachusetts Institute of Technology, Cambridge, Mass.)

AN OVERRIDING CONCLUSION

Let me begin by foreshadowing a major conclusion of this submission.

I believe I speak for virtually all the panelists who addressed themselves to the implications of their analyses for American policy when I say this: Our dangers do not lie primarily in the size of the Soviet economy or its overall rate of growth. Our dangers lie in a particular allocation of Soviet resources; in particular Soviet policies; in the way we Americans now conceive of our problems on the world scene; and, consequently, in the way we allocate our resources, human and material. It will be a grave disservice if the occasion of this distinguished collection of economic analyses obscures this conclusion and perpetuates a somewhat overtechnical and quantitative approach to problems which in the end, come to rest, not in Soviet growth or even in comparative economics, but in American habits of thought and in American polices.

The fate of the United States does not depend on immutable laws of economic growth nor on the curving path of index numbers; it depends upon the actions we Americans take or fail to take; and ultimately it comes to rest on our faith in the democratic process.

Because I believe this to be true, the summary presented below is followed by a statement of policy implications which may appear to transgress the limits of my assigned theme and perhaps, even, the terms of reference of the Joint Committee. But I commend to you this broad interpretation of what we are trying to get at; for I assume we are all concerned here no with a study of the wealth of nations but with the protection of the national interest and the cause of human freedom everywhere.

This paper begins with a brief summary of what the panelists have established; I shall then attempt to place their major findings in a general historical perspective; and, finally, I shall try to identify what appear to me to be the real challenges which lie behind the Soviet statistics and the real implications of this study for American thought, policy, and action.

A SUMMARY OF FINDINGS

Doing some violence to the meticulously stated conclusions of the panelists, the relative position and prospects of the Soviet and American economies may be summarized as follows:

1. Population and working force

Soviet war losses and recent fertility rates set against the rise in the American birth rate have yielded over the past generation a dramatic narrowing in the relative size of the Russian and American populations. Between 1939 and 1959 the Russian margin in population size over the United States decreased from 46 to 18 percent. Although significant shifts in the structure of both populations will occur over the next decade, the gap is not likely to open significantly during this period either for the population as a whole or in those categories most relevant to economic and military activity. With respect to birth rates, there appears to be some stability in the surprisingly high American rate which emerged in the postwar decade, while there are scattered suggestions, at least, that accelerated urbanization and higher living standards may tend to depress somewhat the Soviet rate. In any case, it is important for Americans to realize that the old historic image of Russia—as a nation where the population mass was vastly greater than our own—is no longer correct. We are, roughly speaking, two nations of about the same population size. With respect to the two industrial working forces, there is a similar crude equivalence brought about despite the higher participation of females in Soviet economic activity because of the much higher proportion of the American population in nonagricultural pursuits. In attitudes toward productivity, the Soviet Union has moved away from an earlier concentration on manipulating masses of unskilled labor, in a situation of relative manpower abundance, toward a concern with productivity per man more nearly like that which has historically characterized the United States. This shift is dramatized by the reduction in the role of forced labor in the Soivet economy in recent years, and by the emphasis now placed on mechanization and automation in industry.

2. Agriculture

After a long period of notably sluggish productivity in agriculture, Soviet policy has moved with some success to improve incentives and organization and to increase output of higher grade foods. In addition, a radical increase in the use of commercial fertilizers is apparently now under consideration. Although Soviet productivity per man is likely to remain below the American figures over the next decade (and the Soviet proportion of manpower in agriculture to remain high by American standards) substantial improvements in the productivity of Soviet agriculture and in the food supply are in prospect.

3. Capital

The rate of Soviet gross investment (about 25 percent of GNP) is likely to persist and to remain slightly above the American rate (about 20 percent of GNP including Government investment). Recent changes in investment criteria have probably improved somewhat the efficiency of Soviet investment; and the continued concentration of investment in industrial sectors—as opposed to services, transport, etc.—will probably continue to keep the Soviet rate of increase in GNP higher than the American rate.

4. Transport and power

Transport and power, representing two sectors on which the whole economic structure depend, are useful indexes for comparison. With respect to transport, Russia remains and is likely to remain for the next decade, more heavily dependent than the United States on the intensive use of its railway net. In 1957 less than 40 percent of American intercity traffic moved by rail; the roughly equivalent Soviet figure was 90 percent. Some increase in Soviet road and pipeline transport is planned; but the major technical change appears to be a shift of rail lines to diesel and electric power. Total American freight traffic is about twice the Soviet figure. With respect to energy, both nations are well endowed with resources sufficiently economical to justify only a relatively slow introduction of atomic energy. Both use hydro and steam power in the proportion of about 1 to 4; the United States generated in 1957 about 3½ times as many kilowatt-hours as the U.S.S.R. On the other hand, the United States uses about half its electric power for industrial purposes, the Soviet Union perhaps 80 percent. Technically there appears to be increased emphasis in the U.S.S.R. on thermal rather than hydropower; and the relation of power sources to industrial areas has led to virtuosity in high voltage transmission.

5. Management and incentives

Over the past 30 years the Soviet Union has devised a framework of education and administration, compulsion and incentives which yield men and institutions capable of operating a modern, rapidly growing economy. The working norms and methods of this system differ both from the initial standards of egalitarian communism and from those which have emerged in contemporary American society. Recent efforts have decentralized some areas of Soviet administration, without diminishing the ultimate ability of Moscow to allocate resources. Soviet education for management has typically a higher technological component than the typically more humanistic American general education. Although, to a limited extent, interesting similarities can be noted between Russian and American modes and problems of administration, the Soviet industrialist operates in a setting where his relations to the working force, to the consuming public, to the political process, and to the law are radically different from those of his American counterpart.

6. Industrial output, productivity, national income, and growth rate

Despite enormous difficulties in useful comparative measurement, a high degree of consensus now exists among American experts on the Soviet Union with respect to the overall course and prospects of the Russian economy. In 1955, Soviet industrial output was not more than a third of American, perhaps substantially less; industrial productivity per man, certainly below one-third; and GNP, about 40 percent. Soviet industrial output is likely to continue to increase, despite some factors making for deceleration, at about 8 percent per annum, GNP at about 6 percent. Assuming optimistically a rise of 4.4 percent in the rate of increase of American GNP, the ratio of Soviet to American GNP would rise from its figure of 43 percent in 1958 to 48 percent in 1970, the equivalent per capita figures being

36 and 41 percent. A 3 percent U.S. growth rate would lift Soviet GNP slightly over 50 percent of the American figure by 1970. Given the differences in growth rate this would mean that the Soviet Union would dispose for the first time of a larger annual increment in GNP than the United States, at the end of the coming decade.

7. Standard of living

International comparisons of living standards are the most difficult of all relative measurements. But something like the following appears to be true: Soviet housing standards per family are about a fourth of the American average; food consumption per head somewhat better than one-half; clothing, a bit less than half; medical services, public parks, etc., similar to American standards. In durable consumers' goods and travel, the Soviet standard of living is, as it were, just entering the competition. The prospects for a significant improvement in Soviet food, shelter, and clothing for the next decade are good; and certain types of durable consumers' goods are under rapid expansion. No serious effort is now planned to manufacture and diffuse the automobile on a mass basis; and new housing will remain principally large urban apartment buildings. Except in a few particular categories (e.g., fish, woolen fabrics, and butter) there is little likelihood that Soviet consumption per capita will exceed the American figures, down to 1965. Taken all-in-all, a rise in the Soviet standard of living from something like one-third to about 40 percent of the American level is to be anticipated over the next decade.

8. Military expenditures

When corrected for all the relevant factors, Soviet military expenditures are at about the same level as American outlays; that is to say, the Soviet Government is allocating more than twice the proportion of GNP to military purposes than the American Government.

9. Foreign aid

Although Communist bloc foreign-aid figures in no way measure the scale nor define the nature of the Communist threat in Asia, the Middle East, Africa, and Latin America, Soviet military and economic assistance to underdeveloped areas was about half the level of American assistance in the period 1954–59. In addition, Moscow may have granted important assistance to Communist China over these years, although it is not certain. In 1959, some 4,700 Soviet technicians were engaged on work in the free world, about 75 percent of the number of Americans.

* * * * * * *

THE STAGES OF AMERICAN AND RUSSIAN GROWTH

To make sense of this broad picture, and to pose the questions it raises for American policy, it is important to look far back in the history of the United States and Russia. For in comparing the two countries, we are looking at societies at quite different points in their own evolution. I shall here use, if I may, the concept of stages of growth which I developed last year in some lectures at Cambridge University. This analysis would define societies as falling into the following broad categories: the traditional society; the preconditions for takeoff; the drive to technological maturity; the age of high mass consumption.

The patterns of American and Russian evolution since they underwent the preconditioning for takeoff present both startling similarities and profound and persistent differences. American industrialization took hold seriously in the two decades before the Civil War, although there had been a considerable prior development of modern textile industries, notably in New England. This period of American takeoff centered on the building of a railway net reaching out to the Middle West. This enterprise created a national market and brought to life vigorous modern coal, iron, and heavy engineering industries. In the period after the Civil War, the railway net was thrown out to the Pacific; and from the 1880's down to the first decade of this century, the American economy concentrated on spreading modern technology—rooted in the fabrication of steel—out over the other sectors of the economy. At about 1900, the American economy was technologically mature; that is, the bulk of then existing technology had been applied to our resources. Technological development proceeded, of course, as the new possibilities of electricity, chemicals, and the internal combustion engine unfolded; but Americans turned their minds increasingly to the larger purposes to which this mature establishment should be used.

At about the turn of the century, Americans developed new concepts of their status on the world scene; and in the progressive period they began to soften some of the harshness and to remove some of the inequities which had arisen in the post-Civil War decades, as the economy drove on from the railway age to technological maturity.

But, when the possibilities of technological maturity had been sorted out, Americans, in effect, decided to use their industrial machine to create a new way of life. This way of life was based on the mobility which the mass diffusion of the automobile could afford; on the single family house in the suburbs; and on the ample use of electrical and gas-powered household gadgets, to ease the burdens of the household at a time when it became progressively more difficult to recruit domestic service. This revolutionary change in the American way of life was both permitted by (and it further stimulated) rapid growth in certain important manufacturing industries; notably light engineering, electricity, rubber, oil, and chemicals. The process of diffusion took place in two great periods of expansion: the boom of the 1920's; and the sustained prosperity of the first decade after the Second World War.

During the postwar decade, however, Americans began to behave as if they preferred larger families to an increase in income along the familiar lines. Whatever the underlying human motives involved, it is clear that the rise in the American birth rate and the foreseeable expansion in the American population has become a new central fact in our economy. In addition, as American incomes rose, our people have tended to spend this increase on various kinds of services rather than on manufactured products. Finally, as the great American inner migration proceeded, we have built up vast requirements for social overhead capital: to round out the new suburbs; to reconstruct the old city centers; and to meet the requirements for the enlarging American population.

Russian industrialization took a firm grip some 40 years after the process had begun in the United States—in, say, the 1880's. And the Russian equivalent of the American pre-Civil War takeoff took place in the decades before the First World War. Like the American takeoff, the Russian first phase of industrialization centered about the rapid building of a railway network which, as in the American case, linked agricultural and raw material producing areas to the cities, creating a national market and stimulating modern coal, iron, and heavy engineering sectors. The Russian drive to technological maturity took place, essentially between the end of the 1920's and the 1950's.

In terms of these stages of growth, Russia is now roughly at the level of the United States in the first decade of the 20th century; but it comes to maturity at a different, more advanced level of technology. And Russia, like the United States and nations which have achieved technological maturity, confronts the question, To what larger purposes should its mature establishment be put—to enlarge Russian power on the world scene, to soften the harshness of the drive to maturity, or to enlarge consumption? But before examining the balance that Soviet policy has struck among these three alternatives in the 1950's, let us look back at the principal differences between the evolution of Russian and American growth.

First, Russia faced a far more difficult problem than the United States in preparing itself for industrial growth. It began in the 19th century with a traditional form of autocratic monarchy which, in many ways, obstructed the road to modernization. It faced, as well, intractable problems of land tenure, an illiterate serfdom, overpopulation on the land, the lack of a free-wheeling commercial middle class, a culture which initially placed a low premium on modern productive economic activity. The United States was provided with vigorous, independent landowning farmers, and an ample supply of enterprising men of commerce, as well as a social and political system that took easily to iudustrialization, outside the South. Thus, in order to industrialize, Russia had to overcome the drag of a traditional society, whereas the United States had only to overcome the high attractions of continuing to be a supplier of foodstuffs and raw materials. Contemporary Russian society still bears the marks of this struggle.

Second, throughout this sequence, American consumption per head, at each stage of growth, was higher than in Russia. Basically, this resulted from a more favorable American balance between population and resources; but the tendency was reinforced in both Czarist and Soviet Russia by constraints imposed by the state on the level of mass consumption.

Third, the drive to maturity took place in the United States, after the Civil War, in a setting of relative political freedom in a society tightly linked to the international economy, at a time of peace, and, generally, with rising standards of consumption per head. In Russia it occurred in the three decades after 1928, in a virtually closed economy, against a background of war and preparations for war, which did not slow the spread of technology, but which did limit the rise of consumption; and it occurred with something over 10 million members of the working force regularly in forced labor down to very recent years.

Fourth, the Soviet drive to maturity took place not only with constraints on consumption in general but severe restraints in two major sectors of the economy, not fully represented in indexes of industrial production—agriculture and housing. In housing, the Soviet Union lived substantially off the Czarist capital stock down to recent years, minimizing housing outlays, letting space per family shrink; in agriculture it invested heavily, but within a framework of collectivization that kept productivity pathologically low, once Lenin's N. E. P. was abandoned in 1929. In addition, Russia has invested very little indeed in a modern road system, which has drawn so much American capital.

Thus, the statistical equality in historical pace between Soviet and American industrialization, which Professor Nutter has so well dramatized, has been achieved by a radically higher proportion of Soviet investment in the heavy and metalworking industries than in the United States, imparting a major statistical advantage to Russia in comparison of indexes of industrial growth. And this difference in the pattern of investment was reinforced by the following two further quite real technical factors enjoyed by any latecomer: The ratio of net to gross investment during the industrialization drive was higher in Russia than in the United States, and the pool of unapplied technological possibilities was greater than in the United States. Both of these latter advantages are, essentially, transient; that is, as Russia has come to maturity, it must allocate increased relative proportions of its resources to meet depreciation; and, as it catches up with modern technology over the full range of its resources, it can enjoy, like the United States and the other mature economies, only the annual increment to technology, as it were, rather than a large unapplied backlog.

Nevertheless, as several of your panelists have strongly emphasized, on the eve of the 1960's we must assume that the Russian rate of growth will be higher than the American. This difference stems primarily from the way that Soviet Government has decided since Stalin's death to balance its choice among the three postmaturity alternatives.

Since 1953, the Soviet Union has, to a degree, reduced the harshness of police state rule and cut down on forced labor. To a degree it has increased the level of consumption of the Russian peoples. But its basic decision has been to use the annual increments in production to maintain a very large military establishment and to continue pressing for enlarged power on the world scene. Quite consciously, Soviet policy is postponing the age of the mass automobile and the single family house—the revolution which seized the United States in the 1920's, Western Europe in the 1950's—in order to make a bid for primacy in world power. Technically, this has meant that a much higher proportion of Russian investment than American has continued to go into manufacturing sectors rather than into construction and services. It is this relative concentration of Soviet investment in manufactures—and especially in industry related to military potential, which largely explains the higher Soviet than American rate of growth—now and for the next decade.

In historical terms, the challenge posed for the United States is whether a nation which has gone beyond the age of the automobile and suburbia and is concerning itself with larger families, travel, the refinement and differentiation of consumption, and the various uses of leisure can cope with a nation now arrived at technological maturity, pressing out on the world scene with high ambition, to see how far it can go, even at the expense of postponing the satisfactions (and problems) of the mass automobile and the single family house.

In policy terms, the challenge posed for the United States is symbolized—not defined, but symbolized—by the fact that a nation with less than half our GNP, living at about a third of our standard of welfare, is spending as much on military affairs as we are; putting 75 percent as many technicians and 50 percent as much capital as we are into the non-Communist world, quite aside from its allocations of men and credit within the Communist bloc.

THE MULTIPLE DIMENSIONS OF THE SOVIET CHALLENGE

To understand the real nature of the Soviet challenge—and what the Soviet Government evidently means by "competitive coexistence"—it is necessary now to go beyond economic analysis and consider what Moscow is trying to accomplish.

Although Soviet policy objectives are primarily military, political, and psychological, they are based on an economic fact: the arrival of Russia at technological maturity. This means that the Soviet Union has the resources and technological capacity to mount a wider variety of military and economic programs than in the past. In the immediate postwar years, for example, the Soviet military threat was confined to the power of the Red Army. At the present time, it controls a full spectrum of military power ranging from ICBM's to conventional infantry and, one might add, "volunteers." A decade or so ago, Soviet trade and credit operations as well as technical assistance programs on the present scale would have been unthinkable. At the present time the Soviet Union has the evident capacity to conduct such operations on a regular expanding basis if it chooses to do so.

Here one specific aspect of the Soviet growth rate should be noted. A 6 percent rate of increase in Soviet GNP means that the Government disposes each year of something like the equivalent of $12 billion for whatever purposes it chooses. Although the level of American gross national product is more than twice that of the Soviet Union, an average growth rate of 3 percent means that the American economy as a whole—not the Government—disposes of an increment of, say, only some $15 billion. I shall consider later the implications of the different procedures for allocating this increment; but in the discussion of specific dimensions of Soviet policy which follows, the wide range of capabilities and the flexibility afforded by government control over an annual increment not much less than our own should be borne in mind.

1. The threat of major war

The main weight of Soviet policy is being articulated to the Russian peoples and to the world in terms of a nonmilitary struggle, which is, indeed, being energetically and frankly pursued. But there is no evidence whatsoever that the Soviet military effort is being reduced; and there are no grounds for building American policy on the assumption that if the Soviet Government believed that it enjoyed a sufficient advantage in nuclear weapons to take out American retaliatory power at a blow, it would not do so. Inhibitions may well exist in the Soviet political system against such a course of action; but there is no objective basis for believing that the United States would be safe should the gap in military capabilities be permitted to open to such an extent. Put another way, we Americans have no right before man or God to tempt Moscow's planners with this possibility. At the present time and for some years—until we create a highly dispersed deterrent system—our ability to make this course of action irrational appears to hinge on an ability to get sufficient advance warning of a Soviet missile attack to put our bombers in the air; and on the pace at which we "harden" our bases. These slender threads on which American safety now rests illustrates the dangers of analyzing the Soviet threat in conventional economic terms. Essentially since 1953 when the mounting of a fusion bomb in a rocket became feasible, the Soviet Union has made a plunge for primacy in this particular weapons system. The American military danger arises from the advantage Russia has achieved in this relatively narrow area, rather than from the rough equivalence in American and Soviet total military outlays in recent years. Although it is evident that the Soviet Government is not building its policy on the certainty or even likelihood that it will get far enough ahead of the United States to take out our retaliatory power at a blow, its allocations for military purposes (including air defense) and the military doctrines now developing within the Soviet military establishment are wholly consistent with a missile salvo being regarded as one among several possible routes to world primacy—coexistence or no coexistence.

2. The threat of limited war

Similarly, there is no evidence in Soviet military allocations nor in Soviet military doctrine that the use of arms short of an all-out atomic was has been ruled out. On the contrary, the evidence remains that the Soviet Union has continued to modernize its ground force in ways which would make possible combat with either conventional or tactical atomic weapons. Moreover, just as the Geneva Conference of 1955 was accompanied by the disruptive Czech arms deal with Egypt, the present exploration of the possibilities of arms reduction and control is accompanied by Chinese Communist incursions across their southern border. This lively threat is, again, not illuminated by comparative economic analysis of the Russian and American economies.

And we must look at the problem of building deterrence to limited war in even broader terms.

First, there is the fact that, since 1947—from the threat to Greece and Turkey to the latest attacks on Quemoy and Matsu—we have in the end met limited aggression not by using strategic airpower with nuclear weapons, but by hurriedly mobilizing some form of limited countermeasure. There has been a gap between our emphasis on nuclear weapons in diplomatic theory and budget allocations on the one hand, and our policy when the chips were down, on the other. It is quite likely that if we and our opponents understood better how we would in fact behave, in the face of limited aggression, we would have seen fewer forays across the truce lines since the end of the Second World War. Our concentration on the big weapons has tempted them in the past and may tempt them again.

Second, in Europe we now confront a situation where our allies are increasingly unwilling to accept a situation where limited aggression may still occur and their only recourse is to rely on counterattack with nuclear weapons under circumstances where Soviet missiles could evidently overwhelm them and where the United States would have to reckon on direct attack. Increasingly, thoughtful Europeans have come to understand that stability in that region demands increased nonnuclear strength.

Finally, and perhaps most important of all, we must begin to understand that if we make progress toward placing nuclear weapons under international control, we must have an alternative conventional basis for maintaining security. In the long run, by slow stages, we may well move, if all goes well, to very low levels of armaments of all types. In that process, however, we cannot negotiate confidently and safely unless we can mount alternative forms of defense, should a breakthrough come that would neutralize nuclear weapons.

In short, the nature of the Soviet challenge—including the Soviet challenge to put forward concrete proposals for step-by-step movement toward the control of nuclear armaments—requires that we take the problem of deterring limited aggression much more seriously than we have done in the past 15 years.

3. Diplomatic blackmail

Since the early months of 1956 down through the Berlin crisis, the Soviet Union has on a number of occasions used the threat of its missile capabilities to strengthen the hand of its diplomacy. Again, this is a form of threat which cannot be defined with reference to economic analysis. It comes, in the end, to a simple test of nerve and will.

4. The political penetration of the underdeveloped areas

Soviet policy in Asia, the Middle East, Africa, and Latin America is increasingly discussed under the heading of "The Economic Offensive." This leads to complicated efforts to compare the scale of Soviet and American aid on a quantitative basis. And, indeed, it is quite clear that Soviet technical and economic assistance to underdeveloped areas in the free world as well as Soviet trade policy have been significant forms for creating areas of political influence and sympathy in various parts of the world. But analysis confined to these familiar dimensions misses the main point and the fundamental nature of the Soviet threat. It is quite evident from Communist thought, writing, and policy that their goal in Asia, the Middle East, Africa, and parts of Latin America is a repetition in some form of the story of China from, say, 1927 to 1949; that is, Soviet analysts look to a progressive failure of the non-Communist regimes in these areas to solve the problems of modernization and economic growth, leading to frustration, internal turmoil, and to acceptance of the Communist alternative as a way of organizing these transitional societies. Thus, the central challenge confronting the United States and the Western World in the underdeveloped areas is not, somehow, to outstrip Russian loans and technical assistance. The challenge is to mount our own positive long-term policies designed to maximize the chance that these transitional societies will emerge into modernization without losing their independence and without foreclosing the possibility of progressively more democratic political development. Additional American and free world resources are required in this effort; and Soviet aid and trade policies play some role in the mounting of this challenge—which is, I believe, the route to world power that Moscow now regards as most likely. But to understand and deal with that challenge we must abandon a numbers racket approach and look directly and with insight at the problems of transitional societies and what we can do to help them.

5. The fragmentation of the Atlantic alliance

It is clear that Soviet policy is immensely alert to the possibility of exploiting schisms as among the Western European nations and as beween Western Europe and the United States. Offers of East-West trade play some part in this Soviet policy; but its primary tools are military, political, and psychological—combined with the fact that Moscow controls Eastern Germany and, therefore, the possibility of German unity. This major Soviet effort is only obliquely related to Soviet and American growth rates; and the American response lies in the area of new ideas and institutional arrangements within the Western Alliance—which is now very rich—rather than in new American expenditures.

6. The psychological image

In support of these various efforts to achieve or to prepare for a breakthrough to world primacy, the Soviet Union is mounting a remarkable and sustained effort to project to the external world and to the Russian peoples a quite particular image. That image is of an ardent, energetic, and technically competent competitor closing fast on—and preparing to supersede—a front runner who has lost the capacity to deal with his problems and prefers to go down in the style to whch he has become accustomed rather than to maintain his position. Leaving aside the various American contributions to the persuasiveness of this image in the outside world, this campaign has its foundations in three dimensions of Soviet policy: a somewhat dubious numerical approach to "catching up" with the American economy which, nevertheless, is rooted in the high momentum and technological maturity of the Soviet economy; [1] an exceedingly solid set of Soviet achievements in missiles technology (military and nonmilitary) and a sporadically successful projection of the Soviet Union as the leader in the quest for peace. At home, the building of Soviet policy around the objective of catching up with the United States and with the American standards of living has proved an exceedingly successful device for unifying Soviet society, appealing as it does to three strong motivations evident in the Russian peoples: a deep nationalist pride, a desire for higher standards of living, and a passion for peace. In these dimensions of the Soviet challenge, the high momentum of the Soviet economy has played some part, but it is by no means the sole basis of the challenge.

THE AMERICAN AGENDA

We turn now to the following question: In the light of the purposes of our society, at home and on the world scene, what lines of action are suggested by these multiple Soviet challenges; and what role, if

[1] The professional Soviet literature on "catching up" with the United States suggests the objective in the next decade is to equal or surpass American production in certain key sectors related to military potential (e.g., steel) rather than to exceed American levels of GNP or to exceed American consumption levels on the American pattern.

any, does the growth rate and economic policy play in shaping an effective American response? [2]

The elements in an effective American military and foreign policy are, I suspect, quite clear to us all and likely to command something of a consensus. They come to this. By our military dispositions, we must continue to make either major or limited war an irrational undertaking for Communists. On this basis we must use our economic resources and our political and human insight to the full in doing what we can to insure that the nations of Asia, the Middle East, Africa, and Latin America remain independent and move through their difficult transitions to modernization in ways which keep open the possibility of a democratic evolution for their societies. In order to execute these military and creative missions, we must form up a new set of relationships with the resurgent nations of Western Europe and Japan. And from this solid free world base, we must maintain an endless diplomatic initiative and an endless sympathetic dialog with the Soviet leadership seeking to exploit every serious possibility for movement toward the effective international control of armaments.

In three categories this requires more American public expenditure: to be specific (but not necessarily inclusive) to "harden" American bases in the period of Soviet missile advantage; to provide an adequate airlift for the deterrence of limited war; and to develop an American contribution to an international aid scheme for underdeveloped areas which would be adequate to the task.

I am not prepared to estimate the amount by which American public expenditures need to be increased to cover these three policy objectives; but I would say this much. It is perfectly clear that the United States is not so poor that it cannot pay the bill for an adequate national effort; nor does the difficulty lie in the potentials for American growth over, say, the next decade. The problem lies in the attitudes of mind and the procedures we bring to bear in allocating resources for public purposes; and it lies in the way we are seeking to handle the problem of inflation. It is to these themes that I now turn.

THE POTENTIALS OF AMERICAN GROWTH

The potentials for American growth in the next decade would, I believe, permit us both chronic full employment and one of those surges of growth which transcend the long period average of 3 percent per annum increase in GNP. I am a little skeptical that we can attain 5 percent rate of increase; but a 4 percent rate of increase could be within our grasp if our growth potentials are fully and well used. I hold this view because there are three powerful expansionary forces now operating within the American economy: the rise in population, the acceleration of research and development, and the society's massive requirements for social overhead capital. A 4-percent growth in GNP would yield our society an annual increment for all purposes of well over $20 billion over the next decade. The first proposition is,

---

[2] In this discussion I shall leave aside a question which concerns many Americans, including myself; namely, the question of whether we are allocating enough resources to education, urban reconstruction, roads, water development, and other forms of social overhead capital on whose adequacy the quality of American society partially depends. I shall consider merely the relation between an adequate American response to our position on the world scene and the American economy. However, what is said here about allocation and inflation policy are relevant equally to domestic, military, and foreign policy.

therefore, that I can envisage no increase in American public outlays required to deal with the Soviet threats which could not easily be met by a society with over a $500 billion GNP and a more than $20 billion annual increment in GNP.

The achievement of a high rate of growth is, however, neither automatic nor assured; we shall have to find new ways of handling the inflation problem, and we shall have to take special steps to assure that the potentials for productivity increase are, in fact, exploited. These matters are considered below. But first it is necessary to examine directly our most fundamental problem—the American method for allocating resources between the private and public sectors.

THE ALLOCATION PROBLEM

The root cause of our difficulty lies not in our income or our growth potential but in certain American habits of mind, carried over from earlier phases of our history, and in the workings of the political process, as they affect the allocation of resources. This interplay of intellectual conception and conventional politics conspire to make it difficult for Americans to increase the scale of public outlays except at moments of acute crisis. Here lies a danger to the national interest as well as a threat to the quality of American society.

Specifically, the working concepts of modern economics encourage the view that public outlays should be accommodated to the natural ebb and flow of the private sector, perhaps to be expanded at times of recession but certainly to be restrained when the private sectors exhibit high momentum.[3] This perspective, carried over inappropriately from an era of depression and peace to a time of chronic cold war and secular expansion, constitutes a powerful deterrent to outlays in the public sector, especially at a time of chronic prosperity; for it renders difficult a rational choice between marginal outlays in the public and private sectors, without extraordinary exertions of political leadership which have not been forthcoming. Without such efforts, the calculation takes the form of a crude clash between the total claims of the state as against the individual family budget, in which the latter enjoys an evident prima facie advantage. The existing level of taxation acquires a degree of acceptability as citizens accommodate themselves to its burdens. Familiarity breeds not contempt but stoicism. Lacking a concerted effort of political leadership to dramatize the meaning of marginal shifts from the private to the public sector, it is difficult to generate the political base for tax increases or other forms of restraint on private outlays; e.g., checks on installment spending. This leads politicians, except under acute crisis circumstances, to work out the pattern of public outlays within ceilings determined by what the existing tax schedules—the arbitrary product of the last acute crisis—will yield at existing levels of income, if indeed it does not lead to inappropriate tax reductions.

It is essentially these two features of the American scene which have made our response to the changing directions of challenge in the cold war so sluggish on the one hand and convulsive on the other.

---

[3] For example: "It is true that Federal spending increased much less rapidly than did the Nation's total expenditure after 1954. It may justly be held, however, that there was a need for special restraint on the Government's part at a time when the rest of the economy was displaying extreme exuberance"; see A. F. Burns, "Prosperity Without Inflation," New York, 1957, p. 40.

Neither our concepts of political economy nor our notions of politics have made it possible to deal with threats to the national interest in a forehanded flexible way. We have shifted erratically from the moods and political economy of peace, to those of war. In the interval between, say, mid-1948 and the attack in Korea, for example, men in responsibility came to believe that a military budget beyond $15 billion was a threat to the American way of life. After the convulsive reaction to the Korean war had lifted military outlays more than threefold, this new range became again accepted as a line to be defended with a quite irrational ideological fervor.

The heart of the Soviet challenge lies, then, in presenting us with a situation where our interests may be eroded away, without palpable crisis, to a point where a traditional convulsive American response will no longer suffice. Our conceptions and methods of allocation to the public sector are inappropriate to a world caught up in a technological arms race and a slow grinding struggle for power and ideological conception in the underdeveloped areas. It is not the Soviet growth rate we need fear but a mode of American allocation which tends to imprison us at a level of public outlays determined by our arbitrary response to the last major crisis.

THE INFLATION PROBLEM

The allocation problem has been made more difficult in recent years by the way we have thought and acted with respect to inflation. The debate on inflation in the Western World has been dominated by men whose training has led them to examine prices almost wholly in terms of effective demand. One school says that effective demand must be restrained by fiscal and monetary means if prices are to remain constant, even at the cost of a low rate of growth. The other school says that effective demand must be sufficient to main full employment and rapid growth, even if this means a steady rise in prices. Both lines of thought derive directly from the experiences and concepts of the interwar years.

It is time that we freed ourselves from the vocabulary and concepts and quarrels of an earlier generation. It is time that we looked squarely at the situatiton as it is on the eve of the 1960's. It is time that we accepted the challenge to create a policy of full employment without inflation. Here I would echo Tocqueville's statement: "In politics one perishes from too much memory."

In my view the inflation problem of the 1950's is only superficially to be analyzed as the product of a peculiar wage push or effective demand pull. More fundamentally it arises from a historical change in the institutional methods and attitudes brought to bear in setting industrial and farm prices on the one hand and wages on the other.

These changes have two effects. First they render it difficult to pass along productivity increases in lower prices. The common expectation is that prices can only move in one direction: up. In turn, this throws almost the whole burden of achieving a rise in real wages on money wage negotiations, where the expectation is that money wages also can only rise. This expectation forces businessmen to seek to hedge, in order to protect their profits, and labor leaders to hedge in order to protect the real wages of labor. Wage negotiations are thus complicated because business negotiators must try to discount the effect of probable wage increases and labor negotiators must try to discount the effect on real wages of probable price increases. In trying to hedge against inflation, they perpetuate inflation at the expense of the public interest. The existence, as it were, of a firm price floor is compounded by the second major institutional fact: money wage bargains are struck in a setting largely divorced from price policy—and from the course of average national productivity—where the negotiators feel little responsibility except a short run responsibility to their immediate constituents.

The challenge confronting our democracy is to change the setting in which price and wage policies are established and to make the public interest and public presence felt. We must fashion price and wage policies under chronic high employment conditions, which are judged equitable and which allocate increases in real income by some method other than that we now have; that is, a method where money wage rates are increased more than the rise in average productivity, and then corrected by inflation. There appears to be no way of achieving a better result via conventional fiscal and monetary policy, without also bringing about changes in price policy which would permit a substantial part of the increase in real wages to assume the form of price decreases made possible by higher productivity. In this connection, it is an often forgotten lesson of economic history that periods of relative peace in labor relations have tended also to be periods of declining trend in living costs.

THE RELEVANCE OF THE GROWTH RATE

Having tried to break through the Soviet economic data to identify the concrete dimensions of the Soviet challenge and to break through the American statistics to identify the real nature of our problem, let me say a word about the American growth rate. As Report IV of the Rockefeller Bros. Fund special studies project dramatized, a high rate of growth in gross national product makes it possible to enlarge both private income per head and public outlays, at existing tax rates. Put another way, the higher the growth rate, the less the potential clash between the claims of the two sectors. But, a high rate of growth, in itself, does not guarantee that the public sector will be adequately supplied with resources: for the American allocation system does not automatically maintain constant fixed percentage allocations to various purposes (assuming for a moment that such a system would yield increases adequate to the national interest at high rates of growth in GNP). Without purposeful efforts the natural tendency of the American system is for public outlays to decline as a percentage of total resources, except at intervals of acknowledged crisis.

In fact, as a rough approximation, it is quite accurate to identify the Soviet advantage over the United States as consisting in a more stable percentage allocation to military and foreign policy sectors, starting from a high initial percentage base, at a time of rapid increase in Soviet GNP. Soviet allocations follow a regular path of expansion accommodated to the high rate of growth of GNP. American allocations follow a convulsive path, moving from plateau to (downward sloping) plateau, as crises dictate.

There is every reason for us to seek a higher American rate of growth, and notably an accelerated increase in productivity. Such an achievement could ease the problem of allocation and ease the problem of inflation. But it would not automatically remove from us the hard choices of allocation, nor would it remove the challenge to the democratic process represented by the need to control inflation without stagnation or damping the rate of growth.

THE PROBLEM OF INCREASING AMERICAN PRODUCTIVITY

Here I should like to bring to bear some insights derived from work as an economic historian.

As one examines the story of economic growth in the past, it is possible to identify for each economy, over each substantial period of time, the sectors whose disproportionately rapid growth made it possible for the economy as a whole to continue to grow. These leading sectors have, historically, been connected with new forms of technology: modern cotton textiles, the railroads, steel, electricity, chemicals, and so on. The power of these sectors in affecting the overall rate of growth derived from the fact that they directly and indirectly stimulated productivity in other sectors: they set up new direct demands such as the railway demand for coal, iron, and engineering products; and they also opened up, through what we call external economy effects, wholly new avenues of economic development.

Now economic history also tells us that each cyclical expansion was dominated by a group of leading sectors, whose rapid increase provided the effective demand which brought the economy to full employment. But the leading sectors in a boom were not necessarily also leading growth sectors. For example, some booms have been based mainly on a rapid expansion in housing rather than on the rapid diffusion of new branches of technology. Housing, unfortunately, has not been subjected to a major technological revolution with strong secondary effects on productivity. An expansion in housing will certainly increase effective demand and employment; but it will not, in itself, bring about a strong stimulus to productivity.

This distinction between the effect of leading sectors on productivity and effective demand becomes of peculiar importance to the United States at the present stage of our history. We are emerging, as I suggested earlier, from the process of diffusing a new level and pattern of consumption based on the automobile, electric-powered gadgets, etc. While that process of diffusion proceeded, we collected powerful and general productivity benefits in a wide range of industries directly and indirectly connected with the new patterns of consumption. Moreover, as we look around the world, we can see that Western Europe, Japan, as well as Russia and Eastern Europe are now enjoying or may shortly enjoy the productivity effects which stem from pressing consumption on into the new high ranges which the United States (along with Canada and Scandinavia) first explored.

As nearly as we can make out, Americans, as they have become richer, have tended to allocate their increase in income to larger families and increased outlays on services, rather than to manufactured products. The expansion in population and the increased demand for services will help to maintain full employment in the United States. There is no shortage of effective demand in prospect unless the Government creates it by a dour and persistent deflationary policy. On the other hand, a lateral expansion of our facilities to accommodate a larger population and increased outlays on education, travel, health, and so forth are not likely to induce new technological revolutions with powerful and widespread secondary effects on the Nation's productivity level.

In short, we cannot look to the leading sectors in the next wave of business expansion—the leading sectors in effective demand—also to yield the rapid increases in productivity associated with leading growth sectors. Here, as I say, the American position differs radically from that of Western Europe, Japan, and the Soviet Union, where high income elasticity of demand is still associated more largely with manufacturing sectors, where productivity gains are still to be had. Some such distinction in historical phase now contributes a bit to the present embarrassment of the American balance of payments.

In facing this situation we are not, however, without resource. We all know that we live in a world where science and technology are expanding at an unprecedented rate; and that research and development in industry is expanding at something like 10 percent per annum. Can we not count on these developments to outweigh the consequences of our high income elasticity of demand for babies and services?

I believe there is some reason for caution here. In both scale and apparent effectiveness, industrial research and development has been historically concentrated in a relatively few sectors, linked in their very origins to modern science—electricity, chemicals, and aeronautics. These sectors—as well as atomic energy and electronics—will certainly yield general productivity benefits to the economy, over the next decade; but the concentration in both scale and quality of research and development in a relatively few fields, may not yield us the national result we would like to see. We should beware, particularly in research and development, of global statistics: the general lesson of research and development is that results are proportionate to quality rather than scale. Moreover, a great deal of contemporary research and development is directed to fields of military interest from which the civilian economy benefits only in indirect and uncertain ways.

In my view it would be wholesome, therefore, to place the issue of productivity high on the national agenda. It might be useful, for example, for task forces of private and public authorities jointly and systematically to examine the productivity potentials in various major sectors of the American economy with three objectives in mind. First, to identify the specific technical and institutional boottlenecks which need to be overcome in order to achieve more rapid expansion in productivity. Second, to see whether it might not be in the common interest to allocate increased research and development talent of the first order to those older and less glamorous fields where deceleration or decline has long since set in, but where very substantial proportions of the Nation's resources are still consumed; for example, cotton textiles, railroads, housing construction. The objective would be to correct a little the natural tendency, familiar to economic historians, for the new, rapidly expanding fields to absorb a disproportionate percentage of first-class talent. Third, we might systematically examine the extent to which entrepreneurship in the various sectors is or is not effectively bringing to bear the potentials which already exist for increased productivity, and we might then consider what incentives might be created to bring average levels of productivity closer to best-proved standards.

Among the particular sectors that deserve close examination is what might broadly be called staff work both within government and in the private economy. Some of us hold the view that we Americans have carried over into staff work criteria of specialization derived historically from notions of scientific management which originated in the problems of running a railroad system, an army in peacetime, and a machine shop.[4] This leads to overmanned, overfragmented staffs, with tremendous inertia built into them, consuming their energies in maintaining the status quo, radically damping the pace of innovation. The increasing role of government in all our lives as well as the increasing role of staff work in the private sector, absorbing as staff work does so high a proportion of first rate human capital, may justify a serious examination of this prejudice.

It may seem odd to commend productivity teams to a nation which still leads the world in productivity and which, for so long, has been able to count on high productivity as an almost automatic byproduct of its evolution. But we must bear in mind that high productivity is not enough; it is the pace of increase that will help determine how easy or difficult it will be to meet our domestic and international challenges. And we should also bear in mind that the stage of growth which the United States has attained has altered the old tight connection between areas of high income elasticity of demand and high technological momentum. History appears to have decreed that, in order to remain a front runner, we shall have to continue to pioneer—in this case to pioneer in engineering productivity increases along a broad front. And in facing this challenge we should not complain, for a front runner's status is never automatically sustained. It must be constantly renewed.

CAN THE DEMOCRATIC PROCESS SOLVE THESE PROBLEMS?

The burden of this argument is, then, that the challenge the Nation confronts, finally, have major economic dimensions: The challenges of adequate and forehanded allocation to the public sector; of dealing with inflation without damping the rate of growth; of creating an environment and a public policy which would accelerate the rise of productivity on a broad front.[5] Each of these is a direct challenge to the vitality of the democratic political process in the United States. As members of the Joint Economic Committee are well aware, there are many Americans (including, I would surmise, certain of your panelists) who would take the view that efforts by the American political process to come to grips with them would inevitably result either in more economic loss than the gain sought; or, in political damage to our society which would outweigh the possible economic gain.

---

[4] See, for example, E. E. Morison (ed.), "The American Style," New York. 1958, chapters by George F. Kennan and W. W. Rostow, and the commentary of Richard M. Bissell, Jr.

[5] To this might be added the challenge of dealing with the problem of international reserves and the pressure on the American balance of payments without damaging and, if possible, by strengthening the unity of the free world—the latter by no means an impossible objective. But I have set this problem aside since it arises mainly from the inner dynamics of the free world's economies; although Soviet policy and pressure play a role by forcing the United States to maintain such high levels of dollar outlays abroad.

One can reply that other democratic societies have, at various times, dealt more or less successfully with each of these problems, without losing their fundamental values; for example, the American Marshall plan effort of 1947–48, conducted without the stimulus of military operations, but with strong political leadership which succeeded in getting support for a quite sharp increase in the public budget; for example, the efforts of the Netherlands to accommodate real wages to the average level of productivity increase in the economy; for example, the performance of western Europeans, at our strong urging, in stimulating substantial productivity increases after the Second World War.

But it would be wrong to rest the American case for accepting this tough agenda merely on the basis of analogy. Times are different, nations differ, and problems are never quite the same.

The real case must be negative on the one hand, positive on the other.

Negatively we know that four of our worst mistakes in modern history arose from a fear that our democracy could not deal with the problems it faced, without losing its essence. I refer, of course, to the belief of the Republican administration after 1929 that it could not deal with the great depression without risking unacceptable damage to capitalism; to the belief of isolationists in both parties that we could not deal with Hitler and the Axis without permanently damaging basic qualities in our society; to the belief of the Democratic administration before June 1950 that our society could not afford a military budget of more than $15 billion; and, I would add, the similar belief of the present administration that its overriding mission has been to reduce the public budget it inherited, despite the accelerated challenge it has faced since 1953 in many dimensions.

The lesson of our recent history is that every time the men in authority decided that some problem was too tough for democracy to lick, and that they had to evade the problem in order to save democracy, we have gotten into a quite deep hole; and in all but the fourth case, where the bill is still to be reckoned, democracy was, in the end, much more searchingly and dangerously threatened than if the challenge had been accepted in the first place, at an early stage of the difficulty.

But there is a positive case as well. The positive case is not only that the democratic technique, energetically applied, has proved capable of handling such awkward problems as severe unemployment, major war, and limited war; it is also the simple faith that if any problem is soluble by human beings it is best solved, in the long run, by responsible freemen, subject to the mixture of freedom and self-discipline which is the essence of the democratic process when it works. Without that faith the struggle in which we are engaged lacks meaning.

Our experience of the past century and three quarters should convince us that the democratic process in the United States is tough, resilient, and capable of handling whatever problems the flow of history may place on our agenda.

A CONCLUSION

Now, a final word. Khrushchev's Russia is not the first nation to arrive at technological maturity, feel its oats, look over the field, and decide the old front runner was ripe for the taking. In our own time we have faced such moods and policies from Germany and Japan.

In the past these fast-closing nations have been persuaded to accept the fact that the world was not their oyster and to settle down as part of the international community only by defeat in major war. Major war was then necessary because the older powers did not so conduct themselves as to make major war a totally irrational undertaking.

In Russia we do not face a nation irrevocably committed to pursue power by major war unless we tempt it beyond endurance by our weakness during the period of the missile gap. The main hope for Soviet world leadership lies in various other dimensions, notably in their hope that the Western World and the democratic principle will fail in Asia, the Middle East, Africa, and Latin America. Moreover, I believe that there may well be men in Russia who already perceive that the rise of new nations, in the southern half of the globe, and in China, in a world of atomic weapons, may require a much higher degree of collaboration with the United States than even Khrushchev's challenge to compete peacefully would imply; they may begin to count not on burying us, but on making common cause with us over a widening range of problems. The discussions about ending H-bomb tests, with all they imply about Moscow's worries concerning the spread of atomic weapons, are a small beginning in this direction.

I doubt very much that Mr. Khrushchev is sure exactly where peaceful coexistence will end: in a missile salvo; in a protracted and dangerous struggle in the underdeveloped areas; or in a peace in which Russia accepts its destiny as a very great power, in a world of many diverse substantial powers. The answer lies not in the Kremlin's plans, but in what the free world does or fails to do, notably over the next decade. It is too much to ask of Russians at this stage of their history not to exploit every weakness we may offer. It is the strength and effectiveness of our response to the Soviet challenge—in all of its dimensions—which will determine the final meaning of peaceful coexistence.

Between now and 1970 a decisive test will take place. The real lesson of your panelists' papers is that there is nothing in the structure or growth rates of the two economies that will automatically determine the outcome of this test. The answer lies in whether our political leadership mobilizes the evidently ample resources that lie to hand—resources of will, of skill, of talent, of commitment to the American heritage, as well as goods and services—to do the job.

REFLECTIONS ON THE ECONOMIC RACE

(By Harry Schwartz, the New York Times, New York City)

The Subcommittee on Economic Statistics of the Joint Economic Committee of Congress has performed a major public service by its initiative in focusing public attention on Soviet-American economic comparisons. The two volumes of materials on this issue already released are the richest, systematic treasure trove of information on this subject which have become recently available in the public domain.[1]

I am appreciative both of the honor and of the responsibility involved in being invited to comment on these materials. In offering the comments below, however, I am giving only my own opinions and do not speak for the New York Times, my employer.

A GENERAL STATEMENT

The picture presented by the bulk of materials prepared for the subcommittee may be summarized somewhat as follows: Soviet production is still well below that of the United States, but is increasing far more rapidly and—what should not be forgotten—far more steadily than is that of the United States. Moreover the increasing Soviet output consists to a much larger degree of goods which serve to further the national power of the Soviet Union than does the product and services mix of the U.S. economy. As a result the standard of living of the American people is far higher than that of the Soviet people, but the efficiency of Soviet utilization of resources for power purposes is far greater than cur own. Any long continuation of these trends must pose the most serious questions about the future of our society and our way of life.

George F. Kennan, former U.S. Ambassador to the Soviet Union, has recently stated the issue in words which seem to me to deserve the most serious consideration:

> If you ask me—as a historian, let us say—whether a country in the state this country is in today: With no highly developed sense of national purpose, with the overwhelming accent of life on personal comfort and amusement, with a dearth of public services and a surfeit of privately sold gadgetry, with a chaotic transportation system, with its great urban areas being gradually disintegrated by the head-long switch to motor transportation, with an educational system where quality has been extensively sacrificed to quantity, fanned with insufficient social discipline even to keep its major industries functioning without grievous interruptions—if you ask me whether such a country has over the long run good chances of competing with a purposeful, serious, and disciplined society such as that of the Soviet Union, I must say that the answer is "No."[2]

Behind Mr. Kennan's anxiety, which I share, is I believe this unpleasant fact. The Soviet Union, with a gross national product less than half of ours, is today effectively our military equal and our superior in the most exciting contemporary adventure of the human

---

[1] "Comparisons of the United States and Soviet Economies. Paper Submitted by Panelists Appearing Before the Subcommittee on Economic Statistics." Joint Economic Committee, Congress of the United States. Washington: Government Printing Office, 1959, pts. I and II. These volumes will be cited below simply as pt. I or pt. II as appropriate.

[2] Quotation is taken from the text of Mr. Kennan's speech last Oct. 22.

race: the exploration of space. If Soviet world power and prestige have risen so high on such a relatively small economic base compared to ours, one can only look forward with foreboding to the situation which will develop as Soviet production increases and the economic gap between us and the Soviet Union diminishes, as diminish it will. Moreover in this world where abysmal poverty is still the lot of most of the world's people, the example of superior Soviet speed in raising production is exercising and, if continued, will exercise the greatest attraction upon the masses and leaders of South America, Asia, and Africa where most of the world's people and most of the world's poverty are concentrated.

We know that the rulers of the Soviet Union are dedicated to maximally rapid increase of the production base for their power position. Against the record of their disturbing achievements since 1945 we must expect they will continue to progress relatively rapidly in the years ahead. If we are to remain an effective bulwark for democracy, we must improve our own performance in terms of speed and amount of economic advance. We must also improve the allocation of our resources so as to get a mix of products and services more nearly corresponding to our national needs in this competition for survival.

RECENT AND FUTURE SOVIET INDUSTRIAL GROWTH

The key to the policy problems facing us lies in the speed of the future growth of Soviet heavy industry. On the basis of the evidence already presented to this committee, I think we may assume that other fields of the Soviet economy—agriculture, standard of living, transportation, etc.—will continue to improve at rates which will probably be adequate to keep the Soviet people quiescent, even if still far from fully satisfied, and the Soviet economy operating. Premier Khrushchev's recent speeches in Siberia made clear his knowledge of the desire of the Soviet people for lower prices, more and better goods, and the like. But the concessions already given—for example the increased durable consumer goods production goals for 1961—and those he could make if pressed seem adequate to prevent serious political trouble. But the emphasis on heavy industry continues and will continue.

It seems useful at this point to introduce into the record the latest data on recent growth of Soviet key heavy industrial raw materials production, and the plans for their increased output next year.

Soviet production of key commodities, 1955, 1959, and 1960 plan

Commodity	Units	1955	1959	1960 goal	1960 goal as percent of 1955
Pig iron	Million metric tons	33.3	43.0	47.0	142
Steel	do	45.3	60.3	65.0	143
Coal	do	391.3	507.0	516.0	132
Oil	do	70.8	129.2	144.0	203
Natural gas	Billion cubic meters	10.4	35.0	53.0	510
Electricity	Billion kilowatt-hours	170.2	262.8	291.0	171
Cement	Million metric tons	22.5	38.5	45.5	202

Sources: 1955, Narodnoye Khozyaistvo SSSR v 1958 Godu, pp. 158–165. 1959, Steel, oil and electricity figures from A. I. Mikoyan's speech in Izvestia, Oct. 24, 1959. Remaining figures estimated on basis of 9-month production figures in Pravda, Oct. 15, 1959. 1960 goal, Aleksei N. Kosygin's speech in Pravda, Oct. 28, 1959.

This is not an unimpressive performance, especially when we bear in mind that our recent evidence regarding the principles governing Soviet industrial planning suggests that the 1960 goals shown above have been estimated realistically and will probably be attained or very closely approached. As I have pointed out elsewhere in detail,[3] the published 1960 goals for Soviet industry are—with the exception of oil and gas—below the original goals of the sixth 5-year plan for that year. Those original goals, the data suggest, may be reached in 1961 or 1962 at the latest. But even though the sixth 5-year plan had to be abandoned, the production increase that now appears likely for the 1956–60 period can in no way encourage complacency on our part.

One value of the data above, I believe, is that they provide information useful for making minimum estimates of likely Soviet production of these key commodities in 1965 and 1970. We can do this by adding to the 1960 goals, the apparent absolute increases in outputs of these commodities since 1955. The result is an estimate of Soviet 1965 production on the assumption merely that the indicated absolute increase achieved during 1956–60 will be repeated in the next half decade. This is a minimal estimate of possible 1965 Soviet production because this technique implies immediately a significant slowdown in the rate of growth of the production of these commodities. In addition, it will be a far easier task for the larger Soviet economy of the early 1960's to achieve a given absolute amount of production increase than it was for the smaller Soviet economy of the late 1950's. Adding the same absolute figures for apparent 1956–60 production increase to the minimal 1965 estimates gives us similarly an even more minimal estimate of Soviet production of these commodities in 1970. Let us look at the results of these calculations, and compare them with the official Soviet goals for 1965 and also American production of these commodities in 1958:

Minimum estimates of Soviet output of key commodities in 1965 and 1970, Soviet goals for 1965, and U.S. output in 1958

Commodity	Units	Minimum estimates		Soviet 1965 goals	U.S. 1958 output
		1965	1970		
Pig iron	Million metric tons	60.7	74.4	65–70	52.4
Steel	do	84.7	104.4	86–91	77.2
Coal	do	[1] 600.0	[1] 700.0	596–609	382.8
Oil	do	217.2	290.4	230–240	330.8
Natural gas	Billion cubic meters	95.6	138.2	150	311.9
Electricity	Billion kilowatt-hours	411.8	532.6	500–520	724.0
Cement	Million metric tons	68.5	91.5	75–81	53.1

[1] Arbitrary estimates which are below the minima calculated by the technique otherwise applied in these tables because of announced Soviet intention sharply to reduce growth of coal output.

Sources: Soviet 1965 goals from Izvestia, Nov. 14, 1958. U.S. 1958 output from Survey of Current Business, March and April 1959.

My own belief is that, barring war or unlikely major political disturbance in the Soviet Union, the minimum estimates are very likely to be reached or even exceeded, particularly in 1970, by the dates indicated. Let us look at some of the implications of this belief,

[3] The New York Times, Nov. 2, 1959.

bearing in mind that the minimum estimates for 1965 are very conservative and imply a substantial failure of the current Soviet 7 year plan to reach even its minimum targets for 1965:

1. In 1965 Soviet heavy industry will be producing substantially more than did the corresponding industry of the United States in 1958. It should be noted that the minimum 1965 estimates for pig iron, steel, coal, and cement are all well above actual production in this country last year. Moreover, bearing in mind the fact that Soviet output of automobiles and other consumer durable goods in 1965 will certainly be still far below the corresponding output of these goods here last year, Soviet production of heavy machinery, armaments, and other goods important primarily from the point of view of national power is likely to be far greater in 1965 than was corresponding American production last year. The implications of this for the magnitude of the Soviet challenge in such fields as international trade and foreign economic aid would seem to be both obvious and disturbing.

2. Even on the basis of these minimum estimates, the Soviet output of these commodities is growing so rapidly that within the next very few years it will be perfectly feasible for Soviet production of pig iron, steel, and cement to exceed ours if we have only a moderate recession or suffer anything resembling this year's prolonged steel strike. Last year already the recession-caused reduction in our steel output permitted Soviet steel production to exceed 70 percent of our own for the first time in Soviet history.

3. Looking ahead to 1970, we may note that the estimates of minimum likely Soviet output for that year are, in the case of pig iron and steel, approximately of the magnitude of this country's record production. Bearing in mind too the fact that far less of Soviet electricity output is used for direct consumer needs than is true here, the conclusion seems inescapable that by 1970 the Soviet Union's heavy industry will be capable of producing at least as much as, and probably more than, our heavy industry ever has in our history. And here, too, of course, the differences in product mix between our heavy industry—with its emphasis on consumer durables—and Soviet heavy industry is very pertinent.

The conclusion seems inescapable that we are in the eve of a tremendous increase in Soviet capabilities of all kinds and of a vast expansion in Soviet competitive power against us. It also seems likely that the next decade will see Soviet capabilities outstrip our own in many different fields unless the United States substantially lifts its output not only above the levels of recession-ridden 1958 but also above past record levels, or changes its patterns of resource use, or both.

PRESENT AND FUTURE COMMUNIST BLOC STRENGTH

But it is important to remember that growing Communist capabilities are not restricted by the Soviet Union's potentialities. For many purposes of policy formation it is essential to bear in mind the growing economic strength of the total Communist bloc. Premier Khrushchev has already boasted that in 1965 he expects the Communist nations to be producing over half of the world's industrial output.[4] While we need not accept this prediction as certain of

[4] Izvestia, Nov. 14, 1958.

fulfillment, it is worth taking a brief look at the growing output of the Communist bloc as compared with that of the non-Communist world and also at a minimal estimate of what the Communist bloc output may be in 1965:

Output of the Communist bloc in 1950 and 1958, free world output in 1958, and minimum estimate of Communist bloc output in 1965

Commodity	Units	Communist bloc output			Free world 1958 output
		1950 actual	1958 actual	1965 estimate	
Pig iron	Million metric tons	24.7	64.8	104.9	134.8
Steel	do	36.1	80.1	124.1	189.5
Electricity	Billion kilowatt-hours	140.0	362.5	585.0	[1] 1,400.0
Cement	Million metric tons	21.0	61.6	104.6	[1] 150.0

[1] Very rough estimate.

Sources: Communist bloc 1950 and 1958 figures from Voprosy Ekonomiki No. 9, 1959, p. 76. Free world figures based on U.N. data.

The minimal nature of the 1965 estimates given above must be stressed. The estimates were arrived at rather mechanically by assuming merely that at the very least the Communist bloc economies will be able to increase the absolute amount of output of these commodities as much during the 7-year period 1959–65 as they actually did during the 8-year preceding period 1951–58. Actually, bearing in mind the still vast potentialities of economic growth in Communist China, it would not be at all surprising if in 1965 Communist bloc production equalled or exceeded the following somewhat higher figures: pig iron, 120 million metric tons; steel, 150 million metric tons; electricity, 650 billion kilowatt-hours; and cement, 120 million metric tons. And, of course, in comparing the free world and Communist bloc output totals we must bear in mind how very differently the Communists use their steel and electricity as compared to the way we use them.

But even the rather minimal 1965 estimates given in the table above show that we must be prepared to witness a very great expansion of total Communist bloc production and economic power in the years immediately ahead. The free world as a whole has no more right to complacency than does the United States alone. Moreover, it should be borne in mind that the Communist bloc as a whole has only about half as many people as does the free world. Hence when population is considered even the minimal 1965 estimates of the table above give Communist bloc per capita 1965 production estimates substantially exceeding the actual per capita free world figures for 1958 in the case of pig iron, steel, and cement. This is a useful reminder that the free world consists not only of highly industrialized countries such as our own and the nations of Western Europe, but also of many underdeveloped countries in Asia, Africa, and South America which at present contribute very little indeed to the industrial strength of the non-Communist world.

SOME POLICY IMPLICATIONS

The policy implications of the above analysis obviously depend upon one's assumptions as to the likely future relations between the

Soviet Union and the United States. So far as I can see, the most likely assumption here is that a state of uneasy absence of armed conflict will prevail between these two great states in the foreseeable future. And instead of shooting at each other, the two States—and the kinds of societies they represent—will be competing for the minds of men everywhere in terms of performance. This is what Premier Khrushchev obviously has in mind when he talks of peaceful coexistence and peaceful competition. And he has said often enough that he expects to show the superiority of his way of life by superior performance, most particularly by way of superior performance in raising production.

There would seem already to be in this country a substantial amount of informed and responsible opinion which recognizes that we must meet this challenge and this competition within the framework of our democratic institutions. I take it that this recognition is, at least in part, behind such suggestions as President Eisenhower's proposal last January for a committee to set up long-range national goals as well as last year's recommendation by the Rockefeller Bros. Fund study group on the national economy that this Nation seek to expand its output more rapidly and more regularly than in the past, perhaps by 5 percent per annum. Others, such as Prof. J. K. Galbraith, of Harvard University, in his influential book, "The Affluent Society," have stressed also the need for reallocation of our national resources so that social needs for education, housing, medical care and the like are relatively better met in the future than they have been even in the past prosperous post-World War II decade and a half. It seems to me that these and related trends in our public opinion provide important component parts of any adequate attempt to frame a national policy capable of meeting the massive and growing challenge of the Soviet Union and its allies. Certainly the record of recession-ridden 1958 and of 1959, when roughly 85 percent of our steel capacity was shut down by a strike which lasted almost 4 months, does not inspire confidence that business as usual attitudes have any hope of meeting the challenge.

President Eisenhower has repeatedly called in recent months for national self-discipline. By that I take it the President means that the different elements in our economy and our society must take the Nation's needs into account, as well as their own self-interest, in determining their actions. Certainly the perspectives we meet in facing the challenge of the Soviet Union, where discipline is coercively applied to the entire population, strengthens the importance of the American people heeding the President's appeal.

Against this background it is disturbing to read the statement of Howard C. Petersen.[5] The overall impact of his statement, I am afraid, will be to give aid and comfort to those who would prefer not to compete, to continue business as usual in the Micawberish hope that something will turn up which will change and improve the unhappy perspectives before us. Mr. Petersen properly disparages the "vaguely felt fears that we cannot afford to do what is necessary" for defense and foreign aid. Yet it is precisely those who hold such fears who are likely to be most receptive to Mr. Petersen's not so vague hints that any real attempt to compete economically with the Soviet

[5] Pt. II, pp. 517–527.

Union must inevitably mean the fastening of socialist bondage upon our economy. At least that is my reading of his assertion that any serious effort to raise our growth rate would require "a degree of governmental intervention in economic life that would change the very character of our free economy." The implied notion that the distinguished persons involved in the Rockefeller Brothers Fund report on the national enocomy may be in some way heralds of American socialism is curious, to say the least.

I would suggest that there are at least two basic errors in Mr. Petersen's thinking:

First, I believe Mr. Petersen seriously underestimates the flexibility and viability of our private enterprise economy, and its potentialities for adapting itself to the changing needs of our society. A quarter of a century ago, in the 1930's, there were those who similarly raised the specter of socialist slavery against laws providing for social security, unemployment insurance, wage and hour regulation and the like. With the wisdom of hindsight we have come to understand that these changes strengthened rather than weakened our free economy. I would argue rather that there are still very large and untapped reservoirs of flexibility and adaptation which can be drawn upon for fruitful partnership between all key elements in our economic life and government so as successfully to resist a challenge which threatens the very existence of private enterprise and of freedom. After all, defeat in the economic war could be as disastrous as defeat in a shooting war used to be before nuclear weapons made shooting wars involving their use intolerable.

We have, I would point out, social and political mechanisms which would permit leaders of all key elements in our society to hammer out needed national policy without the Draconian government coercion Mr. Petersen fears. Why cannot the top leaders of Government, business, labor, agriculture, and other key groups meet at the American Assembly or some similar forum to face the serious problems posed before us by the Soviet challenge and come to an agreed set of solutions? The attempt, at least, would seem worthwhile. Obviously if each group in our society puts maximization of its own interest before all other goals, such common policy would be difficult indeed to secure. But in the face of the common danger can we not hope for the voluntary self-discipline of all groups to play a greater role in the future than it has played in the past? We are often told these days, by Walter Lippmann, George Kennan, and others, that as a nation we lack a sense of national purpose. Could not such meetings define the purposes of our Nation and measures to implement those purposes?

To create the climate of public opinion which would make possible fruitful cooperation of the type suggested above obviously requires leadership. That is the challenge before all responsible public figures today. We have recently seen effective leadership exercised in mobilizing public resentment and anger against those who practiced fraud via the television screens in our homes. Is it unreasonable to hope that we may have leadership to mobilize public opinion for solution of the far more serious problem of the future survival of the free society and free economy we treasure?

Mr. Petersen's second error, I believe, lies in his estimate of the order of magnitude of the resources required to raise our rate of growth. On the basis of what he himself recognizes is the flimsiest possible kind of evidence he raises the specter that it would take something like $75 billion a year in extra expenditures to raise our growth rate from 3 to 5 percent annually.

My own suspicion is that Mr. Petersen radically underestimates the potentials for rapid expansion of production in our economy, supposing the markets can be provided to give incentives for maximum production and productivity. Surely Mr. Petersen is aware of the significant fraction of our resources which is inefficiently, wastefully, or partially employed because of lack of markets. Moreover we are living at the beginning of the automation revolution, in an era when technological progress is moving exponentially to give us better ways of making old goods as well as new goods we never had before. We have had some glimpses of the fantastic potentials for production increase in our economy in the performance of our war industry during World War II and in the astonishing rise of our agricultural productivity since 1940.

As will be clear from the above, my belief is that Mr. Petersen takes too static, even unimaginative, a view of our potentialities within the framework of our democratic and private enterprise institutions. Those institutions have successfully met all previous tests in our history, and I see no reason to suppose they cannot meet the present test if we use to the full our resources of imaginativeness, inventiveness, and intelligence. That this will require changes in some of our past practices and habits, is clear, of course, but then all life is a process of change and adaptation to new circumstances. What I do not believe is that the changes we need carry the dangers Mr. Petersen raises so gloomily. And I am particularly baffled by his attitude when I see that in this same statement he supports higher taxes for defense and foreign aid, higher taxes which cannot help—to use his own words—"curtailing the freedom of families to choose between consumption and saving and between work and leisure * * *." The real danger, I fear, is that we will do too little and too late to meet the Soviet economic challenge, rather than that we will engage in any mindless, reckless rush to change our basic institutions.

Some months ago a speaker at the National War College began his lecture by reminding his audience that the barbarian tribes which conquered Rome had a far smaller gross national product than did the rich, effete civilization they overcame. We need not labor the analogy, and of course our Soviet competitors are not barbarians, though there have been barbaric periods in not too distant Soviet history. I shall end by noting that the remark is a useful reminder that what is important for survival is not only the size of total production, but also the composition of that production and what it is used for.

O